STARTING OUT WITH

Visual C#® 2010

Second Edition

STARTING OUT WITH

Visual C#®
2010

Second Edition

Tony Gaddis

Haywood Community College

Addison-Wesley

Boston   Columbus   Indianapolis   New York   San Francisco   Upper Saddle River
Amsterdam   Cape Town   Dubai   London   Madrid   Milan   Munich   Paris   Montreal   Toronto
Delhi   Mexico City   São Paulo   Sydney   Hong Kong   Seoul   Singapore   Taipei   Tokyo

Editorial Director: Marcia Horton
Editor-in-Chief: Michael Hirsch
Editorial Assistant: Stephanie Sellinger
Vice President, Marketing: Patrice Jones
Marketing Manager: Yezan Alayan
Marketing Coordinator: Kathryn Ferranti
Vice President, Production: Vince O'Brien
Managing Editor: Jeff Holcomb
Production Project Manager: Heather McNally
Senior Operations Supervisor: Alan Fischer
Operations Specialist: Lisa McDowell
Art Director: Linda Knowles

Cover Designer: Joyce Cosentino Wells
Photo Researcher: Heather Kemp
Cover Art: © Brunosphoto/istockphoto
Media Editor: Daniel Sandin
Media Project Manager: Wanda Rockwell
Full-Service Project Management: Sherrill Redd,
   Aptara®, Inc.
Composition: Aptara®, Inc.
Printer/Binder: Edwards Brothers
Cover Printer: Phoenix Color
Text Font: Sabon

Credits and acknowledgments borrowed from other sources and reproduced, with permission, in this textbook appear on appropriate page within text, or are listed below.

Photo Credits: Figure 1.3 (page 3): U.S. Army Photo; Figure 1.4 (page 4): Vadim Kolobanov/Shutterstock; Figure 1.5 (page 5): Garsya/Shutterstock

Microsoft® and Windows® are registered trademarks of the Microsoft Corporation in the U.S.A. and other countries. Screen shots and icons reprinted with permission from the Microsoft Corporation. This book is not sponsored or endorsed by or affiliated with the Microsoft Corporation.

Library of Congress Cataloging-in-Publication Data

Gaddis, Tony.
   Starting out with Visual C# 2010/Tony Gaddis.—2nd ed.
     p. cm.
   Includes bibliographical references and index.
   ISBN-10: 0-13-216545-7 (alk. paper)
   ISBN-13: 978-0-13-216545-7 (alk. paper)
   1. C# (Computer program language)   2. Visual programming languages
(Computer science)   I. Title.
   QA76.73.C154G33 2012
   005.13'3—dc22

                                                    2010053541

10 9 8 7 6 5 4 3 2 1—EB—11 12 13 14 15

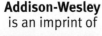

Addison-Wesley
is an imprint of

www.pearsonhighered.com

ISBN 10:   0-13-216545-7
ISBN 13: 978-0-13-216545-7

Brief Contents

Contents

Chapter 4 **Making Decisions 195**

Chapter 5 **Loops, Files, and Random Numbers 265**

Chapter 6 **Modularizing Your Code with Methods   337**

Chapter 7 **Arrays and Lists   387**

Chapter 8 **More about Processing Data   463**

Preface

Welcome to *Starting Out with Visual C# 2010*, Second Edition. This book is intended for an introductory programming course and is ideal for students with no prior experience. Students who are new to programming will appreciate the clear, down-to-earth explanations and the detailed walk-throughs that are provided by the hands-on tutorials. More experienced students will appreciate the depth of detail as they learn about the .NET Framework, databases, and other topics.

As with all the books in the *Starting Out With* series, the hallmark of this text is its clear, friendly, and easy-to-understand writing. In addition, it is rich in example programs that are concise and practical. The programs in this book include short examples that highlight specific programming topics, as well as more involved examples that focus on problem solving. Each chapter provides numerous hands-on tutorials that guide the student through each step of the development of an application. In addition to detailed, step-by-step instructions, the tutorials also provide the application's completed code and screen captures of the completed forms.

New to This Edition

If you have used the First Edition of *Starting Out with Visual C#*, you will recognize that this edition has been completely rewritten. Although the friendly presentation and clear writing style remain the same, many changes and improvements have been made, as summarized here:

GUI-Based Approach. This edition uses a visual, GUI-based approach. From the beginning, students learn to develop Windows Forms applications.

Visual Studio 2010. The book uses Visual Studio 2010 or Visual C# 2010 Express Edition.

New Organization. The book has been completely reorganized to accommodate its new pedagogy of using objects early but writing classes late, and developing GUI applications.

Hands-On Tutorials. Each chapter includes several hands-on tutorials that lead the student through the development of a project.

Lists. Lists are introduced along with arrays.

Exceptions. Simple exception handling is introduced in Chapter 3.

Databases. A new chapter on databases has been added.

A GUI-Based Approach

Beginning students are more motivated to learn programming when their applications have some sort of graphical element, such as a graphical user interface. Students using this book will learn to create GUI-based, event-driven, Visual C# applications. The Visual Studio (or Visual C# Express) environment is used to create forms that are rich with user interface controls and graphical images.

Learn to Use Objects Early, Learn to Write Classes Later

This book explains what objects are very early and shows the student how to create objects from classes that are provided by the .NET Framework. It then introduces the student to the fundamentals of input and output, control structures, methods, arrays and lists, and file I/O. Then the student learns to write his or her own classes and explores the topics of inheritance and polymorphism.

Visual Studio and Visual C# Express Edition

The book can be used with either Visual Studio 2010 or Visual C# 2010 Express Edition. The book is bundled with Microsoft's Visual C# 2010 Express Edition—a streamlined product that captures the best elements of Visual Studio in an ideal format for learning programming. The Express Edition offers an impressive set of tools for developing and debugging Visual C# applications, including those that work with databases and use SQL.

Brief Overview of Each Chapter

Chapter 1: Introduction to Computers and Programming. This chapter begins by giving a very concrete and easy-to-understand explanation of how computers work, how data is stored and manipulated, and why we write programs in high-level languages. In this chapter, the student learns what an object is and sees several examples by studying the objects that make up a program's graphical user interface. The chapter discusses steps in the programming development cycle. It also gives an introduction to the Visual Studio or Visual C# Express environment.

Chapter 2: Introduction to Visual C#. In this chapter the student learns to create forms with labels, buttons, and picture boxes and learns to modify control properties. The student is introduced to C# code, and learns the organizational structure of namespaces, classes, and methods. The student learns to write simple event-driven applications that respond to button clicks or provide interaction through clickable images. The importance of commenting code is also discussed.

Chapter 3: Processing Data. This chapter introduces variables and data types. It discusses the use of local variables and variables declared as fields within a form class. The student learns to create applications that read input from TextBox controls, perform mathematical operations, and produce formatted output. The student learns about the exceptions that can occur when the user enters invalid data into a TextBox and learns to write simple exception-handling code to deal with those problems. Named constants are introduced as a way of representing unchanging values and creating self-documenting, maintainable code. The student also learns more intricacies of creating graphical user interfaces.

Chapter 4: Making Decisions. In this chapter the student learns about relational operators and Boolean expressions and is shown how to control the flow of a program with decision structures. The `if`, `if-else`, and `if-else-if` statements are covered. Nested decision structures, logical operators, and the `switch` statement are also discussed. The student learns to use the `TryParse` family of methods to validate input and prevent exceptions. Radio buttons, check boxes, and list boxes are introduced as ways to let the user select items in a GUI.

Chapter 5: Loops, Files, and Random Numbers. This chapter shows the student how to use loops to create repetition structures. The `while` loop, the `for` loop, and the do-while loop are presented. Counters, accumulators, and running totals are also discussed. This chapter also introduces sequential file input and output and using text files. The student learns various programming techniques for writing data to text files and reading the contents of test files. The chapter concludes with a discussion of pseudorandom numbers, their applications, and how to generate them.

Chapter 6: Modularizing Your Code with Methods. In this chapter the student first learns how to write and call `void` methods. The chapter shows the benefits of using methods to modularize programs and discusses the top-down design approach. Then, the student learns to pass arguments to methods. Passing by value, by reference, and output parameters are discussed. Finally, the student learns to write value-returning methods.

Chapter 7: Arrays and Lists. Arrays and lists are reference-type objects in C#, so this chapter begins by discussing the difference between value type and reference type objects in the C# language. Then, the student learns to create and work with single-dimensional and two-dimensional arrays. The student learns to pass arrays as arguments to methods, transfer data between arrays and files, work with partially filled arrays, and create jagged arrays. Many examples of array processing are provided including examples of finding the sum, average, highest and lowest values in an array. Finally, the student learns to create `List` objects and store data in them.

Chapter 8: More about Processing Data. This chapter presents several diverse topics. Now that the student has studied the fundamentals of Visual C# programming, he or she can use the topics presented in this chapter to perform more advanced operations. First, various string and character processing techniques are introduced. Then the student learns to use structures to encapsulate several variables into a single item. The student next learns to create and use enumerated types. Last, the student learns about the Image-List control, a data structure for storing and retrieving images.

Chapter 9: Classes and Multiform Projects. Up to this point, the student has extensively used objects that are instances of .NET Framework classes. In this chapter the student learns to write classes to create his or her own objects. The student learns to create fields, methods, and constructors and learns to implement properties. Creating arrays of objects and storing objects in a List are also discussed. A primer on finding the classes in a problem as well as their responsibilities is provided. Finally, the chapter shows the student how to create multiple form classes in a project, instantiate those classes, and display them.

Chapter 10: Inheritance and Polymorphism. The study of classes continues in this chapter with the subjects of inheritance and polymorphism. The topics covered include base classes, derived classes, how constructors functions work in inheritance, method overriding, and polymorphism. Abstract classes and abstract methods are also discussed.

Chapter 11: Databases. This chapter introduces the student to basic database concepts. The student first learns about tables, rows, and columns and how to create a SQL Server database in Visual Studio. The student then learns how to connect a database to a Visual C# application and display a table in a DataGridView control, a Details view and other data-bound controls. Finally, the student learns how to write SQL Select statements to retrieve data from a table.

Appendix A: C# Primitive Data Types. This appendix gives an overview of the primitive data types available in C#.

Appendix B: Additional User Interface Controls. This appendix shows how to create a variety of controls such as ToolTips, combo boxes, scroll bars, TabControls, WebBrowser controls, ErrorProvider components, and menu systems.

Appendix C: ASCII/Unicode Characters. This appendix lists the ASCII (American Standard Code for Information Interchange) character set, which is also the Latin Subset of Unicode.

Appendix D: Answers to Checkpoint Questions. This appendix provides the answers to the Checkpoint questions that appear throughout each chapter in the book.

Organization of the Text

The text teaches Visual C# step by step. Each chapter covers a major set of programming topics, introduces controls and GUI elements, and builds knowledge as the student progresses through the book. Although the chapters can be easily taught in their existing sequence, there is some flexibility. Figure P-1 shows the chapter dependencies. As shown in the figure, Chapters 1–7 present the fundamentals of Visual C# programming and should be covered in sequence. Then, you can move directly to Chapter 8, Chapter 9, or Chapter 11. Chapter 10 should be covered after Chapter 9.

Figure P-1 Chapter dependencies

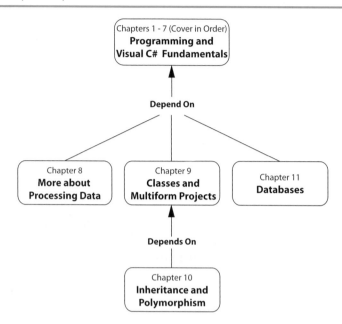

Features of the Text

Concept Statements. Each major section of the text starts with a concept statement. This statement concisely summarizes the main point of the section.

Tutorials. Each chapter has several hands-on tutorials that guide the student through the development of an application. Each tutorial provides detailed, step-by-step instructions, as well as the application's completed code and screen captures of the completed forms.

Example Programs. Each chapter has an abundant number of code examples designed to highlight the current topic.

Notes. Notes appear at several places throughout the text. They are short explanations of interesting or often misunderstood points relevant to the topic at hand.

Tips. Tips advise the student on the best techniques for approaching different programming or animation problems.

Warnings. Warnings caution students about programming techniques or practices that can lead to malfunctioning programs or lost data.

Checkpoints. Checkpoints are questions placed at intervals throughout each chapter. They are designed to query the student's knowledge quickly after learning a new topic. The answers to the Checkpoint questions can be found in Appendix D.

Review Questions. Each chapter presents a thorough and diverse set of Review Questions and Exercises. They include Multiple Choice, True/False, Algorithm Workbench, and Short Answer.

Programming Problems. Each chapter offers a pool of Programming Problems designed to solidify the student's knowledge of the topics currently being studied.

Supplements

Student. The following supplementary material is bundled with the book:

- A student CD-ROM containing the source code and files required for the chapter tutorials.
- A DVD containing Microsoft Visual C# 2010 Express Edition

Instructor. The following supplements are available to qualified instructors:

- Answers to all Review Questions in the text
- Solutions for all Programming Problems in the text
- Completed versions of all tutorials
- PowerPoint presentation slides for every chapter
- Test bank

For information on how to access these supplements, visit the Pearson Education Instructor Resource Center at www.pearsonhighered.com/irc or e-mail computing@pearson.com.

Acknowledgments

I would like to thank my family for their love and support in all my many projects. Thanks also go to Chris Rich for his work on the supplements. I am extremely fortunate to have Michael Hirsch as my editor and Stephanie Sellinger as editorial assistant. Michael's support and encouragement make it a pleasure to write chapters and meet deadlines. I am also fortunate to have Yez Alayan as marketing manager, and Kathryn Ferranti as marketing coordinator. They do a great job getting my books out to the academic community. I had a great production team, led by Jeff Holcomb, Managing Editor, and Heather McNally, Production Project Manager. Thanks to you all!

About the Author

Tony Gaddis is the principal author of the *Starting Out With* series of textbooks. Tony has nearly 20 years experience teaching computer science courses at Haywood Community College in North Carolina. He is a highly acclaimed instructor who was previously selected as the North Carolina Community College Teacher of the Year and has received the Teaching Excellence award from the National Institute for Staff and Organizational Development.

The *Starting Out With* series includes introductory books using the C++ programming language, the Java™ programming language, Microsoft® Visual Basic®, Microsoft® C#®, Python, Programming Logic and Design, and Alice, all published by the Addison-Wesley imprint of Pearson Education.

1 Introduction to Computers and Programming

TOPICS

1.1 Introduction

Think about some of the different ways that people use computers. In school, students use computers for tasks such as writing papers, searching for articles, sending e-mail, and participating in online classes. At work, people use computers to analyze data, make presentations, conduct business transactions, communicate with customers and coworkers, control machines in manufacturing facilities, and do many other things. At home, people use computers for tasks such as paying bills, shopping online, staying connected with friends and family, and playing computer games. And don't forget that smart phones, iPods®, car navigation systems, and many other devices are computers as well. The uses of computers are almost limitless in our everyday lives.

Computers can do such a wide variety of things because they can be programmed, which means that computers are designed not to do just one job, but to do any job that their programs tell them to do. A **program** is a set of instructions that a computer follows to perform a task. For example, Figure 1-1 shows screens from two commonly used Microsoft programs: Word and PowerPoint. Word is a word processing program that allows you to create, edit, and print documents. PowerPoint allows you to create graphical slides and use them as part of a presentation.

Programs are commonly referred to as **software**. Software is essential to a computer because without software, a computer can do nothing. All the software that makes our computers useful is created by individuals known as programmers, or software developers. A **programmer**, or **software developer**, is a person with the training and skills necessary to design, create, and test computer programs. Computer programming is an exciting and rewarding career. Today, programmers work in business, medicine, government, law enforcement, agriculture, academics, entertainment, and almost every other field.

Figure 1-1 A word processing program and a presentation program

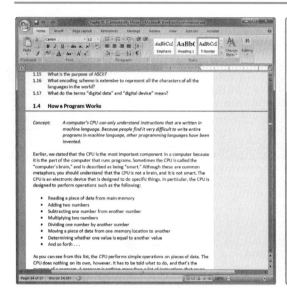 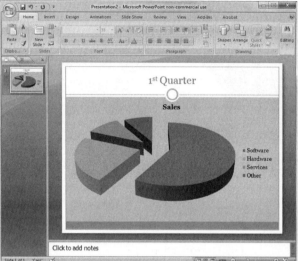

This book introduces you to the fundamental concepts of computer programming using the C# programming language. Before we begin exploring those concepts, you need to understand a few basic things about computers and how they work. This chapter provides a solid foundation of knowledge that you will continually rely on as you study computer science. First, we discuss the physical components that computers are commonly made of. Then, we look at how computers store data and execute programs. Next, we introduce you to two fundamental elements of modern software design: graphical user interfaces and objects. Finally, we give a quick introduction to the software used to write C# programs.

1.2 Hardware and Software

CONCEPT: The physical devices that a computer is made of are referred to as the computer's hardware. The programs that run on a computer are referred to as software.

Hardware

Hardware refers to all the physical devices, or components, of which a computer is made. A computer is not one single device but is a system of devices that all work together. Like the different instruments in a symphony orchestra, each device in a computer plays its own part.

If you have ever shopped for a computer, you have probably seen sales literature listing components such as microprocessors, memory, disk drives, video displays, graphics cards, and so on. Unless you already know a lot about computers or at least have a friend who does, understanding what these different components do can be confusing. As shown in Figure 1-2, a typical computer system consists of the following major components:

- The central processing unit (CPU)
- Main memory
- Secondary storage devices
- Input devices
- Output devices

Let's take a closer look at each of these components.

Figure 1-2 Typical components of a computer system

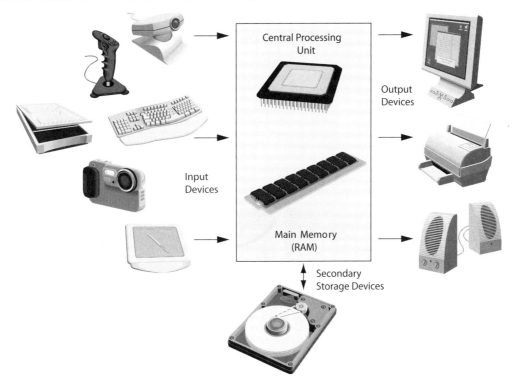

The CPU

When a computer is performing the tasks that a program tells it to do, we say that the computer is **running** or **executing** the program. The **central processing unit**, or CPU, is the part of a computer that actually runs programs. The CPU is the most important component in a computer because without it, the computer could not run software.

In the earliest computers, CPUs were huge devices made of electrical and mechanical components such as vacuum tubes and switches. Figure 1-3 shows such a device. The two

Figure 1-3 The ENIAC computer

women in the photo are working with the historic ENIAC computer. The **ENIAC**, considered by many to be the world's first programmable electronic computer, was built in 1945 to calculate artillery ballistic tables for the U.S. Army. This machine, which was primarily one big CPU, was 8 feet tall and 100 feet long and weighed 30 tons.

Today, CPUs are small chips known as **microprocessors**. Figure 1-4 shows a photo of a lab technician holding a modern-day microprocessor. In addition to being much smaller than the old electromechanical CPUs in early computers, microprocessors are also much more powerful.

Figure 1-4 A lab technician holds a modern microprocessor

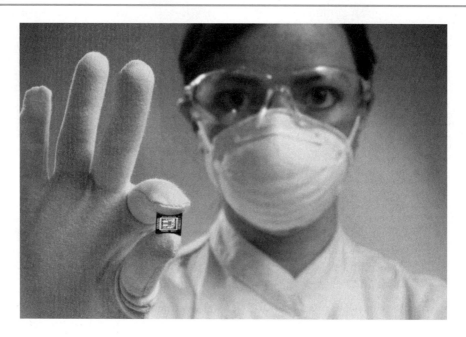

Main Memory

You can think of **main memory** as the computer's work area. This is where the computer stores a program while the program is running, as well as the data that the program is working with. For example, suppose you are using a word processing program to write an essay for one of your classes. While you do this, both the word processing program and the essay are stored in main memory.

Main memory is commonly known as **random-access memory**, or **RAM**. It is called this because the CPU is able to quickly access data stored at any random location in RAM. RAM is usually a **volatile** type of memory that is used only for temporary storage while a program is running. When the computer is turned off, the contents of RAM are erased. Inside your computer, RAM is stored in chips, similar to the ones shown in Figure 1-5.

Secondary Storage Devices

Secondary storage is a type of memory that can hold data for long periods of time, even when there is no power to the computer. Programs are normally stored in secondary

Figure 1-5 Memory chips

memory and loaded into main memory as needed. Important data, such as word processing documents, payroll data, and inventory records, is saved to secondary storage as well.

The most common type of secondary storage device is the disk drive. A **disk drive** stores data by magnetically encoding it onto a circular disk. Most computers have a disk drive mounted inside their case. External disk drives, which connect to one of the computer's communication ports, are also available. External disk drives can be used to create backup copies of important data or to move data to another computer.

In addition to external disk drives, many types of devices have been created for copying data and for moving it to other computers. For many years floppy disk drives were popular. A **floppy disk drive** records data onto a small floppy disk, which can be removed from the drive. Floppy disks have many disadvantages, however. For example, they have limited storage capacity, and are slow to access data. The use of floppy disk drives has declined dramatically in recent years in favor of superior devices such as USB drives. **Universal serial bus (USB) drives** are small devices that plug into the computer's USB port and appear to the system as disk drives. These drives do not actually contain a disk, however. They store data in a special type of memory known as flash memory. USB drives, which are also known as memory sticks and flash drives, are inexpensive, reliable, and small enough to be carried in a pocket.

Optical devices such as the **compact disc (CD)** and the **digital versatile disc (DVD)** are also popular for data storage. Data is not recorded magnetically on an optical disc but is encoded as a series of pits on the disc surface. CD and DVD drives use a laser to detect the pits and thus read the encoded data. Optical discs hold large amounts of data, and because recordable CD and DVD drives are now commonplace, they are good mediums for creating backup copies of data.

Input Devices

Input is any data the computer collects from people and from other devices. The component that collects the data and sends it to the computer is called an **input device**. Common input devices are the keyboard, mouse, scanner, microphone, and digital camera. Disk drives and optical drives can also be considered input devices because programs and data are retrieved from them and loaded into the computer's memory.

Output Devices

Output is any data the computer produces for people or for other devices. It might be a sales report, a list of names, or a graphic image. The data is sent to an **output device**, which formats and presents it. Common output devices are video displays and printers. Disk drives and CD or DVD recorders can also be considered output devices because the system sends data to them in order to be saved.

Software

If a computer is to function, software is not optional. Everything that a computer does, from the time you turn the power switch on until you shut the system down, is under the control of software. There are two general categories of software: system software and application software. Most computer programs clearly fit into one of these two categories. Let's take a closer look at each.

System Software

The programs that control and manage the basic operations of a computer are generally referred to as **system software**. System software typically includes the following types of programs:

Operating Systems

An **operating system** is the most fundamental set of programs on a computer. The operating system controls the internal operations of the computer's hardware, manages all the devices connected to the computer, allows data to be saved to and retrieved from storage devices, and allows other programs to run on the computer.

Utility Programs

A **utility program** performs a specialized task that enhances the computer's operation or safeguards data. Examples of utility programs are virus scanners, file-compression programs, and data-backup programs.

Software Development Tools

The software tools that programmers use to create, modify, and test software are referred to as **software development tools**. Assemblers, compilers, and interpreters, which are discussed later in this chapter, are examples of programs that fall into this category.

Application Software

Programs that make a computer useful for everyday tasks are known as **application software**. These are the programs that people normally spend most of their time running on their computers. Figure 1-1, at the beginning of this chapter, shows screens from two commonly used applications—Microsoft Word, a word processing program, and Microsoft Powerpoint, a presentation program. Some other examples of application software are spreadsheet programs, e-mail programs, Web browsers, and game programs.

 Checkpoint

1.1 What is a program?

1.2 What is hardware?

1.3 List the five major components of a computer system.

1.4 What part of the computer actually runs programs?

1.5 What part of the computer serves as a work area to store a program and its data while the program is running?

1.6 What part of the computer holds data for long periods of time, even when there is no power to the computer?

1.7 What part of the computer collects data from people and from other devices?

1.8 What part of the computer formats and presents data for people or other devices?

1.9   What fundamental set of programs control the internal operations of the computer's hardware?

1.10   What do you call a program that performs a specialized task, such as a virus scanner, a file-compression program, or a data-backup program?

1.11   Word processing programs, spreadsheet programs, e-mail programs, Web browsers, and game programs belong to what category of software?

1.3 How Computers Store Data

CONCEPT: All data stored in a computer is converted to sequences of 0s and 1s.

A computer's memory is divided into tiny storage locations known as bytes. One **byte** is enough memory to store only a letter of the alphabet or a small number. In order to do anything meaningful, a computer has to have lots of bytes. Most computers today have millions, or even billions, of bytes of memory.

Each byte is divided into eight smaller storage locations known as bits. The term **bit** stands for **binary digit**. Computer scientists usually think of bits as tiny switches that can be either on or off. Bits aren't actual "switches," however, at least not in the conventional sense. In most computer systems, bits are tiny electrical components that can hold either a positive or a negative charge. Computer scientists think of a positive charge as a switch in the *on* position and a negative charge as a switch in the *off* position. Figure 1-6 shows the way that a computer scientist might think of a byte of memory: as a collection of switches that are each flipped to either the on or the off position.

Figure 1-6 A byte thought of as eight switches

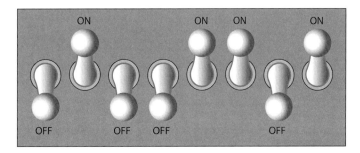

When a piece of data is stored in a byte, the computer sets the eight bits to an on/off pattern that represents the data. For example, the pattern shown on the left in Figure 1-7 shows how the number 77 would be stored in a byte, and the pattern on the right shows how the letter A would be stored in a byte. In a moment you will see how these patterns are determined.

Figure 1-7 Bit patterns for the number 77 and the letter A

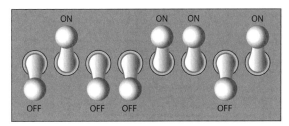
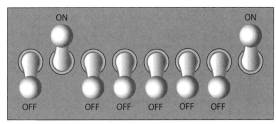

The number 77 stored in a byte.   The letter A stored in a byte.

Storing Numbers

A bit can be used in a very limited way to represent numbers. Depending on whether the bit is turned on or off, it can represent one of two different values. In computer systems, a bit that is turned off represents the number 0 and a bit that is turned on represents the number 1. This corresponds perfectly to the **binary numbering system**. In the binary numbering system (or **binary**, as it is usually called), all numeric values are written as sequences of 0s and 1s. Here is an example of a number that is written in binary:

    10011101

The position of each digit in a binary number has a value assigned to it. Starting with the rightmost digit and moving left, the position values are 2^0, 2^1, 2^2, 2^3, and so forth, as shown in Figure 1-8. Figure 1-9 shows the same diagram with the position values calculated. Starting with the rightmost digit and moving left, the position values are 1, 2, 4, 8, and so forth.

Figure 1-8 The values of binary digits as powers of 2

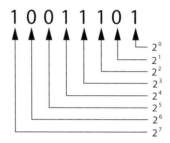

Figure 1-9 The values of binary digits

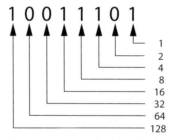

To determine the value of a binary number, you simply add up the position values of all the 1s. For example, in the binary number 10011101, the position values of the 1s are 1, 4, 8, 16, and 128. This is shown in Figure 1-10. The sum of all these position values is 157. So, the value of the binary number 10011101 is 157.

Figure 1-10 Determining the value of 10011101

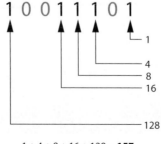

$$1 + 4 + 8 + 16 + 128 = \mathbf{157}$$

Figure 1-11 shows how you can picture the number 157 stored in a byte of memory. Each 1 is represented by a bit in the on position, and each 0 is represented by a bit in the off position.

Figure 1-11 The bit pattern for 157

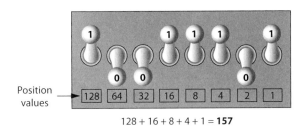

Position values
$$128 + 16 + 8 + 4 + 1 = \mathbf{157}$$

When all the bits in a byte are set to 0 (turned off), then the value of the byte is 0. When all the bits in a byte are set to 1 (turned on), then the byte holds the largest value that can be stored in it. The largest value that can be stored in a byte is 1 + 2 + 4 + 8 + 16 + 32 + 64 + 128 = 255. This limit exists because there are only eight bits in a byte.

What if you need to store a number larger than 255? The answer is simple: use more than 1 byte. For example, suppose we put 2 bytes together. That gives us 16 bits. The position values of those 16 bits would be 2^0, 2^1, 2^2, 2^3, and so forth, up through 2^{15}. As shown in Figure 1-12, the maximum value that can be stored in 2 bytes is 65,535. If you need to store a number larger than this, then more bytes are necessary.

Figure 1-12 Two bytes used for a large number

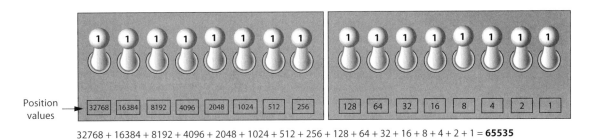

Position values
$$32768 + 16384 + 8192 + 4096 + 2048 + 1024 + 512 + 256 + 128 + 64 + 32 + 16 + 8 + 4 + 2 + 1 = \mathbf{65535}$$

 TIP: In case you're feeling overwhelmed by all this, relax! You will not have to actually convert numbers to binary while programming. Knowing that this process is taking place inside the computer will help you as you learn, and in the long term this knowledge will make you a better programmer.

Storing Characters

Any piece of data that is stored in a computer's memory must be stored as a binary number. That includes characters such as letters and punctuation marks. When a character is stored in memory, it is first converted to a numeric code. The numeric code is then stored in memory as a binary number.

Over the years, different coding schemes have been developed to represent characters in computer memory. Historically, the most important of these coding schemes is **ASCII**, which stands for the **American Standard Code for Information Interchange**. ASCII is a set of 128 numeric codes that represent the English letters, various punctuation marks, and other characters. For example, the ASCII code for the uppercase letter A is 65. When you type an uppercase A on your computer keyboard, the number 65 is stored in memory (as a binary number, of course). This is shown in Figure 1-13.

Figure 1-13 The letter A stored in memory as the number 65

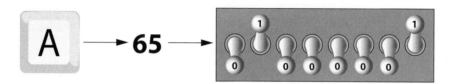

 TIP: The acronym ASCII is pronounced "askee."

In case you are curious, the ASCII code for uppercase B is 66, for uppercase C is 67, and so forth. Appendix C shows all the ASCII codes and the characters they represent.

The ASCII character set was developed in the early 1960s and was eventually adopted by almost all computer manufacturers. ASCII is limited, however, because it defines codes for only 128 characters. To remedy this, the Unicode character set was developed in the early 1990s. **Unicode** is an extensive encoding scheme that is compatible with ASCII and can also represent the characters of many of the world's languages. Today, Unicode is quickly becoming the standard character set used in the computer industry.

Advanced Number Storage

Earlier you saw how numbers are stored in memory. Perhaps it occurred to you then that the binary numbering system can be used to represent only integer numbers, beginning with 0. Negative numbers and real numbers (such as 3.14159) cannot be represented using the simple binary numbering technique we discussed.

Computers are able to store negative numbers and real numbers in memory, but to do so they use encoding schemes along with the binary numbering system. Negative numbers are encoded using a technique known as **two's complement**, and real numbers are encoded in **floating-point notation**. You don't need to know how these encoding schemes work, only that they are used to convert negative numbers and real numbers to binary format.

Other Types of Data

Computers are often referred to as digital devices. The term **digital** can be used to describe anything that uses binary numbers. **Digital data** is data that is stored in binary, and a **digital device** is any device that works with binary data. In this section we have discussed how numbers and characters are stored in binary, but computers also work with many other types of digital data.

For example, consider the pictures that you take with your digital camera. These images are composed of tiny dots of color known as **pixels**. (The term pixel stands for **picture element**.)

As shown in Figure 1-14, each pixel in an image is converted to a numeric code that represents the pixel's color. The numeric code is stored in memory as a binary number.

Figure 1-14 A digital image stored in binary format

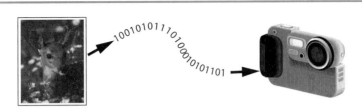

The music that you play on your CD player, iPod, or MP3 player is also digital. A digital song is broken into small pieces known as **samples**. Each sample is converted to a binary number, which can be stored in memory. The more samples that a song is divided into, the more it sounds like the original music when it is played back. A CD-quality song is divided into more than 44,000 samples per second!

 Checkpoint

1.12 What amount of memory is enough to store a letter of the alphabet or a small number?

1.13 What do you call a tiny "switch" that can be set to either on or off?

1.14 In what numbering system are all numeric values written as sequences of 0s and 1s?

1.15 What is the purpose of ASCII?

1.16 What encoding scheme is extensive enough to represent all the characters of many of the languages in the world?

1.17 What do the terms digital data and digital device mean?

1.4 **How a Program Works**

CONCEPT: A computer's CPU can understand only instructions written in machine language. Because people find it very difficult to write entire programs in machine language, other programming languages have been invented.

Earlier, we stated that the CPU is the most important component in a computer because it is the part of the computer that runs programs. Sometimes the CPU is called the "computer's brain," and is described as being "smart." Although these are common metaphors, you should understand that the CPU is not a brain, and it is not smart. The CPU is an electronic device that is designed to do specific things. In particular, the CPU is designed to perform operations such as the following:

- Reading a piece of data from main memory
- Adding two numbers
- Subtracting one number from another number
- Multiplying two numbers
- Dividing one number by another number
- Moving a piece of data from one memory location to another
- Determining whether one value is equal to another value.

As you can see from this list, the CPU performs simple operations on pieces of data. The CPU does nothing on its own, however. It has to be told what to do, which is the purpose of a program. A program is nothing more than a list of instructions that cause the CPU to perform operations.

Each instruction in a program is a command that tells the CPU to perform a specific operation. Here's an example of an instruction that might appear in a program:

```
10110000
```

To you and me, this is only a series of 0s and 1s. To a CPU, however, this is an instruction to perform an operation.[1] It is written in 0s and 1s because CPUs understand only instructions that are written in **machine language**, and machine language instructions are always written in binary.

A machine language instruction exists for each operation that a CPU is capable of performing. For example, there is an instruction for adding numbers; there is an instruction for subtracting one number from another; and so forth. The entire set of instructions that a CPU can execute is known as the CPU's **instruction set**.

> **NOTE:** There are several microprocessor companies today that manufacture CPUs. Some of the more well-known microprocessor companies are Intel, AMD, and Motorola. If you look carefully at your computer, you might find a tag showing a logo for its microprocessor.
>
> Each brand of microprocessor has its own unique instruction set, which is typically understood only by microprocessors of the same brand. For example, Intel microprocessors understand the same instructions, but they do not understand instructions for Motorola microprocessors.

The machine language instruction that was previously shown is an example of only one instruction. It takes a lot more than one instruction, however, for the computer to do anything meaningful. Because the operations that a CPU knows how to perform are so basic in nature, a meaningful task can be accomplished only if the CPU performs many operations. For example, if you want your computer to calculate the amount of interest that you will earn from your savings account this year, the CPU will have to perform a large number of instructions, carried out in the proper sequence. It is not unusual for a program to contain thousands or even a million or more machine language instructions.

Programs are usually stored on a secondary storage device such as a disk drive. When you install a program on your computer, the program is typically copied to your computer's disk drive from a CD-ROM or perhaps downloaded from a Web site.

Although a program can be stored on a secondary storage device such as a disk drive, it has to be copied into main memory, or RAM, each time the CPU executes it. For example, suppose you have a word processing program on your computer's disk. To execute the program, you use the mouse to double-click the program's icon. This causes the program to be copied from the disk into main memory. Then, the computer's CPU executes the copy of the program that is in main memory. This process is illustrated in Figure 1-15.

---

[1]The example shown is an actual instruction for an Intel microprocessor. It tells the microprocessor to move a value into the CPU.

Figure 1-15 A program being copied into main memory and then executed

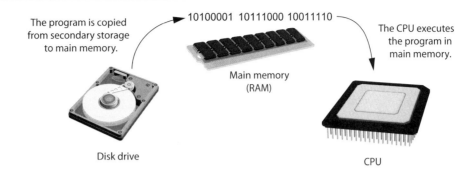

The program is copied from secondary storage to main memory.

10100001 10111000 10011110

The CPU executes the program in main memory.

Main memory (RAM)

Disk drive

CPU

When a CPU executes the instructions in a program, it is engaged in a process that is known as the **fetch-decode-execute cycle**. This cycle, which consists of three steps, is repeated for each instruction in the program. The steps are as follows:

1. **Fetch** A program is a long sequence of machine language instructions. The first step of the cycle is to fetch, or read, the next instruction from memory into the CPU.
2. **Decode** A machine language instruction is a binary number that represents a command that tells the CPU to perform an operation. In this step the CPU decodes the instruction that was just fetched from memory, to determine which operation it should perform.
3. **Execute** The last step in the cycle is to execute, or perform, the operation.

Figure 1-16 illustrates these steps.

Figure 1-16 The fetch-decode-execute cycle

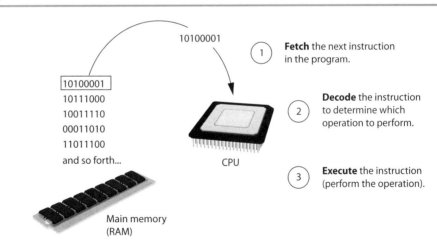

10100001

1 **Fetch** the next instruction in the program.

10100001
10111000
10011110
00011010
11011100
and so forth...

2 **Decode** the instruction to determine which operation to perform.

CPU

3 **Execute** the instruction (perform the operation).

Main memory (RAM)

From Machine Language to Assembly Language

Computers can execute only programs that are written in machine language. As previously mentioned, a program can have thousands or even a million or more binary instructions, and writing such a program would be very tedious and time consuming. Programming in machine language would also be very difficult because putting a 0 or a 1 in the wrong place would cause an error.

Although a computer's CPU understands only machine language, it is impractical for people to write programs in machine language. For this reason, **assembly language** was created in the early days of computing[2] as an alternative to machine language. Instead of using binary numbers for instructions, assembly language uses short words that are known as **mnemonics**. For example, in assembly language, the mnemonic add typically means to add numbers, mul typically means to multiply numbers, and mov typically means to move a value to a location in memory. When a programmer uses assembly language to write a program, he or she can write short mnemonics instead of binary numbers.

> **NOTE:** There are many different versions of assembly language. It was mentioned earlier that each brand of CPU has its own machine language instruction set. Each brand of CPU typically has its own assembly language as well.

Assembly language programs cannot be executed by the CPU, however. The CPU understands only machine language, so a special program known as an **assembler** is used to translate an assembly language program to a machine language program. This process is shown in Figure 1-17. The CPU can then execute the machine language program that the assembler creates.

Figure 1-17 An assembler translating an assembly language program to a machine language program

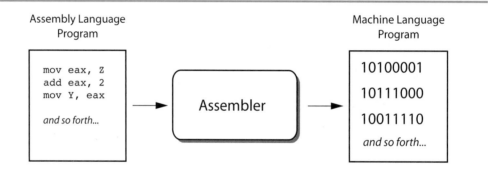

High-Level Languages

Although assembly language makes it unnecessary to write binary machine language instructions, it is not without difficulties. Assembly language is primarily a direct substitute for machine language, and like machine language, it requires that you know a lot about the CPU. Assembly language also requires that you write a large number of instructions for even the simplest program. Because assembly language is so close in nature to machine language, it is referred to as a **low-level language**.

In the 1950s, a new generation of programming languages known as high-level languages began to appear. A **high-level language** allows you to create powerful and complex programs without knowing how the CPU works and without writing large numbers of low-level instructions. In addition, most high-level languages use words that are easy to understand. For example, if a programmer were using COBOL (which was one of the early high-level languages created in the 1950s), he or she would write the following instruction to display the message *Hello world* on the computer screen:

```
DISPLAY "Hello world"
```

---

[2]The first assembly language was most likely developed in the 1940s at Cambridge University for use with a historical computer known as the EDSAC.

Doing the same thing in assembly language would require several instructions and an intimate knowledge of how the CPU interacts with the computer's video circuitry. As you can see from this example, high-level languages allow programmers to concentrate on the tasks they want to perform with their programs rather than the details of how the CPU will execute those programs.

Since the 1950s, thousands of high-level languages have been created. Table 1-1 lists several of the more well-known languages.

Table 1-1 Programming languages

Language	Description
Ada	Ada was created in the 1970s, primarily for applications used by the U.S. Department of Defense. The language is named in honor of Countess Ada Lovelace, an influential and historical figure in the field of computing.
BASIC	**Beginners All-purpose Symbolic Instruction Code** is a general-purpose language that was originally designed in the early 1960s to be simple enough for beginners to learn. Today, there are many different versions of BASIC.
FORTRAN	**FOR**mula **TRAN**slator was the first high-level programming language. It was designed in the 1950s for performing complex mathematical calculations.
COBOL	**Common Business-Oriented Language** was created in the 1950s and was designed for business applications.
Pascal	Pascal was created in 1970 and was originally designed for teaching programming. The language was named in honor of the mathematician, physicist, and philosopher Blaise Pascal.
C and C++	C and C++ (pronounced "c plus plus") are powerful, general-purpose languages developed at Bell Laboratories. The C language was created in 1972, and the C++ language was created in 1983.
C#	Pronounced "c sharp," this language was created by Microsoft around the year 2000 for developing applications based on the Microsoft .NET platform.
Java	Java was created by Sun Microsystems in the early 1990s. It can be used to develop programs that run on a single computer or over the Internet from a Web server.
JavaScript	JavaScript, created in the 1990s, can be used in Web pages. Despite its name, JavaScript is not related to Java.
Python	Python is a general-purpose language created in the early 1990s. It has become popular in business and academic applications.
Ruby	Ruby is a general-purpose language that was created in the 1990s. It is increasingly becoming a popular language for programs that run on Web servers.
Visual Basic	Visual Basic (commonly known as VB) is a Microsoft programming language and software development environment that allows programmers to create Windows-based applications quickly. VB was originally created in the early 1990s.

Keywords, Operators, and Syntax: An Overview

Each high-level language has its own set of predefined words that the programmer must use to write a program. The words that make up a high-level programming language are known as **keywords** or **reserved words**. Each keyword has a specific meaning and cannot be used for any other purpose. Table 1-2 shows the keywords in the C# programming language.

Table 1-2 The C# keywords

abstract	as	base	bool
break	byte	case	catch
char	checked	class	const
continue	decimal	default	delegate
do	double	else	enum
event	explicit	extern	false
finally	fixed	float	for
foreach	goto	if	implicit
in	in	int	interface
internal	is	lock	long
namespace	new	null	object
operator	out	out	override
params	private	protected	public
readonly	ref	return	sbyte
sealed	short	sizeof	stackalloc
static	string	struct	switch
this	throw	true	try
typeof	uint	ulong	unchecked
unsafe	ushort	using	virtual
void	volatile	while	

In addition to keywords, programming languages have **operators** that perform various operations on data. For example, all programming languages have math operators that perform arithmetic. In C#, as well as most other languages, the + sign is an operator that adds two numbers. The following adds 12 and 75:

```
12 + 75
```

There are numerous other operators in the C# language, many of which you will learn about as you progress through this text.

In addition to keywords and operators, each language also has its own **syntax**, which is a set of rules that must be strictly followed when writing a program. The syntax rules dictate how keywords, operators, and various punctuation characters must be used in a program. When you are learning a programming language, you must learn the syntax rules for that particular language.

The individual instructions that you use to write a program in a high-level programming language are called **statements**. A programming statement can consist of keywords, operators, punctuation, and other allowable programming elements, arranged in the proper sequence to perform an operation.

Compilers and Interpreters

Because the CPU understands only machine language instructions, programs that are written in a high-level language must be translated into machine language. Depending on the language in which a program has been written, the programmer will use either a compiler or an interpreter to make the translation.

A **compiler** is a program that translates a high-level language program into a separate machine language program. The machine language program can then be executed any time it is needed. This is shown in Figure 1-18. As shown in the figure, compiling and executing are two different processes.

Figure 1-18 Compiling a high-level program and executing it

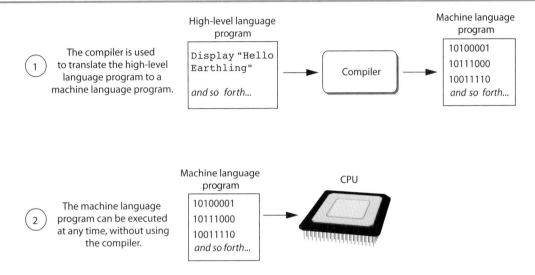

Some programming languages use an **interpreter,** which is a program that both translates and executes the instructions in a high-level language program. As the interpreter reads each individual instruction in the program, it converts it to a machine language instruction and then immediately executes it. This process repeats for every instruction in the program. This process is illustrated in Figure 1-19. Because interpreters combine translation and execution, they typically do not create separate machine language programs.

Figure 1-19 Executing a high-level program with an interpreter

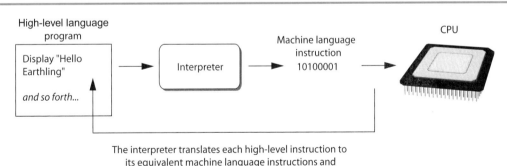

The statements that a programmer writes in a high-level language are called **source code,** or simply **code.** Typically, the programmer types a program's code into a text editor and then saves the code in a file on the computer's disk. Next, the programmer uses a compiler to translate the code into a machine language program or an interpreter to translate and execute the code. If the code contains a syntax error, however, it cannot be translated. A **syntax error** is a mistake such as a misspelled keyword, a missing punctuation character, or the incorrect use of an operator. When this happens, the compiler or interpreter displays an error message, indicating that the program contains a syntax error. The programmer corrects the error and then attempts once again to translate the program.

NOTE: Human languages also have syntax rules. Do you remember when you took your first English class and you learned all those rules about commas, apostrophes, capitalization, and so forth? You were learning the syntax of the English language.

Although people commonly violate the syntax rules of their native language when speaking and writing, other people usually understand what they mean. Unfortunately, compilers and interpreters do not have this ability. If even a single syntax error appears in a program, the program cannot be compiled or executed.

Checkpoint

1.18 A CPU understands instructions that are written only in what language?

1.19 A program has to be copied into what type of memory each time the CPU executes it?

1.20 When a CPU executes the instructions in a program, it is engaged in what process?

1.21 What is assembly language?

1.22 What type of programming language allows you to create powerful and complex programs without knowing how the CPU works?

1.23 Each language has a set of rules that must be strictly followed when writing a program. What is this set of rules called?

1.24 What do you call a program that translates a high-level language program into a separate machine language program?

1.25 What do you call a program that both translates and executes the instructions in a high-level language program?

1.26 What type of mistake is usually caused by a misspelled keyword, a missing punctuation character, or the incorrect use of an operator?

1.5 Graphical User Interfaces

CONCEPT: A graphical user interface allows the user to interact with a program using graphical elements such as icons, buttons, and dialog boxes.

Programmers commonly use the term **user** to describe any hypothetical person that might be using a computer and its programs. A computer's **user interface** is the part of the computer with which the user interacts. One part of the user interface consists of hardware devices, such as the keyboard and the video display. Another part of the user interface involves the way that the computer's operating system and application software accepts commands from the user. For many years, the only way that the user could interact with a computer was through a command line interface. A **command line interface**, which is also known as a **console interface**, requires the user to type commands. If a command is typed correctly, it is executed and the results are displayed. If a command is not typed correctly, an error message is displayed. Figure 1-20 shows the Windows command prompt window, which is an example of a command line interface.

Figure 1-20 A command line interface

```
C:\Windows\system32\cmd.exe

C:\Users\Tony\Images>dir
 Volume in drive C has no label.
 Volume Serial Number is 2414-0F08

 Directory of C:\Users\Tony\Images

03/04/2010  11:54 AM    <DIR>          .
03/04/2010  11:54 AM    <DIR>          ..
09/22/2008  09:12 AM            73,165 Beach.jpg
09/17/2008  01:07 PM           263,212 Boston.jpg
09/25/2008  12:15 PM           230,454 Dog.bmp
09/25/2008  10:21 AM           921,654 Mountains.bmp
09/25/2008  12:23 PM           921,654 Snow.bmp
09/25/2008  10:22 AM           921,654 Station.bmp
               6 File(s)      3,331,793 bytes
               2 Dir(s)  40,247,824,384 bytes free

C:\Users\Tony\Images> _
```

Many computer users, especially beginners, find command line interfaces difficult to use. This is because there are many commands to be learned, and each command has its own syntax, much like a programming statement. If a command isn't entered correctly, it will not work.

In the 1980s, a new type of interface known as a graphical user interface came into use in commercial operating systems. A **graphical user interface**, or **GUI** (pronounced "gooey"), allows the user to interact with the operating system and application programs through graphical elements on the screen. GUIs also popularized the use of the mouse as an input device. Instead of requiring the user to type commands on the keyboard, GUIs allow the user to point at graphical elements and click the mouse button to activate them.

Much of the interaction with a GUI is done through windows that display information and allow the user to perform actions. Figure 1-21 shows an example of a window that allows the user to change the system's Internet settings. Instead of typing cryptic commands, the user interacts with graphical elements such as icons, buttons, and slider bars.

Figure 1-21 A window in a graphical user interface

Event-Driven GUI Programs

In a text-based environment, such as a command line interface, programs determine the order in which things happen. For example, Figure 1-22 shows the interaction that has taken place in a text environment with a program that calculates an employee's gross pay. First, the program told the user to enter the number of hours worked. In the figure, the user entered 40 and pressed the Enter key. Next, the program told the user to enter his or her hourly pay rate. In the figure, the user entered 50.00, and pressed the Enter key. Then, the program displayed the user's gross pay. As the program was running, the user had no choice but to enter the data in the order requested.

Figure 1-22 Interaction with a program in a text environment

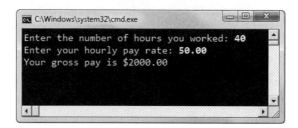

In a GUI environment, however, the user determines the order in which things happen. For example, Figure 1-23 shows a GUI program that calculates an employee's gross pay. Notice that there are boxes in which the user enters the number of hours worked and the hourly pay rate. The user can enter the hours and the pay rate in any order he or she wishes. If the user makes a mistake, the user can erase the data that was entered and re-type it. When the user is ready to calculate the area, he or she uses the mouse to click the *Calculate Gross Pay* button and the program performs the calculation.

Figure 1-23 A GUI program

Because GUI programs must respond to the actions of the user, they are said to be **event driven**. The user causes events, such as the clicking of a button, and the program responds to those events.

This book focuses exclusively on the development of GUI applications using the C# programming language. As you work through this book, you will learn to create applications that interact with the user through windows containing graphical objects. You will also learn how to program your applications to respond to the events that take place as the user interacts with them.

 **Checkpoint**

1.27 What is a user interface?

1.28 How does a command line interface work?

1.29 When the user runs a program in a text-based environment, such as the command line, what determines the order in which things happen?

1.30 What is an event-driven program?

1.6 Objects

CONCEPT: An object is a program component that contains data and performs operations. Programs use objects to perform specific tasks.

Have you ever driven a car? If so, you know that a car is made of a lot of components. A car has a steering wheel, an accelerator pedal, a brake pedal, a gear shifter, a speedometer, and numerous other devices with which the driver interacts. There are also a lot of components under the hood, such as the engine, the battery, the radiator, and so forth. A car is not just one single object, but rather a collection of objects that work together.

This same notion also applies to computer programming. Most programming languages that are used today are **object oriented**. When you use an object-oriented language, you create programs by putting together a collection of objects. In programming, an object is not a physical device, however, like a steering wheel or a brake pedal. Instead, it is a software component that exists in the computer's memory. In software, an object has two general capabilities:

- An object can store data. The data stored in an object are commonly called **fields**, or **properties**.
- An object can perform operations. The operations that an object can perform are called **methods**.

When you write a program using an object-oriented language, you use objects to accomplish specific tasks. Some objects have a visual part that can be seen on the screen. For example, Figure 1-24 shows the wage-calculator program that we discussed in the previous section. The graphical user interface is made of the following objects:

Form object   A window that is displayed on the screen is called a **Form object**. Figure 1-24 shows a Form object that contains several other graphical objects.

Label objects   A **Label** object displays text on a form. The form shown in Figure 1-24 contains two Label objects. One of the Label objects displays the text *Number of Hours Worked* and the other Label object displays the text *Hourly Pay Rate*.

Figure 1-24 Objects used in a GUI

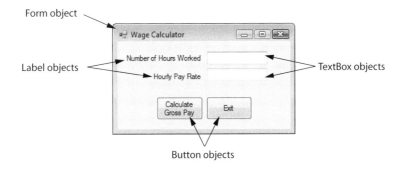

TextBox objects	A **TextBox** object appears as a rectangular region that can accept keyboard input from the user. The form shown in Figure 1-24 has two TextBox objects: one in which the user enters the number of hours worked and another in which the user enters the hourly pay rate.
Button objects	A **Button** object appears on a form as a button with a caption written across its face. When the user clicks a Button object with the mouse, an action takes place. The form in Figure 1-24 has two Button objects. One shows the caption *Calculate Gross Pay*. When the user clicks this button, the program calculates and displays the gross pay. The other button shows the caption *Exit*. When the user clicks this button, the program ends.

Forms, Labels, TextBoxes, and Buttons are just a few of the objects that you will learn to use in C#. As you study this book, you will create applications that incorporate many different types of objects.

Visible versus Invisible Objects

Objects that are visible in a program's graphical user interface are commonly referred to as **controls**. We could say that the form shown in Figure 1-24 contains two Label controls, two TextBox controls, and two Button controls. When an object is referred to as a control, it simply means that the object plays a role in a program's graphical user interface.

Not all objects can be seen on the screen, however. Some objects exist only in memory for the purpose of helping your program perform some task. For example, there are objects that read data from files, objects that generate random numbers, objects that store and sort large collections of data, and so forth. These types of objects help your program perform tasks, but they do not directly display anything on the screen. When you are writing a program, you will use objects that can help your program perform its tasks. Some of the objects that you use will be controls (visible in the program's GUI), and other objects will be invisible.

Classes: Where Objects Come From

Objects are very useful, but they don't just magically appear in your program. Before a specific type of object can be used, that object has to be created in memory. And, before an object can be created in memory, you must have a class for the object.

A **class** is code that describes a particular type of object. It specifies the data that an object can hold (the object's fields and properties), and the actions that an object can perform (the object's methods). You will learn much more about classes as you progress through this book, but for now, just think of a class as a code "blueprint" that can be used to create a particular type of object.

The .NET Framework

C# is a very popular programming language, but there are a lot of things it cannot do by itself. For example, you cannot use C# alone to create a graphical user interface, read data from files, work with databases, or many of the other things that programs commonly need to do. C# provides only the basic keywords and operators that you need to construct a program.

So, if the C# language doesn't provide the classes and other code necessary for creating GUIs and performing many other advanced operations, where do those classes and code come from? The answer is the .NET Framework. The **.NET Framework** is a collection of classes and other code that can be used, along with a programming language such as C#, to create programs for the Windows operating system. For example, the .NET Framework provides classes to create Forms, TextBoxes, Labels, Buttons, and many other types of objects.

When you use Visual C# to write programs, you are using a combination of the C# language and the .NET Framework. As you work through this book you will not only learn C#, but you will also learn about many of the classes and other features provided by the .NET Framework.

Writing Your Own Classes

The .NET Framework provides many prewritten classes ready for use in your programs. There will be times, however, that you will wish you had an object to perform a specific task, and no such class will exist in the .NET Framework. This is not a problem because in C# you can write your own classes that have the specific fields, properties, and methods that you need for any situation. In Chapter 9 you will learn to create classes for the specific objects that you need in your programs.

 Checkpoint

1.31 What is an object?

1.32 What type of language is used to create programs by putting together a collection of objects?

1.33 What two general capabilities does an object have?

1.34 What term is commonly used to refer to objects such as TextBoxes, Labels, and Buttons that are visible in a program's graphical user interface?

1.35 What is the purpose of an object that cannot be seen on the screen and exists only in memory?

1.36 What is a class?

1.37 What is the .NET Framework?

1.38 Why might you need to write your own classes?

 1.7 ## The Program Development Process

CONCEPT: Creating a program requires several steps, which include designing the program's logic, creating the user interface, writing code, testing, and debugging.

The Program Development Cycle

Previously in this chapter you learned that programmers typically use high-level languages such as C# to create programs. There is much more to creating a program than writing code, however. The process of creating a program that works correctly typically requires the six phases shown in Figure 1-25. The entire process is known as the **program development cycle**.

Figure 1-25 The program development cycle

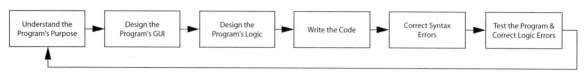

Let's take a closer look at each stage in the cycle.

1. **Understand the Program's Purpose**

   When beginning a new programming project, it is essential that you understand what the program is supposed to do. Most programs perform the following three-step process:

   Step 1. Input is received.
   Step 2. Some process is performed on the input.
   Step 3. Output is produced.

   Input is any data that the program receives while it is running. Once input is received, some process, such as a mathematical calculation, is usually performed on it. The results of the process are then sent out of the program as output. If you can identify these three elements of a program (input, process, and output), then you are on your way to understanding what the program is supposed to do.

   For example, suppose you have been asked to write a program to calculate and display the gross pay for an hourly paid employee. Here is a summary of the program's input, process, and output:

   Input:

   • Input the number of hours that the employee worked.
   • Input the employee's hourly pay rate.

   Process:

   • Multiply the number of hours worked by the hourly pay rate. The result is the employee's gross pay.

   Output:

   • Display the employee's gross pay on the screen.

2. **Design the Graphical User Interface (GUI)**

   Once you clearly understand what the program is supposed to do, you can begin designing its graphical user interface. Often, you will find it helpful to draw a sketch of each form that the program displays. For example, if you are designing a program that calculates gross pay, Figure 1-26 shows how you might sketch the program's form.

   Notice that the sketch identifies each type of control (GUI object) that will appear on the form. The TextBox controls will allow the user to enter input. The user will type the number of hours worked into one of the TextBoxes and the employee's hourly pay rate into the other TextBox. Notice that Label controls are placed on the form to tell the user what data to enter. When the user clicks the Button control that reads *Calculate Gross Pay*, the program will display the employee's gross pay on the screen in a pop-up window. When the user clicks the Button control that reads *Exit*, the program will end.

   Once you are satisfied with the sketches that you have created for the program's forms, you can begin creating the actual forms on the computer. As a Visual C# programmer, you have a powerful environment known as Visual Studio at your disposal. Visual Studio gives you a "what you see is what you get" editor that allows you to visually design a program's forms. You can use Visual Studio to create the program's

Figure 1-26 Form sketch

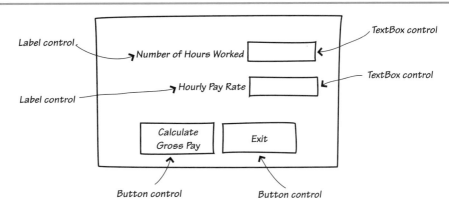

forms, place all the necessary controls on the forms, and set each control's properties so it has the desired appearance. For example, Figure 1-27 shows the actual form that you might create for the wage-calculator program, which calculates gross pay.

Figure 1-27 Form for the wage-calculator program

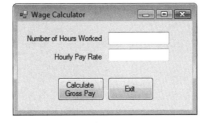

3. **Design the Program's Logic**

In this phase you break down each task that the program must perform into a series of logical steps. For example, if you look back at Figure 1-27, notice that the pay-calculating program's form has a Button control that reads *Calculate Gross Pay*. When the user clicks this button, you want the program to display the employee's gross pay. Here are the steps that the program should take to perform that task:

Step 1. Get the number of hours worked from the appropriate TextBox.
Step 2. Get the hourly pay rate from the appropriate TextBox.
Step 3. Calculate the gross pay as the number of hours worked times the hourly pay rate.
Step 4. Display the gross pay in a pop-up window.

This is an example of an **algorithm**, which is a set of well-defined, logical steps that must be taken to perform a task. An algorithm that is written out in this manner, in plain English statements, is called **pseudocode**. (The word *pseudo* means fake, so pseudocode is fake code.) The process of informally writing out the steps of an algorithm in pseudocode before attempting to write any actual code is very helpful when you are designing a program. Because you do not have to worry about breaking any syntax rules, you can focus on the logical steps that the program must perform.

Flowcharting is another tool that programmers use to design programs. A **flowchart** is a diagram that graphically depicts the steps of an algorithm. Figure 1-28 shows how you might create a flowchart for the wage-calculator algorithm. Notice that there are three types of symbols in the flowchart: ovals, parallelograms, and a rectangle. Each of these symbols represents a step in the algorithm, as described here:

- The ovals, which appear at the top and bottom of the flowchart, are called **terminal symbols**. The **Start terminal** symbol marks the program's starting point and the **End terminal** symbol marks the program's ending point.
- Parallelograms are used as **input symbols** and **output symbols**. They represent steps in which the program reads input or displays output.
- Rectangles are used as **processing symbols**. They represent steps in which the program performs some process on data, such as a mathematical calculation.

Figure 1-28 Flowchart for the wage-calculator program

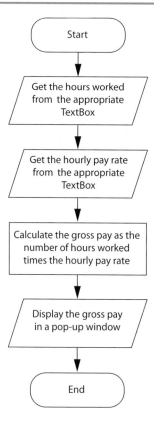

The symbols are connected by arrows that represent the "flow" of the program. To step through the symbols in the proper order, you begin at the *Start* terminal and follow the arrows until you reach the *End* terminal.

4. **Write the Code**

   Once you have created a program's GUI and designed algorithms for the program's tasks, you are ready to start writing code. During this process, you will refer to the pseudocode or flowcharts that you created in Step 3 and use Visual Studio to write C# code.

5. **Correct Syntax Errors**

You previously learned in this chapter that a programming language such as C# has rules, known as syntax, that must be followed when writing a program. A language's syntax rules dictate things such as how key words, operators, and punctuation characters can be used. A syntax error occurs if the programmer violates any of these rules. If the program contains a syntax error or even a simple mistake such as a misspelled key word, the program cannot be compiled or executed.

Virtually all code contains syntax errors when it is first written, so the programmer will typically spend some time correcting these. Once all the syntax errors and simple typing mistakes have been corrected, the program can be compiled and translated into an executable program.

4. **Test the Program and Correct Logic Errors**

Once the code is in an executable form, you must then test it to determine whether any logic errors exist. A **logic error** is a mistake that does not prevent the program from running but causes it to produce incorrect results. (Mathematical mistakes are common causes of logic errors.) If the program produces incorrect results, the programmer must **debug** the code. This means that the programmer finds and corrects logic errors in the program. Sometimes, during this process, the programmer discovers that the program's original design must be changed. In this event, the program development cycle starts over and continues until no errors can be found.

 Checkpoint

1.39 List the six steps in the program development cycle.

1.40 What is an algorithm?

1.41 What is pseudocode?

1.42 What is a flowchart?

1.43 What do each of the following symbols mean in a flowchart?
- Oval
- Parallelogram
- Rectangle

1.8 Getting Started with the Visual Studio Environment

CONCEPT: Visual Studio and Visual C# Express consist of tools that you use to build Visual C# applications. The first step in using Visual C# is learning about these tools.

To follow the tutorials in this book, and create Visual C# applications, you will need to install either Visual Studio 2010 or Visual C# 2010 Express on your computer. **Visual Studio 2010** is a professional **integrated development environment** (IDE), which means that it provides all the necessary tools for creating, testing, and debugging software. It can be used to create applications not only with Visual C#, but also with other languages such as Visual Basic and C++. If you are using a school's computer lab, there's a good chance that Visual Studio 2010 has been installed.

If you do not have access to Visual Studio 2010, you can install **Visual C# 2010 Express**, a free programming environment that is streamlined for Visual C# development. (When this book is purchased new, it has an accompanying Microsoft DVD that contains Visual C# 2010 Express.)

For the purposes of this book, it does not matter whether you are using Visual Studio 2010 or Visual C# 2010 Express. Both products look very similar and work in a similar manner. When there are differences, the book will alert you. To keep things simple, this book will use the term **Visual Studio** to refer to either Visual Studio 2010 or Visual C# 2010 Express. When you are instructed to use Visual Studio to perform some task, use the system that is installed on your computer.

Visual Studio is a customizable environment. If you are working in your school's computer lab, there's a chance that someone else has customized the programming environment to suit his or her own preferences. If this is the case, the screens that you see may not match exactly the ones shown in this book. For that reason it's a good idea to reset the programming environment before you create a Visual C# application. Tutorial 1-1 guides you through the process.

Tutorial 1-1:
Starting Visual Studio and Setting Up the Environment

Step 1: Find out from your instructor whether you are using Visual Studio 2010 or Visual C# 2010 Express. Then, click the *Start* button, open the *All Programs* menu, and perform one of the following:

- If you are using Visual Studio, open the Microsoft Visual Studio 2010 program group and then execute Visual Studio 2010.
- If you are using Visual C# 2010 Express, open the Microsoft Visual Studio 2010 Express program group and then execute Visual C# 2010 Express.

> **NOTE:** If you are using Visual Studio rather than Visual C# Express, the first time you run the software, you will see a window entitled *Choose Default Environment Settings*. Select *Visual C# Development Settings* from the list and click the *Start Visual Studio* button.

Step 2: Figure 1-29 shows the Visual Studio environment. The screen shown in the figure is known as the *Start Page*. By default, the *Start Page* is displayed when you start Visual Studio, but you may not see it because it can be disabled.

Notice the checkbox in the bottom left corner of the *Start Page* that reads *Show page on startup*. If this box is not checked, the *Start Page* will not be displayed when you start Visual Studio. If you do not see the *Start Page*, you can always display it by clicking *View* on the menu bar at the top of the screen and then clicking *Start Page*.

Figure 1-29 Visual Studio *Start Page*

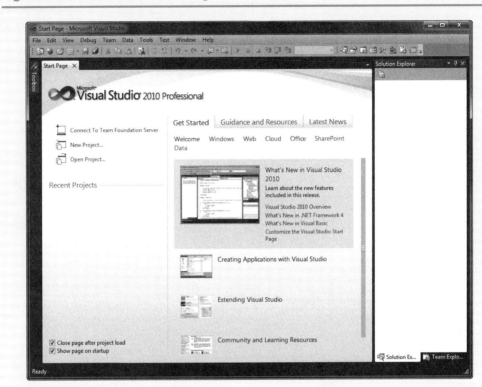

Step 3: This step is applicable *only* if you are using Visual Studio. If you are using Visual C# Express, skip to Step 4. In a school computer lab, it is possible that the Visual Studio environment has been set up for a programming language other than Visual C#. To make sure that Visual Studio looks and behaves as described in this book, you should make sure that Visual C# is selected as the programming environment. Perform the following:

- As shown in Figure 1-30, click *Tools* on the menu bar and then click *Import and Export Settings....*
- On the screen that appears next, select *Reset all settings* and click the *Next >* button.
- On the screen that appears next, select *No, just reset settings, overwriting my current settings*, and then click the *Next >* button.
- The window shown in Figure 1-31 should appear next. Select *Visual C# Development Settings* and then click the *Finish* button.
- After a moment you should see a *Reset Complete* window. Click the *Close* button and continue with the next step in the tutorial.

Step 4: Now you will reset Visual Studio's window layout to the default configuration. As shown in Figure 1-32, click *Window* on the menu bar and then click *Reset Window Layout*. Next you will see a dialog box asking *Are you sure you want to restore the default window layout for the environment?* Click *Yes*.

The Visual Studio environment is now set up so you can follow the remaining tutorials in this book. If you are working in your school's computer lab, it is probably a good idea to go through these steps each time you start Visual Studio. If you are continuing with the next tutorial, leave Visual Studio running. You can exit Visual Studio at any time by clicking *File* on the menu bar and then clicking *Exit*.

Figure 1-30 Selecting *Tools* and then *Import and Export Settings …*

Figure 1-31 Selecting Visual C# Development Settings

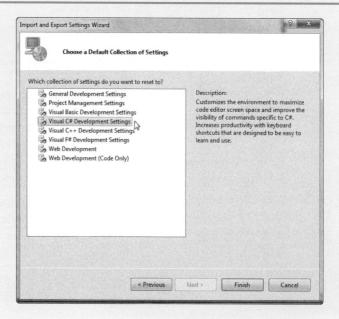

Figure 1-32 Resetting the window layout

Starting a New Project

Each Visual C# application that you create is called a **project**. When you are ready to create a new application, you start a new project. Tutorial 1-2 leads you through the steps of starting a new Visual C# project.

Tutorial 1-2:
Starting a New Visual C# Project

Step 1: If Visual Studio is not already running, start it as you did in Tutorial 1-1.

Step 2: **If you are using Visual Studio 2010:** Click *File* on the menu bar at the top of the screen, then select *New*, and then select *Project*. After doing this, the *New Project* window shown in Figure 1-33 should be displayed.

Figure 1-33 The *New Project* window

If you are using Visual C# 2010 Express: Click *File* on the menu bar at the top of the screen and then select *New Project*. After doing this, a *New Project* window similar to Figure 1-33 should be displayed. (With Visual C# Express, the window will have fewer items than shown in the figure.)

Step 3:   At the left side of the window, under *Installed Templates*, make sure *Visual C#* is selected. (If you are using Visual C# Express, that will be the only choice.) Then, select *Windows Forms Application*, as shown in Figure 1-33.

Step 4:   At the bottom of the *New Project* window, you see a *Name* text box. This is where you enter the name of your project. The *Name* text box will be automatically filled in with a default name. In Figure 1-33 the default name is *WindowsApplication1*. Change the project name to *My First Project*, as shown in Figure 1-34.

Figure 1-34 Changing the project name to *My First Project*

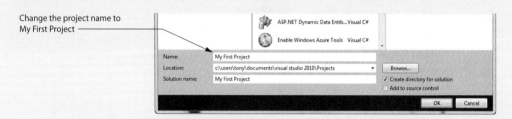

If you are using Visual Studio 2010: Just below the *Name* text box you will see a *Location* text box and a *Solution name* text box.

- The *Location* text box shows where a folder will be created to hold the project. If you wish to change the location, click the *Browse* button and select the desired location.
- A solution is a container that holds a project, and the *Solution name* text box shows the name of the solution that will hold this project. By default, the solution name is the same as the project name. For all the projects that you create in this book, you should keep the solution name the same as the project name.

> **NOTE:** As you work through this book you will create a lot of Visual C# projects. As you do, you will find that default names such as *WindowsApplication1* do not help you remember what each project does. Therefore, you should always change the name of a new project to something that describes the project's purpose.

Step 5:   Click the *OK* button to create the project. It might take a moment for the project to be created. Once it is, the Visual Studio environment should appear, similar to Figure 1-35. Notice that the name of the project, *My First Project*, is displayed in the title bar at the top of the Visual Studio window.

Leave Visual Studio running and complete the next tutorial.

Figure 1-35 The Visual Studio environment with a new project open

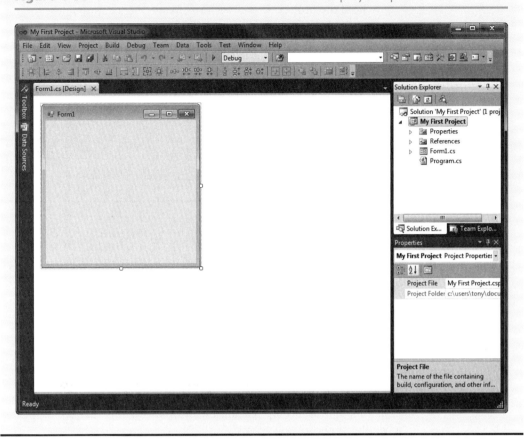

Tutorial 1-3:
Saving and Closing a Project

As you work on a project, you should get into the habit of saving it often. In this tutorial you will save the My First Project application and then close it.

Step 1: Visual Studio should still be running from the previous tutorial. To save the project that is currently open, click *File* on the menu bar and then select *Save All*.

If you are using Visual C# 2010 Express: The first time you save a project, the *Save Project* window will appear, as shown in Figure 1-36.

• The *Name* text box shows the project name that you entered when you created the project. Leave this unchanged.

Figure 1-36 The *Save Project* window in Visual C# 2010 Express

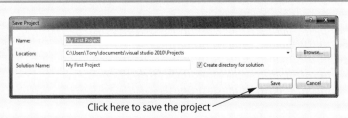

Click here to save the project

- The *Location* text box shows where a folder will be created on your system to hold the project. If you wish to change the location, click the *Browse* button and select the desired drive and folder.
- A solution is a container that holds a project, and the *Solution name* text box shows the name of the solution that will hold this project. By default, the solution name is the same as the project name. For all the projects that you create in this book, you should keep the solution name the same as the project name.

Click the *Save* button to save the project. (If possible, leave Visual Studio running so you can complete the next tutorial.)

Step 2: To close the project, click File on the menu bar and then click *Close Solution*.

The Visual Studio Environment

The Visual Studio environment consists of a number of windows that you will use on a regular basis. Figure 1-37 shows the locations of the following windows that appear within the Visual Studio environment: the **Designer** window, the **Solution Explorer** window, and the **Properties** window. Here is a brief summary of each window's purpose:

- The *Designer* Window

  You use the *Designer* window to create an application's graphical user interface. The Designer window shows the application's form and allows you to visually design its appearance by placing the desired controls that will appear on the form when the application executes.

- The *Solution Explorer* Window

  A solution is a container for holding Visual C# projects. (We discuss solutions in greater detail in a moment.) When you create a new C# project, a new solution is automatically created to contain it. The *Solution Explorer* window allows you to navigate among the files in a Visual C# project.

- The *Properties* Window

  A control's appearance and other characteristics are determined by the control's properties. When you are creating a Visual C# application, you use the *Properties* window to examine and change a control's properties.

  Remember that Visual Studio is a customizable environment. You can move the various windows around, so they may not appear in the exact locations shown in Figure 1-37 on your system.

Displaying the Solution Explorer and Properties Windows

If you do not see the *Solution Explorer* or the *Properties* window, you can follow these steps to make them visible:

- If you do not see the *Solution Explorer* window, click *View* on the menu bar. On the *View* menu, click *Solution Explorer*. (In Visual C# Express, click *View*, *Other Windows*, *Solution Explorer*.) You can also press Ctrl+W, and then press S on the keyboard.

Figure 1-37 The *Designer* window, *Solution Explorer* window, and *Properties* window

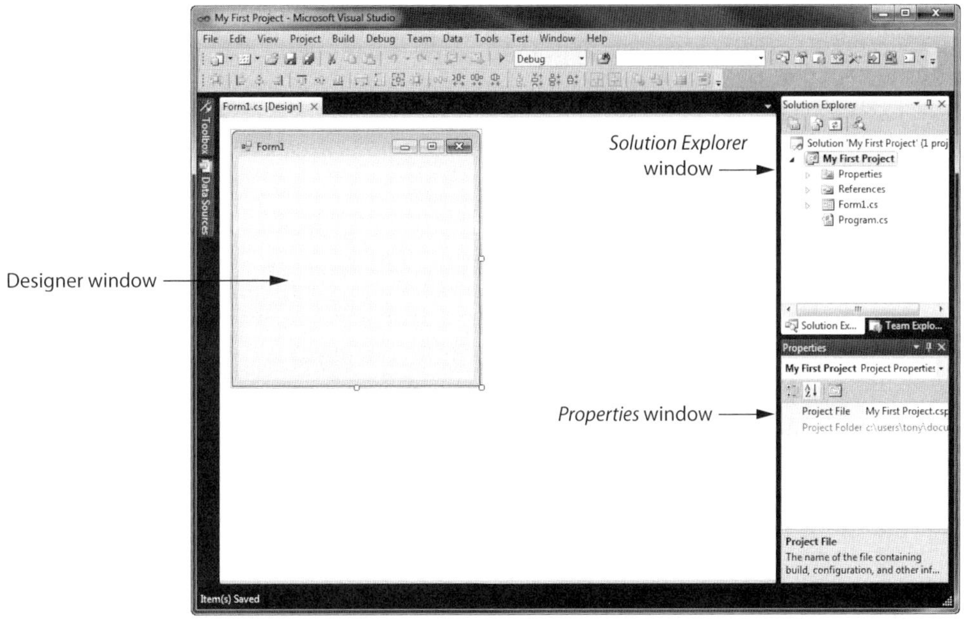

Solution Explorer window

Designer window

Properties window

- If you do not see the *Properties* window, click *View* on the menu bar. On the *View* menu, click *Properties*. (In Visual C# Express, click *View*, *Other Windows*, *Properties*.) You can also press Ctrl+W and then press P on the keyboard.

Using Auto Hide

Many windows in Visual Studio have a feature known as **Auto Hide**. When you see the pushpin icon in a window's title bar, as shown in Figure 1-38, you know that the window has Auto Hide capability. You click the pushpin icon to turn Auto Hide on or off for a window.

Figure 1-38 *Auto Hide* pushpin icon

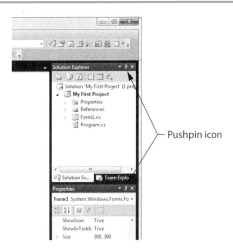

Pushpin icon

When Auto Hide is turned on, the window is displayed only as a tab along one of the edges of the *Visual Studio* environment. This feature gives you more room to view your application's forms and code. Figure 1-39 shows how the *Solution Explorer* and *Properties* windows appear when their Auto Hide feature is turned on. Notice the tabs that read *Solution Explorer* and *Properties* along the right edge of the screen. (Figure 1-39 also shows a *Team Explorer* tab. You might see this tab if you are using Visual Studio 2010. We do not discuss the *Team Explorer* in this book.)

Figure 1-39 The *Solution Explorer* and *Properties* windows hidden

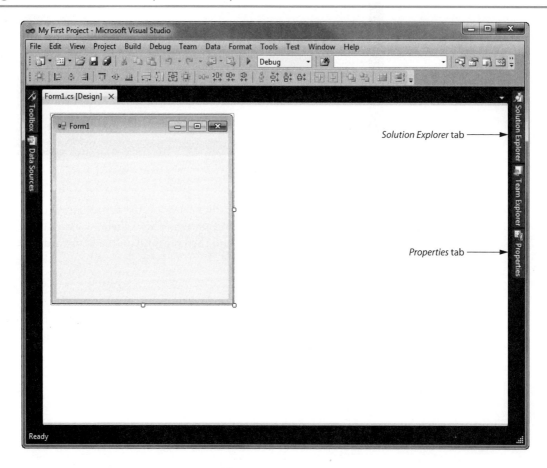

The Menu Bar and the Standard Toolbar

You've already used the Visual Studio menu bar several times. This is the bar at the top of the Visual Studio window that provides menus such as *File*, *Edit*, *View*, *Project*, and so forth. As you progress through this book, you will become familiar with many of the menus.

Below the menu bar is the standard toolbar. The **standard toolbar** contains buttons that execute frequently used commands. All commands that are displayed on the toolbar may also be executed from a menu, but the standard toolbar gives you quicker access to them. Figure 1-40 identifies the standard toolbar buttons that you will use most often, and Table 1-3 gives a brief description of each.

Figure 1-40 Visual Studio toolbar buttons

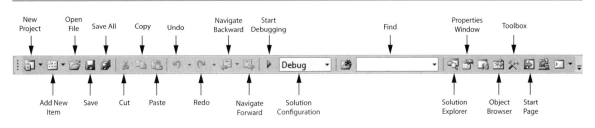

Table 1-3 Visual Basic toolbar buttons

Toolbar Button	Description
New Project	Starts a new project
Add New Item	Adds a new item such as a form to the current project
Open File	Opens an existing file
Save	Saves the file named by *filename*
Save All	Saves all the files in the current project
Cut	Cuts the selected item to the clipboard
Copy	Copies the selected item to the clipboard
Paste	Pastes the contents of the clipboard
Undo	Undoes the most recent operation
Redo	Redoes the most recently undone operation
Navigate Backward	Moves to the previously active tab in the *Designer* window
Navigate Forward	Moves to the next active tab in the *Designer* window
Start Debugging	Starts debugging (running) your program
Solution Configurations	Configures your project's executable code
Find	Searches for text in your application code
Solution Explorer	Opens the *Solution Explorer* window
Properties Window	Opens the *Properties* window
Object Browser	Opens the *Object Browser* window
Toolbox	Opens the *Toolbox* window, displaying, for example, visual controls you can place on Windows forms
Start Page	Displays the Visual Studio Start Page

The *Toolbox*

The *Toolbox* is a window that allows you to select the controls that you want to use in an application's user interface. When you want to place a Button, Label, TextBox, or other control on an application's form, you select it in the *Toolbox*. You will use the *Toolbox* extensively as you develop Visual C# applications.

The *Toolbox* typically appears on the left side of the Visual Studio environment. If the *Toolbox* is in Auto Hide mode, its tab will appear as shown in Figure 1-41. Figure 1-42 shows the *Toolbox* opened, with Auto Hide turned off.

Figure 1-41 The *Toolbox* tab (Auto Hide turned on)

Toolbox tab ———▶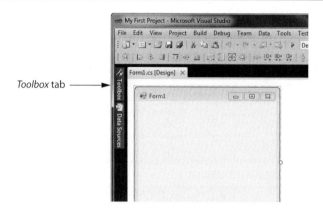

Figure 1-42 The *Toolbox* opened (Auto Hide turned off)

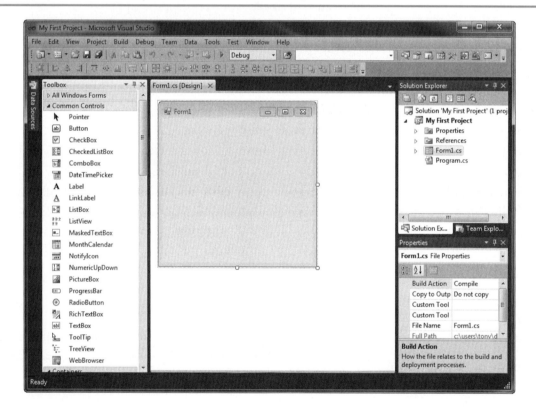

 NOTE: If you do not see the *Toolbox* or its tab along the side of the Visual Studio environment, click *View* on the menu bar and then click *Toolbox*. (In Visual C# Express, click *View* on the menu bar, then click *Other Windows*, and then click *Toolbox*.)

The *Toolbox* is divided into sections, and each section has a name. In Figure 1-42 you can see the *All Windows Forms* and *Common Controls* sections. If you scroll the *Toolbox*, you will see many other sections. Each section can be opened or closed.

If you want to open a section of the *Toolbox*, you simply click on its name tab. To close the section, click on its name tab again. In Figure 1-42, the *Common Controls* section is open. You use the *Common Controls* section to access controls that you frequently need, such as Buttons, Labels, and TextBoxes. You can move any section to the top of the list by dragging its name with the mouse.

Using ToolTips

A **ToolTip** is a small rectangular box that pops up when you hover the mouse pointer over a button on the toolbar or in the *Toolbox* for a few seconds. The ToolTip box contains a short description of the button's purpose. Figure 1-43 shows the ToolTip that appears when the cursor is left sitting on the *Save All* button. Use a ToolTip whenever you cannot remember a particular button's function.

Figure 1-43 *Save All* ToolTip

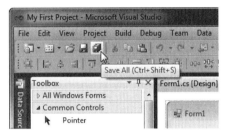

Docked and Floating Windows

Figure 1-42 shows the *Toolbox*, *Solution Explorer*, and *Properties* windows when they are **docked**, which means they are attached to one of the edges of the *Visual Studio* window. Alternatively, the windows can be **floating**. You can control whether a window is docked or floating as follows:

- To change a window from docked to floating, right-click its title bar and select *Float*.
- To change a window from floating to docked, right-click its title bar and select *Dock*.

Figure 1-44 shows Visual Studio with the *Toolbox*, *Solution Explorer*, and *Properties* windows floating. When a window is floating, you can click and drag it by its title bar around the screen. You may use whichever style you prefer—docked or floating. When windows are floating, they behave as normal windows. You may move or resize them to suit your preference.

NOTE: A window cannot float if its Auto Hide feature is turned on.

TIP: Remember, you can always reset the window layout by clicking *Window* on the menu bar and then selecting *Reset Window Layout*. If you accidentally close the Designer window, the *Solution Explorer* window, or the *Properties* window, you can use the *View* menu to redisplay them.

Figure 1-44 *Toolbox, Solution Explorer,* and *Properties* windows floating

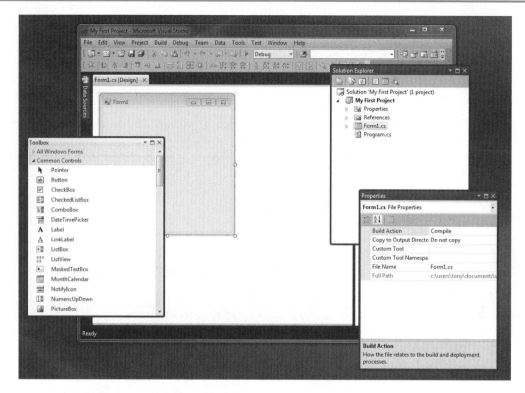

Projects and Solutions

As you learn to program in Visual C#, you will see the terms *project* and *solution* used often. These terms do not mean the same thing, but they are sometimes used interchangeably. Let's briefly discuss the difference between a project and a solution.

Each Visual C# application that you create is called a project. A Visual C# project consists of several files. You can think of a project as a collection of files that belong to a single application.

A **solution** is a container that holds one or more Visual C# projects. If you are developing applications for a large organization, you might find it convenient to store several related projects together in the same solution.

Although it is possible for a solution to hold more than one project, each project that you will create in this book will be saved in its own solution. Each time you create a new project, you will also create a new solution to hold it. Figure 1-45 illustrates this concept. Typically, the solution will be given the same name as the project.

Figure 1-45 Solution and project organization

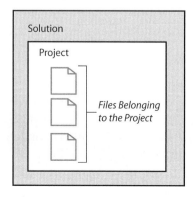

Typical Organization of Solutions and Projects on the Disk

When you create a new project, you specify the project's name, the solution's name, and a location on the disk where the solution should be stored. If you are using Visual Studio, you specify this information at the bottom of the *New Project* window, as shown in Figure 1-46. If you are using Visual C# Express, you specify this information in the *Save Project* window (shown previously in Figure 1-36) the first time you save the project.

Figure 1-46 Specifying the project name, solution name, and location

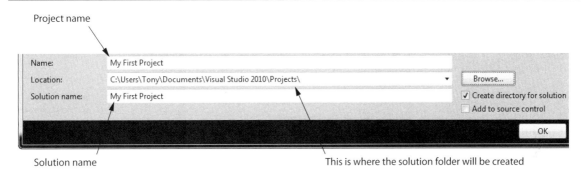

Let's use Figure 1-46 to see an example of how the files for the *My First Project* solution and project will be organized on the disk. Notice that in Figure 1-46, the following location is shown for the solution:

C:\Users\Tony\Documents\Visual Studio 2010\Projects

On your system, the location will not be exactly the same as this, but it will be something similar. At this location, a **solution folder** named *My First Project* will be created. If we use Windows to look inside that folder, we will see the two items shown in Figure 1-47. Notice that one of the items is another folder named *My First Project*. That is the **project folder**, which contains various files related to the project. The other item is the **solution file**. In Windows, you can double-click the solution file to open the project in Visual Studio.

Figure 1-47 Contents of the *My First Project* solution folder

Opening an Existing Project

If Visual Studio is already running, you can perform the following steps to open an existing project:

- Click *File* on the Visual Studio menu bar, then select *Open*, and then select *Project/Solution....*
- The *Open Project* window will appear. Navigate to the desired solution folder, select the solution file, and click *Open*.

In Visual C# Express, perform the following steps to open an existing project:

- Click *File* on the Visual Studio menu bar and then select *Open Project....*
- The *Open Project* window will appear. Navigate to the desired solution folder, select the solution file, and click *Open*.

Tutorial 1-4:
Opening an Existing Project

In this tutorial you will reopen the *My First Project* application that you created in Tutorial 1-2.

Step 1: Visual Studio should still be running from the previous tutorial. Perform one of the following operations to reopen *My First Project*:

If you are using Visual Studio:

Click *File* on the menu bar; select *Open* and then select *Project/Solution....* The *Open Project* window will appear. Navigate to the *My First Project* solution, select the solution file, and click the *Open* button.

If you are using Visual C# Express:

Click *File* on the menu bar, and then select *Open Project....* The *Open Project* window will appear. Navigate to the *My First Project* solution, select the solution file, and click the *Open* button.

After performing this step, *My First Project* should be opened. If you plan to complete the next tutorial, leave Visual Studio running with *My First Project* opened.

Displaying the *Designer* (When It Does Not Automatically Appear)

Sometimes when you open an existing project, the project's form will not be automatically displayed in the *Designer*. Figure 1-48 shows an example of the Visual Studio environment with an opened project but no form displayed in the *Designer*. When this happens, perform the following steps to display the project's form in the *Designer*:

- As shown in Figure 1-49, right-click Form1.cs in the *Solution Explorer*.
- Click *View Designer* in the pop-up menu.

Accessing the Visual Studio Documentation

You can access the documentation for Visual Studio by Clicking *Help* on the menu bar, and then selecting *View Help*. (Or, you can press Ctrl + F1 , and then press V on the keyboard.) This launches your Web browser and opens the online *Microsoft Developer Network*

Figure 1-48 A Project opened with no form displayed in the *Designer*

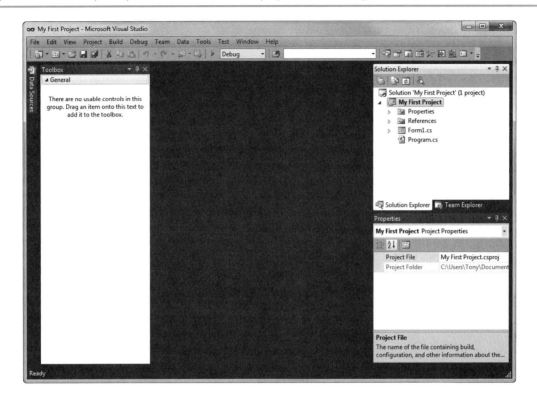

Figure 1-49 Using the *Solution Explorer* to open a form in the *Designer*

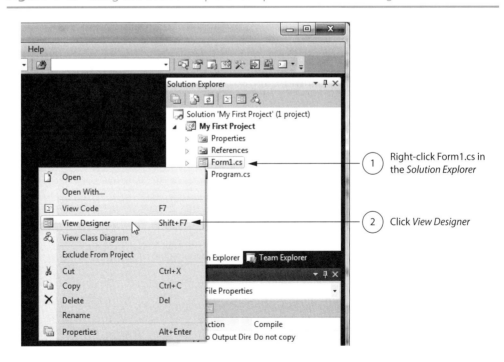

(MSDN) library. The MSDN library provides complete documentation for Visual C# as well as the other programming languages included in Visual Studio. You will also find code samples, tutorials, articles, and access to Microsoft Channel 9 Videos.

Tutorial 1-5:
Getting Familiar with the Visual Studio Environment

This exercise will give you practice interacting with the *Solution Explorer* window, the *Properties* window, and the *Toolbox*.

Step 1:   If Visual Studio is still running on your computer from the previous tutorial, continue to Step 2. If Visual Studio is not running on your computer, repeat the steps in Tutorial 1-4 to open *My First Project*.

Step 2:   Practice turning the *Auto Hide* feature on and off for the *Solution Explorer* window, the *Properties* window, and the *Toolbox*. Recall from our previous discussion that clicking the pushpin icon in each window's title bar turns *Auto Hide* on and off. When you are finished practicing, make sure Auto Hide is turned off for each of these windows. Your screen should look like Figure 1-42.

Step 3:   Practice floating and docking the *Solution Explorer* window, the *Properties* window, and the *Toolbox*. Recall from our previous discussion that you can make any of these windows float by right-clicking its title bar and selecting *Float*. You dock a floating window by right-clicking its title bar and selecting *Dock*.

Step 4:   The *Toolbox, Solution Explorer*, and *Properties* windows each have a *Close* button (⊠) in their upper-right corner. Close each of these windows by clicking their *Close* button.

Step 5:   Do you remember which buttons on the toolbar restore the *Solution Explorer*, *Properties* window, and *Toolbox*? If not, move your mouse cursor over any button on the toolbar and leave it there until the ToolTip appears. Repeat this procedure on different buttons until you find the ones whose ToolTips read *Solution Explorer, Properties Window*, and *Toolbox*. (Refer to Figure 1-40 and Table 1-3 for further assistance.)

Step 6:   Click the appropriate buttons on the toolbar to restore the *Solution Explorer*, the *Properties* window, and the *Toolbox*.

Step 7:   Exit Visual Studio by clicking *File* on the menu bar and then clicking *Exit*. You may see a dialog box asking you if you wish to save changes to a number of items. Click *Yes*.

Checkpoint

1.44 Briefly describe the purpose of the *Solution Explorer* window.

1.45 Briefly describe the purpose of the *Properties* window.

1.46 Briefly describe the purpose of the standard toolbar.

1.47 What is the difference between the toolbar and the *Toolbox*?

1.48 What is a ToolTip?

1.49 What is a project?

1.50 What is a solution?

Key Terms

algorithm

American Standard Code for
   Information Interchange (ASCII)

application software

assembler

assembly language

Auto Hide

binary

binary digit

binary numbering system

bit

Button

byte

class

code

command line interface

compact disc (CD)

compiler

console interface

controls

central processing unit (CPU)

debug

Designer window

digital

digital data

digital device

disk drive

docked (window)

digital versatile disc (DVD)

End lterminal

ENIAC

event driven

executing

fetch-decode-execute cycle

fields

floating (window)

floating-point notation

floppy disk drive

flowchart

Form

graphical user interface (GUI)

hardware

high-level languages

input

input device

input symbols

instruction set

integrated development
   environment (IDE)

interpreter

keywords

Label

logic error

low-level language

machine language

main memory

methods

microprocessors

mnemonics

.NET Framework

object oriented

operating system

operators

output

output device

output symbols

picture element

pixel

processing symbols

program

program development cycle

programmer

project

project folder

properties

Properties window

pseudocode

random-access memory (RAM)

reserved words

running

samples

secondary storage

software

software developer

software development tools

solution

Solution Explorer window

solution file

solution folder

source code

standard toolbar

start terminal

statements

syntax

syntax error

system software

terminal symbol

TextBox

Toolbox

ToolTip

two's complement

Unicode

universal serial bus (USB)	volatile
user	Visual C# 2010 Express
user interface	Visual Studio
utility program	Visual Studio 2010

Review Questions

Multiple Choice

1. A(n) _____ is a set of instructions that a computer follows to perform a task.
   a. compiler
   b. program
   c. interpreter
   d. programming language

2. The physical devices that a computer is made of are referred to as _____.
   a. hardware
   b. software
   c. the operating system
   d. tools

3. The part of a computer that runs programs is called _____.
   a. RAM
   b. secondary storage
   c. main memory
   d. the CPU

4. Today, CPUs are small chips known as _____.
   a. ENIACs
   b. microprocessors
   c. memory chips
   d. operating systems

5. The computer stores a program while the program is running, as well as the data that the program is working with, in _____.
   a. secondary storage
   b. the CPU
   c. main memory
   d. the microprocessor

6. _____ is a volatile type of memory that is used only for temporary storage while a program is running.
   a. RAM
   b. secondary storage
   c. the disk drive
   d. the USB drive

7. A type of memory that can hold data for long periods of time—even when there is no power to the computer—is called _____.
   a. RAM
   b. main memory
   c. secondary storage
   d. CPU storage

8. A component that collects data from people or other devices and sends it to the computer is called _____.

   a. an output device
   b. an input device
   c. a secondary storage device
   d. main memory

9. A video display is a(n) _____ device.

   a. output device
   b. input device
   c. secondary storage device
   d. main memory

10. A _____ is enough memory to store a letter of the alphabet or a small number.

    a. byte
    b. bit
    c. switch
    d. transistor

11. A byte is made up of eight _____.

    a. CPUs
    b. instructions
    c. variables
    d. bits

12. In the _____ numbering system, all numeric values are written as sequences of 0s and 1s.

    a. hexadecimal
    b. binary
    c. octal
    d. decimal

13. A bit that is turned off represents the following value: _____.

    a. 1
    b. −1
    c. 0
    d. "no"

14. A set of 128 numeric codes that represent the English letters, various punctuation marks, and other characters is _____.

    a. binary numbering
    b. ASCII
    c. Unicode
    d. ENIAC

15. An extensive encoding scheme that can represent the characters of many of the languages in the world is _____.

    a. binary numbering
    b. ASCII
    c. Unicode
    d. ENIAC

16. Negative numbers are encoded using the _____ technique.

    a. two's complement
    b. floating point
    c. ASCII
    d. Unicode

17. Real numbers are encoded using the _____ technique.
    a. two's complement
    b. floating point
    c. ASCII
    d. Unicode

18. The tiny dots of color that digital images are composed of are called _____.
    a. bits
    b. bytes
    c. color packets
    d. pixels

19. If you were to look at a machine language program, you would see _____.
    a. C# code
    b. a stream of binary numbers
    c. English words
    d. circuits

20. In the _____ part of the fetch-decode-execute cycle, the CPU determines which operation it should perform.
    a. fetch
    b. decode
    c. execute
    d. immediately after the instruction is executed

21. Computers can execute only programs that are written in _____.
    a. C#
    b. assembly language
    c. machine language
    d. Java

22. The _____ translates an assembly language program to a machine language program.
    a. assembler
    b. compiler
    c. translator
    d. interpreter

23. The words that make up a high-level programming language are called _____.
    a. binary instructions
    b. mnemonics
    c. commands
    d. keywords

24. The rules that must be followed when writing a program are called _____.
    a. syntax
    b. punctuation
    c. keywords
    d. operators

25. A(n) _____ program translates a high-level language program into a separate machine language program.
    a. assembler
    b. compiler
    c. translator
    d. utility

26. A _____ is any hypothetical person using a program and providing input for it.

    a. designer
    b. user
    c. guinea pig
    d. test subject

27. A _____ error does not prevent the program from running but causes it to produce incorrect results.

    a. syntax
    b. hardware
    c. logic
    d. fatal

28. A(n) _____ is a set of well-defined logical steps that must be taken to perform a task.

    a. logarithm
    b. plan of action
    c. logic schedule
    d. algorithm

29. An informal language that has no syntax rules and is not meant to be compiled or executed is called _____.

    a. faux code
    b. pseudocode
    c. C#
    d. a flowchart

30. A _____ is a diagram that graphically depicts the steps that take place in a program.

    a. flowchart
    b. step chart
    c. code graph
    d. program graph

31. Objects that are visible in a program's graphical user interface are commonly referred to as _____.

    a. buttons
    b. controls
    c. forms
    d. windows

32. A _____ is code that describes a particular type of object.

    a. namespace
    b. blueprint
    c. schema
    d. class

33. The _____ is a collection of classes and other code that can be used, along with a programming language such as C#, to create programs for the Windows operating system.

    a. .NET framework
    b. Standard Template Library
    c. GUI framework
    d. MSDN Library

34. The _____ is the part of a computer with which the user interacts.
     a. central processing unit
     b. user interface
     c. control system
     d. interactivity system

35. Before GUIs became popular, the _____ interface was the most commonly used.
     a. command line
     b. remote terminal
     c. sensory
     d. event-driven

36. _____ programs are usually event driven.
     a. command line
     b. text-based
     c. GUI
     d. procedural

True or False

1. Today, CPUs are huge devices made of electrical and mechanical components such as vacuum tubes and switches.

2. Main memory is also known as RAM.

3. Any piece of data that is stored in a computer's memory must be stored as a binary number.

4. Images, such as the ones you make with your digital camera, cannot be stored as binary numbers.

5. Machine language is the only language that a CPU understands.

6. Assembly language is considered a high-level language.

7. An interpreter is a program that both translates and executes the instructions in a high-level language program.

8. A syntax error does not prevent a program from being compiled and executed.

9. Windows, Linux, UNIX, and Mac OS are all examples of application software.

10. Word processing programs, spreadsheet programs, e-mail programs, Web browsers, and games are all examples of utility programs.

11. Programmers must be careful not to make syntax errors when writing pseudocode programs.

12. C# provides only the basic keywords and operators that you need to construct a program.

Short Answer

1. Why is the CPU the most important component in a computer?

2. What number does a bit that is turned on represent? What number does a bit that is turned off represent?

3. What would you call a device that works with binary data?

4. What are the words that make up a high-level programming language called?

5. What are the short words that are used in assembly language called?

6. What is the difference between a compiler and an interpreter?

7. What type of software controls the internal operations of the computer's hardware?

8. What is pseudocode? What is a flowchart?

9. When a program runs in a text-based environment, such as a command line interface, what determines the order in which things happen?

10. What does a class specify about an object?

11. Can you use C# alone to perform advanced operations such as creating GUIs, reading data from a file, or working with databases? Why or why not?

12. Figure 1-50 shows the Visual Studio IDE. What are the names of the four areas that are indicated in the figure?

13. What is the purpose of the Toolbox in the Visual Studio environment?

14. How can you access the documentation for Visual Studio? What resources are provided by the MSDN Library?

15. What steps must you take to open an existing project?

16. How can you view the project's form if it is not automatically displayed in the *Designer*?

Figure 1-50 The Visual Studio IDE

Programming Problems

1. Use what you've learned about the binary numbering system in this chapter to convert the following decimal numbers to binary:

11
65
100
255

2. Use what you've learned about the binary numbering system in this chapter to convert the following binary numbers to decimal:

    1101

    1000

    101011

3. Look at the ASCII chart in Appendix C and determine the codes for each letter of your first name.

4. Suppose your instructor gives three exams during the semester and you want to write a program that calculates your average exam score. Answer the following:

    a. What items of input must the user enter?
    b. Once the input has been entered, how will the program determine the average?
    c. What output will the program display?

2 Introduction to Visual C#

TOPICS

2.1 Getting Started with Forms and Controls

CONCEPT: The first step in creating a Visual C# application is creating the application's GUI. You use the Visual Studio Designer, Toolbox, and Properties window to build the application's form with the desired controls and set each control's properties.

In this chapter you will create your first Visual C# application. Before you start, however, you need to learn some fundamental concepts about creating a GUI in Visual Studio. This section shows the basics of editing forms and creating controls.

The Application's Form

When you start a new Visual C# project, Visual Studio automatically creates an empty form and displays it in the *Designer*. Figure 2-1 shows an example. Think of the empty form as a blank canvas that can be used to create the application's user interface. You can add controls to the form, change the form's size, and modify many of its characteristics. When the application runs, the form will be displayed on the screen.

Figure 2-1 A new project with a blank form displayed in the *Designer*

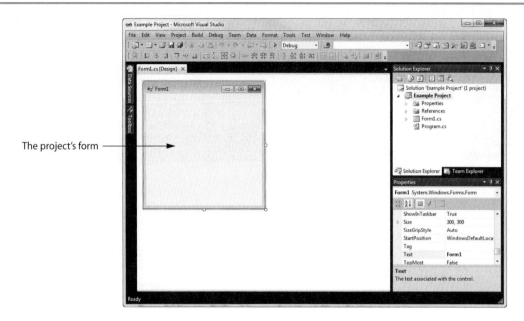

The project's form

If you take a closer look at the form, you will notice that it is enclosed by a thin dotted line, known as a **bounding box**. As shown in Figure 2-2, the bounding box has small **sizing handles**, which appear on the form's right edge, bottom edge, and lower-right corner. When a bounding box appears around an object in the *Designer*, it indicates that the object is selected and is ready for editing.

Figure 2-2 The form's bounding box and sizing handles

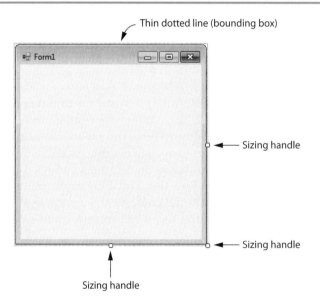

Thin dotted line (bounding box)

Sizing handle

Sizing handle

Sizing handle

Initially the form's size is 300 pixels wide by 300 pixels high. You can easily resize the form with the mouse. When you position the mouse cursor over any edge or corner that has a sizing handle, the cursor changes to a two-headed arrow (⟺). Figure 2-3 shows examples. When the mouse cursor becomes a two-headed arrow, you can click and drag the mouse to resize form.

Figure 2-3 Using the mouse to resize the form

Identifying Forms and Controls by Their Names

An application's GUI is made of forms and various controls. Each form and control in an application's GUI must have a name that identifies it. The blank form that Visual Studio initially creates in a new project is named Form1.

NOTE: Later in this book you will learn how to change a form's name, but for now, you will keep the default name, Form1.

The *Properties* Window

The appearance and other characteristics of a GUI object are determined by the object's properties. When you select an object in the *Designer*, that object's properties are displayed in the *Properties* window. For example, when the Form1 form is selected, it's properties are displayed in the *Properties* window, as shown in Figure 2-4.

TIP: Recall from Chapter 1 that if the *Properties* window is in Auto Hide mode, you can click its tab to open it. If you do not see the *Properties* window, click *View* on the menu bar. On the *View* menu, click *Properties*. (In Visual C# Express, click *View*, *Other Windows*, *Properties*.)

The area at the top of the *Properties* window shows the name of the object that is currently selected. You can see in Figure 2-4 that the name of the selected object is *Form1*. Below that is a scrollable list of properties. The list of properties has two columns: The left column shows each property's name, and the right column shows each property's value. For example, look at the form's Size property in Figure 2-4. Its value is *300, 300*. This means that the form's size is 300 pixels wide by 300 pixels high. Next, look at the form's Text property. The Text property determines the text that is displayed in the form's title bar (the bar that appears at the top of the form). Its current value is Form1, so the text *Form1* is displayed in the form's title bar.

When a form is created, its Text property is initially set to the same value as the form's name. When you start a new project, the blank form that appears in the *Designer* will always be named Form1, so the text *Form1* will always appear in the form's title bar. In most cases you want to change the value of the form's Text property to something more meaningful. For example, assume the Form1 form is currently selected. You can perform the following steps to change its Text property to *My First Program*.

Figure 2-4 The *Properties* window, showing the selected object's properties

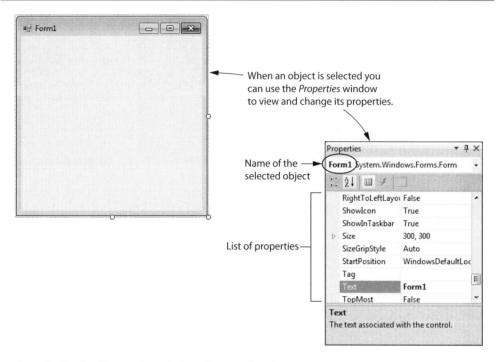

Step 1: In the *Properties* window, locate the Text property.

Step 2: Click inside the area that holds the Text property's value, and then use the $\boxed{\text{Backspace}}$ and/or the $\boxed{\text{Delete}}$ key to delete the word *Form1*.

Step 3: Type *My First Program* in its place and press the $\boxed{\text{Enter}}$ key. The text *My First Program* will now appear in the form's title bar, as shown in Figure 2-5.

 NOTE: Changing an object's Text property does not change the object's name. For example, if you change the Form1 form's Text property to *My First Program*, the form's name is still Form1. You have changed only the text that is displayed in the form's title bar.

Figure 2-5 The form's Text property value displayed in the form's title bar

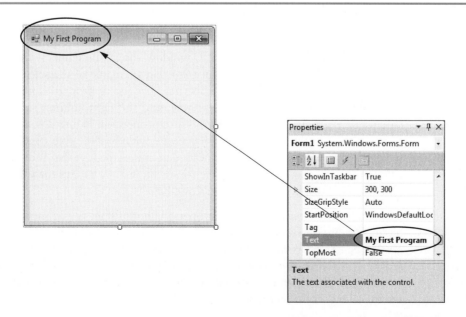

Earlier we discussed how to use the mouse to resize a form in the *Designer*. An alternative method is to change the form's Size property in the *Properties* window. For example, assume the Form1 form is currently selected. You can perform the following steps to change its size to 400 pixels wide by 100 pixels high.

Step 1: In the *Properties* window, locate the Size property.
Step 2: Click inside the area that holds the Size property's value, and then use the Backspace and/or the Delete key to delete the current value.
Step 3: Type *400, 100* in its place and press the Enter key. The form will be resized as shown in Figure 2-6.

Figure 2-6 The form's size changed to 400 by 100

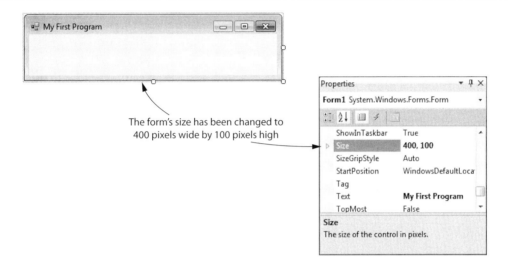

The form's size has been changed to 400 pixels wide by 100 pixels high

 NOTE: Notice in Figure 2-6 that the **Alphabetical button** ( ) is selected near the top of the *Properties* window. This causes the properties to be displayed in alphabetical order. Alternatively, the **Categorized button** ( ) can be selected, which causes the properties to be displayed in groups. The alphabetical listing is the default selection, and most of the time, it makes it is easier to locate specific properties.

Adding Controls to a Form

When you are ready to create controls on the application's form, you use the *Toolbox*. Recall from Chapter 1 that the *Toolbox* usually appears on the left side of the Visual Studio environment. If the Toolbox is in Auto Hide mode, you can click its tab to open it. Figure 2-7 shows an example of how the *Toolbox* typically appears when it is open.

 TIP: Recall from Chapter 1 that if you do not see the *Toolbox* or its tab, click *View* on the menu bar and then click *Toolbox*. (In Visual C# Express, click *View* on the menu bar, then click *Other Windows*, and then click *Toolbox*.)

The *Toolbox* shows a scrollable list of controls that you can add to a form. To add a control to a form, you simply find it in the *Toolbox* and then double-click it. The control will be created on the form. For example, suppose you want to create a Button control on the form. You find it in the *Toolbox*, as shown in Figure 2-8, double-click it, and a Button control will appear on the form.

Figure 2-7 The *Toolbox*

Figure 2-8 Creating a Button control

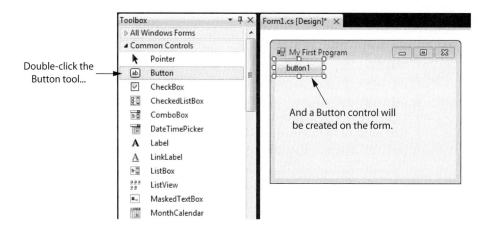

Double-click the Button tool...

And a Button control will be created on the form.

TIP: You can also click and drag controls from the *Toolbox* onto the form.

Resizing and Moving Controls

Take a closer look at the Button control that is shown on the form in Figure 2-8. Notice that it is enclosed in a bounding box with sizing handles. This indicates that the control is currently selected. When a control is selected, you can use the mouse to resize it in the same way that you learned to resize a form earlier. You can also use the mouse to move a control to a new location on the form. Position the mouse cursor inside the control, and when the mouse cursor becomes a four-headed arrow (✛), you can click and drag the control to a new location. Figure 2-9 shows a form with a Button control that has been enlarged and moved.

Figure 2-9 A Button control resized and moved

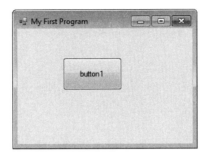

Deleting a Control

Deleting a control is simple: you select it and then press the Delete key on the keyboard.

More About Button Controls

You learned earlier that each form and each control in an application's GUI must have a name that identifies it. When you create Button controls, they are automatically given default names such as button1, button2, and so forth.

Button controls have a Text property, which holds the text that is displayed on the face of the button. When a Button control is created, its Text property is initially set to the same value as the Button control's name. As a result, when you create a Button control, its name will be displayed on the face of the button. For example, the form in Figure 2-10 contains three Button controls named button1, button2, and button3.

Figure 2-10 A form with three Button controls

After you create a Button control, you should always change its Text property. The text that is displayed on a button should indicate what the button will do when it is clicked. For example, a button that calculates an average might have the text *Calculate Average* displayed on it, and a button that prints a report might have the text *Print Report* displayed on it. Here are the steps you perform to change a Button control's Text property:

Step 1: Make sure the Button control is selected. (If you don't see the bounding box and sizing handles around the control, just click the control to select it.)

Step 2: In the *Properties* window, locate the Text property.

Step 3: Click inside the area that holds the Text property's value, and then use the Backspace and/or the Delete key to delete the current value. Then, type the new text in its place and press the Enter key. The new text will be displayed on the button.

Figure 2-11 shows an example of how changing a Button control's Text property changes the text displayed on the face of the button.

Figure 2-11 A Button control's Text property changed

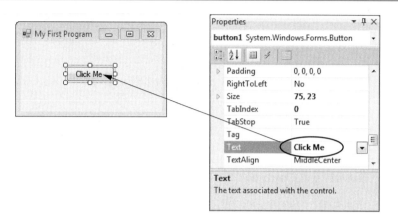

Changing a Control's Name

A control's name identifies the control in the application's code and in the Visual Studio environment. When you create a control on an application's form, you should always change the control's name to something that is more meaningful than the default name that Visual Studio gives it. A control's name should reflect the purpose of the control.

For example, suppose you've created a Button control to calculate an amount of tax. A default name such as button1 does not convey the button's purpose. A name such as calculateTaxButton would be much better. When you are working with the application's code and you see the name calculateTaxButton, you will know precisely which button the code is referring to.

You can change a control's name by changing its Name property. Here are the steps:

Step 1: Make sure the control is selected. (If you do not see the bounding box and sizing handles around the control, just click the control to select it.)

Step 2: In the *Properties* window, scroll up to the top of the list of properties. You should see the Name property, as shown in Figure 2-12. (The Name property is enclosed in parentheses to make it appear near the top of the alphabetical list of properties. This makes it easier to find.)

Step 3: Click inside the area that holds the Name property's value and then use the [Backspace] and/or the [Delete] key to delete the current name. Then, type the new name in its place and press the [Enter] key. You have successfully changed the name of the control.

Figure 2-12 The Name property

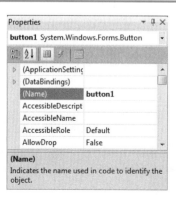

Figure 2-13 shows the *Properties* window after a Button control's name has been changed to calculateTaxButton.

Figure 2-13 The Name property changed to calculateTaxButton

Rules for Naming Controls

Control names are also known as **identifiers**. When naming a control, you must follow these rules for C# identifiers:

- The first character must be one of the letters a through z or A through Z or an underscore character (_).
- After the first character, you may use the letters a through z or A through Z, the digits 0 through 9, or underscores.
- The name cannot contain spaces.

Table 2-1 lists some identifiers that might be used for Button control names and indicates whether each is a legal or illegal identifier in C#.

Table 2-1 Legal and Illegal Identifiers

Identifier	Legal or Illegal?
showDayOfWeekButton	Legal
3rdQuarterButton	Illegal because identifiers cannot begin with a digit.
change*color*Button	Illegal because the * character is not allowed.
displayTotalButton	Legal
calculate Tax Button	Illegal because identifiers cannot contain spaces.

Because a control's name should reflect the control's purpose, programmers often find themselves creating names that are made of multiple words. For example, consider the following Button control names:

```
calculatetaxbutton
printreportbutton
displayanimationbutton
```

Unfortunately, these names are not easily read by the human eye because the words are not separated. Because we cannot have spaces in control names, we need to find another way to separate the words in a multiword control name to make it more readable to the human eye.

Most C# programmers address this problem by using the **camelCase** naming convention for controls. camelCase names are written in the following manner:

- You begin writing the name with lowercase letters.
- The first character of the second and subsequent words is written in uppercase.

For example, the following control names are written in camelCase:

```
calculateTaxButton
printReportButton
displayAnimationButton
```

NOTE: This style of naming is called camelCase because the uppercase characters that appear in a name are sometimes reminiscent of a camel's humps.

 Checkpoint

2.1 When you start a new Visual C# project, what is automatically created and displayed in the *Designer*?

2.2 How can you tell that an object is selected and ready for editing in the *Designer*?

2.3 What is the purpose of an object's sizing handles?

2.4 What must each form and control in an application's GUI have to identify it?

2.5 What is the purpose of the *Properties* window?

2.6 What does the Alphabetical button do when it is selected in the *Properties* window?

2.7 What does the Categorized button do when it is selected in the *Properties* window?

2.8 What does a form's Text property determine?

2.9 What does a form's Size property determine?

2.10 What is shown in the *Toolbox*?

2.11 How do you add a control to a form?

2.12 What should the text that is displayed on a button indicate?

2.13 What are the rules for naming controls?

2.14 What naming convention do most C# programmers use to separate words in a multiword identifier?

2.2 Creating the GUI for Your First Visual C# Application: The *Hello World* Application

When a student is learning computer programming, it is traditional to start by learning to write a *Hello World* program. A **Hello World** program is a simple program that merely displays the words *"Hello World"* on the screen. In this chapter you will create your first Visual C# application, which will be an event-driven *Hello World* program. When the finished application runs, it will display the form shown on the left in Figure 2-14.

Figure 2-14 Screens displayed by the completed *Hello World* program

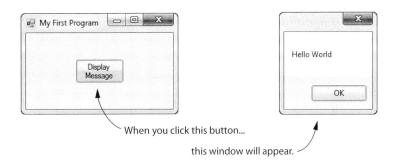

When you click this button...

this window will appear.

Notice that the form contains a button that reads *Display Message*. When you click the button, the window shown on the right in the figure will appear.

The process of creating this application is divided into two parts. First, you will create the application's GUI, and second, you will write the code that causes the *Hello World* message to appear when the user clicks the *Display Message* button. Tutorial 2-1 leads you through the process of creating the GUI.

Tutorial 2-1:
Creating the GUI for the *Hello World* Application

Step 1:   Start Visual Studio (or Visual C# Express).

Step 2:   Start a new project by performing one of the following actions:
   • If you are using Visual Studio, click *File* on the menu bar, then select *New*, and then select *Project....*
   • If you are using Visual C# Express, click *File* on the menu bar and then select *New Project...*

Step 3:   The *New Project* window should appear. At the left side of the window, under *Installed Templates*, make sure *Visual C#* is selected. Then, select *Windows Forms Application* as the type of application. In the *Name* text box (at the bottom of the window), change the name of the project to *Hello World*, and then click the *Ok* button.

Step 4:   Make sure the *Toolbox*, the *Solution Explorer*, and the *Properties* window are visible and that Auto Hide is turned off for each of these windows. The Visual Studio environment should appear as shown in Figure 2-15.

Step 5:   Change the Form1 form's Text property to *My First Program*, as shown in Figure 2-16.

Step 6:   The form's default size is too large for this application, so you need to make it smaller. Use the technique discussed in the previous section to adjust the form's size with the mouse. The form should appear similar to that shown in Figure 2-17. (Don't worry about the form's exact size. Just make it appear similar to Figure 2-17.)

Figure 2-15 The Visual Studio environment

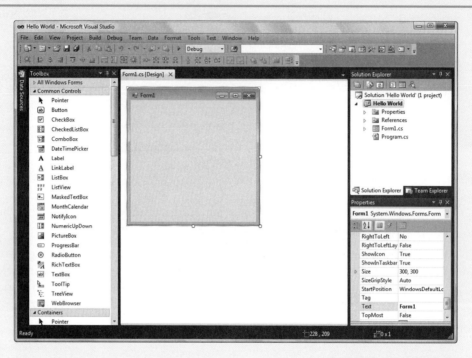

Figure 2-16 The form's Text property changed to *My First Program*

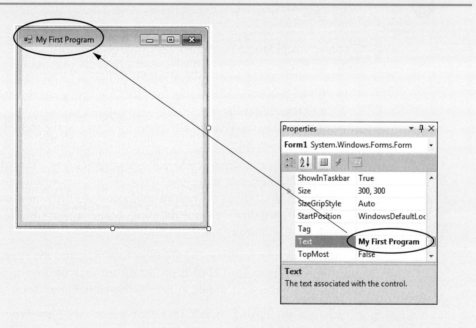

Figure 2-17 The form resized

Step 7: Now you are ready to add a Button control to the form. Locate the Button tool in the *Toolbox* and double-click it. A Button control should appear on the form, as shown in Figure 2-18. Move the Button control so it appears approximately in the center of the form, as shown in Figure 2-19.

Step 8: Change the value of the Button control's Text property to *Display Message*. After doing this, notice that the text displayed on the button has changed, as shown in Figure 2-20.

Figure 2-18 A Button control created on the form

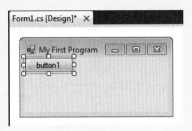

Figure 2-19 The Button control moved

Figure 2-20 The Button control's Text property changed

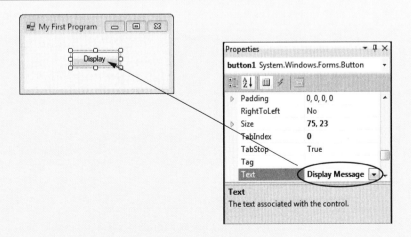

Step 9: The Button control isn't quite large enough to accommodate all of the text that you typed into its Text property, so enlarge the Button control, as shown in Figure 2-21.

Figure 2-21 The Button control enlarged

Step 10: As discussed in the previous section, a control's name should reflect the purpose of the control. The Button control that you created in this application will cause a message to be displayed when it is clicked. The name button1 does not convey that purpose, however. Change the Button control's Name property to messageButton. The Properties window should appear as shown in Figure 2-22.

Figure 2-22 The Button control's Name property changed to messageButton

Step 11: Click *File* on the Visual Studio menu bar and then click *Save All* to save the project. (If you are using Visual C# Express, you will see the *Save Project* dialog box the first time you save the project. Make sure the correct location is selected, and click the *Save* button.)

Step 12: You're only partially finished with the application, but you can run it now to see how the GUI looks on the screen. To run the application, press the F5 key on the keyboard or click the *Start Debugging* button (▶) on the toolbar. This causes the application to be compiled and executed. You will notice the appearance of the Visual Studio environment change somewhat, and you will see the application's form appear on the screen as shown in Figure 2-23.

Figure 2-23 The application running

Click here to end the application.

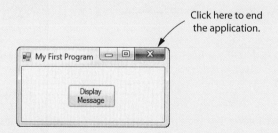

Although the application is running, it is not capable of doing anything other than displaying the form. If you click the *Display Message* button, nothing will happen. That is because you have not yet written the code that executes when the button is clicked. You will do that in the next tutorial. To end the application, click the standard Windows close button (▣) in the form's upper-right corner.

2.3 Introduction to C# Code

CONCEPT: You use the Visual Studio code editor to write an application's code. Much of the code that you will write in an application will be event handlers. Event handlers respond to specific events that take place while an application is running.

In the previous sections of this chapter, you learned the basics of creating an application's GUI. An application is more than a user interface, however. If you want your application to perform any meaningful actions, you have to write code. This section introduces you to Visual C# code and shows how to program an application to respond to button clicks.

A file that contains program code is called a **source code file**. When you start a C# Windows Forms Application project, Visual Studio automatically creates several source code files and adds them to the project. If you look at the *Solution Explorer*, as shown in Figure 2-24, you will see the names of two source code files: Form1.cs and Program.cs. (C# source code files always end with the .cs extension.)

Figure 2-24 Source code files shown in the *Solution Explorer*

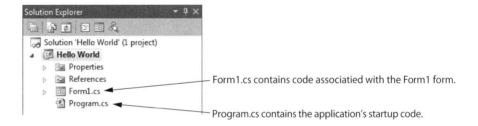

Here is a brief description of the two files:

- The **Program.cs file** contains the application's start-up code, which executes when the application runs. The code in this file performs behind-the-scenes initialization tasks that are necessary to get the application up and running. It is important that you do not modify the contents of this file because doing so could prevent the application from executing.
- The **Form1.cs file** contains code that is associated with the Form1 form. When you write code that defines some action related to Form1 (such as responding to a button click), you will write the code in this file.

The Form1.cs file already contains code that was generated by Visual Studio when the project was created. You can think of this auto-generated code as an outline to which you can add your own code as you develop the application.

Let's take a look at the code. If you still have the *Hello World* project open from the previous tutorial, right-click Form1.cs in the *Solution Explorer*. A pop-up menu will appear, as shown in Figure 2-25. On the pop-up menu, click *View Code*. The file's contents will be displayed in the Visual Studio code editor, as shown in Figure 2-26.

At this point, it's not necessary for you to understand the meaning of the statements that you see in this code. It will be helpful for you to know how this code is organized, however, because later you will add your own code to this file. C# code is primarily organized in three ways: namespaces, classes, and methods. Here's a summary:

- A **namespace** is a container that holds classes.
- A class is a container that holds methods (among other things).

Figure 2-25 Opening Form1.cs in the code editor

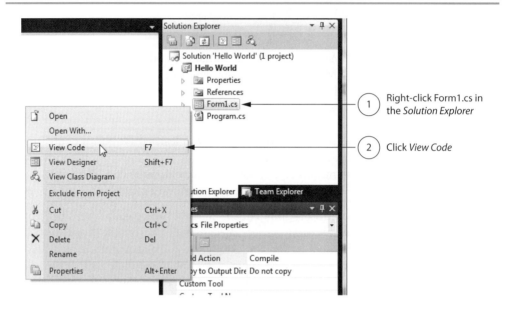

Figure 2-26 Form1.cs code displayed in the Visual Studio code editor

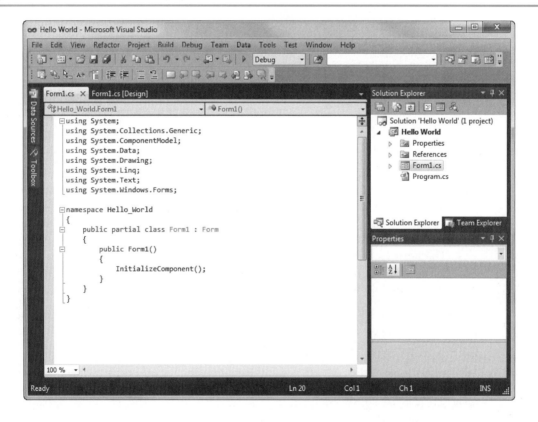

- A method is a group of one or more programming statements that performs some operation.

So, C# code is organized as methods, which are contained inside classes, which are contained inside namespaces. With this organizational structure in mind, look at Figure 2-27.

The figure shows four different sections of the code, marked with the numbers 1, 2, 3, and 4. Let's discuss each section of code.

Figure 2-27 Organization of the Form1.cs code

```
 ┌── using System;
 │   using System.Collections.Generic;
 │   using System.ComponentModel;
(1)  using System.Data;
 │   using System.Drawing;
 │   using System.Linq;
 │   using System.Text;
 └── using System.Windows.Forms;

 ┌── namespace Hello_World
 │   {
 │    ┌── public partial class Form1 : Form
 │    │   {
 │    │    ┌── public Form1()
(2)  (3)  │   {                                   (4)
 │    │    │       InitializeComponent();
 │    │    └── }
 │    │   }
 │    └── }
 └── }
```

① Recall from Chapter 1 that C# applications rely heavily on the .NET Framework, which is a collection of classes and other code. The code in the .NET Framework is organized into namespaces. The series of `using` directives that appears at the top of a C# source code file indicate which namespaces in the .NET Framework the program will use.

② This section of code creates a namespace for the project. The line that reads `namespace Hello_World` marks the beginning of a namespace named `Hello_World`. Notice that the next line contains an opening brace (`{`) and that the last line in the file contains a corresponding closing brace (`}`). All the code that appears between these braces is inside the `Hello_World` namespace.

③ This section of code is a class declaration. The line that reads `public partial class`, and so forth, marks the beginning of the class. The next line contains an opening brace (`{`), and the last line in this section of code contains a corresponding closing brace (`}`). All the code that appears between these braces is inside the class.

④ This section of code is a method. The line that reads `public Form1()` marks the beginning of the method. The next line contains an opening brace (`{`), and the last line in this section of code contains a corresponding closing brace (`}`). The code that appears between these braces is inside the method.

It's important to point out that code containers, such as namespaces, classes, and methods, use **braces** (`{}`) to enclose code. Each opening brace (`{`) must have a corresponding closing brace (`}`) at some later point in the program. Figure 2-28 shows how the braces in Form1.cs are paired.

Figure 2-28 Corresponding braces

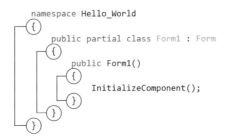

Switching Between the Code Editor and the *Designer*

When you open the code editor, it appears in the same part of the screen as the *Designer*. While developing a Visual C# application, you will often find yourself needing to switch back and forth between the *Designer* and the code editor. One way to quickly switch between the two windows is to use the tabs shown in Figure 2-29. In the figure, notice that the leftmost tab reads *Form1.cs*. That is the tab for the code editor. The rightmost tab reads *Form1.cs [Design]*. That is the tab for the *Designer*. (The tabs may not always appear in this order.) To switch between the *Designer* and the code editor, you simply click the tab for the desired window.

Figure 2-29 Code editor and *Designer* tabs

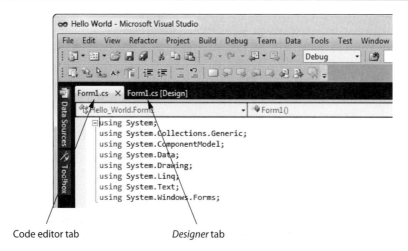

Code editor tab   *Designer* tab

You can also detach the code editor and move it to another part of the screen. This allows you to see the code editor and the *Designer* at the same time. As shown in Figure 2-30, click the code editor tab and drag it to the desired location on the screen. (If you have multiple monitors connected to your computer, you can even drag the code editor to a different monitor.) To return the code editor to its position within the IDE, right-click the code editor window's title bar and select *Dock as Tabbed Document*. This is shown in Figure 2-31.

Figure 2-30 Detaching the code editor by clicking and dragging

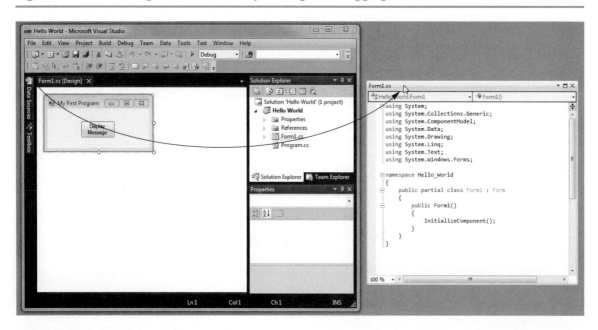

Figure 2-31 Returning the code editor to its docked position

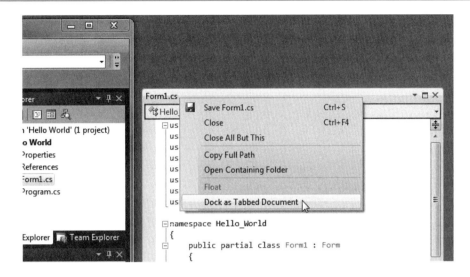

Adding Your Own Code to a Project

Now you are ready to learn how to add your own code to a project. Suppose you have created a project named Code Demo and set up the project's form with a Button control, as shown in Figure 2-32. The Button control's name is myButton, and its Text property is set to *Click Me!*.

Suppose you want the application to display the message *Thanks for clicking the button!* when the user clicks the button. To accomplish that, you need to write a special type of

Figure 2-32 A form with a Button control

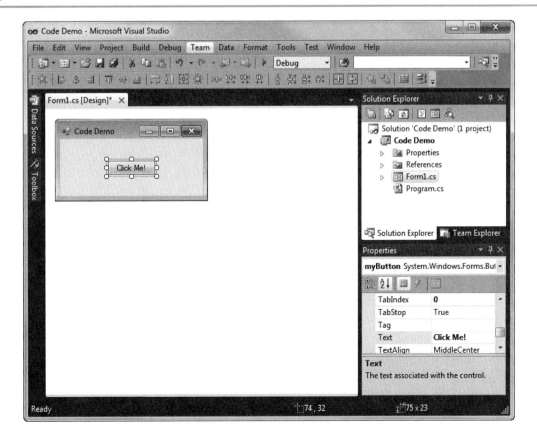

method known as an event handler. An **event handler** is a method that executes when a specific event takes place while an application is running. In this project you need to write an event handler that will execute when the user clicks the myButton control. To create the event handler, you double-click the myButton control in the *Designer*. This opens the Form1.cs file in the code editor, as shown in Figure 2-33, with some new code added to it.

Figure 2-33 The code window opened with event handler code generated

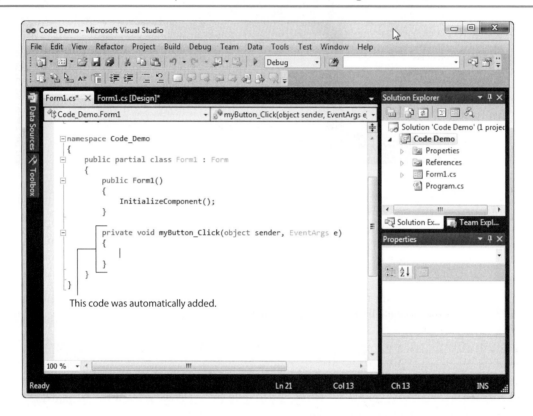

This code was automatically added.

When an application is running and the user clicks a control, we say that a **Click event** has occurred on the control. The code that has been added to the Form1.cs file (shown in Figure 2-33) is an event handler that will execute when a Click event occurs on the myButton control. For now you do not need to understand all parts of the event handler code. At this point you need to understand only the following concepts:

- As shown in Figure 2-34, the event handler's name is myButton_Click. The "myButton" portion of the name indicates that the event handler is associated with the myButton control, and the "Click" portion of the name indicates that the event handler responds to Click events. This is the typical naming convention that Visual Studio uses when it generates event handler code. When you see the name

Figure 2-34 A closer look at the event handler code

The event handler's name

```
private void myButton_Click(object sender, EventArgs e)
{

}
```

Your code goes here, between the braces.

myButton_Click, you understand that it is an event handler that executes when a Click event occurs on the myButton control.

- The event handler that Visual Studio generates doesn't actually do anything. You can think of it as an empty container to which you can add your own code. Notice that the second line of the event handler is an opening brace ({) and the last line is a closing brace (}). Any code that you want executed when the user clicks the myButton control must be written between these braces.

Now you know how to create an empty Click event handler for a Button control. But what code do you write inside the event handler? In this example we write code that displays the message *Thanks for clicking the button!* in a message box, which is a small pop-up window.

Message Boxes

A **message box** is a small window, sometimes referred to as a **dialog box**, that displays a message. Figure 2-35 shows an example of a message box displaying the message *Thanks for clicking the button!* Notice that the message box also has an *OK* button. When the user clicks the *OK* button, the message box closes.

Figure 2-35 A message box

The .NET Framework provides a method named MessageBox.Show that you can use in Visual C# to display a message box. If you want to execute the MessageBox.Show method, you write a statement known as a **method call**. (Programmers refer to the act of executing a method as *calling* the method.) The following statement shows an example of how you would call the MessageBox.Show method to display the message box shown in Figure 2-35:

```
MessageBox.Show("Thanks for clicking the button!");
```

When you call the MessageBox.Show method, you write a string of characters inside the parentheses. (In programming we use the term **string** to mean string of characters.) The string that is written inside the parentheses will be displayed in the message box. In this example the string "Thanks for clicking the button!" is written inside the parentheses.

Notice that the string is enclosed in double quotation marks in the code. When the message is displayed (as shown in Figure 2-35), however, the double quotation marks do not appear. The double quotation marks are required in the code to indicate the beginning and the end of the string.

Also notice that a semicolon appears at the end of the statement. This is required by C# syntax. Just as a period marks the end of a sentence, a **semicolon** marks the end of a programming statement in C#.

Getting back to our Code Demo example project, Figure 2-36 shows how you can call the MessageBox.Show method from the myButton_Click event handler. After typing the statement as shown in the figure, you can press the F5 key on the keyboard, or click the *Start Debugging* button (▶) on the toolbar to compile and run the application. When

Figure 2-36 Event handler code for displaying a message box

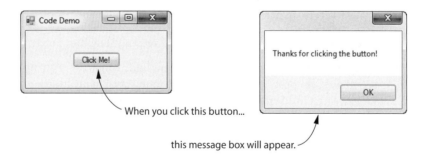

```
Form1.cs*  X  Form1.cs [Design]*

Code_Demo.Form1                                    myButton_Click(object sender, EventArgs e)

using System;
using System.Collections.Generic;
using System.ComponentModel;
using System.Data;
using System.Drawing;
using System.Linq;
using System.Text;
using System.Windows.Forms;

namespace Code_Demo
{
    public partial class Form1 : Form
    {
        public Form1()
        {
            InitializeComponent();
        }

        private void myButton_Click(object sender, EventArgs e)
        {
            MessageBox.Show("Thanks for clicking the button!");
        }
    }
}

100 %
```

the application runs, it will display the form shown on the left in Figure 2-37. When you click the button, the message box shown on the right in the figure will appear. You can click the *OK* button on the message box to close it.

Figure 2-37 The Code Demo project running

When you click this button...

this message box will appear.

> **NOTE:** When writing a Click event handler for a Button control, you might be wondering if it is necessary to first double-click the Button control in the *Designer*, creating the empty event handler code. After all, couldn't you just skip this step and instead open the code editor and write all the event handler code yourself? The answer is no, you cannot skip this step. When you double-click a control in the *Designer*, Visual Studio not only creates an empty event handler, but it also writes some code that you don't see elsewhere in the project. This other code is necessary for the event handler to properly function.

String Literals

Programs almost always work with data of some type. For example, the code shown in Figure 2-36 uses the following string when it calls the `MessageBox.Show` method:

```
"Thanks for clicking the button!"
```

This string is the data that is displayed by the program. When a piece of data is written into a program's code, it's called a **literal** (because the data is *literally* written into the program). When a string is written into a program's code, it's called a *string literal*. In C#, string literals must be enclosed in double quotation marks.

 NOTE: Programmers sometimes say that literals are values that are *hard coded* into a program because the value of a literal cannot change while the program is running.

Multiple Buttons with Event Handlers

The Code Demo project previously shown has only one button with a Click event handler. Many of the applications that you will develop will have multiple buttons, each with its own Click event handler. For example, the form shown in Figure 2-38 has three Button controls. As shown in the figure, the controls are named `firstButton`, `secondButton`, and `thirdButton`.

Figure 2-38 A form with multiple Button controls

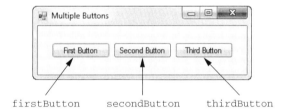

To create Click event handlers for the buttons, you simply double-click each Button control in the *Designer* and an empty event handler will be created in the form's source code file. The names of the Click event handlers will be `firstButton_Click`, `secondButton_Click`, and `thirdButton_Click`. Figure 2-39 shows an example of the form's source code after the three event handlers have been created and a `MessageBox.Show` statement has been added to each one.

Design Time and Run Time

When you have a project open in Visual Studio, the time during which you build the GUI and write the application's code is referred to as **design time**. During design time, you can use the *Designer* and the *Toolbox* to place controls on the form, use the *Properties* window to set property values, use the code editor to write code, and so forth. This is the phase during which you create or modify the application.

When you are ready to run a project that you have open in Visual Studio, you press the `F5` key on the keyboard or click the *Start Debugging* button (▶) on the toolbar. The project will be compiled, and if there were no errors, it will be executed. The time during which an application is executing is referred to as **run time**. During run time, you can

Figure 2-39 Source code with three Click event handlers

```
using System;
using System.Collections.Generic;
using System.ComponentModel;
using System.Data;
using System.Drawing;
using System.Linq;
using System.Text;
using System.Windows.Forms;

namespace Multiple_Buttons
{
    public partial class Form1 : Form
    {
        public Form1()
        {
            InitializeComponent();
        }

        private void firstButton_Click(object sender, EventArgs e)
        {
            MessageBox.Show("You clicked the first button.");
        }

        private void secondButton_Click(object sender, EventArgs e)
        {
            MessageBox.Show("You clicked the second button.");
        }

        private void thirdButton_Click(object sender, EventArgs e)
        {
            MessageBox.Show("You clicked the third button.");
        }
    }
}
```

Click event handler for `firstButton`

Click event handler for `secondButton`

Click event handler for `thirdButton`

interact with the running application, but you cannot use the *Designer*, the *Toolbox*, the *Properties* window, the code editor, or parts of Visual Studio to make changes to it.

NOTE: In computing literature and on the Web, you will see the term run time also spelled as *runtime* or *run-time*. All these variations typically mean the same thing.

Checkpoint

2.15 A file that contains program code is known as what type of file?

2.16 What must you do if you want your application to perform any meaningful actions?

2.17 What does the Program.cs file contain?

2.18 What does the Form1.cs file contain?

2.19 How is C# code organized?

2.20 What is a namespace?

2.21 What characters do code containers, such as namespaces, classes, and methods, use to enclose code?

2.22 How do you switch between the *Designer* and the code editor?

2.23 How do you create an event handler for a button?

2.24 What is a Click event?

2.25 What method do you use in Visual C# to display a message box?

2.26 What is a literal?

2.27 What are string literals enclosed in?

2.28 How do you run a project that you have open in Visual Studio?

2.4 Writing Code for the *Hello World* Application

Now you know everything necessary to complete the *Hello World* project. In Tutorial 2-2 you will open the project and add a Click event handler for the `messageButton` control. The event handler will call the `MessageBox.Show` method to display a message box with the message *Hello World*.

Tutorial 2-2:
Writing Code for the *Hello World* Application

Step 1: If Visual Studio (or Visual C# Express) is not already running, start it. Open the *Hello World* project that you started in Tutorial 2-1.

Step 2: Make sure the Form1 form is visible in the *Designer,* as shown in Figure 2-40. If it is not, right-click Form1.cs in the *Solution Explorer* and then select *View Designer* from the pop-up menu.

Figure 2-40 The *Hello World* project loaded with Form1 shown in the *Designer*

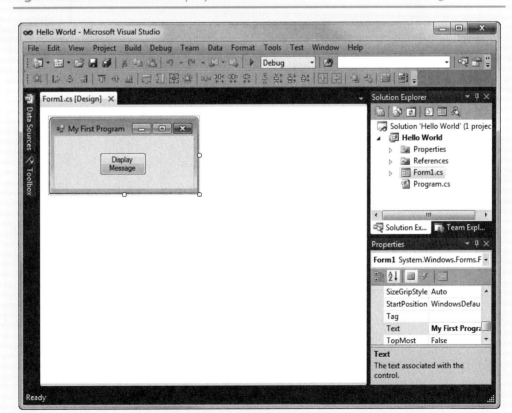

Step 3:   In the *Designer*, double-click the `messageButton` control. This should cause the code editor to appear as shown in Figure 2-41. Notice that an empty event handler named `messageButton_Click` has been created.

Figure 2-41 Code editor with an empty event handler

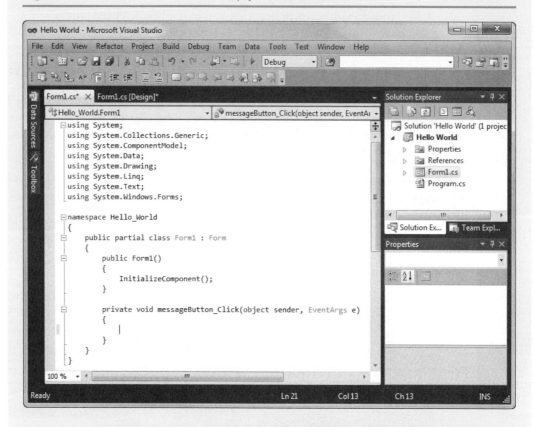

Step 4:   Inside the `messageButton_Click` event handler, type the following statement exactly as it is shown:

```
MessageBox.Show("Hello World");
```

Don't forget to type the semicolon at the end of the statement! When you have finished, the code window should look like Figure 2-42.

Step 5:   Save the project.

Step 6:   Press the [F5] key on the keyboard, or click the *Start Debugging* button (▶) on the toolbar to compile and run the application.

NOTE: If you typed the statement correctly inside the `messageButton_Click` event handler (in Step 4), the application should run. If you did not type the statement correctly, however, a window will appear reporting build errors. If that happens, click the *No* button in the window and then correct the statement so it appears exactly as shown in Figure 2-42.

Figure 2-42 Statement written inside the event handler

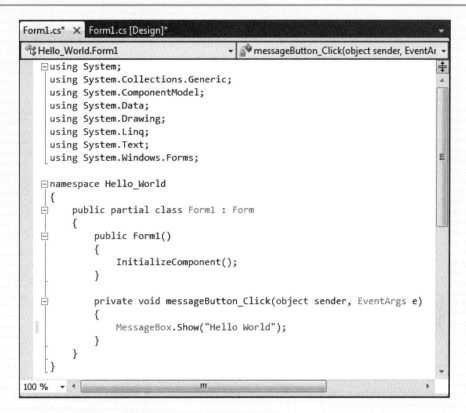

When the application runs, it will display the form shown on the left in Figure 2-43. When you click the *Display Message* button, the message box shown on the right in the figure will appear. You can click the *OK* button on the message box to close it.

Figure 2-43 The *Hello World* application running

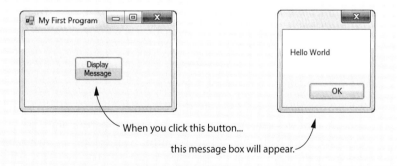

When you click this button...

this message box will appear.

2.5 Label Controls

CONCEPT: A label control displays text on a form. Label controls have various properties that affect the control's appearance. Label controls can be used to display unchanging text, or program output.

When you want to display text on a form, you use a **Label control**. Figure 2-44 shows an example of a form with two Label controls. Once you have placed a Label control on a form, you set its Text property to the text that you want to display. For example, in Figure 2-44, the upper Label control's Text property is set to *Number of Hours Worked*, and the lower Label control's Text property is set to *Hourly Pay Rate*.

Figure 2-44 A form with Label controls

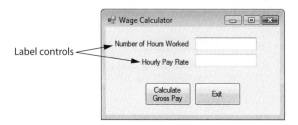

You'll find the Label control tool in the *Common Controls* group of the *Toolbox*, as shown in Figure 2-45. To create a Label control on a form, you double-click the Label control tool in the *Toolbox*. As shown in Figure 2-45, a Label control will be created on the form. (Alternatively, you can click and drag the Label control tool from the *Toolbox* onto the form.) Notice that a bounding box appears around the Label control in the figure. This indicates that the control is currently selected.

Figure 2-45 Creating a Label control

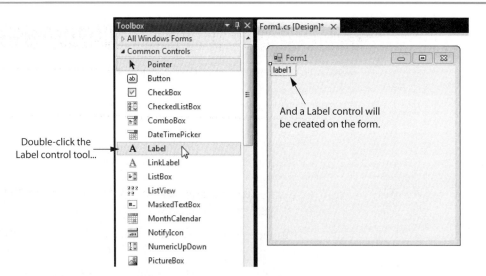

When you create Label controls, they are automatically given default names such as `label1`, `label2`, and so forth. A Label control's Text property is initially set to the same value as the Label control's name. So, a Label control will display its own name when it is created, as shown by the example in Figure 2-45. When a Label control is selected in the Designer, you can use the *Properties* window to change its Text property. Figure 2-46 shows a Label control after its Text property has been changed to *Programming in Visual C# is fun!*

You can also use the Properties window to change a Label control's name. It's always a good idea to change a control's name to something that is more meaningful than the default name that Visual Studio gives it.

The Font Property

If you want to change the appearance of a Label control's text, you can change the control's Font property. The **Font property** allows you to set the font, font style, and size of the con-

Figure 2-46 A Label control displaying a message

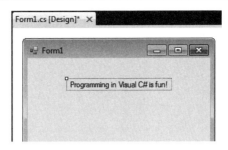

trol's text. When you select the Font property in the Properties window, you will notice that an ellipses button (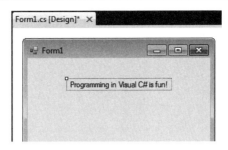) appears next to the property's value, as shown in Figure 2-47. When you click the ellipses button, the *Font* dialog box appears, as shown in Figure 2-48. Select a font, font style, and size, and click *OK*. The text displayed by the control will be updated with the selected attributes. For example, Figure 2-49 shows a Label control with the following Font property attributes:

Font: Lucida Handwriting

Font Style: Italic

Size: 10 point.

Figure 2-47 The Font property

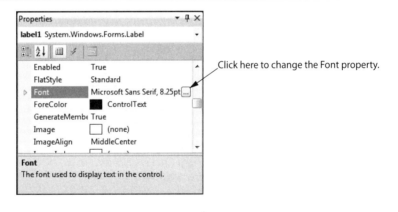

Figure 2-48 The *Font* dialog box

Figure 2-49 A label's appearance with altered font attributes

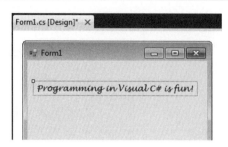

The BorderStyle Property

Label controls have a **BorderStyle property** that allows you to display a border around the control's text. The BorderStyle property may have one of three values: None, FixedSingle, or Fixed3D. The property is set to None by default, which means that no border will appear around the control's text. If the BorderStyle property is set to FixedSingle, the control's text will be outlined with a thin border. If the BorderStyle property is set to Fixed3D, the control's text will have a recessed 3D appearance. Figure 2-50 shows an example of Label controls with each BorderStyle setting.

Figure 2-50 BorderStyle examples

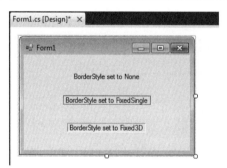

To change the BorderStyle property, select it in the Properties window and then click the down-arrow button ([▼]) that appears next to the property's value. As shown in Figure 2-51, a drop-down list will appear containing the three possible values for this property. Select the desired value and the control's text will be updated.

Figure 2-51 BorderStyle selections

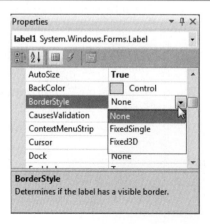

The AutoSize Property

Label controls have an **AutoSize property** that controls the way they can be resized. The AutoSize property is a **Boolean** property, which means that it can be set to one of two possible values: True or False. By default, a Label control's AutoSize property is set to True, which means that the control automatically resizes itself to accommodate the size of the text it displays. For example, look at the three Label controls in Figure 2-52. Each of the controls displays different amounts of text at different font sizes. Because each control's BorderStyle property is set to FixedSingle, you can see that each control is just large enough to accommodate its text.

Figure 2-52 Label controls with AutoSize set to True

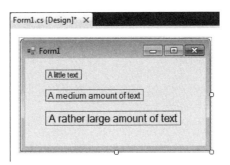

When a Label control's AutoSize property is set to True, you cannot manually change the size of the control by clicking and dragging its bounding box. If you want to manually change the size of a Label control, you have to set its AutoSize property to False. When AutoSize is set to False, sizing handles will appear around the control, allowing you to click and drag the bounding box to resize the control. Figure 2-53 shows an example. In the figure, the Label control has been resized so it is much larger than the text it displays.

Figure 2-53 Label control with AutoSize set to False

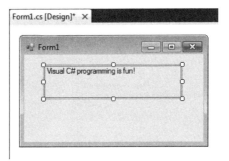

NOTE: When a Label control's AutoSize property is set to True, the label's text will always appear on one line. When the AutoSize property is set to False, the label's text will wrap across multiple lines if it is too long to fit on one line.

The TextAlign Property

When you set a Label control's AutoSize property to False and then manually resize the control, it sometimes becomes necessary to change the way the label's text is aligned. By default, a label's text is aligned with the top and left edges of the label's bounding box. For example, look at the label shown in Figure 2-53. Notice how the text is positioned in the label's upper-left corner.

What if we want the text to be aligned differently within the label? For example, what if we want the text to be centered in the label or positioned in the lower-right corner? We can change the text's alignment in the label with the **TextAlign property**. The TextAlign property may be set to any of the following values: TopLeft, TopCenter, TopRight, MiddleLeft, MiddleCenter, MiddleRight, BottomLeft, BottomCenter, or BottomRight. Figure 2-54 shows nine Label controls, each with a different TextAlign value.

Figure 2-54 Text alignments

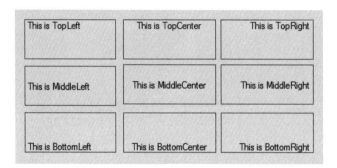

To change the TextAlign property, select it in the *Properties* window and then click the down-arrow button (▼) that appears next to its value. This causes a dialog box with nine buttons, as shown in the left image in Figure 2-55, to appear. As shown in the right image in the figure, the nine buttons represent the valid settings of the TextAlign property.

Figure 2-55 Setting the TextAlign property

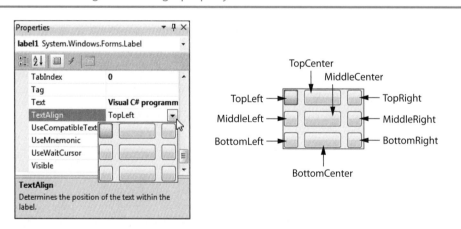

Using Code to Display Output in a Label Control

In addition to displaying unchanging text on a form, Label controls are also useful for displaying output while an application is running. For example, suppose you are creating an application that performs a calculation and you want to display the result of the calculation at a specific location on the form. Using a Label control to display the output would be an ideal solution. Here are the general steps that you would follow:

Step 1: While creating the application's GUI, you place a Label control on the form at the location where you want the result to be displayed. Then, in the *Properties* window, you erase the contents of the Label control's Text property. Because the control's Text property is empty, the control will not initially display anything when the application runs.

Step 2: In the application's code, you write the necessary statements to perform the calculation and then you store the result of the calculation in the Label control's Text property. This causes the result to be displayed on the form in the Label control.

NOTE: We do not discuss calculations until Chapter 3, so in this chapter we look at examples that display nonmathematical data as output in Label controls.

In code, you use an **assignment statement** to store a value in a control's property. For example, suppose you have created a Label control and named it `outputLabel`. The following assignment statement stores the string `"Thank you very much"` in the control's Text property.

```
outputLabel.Text = "Thank you very much";
```

The equal sign (=) is known as the **assignment operator**. It assigns the value that appears on its right side to the item that appears on its left side. In this example, the item on the left side of the assignment operator is the expression `outputLabel.Text`. This is simply the `outputLabel` control's Text property. The value on the right side of the assignment operator is the string `"Thank you very much"`. When this statement executes, the string `"Thank you very much"` is assigned to the `outputLabel` control's Text property. When this statement executes, the text *Thank you very much* is displayed in the Label control.

WARNING! When writing assignment statements, remember that the item receiving the value must be on the left side of the = operator. The following statement, for example, is wrong and will cause an error when you compile the program:

```
"Thank you very much" = outputLabel; ← ERROR!
```

NOTE: The standard notation for referring to a control's property in code is:

ControlName.PropertyName

Let's look at an example application that uses a Label control to display output. In the *Chap02* folder of the Student Sample Programs that accompany this textbook, you will find a project named Presidential Trivia. The purpose of the application is to display a trivia question about a former U.S. president. When the user clicks a button, the answer to the trivia question is displayed on the form. The project's form appears as shown in Figure 2-56.

As shown in the figure, the form has the three controls:

- A Label control named `questionLabel`. This label displays the trivia question.
- A Label control named `answerLabel`. This label initially appears empty, but will be used to display the answer to the trivia question.

Figure 2-56 Presidential Trivia form

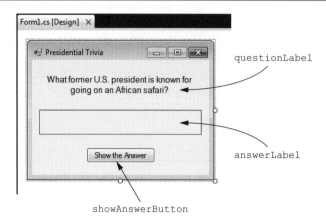

- A Button control named `showAnswerButton`. When the user clicks this button, the answer to the trivia question is displayed.

Table 2-2 lists the property settings for each control of which you should take note.

Table 2-2 Control property settings

Control Name	Control Type	Property Settings
`questionLabel`	Label	**AutoSize:** False **BorderStyle:** None **Font:** Microsoft Sans Serif (Style: Regular, Size: 10 point) **Text:** *What former U.S. president is known for going on an African safari?* **TextAlign:** MiddleCenter
`answerLabel`	Label	**AutoSize:** False **BorderStyle:** FixedSingle **Font:** Microsoft Sans Serif (Style: Bold, Size: 10 point) **Text:** (The contents of the Text property have been erased.) **TextAlign:** MiddleCenter
`showAnswerButton`	Button	**Size:** 110, 23 **Text:** *Show the Answer*

If we open the Form1.cs file in the code editor, we see the code shown in Figure 2-57. (To open the file in the code window, right-click Form1.cs in the *Solution Explorer* and then select *View Code*.) Notice the method named `showAnswerButton_Click`. This is the Click event handler for the `showAnswerButton` control. It contains the following statement:

```
answerLabel.Text = "Theodore Roosevelt";
```

When this statement executes, it assigns the string `"Theodore Roosevelt"` to the `answerLabel` control's Text property. As a result, Theodore Roosevelt is displayed in the label control.

When you run the application, the form appears as shown on the left in Figure 2-58. Click the *Show the Answer* button and the answer to the trivia question appears as shown on the right in the figure.

Figure 2-57 Form1.cs code

```csharp
using System;
using System.Collections.Generic;
using System.ComponentModel;
using System.Data;
using System.Drawing;
using System.Linq;
using System.Text;
using System.Windows.Forms;

namespace Presidential_Trivia
{
    public partial class Form1 : Form
    {
        public Form1()
        {
            InitializeComponent();
        }

        private void showAnswerButton_Click(object sender, EventArgs e)
        {
            answerLabel.Text = "Theodore Roosevelt";
        }
    }
}
```

Figure 2-58 The Presidential Trivia application running

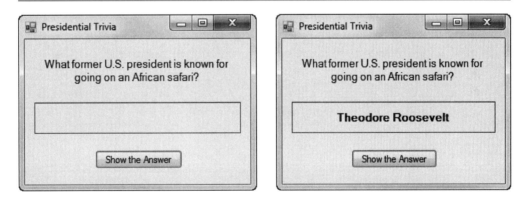

The Text Property Accepts Strings Only

It is important to point out that the Label control's Text property can accept strings only. You cannot assign a number to the Text property. For example, let's assume that an application has a Label control named `resultLabel`. The following statement will cause an error because it is attempting to store the number 5 in the `resultLabel` control's Text property:

```csharp
resultLabel.Text = 5;  ← ERROR!
```

This does not mean that you cannot display a number in a label, however. If you put quotation marks around the number, it becomes a string. The following statement will work:

```csharp
resultLabel.Text = "5";
```

Clearing a Label

In code, if you want to clear the text that is displayed in a Label control, simply assign an empty string (`""`) to the control's Text property, as shown here:

```csharp
answerLabel.Text = "";
```

In Tutorial 2-3 you will work with some of the Label control properties that we have discussed in this section.

Tutorial 2-3:
Creating the Language Translator Application

In this tutorial you will create an application that displays the phrase "Good Morning" in different languages. The form will have three buttons: one for Italian, one for Spanish, and one for German. When the user clicks any of these buttons, the translated phrase will appear in a Label control.

Step 1: Start Visual Studio (or Visual C# Express) and begin a new Windows Forms Application project named Language Translator.

Step 2: Set up the application's form as shown in Figure 2-59. Notice that the form's Text property is set to *Language Translator*. The form has two Label controls and three Button controls. The names of the controls are shown in the figure. As you place each of the controls on the form, refer to Table 2-3 for the relevant property settings.

Figure 2-59 The Language Translator form

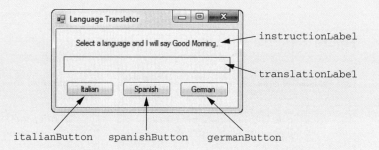

Table 2-3 Control property settings

Control Name	Control Type	Property Settings
instructionLabel	Label	**Text:** *Select a language and I will say Good Morning.*
translationLabel	Label	**AutoSize:** False **BorderStyle:** FixedSingle **Font:** Microsoft Sans Serif (Style: Bold, Size: 10 point) **Text:** (The contents of the Text property have been erased.) **TextAlign:** MiddleCenter
italianButton	Button	**Text:** *Italian*
spanishButton	Button	**Text:** *Spanish*
germanButton	Button	**Text:** *German*

Step 3: Once you have the form and its controls set up, you can create the Click event handlers for the Button controls. In the *Designer*, double-click the italianButton control. This will open the code editor, and you will see an empty event handler

named `italianButton_Click`. Write the following statement inside the event handler:

```
translationLabel.Text = "Buongiorno";
```

Step 4: Switch your view back to the *Designer* and double-click the `spanishButton` control. In the code editor you will see an empty event handler named `spanishButton_Click`. Write the following statement inside the event handler:

```
translationLabel.Text = "Buenos Dias";
```

Step 5: Switch your view back to the *Designer* and double-click the `germanButton` control. In the code editor you will see an empty event handler named `germanButton_Click`. Write the following statement inside the event handler:

```
translationLabel.Text = "Guten Morgen";
```

Step 6: The form's code should now appear as shown in Program 2-1. Note that the line numbers are not part of the code. The line numbers are shown so that you and your instructor can more easily refer to different parts of the program. The lines that appear in boldface are the ones that you typed. Make sure the code you typed appears exactly as shown here. (Don't forget the semicolons!)

Program 2-1 Completed Form1 Code for the *Language Translator* Application

```
 1 using System;
 2 using System.Collections.Generic;
 3 using System.ComponentModel;
 4 using System.Data;
 5 using System.Drawing;
 6 using System.Linq;
 7 using System.Text;
 8 using System.Windows.Forms;
 9
10 namespace Language_Translator
11 {
12    public partial class Form1 : Form
13    {
14      public Form1()
15      {
16          InitializeComponent();
17      }
18
19      private void italianButton_Click(object sender, EventArgs e)
20      {
21          translationLabel.Text = "Buongiorno";
22      }
23
24      private void spanishButton_Click(object sender, EventArgs e)
25      {
26          translationLabel.Text = "Buenos Dias";
27      }
28
29      private void germanButton_Click(object sender, EventArgs e)
30      {
31          translationLabel.Text = "Guten Morgen";
32      }
33    }
34 }
```

Step 7: Save the project. Then, press the $\boxed{F5}$ key on the keyboard or click the *Start Debugging* button ( ) on the toolbar to compile and run the application.

> **NOTE:** If you typed the statements correctly inside the event handlers, the application should run. If you did not type the statements correctly inside the event handlers, a window will appear reporting build errors. If that happens, click the *No* button in the window and then correct the code so it appears exactly as previously shown.

Figure 2-60 shows the application's form when it starts running and after you have clicked each of the Button controls. After you have tested each button, close the application's form.

Figure 2-60 The Language Translator application running

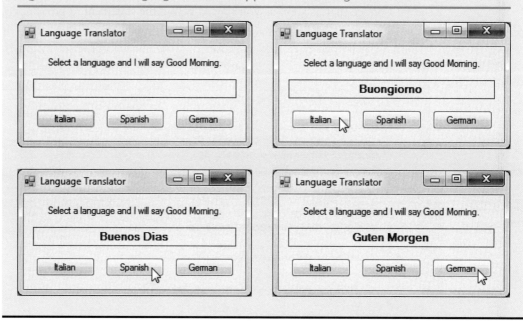

Checkpoint

2.29 In which group of the *Toolbox* can you find the Label control tool?

2.30 Once you have placed a Label control on a form, which property do you use to set the text that you want to display?

2.31 What property can you use to change the appearance of a Label control's text?

2.32 What is the default value of a label's BorderStyle property?

2.33 How do you change the BorderStyle property of a control in the *Properties* window?

2.34 What property determines whether a label can be resized?

2.35 What property determines the way text is aligned in a Label control?

2.36 How can you use a Label control to display output while a program is running?

2.37 What happens if you assign an empty string to a control's Text property in code?

2.6 Making Sense of IntelliSense

CONCEPT: As you type code in the Visual Studio code editor, IntelliSense boxes pop up to assist you. You can use the IntelliSense boxes to automatically complete some programming statements after typing only the first few characters.

IntelliSense is a feature of Visual Studio that provides automatic code completion as you write programming statements. Once you learn how to use IntelliSense, it helps you write code faster. If you've worked through the previous tutorials in this chapter, you've already encountered IntelliSense. For example, in Step 3 of Tutorial 2-3, you were instructed to write the following statement in the `italianButton_Click` event handler:

```
translationLabel.Text = "Buongiorno";
```

Did you notice that as soon as you started typing the statement, a box popped up on the screen? This is known as an IntelliSense list box. The contents of the list box changes as you type. Figure 2-61 shows the IntelliSense list box after you have typed the characters `tra`.

Figure 2-61 IntelliSense list box displayed

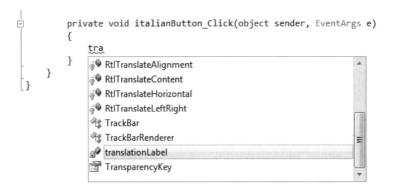

The IntelliSense system is anticipating what you are about to type, and as you type characters, the content of the list box is reduced. The list box shown in Figure 2-61 shows all the names starting with `tra` that might be a candidate for the statement you are typing. Notice that `translationLabel` is selected in the list box. With that item selected, you can press the Tab key on the keyboard, and the `tra` that you previously typed becomes `translationLabel`.

Next, when you type a period, an IntelliSense list pops up showing every property and method belonging to the `translationLabel` control. Type `te` and the Text property becomes selected, as shown in Figure 2-62. When you press the Tab key to select the Text

Figure 2-62 IntelliSense list box after typing ".te"

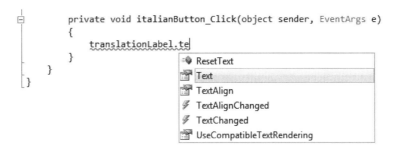

property, your statement automatically becomes translationLabel.Text. At this point, you can continue typing until you have completed the statement.

Now that you have an idea of how IntelliSense works, you are encouraged to experiment with it as you write code in future projects. With a little practice, it will become intuitive.

2.7 PictureBox Controls

CONCEPT: A PictureBox control displays a graphic image on a form. Picture-Box controls have properties for controlling the way the image is displayed. A PictureBox control can have a Click event handler that responds when the user clicks the control at run time.

You can use a **PictureBox control** to display a graphic image on a form. A PictureBox control can display images that have been saved in the bitmap, GIF, JPEG, metafile, or icon graphics formats.

In the *Toolbox*, the PictureBox tool is located in the *Common Controls* group. When you double-click the tool, an empty PictureBox control is created on the form, as shown in Figure 2-63. Although the control does not yet display an image, it has a bounding box that shows its size and location, as well as sizing handles. When you create PictureBox controls, they are automatically given default names such as pictureBox1, pictureBox2, and so forth. You should always change the default name to something more meaningful.

Figure 2-63 An empty PictureBox control

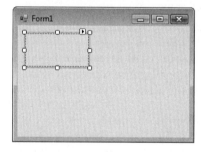

Once you have created a PictureBox control, you use its **Image property** to specify the image that it will display. Follow these steps:

Step 1: Click the Image property in the *Properties* window. An ellipses button (⊡) will appear, as shown on the left in Figure 2-64.

Step 2: Click the ellipses button and the *Select Resource* window, shown on the right in Figure 2-64, will appear.

Step 3: In the *Select Resource* window, click the *Import* button. An *Open* dialog box will appear. Use the dialog box to locate and select the image file that you want to display.

Step 4: After you select an image file, you will see its contents displayed in the *Select Resource* window. This indicates that the image has been imported into the project. Figure 2-65 shows an example of the *Select Resource* window after we have selected and imported an image.

Step 5: Click the *OK* button in the *Select Resource* window, and the selected image will appear in the PictureBox control. Figure 2-66 shows an example. Depending on the size of the image, you might see only part of it displayed. This is the case in Figure 2-66 because the image is larger than the PictureBox control. Your next step is to set the SizeMode property and adjust the size of the control.

Figure 2-64 The Image property's *Select Resource* window

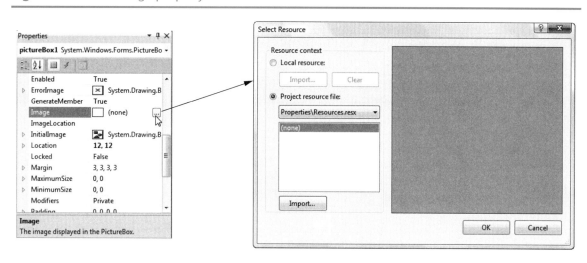

Figure 2-65 An image selected and imported

Figure 2-66 The image displayed in the PictureBox control

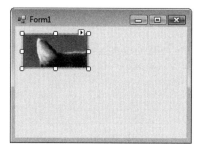

The SizeMode Property

The PictureBox control's **SizeMode property** specifies how the control's image is to be displayed. It can be set to one of the following values:

- **Normal**

  Normal is the default value. The image will be positioned in the upper-left corner of the PictureBox control. If the image is too big to fit in the PictureBox control, it will be clipped.

- **StretchImage**

  StretchImage resizes the image both horizontally and vertically to fit in the PictureBox control. If the image is resized more in one direction than the other, it will appear stretched.

- **AutoSize**

  With AutoSize, the PictureBox control is automatically resized to fit the size of the image.

- **CenterImage**

  CenterImage centers the image in the PictureBox control without resizing it.

- **Zoom**

  Zoom uniformly resizes the image to fit in the PictureBox without losing its original aspect ratio. (**Aspect ratio** is the image's width to height ratio.) This causes the image to be resized without appearing stretched.

Figure 2-67 shows an example of an image displayed in a PictureBox control. The control's SizeMode is set to Zoom, so it can be resized without appearing stretched.

Figure 2-67 An image resized with SizeMode set to Zoom

 NOTE: PictureBox controls also have a BorderStyle property that works just like a Label control's BorderStyle property.

Creating Clickable Images

Buttons aren't the only controls that can respond to Click events. PictureBox controls can, too. That means an application can display an image and perform some action when the user clicks the image.

To make an image clickable, you simply have to create a Click event handler for the PictureBox control that displays the image. You create a Click event handler for a PictureBox control in the same way that you create a Click event handler for a Button control:

- You double-click the PictureBox control in the *Designer*. This creates an empty Click event handler in the form's source code file.
- In the code editor you write statements inside the event handler that you want to execute when the image is clicked.

As an example, look at the Cat project that is in the *Chap02* folder of the Student Sample Programs that accompany this textbook. Figure 2-68 shows the application's form. The PictureBox control's name is `catPictureBox`. Its image is the Cat.jpg file, which is also found in the *Chap02* folder of the Student Sample Programs. The SizeMode property is set to Zoom, and the BorderStyle property is set to FixedSingle.

Open the Form1.cs file in the code editor and you will see that we have already created a Click event handler for the `catPictureBox` control, as shown in Figure 2-69. If you run the application and click the PictureBox, a message box will appear displaying the string *Meow*.

Figure 2-68 The Cat form

Figure 2-69 Code for the Cat project's Form1.cs file

```csharp
using System;
using System.Collections.Generic;
using System.ComponentModel;
using System.Data;
using System.Drawing;
using System.Linq;
using System.Text;
using System.Windows.Forms;

namespace Cat
{
    public partial class Form1 : Form
    {
        public Form1()
        {
            InitializeComponent();
        }

        private void catPictureBox_Click(object sender, EventArgs e)
        {
            MessageBox.Show("Meow");
        }
    }
}
```

Click event handler for the
`catPictureBox` control

Tutorial 2-4 gives you a chance to practice using PictureBox controls. In the tutorial, you will create an application with three clickable PictureBox controls, displaying images that are provided in the Student Sample Program files that accompany this book.

Tutorial 2-4:
Creating the *Flags* Application

In this tutorial you will create an application that displays the flags of Finland, France, and Germany in PictureBox controls. When the user clicks any of these PictureBoxes, the name of that flag's country will appear in a Label control.

Step 1: Start Visual Studio (or Visual C# Express) and begin a new Windows Forms Application project named Flags.

Step 2: Set up the application's form as shown in Figure 2-70. Notice that the form's Text property is set to *Flags*. The names of the controls are shown in the figure. Refer to Table 2-4 for each control's relevant property settings.

Figure 2-70 The Flags form

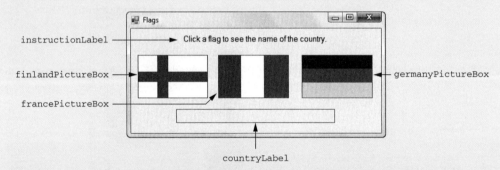

Table 2-4 Control property settings

Control Name	Control Type	Property Settings
instructionLabel	Label	**Text:** *Click a flag to see the name of the country.*
finlandPictureBox	PictureBox	**Image:** Select and import the Finland.bmp file from the *Chap02* folder of the Student Sample Programs. **BorderStyle:** FixedSingle **SizeMode:** AutoSize
francePictureBox	PictureBox	**Image:** Select and import the France.bmp file from the *Chap02* folder of the Student Sample Programs. **BorderStyle:** FixedSingle **SizeMode:** AutoSize
germanyPictureBox	PictureBox	**Image:** Select and import the Germany.bmp file from the *Chap02* folder of the Student Sample Programs. **BorderStyle:** FixedSingle **SizeMode:** AutoSize
countryLabel	Label	**AutoSize:** False **BorderStyle:** FixedSingle **Font:** Microsoft Sans Serif (Style: Bold, Size: 10 point) **Text:** (The contents of the Text property have been erased.) **TextAlign:** MiddleCenter

Step 3: Once you have the form and its controls set up, you can create the Click event handlers for the PictureBox controls. In the *Designer*, double-click the `finlandPictureBox` control. This will open the code editor, and you will see an empty event handler named `finlandPictureBox_Click`. Write the following statement inside the event handler:

```
countryLabel.Text = "Finland";
```

Step 4: Switch your view back to the *Designer* and double-click the `francePictureBox` control. This will open the code editor, and you will see an empty event handler named `francePictureBox_Click`. Write the following statement inside the event handler:

```
countryLabel.Text = "France";
```

Step 5: Switch your view back to the *Designer* and double-click the `germanyPictureBox` control. This will open the code editor, and you will see an empty event handler named `germanyPictureBox_Click`. Write the following statement inside the event handler:

```
countryLabel.Text = "Germany";
```

Step 6: The form's code should now appear as shown in Program 2-2. As was mentioned in the previous tutorial, the line numbers are shown for reference only, and are not part of the code. The lines that appear in boldface are the ones that you typed. Make sure the code you typed appears exactly as shown here. (Don't forget the semicolons!)

Program 2-2 Completed Form1 code for the *Flags* application

```
 1 using System;
 2 using System.Collections.Generic;
 3 using System.ComponentModel;
 4 using System.Data;
 5 using System.Drawing;
 6 using System.Linq;
 7 using System.Text;
 8 using System.Windows.Forms;
 9
10 namespace Flags
11 {
12     public partial class Form1 : Form
13     {
14         public Form1()
15         {
16             InitializeComponent();
17         }
18
19         private void finlandPictureBox_Click(object sender, EventArgs e)
20         {
21             countryLabel.Text = "Finland";
22         }
23
24         private void francePictureBox_Click(object sender, EventArgs e)
25         {
26             countryLabel.Text = "France";
27         }
28
29         private void germanyPictureBox_Click(object sender, EventArgs e)
```

```
30      {
31          countryLabel.Text = "Germany";
32      }
33  }
34 }
```

Step 7: Save the project. Then, press the [F5] key on the keyboard, or click the *Start Debugging* button (▶) on the toolbar to compile and run the application.

> **NOTE:** If you typed the statements correctly inside the event handlers, the application should run. If you did not type the statements inside the event handlers correctly, a window will appear reporting build errors. If that happens, click the *No* button in the window, then correct the code so it appears exactly as previously shown.

Figure 2-71 shows the application's form when it starts running and then after you have clicked each of the PictureBox controls. After you have clicked each flag to make sure the application works correctly, close the form.

Figure 2-71 The Flags application running

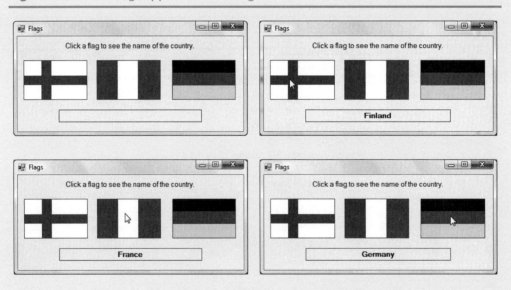

The Visible Property

Most controls have a **Visible property** that determines whether the control is visible on the form at run time. The Visible property is a Boolean property, which means it can be set only to the values True or False. If a control's Visible property is set to True, the control will be visible on the form at run time. If a control's Visible property is set to False, however, the control will not be visible at run time. By default, the Visible property is set to True.

When you use the *Properties* window to change a control's Visible property at design time, the control will still be visible in the *Designer*. When you run the application, however, the control will not be visible on the form. For example, the image on the left in Figure 2-72 shows a form in the *Designer*. The PictureBox control's Visible property is set to False, but the control can still be seen in the *Designer*. The image on the right shows the form while the application is running. At run time, the control is not visible.

Figure 2-72 A PictureBox control with its Visible property set to False

The form in the *Designer*   The form at run time

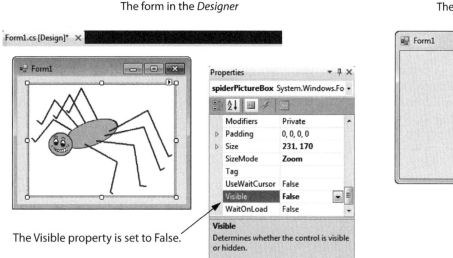
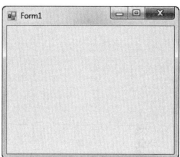

The Visible property is set to False.

A control's Visible property can also be modified in code by an assignment statement, which makes it possible to hide or display a control while the application is running. For example, the PictureBox control shown in Figure 2-72 is named `spiderPictureBox`. The following statement sets the control's Visible property to `true`:

```
spiderPictureBox.Visible = true;
```

When this statement executes, the `spiderPictureBox` control will become visible. Likewise, the following statement sets the control's Visible property to `false`:

```
spiderPictureBox.Visible = false;
```

When this statement executes, the `spiderPictureBox` control will become invisible.

NOTE: When you write the values `true` or `false` in code, as shown in the previous assignment statement, they must be written in all lowercase letters. The words `true` and `false` are C# keywords, and an error will occur if you don't write them in lowercase. However, when you use the *Properties* window to set a Boolean property, such as Visible, the values True and False will be shown with an initial capital. Try not to let this inconsistency confuse you!

In Tutorial 2-5 you will create an application that uses the Visible property of two PictureBox controls to simulate a card being flipped over.

Tutorial 2-5:
Creating the Card Flip Application

In this tutorial you will create an application that simulates a card being flipped over. When the application runs, it will display the form shown on the left in Figure 2-73. The form initially displays the back of a poker card. When the user clicks the *Show the Card Face* button, the card will be flipped over to show its face, as shown in the form on the right. When the user clicks the *Show the Card Back* button, the card is flipped back over to show its back.

The simulation of the card being flipped will be accomplished using the following logic:

- When the user clicks the *Show the Card Face* button, the PictureBox showing the card's back will be made invisible and the PictureBox showing the card's face will be made visible.
- When the user clicks the *Show the Card Back* button, the PictureBox showing the card's face will be made invisible and the PictureBox showing the card's back will be made visible.

Figure 2-73 The Card Flip application

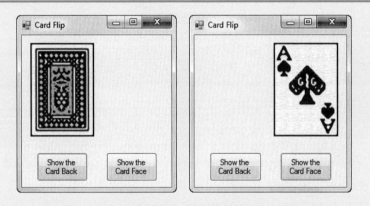

Figure 2-74 The Card Flip form

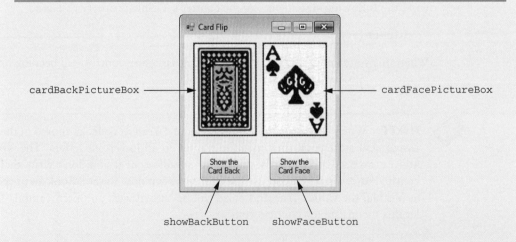

Step 1: Start Visual Studio (or Visual C# Express) and begin a new Windows Forms Application project named Card Flip.

Step 2: Set up the application's form as shown in Figure 2-74. Notice that the form's Text property is set to *Card Flip*. The names of the controls are shown in the figure. Use the Properties window to make the property settings shown in Table 2-5. (In particular, note that the `cardBackPictureBox` control's Visible property is set to True, and the `cardFacePictureBox` control's Visible property is set to False.)

Table 2-5 Control property settings

Control Name	Control Type	Property Settings
cardBackPictureBox	PictureBox	**Image:** Select and import the Backface_Blue.jpg file from the *Chap02* folder of the Student Sample Programs. **Size:** 100, 140 **SizeMode:** Zoom **Visible:** True
cardFacePictureBox	PictureBox	**Image:** Select and import the Ace_Spades.jpg file from the *Chap02* folder of the Student Sample Programs. **Size:** 100, 140 **SizeMode:** Zoom **Visible:** False
showBackButton	Button	**Text:** *Show the Card Back* (Manually resize the button to accommodate the text, as shown in Figure 2-74.)
showFaceButton	Button	**Text:** *Show the Card Face* (Manually resize the button to accommodate the text, as shown in Figure 2-74.)

Step 3: Once you have the form and its controls set up, you can create the Click event handlers for the Button controls. In the *Designer*, double-click the `showBackButton` control. This will open the code editor, and you will see an empty event handler named `showBackButton_Click`. Write the following statements inside the event handler:

```
cardBackPictureBox.Visible = true;
cardFacePictureBox.Visible = false;
```

Step 4: Switch your view back to the *Designer* and double-click the `showFaceButton` control. This will open the code editor, and you will see an empty event handler named `showFaceButton_Click`. Write the following statements inside the event handler:

```
cardBackPictureBox.Visible = false;
cardFacePictureBox.Visible = true;
```

Step 5: The form's code should now appear as shown in Program 2-3. Remember, the line numbers are shown for reference only and are not part of the code. The lines that appear in boldface are the ones that you typed. Make sure the code you typed appears exactly as shown here. (Don't forget the semicolons!)

Program 2-3 Completed Form1 code for the *Card Flip* application

```
 1 using System;
 2 using System.Collections.Generic;
 3 using System.ComponentModel;
 4 using System.Data;
 5 using System.Drawing;
 6 using System.Linq;
 7 using System.Text;
 8 using System.Windows.Forms;
 9
10 namespace Card_Flip
11 {
12    public partial class Form1 : Form
13    {
14       public Form1()
15       {
16          InitializeComponent();
17       }
18
19       private void showBackButton_Click(object sender, EventArgs e)
20       {
21          cardBackPictureBox.Visible = true;
22          cardFacePictureBox.Visible = false;
23       }
24
25       private void showFaceButton_Click(object sender, EventArgs e)
26       {
27          cardBackPictureBox.Visible = false;
28          cardFacePictureBox.Visible = true;
29       }
30    }
31 }
```

Step 6: Save the project. Then, press the F5 key on the keyboard, or click the *Start Debugging* button (▶) on the toolbar to compile and run the application.

Test the application by clicking the buttons. When you click the *Show the Card Face* button you should see the card's face (and the back of the card should be invisible). When you click the *Show the Card Back* button you should see the card's back (and the card's face should be invisible). When you are finished, close the application.

NOTE: If you typed the statements correctly inside the event handlers, the application should run. If you did not type the statements inside the event handlers correctly, a window will appear reporting build errors. If that happens, click the *No* button in the window and then correct the code so it appears exactly as previously shown.

NOTE: In addition to PictureBoxes, many other types of controls have a Visible property. For example, you can make a Label control visible or invisible by setting the value of its Visible property.

Sequential Execution of Statements

In Tutorial 2-5, the event handlers that you created each contained more than one statement. For example, here is the `showBackButton_Click` method:

```
private void showBackButton_Click(object sender, EventArgs e)
{
    cardBackPictureBox.Visible = true;
    cardFacePictureBox.Visible = false;
}
```

This method has two assignment statements. When the method executes, the statements in the method execute in the order that they appear, from the beginning of the method to the end of the method. This statement executes first:

```
cardBackPictureBox.Visible = true;
```

Then this statement executes:

```
cardFacePictureBox.Visible = false;
```

When the application is running, however, you can't really tell that the statements are executing in this order simply by watching the action take place on the screen. When you click the `showBackButton` control, the Click event handler executes so quickly that it appears as though both statements execute simultaneously. It's important for you to understand, however, that the statements execute one at a time, in the order that they appear in the method.

In this particular method, it doesn't really matter which assignment statement is written first. If we reverse the order of the statements, we will not be able to see the difference on the screen because the application executes so quickly. In most applications, however, the order in which you write the statements in the event handlers is critically important. In Chapter 3 you will start writing event handlers that perform several steps, and in most cases, the steps must be performed in a specific order. Otherwise, the program will not produce the correct results.

 ## Checkpoint

2.38   What is a PictureBox control used for?

2.39   Where is the PictureBox tool located in the *Toolbox*?

2.40   How do you display an image in the PictureBox?

2.41   What is the default value of the PictureBox control's SizeMode property?

2.42   How does setting the SizeMode property to Zoom affect the image that is to be displayed in the PictureBox control?

2.43   How do you create a clickable image?

2.44   Does the value of a control's Visible property change how the image appears at run time and design time?

 2.8 ## Comments, Blank Lines, and Indentation

CONCEPT: Comments are brief notes that are placed in a program's source code to explain how parts of the program work. Programmers commonly use blank lines and indentation in program code to give the code visual organization and make it easier to read.

Comments

Comments are short notes that are placed in different parts of a program, explaining how those parts of the program work. Comments are not intended for the compiler. They are intended for any person who is reading the code and trying to understand what it does.

In C# there are three types of comments: line comments, block comments, and documentation comments. A **line comment** appears on one line in a program. You begin a line comment with two forward slashes (//). Everything written after the slashes, to the end of the line, is ignored by the compiler. The following code sample shows how we might use line comments in the showBackButton_Click event handler from Tutorial 2-5. Each line comment explains what the very next line of code does.

```
private void showBackButton_Click(object sender, EventArgs e)
{
    // Make the image of the back of the card visible.
    cardBackPictureBox.Visible = true;

    // Make the image of the face of the card invisible.
    cardFacePictureBox.Visible = false;
}
```

A line comment does not have to occupy an entire line. Anything appearing after the // symbol, to the end of the line, is ignored. So, a comment can appear after an executable statement. The following code sample shows an example.

```
private void showBackButton_Click(object sender, EventArgs e)
{
    cardBackPictureBox.Visible = true;  // Show the card back.
    cardFacePictureBox.Visible = false; // Hide the card face.
}
```

A **block comment** can occupy multiple consecutive lines in a program. A block comment starts with /* (a forward slash followed by an asterisk) and ends with */ (an asterisk followed by a forward slash). Everything between these markers is ignored. The following code sample shows how block comments may be used.

```
/*  Click event handler for the showBackButton control.
    This method makes the image of the back of the card
    visible and makes the image of the card's face
    invisible.
*/

private void showBackButton_Click(object sender, EventArgs e)
{
    cardBackPictureBox.Visible = true;  // Show the card back.
    cardFacePictureBox.Visible = false; // Hide the card face.
}
```

The first five lines in this code sample are a block comment that explains what the showBackButton_Click method does. Block comments make it easier to write long explanations because you do not have to mark every line with a comment symbol.

Remember the following advice when using block comments:

- Be careful not to reverse the beginning symbol (/*) with the ending symbol (*/).
- Do not forget the ending symbol.

Each of these mistakes can be difficult to track down and will prevent the program from compiling correctly.

The third type of comment is known as a documentation comment. **Documentation comments** are used by professional programmers to embed extensive documentation in a

    c. machine language file

    d. source code file

6. A namespace is container that holds _____.

    a. methods

    b. names

    c. spaces

    d. classes

7. A(n) _____ is a method that executes when a specific event takes place while an application is running.

    a. action process

    b. event handler

    c. runtime procedure

    d. event method

8. The statement `MessageBox.Show("Hello World");` is an example of a(n) _____.

    a. method call

    b. namespace

    c. Click event

    d. event handler

9. In programming we use the term string to mean _____.

    a. many lines of code

    b. parallel memory locations

    c. string of characters

    d. virtually anything

10. A(n) _____ marks the end of a programming statement in C#.

    a. semicolon

    b. period

    c. hyphen

    d. underscore

11. A piece of data that is written into a program's code is a(n) _____.

    a. identifier

    b. specifier

    c. keyword

    d. literal

12. The time during which you build the GUI and write the application's code is referred to as _____.

    a. run time

    b. design time

    c. code time

    d. planning

13. The time during which an application is executing is referred to as _____.

    a. go time

    b. design time

    c. execution

    d. run time

14. When you want to display text on a form, you use a _____ control.

    a. Button

    b. PictureBox

    c. Label

    d. TextBox

15. The _____ property allows you to set the font, font style, and size of the control's text.

    a. Style

    b. AutoSize

    c. Text

    d. Font

16. A(n) _____ property can be set to one of two possible values: True or False.

    a. Boolean

    b. Logical

    c. Binary

    d. Dual

17. Label controls have a(n) _____ property that controls the way they can be resized.

    a. Stretch

    b. AutoSize

    c. Dimension

    d. Fixed

18. The _____ property can be used to change the text's alignment in the label.

    a. TextPosition

    b. AutoAlign

    c. TextCenter

    d. TextAlign

19. In code, you use a(n) _____ to store a value in a control's property.

    a. Click event

    b. method call

    c. assignment statement

    d. Boolean value

20. The equal sign (=) is known as the _____.

    a. equality symbol

    b. assignment operator

    c. equality operator

    d. property position

21. The standard notation for referring to a control's property in code is _____.

    a. `ControlName.PropertyName`

    b. `ControlName=PropertyName`

    c. `PropertyName.ControlName`

    d. `PropertyName=ControlName`

22. _____ is a feature of Visual Studio that provides automatic code completion as you write programming statements.

    a. AutoCode

    b. AutoComplete

    c. IntelliSense

    d. IntelliCode

23. You can use a(n) _____ control to display a graphic image on a form.

    a. Graphics

    b. PictureBox

    c. Drawing

    d. ImageBox

24. Once you have created a PictureBox control, you use its _____ property to specify the image that it will display.

    a. Image

    b. Source

    c. DrawSource

    d. ImageList

25. The PictureBox control's _____ property specifies how the control's image is to be displayed.

    a. RenderMode

    b. DrawMode

    c. SizeMode

    d. ImageMode

26. _____ is the image's width to height ratio.

    a. Aspect ratio

    b. Size ratio

    c. Projection ratio

    d. Area ratio

27. Most controls have a _____ property that determines whether the control is visible on the form at run time.

    a. Render

    b. Viewable

    c. Visible

    d. Draw

28. A _____ appears on one line in a program.

    a. inline comment

    b. line comment

    c. forward comment

    d. block comment

29. A _____ can occupy multiple consecutive lines in a program.

    a. block comment

    b. square comment

    c. multiline comment

    d. machine comment

30. Programmers commonly use blank lines and indentations in their code to create a sense of _____.

    a. logic

    b. visual organization

    c. documentation

    d. program flow

31. To close an application's form in code, you use the statement _____.

    a. `Close();`

    b. `Close.This();`

    c. `Close()`

    d. `this.Close();`

True or False

1. Changing an object's Text property also changes the object's name.

2. When a form is created, its Text property is initially set to the same value as the form's name.

3. The form's title is displayed in the bar along the top of a form.

4. C# source code files always end with the .cs extension.

5. You add your own code to the Progam.cs file as you develop an application.

6. C# code is organized as methods, which are contained inside classes, which are contained inside namespaces.

7. In C# code, each opening brace must have a corresponding closing brace at some point later in the program.

8. When you double-click a control in the *Designer*, Visual Studio not only creates an empty event handler, but it also writes some code that you don't see, elsewhere in the project that is necessary for the event handler to properly function.

9. A Label control's Text property is initially set to the same value as the Label control's name.

10. When a Label control's AutoSize property is set to True, you cannot manually change the size of the control by clicking and dragging its bounding box.

11. By default, a label's text is aligned with the bottom and right edges of the label's bounding box.

12. Label controls are useful for displaying output while an application is running.

13. The assignment operator assigns the value that appears on its left side to the item that appears on its right side.

14. PictureBox controls also have a BorderStyle property that works just like a Label control's BorderStyle property.

15. Buttons are the only controls that can respond to Click events.

16. The Visible property is a Binary property, which means it can be set only to the values 1 or 0.

17. When you write the values `true` or `false` in code, they must be written in all lowercase letters.

18. In C# there are three types of comments: line comments, block comments, and documentation comments.

19. To close an application's form in code, you use the statement `Close.This();`

20. The Visual Studio code editor examines each statement as you type it, and reports any syntax errors that are found.

Short Answer

1. What does a bounding box indicate about an object in the *Designer*?

2. What happens when you position the mouse cursor over an edge or corner of a bounding box that has sizing handles?

3. What determines an object's appearance and other characteristics?

4. What is shown by each column in the *Properties* window?

5. What steps must you perform to change a form's Text property?

6. What steps must you perform to change a form's Size property in the *Properties* window?

7. How do you move a control to a new location on the form using the mouse?

8. What steps do you perform to change a Button control's Text property?

9. Briefly describe the contents of the Form1.cs file.

10. In code, what characters do you enclose a string literal in?

11. When creating an event handler for a button, is it possible to skip a step by opening the code editor and writing all the event handler code yourself? Why or why not.

12. Briefly describe the difference between design time and run time.

13. Describe the appearance of a Label control that's BorderStyle property is set to Fixed3D.

14. What does it mean when a Label control's AutoSize property is set to True?

15. What are the values that the TextAlign property may be set to?

16. How do you clear the text that is displayed in a Label control in code?

17. What are the different image formats that a PictureBox control can display?

18. List the values that the SizeMode property of a PictureBox control can be set to.

19. What are the three types of comments you can use in Visual C#?

20. How does Visual Studio help you to quickly correct syntax errors?

Algorithm Workbench

1. What statement would you write to display *Good Afternoon* in a message box?

2. What statement would you write to display your name in a message box?

3. Suppose an application's GUI has a Label control named `dogLabel`. Write a statement that causes *Fido* to be displayed in the `dogLabel` control.

4. Suppose an application's GUI has a Label control named `outputLabel`. Write a statement that clears any text that happens to be displayed by the control.

5. Suppose an application's GUI has a PictureBox control named `myPicture`. Write a statement that makes the control invisible.

Programming Problems

1. Latin Translator

   Look at the following list of Latin words and their meanings.

Latin	English
sinister	left
dexter	right
medium	center

   Create an application that translates the Latin words to English. The form should have three buttons, one for each Latin word. When the user clicks a button, the application should display the English translation in a Label control.

2. **Clickable Number Images**

In the *Chap02* folder, in the Student Sample Program files, you will find the image files shown in Figure 2-79. Create an application that displays these images in PictureBox controls. The application should perform the following actions:

- When the user clicks the 1 image, the application should display the word *One* in a message box.
- When the user clicks the 2 image, the application should display the word *Two* in a message box.
- When the user clicks the 3 image, the application should display the word *Three* in a message box.
- When the user clicks the 4 image, the application should display the word *Four* in a message box.
- When the user clicks the 5 image, the application should display the word *Five* in a message box.

Figure 2-79 Image files

One.bmp   Two.bmp   Three.bmp   Four.bmp   Five.bmp

3. **Card Identifier**

In the Student Sample Programs that accompany this book, you will find a folder named *Images\Cards\Poker Large*. In that folder you will find JPEG image files for a complete deck of poker cards. Create an application with five PictureBox controls. Each PictureBox should display a different card from the set of images. When the user clicks any of the PictureBox controls, the name of the card should be displayed in a Label control. Figure 2-80 shows an example of the application running. The image on the left shows the application's form when it starts running. The image on the right shows the form after the user has clicked the two of clubs card.

Figure 2-80 Card Identifier application

4. **Joke and Punch line**

A joke typically has two parts: a setup and a punch line. For example, this might be the setup for a joke:

How many programmers does it take to change a lightbulb?

And this is the punch line:

None. That's a hardware problem.

Think of your favorite joke and identify its setup and punch line. Then, create an application that has a Label and two buttons on a form. One of the buttons should read "Setup" and the other button should read "Punch line." When the *Setup* button is clicked, display the joke's setup in the Label control. When the *Punch line* button is clicked, display the joke's punch line in the Label control.

5. **Heads or Tails**

In the Student Sample Programs that accompany this book you will find a folder named *Images\Coins* that contains images showing the heads and tails sides of a coin. Create an application with a *Show Heads* button and a *Show Tails* button. When the user clicks the *Show Heads* button, an image of the heads side of a coin should appear. When the user clicks the *Show Tails* button, an image of the tails side of a coin should appear. Figure 2-81 shows examples of how the application's form might appear.

Figure 2-81 The Heads or Tails application

6. **Orion Constellation**

Orion is one of the most famous constellations in the night sky. In the *Chap02* folder of the Student Sample Programs that accompany this book, you will find an image file named Orion.bmp, which contains a diagram of the Orion constellation. Create an application that displays the Orion image in a PictureBox control, as shown on the left in Figure 2-82. The application should have a button that, when clicked, displays the names of each of the stars, as shown on the right in Figure 2-82. The application should have another button that, when clicked, hides the star names. The names of the stars are: *Betelgeuse*, *Meissa*, *Alnitak*, *Alnilam*, *Mintaka*, *Saiph*, and *Rigel*.

Hint: Place the PictureBox control with the Orion image on the form. Then, place Label controls containing the star names on top of the PictureBox. Use the Properties window to set each of the Label control's Visible property to False. That will cause the labels to be invisible when the application runs. The *Show Star Names* button will set each of the Label control's Visible property to `true`, and the *Hide Star Names* button will set each of the Label control's Visible property to `false`.

Figure 2-82 The Orion Constellation application

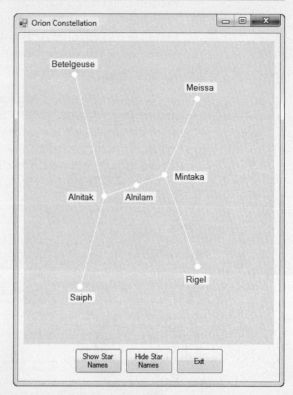

3 Processing Data

3.1 Reading Input with TextBox Controls

CONCEPT: The TextBox control is a rectangular area that can accept keyboard input from the user.

Many of the programs that you will write from this point forward will require the user to enter data. The data entered by the user will then be used in some sort of operation. One of the primary controls that you will use to get data from the user is the TextBox control.

A **TextBox control** appears as a rectangular area on a form. When the application is running, the user can type text into a TextBox control. The program can then retrieve the text that the user entered and use that text in any necessary operations.

In the *Toolbox*, the TextBox tool is located in the *Common Controls* group. When you double-click the tool, a TextBox control is created on the form, as shown in Figure 3-1. When you create TextBox controls, they are automatically given default names such as `textBox1`, `textBox2`, and so forth. As you learned in Chapter 2, you should always change a control's default name to something more meaningful.

When the user types into a TextBox control, the text is stored in the control's Text property. In code, if you want to retrieve the data that has been typed into a TextBox, you simply retrieve the contents of the control's Text property.

Figure 3-1 A TextBox control

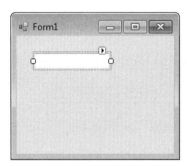

 NOTE: When you retrieve the contents of the Text property, you *always* get a string. Any operation that can be performed on a string can be performed on a control's Text property.

Let's look at an example. In the *Chap03* folder of the Student Sample Program files that accompany this book, you will find a project named TextBox Demo. Figure 3-2 shows the form, with most of the control names specified, and Figure 3-3 shows the form's code. (In Figure 3-3, to conserve space on the page, we have scrolled past the using directives that appear at the top of the code file.)

Notice in Figure 3-3 that the readInputButton control's Click event handler performs the following assignment statement:

```
outputLabel.Text = nameTextBox.Text;
```

This statement assigns the value of the nameTextBox control's Text property to the outputLabel control's Text property. In other words, it gets any text that has been entered by the user into the nameTextBox control and displays it in the outputLabel control. If you run the application, Figure 3-4 shows an example of how the form appears after you have entered *Kathryn Smith* and clicked the readInputButton control.

Figure 3-2 The TextBox Demo application

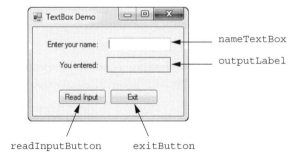

Clearing the Contents of a TextBox Control

You can clear the contents of a TextBox control in the same way that you clear the contents of a Label control: you assign an empty string ("") to the control's Text property. For example, the following statement clears the contents of the nameTextBox control:

```
nameTextBox.Text = "";
```

Figure 3-3 The form's code (excluding the `using` directives)

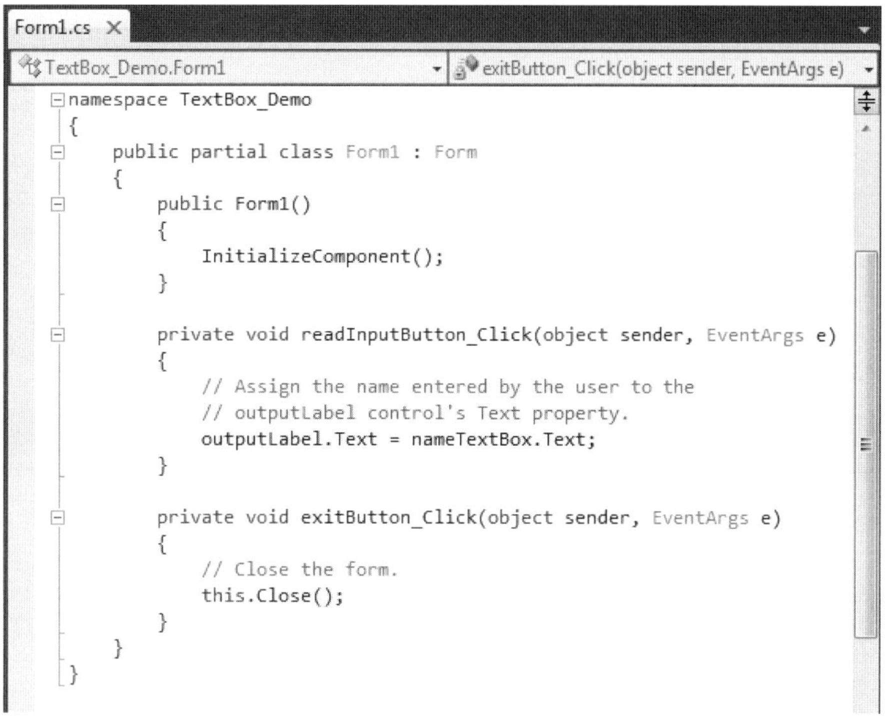

```
Form1.cs ×
TextBox_Demo.Form1                              ▾    exitButton_Click(object sender, EventArgs e)  ▾
namespace TextBox_Demo
{
    public partial class Form1 : Form
    {
        public Form1()
        {
            InitializeComponent();
        }

        private void readInputButton_Click(object sender, EventArgs e)
        {
            // Assign the name entered by the user to the
            // outputLabel control's Text property.
            outputLabel.Text = nameTextBox.Text;
        }

        private void exitButton_Click(object sender, EventArgs e)
        {
            // Close the form.
            this.Close();
        }
    }
}
```

Figure 3-4 The user's name displayed in the label

When this statement executes, the `nameTextBox` control will appear empty on the application's form.

 Checkpoint

> 3.1 What control can be used to gather text input from the user?
>
> 3.2 In code, how do you retrieve data that has been typed into a TextBox control?
>
> 3.3 What type of data does a control's Text property always contain?
>
> 3.4 How do you clear the contents of a TextBox control?

3.2 A First Look at Variables

CONCEPT: A variable is a storage location in memory that is represented by a name.

Most programs store data in the computer's memory and perform operations on that data. For example, consider the typical online shopping experience: you browse a Web site and add the items that you want to purchase to the shopping cart. As you add items to the shopping cart, data about those items is stored in memory. Then, when you click the *checkout* button, a program running on the Web site's computer calculates the cost of all the items you have in your shopping cart, applicable sales taxes, shipping costs, and the total of all these charges. When the program performs these calculations, it stores the results in the computer's memory.

Programs use variables to store data in memory. A **variable** is a storage location in memory that is represented by a name. For example, a program that manages a company's customer mailing list might use a variable named `lastName` to hold a customer's last name, a variable named `firstName` to hold the customer's first name, a variable named `address` to hold the customer's mailing address, and so on.

In C#, you must declare a variable in a program before you can use it to store data. You do this with a **variable declaration**, which specifies two things about the variable:

1. The variable's data type, which is the type of data the variable will hold
2. The variable's name

A variable declaration statement is written in this general format:

    DataType VariableName;

Let's take a closer look at each of these.

Data Type

A variable's **data type** indicates the type of data that the variable will hold. Before you declare a variable, you need to think about the type of value that will be stored in the variable. For example, will the variable hold a string or a number? If it will hold a number, what kind of number will it be, an integer or a real number? When you have determined the kind of data that the variable will hold, you select one of the data types that C# provides for variable.

The C# language provides many data types for storing fundamental types of data, such as strings, integers, and real numbers. These data types are known as **primitive data types**. We will look at several of them in this chapter.

Variable Name

A **variable name** identifies a variable in the program code. When naming a variable, you should always choose a meaningful name that indicates what the variable is used for. For example, a variable that holds the temperature might be named `temperature`, and a variable that holds a car's speed might be named `speed`. You may be tempted to give variables short, nondescript names such as `x` or `b2`, but names such as these give no clue as to the purpose of the variable.

In addition, there are some specific rules that you must follow when naming a variable. The same rules for identifiers that apply to control names also apply to variable names. We discussed these rules in Chapter 2, but we review them now:

- The first character must be one of the letters a through z or A through Z or an underscore character (_).
- After the first character, you may use the letters a through z or A through Z, the digits 0 through 9, or underscores.
- The name cannot contain spaces.

When naming variables, we use the same camelCase naming convention that we introduced in Chapter 2 for control names. For example, if we are declaring a variable to hold an employee's gross pay, we might name it `grossPay`. Or, if are declaring a variable to a customer number, we might name it `customerNumber`.

`string` Variables

The first primitive data type we consider is the `string` data type. A variable of the `string` data type can hold any string of characters, such as a person's name, address, password, and so on. Here is an example of a statement that declares a `string` variable named `productDescription`:

```
string productDescription;
```

After the variable has been declared, you can use the assignment operator (=) to store a value in the variable. Here is an example:

```
productDescription = "Italian Espresso Machine";
```

When this statement executes, the string literal `"Italian Espresso Machine"` is assigned to the `productDescription` variable. When writing an assignment statement, remember that the assignment operator assigns the value that appears on its right side to the variable that appears on its left side.

Once you have assigned a value to a variable, you can use the variable in other operations. For example, assume `productLabel` is the name of a Label control. The following statement assigns the `productDescription` string to the `productLabel` control's Text property:

```
productLabel.Text = productDescription;
```

After this statement executes, the string that is stored in the `productDescription` variable is displayed in the `productLabel` control. The following statement shows another example:

```
MessageBox.Show(productDescription);
```

When this statement executes, the string that is stored in the `productDescription` variable is displayed in a message box.

String Concatenation

A common operation that performed on strings is **concatenation**, or appending one string to the end of another string. In C# you use the + operator to concatenate strings. The + operator produces a string that is the combination of the two strings used as its operands. The following code shows an example:

```
string message;
message = "Hello " + "world";
MessageBox.Show(message);
```

The first statement declares a `string` variable named `message`. The second statement combines the strings `"Hello "` and `"world"` to produce the string `"Hello world"`. The string `"Hello world"` is then assigned to the `message` variable. The third statement displays the contents of the `message` variable in a message box. When the message box is displayed, it shows the string *Hello world*.

Let's look at an application that further demonstrates string concatenation. In the *Chap03* folder of the Student Sample Program files that accompany this book, you will find a project named String Variable Demo. Figure 3-5 shows the form, with most of the control names specified, and Figure 3-6 shows the form's code. (In Figure 3-6, to conserve space on the page, we have scrolled past the `using` directives that appear at the top of the code file.)

Figure 3-5 The String Variable Demo application

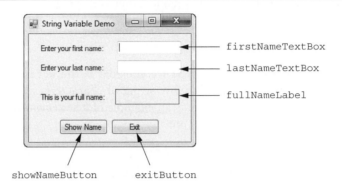

Figure 3-6 The form's code (excluding the `using` directives)

```
Form1.cs  ×
String_Variable_Demo.Form1                    exitButton_Click(object sender, EventArgs e
namespace String_Variable_Demo
{
    public partial class Form1 : Form
    {
        public Form1()
        {
            InitializeComponent();
        }

        private void showNameButton_Click(object sender, EventArgs e)
        {
            // Declare a string variable to hold the full name.
①          string fullName;

            // Combine the names, with a space between them. Assign the
            // result to the fullName variable.
②          fullName = firstNameTextBox.Text + " " + lastNameTextBox.Text;

            // Display the fullName variable in the fullNameLabel control.
③          fullNameLabel.Text = fullName;
        }

        private void exitButton_Click(object sender, EventArgs e)
        {
            // Close the form.
            this.Close();
        }
    }
}
```

In Figure 3-6, three statements in the `showNameButton_Click` event handler are pointed out:

① This statement is a variable declaration. It declares a `string` variable named `fullName`.

② This statement assigns the result of a string concatenation to the `fullName` variable. The string that is assigned to the variable begins with the value of the `firstNameTextBox` control's Text property, followed by a space (`" "`), followed by the value of the `lastNameTextBox` control's Text property. For example, if the user has entered *Joe* into the `firstNameTextBox` control and *Smith* into the `lastNameTextBox` control, this statement will assign the string `"Joe Smith"` to the `fullName` variable.

③ This statement assigns the `fullName` variable to the `fullNameLabel` control's Text property. As a result, the string that is stored in the `fullName` variable is displayed in the `fullNameLabel` control.

If you run the application, Figure 3-7 shows an example of how the form appears after you have entered *Chris* for the first name and *Jones* for the last name and clicked the `showNameButton` control.

Figure 3-7 The user's full name displayed in the label

Declaring Variables Before Using Them

The purpose of a variable declaration statement is to tell the compiler that you plan to use a variable of a specified name to store a particular type of data in the program. A variable declaration statement causes the variable to be created in memory. For this reason, a variable's declaration statement must appear *before* any other statements in the method that use the variable. This makes perfect sense because you cannot store a value in a variable if the variable has not been created in memory.

Local Variables

Notice that the `fullName` variable in Figure 3-6 is declared inside the event handler method. Variables that are declared inside a method are known as local variables. A **local variable** belongs to the method in which it is declared, and only statements inside that method can access the variable. (The term *local* is meant to indicate that the variable can be used only locally, within the method in which it is declared.)

An error will occur if a statement in one method tries to access a local variable that belongs to another method. For example, let's go over the sample code shown in Figure 3-8:

① This statement declares a `string` variable named `myName`. The variable is declared inside the `firstButton_Click` event handler, so it is local to that method.

② This statement, which is also in the `firstButton_Click` event handler, assigns the `nameTextBox` control's Text property to the `myName` variable.

Figure 3-8 One method trying to access a variable that is local to another method

```
private void firstButton_Click(object sender, EventArgs e)
{
    // Declare a string variable.
①  string myName;

    // Assign the nameTextBox control's Text property
    // to the myName variable.
②  myName = nameTextBox.Text;
}

private void secondButton_Click(object sender, EventArgs e)
{
    // Assign the myName variable to the outputLabel
    // control's Text property.
③  outputLabel.Text = myName;    ◄——————— ERROR!
}
```

③ This statement, which is in the `secondButton_Click` event handler, *attempts* to assign the `myName` variable to the `outputLabel` control's Text property. This statement will not work, however, because the `myName` variable is local to the `firstButton_Click` event handler, and statements in the `secondButton_Click` event handler cannot access it.

Scope of a Variable

Programmers use the term **scope** to describe the part of a program in which a variable may be accessed. A variable is visible only to statements inside the variable's scope.

A local variable's scope begins at the variable's declaration and ends at the end of the method in which the variable is declared. As you saw in the previous example, a local variable cannot be accessed by statements that are outside the method. In addition, a local variable cannot be accessed by code that is inside the method but before the variable's declaration.

Lifetime of a Variable

A variable's **lifetime** is the time period during which the variable exists in memory while the program is executing. A local variable is created in memory when the method in which it is declared starts executing. When the method ends, all the method's local variables are destroyed. So, a local variable's lifetime is the time during which the method in which it is declared is executing.

Duplicate Variable Names

You cannot declare two variables with the same name in the same scope. For example, if you declare a variable named `productDescription` in an event handler, you cannot declare another variable with that name in the same event handler. You can, however, have variables of the same name declared in different methods.

Assignment Compatibility

You can assign a value to a variable only if the value is compatible with the variable's data type. Only strings are compatible with the `string` data type, so all the assignments in the following code sample work:

```
 1 // Declare and initialize a string variable.
 2 string productDescription = "Chocolate Truffle";
 3
 4 // Declare another string variable.
 5 string myFavoriteProduct;
 6
 7 // Assign a value to a string variable.
 8 myFavoriteProduct = productDescription;
 9
10 // Assign a value from a TextBox to a string variable.
11 productDescription = userInputTextBox.Text;
```

The following comments explain these lines of code:

- In line 2 we initialize a `string` variable with a string literal. This works because string literals are assignment compatible with `string` variables.
- In line 8 we assign a `string` variable to another `string` variable. This works for the obvious reason that `string` variables are compatible with other `string` variables.

- Assume that the application has a TextBox control named `userInputTextBox`. In line 11 we assign the value of the TextBox control's Text property to a `string` variable. This works because the value in a control's Text property is always a string.

The following code will not work, however, because it attempts to assign a nonstring value to a `string` variable:

```
1 // Declare a string variable.
2 string employeeID;
3
4 // Assign a value to the variable. Will this work?
5 employeeID = 125; ← ERROR!
```

In line 5 we are attempting to assign the number 125 to a `string` variable. Numbers are not assignment compatible with `string` variables, so this statement will cause an error when the code is compiled.

 NOTE: Although you cannot store the number 125 in a `string` variable, you can store the string literal `"125"` in a `string` variable.

A Variable Holds One Value at a Time

Variables can hold different values while a program is running, but they can hold only one value at a time. When you assign a value to a variable, that value will remain in the variable until you assign a different value to the variable. For example, look at the following code sample:

```
1 // Declare a string variable.
2 string productDescription;
3
4 // Assign a value to the variable.
5 productDescription = "Large Medium-roast Coffee";
6
7 // Display the variable's value.
8 MessageBox.Show(productDescription);
9
10 // Assign a different value to the variable.
11 productDescription = "Chocolate Truffle";
12
13 // Display the variable's value.
14 MessageBox.Show(productDescription);
```

The following comments explain what we did:

- Line 2 declares a `string` variable named `productDescription`.
- Line 5 assigns the string `"Large Medium-Roast Coffee"` to the `productDescription` variable.
- Line 8 displays the value of the `productDescription` variable in a message box. (The message box will display *Large Medium-Roast Coffee*.)
- Line 11 assigns a different value to the `productDescription` variable. After this statement executes, the `productDescription` variable will hold the string `"Chocolate Truffle"`.
- Line 14 displays the value of the `productDescription` variable in a message box. (The message box will display *Chocolate Truffle*.)

This code sample illustrates two important characteristics of variables:

- A variable holds only one value at a time.
- When you store a value in a variable, that value replaces the previous value that was in the variable.

Tutorial 3-1 gives you some practice using variables. You will create an application that uses TextBox controls to get input values, stores those values in variables, and uses the variables in operations.

Tutorial 3-1:
The *Birth Date String* Application

In this tutorial you create an application that lets the user enter the following information about his or her birthdate:

- The day of the week (Monday, Tuesday, etc.)
- The name of the month (January, February, etc.)
- The numeric day of the month
- The year

Figure 3-9 shows the application's form, along with the names of all the controls. When the application runs, the user enters each piece of data into a separate TextBox. When the user clicks the *Show Date* button, the application concatenates the contents of the TextBoxes into a string such as *Friday, June 1, 1990.* The string is displayed in the `dateOutputLabel` control. When the user clicks the *Clear* button, the contents of the TextBoxes and the `dateOutputLabel` control are cleared. The *Exit* button closes the application's form.

Figure 3-9 The *Birth Date String* form

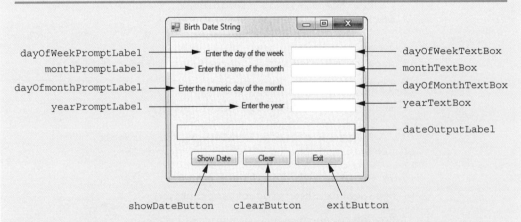

Step 1: Start Visual Studio (or Visual C# Express) and begin a new Windows Forms Application project named *Birth Date String*.

Step 2: Set up the application's form as shown in Figure 3-9. Notice that the form's Text property is set to *Birth Date String*. The names of the controls are shown in the figure. As you place each control on the form, refer to Table 3-1 for the relevant property settings.

Step 3: Once you have set up the form with its controls, you can create the Click event handlers for the Button controls. At the end of this tutorial, Program 3-1 shows the completed code for the form. You will be instructed to refer to Program 3-1

Table 3-1 Control property settings

Control Name	Control Type	Property Settings
dayOfWeekPromptLabel	Label	**Text:** *Enter the day of the week*
monthPromptLabel	Label	**Text:** *Enter the name of the month*
dayOfMonthPromptLabel	Label	**Text:** *Enter the numeric day of the month*
yearPromptLabel	Label	**Text:** *Enter the year*
dayOfWeekTextBox	TextBox	No properties changed
monthTextBox	TextBox	No properties changed
dayOfMonthTextBox	TextBox	No properties changed
yearTextBox	TextBox	No properties changed
dateOutputLabel	Label	**AutoSize:** False **BorderStyle:** FixedSingle **Text:** (The contents of the Text property have been erased.) **TextAlign:** MiddleCenter
showDateButton	Button	**Text:** *Show Date*
clearButton	Button	**Text:** *Clear*
exitButton	Button	**Text:** *Exit*

as you write the event handlers. (Remember, the line numbers that are shown in Program 3-1 are not part of the program. They are shown for reference only.)

In the *Designer*, double-click the showDateButton control. This will open the code editor, and you will see an empty event handler named showDateButton_Click. Complete the showDateButton_Click event handler by typing the code shown in lines 21–31 in Program 3-1.

Let's take a closer look at the code:

Line 22: This statement declares a string variable named output.

Lines 25–28: These lines are actually one long statement, broken up into multiple lines. The statement concatenates the Text properties of the TextBox controls, along with appropriately placed commas and spaces, to create the date string. The resulting string is assigned to the output variable.

For example, suppose the user has entered the following input:

- *Friday* in the dayOfWeekTextBox control.
- *June* in the monthTextBox control.
- *1* in the dayOfMonthTextBox control.
- *1990* in the yearTextBox control.

The concatenation in this statement produces the string "June 1, 1990"; it is assigned to the output variable.

Line 31: This statement assigns the output variable to the dateOutputLabel control's Text property. When this statement executes, the contents of the output variable are displayed in the dateOutputLabel control.

Step 4: Switch your view back to the *Designer* and double-click the clearButton control. In the code editor, you will see an empty event handler named clearButton_Click. Complete the clearButton_Click event handler by typing the code shown in lines 36–43 in Program 3-1.

Let's take a closer look at the code:

Lines 37–40: Each statement assigns an empty string ("") to the Text property of one of the TextBox controls. When these statements have finished executing, the TextBox controls will appear empty.

Line 43: This statement assigns an empty string ("") to the dateOutputLabel control's Text property. After the statement has executed, the label appears empty.

Step 5: Switch your view back to the *Designer* and double-click the exitButton control. In the code editor, you will see an empty event handler named exitButton_Click. Complete the exitButton_Click event handler by typing the code shown in lines 48–49 in Program 3-1.

Step 6: Save the project. Then, press the F5 key on the keyboard, or click the *Start Debugging* button (▶) on the toolbar to compile and run the application. The form will appear as shown in the image on the left in Figure 3-10. Test the application by entering values into the TextBoxes and clicking the *Show Date* button. The date should be displayed, similar to the image shown on the right in the figure. Click the *Clear* button, and the contents of the TextBoxes and the Label control should clear. Click the *Exit* button and the form should close.

Figure 3-10 The *Birth Date String* application

Program 3-1 Completed Form1 code for the *Birth Date String application*

```
1 using System;
2 using System.Collections.Generic;
3 using System.ComponentModel;
4 using System.Data;
5 using System.Drawing;
6 using System.Linq;
7 using System.Text;
8 using System.Windows.Forms;
9
10 namespace Birth_Date_String
11 {
12     public partial class Form1 : Form
13     {
```

```
14          public Form1()
15          {
16              InitializeComponent();
17          }
18
19          private void showDateButton_Click(object sender, EventArgs e)
20          {
21              // Declare a string variable.
22              string output;
23
24              // Concatenate the input and build the output string.
25              output = dayOfWeekTextBox.Text + ", " +
26                  monthTextBox.Text + " " +
27                  dayOfMonthTextBox.Text + ", " +
28                  yearTextBox.Text;
29
30              // Display the output string in the dateOutputLabel control.
31              dateOutputLabel.Text = output;
32          }
33
34          private void clearButton_Click(object sender, EventArgs e)
35          {
36              // Clear the TextBoxes.
37              dayOfWeekTextBox.Text = "";
38              monthTextBox.Text = "";
39              dayOfMonthTextBox.Text = "";
40              yearTextBox.Text = "";
41
42              // Clear the dateOutputLabel control.
43              dateOutputLabel.Text = "";
44          }
45
46          private void exitButton_Click(object sender, EventArgs e)
47          {
48              // Close the form.
49              this.Close();
50          }
51      }
52 }
```

NOTE: In Tutorial 3-1, the statement in lines 25–28 shows an example of how you can break up a statement into multiple lines. Quite often, you will find yourself writing statements that are too long to fit entirely inside the *Code* window. Your code will be hard to read if you have to horizontally scroll the *Code* window to view long statements. In addition, if you or your instructor chooses to print your code, the statements that are too long to fit on one line of the page will wrap around to the next line and make your code look unorganized. For these reasons, it is usually best to break a long statement into multiple lines.

When typing most statements, you can simply press the Enter key when you reach an appropriate point to continue the statement on the next line. Remember, however, that you cannot break up a keyword, a quoted string, or an identifier (such as a variable name or a control name).

Initializing Variables

In C#, a variable must be assigned a value before it can be used. For example, look at this code:

```
string productDescription;
MessageBox.Show(productDescription);
```

This code declares a `string` variable named `productDescription` and then tries to display the variable's value in a message box. The only problem is that we have not assigned a value to the variable. When we compile the application containing this code, we will get an error message such as *Use of unassigned local variable 'productDescription'*. The C# compiler will not compile code that tries to use an unassigned variable.

One way to make sure that a variable has been assigned a value is to **initialize** the variable with a value when you declare it. For example, the following statement declares a `string` variable named `productDescription` and immediately assigns the string literal `"Chocolate Truffle"` to it:

```
string productDescription = "Chocolate Truffle";
```

We say that this statement *initializes* the `productDescription` variable with the string `"Chocolate Truffle"`. Here is another example:

```
string lastName = lastNameTextBox.Text;
```

Assume that this statement belongs to an application that has a TextBox named `lastNameTextBox`. The statement declares a `string` variable named `lastName` and initializes it with the value of the `lastNameTextBox` control's Text property.

Declaring Multiple Variables with One Statement

You can declare multiple variables of the same data type with one declaration statement. Here is an example:

```
string lastName, firstName, middleName;
```

This statement declares three `string` variables named `lastName`, `firstName`, and `middleName`. Notice that commas separate the variable names. Here is an example of how we can declare and initialize the variables with one statement:

```
string lastName = "Jones", firstName = "Jill", middleName = "Rebecca";
```

Remember, you can break up a long statement so it spreads across two or more lines. Sometimes you will see long variable declarations written across multiple lines, like this:

```
string lastName = "Jones",
       firstName = "Jill",
       middleName = "Rebecca";
```

Checkpoint

3.5 What is the purpose of a variable?

3.6 Give an example of a variable declaration that will store the name of your favorite food.

3.7 For each of the following items, determine whether the data type should be an integer, string, or real number.

a. pet name
b. sales tax
c. mailing address
d. video game score

3.8 Indicate whether each of the following is a legal variable name. If it is not, explain why.

a. `pay_Rate`
b. `speed of sound`
c. `totalCost`
d. `2ndPlaceName`

3.9 What will be stored in the `message` variable after the following statement is executed?

```
string message = "He" + "ll" + "o!";
```

3.10 What is the lifetime of a variable that is declared inside of a click event handler?

3.11 Assuming the variable `greeting` has not been assigned a value, what will be the result of the following statement?

```
MessageBox.Show(greeting);
```

3.12 Will the following statement cause an error? Why or why not.

```
string luckyNumber = 7;
```

3.13 Write a single declaration statement for the variables `name`, `city`, and `state`.

3.3 Numeric Data Types and Variables

CONCEPT: If you need to store a number in a variable and use that number in a mathematical operation, the variable must be of a numeric data type. You select a numeric data type that is appropriate for the type of number that you need to store.

In the previous section you read about `string` variables. Variables of the `string` data type can be used to store text, but they cannot store numeric data for the purpose of performing mathematical operations. If you need to store numbers and perform mathematical operations on them, you have to use a numeric data type.

The C# language provides several primitive data types. You can read about all the C# primitive data types in Appendix A. Many of the data types provided by C# are for specialized purposes beyond the scope of this book. When it comes to numeric data, most of the time you will use the three numeric primitive data types described in Table 3-2.

Here are examples of declaring variables of each data type:

```
int speed;
double distance;
decimal grossPay;
```

The first statement declares an `int` variable named `speed`. The second example declares a `double` variable named `distance`. The third statement declares a `decimal` variable named `grossPay`.

Table 3-2 The primitive numeric data types that you will use most often

Data Type	Description
int	A variable of the int data type can hold whole numbers only. For example, an int variable can hold values such as 42, 0, and −99. An int variable cannot hold numbers with a fractional part, such as 22.1 or −4.9.
	The int data type is the primary data type for storing integers. We use it in this book any time we need to store and work with integers. An int variable uses 32 bits of memory and can hold an integer number in the range of −2,147,483,648 through 2,147,483,647.
double	A variable of the double data type can hold real numbers, such as 3.5, −87.95, or 3.0. A number that is stored in a double variable is rounded to 15 digits of precision.
	We use variables of the double data type to store any number that might have a fractional part. The double data type is especially useful for storing extremely great or extremely small numbers.
	In memory a double variable uses 64 bits of memory. It is stored in a format that programmers call *double precision floating-point notation*. Variables of the double data type can hold numbers in the range of $\pm 5.0 \times 10^{2324}$ to $\pm 1.7 \times 10^{308}$.
decimal	A variable of the decimal data type can hold real numbers with greater precision than the double data type. A number that is stored in a decimal variable is rounded to 28 digits of precision.
	Because decimal variables store real numbers with a great deal of precision, they are most commonly used in financial applications. In this book we typically use the decimal data type when storing amounts of money.
	In memory a decimal variable uses 128 bits of memory. It is stored in a format that programmers call *decimal notation*. Variables of the decimal data type can hold numbers in the range of $\pm 1.0 \times 10^{228}$ to $\pm 7.9 \times 10^{28}$.

Numeric Literals

You learned in Chapter 2 that a literal is a piece of data written into a program's code. When you know, at the time that you are writing a program's code, that you want to store a specific value in a variable, you can assign that value as a literal to the variable.

A **numeric literal** is a number that is written into a program's code. For example, the following statement declares an int variable named hoursWorked and initializes it with the value 40:

```
int hoursWorked = 40;
```

In this statement, the number 40 is a numeric literal. The following shows another example:

```
double temperature = 87.6;
```

This statement declares a double variable named temperature and initializes it with the value 87.6. The number 87.6 is a numeric literal.

When you write a numeric literal in a program's code, the numeric literal is assigned a data type. In C#, if a numeric literal is an integer (not written with a decimal point) and it fits within the range of an int (see Table 3-2 for the minimum and maximum values), then the numeric literal is treated as an int. A numeric literal that is treated as an int is called an **integer literal**. For example, each of the following statements initializes a variable with an integer literal:

```
int hoursWorked = 40;
int unitsSold = 650;
int score = -23;
```

If a numeric literal is written with a decimal point and it fits within the range of a double (see Table 3-2 for the minimum and maximum values), then the numeric literal is treated as a double. A numeric literal that is treated as a double is called a **double literal**. For example, each of the following statements initializes a variable with a double literal:

```
double distance = 28.75;
double speed = 87.3;
double temperature = -10.0;
```

When you append the letter M or m to a numeric literal, it is treated as a decimal and is referred to as a **decimal literal**. Here are some examples:

```
decimal payRate = 28.75m;
decimal price = 8.95M;
decimal profit = -50m;
```

> **TIP:** Because decimal is the preferred data type for storing monetary amounts, remembering that "m" stands for "money" might help you to remember that decimal literals must end with the letter M or m.

Assignment Compatibility for int Variables

You can assign int values to int variables, but you cannot assign double or decimal values to int variables. For example, look at the following declarations.

```
int hoursWorked = 40;    ← This works
int unitsSold = 650m;    ← ERROR!
int score = -25.5;       ← ERROR!
```

The first declaration works because we are initializing an int variable with an int value. The second declaration causes an error, however, because you cannot assign a decimal value to an int variable. The third declaration also causes an error because you cannot assign a double value to an int variable.

You cannot assign a double or a decimal value to an int variable because such an assignment could result in a loss of data. Here are the reasons:

- The double and decimal values may be fractional, but int variables can hold only integers. If you were allowed to store a fractional value in an int variable, the fractional part of the value would have to be discarded.

- The double and decimal values may be much larger or much smaller than allowed by the range of an int variable. A double or a decimal number can potentially be so large or so small that it will not fit in an int variable.

Assignment Compatibility for double Variables

You can assign either double or int values to double variables, but you cannot assign decimal values to double variables. For example, look at the following declarations.

```
double distance = 28.75;   ← This works
double speed = 75;         ← This works
double sales = 6500.0m;    ← ERROR!
```

The first declaration works because we are initializing a double variable with a double value. The second declaration works because we are initializing a double variable with an int value. The third declaration causes an error, however, because you cannot assign a decimal value to a double variable.

It makes sense that you are allowed to assign an int value to a double variable because any number that can be stored as an int can be converted to a double with no loss of data. When you assign an int value to a double variable, the int value is implicitly converted to a double.

You cannot assign a decimal value to a double variable because the decimal data type allows for much greater precision than the double data type. A decimal value can have up to 28 digits of precision, whereas a double can provide only 15 digits of precision. Storing a decimal value in a double variable could potentially result in a loss of data.

Assignment Compatibility for decimal Variables

You can assign either decimal or int values to decimal variables, but you cannot assign double values to decimal variables. For example, look at the following declarations.

```
decimal balance = 9280.73m;   ← This works
decimal price = 50;           ← This works
decimal sales = 6500.0;       ← ERROR!
```

The first declaration works because we are initializing a decimal variable with a decimal value. The second declaration works because we are initializing a decimal variable with an int value. When you assign an int value to a decimal variable, the int value is implicitly converted to a decimal with no loss of data. The third declaration causes an error, however, because you cannot assign a double value to a decimal variable. A double value can potentially be much larger or much smaller than allowed by the range of a decimal.

Explicitly Converting Values with Cast Operators

Let's consider a hypothetical situation. Suppose you've written an application that uses a double variable, and for some reason, you need to assign the contents of the double variable to an int variable. In this particular situation, you know that the double variable's value is something that can be safely converted to an int without any loss of data (such as 3.0, or 98.0). However, the C# compiler will not allow you to make the assignment because double values are not assignment compatible with int variables. Isn't there a way to override the C# rules in this particular situation and make the assignment anyway?

The answer is yes, there is a way. You can use a **cast operator** to explicitly convert a value from one numeric data type to another, even if the conversion might result in a loss of data. A cast operator is the name of the desired data type, written inside parentheses and placed to the left of the value that you want to convert. The following code sample demonstrates:

```
1 // Declare an int variable.
2 int wholeNumber;
3
4 // Declare a double variable.
5 double realNumber = 3.0;
6
7 // Assign the double to the int.
8 wholeNumber = (int)realNumber;
```

The following points describe the code:

- Line 2 declares an `int` variable named `wholeNumber`.
- Line 5 declares a `double` variable named `realNumber`, initialized with the value 3.0.
- Line 8 uses a cast operator to convert the value of `realNumber` to an `int` and assigns the converted value to `wholeNumber`. After this statement executes, the `wholeNumber` variable is assigned the value 3.

Table 3-3 shows other code examples involving different types of cast operators.

Table 3-3 Examples of uses of cast operators

Code Example	Description

`int wholeNumber;`
`decimal moneyNumber = 4500m;`
`wholeNumber = (int)moneyNumber;`
	The (`int`) cast operator converts the value of the `moneyNumber` variable to an `int`. The converted value is assigned to the `wholeNumber` variable.

`double realNumber;`
`decimal moneyNumber = 625.70m;`
`realNumber = (double)moneyNumber;`
	The (`double`) cast operator converts the value of the `moneyNumber` variable to a `double`. The converted value is assigned to the `realNumber` variable.

`decimal moneyNumber;`
`double realNumber = 98.9;`
`moneyNumber = (decimal)realNumber;`
	The (`decimal`) cast operator converts the value of the `realNumber` variable to a `decimal`. The converted value is assigned to the `moneyNumber` variable.

When you use a cast operator, you are essentially telling the compiler that you know what you are doing and you are willing to accept the consequences of the conversion. It is still possible that a loss of data can occur. For example, look at the following code sample:

```
int wholeNumber;
double realNumber = 8.9;
wholeNumber = (int)realNumber;
```

In this example, the `double` variable contains a fractional number. When the cast operator converts the fractional number to an `int`, the part of the number that appears after the decimal point is dropped. The process of dropping a number's fractional part is called **truncation**. After this code executes, the `wholeNumber` variable contains the value 8.

It's important to realize that when a cast operator is applied to a variable, it does not change the contents of the variable. The cast operator merely returns the value that is stored in the variable, converted to the specified data type. In the previous code sample, when the (`int`) cast operator is applied to the `realNumber` variable, the cast operator returns the value 8. The `realNumber` variable remains unchanged, however, still containing the value 8.9.

 **Checkpoint**

3.14 Specify the appropriate primitive numeric data type to use for each of the following values.

    a. 24 dollars
    b. 12 bananas
    c. 14.5 inches
    d. 83 cents
    e. 2 concert tickets

3.15 Which of the following variable declarations will cause an error? Why?

```
a. decimal payRate = 24m;
b. int playerScore = 1340.5;
c. double boxWidth = 205.25;
d. string lastName = "Holm";
```

3.16 Write a programming statement that will convert the following `decimal` variable to an `int` and store the result in an `int` variable named `dollars`:

```
decimal deposit = 976.54m;
```

3.17 What value will the `wholePieces` variable contain after the following code executes?

```
double totalPieces = 6.5;
int wholePieces = (int)totalPieces;
```

 ## 3.4 Performing Calculations

CONCEPT: You can use math operators to perform simple calculations. Math expressions can be written using the math operators and parentheses as grouping symbols. The result of a math expression can be assigned to a variable.

Most programs require calculations of some sort to be performed. A programmer's tools for performing calculations are **math operators**. C# provides the math operators shown in Table 3-4.

Table 3-4 Math operators

Operator	Name of the Operator	Description
+	Addition	Adds two numbers
−	Subtraction	Subtracts one number from another
*	Multiplication	Multiplies one number by another
/	Division	Divides one number by another and gives the quotient
%	Modulus	Divides one integer by another and gives the remainder

Programmers use the operators shown in Table 3-4 to create math expressions. A **math expression** performs a calculation and gives a value. The following is an example of a simple math expression:

12 * 2

The values on the right and left of the + operator are called **operands**. These are values that the * operator multiplies together. The value that is given by this expression is 24.

Variables may also be used in a math expression. For example, suppose we have two variables named hoursWorked and payRate. The following math expression uses the * operator to multiply the value in the hoursWorked variable by the value in the payRate variable:

```
hoursWorked * payRate
```

When we use a math expression to calculate a value, we have to do something with the value. Normally we want to save the value in memory so we can use it again in the program. We do this with an assignment statement. For example, suppose we have another variable named grossPay. The following statement assigns the value hoursWorked times payRate to the grossPay variable:

```
grossPay = hoursWorked * payRate;
```

Here are some other examples of statements that assign the result of a math expression to a variable:

```
total = price + tax;
sale = price - discount;
commission = sales * percent;
half = number / 2;
```

The modulus operator (%) performs division between two integers, but instead of returning the quotient, it returns the remainder. The following statement assigns 2 to leftOver:

```
leftOver = 17 % 3;
```

This statement assigns 2 to leftover because 17 divided by 3 is 5 with a remainder of 2. You will not use the modulus operator frequently, but it is useful in some situations. It is commonly used in calculations that detect odd or even numbers, determine the day of the week, or measure the passage of time and in other specialized operations.

The Order of Operations

You can write mathematical expressions with several operators. The following statement assigns the sum of 17, the variable x, 21, and the variable y to the variable answer.

```
answer = 17 + x + 21 + y;
```

Some expressions are not that straightforward, however. Consider the following statement:

```
outcome = 12 + 6 / 3;
```

What value will be stored in outcome? The number 6 is used as an operand for both the addition and division operators. The outcome variable could be assigned either 6 or 14, depending on when the division takes place. The answer is 14 because the **order of operations** dictates that the division operator works before the addition operator does.

The order of operations can be summarized as follows:

1. Perform any operations that are enclosed in parentheses.
2. Perform any multiplications, divisions, or modulus operations as they appear from left to right.
3. Perform any additions or subtractions as they appear from left to right.

Mathematical expressions are evaluated from left to right. Multiplication and division are always performed before addition and subtraction, so the statement

```
outcome = 12 + 6 / 3;
```

works like this:

1. 6 is divided by 3, yielding a result of 2.
2. 12 is added to 2, yielding a result of 14.

It could be diagrammed as shown in Figure 3-11.

Table 3-5 shows some other sample expressions with their values.

Figure 3-11 The order of operations at work

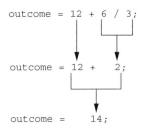

Table 3-5 Some math expressions and their values

Expression	Value
`5 + 2 * 4`	13
`10 / 2 - 3`	2
`8 + 12 * 2 - 4`	28
`6 - 3 * 2 + 7 - 1`	6

Grouping with Parentheses

Parts of a mathematical expression may be grouped with parentheses to force some operations to be performed before others. In the following statement, the variables a and b are added together, and their sum is divided by 4:

```
result = (a + b) / 4;
```

But what if we left the parentheses out, as shown here?

```
result = a + b / 4;
```

We would get a different result. Without the parentheses, b would be divided by 4 and the result added to a. Table 3-6 shows some math expressions that use parentheses and their values.

Table 3-6 More expressions and their values

Expression	Value
`(5 + 2) * 4`	28
`10 / (5 - 3)`	5
`8 + 12 * (6 - 2)`	56
`(6 - 3) * (2 + 7) / 3`	9

Mixing Data Types in a Math Expression

When you perform a math operation on two operands, the data type of the result will depend on the data type of the operands. If the operands are of the same data type, the result will also be of that data type. For example:

- When an operation is performed on two `int` values, the result will be an `int`.
- When an operation is performed on two `double` values, the result will be a `double`.
- When an operation is performed on two `decimal` values, the result will be a `decimal`.

It's not uncommon, however, for a math expression to have operands of different data types. C# handles operations involving `int`, `double`, and `decimal` operands in the following ways:

- When a math expression involves an `int` and a `double`, the `int` is temporarily converted to a `double`, and the result is a `double`.
- When a math expression involves an `int` and a `decimal`, the `int` is temporarily converted to a `decimal`, and the result is a `decimal`.
- Math expressions involving a `double` and a `decimal` are not allowed unless a cast operator is used to convert one of the operands.

For example, suppose a pay-calculating program has the following variable declarations:

```
int hoursWorked;   // To hold the number of hours worked
decimal payRate;   // To hold the hourly pay rate
decimal grossPay;  // To hold the gross pay
```

Then, later in the program this statement appears:

```
grossPay = hoursWorked * payRate;
```

The math expression on the right side of the = operator multiplies an `int` by a `decimal`. When the statement executes, the value of the `hoursWorked` variable is temporarily converted to a `decimal` and then multiplied by the `payRate` variable. The result is a `decimal` and is assigned to the `grossPay` variable.

When possible, you should avoid math operations that use a mixture of `double` and `decimal` operands. C# does not allow operations involving these two types unless you use a cast operator to explicitly convert one of the operands. For example, suppose a program that calculates the cost of a product has the following variable declarations:

```
double weight;          // The product weight
decimal pricePerPound;  // The price per pound
decimal total;          // The total cost
```

Later in the program you need to calculate the total cost, like this:

```
total = weight * pricePerPound;  ← ERROR!
```

The compiler will not allow this statement because `weight` is a `double` and `pricePerPound` is a `decimal`. To fix the statement, you can insert a cast operator, as shown here:

```
total = (decimal)weight * pricePerPound;
```

The cast operator converts the value of the `weight` variable to a `decimal`, and the converted value is multiplied by `pricePerPound`. The result of the expression is a `decimal` and is assigned to `total`.

Integer Division

When you divide an integer by an integer in C#, the result is always given as an integer. If the result has a fractional part, it is truncated. For example, look at the following code:

```
int length;        // Declare length as an int
double half;       // Declare half as a double
length = 75;       // Assign 75 to length
half = length / 2; // Calculate half the length
```

The last statement divides the value of length by 2 and assigns the result to half. Mathematically, the result of 75 divided by 2 is 37.5. However, that is not the result that we get from the math expression. The length variable is an int, and it is being divided by the numeric literal 2, which is also treated as an int. The result of the division is truncated, giving the value 37. This is the value that is assigned to the half variable. It does not matter that the half variable is declared as a double. The fractional part of the result is truncated before the assignment takes place.

Combined Assignment Operators

Sometimes you want to increase a variable's value by a certain amount. For example, suppose you have a variable named number and you want to increase its value by 1. You can accomplish that with the following statement:

```
number = number + 1;
```

The expression on the right side of the assignment operator calculates the value of number plus 1. The result is then assigned to number, replacing the value that was previously stored there. This statement effectively adds 1 to number. For example, if number is equal to 6 before this statement executes, it is equal to 7 after the statement executes.

Similarly, the following statement subtracts 5 from number:

```
number = number - 5;
```

If number is equal to 15 before this statement executes, it is equal to 10 after the statement executes. Here's another example. The following statement doubles the value of the number variable:

```
number = number * 2;
```

If number is equal to 4 before this statement executes, it is equal to 8 after the statement executes.

These types of operations are very common in programming. For convenience, C# offers a special set of operators known as **combined assignment operators** that are designed specifically for these jobs. Table 3-7 shows the combined assignment operators.

Table 3-7 Combined assignment operators

Operator	Example Usage	Equivalence
+=	x += 5;	x = x + 5;
-=	y -= 2;	y = y - 2;
*=	z *= 10;	z = z * 10;
/=	a /= b;	a = a / b;
%=	c %= 3;	c = c % 3;

As you can see, the combined assignment operators do not require the programmer to type the variable name twice. Also, they give a clear indication of what is happening in the statement.

Checkpoint

3.18 List the operands for the following math expression.

```
length * width
```

3.19 Summarize the mathematical order of operations.

3.20 Rewrite the following code segment so that it does not cause an error.

```
decimal pricePerFoot = 2.99m;
double boardLength = 10.5;
decimal totalCost = boardLength * pricePerFoot;
```

3.21 Assume `result` is a double variable. When the following statement executes, what value will be stored in `result`?

```
result = 4 + 10 / 2;
```

3.22 Assume `result` is a an int variable. When the following statement executes, what value will be stored in `result`?

```
result = (2 + 5) * 10;
```

3.23 Assume `result` is a double variable. When the following statement executes, what value will be stored in `result`?

```
result = 5 / 2;
```

3.24 Rewrite the following statements using combined assignment operators:

```
a. count = count + 1;
b. amount = amount − 5;
c. radius = radius * 10;
d. length = length / 2;
```

3.5 Inputting and Outputting Numeric Values

CONCEPT: If the user has entered a number into a TextBox, the number will be stored as a string in the TextBox's Text property. If you want to store that number in a numeric variable, you have to convert it to the appropriate numeric data type. When you want to display the value of a numeric variable in a Label control or a message box, you have to convert it to a string.

Getting a Number from a TextBox

GUI applications typically use TextBox controls to read keyboard input. Any data that the user enters into a TextBox control is stored in the control's Text property as a string, even if it is a number. For example, if the user enters the number 72 into a TextBox control, the input is stored as the string "72" in the control's Text property.

If the user has entered a numeric value into a TextBox control and you want to assign that value to a numeric variable, you have to convert the control's Text property to the desired numeric data type. Unfortunately, you cannot use a cast operator to convert a string to a numeric type.

To convert a string to any of the numeric data types, we use a family of methods in the .NET Framework known as the **Parse methods**. In computer science, the term **parse** typically means to analyze a string of characters for some purpose. The Parse methods are used to convert a string to a specific data type. There are several Parse methods in the .NET Framework, but because we are primarily using the int, double, and decimal numeric data types, we need only three of them:

- We use the **int.Parse method** to convert a string to an int.
- We use the **double.Parse method** to convert a string to a double.
- We use the **decimal.Parse method** to convert a string to a decimal.

When you call one of the Parse methods, you pass a piece of data known as an **argument** into the method, and the method returns a piece of data back to you. The argument that you pass to the method is the string that you want to convert, and the piece of data that the method returns back to you is the converted value. Figure 3-12 illustrates this concept using the int.Parse method as an example.

Figure 3-12 The int.Parse method

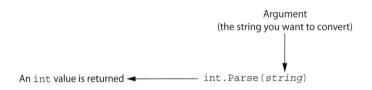

The following code sample shows how to use the int.Parse method to convert a control's Text property to an int. Assume that hoursWorkedTextBox is the name of a TextBox control.

```
1 // Declare an int variable to hold the hours worked.
2 int hoursWorked;
3
4 // Get the hours worked from the TextBox.
5 hoursWorked = int.Parse(hoursWorkedTextBox.Text);
```

Let's assume that the user has entered the value 40 into the hoursWorkedTextBox control. In line 5 of the code sample, on the right side of the = operator is the expression int.Parse(hoursWorkedTextBox.Text). This expression calls the int.Parse method, passing the value of hoursWorkedTextBox.Text as an argument. Because the user has entered 40 into the TextBox, the string "40" is the value that is passed as the argument. The method converts the string "40" to the int value 40. The int value 40 is returned from the method and the = operator assigns it to the hoursWorked variable. Figure 3-13 illustrates this process.

The following code sample demonstrates the double.Parse method. Assume that temperatureTextBox is the name of a TextBox control.

```
1 // Declare a double variable to hold the temperature.
2 double temperature;
3
4 // Get the temperature from the TextBox.
5 temperature = double.Parse(temperatureTextBox.Text);
```

Line 5 passes temperatureTextBox.Text as an argument to the double.Parse method. That value is converted to a double, returned from the double.parse method, and assigned to the temperature variable.

The following code sample demonstrates the decimal.Parse method. Assume that moneyTextBox is the name of a TextBox control.

Figure 3-13 Converting TextBox input to an `int`

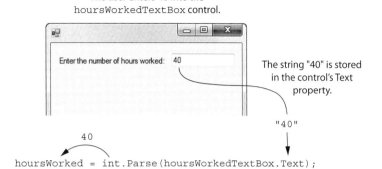

The user enters 40 into the
`hoursWorkedTextBox` control.

Enter the number of hours worked: 40

The string "40" is stored
in the control's Text
property.

"40"

40

`hoursWorked = int.Parse(hoursWorkedTextBox.Text);`

The `int` value 40 is returned
from the `int.Parse` method
and assigned to the `hoursWorked`
variable.

```
1 // Declare a decimal variable to hold an amount of money.
2 decimal money;
3
4 // Get an amount from the TextBox.
5 money = decimal.Parse(moneyTextBox.Text);
```

Line 5 passes `moneyTextBox.Text` as an argument to the `decimal.Parse` method. That value is converted to a `decimal`, returned from the `decimal.parse` method, and assigned to the `money` variable.

NOTE: If you look at the top of a form's source code in the code editor, you should see a directive that reads `using System;`. That directive is required for any program that uses the `Parse` methods.

Invalid Conversions

The `Parse` methods work only if the string that is being converted contains a valid numeric value. If the string contains invalid characters or contains a number that cannot be converted to the specified data type, an error known as an exception occurs. An **exception** is an unexpected error that occurs while a program is running, causing the program to halt if the error is not properly dealt with.

For example, assume that `hoursWorked` is an `int` variable and `hoursWorkedTextBox` is a TextBox control. Suppose the user has entered *xyz* into the TextBox and the following statement executes:

```
hoursWorked = int.Parse(hoursWorkedTextBox.Text);
```

Obviously, the string `"xyz"` cannot be converted to an `int`, so an exception occurs. (When an exception occurs, programmers say an exception is "thrown.") Depending on how you execute the application, you will see one of the windows displayed in Figure 3-14 or Figure 3-15.

- If you see the window in Figure 3-14, you can stop the application by clicking the Stop Debugging button (■), or by pressing [Shift] + [F5], or by clicking *Debug* and then *Stop Debugging*.
- When you see the window shown in Figure 3-15, in most situations you should click the *Quit* button to stop the application.

Figure 3-14 Exception reported

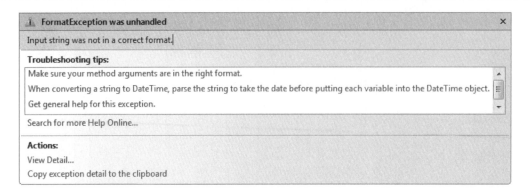

Figure 3-15 Exception reported

Later in this chapter you will learn how to catch errors like this and prevent the program from halting.

Displaying Numeric Values

Suppose an application has a `decimal` variable named `grossPay` and a Label control named `grossPayLabel`. You want to display the variable's value in the Label control. To accomplish this, you must somehow get the value of the `grossPay` variable into the `grossPayLabel` control's Text property. The following assignment statement will not work, however:

```
grossPayLabel.Text = grossPay;  ← ERROR!
```

You cannot assign a numeric value to a control's Text property because only strings can be assigned to the Text property. If you want to display the value of a numeric variable in a Label control, you have to convert the variable's value to a string.

Luckily, all variables have a **ToString** method that you can call to convert the variable's value to a string. You call the `ToString` method using the following general format:

```
variableName.ToString()
```

In the general format, *variableName* is the name of any variable. The expression returns the variable's value as a string. Here is a code sample that demonstrates:

```
decimal grossPay = 1550.0m;
grossPayLabel.Text = grossPay.ToString();
```

The first statement declares a `decimal` variable named `grossPay` initialized with the value 1,550.0. In the second statement, the expression on the right side of the = operator calls the `grossPay` variable's `ToString` method. The method returns the string

"1550.0". The = operator then assigns the string "1550.0" to the grossPayLabel control's Text property. As a result, the value *1550.0* is displayed in the grossPayLabel control. This process is illustrated in Figure 3-16.

Figure 3-16 Displaying numeric data in a Label control

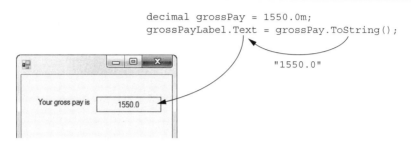

You must also convert a numeric variable to a string before passing it to the MessageBox.Show method. The following example shows how an int variable's value can be converted to a string and displayed in a message box:

```
int myNumber = 123;
MessageBox.Show(myNumber.ToString());
```

The first statement declares an int variable named myNumber, initialized with the value 123. In the second statement the following takes place:

- The myNumber variable's ToString method is called. The method returns the string "123".
- The string "123" is passed to the MessageBox.Show method. As a result, the value *123* is displayed in a message box.

Implicit String Conversion with the + Operator

In this chapter you've learned that the + operator has two uses: string concatenation and numeric addition. If you write an expression using the + operator and both operands are strings, the + operator concatenates the strings. If both operands are numbers of compatible types, then the + operator adds the two numbers. But what happens if one operand is a string and the other operand is a number? The number will be implicitly converted to a string, and both operands will be concatenated. Here's an example:

```
int idNumber = 1044;
string output = "Your ID number is " + idNumber;
```

In the second statement, the string variable output is initialized with the string "Your ID number is 1044". Here is another example:

```
double testScore = 88.5;
MessageBox.Show("Your test score is " + testScore);
```

The second statement displays a message box showing the string "Your test score is 88.5".

In Tutorial 3-2 you will use some of the techniques discussed in this section. You will create an application that reads numeric input from TextBox controls, and displays numeric output in a Label control.

Tutorial 3-2:
Calculating Fuel Economy

In the United States, a car's fuel economy is measured in miles per gallon, or MPG. You use the following formula to calculate a car's MPG:

$$MPG = Miles\ driven \div Gallons\ of\ gas\ used$$

In this tutorial you will create an application that lets the user enter the number of miles he or she has driven and the gallons of gas used. The application will calculate and display the car's MPG.

Figure 3-17 shows the application's form, with the names of all the controls. When the application runs, the user enter the number of miles driven into the `milesTextBox` control and the gallons of gas used into the `gallonsTextBox` control. When the user clicks the `calculateButton` control the application calculates the car's MPG and displays the result in the `mpgLabel` control. The `exitButton` control closes the application's form.

Figure 3-17 The *Fuel Economy* form

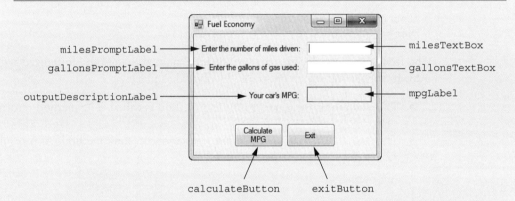

Step 1: Start Visual Studio (or Visual C# Express) and begin a new Windows Forms Application project named *Fuel Economy*.

Step 2: Set up the application's form as shown in Figure 3-17. Notice that the form's Text property is set to *Fuel Economy*. The names of the controls are shown in the figure. As you place each of the controls on the form, refer to Table 3-8 for the relevant property settings.

Step 3: Once you have set up the form with its controls, you can create the Click event handlers for the Button controls. At the end of this tutorial, Program 3-2 shows the completed code for the form. You will be instructed to refer to Program 3-2 as you write the event handlers. (Remember, the line numbers that are shown in Program 3-2 are not part of the program. They are shown for reference only.)

In the *Designer*, double-click the `calculateButton` control. This opens the code editor, and you will see an empty event handler named `calculateButton_Click`. Complete the `calculateButton_Click` event handler by typing the code shown in lines 21–37 in Program 3-2.

Let's take a closer look at the code:

Line 21: This statement declares a `double` variable named `miles`. This variable is used to hold the number of miles driven.

Line 22: This statement declares a `double` variable named `gallons`. This variable is used to hold the number of gallons used.

Table 3-8 Control property settings

Control Name	Control Type	Property Settings
milesPromptLabel	Label	**Text:** *Enter the number of miles driven:*
gasPromptLabel	Label	**Text:** *Enter the gallons of gas used:*
outputDescriptionLabel	Label	**Text:** *Your car's MPG:*
milesTextBox	TextBox	No properties changed
gallonsTextBox	TextBox	No properties changed
mpgLabel	Label	**AutoSize:** False **BorderStyle:** FixedSingle **Text:** (The contents of the Text property have been erased.) **TextAlign:** MiddleCenter
calculateButton	Button	**Text:** *Calculate MPG*
exitButton	Button	**Text:** *Exit*

Line 23: This statement declares a `double` variable named `mpg`. This variable is used to hold the MPG, which will be calculated.

Line 27: This statement converts the `milesTextBox` control's Text property to a `double` and assigns the result to the `miles` variable.

Line 31: This statement converts the `gallonsTextBox` control's Text property to a `double` and assigns the result to the `gallons` variable.

Line 34: This statement calculates MPG. It divides the `miles` variable by the `gallons` variable and assigns the result to the `mpg` variable.

Line 37: This statement converts the `mpg` variable to a string and assigns the result to the `mpgLabel` control's Text property. This causes the value of the `mpg` variable to be displayed in the `mpgLabel` control.

Step 4: Switch your view back to the *Designer* and double-click the `exitButton` control. In the code editor you will see an empty event handler named `exitButton_Click`. Complete the `exitButton_Click` event handler by typing the code shown in lines 42– 43 in Program 3-2.

Step 5: Save the project. Then, press the F5 key on the keyboard or click the *Start Debugging* button (▶) on the toolbar to compile and run the application. Test the application by entering values into the TextBoxes and clicking the *Calculate MPG* button. The MPG should be displayed, similar to Figure 3-18. Click the *Exit* button and the form should close.

Figure 3-18 The *Fuel Economy* application

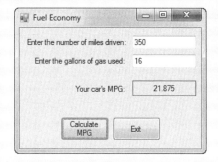

Program 3-2 Completed Form1 code for the *Fuel Economy* application

```csharp
 1 using System;
 2 using System.Collections.Generic;
 3 using System.ComponentModel;
 4 using System.Data;
 5 using System.Drawing;
 6 using System.Linq;
 7 using System.Text;
 8 using System.Windows.Forms;
 9
10 namespace Fuel_Economy
11 {
12   public partial class Form1 : Form
13   {
14     public Form1()
15     {
16       InitializeComponent();
17     }
18
19     private void calculateButton_Click(object sender, EventArgs e)
20     {
21       double miles;   // To hold miles driven
22       double gallons; // To hold gallons used
23       double mpg;     // To hold MPG
24
25       // Get the miles driven and assign it to
26       // the miles variable.
27       miles = double.Parse(milesTextBox.Text);
28
29       // Get the gallons used and assign it to
30       // the gallons variable.
31       gallons = double.Parse(gallonsTextBox.Text);
32
33       // Calculate MPG.
34       mpg = miles / gallons;
35
36       // Display the MPG in the mpgLabel control.
37       mpgLabel.Text = mpg.ToString();
38     }
39
40     private void exitButton_Click(object sender, EventArgs e)
41     {
42       // Close the form.
43       this.Close();
44     }
45   }
46 }
```

 **Checkpoint**

3.25 What method converts the string literal "40" to a value of the int data type?

3.26 Write a statement that converts each of the following string values to the decimal data type using the decimal.Parse method.

a. "9.05"
b. grandTotal
c. "50"
d. priceTextBox.Text

3.27 Suppose an application has a decimal variable named total and a Label control named totalLabel. What will be the result when the following assignment statement is executed?

```
totalLabel.Text = total;
```

3.28 Write a statement that displays each of the following numeric variables in a message box.

a. grandTotal
b. highScore
c. sum
d. width

3.29 Write a statement that will store the value of an int variable named result in the Text property of a Label control named resultLabel.

3.6 Formatting Numbers with the ToString Method

CONCEPT: The ToString method can optionally format a number to appear in a specific way.

When you display large numbers, you usually want to format them with commas so they are easy to read. For example, 487,634,789.0 is easier to read than 487634789.0. Also, when you display amounts of money, you usually want to round them to two decimal places and display a currency symbol, such as a dollar sign ($).

When you call the ToString method, you can optionally pass a formatting string as an argument to the method. The **formatting string** indicates that you want the number to appear formatted in a specific way when it is returned as a string from the method. For example, when you pass the formatting string "c" to the ToString method, the number is returned formatted as currency. Assuming that you are in the United States, numbers formatted as currency are preceded by a dollar sign ($), are rounded to two decimal places, and have comma separators inserted as necessary. The following code sample demonstrates:

```
decimal amount = 123456789.45678m;
MessageBox.Show(amount.ToString("c"));
```

Notice in the second statement that the "c" formatting string is passed to the amount variable's ToString method. The message box that the statement displays appears as shown in Figure 3-19.

There are several other format strings that you can use with the ToString method, and each produces a different type of formatting. Table 3-9 shows a few of them.

Figure 3-19 A number formatted as currency

Table 3-9 A few of the formatting strings

Format String	Description
"N" or "n"	Number format
"F" or "f"	Fixed-point scientific format
"E" or "e"	Exponential scientific format
"C" or "c"	Currency format
"P" or "p"	Percent format

Number Format

Number format ("n" or "N") displays numeric values with comma separators and a decimal point. By default, two digits display to the right of the decimal point. Negative values are displayed with a leading minus sign. An example is −2,345.67.

Fixed-Point Format

Fixed-point format ("f" or "F") displays numeric values with no thousands separator and a decimal point. By default, two digits display to the right of the decimal point. Negative values are displayed with a leading minus (−) sign. An example is −2345.67.

Exponential Format

Exponential format ("e" or "E") displays numeric values in scientific notation. The number is displayed with a single digit to the left of the decimal point. The letter e appears in front of the exponent, and the exponent has a leading + or − sign. By default, six digits display to the right of the decimal point, and a leading minus sign is used if the number is negative.

An example is −2.345670e+003.

Currency Format

Currency format ("c" or "C") displays a leading currency symbol (such as $), digits, comma separators, and a decimal point. By default, two digits display to the right of the decimal point. Negative values are surrounded by parentheses. An example of a negative value is ($2,345.67).

Using Percent Format

Percent format ("p" or "P") causes the number to be multiplied by 100 and displayed with a trailing space and % sign. By default, two digits display to the right of the decimal point. Negative values are displayed with a leading minus sign. For example, the number 0.125 would be formatted as `12.5 %` and the number −0.2345 would be formatted as `-23.45 %`.

Specifying the Precision

Each numeric format string can optionally be followed by an integer that indicates how many digits to display after the decimal point. For example, the format `"n3"` displays three digits after the decimal point. Table 3-10 shows a variety of numeric formatting examples, based on the North American locale.

Table 3-10 Numeric formatting examples (North American locale)

Number	Format String	`ToString( )` Return Value
12.3	"n3"	12.300
12.348	"n2"	12.35
1234567.1	"N"	1,234,567.10
123456.0	"f2"	123456.00
123456.0	"e3"	1.235e+005
.234	"P"	23.40 %
−1234567.8	"C"	($1,234,567.80)

Rounding

Rounding can occur when the number of digits you have specified after the decimal point in the format string is smaller than the precision of the numeric value. Suppose, for example, that the value 1.235 were displayed with a format string of `"n2"`. Then the displayed value would be 1.24. If the next digit after the last displayed digit is 5 or higher, the last displayed digit is rounded *away from zero*. Table 3-11 shows examples of rounding using a format string of `"n2"`.

Table 3-11 Rounding examples using the `"n2"` display format string

Number	Formatted As
1.234	1.23
1.235	1.24
1.238	1.24
−1.234	−1.23
−1.235	−1.24
−1.238	−1.24

Using Leading Zeros with Integer Values

You can use the `"d"` or `"D"` formatting strings with integers to specify the minimum width for displaying the number. Leading zeros are inserted if necessary. Table 3-12 shows examples.

In Tutorial 3-3 you will create an application that uses currency formatting to display a dollar amount.

Table 3-12 Formatting integers using the `"d"` or `"D"` formatting strings

Integer Value	Format String	Formatted As
23	`"d"`	23
23	`"d4"`	0023
1	`"d2"`	01

Tutorial 3-3:

Creating the *Sale Price Calculator* Application with Currency Formatting

If you are writing a program that works with a percentage, you have to make sure that the percentage's decimal point is in the correct location before doing any math with the percentage. This is especially true when the user enters a percentage as input. Most users will enter the number 50 to mean 50 percent, 20 to mean 20 percent, and so forth. Before you perform any calculations with such a percentage, you have to divide it by 100 to move its decimal point to the left two places.

Suppose a retail business is planning to have a storewide sale in which the prices of all items will be reduced by a specified percentage. In this tutorial you will create an application to calculate the sale price of an item after the discount is subtracted. Here is the algorithm, expressed as pseudocode:

1. *Get the original price of the item.*
2. *Get the discount percentage. (For example, 20 is entered for 20 percent.)*
3. *Divide the percentage amount by 100 to move the decimal point to the correct location.*
4. *Multiply the percentage by the original price. This is the amount of the discount.*
5. *Subtract the discount from the original price. This is the sale price.*
6. *Display the sale price.*

Figure 3-20 shows the application's form, with the names of all the controls. When the application runs, the user enters an item's original price into the `originalPriceTextBox` control and the discount percentage into the `discountPercentageTextBox` control. When the user clicks the `calculateButton` control, the application calculates the item's sale price and displays the result in the `salePriceLabel` control. The `exitButton` control closes the application's form.

Figure 3-20 The *Sale Price Calculator* form

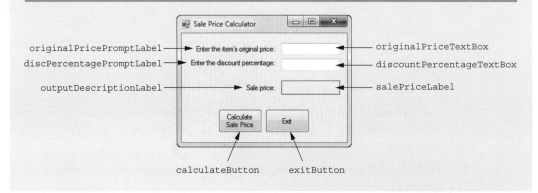

Step 1: Start Visual Studio (or Visual C# Express) and begin a new Windows Forms Application project named *Sale Price Calculator*.

Step 2: Set up the application's form, as shown in Figure 3-20. Notice that the form's Text property is set to *Sale Price Calculator*. The names of the controls are shown in the figure. As you place each of the controls on the form, refer to Table 3-13 for the relevant property settings.

Table 3-13 Control property settings

Control Name	Control Type	Property Settings
originalPricePromptLabel	Label	**Text:** *Enter the item's original price:*
discPercentagePromptLabel	Label	**Text:** *Enter the discount percentage:*
outputDescriptionLabel	Label	**Text:** *Sale price:*
originalPriceTextBox	TextBox	No properties changed
discountPercentageTextBox	TextBox	No properties changed
salePriceLabel	Label	**AutoSize:** False **BorderStyle:** FixedSingle **Text:** (The contents of the Text property have been erased.) **TextAlign:** MiddleCenter
calculateButton	Button	**Text:** *Calculate Sale Price*
exitButton	Button	**Text:** *Exit*

Step 3: Once you have set up the form with its controls, you can create the Click event handlers for the Button controls. At the end of this tutorial, Program 3-3 shows the completed code for the form. You will be instructed to refer to Program 3-3 as you write the event handlers. (Remember, the line numbers that are shown in Program 3-3 are not part of the program. They are shown for reference only.)

In the *Designer*, double-click the `calculateButton` control. This will open the code editor, and you will see an empty event handler named `calculateButton_Click`. Complete the `calculateButton_Click` event handler by typing the code shown in lines 21–37 in Program 3-3.

Let's take a closer look at the code:

Line 21: This statement declares a `decimal` variable named `originalPrice`. This variable will hold the item's original price.

Line 22: This statement declares a `decimal` variable named `discountPercentage`. This variable will hold the discount percentage.

Line 23: This statement declares a `decimal` variable named `discountAmount`. This variable will hold the amount of discount that will be taken from the item's original price. This amount will be calculated.

Line 24: This statement declares a `decimal` variable named `salePrice`. This variable will hold the item's sale price. This amount will be calculated.

Line 27: This statement converts the `originalPriceTextBox` control's Text property to a `decimal` and assigns the result to the `originalPrice` variable.

Line 30: This statement converts the `discountPercentageTextBox` control's Text property to a `decimal` and assigns the result to the `discountPercentage` variable.

Line 33: This statement divides `discountPercentage` by 100 and stores the result back in `discountPercentage`. This moves the decimal point in the `discountPercentage` variable to the left two places.

Line 36: This statement calculates the amount of the discount. It multiplies `originalPrice` by `discountPercentage` and assigns the result to `discountAmount`.

Line 39: This statement calculates the item's sale price. It subtracts the `discountAmount` variable from the `originalPrice` variable and assigns the result to the `salePrice` variable.

Line 42: This statement displays the item's sale price as a currency amount. It converts the `salePrice` variable to a string and assigns the result to the `salePriceLabel` control's Text property. Notice that the format string `"c"` is passed to the `salePrice` variable's `ToString` method.

Step 4: Switch your view back to the *Designer* and double-click the `exitButton` control. In the code editor you will see an empty event handler named `exitButton_Click`. Complete the `exitButton_Click` event handler by typing the code shown in lines 47–48 in Program 3-3.

Step 5: Save the project. Then, press the `F5` key on the keyboard or click the *Start Debugging* button (▶) on the toolbar to compile and run the application. Test the application by entering values into the TextBoxes and clicking the *Calculate Sale Price* button. The sale price is displayed, similar to Figure 3-21. Click the *Exit* button and the form closes.

Figure 3-21 The *Sale Price Calculator* application

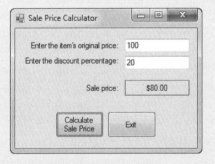

Program 3-3 Completed Form1 code for the *Sale Price Calculator* application

```
1 using System;
2 using System.Collections.Generic;
3 using System.ComponentModel;
4 using System.Data;
5 using System.Drawing;
6 using System.Linq;
7 using System.Text;
8 using System.Windows.Forms;
9
10 namespace Sale_Price_Calculator
```

```
11 {
12    public partial class Form1 : Form
13    {
14       public Form1()
15       {
16          InitializeComponent();
17       }
18
19       private void calculateButton_Click(object sender, EventArgs e)
20       {
21          decimal originalPrice;      // The item's original price
22          decimal discountPercentage; // The discount percentage
23          decimal discountAmount;     // The amount of discount
24          decimal salePrice;          // The item's sale price
25
26          // Get the item's original price.
27          originalPrice = decimal.Parse(originalPriceTextBox. Text);
28
29          // Get the discount percentage.
30          discountPercentage = decimal.Parse(discountPercentageTextBox.Text);
31
32          // Move the percentage's decimal point left two spaces.
33          discountPercentage = discountPercentage / 100;
34
35          // Calculate the amount of the discount.
36          discountAmount = originalPrice * discountPercentage;
37
38          // Calculate the sale price.
39          salePrice = originalPrice - discountAmount;
40
41          // Display the sale price.
42          salePriceLabel.Text = salePrice.ToString("c");
43       }
44
45       private void exitButton_Click(object sender, EventArgs e)
46       {
47          // Close the form.
48          this.Close();
49       }
50    }
51 }
```

Checkpoint

3.30 Write a programming statement that displays the string value of a variable named
salary in a message box using currency format.

3.31 The following variable names give an indication of the data each stores. For each
variable, specify the format string that you think is most appropriate.
a. discountPercentage
b. atomicWeight
c. retailPrice
d. quantityPurchased
e. degreesKelvin

3.32 What value will be displayed in the message box when the following code segment is executed?

```
double apples = 12.0;
MessageBox.Show(apples.ToString("n0"));
```

3.33 Examine the following integer variables and specify the number of leading zeros to use with the d or D format strings so that all the numbers are equal in width.

```
int valueA = 234, valueB = 56, valueC = 7, valueD = 89123;
```

3.34 Write a programming statement that uses the ToString method of a variable named millimeters so that it displays a precision of four digits after the decimal point in fixed-point scientific format.

3.7 Simple Exception Handling

CONCEPT: An exception is an unexpected error that happens while a program is running. If an exception is not handled by the program, the program will abruptly halt.

An exception is an unexpected error that occurs while a program is running, causing the program to halt if the error is not properly dealt with. Exceptions are usually caused by circumstances that are beyond the programmer's control. For example, suppose the user has entered a value into a TextBox, and that value is expected to be a number. The program uses one of the Parse methods to convert the control's Text property to a numeric data type, but the string contains invalid characters and it cannot be converted. The Parse method cannot continue, so an exception occurs. (To use the proper terminology, we say that a method throws an exception when an unexpected error occurs and it cannot continue operating.)

Let's look at an example. If you have completed the *Fuel Economy* project from Tutorial 3-2, open it in Visual Studio and then either click the Start Debugging button (▶) or press F5 to run the application. On the application's form, enter *300* for the number of miles driven and then enter a nonnumeric sequence of characters for the gallons of gas used. Figure 3-22 shows an example where the user has entered *wxyz*. Then, click the *Calculate MPG* button. Because the invalid string that you entered for the gallons of gas cannot be converted to a double, an exception is thrown. The application stops running and Visual Studio goes into a special mode known as **break mode**. The window shown in Figure 3-23 is displayed, and the line of code that was executing when the exception was thrown is highlighted.

Figure 3-22 Invalid data entered for gallons

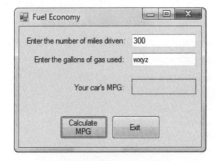

Figure 3-23 Exception reported

```
// Get the gallons used and assign it to
// the gallons variable.
gallons = double.Parse(gallonsTextBox.Text);

// Calculate MPG.
mpg = miles / gallons;

// Display the MPG in the
mpgLabel.Text = mpg.ToStr
}

private void exitButton_Click
{
    // Close the form.
    this.Close();
}
```

i **FormatException was unhandled**   ×

Input string was not in a correct format.

Troubleshooting tips:

Make sure your method arguments are in the right format.

When converting a string to DateTime, parse the string to take the date before putting each variable into the DateTime object.

Get general help for this exception.

Search for more Help Online...

Actions:

View Detail...

Copy exception detail to the clipboard

The exception window that is shown in Figure 3-23 displays a lot of information, but if you look at the line just below the window's title bar, you see the message *Input string was not in a correct format.* That is a description of what happened to cause the exception. To get out of break mode, click the Stop Debugging button (▪), or press ⏍Shift⏍ + ⏍F5⏍. Visual Studio to return it to its normal mode.

Handling Exceptions

C#, like most modern programming languages, allows you to write code that responds to exceptions when they are thrown and prevents the program from abruptly crashing. Such code is called an **exception handler**, and is written with the **try-catch** statement. There are several ways to write a `try-catch` statement, but the following general format is the simplest variation:

```
try
{
    statement;
    statement;
    etc.
}
catch
{
    statement;
    statement;
    etc.
}
```

First the key word `try` appears, followed by a group of one or more statements that appears inside a set of braces. This group of statements is known as a **try block**. One or more of the statements inside the try block can potentially throw an exception.

After the try block, a **catch clause** appears. The `catch` clause is followed by a group of one or more statements enclosed inside a set of braces. This group of statements is known as a **catch block**.

When a `try-catch` statement executes, the statements in the try block are executed in the order that they appear. If a statement in the try block throws an exception, the program immediately jumps to the `catch` clause and executes the statements in the catch block. If all the statements in the try block execute with no exception, the catch block is skipped.

Let's see how a `try-catch` statement can be used in the *Fuel Economy* application. Here is a modified version of the application's `calculateButton_Click` event handler:

```
1 private void calculateButton_Click(object sender, EventArgs e)
2 {
3    try
4    {
5       double miles;    // To hold miles driven
6       double gallons;  // To hold gallons used
7       double mpg;      // To hold MPG
8
9       // Get the miles driven and assign it to
10      // the miles variable.
11      miles = double.Parse(milesTextBox.Text);
12
13      // Get the gallons used and assign it to
14      // the gallons variable.
15      gallons = double.Parse(gallonsTextBox.Text);
16
17      // Calculate MPG.
18      mpg = miles / gallons;
19
20      // Display the MPG in the mpgLabel control.
21      mpgLabel.Text = mpg.ToString();
22    }
23    catch
24    {
25       // Display an error message.
26       MessageBox.Show("Invalid data was entered.");
27    }
28 }
```

When you write a `try-catch` statement, you put all the code that might throw an exception inside the try block. In this version of the event handler, the try block appears in lines 5–21. (In this example, we have put all the statements that previously appeared in the event handler inside the try block.) If any statement inside the try block throws an exception, the program will immediately jump to the catch clause in line 23. Then, the statements in the catch block (lines 25–26) will execute.

Let's say that the application is running and the user enters invalid input into the `milesTextBox` control. When the event handler executes, the statement in line 11 throws an exception because the `double.Parse` method is not able to convert the control's Text property to a `double`. The program will immediately jump to the catch clause in line 23 and then execute the statements inside the catch block. Line 26 displays a message box with an error message. Figure 3-24 illustrates this process.

On the other hand, if all the statements inside the try block execute and no exceptions are thrown, the catch block will be skipped.

Displaying an Exception's Default Error Message

When an exception is thrown, an object known as an **exception object** is created in memory. The exception object has various properties that contain data about the exception. When you write a catch clause, you can optionally assign a name to the exception object, as shown here:

```
catch (Exception ex)
```

The expression that appears inside the parentheses specifies that we are assigning the name ex to the exception object. (There is nothing special about the name ex. That is simply the name that we've chosen for the examples. You can use any name that you wish.)

Figure 3-24 Handling an exception

```
                    private void calculateButton_Click(object sender, EventArgs e)
                    {
                        try
                        {
                            double miles;      // To hold miles driven
                            double gallons;    // To hold gallons used
                            double mpg;        // To hold MPG

If this statement throws    // Get the miles driven and assign it to
an exception...             // the miles variable.
                            miles = double.Parse(milesTextBox.Text);

                            // Get the gallons used and assign it to
The program jumps           // the gallons variable.
to the catch clause         gallons = double.Parse(gallonsTextBox.Text);
and executes the
statements in the           // Calculate MPG.
catch block.                mpg = miles / gallons;

                            // Display the MPG in the mpgLabel control.
                            mpgLabel.Text = mpg.ToString();
                        }
                        catch
                        {
                            // Display an error message.
                            MessageBox.Show("Invalid data was entered.");
                        }
                    }
```

Inside the catch block, we can use the name ex to access the exception object's properties. One of these is the Message property, which contains the exception's default error message. The following code shows how this can be done. This is another modification of the *Fuel Economy* project's calculateButton_Click event handler.

```
 1 private void calculateButton_Click(object sender, EventArgs e)
 2 {
 3    try
 4    {
 5       double miles;    // To hold miles driven
 6       double gallons;  // To hold gallons used
 7       double mpg;      // To hold MPG
 8
 9       // Get the miles driven and assign it to
10       // the miles variable.
11       miles = double.Parse(milesTextBox.Text);
12
13       // Get the gallons used and assign it to
14       // the gallons variable.
15       gallons = double.Parse(gallonsTextBox.Text);
16
17       // Calculate MPG.
18       mpg = miles / gallons;
19
20       // Display the MPG in the mpgLabel control.
21       mpgLabel.Text = mpg.ToString();
22    }
23    catch (Exception ex)
24    {
25       // Display the default error message.
26       MessageBox.Show(ex.Message);
27    }
28 }
```

The statement in line 26 simply passes the exception object's Message property to the `MessageBox.Show` method. This causes the default error message to be displayed in a message box. Figure 3-25 shows an example of the message that is displayed as a result of the user entering invalid input for either the `milesTextBox` or the `gallonsTextBox` controls.

Figure 3-25 A message box showing an exception's default error message

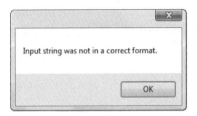

In Tutorial 3-4 you create an application that uses a `try-catch` statement to handle exceptions that are thrown when the user enters invalid data into a TextBox control.

Tutorial 3-4:
Creating the *Test Average* Application with Exception Handling

Determining the average of a group of values is a simple calculation: You add all the values and then divide the sum by the number of values. Although this is a straightforward calculation, it is easy to make a mistake when writing a program that calculates an average. For example, let's assume that the variables a, b, and c each hold a value and we want to calculate the average of those values. If we are careless, we might write a statement such as the following to perform the calculation:

```
average = a + b + c / 3.0;
```

Can you see the error in this statement? When it executes, the division will take place first. The value in c will be divided by 3, and then the result will be added to a + b. That is not the correct way to calculate an average. To correct this error we need to put parentheses around a + b + c, as shown here:

```
average = (a + b + c) / 3.0;
```

In this tutorial you will create an application that calculates the average of three test scores. Figure 3-26 shows the application's form, with the names of all the controls. When

Figure 3-26 The *Test Average* form

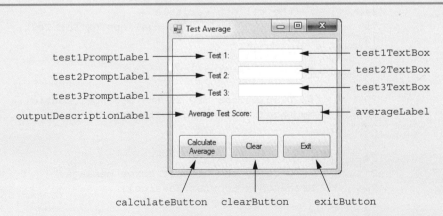

the application runs, the user will enter the test scores into the TextBox controls. When the user clicks the `calculateButton` control, the application will calculate the average test score and display the result in the `averageLabel` control. The `clearButton` control will clear the contents of the TextBoxes and the `averageLabel` control. The `exitButton` control closes the application's form.

Step 1: Start Visual Studio (or Visual C# Express) and begin a new Windows Forms Application project named *Test Average*.

Step 2: Set up the application's form as shown in Figure 3-26. Notice that the form's Text property is set to *Test Average*. The names of the controls are shown in the figure. As you place each of the controls on the form, refer to Table 3-14 for the relevant property settings.

Table 3-14 Control property settings

Control Name	Control Type	Property Settings
test1PromptLabel	Label	**Text:** *Test 1:*
test2PromptLabel	Label	**Text:** *Test 2:*
test3PromptLabel	Label	**Text:** *Test 3:*
outputDescriptionLabel	Label	**Text:** *Average Test Score:*
test1TextBox	TextBox	No properties changed
test2TextBox	TextBox	No properties changed
test3TextBox	TextBox	No properties changed
averageLabel	Label	**AutoSize:** False **BorderStyle:** FixedSingle **Text:** (The contents of the Text property have been erased.) **TextAlign:** MiddleCenter
calculateButton	Button	**Text:** *Calculate Sale Price*
clearButton	Button	**Text:** *Clear*
exitButton	Button	**Text:** *Exit*

Step 3: Once you have set up the form with its controls, you can create the Click event handlers for the Button controls. At the end of this tutorial, Program 3-4 shows the completed code for the form. You will be instructed to refer to Program 3-4 as you write the event handlers. (Remember, the line numbers that are shown in Program 3-4 are not part of the program. They are shown for reference only.)

In the *Designer*, double-click the `calculateButton` control. This will open the code editor, and you will see an empty event handler named `calculateButton_Click`. Complete the `calculateButton_Click` event handler by typing the code shown in lines 21–44 in Program 3-4. Let's take a closer look at the code:

Line 21: This is the beginning of a `try-catch` statement. The try block appears in lines 23–38, and the catch block appears in lines 42–43.

Lines 23–26: These statements declare the following `double` variables: `test1`, `test2`, `test3`, and `average`. The variables will hold the three test scores and the average test score.

Line 29: This statement converts the `test1TextBox` control's Text property to a `double` and assigns the result to the `test1` variable.

Line 30: This statement converts the `test2TextBox` control's Text property to a `double` and assigns the result to the `test2` variable.

Line 31: This statement converts the `test3TextBox` control's Text property to a `double` and assigns the result to the `test3` variable.

Line 34: This statement calculates the average of the `test1`, `test2`, and `test3` variables and assigns the result to the `average` variable.

Line 38: This statement converts the `average` variable to a string and assigns the result to the `averageLabel` control's Text property. Notice that the `"n1"` format string is passed as an argument to the `ToString` method. This causes the number to be rounded to one decimal point.

Step 4: Switch your view back to the *Designer* and double-click the `clearButton` control. In the code editor you will see an empty event handler named `clearButton_Click`. Complete the `clearButton_Click` event handler by typing the code shown in lines 49–53 in Program 3-4.

Lines 50–52: Each of these statements assigns an empty string (`""`) to the Text property of one of the TextBox controls. When these statements have finished executing, the TextBox controls appear empty.

Line 53: This statement assigns an empty string (`""`) to the `averageLabel` control's Text property. After the statement has executed, the label appears empty.

Step 5: Switch your view back to the *Designer* and double-click the `exitButton` control. In the code editor you will see an empty event handler named `exitButton_Click`. Complete the `exitButton_Click` event handler by typing the code shown in lines 58–59 in Program 3-4.

Step 6: Save the project. Then, press the F5 key on the keyboard or click the *Start Debugging* button (▶) on the toolbar to compile and run the application.

First, test the application by entering valid numeric values into the TextBoxes and clicking the *Calculate Average* button. A test average should be displayed, similar to the image shown on the left in Figure 3-27.

Figure 3-27 The *Test Average* application

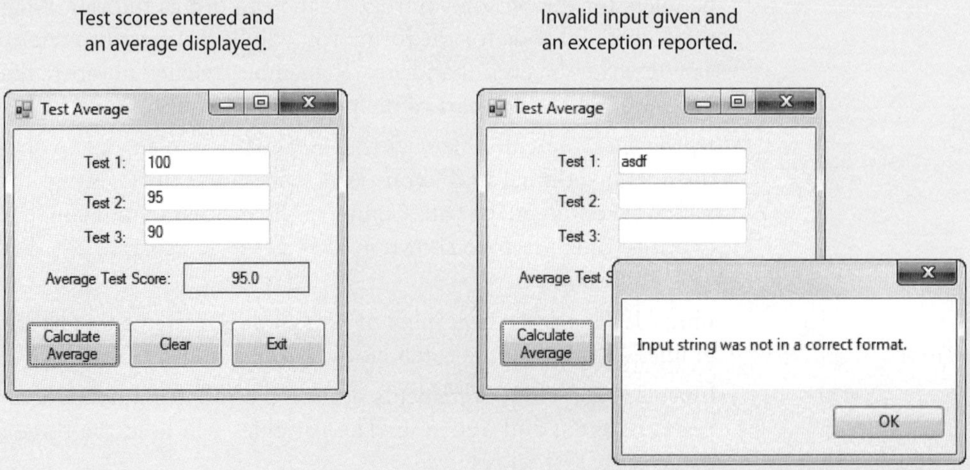

Next, click the *Clear* button to clear the TextBoxes and the average. Then enter a nonnumeric value for test 1, and click the *Calculate Average* button. An exception will be thrown, and you should see the message box shown in the image on the right in Figure 3-27.

Continue to test the application as you wish. When you are finished, click the *Exit* button and the form should close.

Program 3-4 Completed Form1 code for the *Test Average* application

```csharp
 1 using System;
 2 using System.Collections.Generic;
 3 using System.ComponentModel;
 4 using System.Data;
 5 using System.Drawing;
 6 using System.Linq;
 7 using System.Text;
 8 using System.Windows.Forms;
 9
10 namespace Test_Average
11 {
12     public partial class Form1 : Form
13     {
14         public Form1()
15         {
16             InitializeComponent();
17         }
18
19         private void calculateButton_Click(object sender, EventArgs e)
20         {
21             try
22             {
23                 double test1;   // To hold test score #1
24                 double test2;   // To hold test score #2
25                 double test3;   // To hold test score #3
26                 double average; // To hold the average test score
27
28                 // Get the three test scores.
29                 test1 = double.Parse(test1TextBox.Text);
30                 test2 = double.Parse(test2TextBox.Text);
31                 test3 = double.Parse(test3TextBox.Text);
32
33                 // Calculate the average test score.
34                 average = (test1 + test2 + test3) / 3.0;
35
36                 // Display the average test score, with
37                 // the output rounded to 1 decimal point.
38                 averageLabel.Text = average.ToString("n1");
39             }
40             catch (Exception ex)
41             {
42                 // Display the default error message.
43                 MessageBox.Show(ex.Message);
44             }
45         }
46
```

```
47            private void clearButton_Click(object sender, EventArgs e)
48            {
49                // Clear the input and output controls.
50                test1TextBox.Text = "";
51                test2TextBox.Text = "";
52                test3TextBox.Text = "";
53                averageLabel.Text = "";
54            }
55
56            private void exitButton_Click(object sender, EventArgs e)
57            {
58                // Close the form.
59                this.Close();
60            }
61        }
62 }
```

Checkpoint

3.35 What can cause an application to throw an exception?

3.36 How do you get out of break mode when an exception is thrown?

3.37 What kind of code does the try block of a try-catch statement contain?

3.38 What causes the program to jump to the catch clause and execute the catch block of a try-catch statement?

3.39 How can you display the default error message when an exception is thrown?

3.40 Write a try-catch statement for an application that calculates the sum of two whole numbers and displays the result. The application uses two TextBox controls named value1TextBox and value2TextBox to gather the input and a Label control named sumLabel to display the result.

3.8 Using Named Constants

CONCEPT: A named constant is a name that represents a value that cannot be changed during the program's execution.

Assume that the following statement appears in a banking program that calculates data pertaining to loans:

```
amount = balance * 0.069;
```

In such a program, two potential problems arise. First, it is not clear to anyone other than the original programmer what 0.069 is. It appears to be an interest rate, but in some situations there are fees associated with loan payments. How can the purpose of this statement be determined without painstakingly checking the rest of the program?

The second problem occurs if this number is used in other calculations throughout the program and must be changed periodically. Assuming the number is an interest rate, what if the rate changes from 6.9 percent to 7.2 percent? The programmer would have to search through the source code for every occurrence of the number.

Both these problems can be addressed by using named constants. A **named constant** is a name that represents a value that cannot be changed during the program's execution. The following is an example of how you can declare a named constant in C#:

```
const double INTEREST_RATE = 0.129;
```

This statement declares a named constant named `INTEREST_RATE` initialized with the value 0.129. It looks like a regular variable declaration, except that the word `const` appears before the data type name and the name of the variable is written in uppercase characters. The keyword `const` is a qualifier that tells the compiler to make the variable read only. If a statement attempts to change the constant's value, an error will occur when the program is being compiled. When you declare a named constant, an initialization value is required.

It is not required that the constant name be written in uppercase letters, but many programmers prefer to write them this way so they are easily distinguishable from regular variable names. When you are reading a program's code and you see an uppercase identifier, you know instantly that it is a constant.

NOTE: Writing the names of constants in uppercase letters is traditional in many programming languages, and that practice is followed in this book. Within the C# community, some programmers adhere to this practice and some do not. In the classroom, you should use the naming convention that your instructor prefers.

An advantage of using named constants is that they make programs more self-explanatory. The statement

```
amount = balance * 0.069;
```

can be changed to read

```
amount = balance * INTEREST_RATE;
```

A new programmer can read the second statement and know what is happening. It is evident that `balance` is being multiplied by the interest rate. Another advantage to this approach is that widespread changes can easily be made to the program. Let's say the interest rate appears in a dozen different statements throughout the program. When the rate changes, the initialization value in the declaration of the named constant is the only value that needs to be modified. If the rate increases to 7.2 percent, the declaration can be changed to the following:

```
const double INTEREST_RATE = 0.072;
```

The new value of 0.072 will then be used in each statement that uses the `INTEREST_RATE` constant. In Tutorial 3-5 you will create an application that uses named constants.

3.9 Declaring Variables as Fields

CONCEPT: A field is a variable that is declared at the class level. A field's scope is the entire class.

So far in this chapter, all the variables with which we have worked have been local variables. A local variable is declared inside a method and is visible only to statements in that method. Another type of variable is a **field**, which is a variable that is declared inside a class but not inside of any method. A field's scope is the entire class, so when you declare a field, all the methods in the class can access the variable.

Typically, fields are declared at the top of a class declaration, before any methods. Figure 3-28 shows where you would write field declarations inside a form class. When you are about to write a field declaration, you can insert some blank lines after the class's opening brace ({) and write the field declaration in that space.

Figure 3-28 Where to insert field declarations

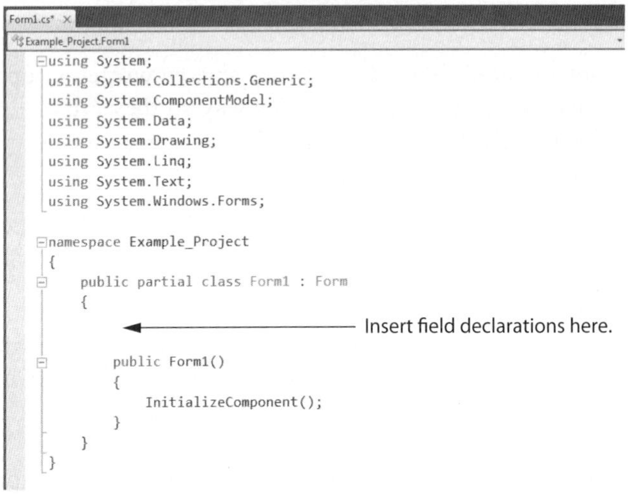

Let's look at an example of a field declaration. Assume that the following statement appears inside a class declaration but not inside any methods. This statement declares an `int` field named `number`, initialized with the value 0:

```
private int number = 0;
```

Field declarations are written like any other variable declaration, except that an access modifier usually appears before the data type. In this example, the keyword `private` is the access modifier. An **access modifier** specifies how a class member can be accessed by code outside the class. When you use the `private` access modifier in a field declaration, the field cannot be accessed by code outside the class. It can be accessed only by the methods that are inside the class.

It is a good programming practice to make fields `private` because `private` fields are hidden from code outside the class. That prevents code outside the class from changing the values of a class's fields and helps prevent bugs from creeping into your program. You will learn more about this in Chapter 10. Until then, if you declare fields in a class, you should get in the habit of making them `private`.

NOTE: There are other access modifiers, as you will learn later in this book. If you don't write an access modifier in a field declaration, C# will automatically make the field `private`. It is still a good idea to write the `private` access modifier because it makes it evident to anyone reading the code that the field is indeed `private`.

In the previous field-declaration example, the number field is initialized with the value 0. If a field is a variable of a numeric data type (such as int, double, or decimal), it will be initialized to 0 by default if you do not explicitly initialize it with a value. It is always a good idea to explicitly initialize a field, however, even if you want it to begin with the value 0. This clearly indicates the field's starting value for anyone reading the code.

 WARNING! If you do not initialize a string field, it begins with a special value known as null. An error will occur if you attempt to use a string that is set to null.

In a form, fields are useful for storing pieces of data that must be shared among the form's event handlers. For example, in the *Chap03* folder of the Student Sample Program files that accompany this book, you will find a project named *Field Demo*. Figure 3-29 shows the application's form, along with the names of the Button controls.

Figure 3-29 The *Field Demo* form

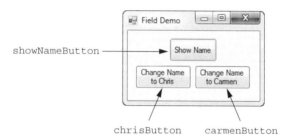

Program 3-5 shows the Form1 code. Notice that in line 15 a string variable named name is declared as a field and initialized with the value "Charles". Next look at the button event handlers:

- In the showNameButton_Click event handler, line 24 displays a message box showing the value of the name variable.
- In the chrisButton_Click event handler, line 29 changes the value of the name variable to "Chris".
- In the carmenButton_Click event handler, line 34 changes the value of the name variable to "Carmen".

As you can see, all of the event handlers in the Form1 class have access to the name variable. If you run the application and click the *Show Name* button, a message box will appear displaying *Charles*, which is the name field's initial value. If you click the *Change Name to Chris* button and then click the *Show Name* button, a message box will appear displaying *Chris*. If you click the *Change Name to Carmen* button and then click the *Show Name* button, a message box will appear displaying *Carmen*.

Program 3-5 Form1 code for the *Field Demo* application

```
 1 using System;
 2 using System.Collections.Generic;
 3 using System.ComponentModel;
 4 using System.Data;
 5 using System.Drawing;
 6 using System.Linq;
 7 using System.Text;
 8 using System.Windows.Forms;
 9
10 namespace Field_Demo
```

```
11 {
12     public partial class Form1 : Form
13     {
14         // Declare a private field to hold a name.
15         private string name = "Charles";
16
17         public Form1()
18         {
19             InitializeComponent();
20         }
21
22         private void showNameButton_Click(object sender, EventArgs e)
23         {
24             MessageBox.Show(name);
25         }
26
27         private void chrisButton_Click(object sender, EventArgs e)
28         {
29             name = "Chris";
30         }
31
32         private void carmenButton_Click(object sender, EventArgs e)
33         {
34             name = "Carmen";
35         }
36     }
37 }
```

The Lifetime of a Field in a Form Class

When you declare a field in a form class, the field's lifetime is the time during which the form exists. This means that the field will exist in memory as long as the form exists. This is different than the lifetime of a local variable, which exists only while the method in which it is declared is executing. Local variables come and go in memory, but a form's fields exist as long as the form exists.

You can see this in the *Field Demo* application. The name field is created in memory when the Form1 form is created, and it continues to exist as long as Form1 exists. When one of the event handlers stores a value in the field, that value remains in the field until it is changed again, perhaps by different event handler. So, fields give you a way of storing values that must not disappear when a particular method ends.

Precautions

Although fields make it easy to share data among the methods in a class, you should be careful about using them. The overuse of fields can make debugging a class's code difficult, especially if the class has many methods. If an incorrect value is being stored in a field, you will have to track down every statement in the class that accesses the field to determine where the incorrect value is coming from. In most cases, fields should be used only for data that must be shared among multiple methods and must continue to exist in memory when the methods are not executing.

Constant Fields

A **constant field** is a field that cannot be changed by any statement in the class. An error will occur if the compiler finds a statement that tries to change the value of a constant field. A constant field is declared with the `const` keyword and initialized with a value. Here is an example:

```
private const decimal INTEREST_RATE = 0.075m;
```

This statement declares a constant `decimal` field named `INTEREST_RATE`, initialized with the value 0.075. Constant fields are typically used to represent unchanging values that are needed by many of a class's methods. For example, suppose a banking program uses a constant field to represent an interest rate. If the interest rate is used in several methods, it is easier to create a constant field, rather than a local named constant in each method. This also simplifies maintenance of the code. If the interest rate changes, only the declaration of the constant field has to be changed, instead of several local declarations.

> **NOTE:** Because a constant field's value cannot be changed by other statements in the class, you do not have to worry about many of the potential debugging problems that are associated with the overuse of regular, nonconstant fields.

In Tutorial 3-5 you will create an application that uses a field in a form class to hold data, as well as constant fields to represent nonchanging values.

Tutorial 3-5:
Creating the *Change Counter* Application

In this tutorial you will create the *Change Counter* application. The application displays images of four coins, having the values 5 cents, 10 cents, 25 cents, and 50 cents. Each time the user clicks on a coin image, the value of that coin is added to a total, and the total is displayed. Figure 3-30 shows the application's form, with the names of all the controls.

Figure 3-30 The *Change Counter* form

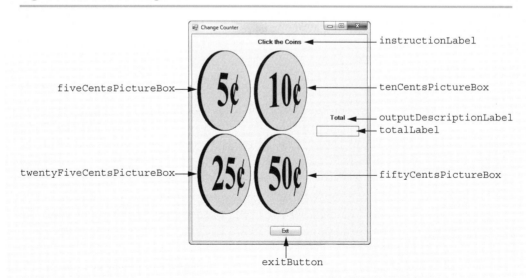

Step 1: Start Visual Studio (or Visual C# Express) and begin a new Windows Forms Application project named *Sale Price Calculator*.

Step 2: Set up the application's form as shown in Figure 3-30. Notice that the form's Text property is set to *Change Counter*. The names of the controls are shown in the figure. As you place each of the controls on the form, refer to Table 3-15 for the relevant property settings.

Table 3-15 Control property settings

Control Name	Control Type	Property Settings
instructionLabel	Label	**Font:** Microsoft Sans Serif (Style: Bold, Size: 10 point) **Text:** *Click the Coins*
fiveCentsPictureBox	PictureBox	**Image:** Select and import the 5cents.png file from the *Chap02* folder of the Student Sample Programs. **SizeMode:** AutoSize
tenCentsPictureBox	PictureBox	**Image:** Select and import the 10cents.png file from the *Chap02* folder of the Student Sample Programs. **SizeMode:** AutoSize
twentyFiveCentsPictureBox	PictureBox	**Image:** Select and import the 25cents.png file from the *Chap02* folder of the Student Sample Programs. **SizeMode:** AutoSize
fiftyCentsPictureBox	PictureBox	**Image:** Select and import the 50cents.png file from the *Chap02* folder of the Student Sample Programs. **SizeMode:** AutoSize
outputDescriptionLabel	Label	**Font:** Microsoft Sans Serif (Style: Bold, Size: 10 point) **Text:** *Total*
totalLabel	Label	**AutoSize:** False **BorderStyle:** FixedSingle **Text:** (The contents of the Text property have been erased.) **TextAlign:** MiddleCenter
exitButton	Button	**Text:** *Exit*

Step 3: Once you have set up the form with its controls, you can begin writing code. At the end of this tutorial, Program 3-6 shows the completed code for the form. You will be instructed to refer to Program 3-6 as you write the form's code. (Remember, the line numbers that are shown in Program 3-6 are not part of the program. They are shown for reference only.)

First, you write the declarations for the fields. Switch your view to the code editor (right-click *Form1.cs* in the *Solution Explorer* and select *View Code* from the pop-up menu). Write the declarations shown in lines 15–22 in Program 3-6. Let's take a closer look at the code:

Line 15: This statement declares a constant `decimal` field named `FIVE_CENTS_VALUE`, initialized with the value 0.05. This constant represents the value of the 5-cent coin.

Line 16: This statement declares a constant `decimal` field named `TEN_CENTS_VALUE`, initialized with the value 0.10. This constant represents the value of the 10-cent coin.

Line 17: This statement declares a constant `decimal` field named `TWENTY_FIVE_CENTS_VALUE`, initialized with the value 0.25. This constant represents the value of the 25-cent coin.

Line 18: This statement declares a constant `decimal` field named `FIFTY_CENTS_VALUE`, initialized with the value 0.50. This constant represents the value of the 50-cent coin.

Line 22: This statement declares a `decimal` field named `total`, initialized with the value 0. This field is used to keep the total value of the coins that the user clicks.

Step 4: Now you can create the Click event handlers for the PictureBox controls. Switch your view back to the *Designer* and double-click the `fiveCentsPictureBox` control. This opens the code editor, and you will see an empty event handler named `fiveCentsPictureBox_Click`. Complete the `fiveCentsPictureBox_Click` event handler by typing the code shown in lines 31–35 in Program 3-6. Let's take a closer look at the code:

Line 32: This statement adds the value of the `FIVE_CENTS_VALUE` constant to the `total` field.

Line 35: This statement converts the `total` variable to a string and assigns the result to the `totalLabel` control's Text property. The `"c"` format string causes the number to be formatted as currency.

Step 5: Switch your view back to the *Designer* and double-click the `tenCentsPictureBox` control. This opens the code editor, and you will see an empty event handler named `tenCentsPictureBox_Click`. Complete the `tenCentsPictureBox_Click` event handler by typing the code shown in lines 40–44 in Program 3-6. Let's take a closer look at the code:

Line 41: This statement adds the value of the `TEN_CENTS_VALUE` constant to the `total` field.

Line 44: This statement converts the `total` variable to a string and assigns the result to the `totalLabel` control's Text property. The `"c"` format string causes the number to be formatted as currency.

Step 6: Switch your view back to the *Designer* and double-click the `twentyFiveCentsPictureBox` control. This opens the code editor, and you will see an empty event handler named `twentyFiveCentsPictureBox_Click`. Complete the `twentyFiveCentsPictureBox_Click` event handler by typing the code shown in lines 49–53 in Program 3-6. Let's take a closer look at the code:

Line 50: This statement adds the value of the `TWENTY_FIVE_CENTS_VALUE` constant to the `total` field.

Line 53: This statement converts the `total` variable to a string and assigns the result to the `totalLabel` control's Text property. The `"c"` format string causes the number to be formatted as currency.

Step 7: Switch your view back to the *Designer* and double-click the `fiftyCentsPictureBox` control. This opens the code editor, and you will see an empty event handler named `fiftyCentsPictureBox_Click`. Complete the `fiftyCentsPictureBox_Click` event handler by typing the code shown in lines 58–62 in Program 3-6. Let's take a closer look at the code:

Line 59: This statement adds the value of the `FIFTY_CENTS_VALUE` constant to the `total` field.

Line 62: This statement converts the `total` variable to a string and assigns the result to the `totalLabel` control's Text property. The `"c"` format string causes the number to be formatted as currency.

Step 8:   Now you write the event handler for the *Exit* button. Switch your view back to the *Designer* and double-click the exitButton control. This opens the code editor, and you will see an empty event handler named exitButton_Click. Complete the exitButton_Click event handler by typing the code shown in lines 67–68 in Program 3-6.

Step 9:   Save the project. Then, press the ⌊F5⌋ key on the keyboard or click the *Start Debugging* button (▶) on the toolbar to compile and run the application. Test the application by clicking the coin images in any order you wish. The total shown on the form should update by the correct amount each time you click a coin. When you are finished, click the *Exit* button and the form should close.

Program 3-6 Completed Form1 code for the *Change Counter* application

```
 1 using System;
 2 using System.Collections.Generic;
 3 using System.ComponentModel;
 4 using System.Data;
 5 using System.Drawing;
 6 using System.Linq;
 7 using System.Text;
 8 using System.Windows.Forms;
 9
10 namespace Change_Counter
11 {
12     public partial class Form1 : Form
13     {
14         // Constant fields
15         private const decimal FIVE_CENTS_VALUE = 0.05m;
16         private const decimal TEN_CENTS_VALUE = 0.10m;
17         private const decimal TWENTY_FIVE_CENTS_VALUE = 0.25m;
18         private const decimal FIFTY_CENTS_VALUE = 0.50m;
19
20         // Field variable to hold the total,
21         // initialized with 0.
22         private decimal total = 0m;
23
24         public Form1()
25         {
26             InitializeComponent();
27         }
28
29         private void fiveCentsPictureBox_Click(object sender, EventArgs e)
30         {
31             // Add the value of 5 cents to the total.
32             total += FIVE_CENTS_VALUE;
33
34             // Display the total, formatted as currency.
35             totalLabel.Text = total.ToString("c");
36         }
37
38         private void tenCentsPictureBox_Click(object sender, EventArgs e)
39         {
40             // Add the value of 10 cents to the total.
41             total += TEN_CENTS_VALUE;
42
```

```
43              // Display the total, formatted as currency.
44              totalLabel.Text = total.ToString("c");
45          }
46
47          private void twentyFiveCentsPictureBox_Click(object sender, EventArgs e)
48          {
49              // Add the value of 25 cents to the total.
50              total += TWENTY_FIVE_CENTS_VALUE;
51
52              // Display the total, formatted as currency.
53              totalLabel.Text = total.ToString("c");
54          }
55
56          private void fiftyCentsPictureBox_Click(object sender, EventArgs e)
57          {
58              // Add the value of 50 cents to the total.
59              total += FIFTY_CENTS_VALUE;
60
61              // Display the total, formatted as currency.
62              totalLabel.Text = total.ToString("c");
63          }
64
65          private void exitButton_Click(object sender, EventArgs e)
66          {
67              // Close the form.
68              this.Close();
69          }
70      }
71 }
```

✅ Checkpoint

3.41 What are two advantages of using named constants?

3.42 Write a programming statement that declares a named constant for a 10 percent discount.

3.43 Where should you place field declarations in a program?

3.44 What access modifier should you use when declaring a field? Why?

3.45 How is the lifetime of a field different from the lifetime of a local variable?

3.46 Write a programming statement that declares a constant field for a 5.9 percent interest rate.

3.10 Using the Math Class

CONCEPT: The .NET Framework's Math class provides several methods for performing complex mathematical calculations.

The .NET Framework provides a class named Math, which contains numerous methods that are useful for performing advanced mathematical operations. Table 3-16 gives a summary of several of the Math class methods. (For a comprehensive list of all the methods

Table 3-16 Many of the `Math` class methods

Math Class Method	Description
`Math.Abs(x)`	Returns the absolute value of *x*.
`Math.Acos(x)`	Returns the arccosine of *x*, *in radians*. The argument *x* is a `double`, and the value that is returned is a `double`.
`Math.Asin(x)`	Returns the arcsine of *x*, *in radians*. The argument *x* is a `double`, and the value that is returned is a `double`.
`Math.Atan(x)`	Returns the arctangent of *x*, *in radians*. The argument *x* is a `double`, and the value that is returned is a `double`.
`Math.Ceiling(x)`	Returns the least integer that is greater than or equal to *x* (a `decimal` or a `double`).
`Math.Cos(x)`	Returns the cosine of *x* in radians. The argument *x* is a `double`, and the value that is returned is a `double`.
`Math.Exp(x)`	Returns e^x. The argument *x* is a `double`, and the value that is returned is a `double`.
`Math.Floor(x)`	Returns the greatest integer that is less than or equal to *x* (a `decimal` or a `double`).
`Math.Log(x)`	Returns the natural logarithm of *x*. The argument *x* is a `double`, and the value that is returned is a `double`.
`Math.Log10(x)`	Returns the base-10 logarithm of *x*. The argument *x* is a `double`, and the value that is returned is a `double`.
`Math.Max(x, y)`	Returns the greater of the two values *x* and *y*.
`Math.Min(x, y)`	Returns the lesser of the two values *x* and *y*.
`Math.Pow(x, y)`	Returns the value of *x* (a `double`) raised to the power of *y* (also a `double`). The value that is returned is a `double`.
`Math.Round(x)`	Returns the value of *x* (a `double` or a `decimal`) rounded to the nearest integer.
`Math.Sin(x)`	Returns the sine of *x* in radians.
`Math.Sqrt(x)`	Returns the square root of *x* (a `double`). The value that is returned is a `double`.
`Math.Tan(x)`	Returns the tangent of *x* in radians. The argument *x* is a `double`, and the value that is returned is a `double`.
`Math.Truncate(x)`	Returns the integer part of *x* (a `double` or a `decimal`).

provided by the `Math` class and more details on any of the methods, just search for *Math class* in the MSDN help system.)

These methods typically accept one or more values as arguments, perform a mathematical operation using the arguments, and return the result. For example, the `Math.Pow` method raises a number to a power. Here is an example of how the method is called:

```
double result;
result = Math.Sqrt(4.0, 2.0);
```

The method takes two `double` arguments. It raises the first argument to the power of the second argument and returns the result as a `double`. In this example, 4.0 is raised to the power of 2.0. This statement is equivalent to the following algebraic statement:

```
result = 4²
```

The following code sample shows another example of a statement using the `Math.Pow` method. It assigns 3 times 6^3 to x:

```
double x;
x = 3 * Math.pow(6.0, 3.0);
```

The `Math.Sqrt` method accepts an argument and returns the square root of the argument. Here is an example of how it is used:

```
double result;
result = Math.Sqrt(16.0);
```

The statement that calls the `Math.Sqrt` method passes 16.0 as an argument. The method returns the square root of 16.0 (as a `double`), which is then assigned to the `result` variable.

The `Math.PI` and `Math.E` Named Constants

The `Math` class also provides two predefined named constants, `Math.PI` and `Math.E`, which are assigned mathematical values for *pi* and *e*. You can use these variables in equations that require their values. For example, the following statement, which calculates the area of a circle, uses `Math.PI`.

```
area = Math.PI * radius * radius;
```

 NOTE: If you look at the top of a form's source code in the code editor, you should see a directive that reads `using System;`. That directive is required for any program that uses the `Math` class.

 ### Checkpoint

3.47 Write a programming statement that uses the `Math.Pow` method to square the number 12 and store the result in a `double` variable named `product`.

3.48 What method of the `Math` class can be used to determine the larger of two values?

3.49 What method of the `Math` class can be used to determine the smaller of two values?

 ## 3.11 More GUI Details

In Chapter 2 you learned the basics of creating a GUI by placing controls on a form and setting various properties. In this section you learn to fine-tune many aspects of an application's GUI.

Controlling a Form's Tab Order

When an application is running and a form is displayed, one of the form's controls always has the focus. The control having the **focus** is the one that receives the user's keyboard input. For example, when a TextBox control has the focus, it receives the characters that the user enters on the keyboard. When a button has the focus, pressing the Enter key executes the button's Click event handler.

> **NOTE:** Only controls capable of receiving some sort of input, such as text boxes and buttons, may have the focus.

You can tell which control has the focus by looking at the form at run time. When a TextBox control has the focus, a blinking text cursor appears inside it, or the text inside the TextBox control might appear highlighted. When a button has the focus, a thin dotted line usually appears around the control.

When an application is running, pressing the Tab key changes the focus from one control to another. The order in which controls receive the focus is called the **tab order**. When you place controls on a form in Visual C#, the tab order is in the same sequence in which you created the controls. In many cases this is the tab order you want, but sometimes you rearrange controls on a form, delete controls, and add new ones. These modifications often lead to a disorganized tab order, which can confuse and irritate the users of your application.

Users want to tab smoothly from one control to the next, in a logical sequence. You can modify the tab order by changing a control's TabIndex property. The **TabIndex property** contains a numeric value, which indicates the control's position in the tab order. When you create a control, Visual C# automatically assigns a value to its TabIndex property. The first control you create on a form has a TabIndex of 0, the second has a TabIndex of 1, and so on. The control with a TabIndex of 0 is the first control in the tab order. The next control in the tab order is the one with a TabIndex of 1. The tab order continues in this sequence.

You may change the tab order of a form's controls by selecting them, one by one, and changing their TabIndex property in the *Properties* window. An easier method, however, is to click *View* on the Visual Studio menu bar and then click *Tab Order*. This causes the form to be displayed in **tab order selection mode**. The image on the left in Figure 3-31 shows a form in the normal view, and the image on the right shows the form in tab order selection mode. We have also inserted the names of the TextBox and Button controls in the image on the right for reference purposes.

Figure 3-31 A form displayed in tab order selection mode

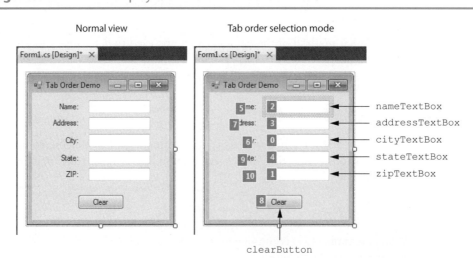

In tab order selection mode, each control's existing TabIndex value is displayed in a small box in the control's upper-left corner. Notice the following in the image on the right in Figure 3-31:

- The `nameTextBox` control's TabIndex is 2.
- The `addressTextBox` control's TabIndex is 3.
- The `cityTextBox` control's TabIndex is 0.
- The `stateTextBox` control's TabIndex is 4.
- The `zipTextBox` control's TabIndex is 1.
- The `clearButton` control's TabIndex is 8.

NOTE: Although the Label controls have TabIndex values, those values are irrelevant in this example because Label controls cannot receive the focus.

As you look at Figure 3-31, think about the order in which the controls will receive the focus when the application runs.

- The `cityTextBox` control has the lowest TabIndex value (0), so it will receive the focus first.
- If you press the Tab key, the focus will jump to the `zipTextBox` control because it has the next lowest TabIndex value (1).
- Press the Tab key again and the focus will jump to the `nameTextBox` control (TabIndex is set to 2).
- Press the Tab key again and the focus will jump to the `addressTextBox` control (TabIndex is set to 3).
- Press the Tab key again and the focus will jump to the `stateTextBox` control (TabIndex is set to 4).
- Press the Tab key again and the focus will jump to the `clearButton` control (TabIndex is set to 8).

This is a very confusing tab order and should be rearranged. When a form is displayed in tab order selection mode, you establish a new tab order by simply clicking the controls with the mouse in the order you want. To fix the disorganized tab order shown in Figure 3-31, we perform the following:

- First, click the `nameTextBox` control. The control's TabIndex value changes to 0.
- Next, click the `addressTextBox` control. The control's TabIndex value changes to 1.
- Then, click the `cityTextBox` control. The control's TabIndex value changes to 2.
- Next, click the `stateTextBox` control. The control's TabIndex value changes to 3.
- Then, click the `zipTextBox` control. The control's TabIndex value changes to 4.
- Finally, click the `clearButton` control. The control's TabIndex value changes to 5.

When you are finished, exit tab order selection mode by pressing the Esc key. Now when the application runs, the focus will shift smoothly in an order that makes sense to the user.

Changing the Focus with the `Focus` Method

Often, you want to make sure a particular control has the focus. For example, look at the form shown in Figure 3-31. The purpose of the *Clear* button is to clear any input that the user has entered and reset the form so it is ready to accept a new set of input. When the *Clear* button is clicked, the TextBox controls should be cleared and the focus should return to the `nameTextBox` control. This would make it unnecessary for the user to click the TextBox control in order to start entering another set of information.

In code, you move the focus to a control by calling the **Focus method**. The method's general syntax is:

```
ControlName.Focus();
```

where *ControlName* is the name of the control. For instance, you move the focus to the nameTextBox control with this statement:

```
nameTextBox.Focus();
```

After the statement executes, the nameTextBox control will have the focus. Here is an example of how the clearButton control's Click event handler could be written:

```
 1 private void clearButton_Click(object sender, EventArgs e)
 2 {
 3     // Clear the TextBox controls.
 4     nameTextBox.Text = "";
 5     addressTextBox.Text = "";
 6     cityTextBox.Text = "";
 7     stateTextBox.Text = "";
 8     zipTextBox.Text = "";
 9
10     // Set the focus to nameTextBox.
11     nameTextBox.Focus();
12 }
```

The statements in lines 4–8 clear the contents of the TextBox controls. Then, the statement in line 11 sets the focus to the nameTextBox control.

Assigning Keyboard Access Keys to Buttons

An **access key,** also known as a **mnemonic,** is a key that is pressed in combination with the Alt key to access quickly a control such as a button. When you assign an access key to a button, the user can trigger a Click event either by clicking the button with the mouse or by using the access key. Users who are quick with the keyboard prefer to use access keys instead of the mouse.

You assign an access key to a button through its Text property. For example, assume an application has a button whose Text property is set to *Exit*. You wish to assign the access key [Alt] + [X] to the button so the user may trigger the button's Click event by pressing [Alt] + [X] on the keyboard. To make the assignment, place an ampersand (&) before the letter *x* in the button's Text property: E&xit. Figure 3-32 shows how the Text property appears in the *Properties* window.

Figure 3-32 Text property E&xit

Although the ampersand is part of the Button control's Text property, it is not displayed on the button. With the ampersand in front of the letter *x*, the letter will appear underlined as shown in Figure 3-33. This indicates that the button may be clicked by pressing [Alt] + [X] on the keyboard. (You will see the underlining at design time. At run time, however, the underlining may not appear until the user presses the Alt key.)

Figure 3-33 Button control with `E&xit` Text property

 NOTE: Access keys do not distinguish between uppercase and lowercase characters. There is no difference between [Alt] + [X] and [Alt] + [x].

Suppose we store the value `&Exit` in the button's Text property. The ampersand is in front of the letter *E*, so [Alt] + [E] becomes the access key. The button will appear as shown in Figure 3-34.

Figure 3-34 Button control with `&Exit` Text property

Assigning the Same Access Key to Multiple Buttons

Be careful not to assign the same access key to two or more buttons on the same form. If two or more buttons share the same access key, a Click event is triggered for the first button created when the user presses the access key.

Displaying the & Character on a Button

If you want to display an ampersand character on a button, use two ampersands (`&&`) in the Text property. Using two ampersands causes a single ampersand to display and does not define an access key. For example, if a button's Text property is set to `Save && Exit`, the button will appear as shown in Figure 3-35.

Figure 3-35 Button control with `Save && Exit` Text property

Accept Buttons and Cancel Buttons

An **accept button** is a button on a form that is automatically clicked when the user presses the Enter key. A **cancel button** is a button on a form that is automatically clicked when the user presses the Esc key. Forms have two properties, AcceptButton and CancelButton, which allow you to designate an accept button and a cancel button. When you select these properties in the *Properties* window, a down-arrow button (▾) appears, which displays a drop-down list when clicked. The list contains the names of all the buttons on the form. You select the button that you want to designate as the accept button or cancel button.

Any button that is frequently clicked should probably be selected as the accept button. This will allow keyboard users to access the button quickly and easily. *Exit* or *Cancel* buttons are likely candidates to become cancel buttons.

The BackColor Property

Forms and most controls have a **BackColor property** that allows you to change the object's background color. When you select an object's BackColor property in the *Properties* window, a down-arrow button ( ) appears, which displays a drop-down list of available colors when clicked, as shown in Figure 3-36.

The drop-down list has three tabs: *Custom*, *Web*, and *System*. The *System* tab lists colors defined in the current Windows configuration. The *Web* tab lists colors displayed with consistency in Web browsers. The *Custom* tab displays a color palette. Select a color from one of the tabs and the object's background color will be set to that color.

The ForeColor Property

Controls that display text have a **ForeColor** property that allows you to change the color of the text. When you select a control's ForeColor property in the *Properties* window, a down-arrow button ( ) appears, which displays the drop-down list of available colors shown in Figure 3-36 when clicked. Select a color from one of the tabs and the text that is displayed by the control will be set to that color.

Figure 3-36 Drop-down list of colors

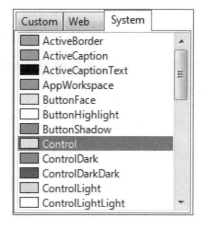

Setting Colors in Code

In addition to using the *Properties* window, you can also set the values of the BackColor and ForeColor properties with code. The .NET Framework provides numerous values that represent colors and can be assigned to the ForeColor and BackColor properties in code. The following are a few of the values:

```
Color.Black
Color.Blue
Color.Cyan
Color.Green
Color.Magenta
Color.Red
Color.White
Color.Yellow
```

For example, assume an application has a Label control named `messageLabel`. The following code sets the label's background color to black and foreground color to yellow:

```
messageLabel.BackColor = Color.Black;
messageLabel.ForeColor = Color.Yellow;
```

The .NET Framework also provides values that represent default colors on your system. For example, the value `SystemColors.Control` represents the default control background color and `SystemColors.ControlText` represents the default control text color. The following statements set the `messageLabel` control's background and foreground to the default colors.

```
messageLabel.BackColor = SystemColors.Control
messageLabel.ForeColor = SystemColors.ControlText
```

NOTE: If you have an event handler in a form's source code file and you want the event handler to change the form's BackColor property, use the `this` keyword to refer to the form. For example, the following statement changes the color of the form to blue:

```
this.BackColor = Color.Blue;
```

Background Images for Forms

In Chapter 2 you learned about displaying images with PictureBox controls. An image can also be displayed as the background for a form. Forms have a property named BackgroundImage that allows you to import and display an image on the form. If you know how to use the PictureBox control's Image property, then you already know how to use a form's BackgroundImage property. They both work the same way:

- Click the BackgroundImage property in the *Properties* window. An ellipses button ( ) will appear.
- Click the ellipses button and the *Select Resource* window will appear.
- In the *Select Resource* window, click the *Import* button. An *Open* dialog box will appear. Use the dialog box to locate and select the image file that you want to display.
- Click the *OK* button in the *Select Resource* window, and the selected image will appear as the form's background.

A form's BackgroundImageLayout property is similar to the PictureBox control's Size-Mode property. It specifies how the background image is to be displayed. It can be set to one of the following values:

- **None**

  The image is positioned in the upper-left corner of the form. If the image is too big to fit in the form, it is clipped.

- **Tile**

  This is the default value. The image is tiled (repeatedly displayed) across the form.

- **Center**

  The image is centered in the form without being resized.

- **Stretch**

  The image is resized both horizontally and vertically to fit in the form. If the image is resized more in one direction than the other, it appears stretched.

- **Zoom**

  The image is uniformly resized to fit in the form without losing its original aspect ratio. This causes the image to be resized without appearing stretched.

Figure 3-37 shows examples of each of these settings.

Figure 3-37 Different settings for the BackgroundImageLayout property

BackgroundImageLayout set to None

BackgroundImageLayout set to Tile

BackgroundImageLayout set to Center

BackgroundImageLayout set to Stretch

BackgroundImageLayout set to Zoom

Organizing Controls with GroupBoxes and Panels

A **GroupBox control** is a rectangular control that appears with a thin border and an optional title in its upper-left corner. It is a container that can hold other controls. You can use GroupBoxes to create a sense of visual organization on a form.

The GroupBox control is found in the *Toolbox*, in the *Containers* section. When you create a GroupBox control, you can set its Title property to the text that you want displayed in the GroupBox's upper-left corner. If you don't want a title displayed on the GroupBox, you can clear the contents of its Text property.

Figure 3-38 shows a GroupBox control. The control's Text property is set to *Personal Data*, and several other controls are inside the GroupBox.

Figure 3-38 A GroupBox containing other controls

Creating a Group Box and Adding Controls to It

Suppose you've just created a GroupBox control. To add another control to the Group-Box, select the GroupBox control and then double-click the desired tool in the Toolbox to place another control inside the group box.

Moving an Existing Control to a Group Box

If an existing control is not inside a GroupBox but you want to move it to the GroupBox, follow these steps:

1. Select the control you wish to add to the GroupBox.
2. Cut the control to the clipboard.
3. Select the GroupBox.
4. Paste the control.

Moving and Resizing a GroupBox

If a GroupBox is selected in the *Designer*, a four-headed arrow (✥) will appear in the GroupBox's upper-left corner. Click and drag the four-headed arrow to move the Group-Box. Any controls inside the GroupBox move with it.

Deleting a GroupBox

To delete a GroupBox, simply select it in the *Designer* and then press the (Delete) key. Any controls inside the GroupBox are deleted as well.

Group Box Tab Order

The value of a control's TabIndex property is handled differently when the control is placed inside a GroupBox control. GroupBox controls have their own TabIndex property, and the TabIndex value of the controls inside the group box are relative to the GroupBox control's TabIndex property. For example, Figure 3-39 shows a GroupBox control displayed in tab order selection mode. As you can see, the GroupBox control's TabIndex is set to 0. The TabIndex of the controls inside the group box is displayed as 0.0, 0.1, 0.2, and so on.

Figure 3-39 GroupBox TabIndex values

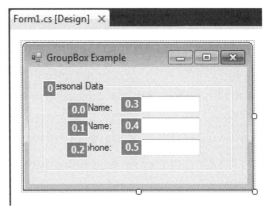

 NOTE: The TabIndex properties of the controls inside the group box will not appear this way in the *Properties* window. They will appear as 0, 1, 2, and so on.

A **Panel control** is a rectangular container for other controls, like a GroupBox. There are several primary differences between a Panel and GroupBox:

- A Panel cannot display a title and does not have a Text property.
- A Panel's border can be specified by its BorderStyle property. The available settings are None, FixedSingle, and Fixed3D. The property is set to None by default, which means that no border will appear. If the BorderStyle property is set to FixedSingle, the control will be outlined with a thin border. If the BorderStyle property is set to Fixed3D, the control will have a recessed 3D appearance.

Figure 3-40 shows an example of a form with a Panel. The Panel's BorderStyle property is set to Fixed3D.

Figure 3-40 A Panel containing other controls

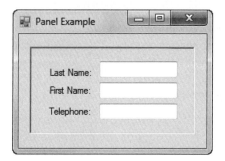

 Checkpoint

3.50 What happens if you press the Enter key while a Button control has the focus?

3.51 How do you display a form in tab order selection mode? How do you exit tab order selection mode?

3.52 Write a programming statement that gives the focus to a TextBox control named `numberTextBox`.

3.53 How do you assign an access key to a Button control?

3.54 How do you display an ampersand (&) character on a Button control?

3.55 Write the code that will change the BackColor property of a Label control named `resultLabel` to the color white and the ForeColor property to the color red.

3.56 List the different values of a form's BackgroundImageLayout property.

3.57 When a GroupBox control is deleted, what happens to the controls that are inside?

3.58 How are the TabIndex properties of the controls inside the group box organized?

3.59 How is a Panel control different from a GroupBox control?

Key Terms

accept button	`int.Parse` method
access key	integer literal
access modifier	lifetime
argument	local variable
BackColor property	math expression
break mode	math operators
cancel button	mnemonic
cast operator	named constant
catch block	numeric literal
`catch` clause	operands
combined assignment operators	order of operations
concatenation	Panel control
constant field	parse
data type	`Parse` methods
`decimal` literal	primitive data types
`decimal.Parse` method	scope
`double` literal	tab order
`double.Parse` method	tab order selection mode
exception	TabIndex property
exception handler	TextBox control
exception object	`ToString` method
field	truncation
focus	try block
`Focus` method	`try-catch` statement
ForeColor	variable
formatting string	variable declaration
GroupBox Control	variable name
initialize	

Review Questions

1. When the user types into a TextBox control, the text is stored in the control's _____ property.

   a. Input
   b. Text
   c. String
   d. Data

2. A _____ is a storage location in memory that is represented by a name.

   a. mnemonic
   b. data type
   c. namespace
   d. variable

3. In C#, you must _____ a variable before you can use it to store data.

   a. cite
   b. associate
   c. declare
   d. instance

4. A variable's _____ indicates the type of data that the variable will hold.

   a. name
   b. data type
   c. scope
   d. value

5. Fundamental types of data, such as strings, integers, and real numbers, are known as _____.

   a. primitive data types
   b. fundamental variables
   c. logical digits
   d. literal data types

6. A _____ identifies a variable in the program code.

   a. binary number
   b. variable name
   c. unique global identifier
   d. hexadecimal value

7. A common operation performed on strings is _____, or appending one string to the end of another string.

   a. addition
   b. merging
   c. concatenation
   d. tying

8. A _____ belongs to the method in which it is declared, and only statements inside that method can access the variable.

   a. method variable
   b. primitive variable
   c. temporary variable
   d. local variable

9. Programmers use the term _____ to describe the part of a program in which a variable may be accessed.

   a. range
   b. scope
   c. focus
   d. field

10. A variable's _____ is the time period during which the variable exists in memory while the program is executing.

    a. lifetime
    b. run time
    c. time to live
    d. half life

11. One way to make sure that a variable has been assigned a value is to _____ the variable with a value when you declare it.

    a. concatenate
    b. initialize
    c. delimit
    d. restrict

12. You can use a _____ to explicitly convert a value from one numeric data type to another, even if the conversion might result in a loss of data.

    a. transpose statement
    b. cast operator
    c. conversion operator
    d. literal conversion

13. The process of dropping a number's fractional part is called _____.

    a. shifting
    b. twos complement
    c. numeric rounding
    d. truncation

14. A programmer's tools for performing calculations are _____.

    a. math operators
    b. numeric literals
    c. local variables
    d. parsed literals

15. A _____ performs a calculation and gives a value.

    a. numeric literal
    b. math expression
    c. machine instruction
    d. programming statement

16. C# offers a special set of operators known as _____ that are designed specifically for changing the value of a variable without having to type the variable name twice.

    a. combined assignment operators
    b. advanced math operators
    c. variable modifiers
    d. assignment sequencers

17. In computer science, the term _____ typically means to analyze a string of characters for some purpose.

    a. compile
    b. compute
    c. debug
    d. parse

18. A(n) _____ is a piece of data that is passed into a method.

    a. variable
    b. argument
    c. string
    d. literal

19. A(n) _____ is an unexpected error that occurs while a program is running, causing the program to halt if the error is not properly dealt with.

    a. breakpoint
    b. bug
    c. syntax error
    d. exception

20. The _____ indicates that you want the number to appear formatted in a specific way when it is returned as a string from the `ToString` method.
    a. formatting string
    b. `insert` method
    c. data type
    d. variable name

21. You have started an application by clicking the start Debugging button (▶) or by pressing [F5] on the keyboard. If an exception is thrown, the application stops running and Visual Studio goes into a special mode known as _____.
    a. exception mode
    b. break mode
    c. debug mode
    d. crash mode

22. Code that responds to exceptions when they are thrown and prevents the program from abruptly crashing is called a(n) _____.
    a. exit strategy
    b. fail safe
    c. event handler
    d. exception handler

23. A _____ is a name that represents a value that cannot be changed during the program's execution.
    a. named literal
    b. named constant
    c. variable signature
    d. key term

24. A _____ is a variable that is declared inside a class but not inside any method.
    a. term
    b. class variable
    c. field
    d. mnemonic

25. A(n) _____ specifies how a class member can be accessed by code outside the class.
    a. namespace
    b. access modifier
    c. scope delimiter
    d. class directive

26. A _____ is a field that cannot be changed by any statement in the class.
    a. static field
    b. class name
    c. key field
    d. constant field

27. The .NET Framework provides a class named _____, which contains numerous methods that are useful for performing advanced mathematical operations.
    a. `Math`
    b. `Calc`
    c. `Trig`
    d. `Linq`

28. When a control has the _____, it receives the user's keyboard input.
    a. text
    b. tab order
    c. focus
    d. input allocator

29. The order in which controls receive the focus is called the _____.
    a. order of operations
    b. program flow
    c. execution sequence
    d. tab order

30. The _____ contains a numeric value, which indicates the control's position in the tab order.
    a. IndexOf property
    b. TabIndex property
    c. ControlOrder property
    d. TabOrder property

True or False

1. You can clear the contents of a TextBox control in the same way that you clear the contents of a Label control.

2. In C#, you must declare a variable in a program before you can use it to store data.

3. You can declare multiple variables of different data types with one declaration.

4. When you append the letter D or d to a numeric literal, it is treated as a `decimal` and is referred to as a `decimal` literal.

5. The order of operations dictates that the division operator works before the addition operator does.

6. All variables have a `ToString` method that you can call to convert the variable's value to a string.

7. When you pass the formatting string `"C"` or `"c"` to the `ToString` method, the number is returned formatted as currency.

8. When you declare a named constant, an initialization value is required.

9. An error will occur if the compiler finds a statement that tries to change the value of a constant field.

10. Forms and most controls have a Preferences property that allows you to change the object's background color.

Short Answer

1. In the *Toolbox*, in which group is the TextBox tool located?

2. What two things does a variable declaration specify about a variable?

3. Give an example of a programming statement that uses string concatenation.

4. What is the term used for a number that is written into a program's code.

5. Write a programming statement that assigns an integer literal to a variable.

6. What are the values on the right and left of an operator called?

7. Name the family of methods in the .NET Framework that can be used to convert a string to any of the numeric data types.

8. What object is created in memory when an exception is thrown and has various properties that contain data about the exception?

9. What is the purpose of a `try-catch` statement?

10. Which class in the .NET Framework provides predefined named constants that are assigned the mathematical values for *pi* and *e*?

11. In code, what function do you call to move the focus to a control?

12. What property allows you to change the color of a control's text?

Algorithm Workbench

Programming Problems

1. **Name Formatter**

    Create an application that lets the user enter the following pieces of data:

    -   The user's first name
    -   The user's middle name
    -   The user's last name
    -   The user's preferred title (Mr., Mrs., Ms., Dr., etc.)

    Assume the user has entered the following data:

    -   First name: *Kelly*
    -   Middle name: *Jane*
    -   Last name: *Smith*
    -   Title: *Ms.*

    The application should have buttons that display the user's name formatted in the following ways:

    Ms. Kelly Jane Smith
    Kelly Jane Smith
    Kelly Smith
    Smith, Kelly Jane, Ms.
    Smith, Kelly Jane
    Smith, Kelly

2. **Tip, Tax, and Total**

    Create an application that lets the user enter the food charge for a meal at a restaurant. When a button is clicked, the application should calculate and display the amount of a 15 percent tip, 7 percent sales tax, and the total of all three amounts.

3. **Distance Traveled**

    Assuming there are no accidents or delays, the distance that a car travels down an interstate highway can be calculated with the following formula:

    $$Distance = Speed \times Time$$

    Create an application that allows the user to enter a car's speed in miles per hour.

    The application should have buttons that display the following:

    -   The distance the car will travel in 5 hours
    -   The distance the car will travel in 8 hours
    -   The distance the car will travel in 12 hours

4. **Sales Tax and Total**

    Create an application that allows the user to enter the amount of a purchase. The program should then calculate the state and county sales tax. Assume the state sales tax is 4 percent and the county sales tax is 2 percent. The program should display the amount of the purchase, the state sales tax, the county sales tax, the total sales tax, and the total of the sale (which is the sum of the amount of purchase plus the total sales tax).

5. **Celsius and Fahrenheit Temperature Converter**

   Assuming that C is a Celsius temperature, the following formula converts the temperature to Fahrenheit:

   $$F = \frac{9}{5}C + 32$$

   Assuming that F is a Fahrenheit temperature, the following formula converts the temperature to Celsius:

   $$C = \frac{5}{9}(F - 32)$$

   Create an application that allows the user to enter a temperature. The application should have Button controls described as follows:

   - A button that reads *Convert to Fahrenheit*. If the user clicks this button, the application should treat the temperature that is entered as a Celsius temperature and convert it to Fahrenheit.
   - A button that reads *Convert to Celsius*. If the user clicks this button, the application should treat the temperature that is entered as a Fahrenheit temperature, and convert it to Celsius.

6. **Body Mass Index**

   Create an application that lets the user enter his or her weight (in pounds) and height (in inches). The application should display the user's body mass index (BMI). The BMI is often used to determine whether a person is overweight or underweight for his or her height. A person's BMI is calculated with the following formula:

   $$BMI = weight \times 703 \div height^2$$

7. **Sentence Builder**

   The form in Figure 3-41 contains buttons showing various words, phrases, and punctuation. Create an application with a form similar to this one. When the application runs, the user clicks the buttons to build a sentence, which is shown in a Label control. You can use the same buttons as shown in the figure or make up your own. The *Reset* button should clear the sentence so the user can start over.

Figure 3-41 The *Sentence Builder* form

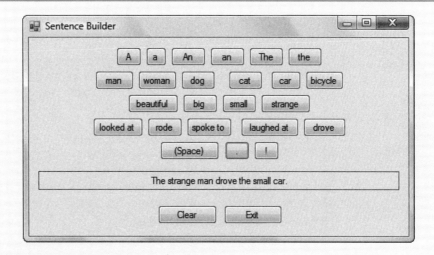

8. **How Much Insurance?**

Many financial experts advise that property owners should insure their homes or buildings for at least 80 percent of the amount it would cost to replace the structure. Create an application that lets the user enter the replacement cost of a building and then displays the minimum amount of insurance he or she should buy for the property.

9. **Cookie Calories**

A bag of cookies holds 40 cookies. The calorie information on the bag claims that there are 10 servings in the bag and that a serving equals 300 calories. Create an application that lets the user enter the number of cookies he or she actually ate and then reports the number of total calories consumed.

10. **Calorie Counter**

Create an application with a form that resembles Figure 3-42. The PictureBox controls display the images of four fruits (a banana, an apple, an orange, and a pear) and each fruit's calories. You can find these images in the *Chap03* folder of the Student Sample Programs.

When the application starts, the total calories displayed should be zero. Each time the user clicks one of the PictureBoxes, the calories for that fruit should be added to the total calories, and the total calories should be displayed. When the user clicks the *Reset* button, the total calories should be reset to zero.

Figure 3-42 *Calorie Counter* form

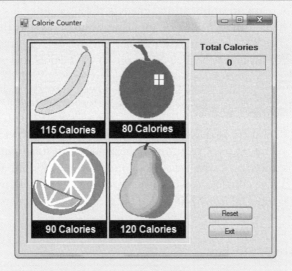

11. **Automobile Costs**

Create an application that lets the user enter the monthly costs for the following expenses incurred from operating his or her automobile: loan payment, insurance, gas, oil, tires, and maintenance. The program should then display the total monthly cost of these expenses and the total annual cost of these expenses.

12. **Paint Job Estimator**

A painting company has determined that for every 115 square feet of wall space, 1 gallon of paint and 8 hours of labor will be required. The company charges $20.00 per hour for labor. Create an application that allows the user to enter the square feet of wall space to be painted and the price of the paint per gallon. The program should display the following data:

- The number of gallons of paint required
- The hours of labor required

- The cost of the paint
- The labor charges
- The total cost of the paint job

13. **Property Tax**

If you own real estate in a particular county, the property tax that you owe each year is calculated as 64 cents per $100 of the property's value. For example, if the property's value is $10,000, then the property tax is calculated as follows:

$$Tax = \$10,000 \div 100 \times 0.64$$

Create an application that allows the user to enter a property's value and displays the sales tax on that property.

14. **Stadium Seating**

There are three seating categories at an athletic stadium. For a baseball game, Class A seats cost $15 each, Class B seats cost $12 each, and Class C seats cost $9 each. Create an application that allows the user to enter the number of tickets sold for each class. The application should be able to display the amount of income generated from each class of ticket sales and the total revenue generated. The application's form should resemble the one shown in Figure 3-43.

Figure 3-43 *Stadium Seating* form

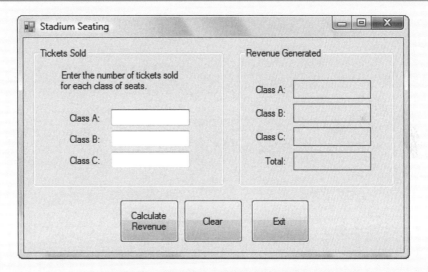

Use the following sets of test data to determine if the application is calculating properly:

Ticket Sales	Revenue
Class A: 320	Class A: $4,800.00
Class B: 570	Class B: $6,840.00
Class C: 890	Class C: $8,010.00
	Total Revenue: $19,650.00
Class A: 500	Class A: $7,500.00
Class B: 750	Class B: $9,000.00
Class C: 1,200	Class C: $10,800.00
	Total Revenue: $27,300.00
Class A: 100	Class A: $1,500.00
Class B: 300	Class B: $3,600.00
Class C: 500	Class C: $4,500.00
	Total Revenue: $9,600.00

4 Making Decisions

4.1 Decision Structures and the `if` Statement

CONCEPT: A decision structure allows a program to perform actions only under certain conditions. In code, you can use the `if` statement to write a simple decision structure.

A **control structure** is a logical design that controls the order in which a set of statements execute. So far in this book we have used only the simplest type of control structure: the sequence structure. A **sequence structure** is a set of statements that execute in the order that they appear. For example, the following code sample is a sequence structure because the statements execute from top to bottom.

```
int ageInYears, ageInDays;
ageInYears = int.Parse(ageTextBox.Text);
ageInDays = ageInYears * 365;
daysLabel = ageInDays.ToString();
```

Although the sequence structure is heavily used in programming, it cannot handle every type of task. Some problems simply cannot be solved by performing a set of ordered steps, one after the other. For example, consider a pay-calculating program that determines whether an employee has worked overtime. If the employee has worked more than 40 hours, he or she gets paid extra for all hours over 40. Otherwise, the overtime calculation should be skipped. Programs like this require a different type of control structure: one that can execute a set of statements only under certain circumstances. This can be accomplished with a **decision structure**. (Decision structures are also known as **selection structures**.)

In a decision structure's simplest form, a specific action is performed only if a certain condition exists. If the condition does not exist, the action is not performed. The flowchart shown in Figure 4-1 shows how the logic of an everyday decision can be diagrammed as a decision structure. The diamond symbol represents a true-false condition. If the condition is true, we follow one path, which leads to an action being performed. If the condition is false, we follow another path, which skips the action.

Figure 4-1 A simple decision structure

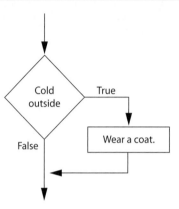

In the flowchart, the diamond symbol indicates some condition that must be tested. In this case, we are determining whether the condition *Cold outside* is true or false. If this condition is true, the action *Wear a coat* is performed. If the condition is false, the action is skipped. The action is **conditionally executed** because it is performed only when a certain condition is true.

Programmers call the type of decision structure shown in Figure 4-1 a **single-alternative decision structure** because it provides only one alternative path of execution. If the condition in the diamond symbol is true, we take the alternative path. Otherwise, we exit the structure. Figure 4-2 shows a more elaborate example, where three actions are taken only when it is cold outside.

Figure 4-2 A decision structure that performs three actions if it is cold outside

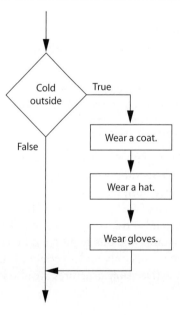

In C#, you use the if statement to write a single-alternative decision structure. Here is the general format of the if statement:

```
if (expression)
{
    statement;
    statement;
    etc;
}
```

The statement begins with the word if, followed by an *expression* enclosed in a set of parentheses. Beginning on the next line is a set of statements enclosed in curly braces.

The *expression* that appears inside the parentheses is a Boolean expression. A **Boolean expression** is an expression that can be evaluated as either true or false. When the if statement executes, the Boolean expression is tested. If it is true, the statements that appear inside the curly braces are executed. If the Boolean expression is false, however, the statements inside the curly braces are skipped. We say that the statements inside the curly braces are *conditionally executed* because they are executed only if the Boolean expression is true.

If you are writing an if statement that has only one conditionally executed statement, you do not have to enclose the conditionally executed statement inside curly braces. Such an if statement can be written in the following general format:

```
if (expression)
    statement;
```

When an if statement written in this format executes, the Boolean expression is tested. If it is true, the one statement that appears on the next line is executed. If the Boolean expression is false, however, that one statement is skipped.

Although the curly braces are not required when there is only one conditionally executed statement, it is still a good idea to use them, as shown in the following general format:

```
if (expression)
{
    statement;
}
```

This is a good style for writing if statements because it minimizes errors. Remember, if you have more than one conditionally executed statement, those statements *must* be enclosed in curly braces. If you get into the habit of always enclosing the conditionally executed statements in a set of curly braces, it's less likely that you will forget them.

Boolean Expressions and Relational Operators

Boolean expressions are named in honor of the English mathematician George Boole. In the 1800s, Boole invented a system of mathematics in which the abstract concepts of true and false can be used in computations.

Typically, the Boolean expression that is tested by an if statement is formed with a relational operator. A **relational operator** determines whether a specific relationship exists between two values. For example, the greater than operator (>) determines whether one value is greater than another. The equal to operator (==) determines whether two values are equal. Table 4-1 lists the relational operators that are available in C#.

The following is an example of an expression that uses the greater than (>) operator to compare two variables, length and width:

```
length > width
```

Table 4-1 Relational operators

Operator	Meaning
>	Greater than
<	Less than
>=	Greater than or equal to
<=	Less than or equal to
==	Equal to
!=	Not equal to

This expression determines whether the value of the length variable is greater than the value of the width variable. If length is greater than width, the value of the expression is true. Otherwise, the value of the expression is false. The following expression uses the less than operator (<) to determine whether length is less than width:

```
length < width
```

Table 4-2 shows examples of several Boolean expressions that compare the variables x and y.

Table 4-2 Boolean expressions using relational operators

Expression	Meaning
x > y	Is x greater than y?
x < y	Is x less than y?
x >= y	Is x greater than or equal to y?
x <= y	Is x less than or equal to y?
x == y	Is x equal to y?
x != y	Is x not equal to y?

The >= and <= Operators

Two of the operators, >= and <=, test for more than one relationship. The >= operator determines whether the operand on its left is greater than *or* equal to the operand on its right. The <= operator determines whether the operand on its left is less than *or* equal to the operand on its right.

For example, assume the variable a is assigned 4. All the following expressions are true:

```
a >= 4
a >= 2
8 >= a
a <= 4
a <= 9
4 <= a
```

The == Operator

The == operator determines whether the operand on its left is equal to the operand on its right. If the values of both operands are the same, the expression is true. Assuming that a is 4, the expression a == 4 is true and the expression a == 2 is false.

NOTE: The equality operator is two = symbols together. Don't confuse this operator with the assignment operator, which is one = symbol.

The `!=` Operator

The `!=` operator is the not equal to operator. It determines whether the operand on its left is not equal to the operand on its right, which is the opposite of the `==` operator. As before, assuming a is 4, b is 6, and c is 4, both a `!=` b and b `!=` c are true because a is not equal to b and b is not equal to c. However, a `!=` c is false because a is equal to c.

Putting It All Together

Let's look at the following example of the `if` statement:

```
if (sales > 50000)
{
    bonus = 500;
}
```

This statement uses the > operator to determine whether `sales` is greater than 50,000. If the expression `sales > 50000` is true, the variable `bonus` is assigned 500. If the expression is false, however, the assignment statement is skipped. Figure 4-3 shows a flowchart for this section of code.

Figure 4-3 Example decision structure

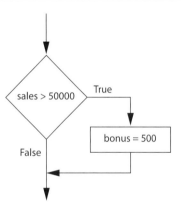

The following code sample conditionally executes three statements. Figure 4-4 shows a flowchart for this section of code.

```
if (sales > 50000)
{
    bonus = 500;
    commissionRate = 0.12;
    MessageBox.Show("You met your sales quota!");
}
```

When you write an `if` statement, Visual Studio automatically indents the conditionally executed statements, as shown in the previous examples. The indentation is not required, but it makes the code easier to read and debug. By indenting the conditionally executed statements, you visually set them apart from the surrounding code. This allows you to tell at a glance what part of the program is controlled by the `if` statement. Most programmers use this style of indentation when writing `if` statements.

Figure 4-4 Example decision structure

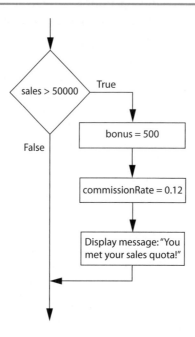

Tutorial 4-1:

Completing the *Test Score Average* Application

In this tutorial you will complete an application that allows the user to enter three test scores and calculates the average of the test scores. If the average is greater than 95, the application also displays a message congratulating the user.

To save time, the project has already been started for you, and the application's form has already been created. To complete the project, follow the steps in this tutorial.

Step 1: Start Visual Studio (or Visual C# Express). Open the project named *Test Score Average* in the *Chap04* folder of the Student Sample Programs that accompany this book.

Step 2: Open the Form1 form in the *Designer*. The form is shown, along with the names of the important controls, in Figure 4-5.

Figure 4-5 The *Test Score Average* form

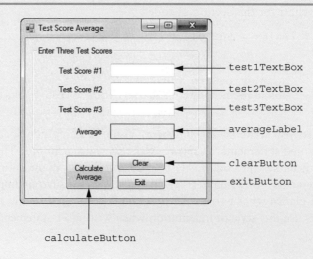

The decision structure in the flowchart tests the expression `temperature < 40`. If this expression is true, the message "A little cold, isn't it?" is displayed. If the expression is false, the message "Nice weather we're having." is displayed.

In code we write a dual-alternative decision structure as an `if-else` statement. Here is the general format of the `if-else` statement:

```
if (expression)
{
    statement;
    statement;      }———  If the Boolean expression is true,
    etc;                  this set of statements is executed.
}
else
{
    statement;
    statement;      }———  If the Boolean expression is false,
    etc;                  this set of statements is executed.
}
```

An `if-else` statement has two parts: an `if` clause and an `else` clause. Just like a regular `if` statement, the `if-else` statement tests a Boolean expression. If the Boolean expression is true, the set of statements following the `if` clause is executed. If the Boolean expression is false, the set of statements following the `else` clause is executed.

The `if-else` statement has two sets of conditionally executed statements. One set is executed only under the condition that the Boolean expression is true, and the other set is executed only under the condition that the Boolean expression is false. Under no circumstances are both sets of conditionally executed statements executed.

If either set of conditionally executed statements contains only one statement, the curly braces are not required. For example, the following general format shows only one statement following the `if` clause and only one statement following the `else` clause:

```
if (expression)
    statement;
else
    statement;
```

Although the curly braces are not required when there is only one conditionally executed statement, it is still a good idea to use them, as shown in the following general format:

```
if (expression)
{
    statement;
}
else
{
    statement;
}
```

When we discussed the regular `if` statement, we mentioned that this is a good style of programming because it cuts down on errors. If there is more than one conditionally executed statement following either the `if` clause or the `else` clause, those statements *must* be enclosed in curly braces. If you get into the habit of always enclosing the conditionally executed statements in a set of curly braces, it's less likely that you will forget them.

In Tutorial 4-2 you will complete an application that uses an `if-else` statement.

Tutorial 4-2:
Completing the *Payroll with Overtime* Application

At a particular business, if an employee works more than 40 hours in a week, it is said that the employee has worked *overtime*. For example, an employee that has worked 45 hours in a week has worked 5 overtime hours. Employees that work overtime get paid their regular hourly pay rate for the first 40 hours plus 1.5 times their regular hourly pay rate for all hours over 40. In this tutorial you will complete a payroll application that calculates an employee's gross pay, including overtime pay.

The application allows the user to enter the number of hours worked and the hourly pay rate into TextBoxes. When the user clicks a button, the gross pay is calculated in the following manner:

If the hours worked is greater than 40:

>   base pay = hourly pay rate × 40
>   overtime hours = hours worked − 40
>   overtime pay = overtime hours × hourly pay rate × 1.5
>   gross pay = base pay + overtime pay

Else:

>   gross pay = hours worked × hourly pay rate

To save time, the project has already been started for you, and the application's form has already been created. To complete the project, follow the steps in this tutorial.

Step 1: Start Visual Studio (or Visual C# Express). Open the project named *Payroll with Overtime* in the *Chap04* folder of the Student Sample Programs that accompany this book.

Step 2: Open the Form1 form in the *Designer*. The form is shown, along with the names of the important controls, in Figure 4-9.

Figure 4-9 The *Payroll with Overtime* form

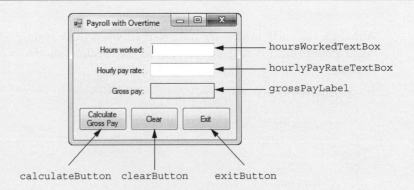

Step 3: Now you will create the Click event handlers for the Button controls. At the end of this tutorial, Program 4-2 shows the completed code for the form. You will be instructed to refer to Program 4-2 as you write the event handlers.

In the *Designer*, double-click the `calculateButton` control. This opens the code editor, and you see an empty event handler named `calculateButton_Click`. Complete the `calculateButton_Click` event handler by typing the code shown in lines 21– 68 in Program 4-2.

Let's take a closer look at the code:

Line 21: This is the beginning of a `try-catch` statement. The try block appears in lines 23–42, and the catch block appears in lines 46–47. The purpose of this `try-catch` statement is to gracefully respond if the user enters invalid input. If an exception is thrown by any statement inside the try block, the program jumps to the catch block, and line 67 displays an error message.

Lines 24–25: These statements declare the following named constants:

- `BASE_HOURS`, a constant `decimal` set to the value 40. This is the number of hours an employee can work in a week without getting overtime pay.
- `OT_MULTIPLIER`, a constant `decimal` set to the value 1.5. This is the pay rate multiplier for overtime hours.

Lines 24–33: These statements declare the following variables:

- `hoursWorked`, a `decimal` variable to hold the number of hours worked
- `hourlyPayRate`, a `decimal` variable to hold the hourly pay rate
- `basePay`, a `decimal` variable to hold the pay for 40 or less hours
- `overtimeHours`, a `decimal` variable to hold the number of overtime hours worked
- `overtimePay`, a `decimal` variable to hold the amount of overtime pay
- `grossPay`, a `decimal` variable to hold the gross pay

Line 36: This statement converts the `hoursWorkedTextBox` control's Text property to a `decimal` and assigns the result to the `hoursWorked` variable.

Line 37: This statement converts the `hourlyPayRateTextBox` control's Text property to a `decimal` and assigns the result to the `hourlyPayRate` variable.

Line 40: This `if` statement determines whether `hoursWorked` is greater than `BASE_HOURS` (40). If so, the statements in lines 42–53 are executed. Otherwise, the statements in lines 57–58 are executed.

Lines 42–53: These statements, which are executed only if the hours worked are greater than 40, make all the necessary calculations to determine gross pay with overtime:

- Line 43 calculates the base pay, which is the amount of pay for the first 40 hours.
- Line 46 calculates the number of overtime hours, which is the number of hours over 40.
- Lines 49 and 50 calculate the amount of overtime pay, which is the pay for the hours over 40.
- Line 53 calculates the gross pay, which is the amount of base pay plus the amount of overtime pay. The result is assigned to the `grossPay` variable.

Line 58: This statement, which is executed only if the hours worked are 40 or less, calculates the gross pay and assigns the result to the `grossPay` variable.

Line 62: This statement converts the value of the `grossPay` variable to a string, formatted as currency, and assigns the result to the `grossPayLabel` control's Text property.

Step 4: Switch your view back to the *Designer* and double-click the `clearButton` control. In the code editor you see an empty event handler named `clearButton_Click`. Complete the `clearButton_Click` event handler by typing the code shown in lines 73–79 in Program 4-2. These statements clear the TextBoxes and the `grossPayLabel` control and sets the focus to the `hoursWorkedTextBox` control.

Step 5: Switch your view back to the *Designer* and double-click the exitButton control. In the code editor you see an empty event handler named exitButton_Click. Complete the exitButton_Click event handler by typing the code shown in lines 84–85 in Program 4-2.

Step 6: Save the project and run the application. First, enter 40 for the number of hours worked and 20 for the hourly pay rate. Click the *Calculate Gross Pay* button, and the application should display $800.00 as the gross pay. No overtime hours were worked, so the gross pay is simply calculated as hours worked × hourly pay rate.

Click the *Clear* button. Enter 50 for the number of hours worked and 20 for the hourly pay rate. Click the *Calculate Gross Pay* button, and the application should display $1,100.00 as the gross pay. This time, more than 40 hours were worked, so the application calculated the gross pay to include overtime pay.

Continue to test the application as you wish. When you are finished, click the *Exit* button and the form should close.

Program 4-2 Completed Form1 code for the *Payroll with Overtime application*

```
 1 using System;
 2 using System.Collections.Generic;
 3 using System.ComponentModel;
 4 using System.Data;
 5 using System.Drawing;
 6 using System.Linq;
 7 using System.Text;
 8 using System.Windows.Forms;
 9
10 namespace Payroll_with_Overtime
11 {
12     public partial class Form1 : Form
13     {
14         public Form1()
15         {
16             InitializeComponent();
17         }
18
19         private void calculateButton_Click(object sender, EventArgs e)
20         {
21             try
22             {
23                 // Named constants
24                 const decimal BASE_HOURS = 40m;
25                 const decimal OT_MULTIPLIER = 1.5m;
26
27                 // Local variables
28                 decimal hoursWorked;        // Number of hours worked
29                 decimal hourlyPayRate;      // Hourly pay rate
30                 decimal basePay;            // Pay not including overtime
31                 decimal overtimeHours;      // overtime hours worked
32                 decimal overtimePay;        // overtime pay
33                 decimal grossPay;           // total gross pay
34
35                 // Get the hours worked and hourly pay rate.
36                 hoursWorked = decimal.Parse(hoursWorkedTextBox.Text);
37                 hourlyPayRate = decimal.Parse(hourlyPayRateTextBox.Text);
38
```

```
39                  // Determine the gross pay.
40                  if (hoursWorked > BASE_HOURS)
41                  {
42                      // Calculate the base pay (without overtime).
43                      basePay = hourlyPayRate * BASE_HOURS;
44
45                      // Calculate the number of overtime hours.
46                      overtimeHours = hoursWorked - BASE_HOURS;
47
48                      // Calculate the overtime pay.
49                      overtimePay = overtimeHours * hourlyPayRate *
50                          OT_MULTIPLIER;
51
52                      // Calculate the gross pay.
53                      grossPay = basePay + overtimePay;
54                  }
55                  else
56                  {
57                      // Calculate the gross pay.
58                      grossPay = hoursWorked * hourlyPayRate;
59                  }
60
61                  // Display the gross pay.
62                  grossPayLabel.Text = grossPay.ToString("c");
63              }
64              catch (Exception ex)
65              {
66                  // Display an error message.
67                  MessageBox.Show(ex.Message);
68              }
69          }
70
71          private void clearButton_Click(object sender, EventArgs e)
72          {
73              // Clear the TextBoxes and gross pay label.
74              hoursWorkedTextBox.Text = "";
75              hourlyPayRateTextBox.Text = "";
76              grossPayLabel.Text = "";
77
78              // Reset the focus.
79              hoursWorkedTextBox.Focus();
80          }
81
82          private void exitButton_Click(object sender, EventArgs e)
83          {
84              // Close the form.
85              this.Close();
86          }
87      }
88 }
```

Checkpoint

4.8 Describe how a dual alternative decision structure works.

4.9 In an if-else statement, under what circumstances do the statements that appear after the else clause execute?

4.10 Write an if-else statement that works like this: If the `sales` variable is greater-than or equal-to 50,000, the `commissionRate` variable should be assigned the value 0.2. Otherwise, the `commissionRate` variable should be assigned the value 0.1.

4.3 Nested Decision Structures

CONCEPT: To test more than one condition, a decision structure can be nested inside another decision structure.

In Section 4.1, we mentioned that a control structure determines the order in which a set of statements execute. Programs are usually designed as combinations of different control structures. For example, Figure 4-10 shows a flowchart that combines a decision structure with two sequence structures.

Figure 4-10 Combining sequence structures with a decision structure

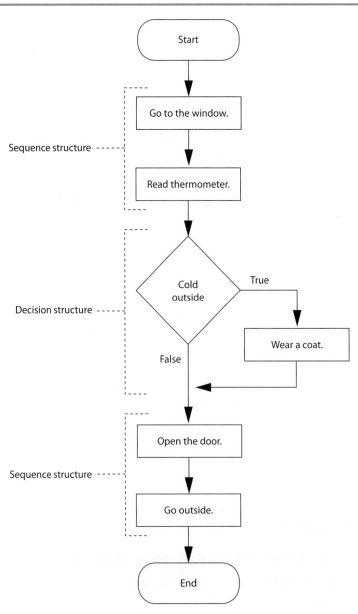

The flowchart in Figure 4-10 starts with a sequence structure. Assuming you have an outdoor thermometer in your window, the first step is *Go to the window*, and the next step is *Read thermometer*. A decision structure appears next, testing the condition *Cold outside*. If this is true, the action *Wear a coat* is performed. Another sequence structure appears next. The step *Open the door* is performed, followed by *Go outside*.

Quite often, structures must be nested inside other structures. For example, look at the partial flowchart in Figure 4-11. It shows a decision structure with a sequence structure nested inside. The decision structure tests the condition *Cold outside*. If that condition is true, the steps in the sequence structure are executed.

Figure 4-11 A sequence structure nested inside a decision structure

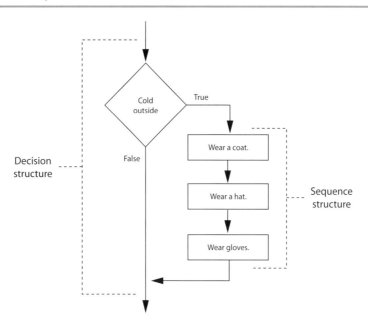

You can also have **nested decision structures**, which are decision structures that appear inside other decision structures. This is commonly done in programs that need to test more than one condition. For example, consider a program that determines whether a bank customer qualifies for a loan. To qualify, two conditions must exist: (1) The customer must earn at least $40,000 per year, and (2) the customer must have been employed at his or her current job for at least 2 years. Figure 4-12 shows a flowchart for an algorithm that could be used in such a program. Assume that the `salary` variable contains the customer's annual salary, and the `yearsOnJob` variable contains the number of years that the customer has worked on his or her current job.

If we follow the flow of execution, we see that the Boolean expression `salary >= 40000` is tested. If this expression is false, there is no need to perform further tests; we know that the customer does not qualify for the loan. If the expression is true, however, we need to test the second condition. This is done with a nested decision structure that tests the Boolean expression `yearsOnJob >= 2`. If this expression is true, then the customer qualifies for the loan. If this expression is false, then the customer does not qualify. In Tutorial 4-3 you create an application that performs this algorithm.

Figure 4-12 A nested decision structure

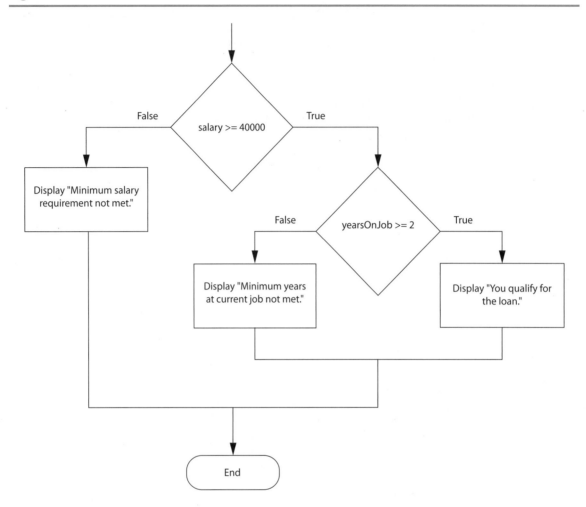

Tutorial 4-3:
Completing the *Loan Qualifier* Application

In this tutorial you complete an application that determines whether a person qualifies for a loan. To qualify for the loan, the person must earn a salary of at least $40,000 and must have been employed at his or her current job for at least 2 years.

To save time, the project has already been started for you, and the application's form has already been created. To complete the project, follow the steps in this tutorial.

Step 1: Start Visual Studio (or Visual C# Express). Open the project named *Loan Qualifier* in the *Chap04* folder of the Student Sample Programs that accompany this book.

Step 2: Open the Form1 form in the *Designer*. The form is shown, along with the names of the important controls, in Figure 4-13.

Step 3: Now you will create the Click event handlers for the Button controls. At the end of this tutorial, Program 4-3 shows the completed code for the form. You will be instructed to refer to Program 4-3 as you write the event handlers.

Figure 4-13 The *Loan Qualifier* form

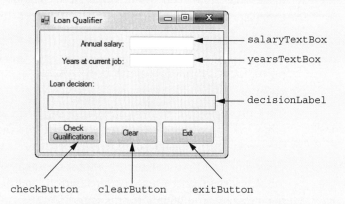

In the *Designer*, double-click the `checkButton` control. This opens the code editor, and you see an empty event handler named `checkButton_Click`. Complete the `checkButton_Click` event handler by typing the code shown in lines 21–61 in Program 4-3. Let's take a closer look at the code:

Line 21: This is the beginning of a `try-catch` statement. The try block appears in lines 23–55, and the catch block appears in lines 59–60. The purpose of this `try-catch` statement is to gracefully respond if the user enters invalid input. If an exception is thrown by any statement inside the try block, the program jumps to the catch block, and line 60 displays an error message.

Lines 24–25: These statements declare the following named constants:

- `MINIMUM_SALARY`, a constant `decimal` set to the value 40,000, which is the minimum salary a person must earn to qualify for the loan
- `MINIMUM_YEARS_ON_JOB`, a constant `int` set to the value 2, which is the minimum number of years a person must have been at his or her current job to qualify for the loan

Lines 28–29: These statements declare the following variables:

- `salary`, a `decimal` variable to hold the salary
- `yearsOnJob`, an `int` variable to hold the number of years at the current job

Lines 32–33: These statements get the salary and years at the current job from the TextBox controls and assign those values to the `salary` and `yearsOnJob` variables.

Line 36: This `if` statement determines whether `salary` is greater than or equal to `MINIMUM_SALARY`. If so, the program continues at line 38. Otherwise, the program jumps to the `else` clause in line 50, and in lines 53–54 the string "Minimum salary requirements not met." is assigned to the `decisionLabel` control's Text property.

Line 38: This `if` statement determines whether `yearsOnJob` is greater than or equal to `MINIMUM_YEARS_ON_JOB`. If so, the program continues at line 41, where the string "You qualify for the loan." is assigned to the `decisionLabel` control's Text property. Otherwise, the program jumps to the `else` clause in line 43, and in lines 46–47 the string "Minimum years at current job not met." is assigned to the `decisionLabel` control's Text property.

Step 4: Switch your view back to the *Designer* and double-click the `clearButton` control. In the code editor you see an empty event handler named `clearButton_Click`. Complete the `clearButton_Click` event handler by typing the code shown in lines 66–72 in Program 4-3.

Step 5: Switch your view back to the *Designer* and double-click the exitButton control. In the code editor you see an empty event handler named exitButton_Click. Complete the exitButton_Click event handler by typing the code shown in lines 77–89 in Program 4-3.

Step 6: Save the project and run the application. First, enter 45000 for the salary and 1 for the years at current job. Click the *Check Qualifications* button, and the application should display the message "Minimum years at current job not met."

Click the *Clear* button. Enter 35000 for the salary and 5 for the years at current job. Click the *Check Qualifications* button, and the application should display the message "Minimum salary requirement not met."

Click the *Clear* button. Enter 45000 for the salary and 5 for the years at current job. Click the *Check Qualifications* button, and the application should display the message "You qualify for the loan."

Continue to test the application as you wish. When you are finished, click the *Exit* button and the form should close.

Program 4-3 Completed Form1 code for the *Loan Qualifier* application

```
 1  using System;
 2  using System.Collections.Generic;
 3  using System.ComponentModel;
 4  using System.Data;
 5  using System.Drawing;
 6  using System.Linq;
 7  using System.Text;
 8  using System.Windows.Forms;
 9
10  namespace Loan_Qualifier
11  {
12      public partial class Form1 : Form
13      {
14          public Form1()
15          {
16              InitializeComponent();
17          }
18
19          private void checkButton_Click(object sender, EventArgs e)
20          {
21              try
22              {
23                  // Names constants
24                  const decimal MINIMUM_SALARY = 40000m;
25                  const int MINIMUM_YEARS_ON_JOB = 2;
26
27                  // Local variables
28                  decimal salary;
29                  int yearsOnJob;
30
31                  // Get the salary and years on the job.
32                  salary = decimal.Parse(salaryTextBox.Text);
33                  yearsOnJob = int.Parse(yearsTextBox.Text);
34
35                  // Determine whether the user qualifies.
36                  if (salary >= MINIMUM_SALARY)
37                  {
```

```
38                  if (yearsOnJob >= MINIMUM_YEARS_ON_JOB)
39                  {
40                      // The user qualifies.
41                      decisionLabel.Text = "You qualify for the loan.";
42                  }
43                  else
44                  {
45                      // The user does not qualify.
46                      decisionLabel.Text = "Minimum years at current " +
47                          "job not met.";
48                  }
49              }
50              else
51              {
52                  // The user does not qualify.
53                  decisionLabel.Text = "Minimum salary requirement " +
54                      "not met.";
55              }
56          }
57          catch (Exception ex)
58          {
59              // Display an error message.
60              MessageBox.Show(ex.Message);
61          }
62      }
63
64      private void clearButton_Click(object sender, EventArgs e)
65      {
66          // Clear the TextBoxes and the decisionLabel.
67          salaryTextBox.Text = "";
68          yearsTextBox.Text = "";
69          decisionLabel.Text = "";
70
71          // Reset the focus.
72          salaryTextBox.Focus();
73      }
74
75      private void exitButton_Click(object sender, EventArgs e)
76      {
77          // Close the form.
78          this.Close();
79      }
80  }
81 }
```

Indentation and Alignment in Nested Decision Structures

For debugging purposes, it's important to use proper alignment and indentation in a nested if statement. This makes it easier to see which actions are performed by each part of the structure. For example, the following code is functionally equivalent to lines 36–55 in Program 4-3. Although this code is logically correct, it would be very difficult to debug because it is not properly indented.

```
if (salary >= MINIMUM_SALARY)
{
if (yearsOnJob >= MINIMUM_YEARS_ON_JOB)
{
// The user qualifies.
decisionLabel.Text = "You qualify for the loan.";
}
else
{
// The user does not qualify.
decisionLabel.Text = "Minimum years at current " +
    "job not met.";
}
}
else
{
// The user does not qualify.
decisionLabel.Text = "Minimum salary requirement " +
    "not met.";
}
```

Fortunately, Visual Studio automatically indents and aligns the statements in a decision structure. Proper indentation and alignment makes it easier to see which `if` and `else` clauses belong together, as shown in Figure 4-14.

Figure 4-14 Alignment of `if` and `else` clauses

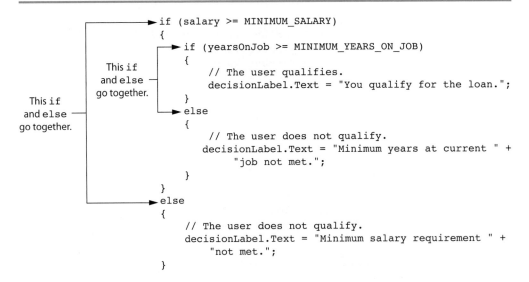

Testing a Series of Conditions

In Tutorial 4-3 you saw how a program can use nested decision structures to test more than one Boolean expression. It is not uncommon for a program to have a series of Boolean expressions to test and then perform an action, depending on which expression is true. One way to accomplish this it to have a decision structure with numerous other decision structures nested inside it. For example, look at the *Grader* application in the *Chap04* folder of the Student Sample Programs that accompany this book.

Figure 4-15 shows the application's form, with the names of several controls. When you run the application, you enter a numeric test score into the `testScoreTexBox` control and click the `determineGradeButton` control; a grade is then displayed in the `gradeLabel` control.

Figure 4-15 The *Grader* application's form

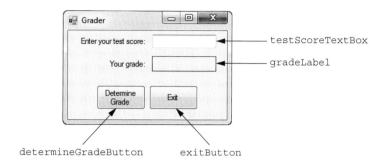

The following 10-point grading scale is used to determine the grade:

Test Score	Grade
90 and above	A
80–89	B
70–79	C
60–69	D
Below 60	F

The logic of determining the grade can be expressed like this:

> If the test score is less than 60, then the grade is "F."
>> Otherwise, if the test score is less than 70, then the grade is "D."
>>> Otherwise, if the test score is less than 80, then the grade is "C."
>>>> Otherwise, if the test score is less than 90, then the grade is "B."
>>>>> Otherwise, the grade is "A."

This logic requires several nested decision structures, as shown in the flowchart in Figure 4-16.

Figure 4-16 Nested decision structure to determine a grade

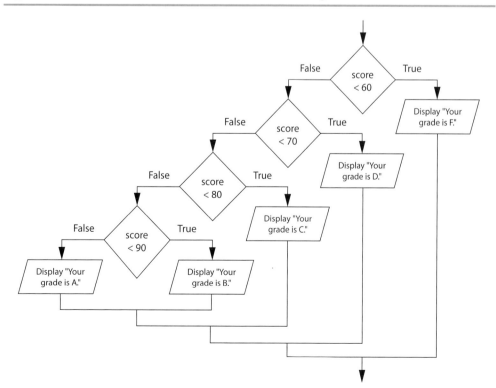

Open the code editor and look at the determineGradeButton_Click event handler, shown in the following code sample. The nested decision structure appears in lines 12–41.

```
 1 private void determineGradeButton_Click(object sender, EventArgs e)
 2 {
 3     try
 4     {
 5         // Variable to hold the test score.
 6         double testScore;
 7
 8         // Get the test score.
 9         testScore = double.Parse(testScoreTextBox.Text);
10
11         // Determine the grade.
12         if (testScore < 60)
13         {
14             gradeLabel.Text = "F";
15         }
16         else
17         {
18             if (testScore < 70)
19             {
20                 gradeLabel.Text = "D";
21             }
22             else
23             {
24                 if (testScore < 80)
25                 {
26                     gradeLabel.Text = "C";
27                 }
28                 else
29                 {
30                     if (testScore < 90)
31                     {
32                         gradeLabel.Text = "B";
33                     }
34                     else
35                     {
36                         gradeLabel.Text = "A";
37                     }
38                 }
39             }
40         }
41     }
42     catch (Exception ex)
43     {
44         // Display an error message.
45         MessageBox.Show(ex.Message);
46     }
47 }
```

The `if-else-if` Statement

Even though the *Grader* application previously shown is a simple example, the logic of the nested decision structure is fairly complex. C# provides a special version of the decision structure known as the **if-else-if statement**, which makes this type of logic simpler to write. You write the if-else-if statement using the following general format:

```
if (BooleanExpression_1)
{
    statement;              If BooleanExpression_1 is true, this
    statement;              set of statements is executed.
    etc.
}
else if (BooleanExpression_2)
{
    statement;              If BooleanExpression_2 is true, this
    statement;              set of statements is executed.
    etc.
}
```

Insert as many else if *clauses as necessary...*

```
else
{
    statement;              This set of statements is executed if
    statement;              none of the Boolean expressions
    etc.                    are true.
}
```

When the statement executes, `BooleanExpression_1` is tested. If `BooleanExpression_1` is true, the set of statements that immediately follows is executed, and the rest of the structure is skipped. If `BooleanExpression_1` is false, however, the program jumps to the very next `else if` clause and tests `BooleanExpression_2`. If it is true, the set of statements that immediately follows is executed, and the rest of the structure is then skipped. This process continues until a Boolean expression is found to be true, or no more `else if` clauses are left. If none of the Boolean expressions are true, the set of statements following the final `else` clause is executed.

For example, look at the *Grader2* application in the *Chap04* folder of the Student Sample Programs that accompany this book. This application works just like the *Grader* application that was previously discussed. The user enters a numeric test score, and the application displays a grade. It's form is identical to the form shown in Figure 4-15. The *Grader2* application, however, uses an `if-else-if` statement to determine the grade instead of nested `if-else` statements. The *Grader2* application's `determineGradeButton_Click` event handler is shown here:

```
 1 private void determineGradeButton_Click(object sender, EventArgs e)
 2 {
 3     try
 4     {
 5         // Variable to hold the test score.
 6         double testScore;
 7
 8         // Get the test score.
 9         testScore = double.Parse(testScoreTextBox.Text);
10
11         // Determine the grade.
12         if (testScore < 60)
13         {
14             gradeLabel.Text = "F";
15         }
16         else if (testScore < 70)
17         {
18             gradeLabel.Text = "D";
19         }
20         else if (testScore < 80)
21         {
22             gradeLabel.Text = "C";
23         }
24         else if (testScore < 90)
25         {
26             gradeLabel.Text = "B";
27         }
28         else
```

```
29          {
30              gradeLabel.Text = "A";
31          }
32      }
33      catch (Exception ex)
34      {
35          // Display an error message.
36          MessageBox.Show(ex.Message);
37      }
38 }
```

Notice the alignment and indentation that is used with the `if-else-if` statement: The `if`, `else if`, and `else` clauses are all aligned, and the conditionally executed statements are indented.

You never have to use the `if-else-if` statement because its logic can be coded with nested `if-else` statements. However, a long series of nested `if-else` statements has two particular disadvantages when you are debugging code:

- The code can grow complex and become difficult to understand.
- Because indenting is important in nested statements, a long series of nested `if-else` statements can become too long to be displayed on the computer screen without horizontal scrolling. Also, long statements tend to wrap around when printed on paper, making the code even more difficult to read.

The logic of an `if-else-if` statement is usually easier to follow than a long series of nested `if-else` statements. And, because all the clauses are aligned in an `if-else-if` statement, the lengths of the lines in the statement tend to be shorter.

 Checkpoint

4.11 Convert the following set of nested `if-else` statements to an `if-else if` statement:

```
if (number == 1)
{
    MessageBox.Show("One");
}
else
{
    if (number == 2)
    {
        MessageBox.Show("Two");
    }
    else
    {
        if (number == 3)
        {
            MessageBox.Show("Three");
        }
        else
        {
            MessageBox.Show("Unknown");
        }
    }
}
```

4.4 ## Logical Operators

CONCEPT: The logical AND operator (`&&`) and the logical OR operator (`||`) allow you to connect multiple Boolean expressions to create a compound expression. The logical NOT operator (`!`) reverses the truth of a Boolean expression.

The C# language provides a set of operators known as **logical operators**, which you can use to create complex Boolean expressions. Table 4-3 describes these operators.

Table 4-3 Logical operators

Operator	Meaning
`&&`	This is the logical AND operator. It connects two Boolean expressions into one compound expression. Both subexpressions must be true for the compound expression to be true.
`||`	This is the logical OR operator. It connects two Boolean expressions into one compound expression. One or both subexpressions must be true for the compound expression to be true. It is necessary for only one of the subexpressions to be true, and it does not matter which.
`!`	This is the logical NOT operator. It is a unary operator, meaning it works with only one operand. The operand must be a Boolean expression. The not operator reverses the truth of its operand. If it is applied to an expression that is true, the operator returns false. If it is applied to an expression that is false, the operator returns true.

Table 4-4 shows examples of several compound Boolean expressions that use logical operators.

Table 4-4 Compound Boolean expressions using logical operators

Expression	Meaning
`x > y && a < b`	Is x greater than y *AND* is a less than b?
`x == y || x == z`	Is x equal to y *OR* is x equal to z?
`! (x > y)`	Is the expression x > y *NOT* true?

The `&&` Operator

The `&&` operator is the **logical AND operator**. It takes two Boolean expressions as operands and creates a compound Boolean expression that is true only when both subexpressions are true. The following is an example of an `if` statement that uses the `&&` operator:

```
if (temperature < 20 && minutes > 12)
{
    MessageBox.Show("The temperature is in the danger zone.");
}
```

In this statement, the two Boolean expressions `temperature < 20` and `minutes > 12` are combined into a compound expression. The `MessageBox.Show` statement is executed only if `temperature` is less than 20 *and* `minutes` is greater than 12. If either of the Boolean subexpressions is false, the compound expression is false and the message is not displayed.

Table 4-5 shows a truth table for the && operator. The truth table lists expressions showing all the possible combinations of true and false connected with the && operator. The resulting values of the expressions are also shown.

Table 4-5 Truth table for the AND operator

Expression	Value of the Expression
true && false	false
false && true	false
false && false	false
true && true	true

As the table shows, both sides of the && operator must be true for the operator to return a true value.

The || Operator

The **||** operator is the **logical OR operator**. It takes two Boolean expressions as operands and creates a compound Boolean expression that is true when either of the subexpressions is true. The following is an example of an if statement that uses the || operator:

```
if (temperature < 20 || temperature > 100)
{
    MessageBox.Show("The temperature is in the danger zone.");
}
```

The MessageBox.Show statement executes only if temperature is less than 20 *or* temperature is greater than 100. If either subexpression is true, the compound expression is true. Table 4-6 shows a truth table for the || operator.

Table 4-6 Truth table for the || operator

Expression	Value of the Expression
true || false	true
false || true	true
false || false	false
true || true	true

All it takes for an || expression to be true is for one side of the || operator to be true. It doesn't matter if the other side is false or true.

Short-Circuit Evaluation

Both the && and || operators perform **short-circuit evaluation**. Here is how it works with the && operator: if the expression on the left side of the && operator is false, the expression on the right side is not checked. Because the compound expression is false if only one of the subexpressions is false, it would waste CPU time to check the remaining expression. So, when the && operator finds that the expression on its left is false, it short-circuits and does not evaluate the expression on its right.

Here's how short-circuit evaluation works with the || operator: if the expression on the left side of the || operator is true, the expression on the right side is not checked. Because it is necessary for only one of the expressions to be true, it would waste CPU time to check the remaining expression.

The ! Operator

The ! **operator** is the **logical NOT operator**. It is a unary operator that takes a Boolean expression as its operand and reverses its logical value. In other words, if the expression is true, the ! operator returns false, and if the expression is false, the ! operator returns true. The following is an `if` statement using the NOT operator:

```
if ( !(temperature > 100) )
{
    MessageBox.Show("This is below the maximum temperature.");
}
```

First, the expression (`temperature > 100`) is tested and a value of either true or false is the result. Then the ! operator is applied to that value. If the expression (`temperature > 100`) is true, the ! operator returns false. If the expression (`temperature > 100`) is false, the ! operator returns true. The previous code is equivalent to asking "Is the temperature not greater than 100?"

Notice that in this example, we have put parentheses around the expression `temperature > 100`. This is necessary because the ! operator has higher precedence than the relational operators. If we do not put the parentheses around the expression `temperature > 100`, the ! operator will be applied just to the `temperature` variable.

Table 4-7 shows a truth table for the ! operator.

Table 4-7 Truth table for the ! operator

Expression	Value of the Expression
! true	false
! false	true

Precedence of the Logical Operators

We mentioned earlier that the ! operator has higher precedence than the relational operators. The `&&` and `||` logical operators have lower precedence than the relational operators. For example, look at the following expression:

```
creditScore > 700 || accountBalance > 9000
```

When this expression is evaluated, the `>` operators work first, and then the `||` operator works. The expression is the same as the following:

```
(creditScore > 700) || (accountBalance > 9000)
```

Many programmers choose to enclose the expressions that are to the left and the right of a logical operator in parentheses, as shown here. Even though the parentheses are not required in many situations, using them makes the compound expression easier to understand.

Checking Numeric Ranges with Logical Operators

Sometimes you need to write code that determines whether a numeric value is within a specific range of values or outside a specific range of values. When determining whether a number is inside a range, it is best to use the `&&` operator. For example, the following `if` statement checks the value in `x` to determine whether it is in the range of 20 through 40:

```
if (x > 20 && x < 40)
{
    MessageBox.Show("The value is in the acceptable range.");
}
```

The compound Boolean expression being tested by this statement is true only when x is greater than 20 *and* less than 40. The value in x must be between the values of 20 and 40 for this compound expression to be true.

When determining whether a number is outside a range, it is best to use the || operator. The following statement determines whether x is outside the range of 20 through 40:

```
if (x < 20 || x > 40)
{
    MessageBox.Show("The value is outside the acceptable range.");
}
```

It is important not to get the logic of the logical operators confused when testing for a range of numbers. For example, the compound Boolean expression in the following code would never test true:

```
// This is an error!
if (x < 20 && x > 40)
{
    MessageBox.Show("The value is outside the acceptable range.");
}
```

Obviously, x cannot be less than 20 and at the same time be greater than 40.

Let's look at an example application that checks the range of a value entered by the user. Open the *Range Checker* application in the *Chap04* folder of the Student Sample Programs that accompany this book. Figure 4-17 shows the application's form, along with the names of some of the controls. When you run the application, you enter an integer into the inputTexBox control and click the checkButton control. If you enter a number in the range of 1 through 10, a message box appears letting you know that the number is acceptable. Otherwise, a message box appears letting you know that the number is *not* acceptable.

Figure 4-17 The *Range Checker* application's form

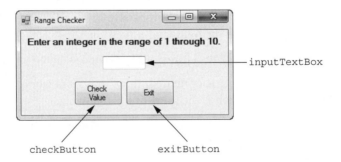

The following code sample shows the checkButton_Click event handler. Line 7 declares an int variable named number, initialized with the value that has been entered into the inputTextBox control. The if statement that begins in line 10 determines whether number is greater than or equal to 1 *AND* number is less than or equal to 10. If the Boolean expression is true, the statement in line 12 executes. Otherwise, the statement in line 16 executes.

```
1 private void checkButton_Click(object sender, EventArgs e)
2 {
3     try
4     {
5         // Declare a variable and initialize it with
6         // the user's input.
```

```
 7          int number = int.Parse(inputTextBox.Text);
 8
 9          // Check the number's range.
10          if (number >= 1 && number <= 10)
11          {
12              MessageBox.Show("That number is acceptable.");
13          }
14          else
15          {
16              MessageBox.Show("That number is NOT acceptable.");
17          }
18      }
19      catch (Exception ex)
20      {
21          // Display an error message.
22          MessageBox.Show(ex.Message);
23      }
24 }
```

 Checkpoint

4.12 What is a compound Boolean expression?

4.13 The following truth table shows various combinations of the values `true` and `false` connected by a logical operator. Complete the table by circling T or F to indicate whether the result of such a combination is `true` or `false`.

Logical Expression	Result (circle T or F)	
`true && false`	T	F
`true && true`	T	F
`false && true`	T	F
`false && false`	T	F
`true || false`	T	F
`true || true`	T	F
`false || true`	T	F
`false || false`	T	F
`! true`	T	F
`! false`	T	F

4.14 Assume the variables a = 2, b = 4, and c = 6. Circle T or F for each of the following conditions to indicate if it is true or false.

`a == 4 || b > 2`	T	F
`6 <= c && a > 3`	T	F
`1 != b && c != 3`	T	F
`a >= -1 || a <= b`	T	F
`!(a > 2)`	T	F

4.15 Explain how short-circuit evaluation works with the `&&` and `||` operators.

4.16 Write an `if` statement that displays the message "The number is valid" in a message box if the variable `speed` is within the range 0 through 200.

4.17 Write an `if` statement that displays the message "The number is not valid" in a message box if the variable `speed` is outside the range 0 through 200.

4.5 bool Variables and Flags

CONCEPT: You can store the values **true** and **false** in **bool** variables, which are commonly used as flags.

The C# language provides the **bool data type** that you can use to create variables that hold true or false values. Here is an example of the declaration of a bool variable:

```
bool grandMaster;
```

This declares a bool variable named grandMaster. In the program we can assign the values true or false to the variable, as shown here:

```
if (points > 5000)
{
    grandMaster = true;
}
else
{
    grandMaster = false;
}
```

Variables of the bool data type are commonly used as flags. A **flag** is a variable that signals when some condition exists in the program. When the flag variable is set to false, it indicates that the condition does not yet exist. When the flag variable is set to true, it means the condition does exist. For example, the previous code might be used in a game to determine whether the user is a "grand master." If he or she has earned more than 5,000 points, we set the grandMaster variable to true. Otherwise, we set the variable to false. Later in the program we can test the grandMaster variable, like this:

```
if (grandMaster)
{
    powerLevel += 500;
}
```

This code performs the following: if grandMaster is true, add 500 to powerLevel. Here is another example:

```
if (!grandMaster)
{
    powerLevel = 100;
}
```

This code performs the following: if grandMaster is not true, set powerLevel to 100.

Checkpoint

4.18 What special values can you store in a bool variable?

4.19 What is a flag variable?

4.6 Comparing Strings

CONCEPT: You can use certain relational operators and methods to compare strings.

You can use the == operator to compare two strings. For example, look at the following code sample:

```
string name1 = "Mary";
string name2 = "Mark";

if (name1 == name2)
{
    MessageBox.Show("The names are the same.");
}
else
{
    MessageBox.Show("The names are NOT the same.");
}
```

The == operator compares name1 and name2 to determine whether they are equal. Because the strings "Mary" and "Mark" are not equal, the else clause displays the message "The names are NOT the same."

You can compare string variables with string literals as well. Assume month is a string variable. The following code sample uses the != operator to determine whether month is not equal to "October".

```
if (month != "October")
{
    statement;
}
```

Look at the *Secret Word* application in the *Chap04* folder of the Student Sample Programs that accompany this book. Figure 4-18 shows the application's form, with the names of some of the controls. The form prompts you to enter the secret word into the inputTexBox control. When you click the checkButton control, the application compares the string that you entered to "Ariel."

Figure 4-18 The *Secret Word* application's form

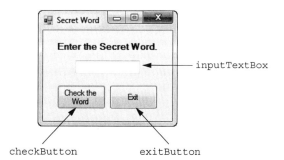

The following code sample shows the checkButton_Click event handler. Line 5 declares a string variable named secretWord, initialized with the value that has been entered into the inputTextBox control. The if statement that begins in line 8 compares the secretWord variable to the string literal "Ariel". If the two are equal, the statement in line 10 executes. Otherwise, the statement in line 14 executes.

```
1 private void checkButton_Click(object sender, EventArgs e)
2 {
3      // Declare a string variable and initialize it with
4      // the user's input.
5      string secretWord = inputTextBox.Text;
6
7      // Did the user enter the correct secret word?
8      if (secretWord == "Ariel")
```

```
 9    {
10         MessageBox.Show("That is the correct secret word.");
11    }
12    else
13    {
14         MessageBox.Show("Sorry, that is NOT the secret word.");
15    }
16 }
```

Other String Comparisons

In addition to determining whether strings are equal or not equal, you can use the `String.Compare` method to determine whether one string is greater than or less than another string. This is a useful capability because sometimes you need to sort strings in some order. Before we look at how the method works, we should review how characters are stored in memory.

Recall from Chapter 1 that computers do not actually store characters, such as *A*, *B*, *C*, and so on, in memory. Instead, they store numeric codes that represent the characters. We mentioned in Chapter 1 that C# uses Unicode to represent characters. Here are some facts about the Unicode system:

- The uppercase characters *A* through *Z* are represented by the numbers 65 through 90.
- The lowercase characters *a* through *z* are represented by the numbers 97 through 122.
- When the digits 0 through 9 are stored in memory as characters, they are represented by the numeric codes 48 through 57. (For example, the string "abc123" is stored in memory as the codes 97, 98, 99, 49, 50, and 51.)
- A blank space is represented by the number 32.

In addition to establishing a set of numeric codes to represent characters in memory, Unicode also establishes an order for characters. The character *A* comes before the character *B*, which comes before the character *C*, and so on.

When a program compares characters, it actually compares the codes for the characters. The character *A* would be considered less than the character *B* because the character *A*'s numeric code is less than the character *B*'s numeric code.

Let's look at how strings containing more than one character are compared. Suppose we have the strings "Mary" and "Mark" stored in memory, as follows:

```
string name1 = "Mary";
string name2 = "Mark";
```

Figure 4-19 shows how the strings "Mary" and "Mark" are stored in memory using character codes.

Figure 4-19 Character codes for the strings "Mary" and "Mark"

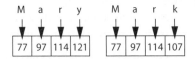

When you compare these strings in a program, they are compared character-by-character, beginning with the first, or leftmost, characters. This is shown in Figure 4-20.

Figure 4-20 Comparing each character in a string

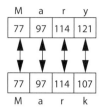

Here is how the comparison takes place:

1. The *M* in "Mary" is compared with the *M* in "Mark." These are the same, so the next characters are compared.
2. The *a* in "Mary" is compared with the *a* in "Mark." Because these are the same, the next characters are compared.
3. The *r* in "Mary" is compared with the *r* in "Mark." These are the same, so the next characters are compared.
4. The *y* in "Mary" is compared with the *k* in "Mark." Because these are not the same, the two strings are not equal. The character *y* has a higher character code (121) than *k* (107), so it is determined that the string "Mary" is greater than the string "Mark."

If one of the strings in a comparison is shorter than the other, only the corresponding characters are compared. If the corresponding characters are identical, then the shorter string is considered less than the longer string. For example, suppose the strings "High" and "Hi" are compared. The string "Hi" is considered less than "High" because it is shorter.

In C# you cannot use relational operators to determine whether one string is greater than or less than another string. Instead, you use the `String.Compare` method. You use the following general format to call the method:

```
String.Compare(string1, string2)
```

In the general format, *string1* and *string2* are the strings that are being compared. The method returns an integer value indicating the result of the comparison. The integer value will be one of the following:

- Greater than zero if *string1* is greater than *string2*.
- Zero if *string1* is equal to *string2*.
- Less than zero if *string1* is less than *string2*.

Here is a code sample that uses the method to display two names in alphabetical order:

```
1 string str1 = "Joe";
2 string str2 = "Kerry";
3
4 if (String.Compare(str1, str2) < 0)
5 {
6     MessageBox.Show(str1 + " " + str2);
7 }
8 else
9 {
10     MessageBox.Show(str2 + " " + str1);
11 }
```

The `if` statement in line 4 calls the `String.Compare` method, passing `str1` and `str2` as arguments. If we execute this code, the method will return a value that is less than 0 because the string "Joe" is less than the string "Kerry". As a result, the statement in line 6 will display *Joe Kerry*.

The `String.Compare` method performs a case sensitive comparison, which means that uppercase characters are not considered the same as their lowercase counterparts. For example, the strings "Joe" and "joe" are not equal because the case of the first character is different in each. You can pass the Boolean value `true` as an optional third argument to the `String.Compare` method if you want it to perform a case insensitive comparison. Here is an example:

```
1 string str1 = "JOE";
2 string str2 = "joe";
3
4 if (String.Compare(str1, str2, true) == 0)
5 {
6     MessageBox.Show(str1 + " and " + str2 + " are equal.");
7 }
8 else
9 {
10     MessageBox.Show(str1 + " and " + str2 + " are NOT equal.");
11 }
```

Notice that the `if` statement in line 4 passes true as the third argument to the `String.Compare` method. This specifies that we want a case insensitive comparison. As a result, the method will return 0 and the statement in line 6 will display *JOE and joe are equal.*

 Checkpoint

4.20 If the following code were part of a complete program, what would it display?

```
if (String.Compare("z", "a") < 0)
{
    MessageBox.Show("z is less than a.");
}
else
{
    MessageBox.Show("z is not less than a.");
}
```

4.21 If the following code were part of a complete program, what would it display?

```
string s1 = "New York";
string s2 = "Boston";
if (String.Compare(s1, s2) > 0)
{
    MessageBox.Show(s2);
    MessageBox.Show(s1);
}
else
{
    MessageBox.Show(s1);
    MessageBox.Show(s2);
}
```

 4.7 **Preventing Data Conversion Exceptions with the `TryParse` Methods**

CONCEPT: Exceptions should be prevented when possible. You can use the **TryParse** methods to prevent exceptions as a result of the user entering invalid data.

In Chapter 3 you learned that the `Parse` methods throw an exception when you try to use them to convert nonnumeric data to a numeric data type. If you use one of the `Parse` methods to convert a TextBox control's Text property to a number, there is always the possibility of an exception being thrown. After all, the user is free to enter anything he or she wants into a TextBox control. To handle the exceptions that are caused by the `Parse` methods, we have been using the `try-catch` statement.

Although many exceptions happen for reasons that the programmer cannot anticipate (such as a system malfunction), some exceptions are predictable. For example, you know that using a `Parse` method to convert nonnumeric input to a numeric data type will throw an exception. In situations like that, where an exception is predictable, you should write your code to prevent the exception. It is a better programming practice to prevent an exception instead of allowing it to happen and then letting a `try-catch` statement react to it. You should use `try-catch` statements primarily for those exceptions that are beyond your control.

> **NOTE:** Until now, we've simply been allowing exceptions to happen and letting a `try-catch` statement respond to them. After reading the previous paragraph, you might be wondering why we haven't been preventing exceptions all along. The reason is that you need to know how to write `if` statements to perform the techniques that we discuss in this section. Now that you know how to write `if` statements, you can add more sophistication to your code.

Now that you know how to write `if` statements, you can use a family of methods in the .NET Framework known as the `TryParse` methods. With the **`TryParse` methods**, you can determine whether a string (such as a control's Text property) contains a value that can be converted to a specific data type *before* it is converted to that data type. The `TryParse` methods do not throw an exception, so you can use them without a `try-catch` statement.

There are several `TryParse` methods in the .NET Framework. For now, we are using the `int`, `double`, and `decimal` numeric data types, so we will discuss three of them:

- We use the **`int.TryParse` method** to convert a string to an `int`.
- We use the **`double.TryParse` method** to convert a string to a `double`.
- We use the **`decimal.TryParse` method** to convert a string to a `decimal`.

When you call one of the `TryParse` methods, you pass two arguments: (1) the string that you want to convert, and (2) the name of the variable in which you want to store the converted value. First, let's look at the `int.TryParse` method. Here is the general format of how the `int.TryParse` method is called:

```
int.TryParse(string, out targetVariable)
```

In the general format, *string* is the string that you want to convert, and *targetVariable* is the name of an `int` variable. The method tries to convert the *string* argument to an `int`. If the conversion is successful, the converted value is stored in the *targetVariable*, and the method returns the Boolean value `true` to indicate that the conversion was successful. If the conversion is not successful, the method does not throw an exception. Instead, it stores 0 in the *targetVariable* and returns the Boolean value `false` to indicate that the *string* could not be converted.

Look carefully at the general format and notice that the word `out` appears before the *targetVariable*. The **`out` keyword** is required, and it specifies that the *targetVariable* is an output variable. An **output variable** is a variable that is passed as an argument to a method, and when the method is finished, a value is stored in the variable.

Because the `TryParse` methods return either `true` or `false`, they are commonly called as the Boolean expression in an `if` statement. The following code shows an example using the `int.TryParse` method. In the example, assume that `inputTextBox` is the name of a TextBox control.

```
 1 int number;
 2
 3 if (int.TryParse(inputTextBox.Text, out number))
 4 {
 5     MessageBox.Show("Success!");
 6 }
 7 else
 8 {
 9     MessageBox.Show("Enter a valid integer.");
10 }
```

The purpose of this code sample is to convert the value of the `inputTextBox` control's Text property to an `int` and assign that value to the `number` variable. In line 3, the `if` statement calls the `int.TryParse` method, passing `inputTextBox.Text` as argument 1 and `number` as argument 2. Here's what happens:

- If `inputTextBox.Text` is successfully converted to an `int`, the resulting value is assigned to the `number` variable, and the method returns `true`. That causes the statement in line 5 to execute.
- If `inputTextBox.Text` cannot be converted to an `int`, the value 0 is assigned to the `number` variable, and the method returns `false`. That causes the statement in line 9 (after the `else` clause) to execute.

The other `TryParse` methods work in a similar manner. Here is the general format of how the `double.TryParse` method is called:

```
double.TryParse(string, out targetVariable)
```

In the general format, *string* is the string that you want to convert, and *targetVariable* is the name of a `double` variable. If the *string* can be converted to a `double`, its value is stored in the *targetVariable*, and the method returns the Boolean value `true` to indicate that the conversion was successful. If the conversion was not successful, the method stores 0 in the *targetVariable* and returns the Boolean value `false` to indicate that the *string* could not be converted.

The following code shows an example using the `double.TryParse` method. In the example, assume that `inputTextBox` is the name of a TextBox control.

```
 1 double number;
 2
 3 if (double.TryParse(inputTextBox.Text, out number))
 4 {
 5     MessageBox.Show("Success!");
 6 }
 7 else
 8 {
 9     MessageBox.Show("Enter a valid double.");
10 }
```

Here is the general format of how the `decimal.TryParse` method is called:

```
decimal.TryParse(string, out targetVariable)
```

In the general format, *string* is the string that you want to convert, and *targetVariable* is the name of a `decimal` variable. If the *string* can be converted to a `decimal`, its value is stored in the *targetVariable*, and the method returns the Boolean value `true` to indicate that the conversion was successful. If the conversion was not successful, the method stores 0 in the *targetVariable* and returns the Boolean value `false` to indicate that the *string* could not be converted.

The following code shows an example using the `decimal.TryParse` method. In the example, assume that `inputTextBox` is the name of a TextBox control.

```
 1 decimal number;
 2
 3 if (decimal.TryParse(inputTextBox.Text, out number))
 4 {
 5     MessageBox.Show("Success!");
 6 }
 7 else
 8 {
 9     MessageBox.Show("Enter a valid decimal.");
10 }
```

Validating the Data in Multiple TextBoxes

If a form has multiple TextBoxes, then the user has multiple opportunities to enter an invalid piece of data. A well-designed program should validate the contents of each TextBox individually. When a piece of invalid data is found, the program should display an error message that tells the user specifically which TextBox contains the bad input.

This technique requires a set of nested `if` statements. For example, suppose a form has two TextBoxes. The following pseudocode shows the logic for validating each TextBox. (In the pseudocode, a set of dotted lines connects each If statement with its corresponding Else clause and its ending.)

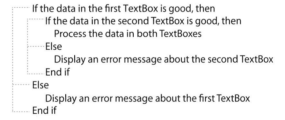

```
If the data in the first TextBox is good, then
    If the data in the second TextBox is good, then
        Process the data in both TextBoxes
    Else
        Display an error message about the second TextBox
    End if
Else
    Display an error message about the first TextBox
End if
```

Let's see how that logic looks in actual C# code. In the *Chap04* folder of the Student Sample Programs that accompany this book, you will find a project named *Add Two Numbers*. The application's form is shown in Figure 4-21. When you run the application, enter an integer into each of the TextBox controls and then click the *Add* button. A message box will appear showing the sum of the two numbers. If you enter anything other than an integer into either TextBox, an error message will appear telling you which TextBox contains the invalid data.

Figure 4-21 The *Add Two Numbers* form

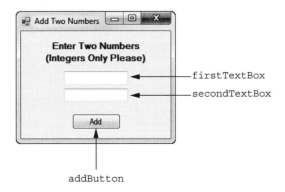

Here is the code for the addButton_Click event handler:

```
 1 private void addButton_Click(object sender, EventArgs e)
 2 {
 3     // Local variables
 4     int first, second, sum;
 5
 6     if (int.TryParse(firstTextBox.Text, out first))
 7     {
 8         if (int.TryParse(secondTextBox.Text, out second))
 9         {
10             // Add the two numbers and display the sum.
11             sum = first + second;
12             MessageBox.Show(sum.ToString());
13         }
14         else
15         {
16             // Display an error message about the second TextBox.
17             MessageBox.Show("The second TextBox contains invalid data.");
18         }
19     }
20     else
21     {
22         // Display an error message about the first TextBox.
23         MessageBox.Show("The first TextBox contains invalid data.");
24     }
25 }
```

Let's take a closer look:

- Line 4 declares three int variables: first, second, and sum.
- The if statement in line 6 tries to convert firstTextBox.Text to an int. If the conversion is successful, the result is stored in the first variable, and the program continues executing at line 8. If the conversion is not successful, the program jumps to the else clause in line 20, and line 23 displays an error message regarding the first TextBox control.
- The if statement in line 8 tries to convert secondTextBox.Text to an int. If the conversion is successful, the result is stored in the second variable, and the program continues executing at line 10. If the conversion is not successful, the program jumps to the else clause in line 14, and line 17 displays an error message regarding the second TextBox control.
- The statements in lines 11 and 12 execute only if both TextBox controls contain valid integer values. These statements add the first and second variables and displays their sum.

If you need to validate three TextBox controls, you will write a set of three nested if statements. Here's the pseudocode:

```
If the data in the first TextBox is good, then
    If the data in the second TextBox is good, then
        If the data in the third TextBox is good, then
            Process the data in all three TextBoxes
        Else
            Display an error message about the third TextBox
        End if
    Else
        Display an error message about the second TextBox
    End if
Else
    Display an error message about the first TextBox
End if
```

In Tutorial 4-4 you will complete an application that uses the `TryParse` methods to validate data entered into two TextBox controls.

Tutorial 4-4:
Calculating Fuel Economy

In Tutorial 3-2, you created an application that calculates a car's fuel economy in miles per gallon (MPG). Recall that the application lets the user enter the number of miles he or she has driven and the gallons of gas used. The application calculates and displays the car's MPG. In this tutorial you will create a new version of the application that validates the data entered by the user.

To save time, the project has already been started for you, and the application's form has already been created. To complete the project, follow the steps in this tutorial.

Step 1: Start Visual Studio (or Visual C# Express). Open the project named *Fuel Economy with TryParse* in the *Chap04* folder of the Student Sample Programs that accompany this book.

Step 2: Open the Form1 form in the *Designer*. The form is shown, along with the names of the important controls, in Figure 4-22.

Figure 4-22 The *Fuel Economy* form

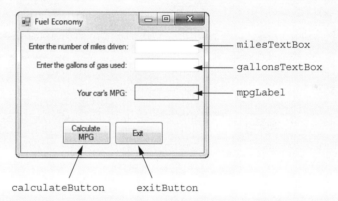

Step 3: Now you will create the Click event handlers for the Button controls. At the end of this tutorial, Program 4-4 shows the completed code for the form. You will be instructed to refer to Program 4-4 as you write the event handlers.

In the *Designer*, double-click the `calculateButton` control. This will open the code editor, and you see an empty event handler named `calculateButton_Click`. Complete the `calculateButton_Click` event handler by typing the code shown in lines 21–47 in Program 4-4.

Let's take a closer look at the code:

Lines 21–23: These lines declare the `double` variables `miles`, `gallons`, and `mpg`. The variables hold the miles driven, the gallons of gas used, and the MPG, respectively.

Line 26: This `if` statement tries to convert `milesTextBox.Text` to a `double`. If the conversion is successful, the result is stored in the `miles` variable, and the program continues executing at line 28. If the conversion is not successful, the program jumps to the `else` clause in line 43, and line 46 displays the error message "Invalid input for miles."

Line 29: This `if` statement tries to convert `gallonsTextBox.Text` to a double. If the conversion is successful, the result is stored in the `gallons` variable, and the program continues executing at line 31. If the conversion is not successful, the program jumps to the `else` clause in line 37, and line 40 displays the error message "Invalid input for gallons."

Lines 31–35: These lines are executed only if both the `milesTextBox` and `gallonsTextBox` contain valid data. Line 32 calculates MPG and assigns the result to the `mpg` variable, and line 35 displays the value of the `mpg` variable in the `mpgLabel` control.

Step 4: Switch your view back to the *Designer* and double-click the `exitButton` control. In the code editor you see an empty event handler named `exitButton_Click`. Complete the `exitButton_Click` event handler by typing the code shown in lines 52–53 in Program 4-4.

Step 5: Save the project and run the application. First, enter 300 for the miles and 10 for the gallons. Click the *Calculate MPG* button, and the application should display 30.0 as the MPG.

Now change the miles to an invalid entry, such as *123xyz*, and click the *Calculate MPG* button. The message "Invalid input for miles" should appear in a message box, as shown on the left in Figure 4-23.

Figure 4-23 Invalid input entered and the resulting error messages

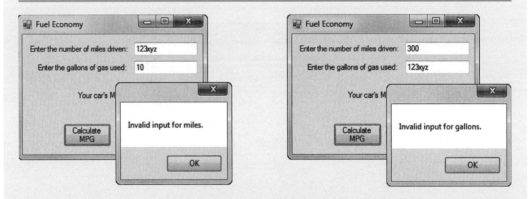

Now change the miles back to 300, change the gallons to an invalid entry, such as *123xyz*, and click the *Calculate MPG* button. The message *Invalid input for gallons* should appear in a message box, as shown on the right in Figure 4-23.

Continue to test the application as you wish. When you are finished, click the *Exit* button and the form should close.

Program 4-4 Completed Form1 code for the *Fuel Economy with TryParse* application

```
1 using System;
2 using System.Collections.Generic;
3 using System.ComponentModel;
4 using System.Data;
5 using System.Drawing;
6 using System.Linq;
7 using System.Text;
8 using System.Windows.Forms;
9
10 namespace Fuel_Economy_with_TryParse
11 {
12     public partial class Form1 : Form
```

```
13    {
14        public Form1()
15        {
16            InitializeComponent();
17        }
18
19        private void calculateButton_Click(object sender, EventArgs e)
20        {
21            double miles;      // To hold miles driven
22            double gallons;    // To hold gallons used
23            double mpg;        // To hold MPG
24
25            // Validate the milesTextBox control.
26            if (double.TryParse(milesTextBox.Text, out miles))
27            {
28                // Validate the gallonsTextBox control.
29                if (double.TryParse(gallonsTextBox.Text, out gallons))
30                {
31                    // Calculate MPG.
32                    mpg = miles / gallons;
33
34                    // Display the MPG in the mpgLabel control.
35                    mpgLabel.Text = mpg.ToString("n1");
36                }
37                else
38                {
39                    // Display an error message for gallonsTextBox.
40                    MessageBox.Show("Invalid input for gallons.");
41                }
42            }
43            else
44            {
45                // Display an error message for milesTextBox.
46                MessageBox.Show("Invalid input for miles.");
47            }
48        }
49
50        private void exitButton_Click(object sender, EventArgs e)
51        {
52            // Close the form.
53            this.Close();
54        }
55    }
56 }
```

Checkpoint

4.22 What value does a TryParse method return if the string argument is successfully converted? What value does it return if the string is not converted?

4.23 If a TryParse method successfully converts the string argument, where is the result stored?

4.24 If a TryParse method cannot convert the string argument, what is stored in the second argument?

4.25 What does the keyword out mean when it is written before an argument to a method call?

4.8 Input Validation

CONCEPT: Input validation is the process of inspecting data that has been input to a program to make sure it is valid before it is used in a computation.

In the previous section you learned about using the `TryParse` methods to validate the type of data entered by the user. You should also validate the accuracy of the data that is entered by the user. One of the most famous sayings among computer programmers is "garbage in, garbage out." This saying, sometimes abbreviated as *GIGO*, refers to the fact that computers cannot tell the difference between good input and bad input. If a user provides bad data as input to a program, the program will process that bad data and, as a result, will produce bad data as output.

For example, consider a payroll program that accepts the number of hours that an employee has worked in a given week as input. If the payroll clerk accidentally enters 400 hours instead of 40 hours, an unusually large check will be written because there are less than 400 hours in a week! The computer, however, is unaware of this fact, and unless the program is written to catch such errors, it will process the bad data just as if it were good data.

Sometimes stories are reported in the news about computer errors that mistakenly cause people to be charged thousands of dollars for small purchases or to receive large tax refunds to which they were not entitled. These "computer errors" are rarely caused by a computer, however; they are more commonly caused by software bugs or bad data that was read into a program as input.

The integrity of a program's output is only as good as the integrity of its input. For this reason, you should write your programs in such a way that bad input is never accepted. When input is given to a program, it should be inspected before it is processed. If the input is invalid, the program should discard it and prompt the user to enter the correct data. This process is known as **input validation**.

For example, in a payroll program we might validate the number of hours worked like this:

```
1  if (int.TryParse(hoursWorkedTextBox.Text, out hours))
2  {
3      if (hours > 0 && hours <= 168)
4      {
5          // Continue to process the input.
6      }
7      else
8      {
9          MessageBox.Show("Invalid number of hours entered.");
10     }
11 }
12 else
13 {
14     MessageBox.Show("The hours worked must be an integer.");
15 }
```

Let's assume the application uses a TextBox named `hoursWorkedTextBox` to get the hours worked. Also assume that the variable `hours` has already been declared as an `int`. The outer `if` statement (line 1) uses the `int.TryParse` method to make sure the user has entered an integer. If so, the value is stored in the `hours` variable and the program continues to the inner `if` statement (line 3). The inner `if` statement ensures that we process the input only if `hours` is greater than 0 *and* `hours` is less than or equal to 168. This is because we cannot write a paycheck for 0 hours worked, and 168 is the maximum number of hours in a week.

Let's look at another example. The following code comes from an application that gets a test score as input. A valid test score is an integer in the range of 0 through 100.

```
 1 if (int.TryParse(testScoreTextBox.Text, out testScore))
 2 {
 3     if (testScore >= 0 && testScore <= 100)
 4     {
 5         // Continue to process the input.
 6     }
 7     else
 8     {
 9         MessageBox.Show("Test score must be in the range 0 - 100.");
10     }
11 }
12 else
13 {
14     MessageBox.Show("The test score must be an integer.");
15 }
```

Let's assume the application uses a TextBox named `testScoreTextBox` to get the test score. Also assume that the variable `testScore` has already been declared as an `int`. The outer `if` statement (line 1) uses the `int.TryParse` method to make sure the user has entered an integer. If so, the value is stored in the `testScore` variable and the program continues to the inner `if` statement (line 3). The inner `if` statement ensures that we process the input only if `testScore` is greater than or equal to 0 *and* `testScore` is less than or equal to 100.

4.9 Radio Buttons and Check Boxes

CONCEPT: GUIs commonly use radio buttons and check boxes to let the user select items.

Radio Buttons

Radio buttons are useful when you want the user to select one choice from several possible choices. Figure 4-24 shows a form with a group of three radio buttons. The radio buttons in the figure allow the user to select *Coffee*, *Tea*, or *Soft Drink*.

Figure 4-24 Radio buttons

A radio button may be either selected or deselected. Each radio button has a small circle that appears filled in when the radio button is selected, and appears empty when the radio button is deselected. In Figure 4-24, the *Coffee* radio button is selected and the other radio buttons are deselected.

At run time, only one radio button in a group may be selected at a time. Clicking on a radio button selects it, and automatically deselects any other radio button in the same group. We call this **mutually exclusive selection**.

NOTE: The name *radio button* refers to the old car radios that had push buttons for selecting stations. Only one button could be pushed in at a time. When you pushed a button, it automatically popped out the currently selected button.

When you want to create a group of radio buttons on a form, you use the **RadioButton control**, which is found in the *Common Controls* section of the *Toolbox*. RadioButton controls are normally grouped in one of the following ways:

- You place them inside a GroupBox control. All RadioButton controls that are inside a GroupBox are members of the same group.
- You place them inside a Panel control. All RadioButton controls that are inside a Panel are members of the same group.
- You place them on a form but not inside a GroupBox or a Panel. All RadioButton controls that are on a form but not inside a GroupBox or Panel are members of the same group.

Figure 4-25 shows a form with two groups of RadioButton controls. The group on the left is inside a GroupBox control, and the group on the right is inside a Panel control. When the application runs, the user will be able to select only one RadioButton from each group. In the figure, *Coffee* is selected in the left group and *Lunch* is selected in the right group.

Figure 4-25 A form with two groups of RadioButton controls

The RadioButton Control's Text Property

RadioButton controls have a Text property, which holds the text that is displayed next to the radio button's circle. For example, the radio buttons shown in Figure 4-24 have their Text properties set to *Coffee*, *Tea*, and *Soft Drink*.

The RadioButton Control's Checked Property

RadioButton controls have a **Checked property** that determines whether the control is selected or deselected. The Checked property is a Boolean property, which means that it may be set to either True or False. When the Checked property is set to True, the RadioButton is selected, and when the Checked property is set to False, the RadioButton is deselected. By default, the Checked property is set to False.

You can use the *Properties* window to set the initial value of a RadioButton control's Checked property. Keep in mind that the Checked property of only one RadioButton in a group can be set to True at a given time. When you set a RadioButton control's Checked property to True in the *Properties* window, the Checked properties of all the other RadioButtons in the same group automatically are set to False.

TIP: When you create a group of RadioButton controls, you should always set one of the control's Checked property to True in the *Properties* window. If all the RadioButtons in a group have their Checked property set to False, then the Checked property of the RadioButton with the lowest TabIndex value will automatically be set to True when you run the application.

Working with Radio Buttons in Code

In code, you can determine whether a RadioButton control is selected by testing its Checked property. For example, suppose a form has a RadioButton control named `choice1RadioButton`. The following `if` statement determines whether it is selected:

```
if (choice1RadioButton.Checked)
{
    MessageBox.Show("You selected Choice 1");
}
```

Notice that we did not have to use the `==` operator to explicitly compare the Checked property to the value `true`. This code is equivalent to the following:

```
if (choice1RadioButton.Checked == true)
{
    MessageBox.Show("You selected Choice 1.");
}
```

Let's look at an example using multiple RadioButton controls. Open the *RadioButton* project in the *Chap04* folder of the Student Sample Programs that accompany this book. The application's form is shown in Figure 4-26. When you run the application, select one of the radio buttons and then click the *OK* button. A message box appears showing the sport that you selected.

Figure 4-26 The *RadioButton Example* form

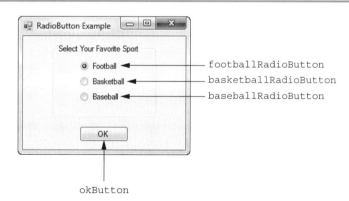

Here is the code for the `okButton_Click` event handler:

```
1 private void okButton_Click(object sender, EventArgs e)
2 {
3     if (footballRadioButton.Checked)
4     {
5         MessageBox.Show("You selected Football.");
6     }
7     else if (basketballRadioButton.Checked)
8     {
9         MessageBox.Show("You selected Basketball.");
10    }
11    else if (baseballRadioButton.Checked)
```

```
12      {
13          MessageBox.Show("You selected Baseball.");
14      }
15 }
```

When the event handler executes, the `if` statement in line 3 determines whether the `footballRadioButton` control's Checked property is true. If it is, the message *You selected Football* is displayed in line 5. Otherwise, line 7 determines whether the `basketballRadioButton` control's Checked property is true. If it is, the message *You selected Basketball* is displayed in line 9. Otherwise, line 11 determines whether the `baseballRadioButton` control's Checked property is true. If it is, the message *You selected Baseball* is displayed in line 13.

Check Boxes

A **check box** appears as a small box with some accompanying text. Figure 4-27 shows an example. They are called check boxes because clicking on an empty check box causes a check mark to appear in it. If a check mark already appears in a check box, clicking it removes the check mark.

Figure 4-27 A check box

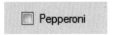

Check boxes are similar to radio buttons, except that check boxes are not mutually exclusive. You can have one or more check boxes in a group, and any number of them can be selected at any given time. When you want to create a check box on a form, you use the **CheckBox control**, which is found in the *Common Controls* section of the *Toolbox*.

The CheckBox Control's Text Property

CheckBox controls have a Text property, which holds the text that is displayed next to the check box. For example, the CheckBox control shown in Figure 4-27 has its Text property set to *Pepperoni*.

The CheckBox Control's Checked Property

Like radio buttons, CheckBox controls have a Checked property. When a CheckBox control is selected, or checked, its Checked property is set to True. When a CheckBox control is deselected, or unchecked, its Checked property is set to False.

Working with CheckBox Controls in Code

In code, you can determine whether a CheckBox control is selected by testing its Checked property. For example, suppose a form has a CheckBox control named `option1CheckBox`. The following `if` statement determines whether it is selected:

```
if (option1CheckBox.Checked)
{
    MessageBox.Show("You selected Option 1.");
}
```

Let's look at an example program. Open the *CheckBox* project in the *Chap04* folder of the Student Sample Programs that accompany this book. The application's form is shown in Figure 4-28. When you run the application, select any of the check boxes and then click the *OK* button. One or more message boxes will appear, showing you the items that you selected.

Figure 4-28 The *CheckBox Example* form

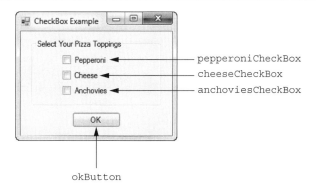

Here is the code for the okButton_Click event handler:

```
 1 private void okButton_Click(object sender, EventArgs e)
 2 {
 3     if (pepperoniCheckBox.Checked)
 4     {
 5         MessageBox.Show("You selected Pepperoni.");
 6     }
 7
 8     if (cheeseCheckBox.Checked)
 9     {
10         MessageBox.Show("You selected Cheese.");
11     }
12
13     if (anchoviesCheckBox.Checked)
14     {
15         MessageBox.Show("You selected Anchovies.");
16     }
17 }
```

Notice that we have three separate if statements. The if statement in line 3 determines whether the pepperoniCheckBox control is selected. If so, line 5 displays the message *You selected Pepperoni*. The if statement in line 8 determines whether the cheeseCheckBox control is selected. If so, line 10 displays the message *You selected Cheese*. The if statement in line 13 determines whether the anchoviesCheckBox control is selected. If so, line 15 displays the message *You selected Anchovies*.

The CheckedChanged Event

Anytime a RadioButton or a CheckBox control's Checked property changes, a **CheckedChanged event** happens for that control. If you want some action to immediately take place when the user selects (or deselects) a RadioButton or CheckBox control, you can create a CheckedChanged event handler for the control and write the desired code in that event handler.

To create a CheckedChanged event handler for a RadioButton or a CheckBox, simply double-click the control in the *Designer*. An empty CheckedChanged event handler is created in the code editor. You can then write code inside the event handler. Tutorial 4-5 leads you through the process.

Tutorial 4-5:
Creating the *Color Theme* Application

In this tutorial you create an application that allows the user to select a color using RadioButton controls. When the user selects a color, the form's background color is changed to that color immediately. Figure 4-29 shows the application's form, with the names of all the controls.

Figure 4-29 The *Color Theme* form

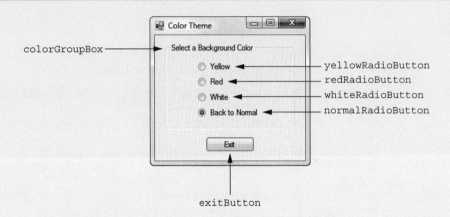

Step 1: Start Visual Studio (or Visual C# Express) and begin a new Windows Forms Application project named *Color Theme*.

Step 2: Set up the application's form as shown in Figure 4-29. Notice that the form's Text property is set to *Color Theme*. The names of the controls are shown in the figure. As you place each of the controls on the form, refer to Table 4-8 for the relevant property settings.

Table 4-8 Control property settings

Control Name	Control Type	Property Settings
colorGroupBox	GroupBox	**Text:** *Select a Background Color*
yellowRadioButton	RadioButton	**Text:** *Yellow* **Checked:** False
redRadioButton	RadioButton	**Text:** *Red* **Checked:** False
whiteRadioButton	RadioButton	**Text:** *White* **Checked:** False
normalRadioButton	RadioButton	**Text:** *Back to Normal* **Checked:** True
exitButton	Button	**Text:** *Exit*

Step 3: Once you have set up the form with its controls, you can create the Checked-Changed event handlers for the RadioButton controls. At the end of this tutorial, Program 4-5 shows the completed code for the form. You will be instructed to refer to Program 4-5 as you write the event handlers.

In the *Designer*, double-click the yellowRadioButton control. This opens the code editor, and you see an empty event handler named yellowRadioButton_CheckedChanged. Complete the yellowRadioButton_CheckedChanged event handler by typing the code shown in lines 21–24 in Program 4-5.

The event handler is easy to understand. The `if` statement in line 21 determines whether the `yellowRadioButton` control is checked. If so, line 23 sets the form's background to yellow.

Step 4: Switch your view back to the *Designer* and double-click the `redRadioButton` control. This opens the code editor, and you see an empty event handler named `redRadioButton_CheckedChanged`. Complete the `redRadioButton_CheckedChanged` event handler by typing the code shown in lines 29–32 in Program 4-5.

Step 5: Switch your view back to the *Designer* and double-click the `whiteRadioButton` control. This opens the code editor, and you see an empty event handler named `whiteRadioButton_CheckedChanged`. Complete the `whiteRadioButton_CheckedChanged` event handler by typing the code shown in lines 37–40 in Program 4-5.

Step 6: Switch your view back to the *Designer* and double-click the `normalRadioButton` control. This opens the code editor, and you see an empty event handler named `normalRadioButton_CheckedChanged`. Complete the `normalRadioButton_CheckedChanged` event handler by typing the code shown in lines 45–48 in Program 4-5.

Step 7: Switch your view back to the *Designer* and double-click the `exitButton` control. In the code editor you see an empty event handler named `exitButton_Click`. Complete the `exitButton_Click` event handler by typing the code shown in lines 53–54 in Program 4-5.

Step 8: Save the project and run the application. Notice that the *Back to Normal* radio button is initially selected. That's because you set its Checked property to True in the Properties window. Click the other *Radio* buttons and notice that the form's background color changes immediately. When you are finished testing the application, click the *Exit* button to close it.

Program 4-5 Completed Form1 code for the *Color Theme* application

```
 1 using System;
 2 using System.Collections.Generic;
 3 using System.ComponentModel;
 4 using System.Data;
 5 using System.Drawing;
 6 using System.Linq;
 7 using System.Text;
 8 using System.Windows.Forms;
 9
10 namespace Color_Theme
11 {
12     public partial class Form1 : Form
13     {
14         public Form1()
15         {
16             InitializeComponent();
17         }
18
19         private void yellowRadioButton_CheckedChanged(object sender, EventArgs e)
20         {
21             if (yellowRadioButton.Checked)
22             {
```

```
23                     this.BackColor = Color.Yellow;
24                 }
25             }
26
27         private void redRadioButton_CheckedChanged(object sender, EventArgs e)
28         {
29             if (redRadioButton.Checked)
30             {
31                 this.BackColor = Color.Red;
32             }
33         }
34
35         private void whiteRadioButton_CheckedChanged(object sender, EventArgs e)
36         {
37             if (whiteRadioButton.Checked)
38             {
39                 this.BackColor = Color.White;
40             }
41         }
42
43         private void normalRadioButton_CheckedChanged(object sender, EventArgs e)
44         {
45             if (normalRadioButton.Checked)
46             {
47                 this.BackColor = SystemColors.Control;
48             }
49         }
50
51         private void exitButton_Click(object sender, EventArgs e)
52         {
53             // Close the form.
54             this.Close();
55         }
56     }
57 }
```

 Checkpoint

4.26 If several RadioButton controls have been created in the same GroupBox, how many of them may be selected at one time?

4.27 If several CheckBox controls have been created in the same GroupBox, how many of them may be selected at one time?

4.28 In code, how do you determine whether a RadioButton or a CheckBox control has been selected?

4.10   The switch Statement

CONCEPT: The switch statement lets the value of a variable or an expression determine which path of execution the program will take.

The **switch statement** is a **multiple-alternative decision structure**. It allows you to test the value of a variable or an expression and then use that value to determine which statement or set of statements to execute. Figure 4-30 shows an example of how a multiple alternative decision structure looks in a flowchart.

Figure 4-30 A multiple alternative decision structure

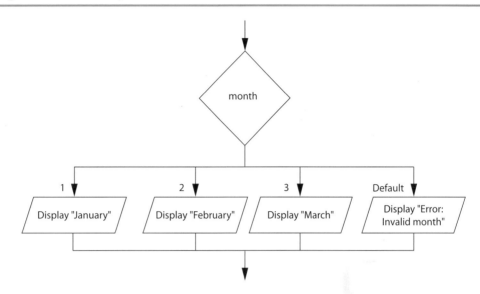

In the flowchart, the diamond symbol shows month, which is the name of a variable. If the month variable contains the value 1, the program displays "January." If the month variable contains the value 2, the program displays "February." If the month variable contains the value 3, the program displays "March." If the month variable contains none of these values, the action that is labeled Default is executed. In this case, the program displays "Error: Invalid month."

Here is the general format of a switch statement in C# code:

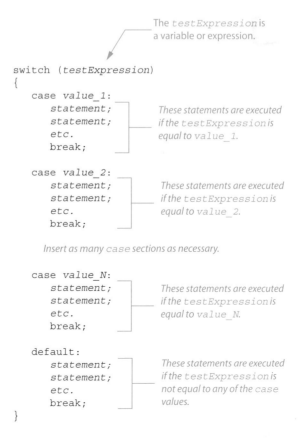

The first line of the statement starts with the word switch, followed by a *testExpression*, which is enclosed in parentheses. The *testExpression* is a variable or an expression that gives an integer, string, or bool value. (Several other data types that we have not discussed yet are also permissible. The important thing to remember is that the *testExpression* cannot be a floating-point or decimal value.)

Beginning at the next line is a block of code enclosed in curly braces. Inside this block of code are one or more case sections. A case section begins with the word case, followed by a value, followed by a colon. Each case section contains one or more statements, followed by a break statement. Each case section must end with a break statement. At the end is an optional default section. The default section must also end with a break statement.

When the switch statement executes, it compares the value of the *testExpression* with the values that follow each of the case statements (from top to bottom). When it finds a case value that matches the *testExpression*'s value, the program branches to the case statement. The statements that follow the case statement are executed, until a break statement is encountered. At that point the program jumps out of the switch statement. If the *testExpression* does not match any of the case values, the program branches to the default statement and executes the statements that immediately follow it.

For example, the following code performs the same operation as the flowchart in Figure 4-30:

```
switch (month)
{
    case 1:
        MessageBox.Show("January");
        break;

    case 2:
        MessageBox.Show("February");
        break;

    case 3:
        MessageBox.Show("March");
        break;

    default:
        MessageBox.Show("Error: Invalid month");
        break;
}
```

In this example the *testExpression* is the month variable. If the value in the month variable is 1, the program branches to the case 1: section and executes the MessageBox.Show("January") statement that immediately follows it. If the value in the month variable is 2, the program branches to the case 2: section and executes the MessageBox.Show("February") statement that immediately follows it. If the value in the month variable is 3, the program branches to the case 3: section and executes the MessageBox.Show("March") statement that immediately follows it. If the value in the month variable is not 1, 2, or 3, the program branches to the default: section and executes the MessageBox.Show("Error: Invalid month") statement that immediately follows it.

The switch statement can be used as an alternative to an if-else-if statement that tests the same variable or expression for several different values. For example, the previously shown switch statement works like this if-else-if statement:

```
if (month == 1)
{
    MessageBox.Show("January");
}
else if (month == 2)
{
    MessageBox.Show("February");
}
else if (month == 3)
{
    MessageBox.Show("March");
}
else
{
    MessageBox.Show("Error: Invalid month");
}
```

To see an application that uses a `switch` statement, look at the *Switch Example* project in the *Chap04* folder of the Student Sample Programs that accompany this book.

Checkpoint

4.29 Convert the following `if-else-if` code to a `switch` statement.

```
if (choice == 1)
{
    MessageBox.Show("You chose 1.");
}
else if (choice == 2)
{
    MessageBox.Show("You chose 2.");
}
else if (choice == 3)
{
    MessageBox.Show("You chose 3.");
}
else
{
    MessageBox.Show("Make another choice.");
}
```

 4.11 **Introduction to List Boxes**

> **CONCEPT:** List boxes display a list of items and allow the user to select an item from the list.

A list box displays a list of items and allows the user to select one or more items from the list. In Visual C# you use the **ListBox control** to create a list box on an application's form. Figure 4-31 shows a form with two ListBox controls. At run time, the user may select one of the items, causing the item to appear selected.

The topmost ListBox in Figure 4-31 does not have a scroll bar, but the bottom one does. A scroll bar appears when a ListBox contains more items than can be displayed in the

Figure 4-31 ListBox examples

space provided. In the figure, the top ListBox has four items (Poodle, Great Dane, German Shepherd, and Terrier), and all items are displayed. The bottom ListBox shows four items (Siamese, Persian, Bobtail, and Burmese), but because it has a scroll bar, we know there are more items in the ListBox than those four.

You will find the ListBox control in the *Common Controls* section of the *Toolbox*. Once you create a ListBox control, you add items to its **Items property**. The items that you add to a ListBox's Items property are displayed in the ListBox.

To store values in the Items property at design time, follow these steps:

1. Select the ListBox control in the *Designer* window.
2. In the *Properties* window, the setting for the Items property is displayed as *(Collection)*. When you select the Items property, an ellipsis button (⊡) appears.
3. Click the ellipsis button. The *String Collection Editor* dialog box appears, as shown in Figure 4-32.
4. Type the values that are to appear in the ListBox into the *String Collection Editor* dialog box. Type each value on a separate line by pressing the Enter key after each entry.
5. When you have entered all the values, click the *OK* button.

Figure 4-32 The *String Collection Editor* dialog box

 NOTE: Once you acquire the necessary skills, you will be able to fill the Items collection of list boxes from external data sources (such as databases).

The SelectedItem Property

When the user selects an item in a ListBox, the item is stored in the ListBox's **SelectedItem property**. For example, suppose an application has a ListBox control named `fruitListBox` and a `string` variable named `selectedFruit`. The `fruitListBox` control contains the items *Apples*, *Pears*, and *Bananas*. If the user has selected *Pears*, the following statement assigns the string `"Pears"` to the variable `selectedFruit`:

```
selectedFruit = fruitListBox.SelectedItem.ToString();
```

Notice that you have to call the SelectedItem property's `ToString` method to retrieve the value as a string.

Determining Whether an Item Is Selected

An exception will occur if you try to get the value of a ListBox's SelectedItem property when no item is selected in the ListBox. For that reason, you should always make sure that an item is selected before reading the SelectedItem property. You do this with the SelectedIndex property.

The items that are stored in a ListBox each have an index. The **index** is simply a number that identifies the item's position in the ListBox. The first item has the index 0, the next has the index 1, and so on. The last index value is $n - 1$, where n is the number of items in the ListBox. When the user selects an item in a ListBox, the item's index is stored in the ListBox's **SelectedIndex property**. If no item is selected in the ListBox, the SelectedIndex property is set to -1.

You can use the SelectedIndex property to make sure that an item is selected in a ListBox before you try to get the value of the SelectedItem property. You simply make sure the SelectedIndex property is not set to -1 before trying to read the SelectedItem property. Here is an example:

```
if (fruitListBox.SelectedIndex != -1)
{
    selectedFruit = fruitListBox.SelectedItem.ToString();
}
```

In Tutorial 4-6 you will create an application that lets the user select an item from a ListBox control.

Tutorial 4-6:
Creating the *Time Zone* Application

In this tutorial you create an application that allows the user to select a city from a List-Box control. When the user clicks a button, the application displays the name of the city's time zone. Figure 4-33 shows the application's form, with the names of all the controls.

Step 1: Start Visual Studio (or Visual C# Express) and begin a new Windows Forms Application project named *Time Zone*.

Step 2: Set up the application's form, as shown in Figure 4-33. Notice that the form's Text property is set to *Color Theme*. The names of the controls are shown in the figure. As you place each of the controls on the form, refer to Table 4-9 for the relevant property settings.

Figure 4-33 The *Color Theme* form

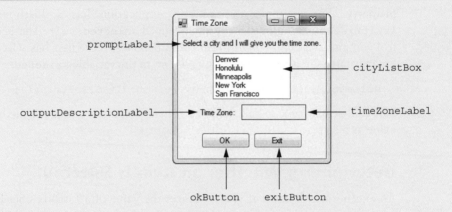

Table 4-9 Control property settings

Control Name	Control Type	Property Settings
promptLabel	Label	**Text:** *Select a city and I will give you the time zone.*
cityListBox	ListBox	**Items:** *Denver* *Honolulu* *Minneapolis* *New York* *San Francisco*
outputDescriptionLabel	Label	**Text:** *Time Zone:*
timeZoneLabel	Label	**AutoSize:** False **BorderStyle:** FixedSingle **Text:** (The contents of the Text property have been erased.) **TextAlign:** MiddleCenter
okButton	Button	**Text:** *OK*
exitButton	Button	**Text:** *Exit*

Step 3: Once you have set up the form with its controls, you can create the Click event handlers for the Button controls. At the end of this tutorial, Program 4-6 shows the completed code for the form. You will be instructed to refer to Program 4-6 as you write the event handlers.

In the *Designer*, double-click the okButton control. This opens the code editor, and you see an empty event handler named okButton_Click. Complete the okButton_Click event handler by typing the code shown in lines 21–52 in Program 4-6. Let's take a closer look at the code:

Line 21: This line declares a string variable named city. It is used to hold the name of the city that the user selects from the ListBox.

Line 23: This if statement determines whether the user has selected an item in the cityListBox control. If an item is selected, the control's SelectedIndex property is set to the item's index (a value of 0 or greater), and the program continues to line 25. If no item is selected, however, the control's SelectedIndex property is set to −1, and the program jumps to the else clause in line 48.

Line 26: This statement gets the selected item from the ListBox and assigns it to the `city` variable.

Line 29: This `switch` statement tests the city variable and branches to one of its case statements, depending on the variable's value:

- If the `city` variable equals `"Honolulu"`, the program jumps to the `case` statement in line 31.
- If the `city` variable equals `"San Francisco"`, the program jumps to the case statement in line 34.
- If the `city` variable equals `"Denver"`, the program jumps to the `case` statement in line 37.
- If the `city` variable equals `"Minneapolis"`, the program jumps to the `case` statement in line 40.
- If the `city` variable equals `"New York"`, the program jumps to the `case` statement in line 43.

Step 4: Switch your view back to the *Designer* and double-click the `exitButton` control. In the code editor you see an empty event handler named `exitButton_Click`. Complete the `exitButton_Click` event handler by typing the code shown in lines 57–58 in Program 4-6.

Step 5: Save the project and run the application. Select a city in the ListBox control and click the *OK* button to see its time zone. Test each city, and when you are finished, click the *Exit* button and the form should close.

Program 4-6 Completed Form1 code for the *Time Zone* application

```
 1 using System;
 2 using System.Collections.Generic;
 3 using System.ComponentModel;
 4 using System.Data;
 5 using System.Drawing;
 6 using System.Linq;
 7 using System.Text;
 8 using System.Windows.Forms;
 9
10 namespace Time_Zone
11 {
12     public partial class Form1 : Form
13     {
14         public Form1()
15         {
16             InitializeComponent();
17         }
18
19         private void okButton_Click(object sender, EventArgs e)
20         {
21             string city;    // To hold the name of a city
22
23             if (cityListBox.SelectedIndex != -1)
24             {
25                 // Get the selected item.
26                 city = cityListBox.SelectedItem.ToString();
27
28                 // Determine the time zone.
29                 switch (city)
```

```
30                       {
31                           case "Honolulu":
32                               timeZoneLabel.Text = "Hawaii-Aleutian";
33                               break;
34                           case "San Francisco":
35                               timeZoneLabel.Text = "Pacific";
36                               break;
37                           case "Denver":
38                               timeZoneLabel.Text = "Mountain";
39                               break;
40                           case "Minneapolis":
41                               timeZoneLabel.Text = "Central";
42                               break;
43                           case "New York":
44                               timeZoneLabel.Text = "Eastern";
45                               break;
46                       }
47                   }
48               else
49               {
50                   // No city was selected.
51                   MessageBox.Show("Select a city.");
52               }
53           }
54
55           private void exitButton_Click(object sender, EventArgs e)
56           {
57               // Close the form.
58               this.Close();
59           }
60       }
61 }
```

✓ Checkpoint

4.30 How do you add items to a ListBox control using the *Properties* window?

4.31 How do you get the item that is selected in a ListBox?

4.32 How can you determine whether an item has been selected in a ListBox?

Key Terms

! operator	logical AND operator
&& operator	logical NOT operator
|| operator	logical operator
bool data type	logical OR operator
Boolean expression	multiple-alternative decision
check box	structure
CheckBox control	mutually exclusive selection
Checked property	nested decision structure
CheckedChanged event	out keyword
conditionally executed	output variable
control structure	radio buttons
decimal.TryParse method	RadioButton control
decision structure	relational operator
double.TryParse method	SelectedIndex property
dual-alternative decision structure	Selecteditem property
flag	selection structure
if-else statement	sequence structure
if-else-if statement	short-circuit evaluation
index	single-alternative decision
input validation	structure
int.Tryparse method	switch statement
Items property	TryParse method
ListBox control	

Review Questions

Multiple Choice

1. A _____ structure executes a set of statements only under certain circumstances.

   a. sequence
   b. circumstantial
   c. decision
   d. Boolean

2. A _____ structure provides one alternative path of execution.

   a. sequence
   b. single-alternative decision
   c. one-path alternative
   d. single-execution decision

3. A(n) _____ expression has a value of either true or false.

   a. binary
   b. decision
   c. unconditional
   d. Boolean

4. The symbols >, <, and == are all _____ operators.

   a. relational
   b. logical
   c. conditional
   d. ternary

5. A(n) _____ structure tests a condition and then takes one path if the condition is true or another path if the condition is false.

    a. multibranch statement
    b. single-alternative decision
    c. dual-alternative decision
    d. sequence

6. You use a(n) _____ statement to write a single-alternative decision structure.

    a. `test-jump`
    b. `if`
    c. `if-else`
    d. `if-call`

7. You use a(n) _____ statement to write a dual alternative decision structure.

    a. `test-jump`
    b. `if`
    c. `if-else`
    d. `if-call`

8. A _____ decision structure is written inside another decision structure.

    a. nested
    b. tiered
    c. dislodged
    d. hierarchical

9. `&&`, `||`, and `!` are _____ operators.

    a. relational
    b. logical
    c. conditional
    d. ternary

10. A compound Boolean expression created with the _____ operator is true only if both of its subexpressions are true.

    a. `&&`
    b. `||`
    c. `!`
    d. `both`

11. A compound Boolean expression created with the _____ operator is true if either of its subexpressions is true.

    a. `&&`
    b. `||`
    c. `!`
    d. `either`

12. The _____ operator takes a Boolean expression as its operand and reverses its logical value.

    a. `&&`
    b. `||`
    c. `!`
    d. `either`

13. A _____ is a Boolean variable that signals when some condition exists in the program.

    a. flag
    b. signal

    c.   sentinel

    d.   siren

14.   The _____ family of methods can be used to convert a string to a specific data type without throwing an exception.

    a.   `TryConvert`

    b.   `Parse`

    c.   `TryParse`

    d.   `SafeConvert`

15.   If several _____ controls exist in a GroupBox, only one of them may be selected at a time.

    a.   CheckBox

    b.   RadioButton

    c.   ListBox

    d.   SelectionButton

16.   You use the _____ statement to create a multiple alternative decision structure.

    a.   `menu`

    b.   `branch`

    c.   `select`

    d.   `switch`

17.   The _____ section of a `switch` statement is branched to if none of the `case` values match the test expression.

    a.   `else`

    b.   `default`

    c.   `case`

    d.   `otherwise`

18.   A ListBox's index numbering starts at _____.

    a.   0

    b.   1

    c.   −1

    d.   any value you specify

19.   You can use the _____ property to determine whether an item is selected in a ListBox.

    a.   Index

    b.   SelectedItem

    c.   SelectedIndex

    d.   Items.SelectedIndex

20.   The _____ property holds the item that is selected in a ListBox control.

    a.   Index

    b.   SelectedItem

    c.   SelectedIndex

    d.   Items.SelectedIndex

True or False

1.   You can write any program using only sequence structures.

2.   A single-alternative decision structure tests a condition and then takes one path if the condition is true or another path if the condition is false.

3.   The `if-else` statement is a dual-alternative decision structure.

4. A decision structure can be nested inside another decision structure.

5. A compound Boolean expression created with the `&&` operator is true only when both subexpressions are true.

6. The `TryParse` methods throw an exception if the string argument cannot be converted.

7. Multiple CheckBox controls in the same GroupBox can be selected at the same time.

8. The test expression in a `switch` statement can be a `double` or a `decimal` value.

9. If an item is not selected in a ListBox, the control's SelectedIndex property will be set to 0.

10. To store items in a ListBox, you add them to the control's Text property.

Short Answer

1. What is meant by the term *conditionally executed*?

2. You need to test a condition and then execute one set of statements if the condition is true. If the condition is false, you need to execute a different set of statements. What structure will you use?

3. Briefly describe how the `&&` operator works.

4. Briefly describe how the `||` operator works.

5. When determining whether a number is inside a range, which logical operator is it best to use?

6. What is a flag and how does it work?

7. What are the two arguments that you pass to a `TryParse` method?

8. How do you determine in code whether a RadioButton control or a CheckBox control is selected?

9. How do you add items to a ListBox using the *Properties* window?

10. How can you read the selected item from a ListBox, while preventing an exception from occurring if no item is selected?

Algorithm Workbench

1. Write an `if` statement that assigns 20 to the variable y and assigns 40 to the variable z if the variable x is greater than 100.

2. Write an `if` statement that assigns 0 to the variable b and assigns 1 to the variable c if the variable a is less than 10.

3. Write an `if-else` statement that assigns 0 to the variable b if the variable a is less than 10. Otherwise, it should assign 99 to the variable b.

4. Write nested decision structures that perform the following: if `amount1` is greater than 10 and `amount2` is less than 100, display the greater of `amount1` and `amount2`.

5. Write an `if-else` statement that displays "Speed is normal" if the value of the speed variable is at least 24 but no more than 56. If the speed variable's value is outside this range, display "Speed is abnormal."

6. Write an `if-else` statement that determines whether the value of the `points` variable is less than 9 or greater than 51. If this is true, display "Invalid points." Otherwise, display "Valid points."

7. Assume `pointsTextBox` is the name of a TextBox control and `points` is the name of an `int` variable. Write an `if-else` statement that uses one of the `TryParse` methods to convert the `pointsTextBox` control's Text property to an `int` and stores the result in the `points` variable. If the conversion is not successful, display an error message in a message box.

8. Rewrite the following `if-else-if` statement as a `switch` statement.

```
if (selection == 1)
{
    MessageBox.Show("You selected 1.");
}
else if (selection == 2)
{
    MessageBox.Show("You selected 2.");
}
else if (selection == 3)
{
    MessageBox.Show("You selected 3.");
}
else if (selection == 4)
{
    MessageBox.Show("You selected 4.");
}
else
{
    Display "Not good with numbers, eh?"
}
```

9. Assume `nameListBox` is a ListBox control. Write code that reads the selected item from the ListBox. Be sure to prevent an exception from occurring in case no item has been selected.

Programming Problems

1. **Roman Numeral Converter**

   Create an application that allows the user to enter an integer between 1 and 10 into a TextBox control. The program should display the Roman numeral version of that number. If the number is outside the range of 1 through 10, the program should display an error message.

   The following table lists the Roman numerals for the numbers 1 through 10.

Number	Roman Numeral
1	I
2	II
3	III
4	IV
5	V
6	VI
7	VII
8	VIII
9	IX
10	X

2. **Mass and Weight**

Scientists measure an object's mass in kilograms and its weight in Newtons. If you know the amount of mass of an object, you can calculate its weight, in Newtons, with the following formula:

$$Weight = Mass \times 9.8$$

Create an application that lets the user enter an object's mass and then calculates its weight. If the object weighs more than 1000 Newtons, display a message indicating that it is too heavy. If the object weighs less than 10 Newtons, display a message indicating that it is too light.

3. **Magic Dates**

The date June 10, 1960, is special because when it is written in the following format, the month times the day equals the year:

6/10/60

Create an application that lets the user enter a month (in numeric form), a day, and a two-digit year. The program should then determine whether the month times the day equals the year. If so, it should display a message saying the date is magic. Otherwise, it should display a message saying the date is not magic.

4. **Color Mixer**

The colors red, blue, and yellow are known as the primary colors because they cannot be made by mixing other colors. When you mix two primary colors, you get a secondary color, as shown here:

- When you mix red and blue, you get purple.
- When you mix red and yellow, you get orange.
- When you mix blue and yellow, you get green.

Create an application that lets the user select two primary colors from two different sets of *Radio* buttons. The form should also have a *Mix* button. When the user clicks the *Mix* button, the form's background should change to the color that you get when you mix the two selected primary colors. Figure 4-34 shows an example of how the form should appear.

Figure 4-34 The *Color Mixer* form

Note: If the user picks the same color from both sets of *Radio* buttons, set the form's background to that color.

5. **Distance Converter**

In the English measurement system, 1 yard equals 3 feet and 1 foot equals 12 inches. Use this information to create an application that lets the user convert distances to and from inches, feet, and yards.

Figure 4-35 shows an example of how the application's form might appear. In the example, the user enters the distance to be converted into a TextBox. A ListBox allows the user to select the units being converted from, and another ListBox allows the user to select the units being converted to.

Figure 4-35 The *Distance Converter* form

Note: Be sure to handle the situation where the user picks the same units from both list boxes. The converted value will be the same as the value entered.

6. **Book Club Points**

Serendipity Booksellers has a book club that awards points to its customers based on the number of books purchased each month. The points are awarded as follows:

- If a customer purchases 0 books, he or she earns 0 points.
- If a customer purchases 1 book, he or she earns 5 points.
- If a customer purchases 2 books, he or she earns 15 points.
- If a customer purchases 3 books, he or she earns 30 points.
- If a customer purchases 4 or more books, he or she earns 60 points.

Create an application that lets the user enter the number of books that he or she has purchased this month and displays the number of points awarded.

7. **Software Sales**

A software company sells a package that retails for $99. Quantity discounts are given according to the following table:

Quantity	Discount
10–19	20%
20–49	30%
50–99	40%
100 or more	50%

Create an application that lets the user enter the number of packages purchased. The program should then display the amount of the discount (if any) and the total amount of the purchase after the discount.

8. **Body Mass Index Program Enhancement**

In Programming Exercise 6 in Chapter 3, you were asked to create an application that calculates a person's body mass index (BMI). Recall from that exercise that the BMI is often used to determine whether a person is overweight or underweight for their height. A person's BMI is calculated with the following formula:

$$BMI = Weight \times 703 \div Height^2$$

In the formula, weight is measured in pounds and height is measured in inches. Enhance the program so it displays a message indicating whether the person has optimal weight, is underweight, or is overweight. A person's weight is considered to be optimal if his or her BMI is between 18.5 and 25. If the BMI is less than 18.5, the person is considered to be underweight. If the BMI value is greater than 25, the person is considered to be overweight.

9. **Change for a Dollar Game**

   Create a change-counting game that gets the user to enter the number of coins required to make exactly one dollar. The program should let the user enter the number of pennies, nickels, dimes, and quarters. If the total value of the coins entered is equal to one dollar, the program should congratulate the user for winning the game. Otherwise, the program should display a message indicating whether the amount entered was more than or less than one dollar.

10. **Fat Percentage Calculator**

    One gram of fat has 9 calories. If you know the number of fat grams in a particular food, you can use the following formula to calculate the number of calories that come from fat in that food:

    $$Calories\ from\ fat = fat\ grams \times 9$$

    If you know the food's total calories, you can use the following formula to calculate the percentage of calories from fat:

    $$Percentage\ of\ calories\ from\ fat = Calories\ from\ fat \div total\ calories$$

    Create an application that allows the user to enter:

    - The total number of calories for a food item
    - The number of fat grams in that food item

    The application should calculate and display:

    - The number of calories from fat
    - The percentage of calories that come from fat

    Also, the application's form should have a CheckBox that the user can check if he or she wants to know whether the food is considered low fat. (If the calories from fat are less than 30% of the total calories of the food, the food is considered low fat.)

    Use the following test data to determine if the application is calculating properly:

Calories and Fat	Percentage Fat
200 calories, 8 fat grams	Percentage of calories from fat: 36%
150 calories, 2 fat grams	Percentage of calories from fat: 12% (a low-fat food)
500 calories, 30 fat grams	Percentage of calories from fat: 54%

    Note: Make sure the number of calories and fat grams are not less than 0. Also, the number of calories from fat cannot be greater than the total number of calories. If that happens, display an error message indicating that either the calories or fat grams were incorrectly entered.

11. **Time Calculator**

    Create an application that lets the user enter a number of seconds and works as follows:

    - There are 60 seconds in a minute. If the number of seconds entered by the user is greater than or equal to 60, the program should display the number of minutes in that many seconds.
    - There are 3,600 seconds in an hour. If the number of seconds entered by the user is greater than or equal to 3,600, the program should display the number of hours in that many seconds.
    - There are 86,400 seconds in a day. If the number of seconds entered by the user is greater than or equal to 86,400, the program should display the number of days in that many seconds.

12. **Workshop Selector**

The following table shows a training company's workshops, the number of days of each, and their registration fees.

Workshop	Number of Days	Registration Fee
Handling Stress	3	$1,000
Time Management	3	$800
Supervision Skills	3	$1,500
Negotiation	5	$1,300
How to Interview	1	$500

The training company conducts its workshops in the six locations shown in the following table. The table also shows the lodging fees per day at each location.

Location	Lodging Fees per Day
Austin	$150
Chicago	$225
Dallas	$175
Orlando	$300
Phoenix	$175
Raleigh	$150

When a customer registers for a workshop, he or she must pay the registration fee plus the lodging fees for the selected location. For example, here are the charges to attend the Supervision Skills workshop in Orlando:

Registration: $1,500
Lodging: $300 × 3 days = $900
Total: $2,400

Create an application that lets the user select a workshop from one ListBox and a location from another ListBox. When the user clicks a button, the application should calculate and display the registration cost, the lodging cost, and the total cost.

5.1   More About ListBoxes

CONCEPT: ListBox controls have various methods and properties that you can use in code to manipulate the ListBox's contents.

In Chapter 4 we introduced the ListBox control, which displays a list of items and allows the user to select one or more items from the list. In this chapter we use ListBox controls to display output. Many of the algorithms that you will see in this chapter generate lists of data and then display those lists in ListBox controls.

Recall from Chapter 4 that you add items to a ListBox control's Items property, and those items are displayed in the ListBox. At design time, you can use the *Properties* window to add items to the control's Items property. You can also write code that adds items to a ListBox control at run time. To add an item to a ListBox control with code, you call the control's **Items.Add** method. Here is the method's general format:

```
ListBoxName.Items.Add(Item);
```

ListBoxName is the name of the ListBox control. *Item* is the value to be added to the Items property. For example, in the *Chap05* folder of the Student Sample Programs that accompany this book, you will find a project named *Name List*. Figure 5-1 shows the application's form. As shown in the image on the left, the ListBox's name is nameListBox and the Button control's name is addButton. At run time, when you click the addButton control, the names shown in the image on the right are added to the nameListBox control.

Figure 5-1 The *Name List* application

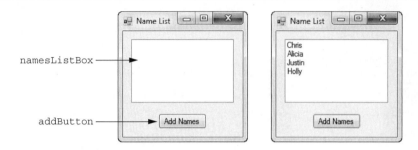

Here is the code for the addButton_Click event handler:

```
1 private void addButton_Click(object sender, EventArgs e)
2 {
3     namesListBox.Items.Add("Chris");
4     namesListBox.Items.Add("Alicia");
5     namesListBox.Items.Add("Justin");
6     namesListBox.Items.Add("Holly");
7 }
```

You can add values of other types as well. In the *Chap05* folder of the book's Student Sample Programs, you will find a project named *Number List*. Figure 5-2 shows the application's form. As shown in the image on the left, the ListBox's name is numberListBox and the Button control's name is addButton. At run time, when you click the addButton control, the numbers shown in the image on the right are added to the numberListBox control.

Figure 5-2 The *Number List* application

Here is the code for the addButton_Click event handler:

```
1 private void addButton_Click(object sender, EventArgs e)
2 {
3     numberListBox.Items.Add(10);
4     numberListBox.Items.Add(20);
5     numberListBox.Items.Add(30);
6     numberListBox.Items.Add(40);
7 }
```

The Items.Count Property

ListBox controls have an **Items.Count property** that reports the number of items stored in the ListBox. If the ListBox is empty, the Items.Count property equals 0. For example, assume an application has a ListBox control named `employeesListBox`. The following `if` statement displays a message box if there are no items in the ListBox:

```
if (employeesListBox.Items.Count == 0)
{
    MessageBox.Show("There are no items in the list!");
}
```

The Items.Count property holds an integer value. Assuming `numEmployees` is an `int` variable, the following statement assigns the number of items in the `employeesListBox` to the `numEmployees` variable:

```
numEmployees = employeesListBox.Items.Count;
```

The `Items.Clear` Method

ListBox controls have an `Items.Clear` **method** that erases all the items in the Items property. Here is the method's general format:

```
ListBoxName.Items.Clear();
```

For example, assume an application has a ListBox control named `employeesListBox`. The following statement clears all the items in the list.

```
employeesListBox.Items.Clear();
```

 Checkpoint

> 5.1 In code, how do you add an item to a ListBox control?
>
> 5.2 How do you determine the number of items that are stored in a ListBox control?
>
> 5.3 How do you erase the contents of a ListBox control?

 ## 5.2 The `while` Loop

CONCEPT: The `while` loop causes a statement or set of statements to repeat as long as a Boolean expression is true.

The `while` loop gets its name from the way it works: *While a Boolean expression is true, do some task*. The loop has two parts: (1) a Boolean expression that is tested for a true or false value and (2) a statement or set of statements that is repeated as long as the Boolean expression is true. Figure 5-3 shows the logic of a `while` loop.

Figure 5-3 The logic of a `while` loop

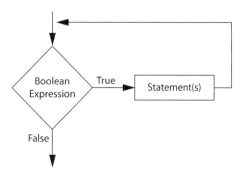

The diamond symbol represents the Boolean expression that is tested. Notice what happens if the expression is true: One or more statements are executed and the program's execution flows back to the point just above the diamond symbol. The Boolean expression is tested again, and if it is true, the process repeats. If the Boolean expression is false, the program exits the loop. Each time the loop executes its statement or statements, we say the loop is iterating, or performing an **iteration**.

Here is the general format of the `while` loop:

```
while (BooleanExpression)
{
    statement;          ⎤  This set of statements are repeated
    statement;          ⎦  while the Boolean expression is true.
    etc;
}
```

We refer to the first line as the **while clause**. The `while` clause begins with the word `while`, followed by a Boolean expression that is enclosed in parentheses. Beginning on the next line is a set of statements enclosed in curly braces. This block of statements is known as the **body** of the loop.

When the `while` loop executes, the Boolean expression is tested. If the Boolean expression is true, the statements that appear in the body of the loop are executed, and then the loop starts over. If the Boolean expression is false, the loop ends and the program resumes execution at the statement immediately following the loop.

We say that the statements in the body of the loop are conditionally executed because they are executed only under the condition that the Boolean expression is true. If you are writing a `while` loop that has only one statement in its body, you do not have to enclose the statement inside curly braces. Such a loop can be written in the following general format:

```
while (BooleanExpression)
    statement;
```

When a `while` loop written in this format executes, the Boolean expression is tested. If it is true, the one statement that appears on the next line is executed, and then the loop starts over. If the Boolean expression is false, however, the loop ends.

Although the curly braces are not required when there is only one statement in the loop's body, it is still a good idea to use them, as shown in the following general format:

```
while (BooleanExpression)
{
    statement;
}
```

When we discussed the various `if` statements in Chapter 4, we mentioned that this is a good style of programming because it cuts down on errors. If you have more than one statement in the body of a loop, those statements *must* be enclosed in curly braces. If you get into the habit of always enclosing the conditionally executed statements in a set of curly braces, it's less likely that you will forget them.

You should also notice that the statements in the body of the loop are indented. As with `if` statements, this indentation makes the code easier to read and debug. By indenting the statements in the body of the loop, you visually set them apart from the surrounding code.

Let's look at an example. In the *Chap05* folder of the Student Sample Programs that accompany this book you will find a project named *while Loop Demo*. Figure 5-4 shows the application's form. As shown in the image on the left, the Button control's name is `goButton`. At run time, when you click the `goButton` control, the message box shown in the image on the right is displayed. When you click the *OK* button to close the message

Figure 5-4 The *while Loop Demo* application

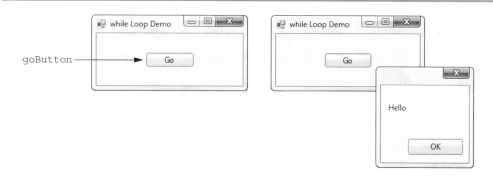

box, another identical message box is displayed. The message box is displayed a total of five times.

Here is the code for the `goButton_Click` event handler:

```
 1 private void goButton_Click(object sender, EventArgs e)
 2 {
 3     // Declare a variable to count the loop iterations.
 4     int count = 1;
 5
 6     // Display "Hello" in a message box five times.
 7     while (count <= 5)
 8     {
 9         // Display the message box.
10         MessageBox.Show("Hello");
11
12         // Add one to count.
13         count = count + 1;
14     }
15 }
```

Let's take a closer look at this code. In line 4 an int variable named count is declared and initialized with the value 1. A while loop begins in line 7. Notice that the while loop tests the expression count <= 5. The statements in the body of the while loop repeat as long as the count variable is less than or equal to 5. Inside the body of the loop, line 10 displays "Hello" in a message box, and then line 13 adds one to the count variable. This is the last statement in the body of the loop, so after it executes, the loop starts over. It tests the Boolean expression again, and if it is true, the statements in the body of the loop are executed. This cycle repeats until the Boolean expression count <= 5 is false, as illustrated in Figure 5-5. A flowchart for the loop is shown in Figure 5-6.

Figure 5-5 The while Loop

① Test this Boolean expression.

```
  while (count <= 5)
  {
      // Display the message box.
      MessageBox.Show("Hello");

      // Add one to count.
      count = count + 1;
  }
```

③ After executing the body of the loop, start over.

② If the Boolean expression is true, perform these statements. Otherwise, the loop ends.

Figure 5-6 Flowchart for the `while` Loop

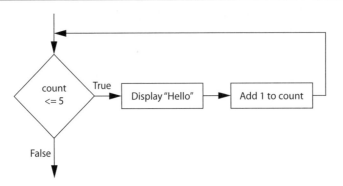

The `while` Loop is a Pretest Loop

The `while` loop is known as a **pretest loop**, which means it tests its condition *before* performing an iteration. Because the test is done at the beginning of the loop, you usually have to perform some steps prior to the loop to make sure that the loop executes at least once. Notice the declaration of the `count` variable in the *while Loop Demo* program:

```
int count = 1;
```

The `count` variable is initialized with the value 1. If `count` had been initialized with a value that is greater than 5, as shown in the following program sample, the loop would never execute:

```
 1 private void goButton_Click(object sender, EventArgs e)
 2 {
 3     // Declare a variable to count the loop iterations.
 4     int count = 6;
 5
 6     // This loop will never iterate!
 7     while (count <= 5)
 8     {
 9         // Display the message box.
10         MessageBox.Show("Hello");
11
12         // Add one to count.
13         count = count + 1;
14     }
15 }
```

An important characteristic of the `while` loop is that the loop will never iterate if the Boolean expression is false to start with. If you want to be sure that a `while` loop executes the first time, you must initialize the relevant data in such a way that the Boolean expression starts out as true.

Counter Variables

In the *while Loop Demo* application, the variable `count` is initialized with the value 1, and then 1 is added to the variable `count` during each loop iteration. The loop executes as long as `count` is less than or equal to 5. The variable `count` is used as a **counter variable**, which means it is regularly incremented in each loop iteration. In essence, the `count` variable keeps count of the number of iterations the loop has performed. Counter variables are commonly used to control the number of times that a loop iterates.

Tutorial 5-1 will give you some practice writing a loop, and using a counter variable. In the tutorial you will write a `while` loop that calculates the amount of interest earned by a bank account each month for a number of months.

Tutorial 5-1:
Using a Loop to Calculate an Account Balance

In this tutorial you complete the *Ending Balance* application. The project has already been started for you and is located in the *Chap05* folder of the Student Sample Programs that accompany this book. The application's form is shown in Figure 5-7.

Figure 5-7 The *Ending Balance* form

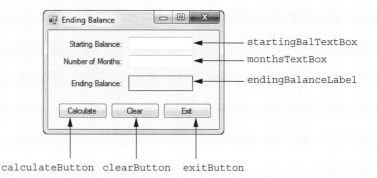

When you complete the application, it will allow the user to enter an account's starting balance into the `startingBalTextBox` control and the number of months that the account will be left to earn interest into the `monthsTextBox` control. When the user clicks the `calculateButton` control, the application calculates the account's balance at the end of the time period. The account's monthly interest rate is 0.005, and the interest is compounded monthly.

Step 1: Start Visual Studio (or Visual C# Express). Open the project named *Ending Balance* in the *Chap05* folder of the Student Sample Programs that accompany this book.

Step 2: Open the Form1 form in the *Designer*. The form is shown, along with the names of the important controls, in Figure 5-7.

Step 3: Now you will create the Click event handlers for the Button controls. At the end of this tutorial, Program 5-1 shows the completed code for the form. You will be instructed to refer to Program 5-1 as you write the event handlers.

In the *Designer*, double-click the `calculateButton` control. This opens the code editor, and you will see an empty event handler named `calculateButton_Click`. Complete the `calculateButton_Click` event handler by typing the code shown in lines 21–58 in Program 5-1. Let's take a closer look at the code:

Line 22: This statement declares a constant `decimal` named `INTEREST_RATE`, set to the value 0.005. This is the monthly interest rate.

Lines 25–27: These statements declare the following variables:

- `balance`, a `decimal` variable to hold the account balance.
- `months`, an `int` variable to hold the number of months that the account will be left to earn interest.
- `count`, an `int` that is used to count the months as a loop iterates. Notice that the `count` variable is initialized with the value 1.

Line 30: This `if` statement tries to convert `startingBalTextBox.Text` to a `decimal`. If the conversion is successful, the result is stored in the `balance` variable, and the program continues executing at line 32. If the conversion is not successful, the program jumps to the `else` clause in line 54, and line 57 displays the error message *Invalid value for starting balance*.

Line 33: This `if` statement tries to convert `monthsTextBox.Text` to an `int`. If the conversion is successful, the result is stored in the `months` variable, and the program continues executing at line 35. If the conversion is not successful, the program jumps to the `else` clause in line 48, and line 51 displays the error message *Invalid value for months*.

Line 36: This is the beginning of a `while` loop. The loop executes as long as the expression `count <= months` is true.

Lines 38–42: These statements are the body of the loop. Line 39 calculates the monthly interest and adds it to the `balance` variable. Line 42 adds 1 to the `count` variable.

Line 46: This statement executes after the loop has finished all of its iterations. It converts the value of the `balance` variable to a string (formatted as currency) and assigns the resulting string to the `endingBalanceLabel` control's Text property.

Step 4: Switch your view back to the *Designer* and double-click the `clearButton` control. In the code editor you will see an empty event handler named `clearButton_Click`. Complete the `clearButton_Click` event handler by typing the code shown in lines 63–69 in Program 5-1.

Step 5: Switch your view back to the *Designer* and double-click the `exitButton` control. In the code editor you will see an empty event handler named `exitButton_Click`. Complete the `exitButton_Click` event handler by typing the code shown in lines 74–75 in Program 5-1.

Step 6: Save the project. Then, press F5 on the keyboard, or click the *Start Debugging* button (▶) on the toolbar to compile and run the application.

First, enter *1000* as the starting balance and *48* as the number of months. Click the *Calculate Average* button and $1,270.49 should appear as the ending balance. Think about the value that you entered for the number of months. How many times did the `while` loop in line 36 iterate? (Answer: 48 times.)

Next, click the *Clear* button to clear the TextBoxes and the ending balance. Now, enter *100* as the starting balance and *1* as the number of months. Click the *Calculate Average* button and $100.50 should appear as the ending balance. How many times did the while loop iterate this time? (Answer: 1 time).

Continue to test the application as you wish. When you are finished, click the *Exit* button and the form should close. (If you plan to continue to the next tutorial, leave this project open in Visual Studio.)

Program 5-1 Completed Form1 code for the *Ending Balance* application

```
1 using System;
2 using System.Collections.Generic;
3 using System.ComponentModel;
4 using System.Data;
5 using System.Drawing;
```

```
 6 using System.Linq;
 7 using System.Text;
 8 using System.Windows.Forms;
 9
10 namespace Ending_Balance
11 {
12     public partial class Form1 : Form
13     {
14         public Form1()
15         {
16             InitializeComponent();
17         }
18
19         private void calculateButton_Click(object sender, EventArgs e)
20         {
21             // Constant for the monthly interest rate.
22             const decimal INTEREST_RATE = 0.005m;
23
24             // Local variables
25             decimal balance;      // The account balance
26             int months;           // The number of months
27             int count = 1;        // Loop counter, initialized with 1
28
29             // Get the starting balance.
30             if (decimal.TryParse(startingBalTextBox.Text, out balance))
31             {
32                 // Get the number of months.
33                 if (int.TryParse(monthsTextBox.Text, out months))
34                 {
35                     // The following loop calculates the ending balance.
36                     while (count <= months)
37                     {
38                         // Add this month's interest to the balance.
39                         balance = balance + (INTEREST_RATE * balance);
40
41                         // Add one to the loop counter.
42                         count = count + 1;
43                     }
44
45                     // Display the ending balance.
46                     endingBalanceLabel.Text = balance.ToString("c");
47                 }
48                 else
49                 {
50                     // Invalid number of months was entered.
51                     MessageBox.Show("Invalid value for months.");
52                 }
53             }
54             else
55             {
56                 // Invalid starting balance was entered.
57                 MessageBox.Show("Invalid value for starting balance.");
58             }
59         }
60
61         private void clearButton_Click(object sender, EventArgs e)
62         {
63             // Clear the TextBoxes and the endingBalanceLabel control.
64             startingBalanceTextBox.Text = "";
```

```
65              monthsTextBox.Text = "";
66              endingBalanceLabel.Text = "";
67
68              // Reset the focus.
69              startingBalanceTextBox.Focus();
70          }
71
72          private void exitButton_Click(object sender, EventArgs e)
73          {
74              // Close the form.
75              this.Close();
76          }
77      }
78 }
```

Tutorial 5-2:
Enhancing the *Ending Balance* Application

In this tutorial you enhance the *Ending Balance* application that you created in Tutorial 5-1. First, add a ListBox control to the application's form, as shown in Figure 5-8. Then modify the `calculateButton_Click` event handler so it displays each month's ending balance in the ListBox. Figure 5-9 shows an example of how the form will appear when the user has entered 1000 for the starting balance and 8 for the months.

Figure 5-8 The modified *Ending Balance* form

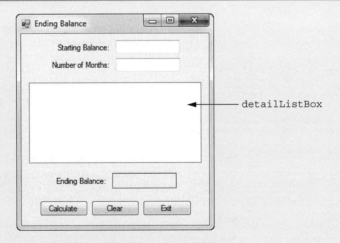

Step 1: Start Visual Studio (or Visual C# Express) and open the *Ending Balance* project that you completed in Tutorial 5-1.

Step 2: Enlarge the form so it is roughly the size shown in Figure 5-8. (310 pixels wide by 325 pixels high should be sufficient.)

Step 3: Create a ListBox control named `detailListBox`. Resize the ListBox as shown in Figure 5-8.

Figure 5-9 Example output

Step 4: Switch to the code editor and insert the code shown in lines 41–44 in Program 5-2. (The new lines of code are shown in bold.) The statement in lines 42–44 adds a string to the `detailListBox` control. If you examine the statement carefully, you will see that it uses concatenation to create a string in the following format:

The ending balance for month *count* is *balance*

In the actual string that is created, *count* will be the value of the `count` variable and *balance* will be the value of the `balance` variable, formatted as currency.

Step 5: Find the `clearButton_Click` event handler in the code editor. Update the comment as shown in lines 68–69, and insert the line of code shown in line 73. (The lines are shown in bold.) The statement in line 73 clears the contents of the `detailListBox` control.

Step 6: Save the project. Then, press F5 on the keyboard or click the *Start Debugging* button (▶) on the toolbar to compile and run the application.

As shown in Figure 5-9, enter *1000* as the starting balance and *8* as the number of months. Click the *Calculate Average* button. Your output should look like that shown in Figure 5-9. Click the *Clear* button and enter any other values you wish to test the application further. When you are finished, click the *Exit* button and the form should close.

Program 5-2 Completed Form1 code for the *Ending Balance* application

```
1 using System;
2 using System.Collections.Generic;
3 using System.ComponentModel;
4 using System.Data;
5 using System.Drawing;
6 using System.Linq;
7 using System.Text;
8 using System.Windows.Forms;
9
10 namespace Ending_Balance
11 {
```

```
12    public partial class Form1 : Form
13    {
14        public Form1()
15        {
16            InitializeComponent();
17        }
18
19        private void calculateButton_Click(object sender, EventArgs e)
20        {
21            // Constant for the monthly interest rate.
22            const decimal INTEREST_RATE = 0.005m;
23
24            // Local variables
25            decimal balance;      // The account balance
26            int months;           // The number of months
27            int count = 1;        // Loop counter, initialized with 1
28
29            // Get the starting balance.
30            if (decimal.TryParse(startingBalTextBox.Text, out balance))
31            {
32                // Get the number of months.
33                if (int.TryParse(monthsTextBox.Text, out months))
34                {
35                    // The following loop calculates the ending balance.
36                    while (count <= months)
37                    {
38                        // Add this month's interest to the balance.
39                        balance = balance + (INTEREST_RATE * balance);
40
41                        // Display this month's ending balance.
42                        detailListBox.Items.Add("The ending balance " +
43                            "for month " + count + " is " +
44                            balance.ToString("c"));
45
46                        // Add one to the loop counter.
47                        count = count + 1;
48                    }
49
50                    // Display the ending balance.
51                    endingBalanceLabel.Text = balance.ToString("c");
52                }
53                else
54                {
55                    // Invalid number of months was entered.
56                    MessageBox.Show("Invalid value for months.");
57                }
58            }
59            else
60            {
61                // Invalid starting balance was entered.
62                MessageBox.Show("Invalid value for starting balance.");
63            }
64        }
65
66        private void clearButton_Click(object sender, EventArgs e)
67        {
68            // Clear the TextBoxes, the endingBalanceLabel control,
69            // and the ListBox.
70            startingBalTextBox.Text = "";
```

```
71              monthsTextBox.Text = "";
72              endingBalanceLabel.Text = "";
73              detailListBox.Items.Clear();
74
75              // Reset the focus.
76              startingBalTextBox.Focus();
77          }
78
79          private void exitButton_Click(object sender, EventArgs e)
80          {
81              // Close the form.
82              this.Close();
83          }
84      }
85 }
```

Infinite Loops

In all but rare cases, loops must contain a way to terminate within themselves. This means that something inside the loop must eventually make the loop's Boolean expression false. The loop in Program 5-2 stops when the expression count <= months is false. If a loop does not have a way of stopping, it is called an infinite loop. An *infinite loop* continues to repeat until the program is interrupted. Infinite loops usually occur when the programmer forgets to write code inside the loop that makes the test condition false. In most circumstances you should avoid writing infinite loops.

The following code sample demonstrates an infinite loop. In line 1 the count variable is declared and initialized with the value 1. The while loop that begins in line 5 executes as long as count is less than or equal to 5. There is no code inside the loop to change the count variable's value, so the expression count <= 5 in line 5 is always true. As a consequence, the loop has no way of stopping.

```
1 // Declare a variable to count the loop iterations.
2 int count = 1;
3
4 // How many times will this loop iterate?
5 while (count <= 5)
6 {
7     // Display the message box.
8     MessageBox.Show("Hello");
9 }
```

Checkpoint

5.4 What is a loop iteration?

5.5 What is a counter variable?

5.6 What is a pretest loop?

5.7 Does the while loop test its condition before or after it performs an iteration?

5.8 What is an infinite loop?

5.3 The ++ and -- operators

CONCEPT: To increment a variable means to increase its value, and to decrement a variable means to decrease its value. C# provides special operators to increment and decrement variables.

To **increment** a variable means to increase its value and to **decrement** a variable means to decrease its value. Both of the following statements increment the variable num by 1:

```
num = num + 1;
num += 1;
```

And num is decremented by 1 in both the following statements:

```
num = num - 1;
num -= 1;
```

Incrementing and decrementing is so commonly done in programs that C# provides a set of simple unary operators designed just for incrementing and decrementing variables. The increment operator is ++, and the decrement operator is --. The following statement uses the ++ operator to add 1 to num:

```
num++;
```

After this statement executes, the value of num is increased by 1. The following statement uses the -- operator to subtract 1 from num:

```
num--;
```

NOTE: The ++ operator is pronounced "plus plus," and the -- operator is pronounced "minus minus." The expression num++ is pronounced "num plus plus," and the expression num-- is pronounced "num minus minus."

In these examples, we have written the ++ and -- operators after their operands (or, on the right side of their operands). This is called **postfix mode**. The operators can also be written before (or, on the left side) of their operands, which is called **prefix mode**. Here are examples:

```
++num;
--num;
```

When you write a simple statement to increment or decrement a variable, such as the ones shown here, it doesn't matter if you use prefix mode or postfix mode. The operators do the same thing in either mode. However, if you write statements that mix these operators with other operators or with other operations, there is a difference in the way the two modes work. Such complex code can be difficult to understand and debug. When we use the increment and decrement operators, we will do so only in ways that are straightforward and easy to understand, such as the statements previously shown.

We introduce these operators at this point because they are commonly used in loops. The following code segment shows an example. In the code, the count variable is initialized with the value 1. The while loop that begins in line 5 iterates as long as count is less than or equal to 5. The statement in line 11 increments count. The loop will iterate 5 times.

```
1 // Declare a variable to count the loop iterations.
2 int count = 1;
```

```
 3
 4 // Display "Hello" in a message box five times.
 5 while (count <= 5)
 6 {
 7     // Display the message box.
 8     MessageBox.Show("Hello");
 9
10     // Increment count.
11     count++;
12 }
```

In the next section, which discusses the `for` loop, you will see these operators used often.

Checkpoint

5.9 What messages will the following code sample display?

```
int number = 5;
number++;
MessageBox.Show(number.ToString());
number--;
MessageBox.Show(number.ToString());
```

5.10 How many times will the following loop iterate?

```
int count = 0;
while (count < 4)
{
    MessageBox.Show(count.ToString());
    count++;
}
```

5.4 The `for` Loop

CONCEPT: The `for` loop is ideal for performing a known number of iterations.

The `for` loop is specifically designed for situations requiring a counter variable to control the number of times that a loop iterates. When you write a `for` loop, you specify three actions:

- **Initialization:** This action takes place when the loop begins. It happens only once.
- **Test:** A Boolean expression is tested. If the expression is true, the loop iterates. Otherwise, the loop stops.
- **Update:** This action takes place at the end of each loop iteration.

Figure 5-10 shows how these three actions are used in the logic of a `for` loop.

Here is the general format of the `for` loop:

```
for (InitializationExpression; TestExpression; UpdateExpression)
{
    statement;
    statement;
    etc.
}
```

The statements that appear inside the curly braces are the body of the loop. These are the statements that are executed each time the loop iterates. As with other control structures,

Figure 5-10 Logic of a `for` loop

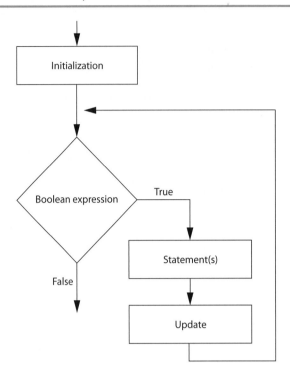

the curly braces are optional if the body of the loop contains only one statement, as shown in the following general format:

```
for (InitializationExpression; TestExpression; UpdateExpression)
    statement;
```

The first line of the `for` loop is the *loop header*. After the key word `for`, there are three expressions inside the parentheses, separated by semicolons. (Notice that there is not a semicolon after the third expression.)

The first expression is the **initialization expression**. It is normally used to initialize a counter variable to its starting value. This is the first action performed by the loop, and it is only done once. The second expression is the **test expression**. This is a Boolean expression that controls the execution of the loop. As long as this expression is true, the body of the `for` loop will repeat. The `for` loop is a pretest loop, so it evaluates the test expression before each iteration. The third expression is the **update expression**. It executes at the end of each iteration. Typically, this is a statement that increments the loop's counter variable.

Let's assume that `count` is an `int` variable that has already been declared. Here is an example of a simple `for` loop that displays "Hello" in a message box 5 times:

```
for (count = 1; count <= 5; count++)
{
    MessageBox.Show("Hello");
}
```

In this loop, the initialization expression is `count = 1`, the test expression is `count <= 5`, and the increment expression is `count++`. The body of the loop has one statement, which is the call to `MessageBox.Show` method. This is a summary of what happens when this loop executes:

1. The initialization expression `count = 1` is executed. This assigns 1 to the `count` variable.
2. The expression `count <= 5` is tested. If the expression is true, continue with Step 3. Otherwise, the loop is finished.
3. The statement `MessageBox.Show("Hello");` is executed.
4. The update expression `count++` is executed. This adds 1 to the `count` variable.
5. Go back to Step 2.

Figure 5-11 illustrates this sequence of events. Notice that Steps 2–4 are repeated as long as the test expression is true. Figure 5-12 shows the logic of the loop as a flowchart.

Figure 5-11 Sequence of events in the for loop

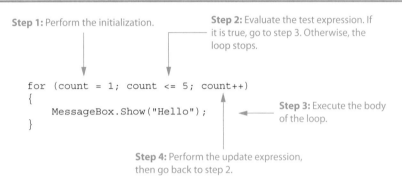

Figure 5-12 Logic of the for loop

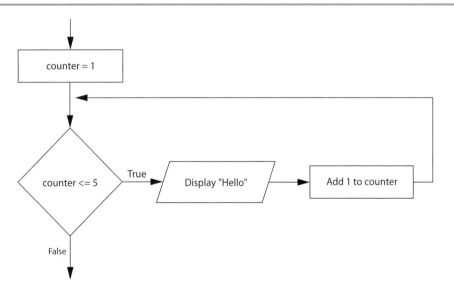

Let's look at a complete application that uses a `for` loop. In the *Chap05* folder of the Student Sample Programs that accompany this book, you will find a project named *Squares*. The purpose of the application is to display the numbers 1–10 and their squares. Figure 5-13 shows the application's form. As shown in the image on the left, the ListBox's name is `outputListBox` and the Button control's name is `goButton`. At run time, when you click the `goButton` control, the `outputListBox` control displays the program's output, as shown in the image on the right.

Figure 5-13 The *Squares* application

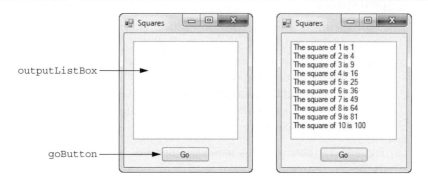

Here is the code for the `goButton_Click` event handler:

```
 1 private void goButton_Click(object sender, EventArgs e)
 2 {
 3     // Constant for the maximum number
 4     const int MAX_VALUE = 10;
 5
 6     // Loop counter
 7     int number;
 8
 9     // Display the list of numbers and their squares.
10     for (number = 1; number <= MAX_VALUE; number++)
11     {
12         outputListBox.Items.Add("The square of " +
13             number + " is " + (number * number));
14     }
15 }
```

Let's take a closer look at the code:

- Line 4 declares an `int` constant named `MAX_VALUE`, set to the value 10. This is the maximum number that we will use to calculate a square.
- Line 7 declares an `int` variable named `number`. This variable is used both as a counter variable and in the calculation of squares.
- Line 10 is the beginning of a `for` loop. You can see from this line that the loop works in the following way:

  Initialization: The `number` variable is initialized with the value 1.
  Test: The expression `number <= MAX_VALUE` is tested at the beginning of each iteration.
  Update: The expression `number++` is executed at the end of each iteration.
- Since the `MAX_VALUE` constant is set to the value 10, the `number` variable will be assigned the values 1 through 10 as the loop iterates.
- Lines 12 and 13: This statement adds a line to the ListBox showing the current value of the `number` variable, and the square of that value.

The `for` Loop Is a Pretest Loop

Because the `for` loop tests its Boolean expression before it performs an iteration, it is a pretest loop. It is possible to write a `for` loop in such a way that it will never iterate. Here is an example:

```
for (count = 6; count <= 5; count++)
{
    MessageBox.Show("Hello");
}
```

Because the variable count is initialized to a value that makes the Boolean expression false from the beginning, this loop terminates as soon as it begins.

Declaring the Counter Variable in the Initialization Expression

Not only may the counter variable be initialized in the initialization expression, but it may also be declared there. The following code shows an example:

```
for (int count = 1; count <= 5; count++)
{
    MessageBox.Show("Hello");
}
```

In this loop, the count variable is both declared and initialized in the initialization expression. If the variable is used only in the loop, it makes sense to define it in the loop header. This makes the variable's purpose clearer.

When a variable is declared in the initialization expression of a for loop, the scope of the variable is limited to the loop. This means you cannot access the variable in statements outside the loop. For example, the following code would cause a compiler error because the statement in line 6 cannot access the count variable.

```
1 for (int count = 1; count <= 5; count++)
2 {
3     MessageBox.Show("Hello");
4 }
5
6 MessageBox.Show("The value of count is " + count);
```

Other Forms of the Update Expression

In the update expression, the counter variable is typically incremented by 1. This makes it convenient to use the ++ operator in the increment expression. This is not a requirement, however. You can write virtually any expression you wish as the update expression. For example, the following loop increments count by 10.

```
for (int count = 0; count <= 100; count += 10)
{
    MessageBox.Show(count.ToString());
}
```

Notice that in this example the increment expression is count += 10. This means that at the end of each iteration, 10 is added to count. During the first iteration count is set to 0, during the second iteration count is set to 10, during the third iteration count is set to 20, and so forth.

Counting Backward by Decrementing the Counter Variable

Although the counter variable is usually incremented in a count-controlled loop, you can alternatively decrement the counter variable. For example, look at the following code:

```
for (int count = 10; count >= 0; count--)
{
    MessageBox.Show(count.ToString());
}
MessageBox.Show("Blastoff!");
```

In this loop the count variable is initialized with the value 10. The loop iterates as long as count is greater than or equal to 0. At the end of each iteration, count is decremented by 1.

During the first iteration count is 10, during the second iteration count is 9, and so forth. If this were in an actual program, it would display the numbers 10, 9, 8, and so forth, down to 0, and then display Blastoff!

Avoiding Modifying the Counter Variable in the Body of the `for` Loop

Be careful not to place a statement that modifies the counter variable in the body of the `for` loop. All modifications of the control variable should take place in the update expression, which is automatically executed at the end of each iteration. If a statement in the body of the loop also modifies the counter variable, the loop probably will not terminate when you expect it to. The following loop, for example, increments count twice for each iteration:

```
for (int count = 1; count <= 10; count++)
{
    MessageBox.Show(count.ToString());
    count++; // Wrong!
}
```

You have seen several examples of the `for` loop. Tutorial 5-3 gives you an opportunity to write one. In the tutorial you will complete an application that uses a `for` loop to convert a series of measurements from the metric system to the English system.

Tutorial 5-3:
Using the `for` Loop

Your friend Amanda just inherited a European sports car from her uncle. Amanda lives in the United States, and she is afraid she will get a speeding ticket because the car's speedometer works in kilometers per hour. She has asked you to write a program that displays a table of speeds in kilometers per hour with their values converted to miles per hour. The formula for converting kilometers per hour to miles per hour is:

$$MPH = KPH * 0.6214$$

In the formula, MPH is the speed in miles per hour and KPH is the speed in kilometers per hour.

The table that your program displays should show speeds from 60 kilometers per hour through 130 kilometers per hour, in increments of 10, along with their values converted to miles per hour. The table should look something like this:

KPH	MPH
60	37.284
70	43.498
80	49.712
etc. . . .	

After thinking about this table of values, you decide that you will write a `for` loop that uses a counter variable to hold the kilometers-per-hour speeds. The counter's starting value will be 60, its ending value will be 130, and you will increase its value by 10 in the update expression. Inside the loop you will use the counter variable to calculate a speed in miles per hour.

The project, which is named *Speed Converter*, has already been started for you. It is located in the *Chap05* folder of the Student Sample Programs that accompany this book. The application's form is shown in Figure 5-14. The image on the left in the figure shows the names of the controls. The image on the right shows how the form appears after the user clicks the *Display Speeds* button.

Figure 5-14 The *Speed Converter* form

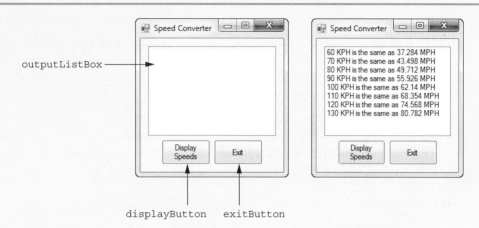

Step 1: Start Visual Studio (or Visual C# Express). Open the project named *Speed Converter* in the *Chap05* folder of the Student Sample Programs that accompany this book.

Step 2: Open the Form1 form in the *Designer*.

Step 3: In the *Designer*, double-click the displayButton control. This opens the code editor, and you will see an empty event handler named displayButton_Click. Complete the displayButton_Click event handler by typing the code shown in lines 21–40 in Program 5-3 (at the end of this tutorial). Let's take a closer look at the code:

Lines 22–25: These statements declare the following named constants:

- START_SPEED, an int constant set to 60. This is the starting speed for the list of conversions and the value with which the loop's counter variable is initialized.
- END_SPEED, an int constant set to 130. This is the ending speed for the list of conversions. When the counter variable exceeds this value, the loop stops.
- INTERVAL, an int constant set to 10. This is the amount that you add to loop's counter variable after each iteration.
- CONVERSION_FACTOR, a double constant set to 0.6214. This is the conversion factor that you use in the formula to convert KPH to MPH.

Lines 28–29: These statements declare the following variables:
- kph, an int variable to hold the speed in kilometers per hour.
- mph, a double variable to hold the speed in miles per hour.

Line 32: This is the beginning of a for loop that works in the following way:

Initialization: The kph variable is initialized with the value of START_SPEED, which is 60.

Test: The expression kph <= END_SPEED is tested at the beginning of each iteration.

Update: The expression kph += INTERVAL is executed at the end of each iteration. This adds the value of INTERVAL (which is 10) to the kph variable.

As the loop iterates, the kph variable is assigned the values 60, 70, 80, and so forth, through 130.

Line 35: This statement converts the value of the kph variable to miles per hour and assigns the result to the mph variable.

Lines 38–39: This statement adds a line to the outputListBox control showing the current value of the kph variable and the equivalent value in miles per hour.

Step 4: Switch your view back to the *Designer* and double-click the exitButton control. In the code editor you will see an empty event handler named exitButton_Click. Complete the exitButton_Click event handler by typing the code shown in lines 45–46 in Program 5-3.

Step 5: Save the project. Then, press F5 on the keyboard or click the *Start Debugging* button (▶) on the toolbar to compile and run the application. Click the *Display Speeds* button, and you should see the output shown in the image on the right in Figure 5-14. Click the exit button to close the form.

Program 5-3 Completed Form1 code for the *Speed Converter* application

```
 1 using System;
 2 using System.Collections.Generic;
 3 using System.ComponentModel;
 4 using System.Data;
 5 using System.Drawing;
 6 using System.Linq;
 7 using System.Text;
 8 using System.Windows.Forms;
 9
10 namespace Speed_Converter
11 {
12     public partial class Form1 : Form
13     {
14         public Form1()
15         {
16             InitializeComponent();
17         }
18
19         private void displayButton_Click(object sender, EventArgs e)
20         {
21             // Constants
22             const int START_SPEED = 60;
23             const int END_SPEED = 130;
24             const int INTERVAL = 10;
25             const double CONVERSION_FACTOR = 0.6214;
26
27             // Variables
28             int kph;        // Kilometers per hour
29             double mph;     // Miles per hour
30
31             // Display the table of speeds.
32             for (kph = START_SPEED; kph <= END_SPEED; kph += INTERVAL)
33             {
```

```
34                          // Calculate miles per hour.
35                          mph = kph * CONVERSION_FACTOR;
36
37                          // Display the conversion.
38                          outputListBox.Items.Add(kph + " KPH is the same as " +
39                              mph + " MPH");
40                  }
41              }
42
43          private void exitButton_Click(object sender, EventArgs e)
44          {
45                  // Close the form.
46                  this.Close();
47          }
48      }
49 }
```

 Checkpoint

5.11 Name the three expressions that appear inside the parentheses in the first line of a for loop.

5.12 You want to write a for loop that displays *I love to program* 50 times. Assume that you will use a variable named count as the counter variable.

    a. What initialization expression will you use?
    b. What test expression will you use?
    c. What update expression will you use?
    d. Write the loop.

5.13 What would the following code display?

```
for (int count = 1; count <= 5; count++)
{
    MessageBox.Show(count.ToString());
}
```

5.14 What would the following code display?

```
for (int count = 0; count <= 500; count += 100)
{
    MessageBox.Show(count.ToString());
}
```

5.5 The do-while Loop

CONCEPT: The do-while loop is a posttest loop, which means it performs an iteration before testing its Boolean expression.

You have learned that the while loop and the for are pretest loops, which means they test their Boolean expressions before performing an iteration. The do-while loop is a **posttest loop**. This means it performs an iteration before testing its Boolean expression. As a result, the do-while loop always performs at least one iteration, even if its Boolean expression is false to begin with. The logic of a do-while loop is shown in Figure 5-15.

Figure 5-15 The logic of a do—while loop

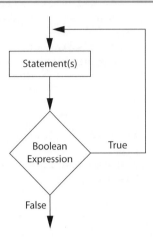

In the flowchart, one or more statements are executed, and then a Boolean expression is tested. If the Boolean expression is true, the program's execution flows back to the point just above the first statement in the body of the loop, and this process repeats. If the Boolean expression is false, the program exits the loop.

In code, the do-while loop looks something like an inverted while loop. Here is the general format of the do-while loop:

```
do
{
    statement;
    statement;
    etc;
} while (BooleanExpression);
```

As with the while loop, the braces are optional if there is only one statement in the body of the loop. This is the general format of the do-while loop with only one conditionally executed statement:

```
do
    statement;
while (BooleanExpression);
```

Notice that a semicolon appears at the very end of the do-while statement. This semicolon is required; leaving it out is a common error.

The do-while loop is a *posttest* loop. This means it does not test its Boolean expression until it has completed an iteration. As a result, the do-while loop always performs at least one iteration, even if the expression is false to begin with. This differs from the behavior of a while loop. For example, in the following while loop, the statement that calls MessageBox.Show will not execute at all:

```
int number = 1;
while (number < 0)
{
    MessageBox.Show(number.ToString());
}
```

But, the statement that calls MessageBox.Show in the following do-while loop executes one time because the do-while loop does not test the expression number < 0 until the end of the iteration.

```
int number = 1;
do
```

```
    {
        MessageBox.Show(number.ToString());
    } while (number < 0);
```

 Checkpoint

5.15 What is a posttest loop?

5.16 What is the difference between the `while` loop and the `do-while` loop?

5.17 How many times will the following loop iterate?
```
int count = 0;
do
{
    MessageBox.Show(count.ToString());
    count++;
} while (count < 0);
```

5.6 Using Files for Data Storage

CONCEPT: When a program needs to save data for later use, it writes the data in a file. The data can be read from the file at a later time.

The programs you have written so far require the user to reenter data each time the program runs because data kept in variables and control properties is stored in RAM and disappears once the program stops running. If a program is to retain data between the times it runs, it must have a way of saving it. Data is saved in a file, which is usually stored on a computer's disk. Once the data is saved in a file, it will remain there after the program stops running. Data that is stored in a file can be retrieved and used at a later time.

Most of the commercial software that you use on a day-to-day basis store data in files. The following are a few examples.

- **Word processors:** Word processing programs are used to write letters, memos, reports, and other documents. The documents are then saved in files so they can be edited and printed.
- **Image editors:** Image-editing programs are used to draw graphics and edit images, such as the ones that you take with a digital camera. The images that you create or edit with an image editor are saved in files.
- **Spreadsheets:** Spreadsheet programs are used to work with numerical data. Numbers and mathematical formulas can be inserted into the rows and columns of the spreadsheet. The spreadsheet can then be saved in a file for use later.
- **Games:** Many computer games keep data stored in files. For example, some games keep a list of player names with their scores stored in a file. These games typically display the players' names in order of their scores, from highest to lowest. Some games also allow you to save your current game status in a file so you can quit the game and then resume playing it later without having to start from the beginning.
- **Web browsers:** Sometimes when you visit a Web page, the browser stores a small file known as a *cookie* on your computer. Cookies typically contain information about the browsing session, such as the contents of a shopping cart.

Programs that are used in daily business operations rely extensively on files. Payroll programs keep employee data in files, inventory programs keep data about a company's products in files, accounting systems keep data about a company's financial operations in files, and so on.

Programmers usually refer to the process of saving data in a file as *writing data* to the file. When a piece of data is written to a file, it is copied from a variable in RAM to the file. This is illustrated in Figure 5-16. The term **output file** is used to describe a file to which data is written. It is called an output file because the program stores output in it.

Figure 5-16 Writing data to a file

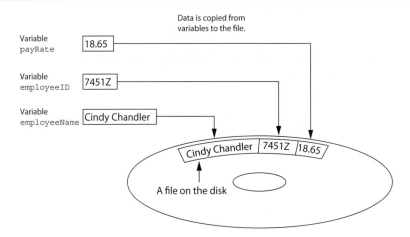

The process of retrieving data from a file is known as *reading data* from the file. When a piece of data is read from a file, it is copied from the file into a variable in RAM. Figure 5-17 illustrates this. The term **input file** is used to describe a file from which data is read. It is called an input file because the program gets input from the file.

Figure 5-17 Reading data from a file

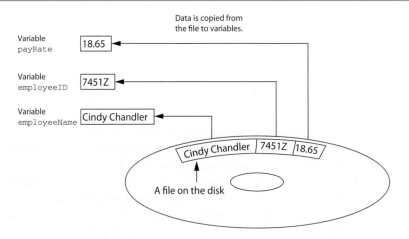

In this section we discuss ways to create programs that write data to files and read data from files. There are always three steps that must be taken when a file is used by a program.

1. **Open the file**—Opening a file creates a connection between the file and the program. Opening an output file usually creates the file on the disk and allows the program to write data to it. Opening an input file allows the program to read data from the file.
2. **Process the file**—In this step data is either written to the file (if it is an output file) or read from the file (if it is an input file).
3. **Close the file**—When the program is finished using the file, the file must be closed. Closing a file disconnects the file from the program.

Types of Files

In general, there are two types of files: text and binary. A **text file** contains data that has been encoded as text using a scheme such as Unicode. Even if the file contains numbers, those numbers are stored in the file as a series of characters. As a result, the file may be opened and viewed in a text editor such as Notepad. A **binary file** contains data that has not been converted to text. As a consequence, you cannot view the contents of a binary file with a text editor. In this chapter we work only with text files.

File Access Methods

Most programming languages provide two different ways to access data stored in a file: sequential access and direct access. When you work with a **sequential access file**, you access data from the beginning of the file to the end of the file. If you want to read a piece of data that is stored at the very end of the file, you have to read all the data that comes before it—you cannot jump directly to the desired data. This is similar to the way cassette tape players work. If you want to listen to the last song on a cassette tape, you have to either fast-forward over all of the songs that come before it or listen to them. There is no way to jump directly to a specific song.

When you work with a **direct access file** (which is also known as a **random access file**), you can jump directly to any piece of data in the file without reading the data that comes before it. This is similar to the way a CD player or an MP3 player works. You can jump directly to any song you want to listen to.

This chapter focuses on sequential access files. Sequential access files are easy to work with, and you can use them to gain an understanding of basic file operations.

Filenames and File Objects

Files on a disk are identified by a **filename**. For example, when you create a document with a word processor and then save the document in a file, you have to specify a filename. When you use a utility such as Windows Explorer to examine the contents of your disk, you see a list of filenames. Figure 5-18 shows how three files named cat.jpg, notes.txt, and resume.doc might be represented in Windows Explorer.

Figure 5-18 Three files

cat.jpg   notes.txt   resume.doc

Each operating system has its own rules for naming files. Many systems, including Windows, support the use of **filename extensions**, which are short sequences of characters that appear at the end of a filename and are preceded by a period (which is known as a "dot"). For example, the files depicted in Figure 5-18 have the extensions .jpg, .txt, and .doc. The extension usually indicates the type of data stored in the file. For example, the .jpg extension usually indicates that the file contains a graphic image that is compressed according to the JPEG image standard. The .txt extension usually indicates that the file contains text. The .doc extension usually indicates that the file contains a Microsoft Word document.

In order for a program to work with a file on the computer's disk, the program must create a file object in memory. A **file object** is an object that is associated with a specific file and provides a way for the program to work with that file. In the program, a variable is linked with the file object. We say that the variable *references* the object. This variable is used to carry out any operations that are performed on the file. This concept is shown in Figure 5-19.

Figure 5-19 A variable referencing a file object that is associated with a file

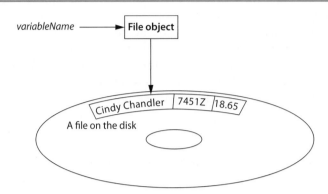

You will be using two classes from the .NET Framework to create file objects. When you want to write data to a text file, you use the **StreamWriter** class, and when you want to read data from a text file you use the **StreamReader** class. These classes are in the System.IO namespace in the .NET Framework, so you will need to write the following directive at the top of your programs:

```
using System.IO;
```

NOTE: In programming terminology, files are considered streams of data. In C# you use a StreamWriter object to open a stream, such as a file, and write data to it. You use a StreamReader object to open a stream, such as a file, and read data from it.

Writing Data to a File with a StreamWriter Object

You can use the StreamWriter class's **WriteLine** method to write a line of text to a file. Let's suppose you want to write a program that creates a text file named courses.txt and writes the names of the courses you are taking to the file. The following code sample shows how you can this:

```
1 StreamWriter outputFile;
2 outputFile = File.CreateText("courses.txt");
3
4 outputFile.WriteLine("Intro to Computer Science");
5 outputFile.WriteLine("English Composition");
6 outputFile.WriteLine("Calculus I");
7 outputFile.WriteLine("Music Appreciation");
8
9 outputFile.Close();
```

Let's look at each line of code.

Line 1: This statement declares a variable named outputFile, which can be used to reference a StreamWriter object.

Line 2: In a nutshell, this statement opens the file to which you will be writing data. It does so by calling the File.CreateText method, passing the string "courses.txt" as an argument. The File.CreateText method does the following:

- It creates a text file with the name specified by the argument. If the file already exists, its contents are erased.
- It creates a StreamWriter object in memory, associated with the file.
- It returns a reference to the StreamWriter object.

Notice that an assignment operator assigns the value returned from the `File.CreateText` method to the `outputFile` variable. This causes the `outputFile` variable to reference the `StreamWriter` object that was created by the method.

After the statement in line 2 executes, the courses.txt file is created on the disk, a `StreamWriter` object associated with the file exists in memory, and the `outputFile` variable references that object.

Line 4: This statement writes the string `"Intro to Computer Science"` to the courses.txt file. It does that by calling the `StreamWriter` class's `WriteLine` method, passing the string that is to be written to the file as an argument. When the `WriteLine` method writes data to a file, it writes a newline character immediately following the data. A **newline character** is an invisible character that specifies the end of a line of text.

Line 5: This statement writes the string `"English Composition"` to the courses.txt file.

Line 6: This statement writes the string `"Calculus I"` to the courses.txt file.

Line 7: This statement writes the string `"Music Appreciation"` to the courses.txt file.

Line 9: This statement closes the courses.txt file. It does that by calling the `StreamWriter` class's `Close` method.

After this code has executed, we can open the courses.txt file using a text editor and look at its contents. Figure 5-20 show how the file's contents will appear in Notepad.

Figure 5-20 Contents of the courses.txt file shown in Notepad

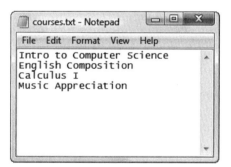

Writing Data with the `Write` Method

Earlier you read that the `StreamWriter` class's `WriteLine` method writes an item of data to a file and then writes a newline character. The newline character specifies the end of a line of text. For example, the following code sample opens a file named Example.txt and then uses the `WriteLine` method to write the strings `"One"`, `"Two"`, and `"Three"` to the file. Because a newline character is written after each string, the strings appear on separate lines when viewed in a text editor. The screen shown on the left in Figure 5-21 shows how the file would appear in Notepad.

```
1 StreamWriter outputFile;
2 outputFile = File.CreateText("Example.txt");
3
4 outputFile.WriteLine("One");
5 outputFile.WriteLine("Two");
6 outputFile.WriteLine("Three");
7
8 outputFile.Close();
```

Figure 5-21 Items written with the `WriteLine` and `Write` methods

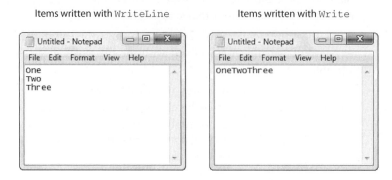

Items written with `WriteLine`   Items written with `Write`

In some situations you might want to write an item to a file without a newline character immediately following it. The `StreamWriter` class provides the **Write method** for this purpose. It writes an item of data to a text file without writing a newline character. The following code sample demonstrates. The screen shown on the right in Figure 5-21 shows how the resulting file would appear in Notepad.

```
1 StreamWriter outputFile;
2 outputFile = File.CreateText("Example.txt");
3
4 outputFile.Write("One");
5 outputFile.Write("Two");
6 outputFile.Write("Three");
7
8 outputFile.Close();
```

Handling File-Related Exceptions

Unexpected problems can potentially occur when working with files. For example, your program might not have sufficient rights to create a file when it calls the `File.CreateText` method, or the disk might be full when you call the `StreamWriter` class's `WriteLine` method. When unexpected errors such as these occur, an exception is thrown. To handle such exceptions, you can write a `try-catch` statement, with the code that performs file operations placed in the try block. Here is an example:

```
1 try
2 {
3     StreamWriter outputFile;
4     outputFile = File.CreateText("courses.txt");
5
6     outputFile.WriteLine("Intro to Computer Science");
7     outputFile.WriteLine("English Composition");
8     outputFile.WriteLine("Calculus I");
9     outputFile.WriteLine("Music Appreciation");
10
11     outputFile.Close();
12 }
13 catch (Exception ex)
14 {
15     // Display an error message.
16     MessageBox.Show(ex.Message);
17 }
```

In Tutorial 5-4 you will complete an application that reads input from a TextBox control and writes the input to a file.

Tutorial 5-4:
Writing Data to a Text File

In this tutorial you complete the *Friend File* application. The project has already been started for you and is located in the *Chap05* folder of the Student Sample Programs that accompany this book. The application's form is shown in Figure 5-22.

Figure 5-22 The *Friend File* form

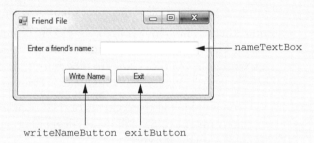

When you complete the application, it will allow the user to enter a name into the `nameTextBox` control. When the user clicks the `writeNameButton` control, the application opens a text file named Friend.txt, writes the name that was entered into the TextBox control to the file, and then closes the file.

Step 1: Start Visual Studio (or Visual C# Express). Open the project named *Ending Balance* in the *Chap05* folder of the Student Sample Programs that accompany this book.

Step 2: Open the Form1 form's code in the code editor. Insert the **using System.IO;** directive shown in line 9 of Program 5-4 at the end of this tutorial. This statement is necessary because the `StreamWriter` class is part of the `System.IO` namespace in the .NET Framework.

Step 3: Open the Form1 form in the *Designer*. The form is shown, along with the names of the important controls, in Figure 5-22. Double-click the `writeNameButton` control. This opens the code editor, and you will see an empty event handler named `writeNameButton_Click`. Complete the `writeNameButton_Click` event handler by typing the code shown in lines 22–35 in Program 5-4. Let's take a closer look at the code:

Line 22: This is the beginning of a `try-catch` statement. The try block appears in lines 24–37, and the catch block appears in lines 41–42. If an exception is thrown by any statement in the try block, the program jumps to the catch block, and line 42 displays an error message.

Line 25: This statement declares a `StreamWriter` variable named `outputFile`. You use this variable to reference a `StreamWriter` object.

Line 28: This statement calls the `File.CreateText` method to create a text file named Friend.txt. The method also creates a `StreamWriter` object in memory associated with the file. The method returns a reference to that object, which is assigned to the `outputFile` variable. As a result, the `outputFile` variable references the `StreamWriter` object. You will be able to use the `outputFile` variable to perform operations on the Friend.txt file.

Line 31: This statement uses the `outputFile` variable to call the `StreamWriter` class's `WriteLine` method. The `nameTextBox` control's Text property is passed as an argument. As a result, the value entered into the TextBox is written to the Friend.txt file.

Line 34: This statement closes the Friend.txt file.

Line 37: This statement displays a message box to let the user know that the name was written to the file.

Step 4: Switch your view back to the *Designer* and double-click the `exitButton` control. In the code editor you will see an empty event handler named `exitButton_Click`. Complete the `exitButton_Click` event handler by typing the code shown in lines 48–49 in Program 5-4.

Step 5: Save the project. Then, press `F5` on the keyboard or click the *Start Debugging* button (▶) on the toolbar to compile and run the application.

Enter a name into the `nameTextBox` control, and then click the *Write Name* button. You should see a message box appear letting you know that the name was written to the file. Click the *OK* button to dismiss the message box; then click the *Exit* button on the application's form to end the application.

Step 6: Now you will look at the contents of the Friend.txt file that the application created. Perform one of the following, depending on whether you are using Visual Studio or Visual C# Express:

- If you are using Visual Studio, click *File* on the menu bar, then click *Open*, and then click *File*.

- If you are using Visual C# Express, click *File* on the menu bar, and then click *Open File*.

Step 7: You should now see the *Open File* window, viewing the contents of the *Friend File* project folder. As shown in Figure 5-23, open the *bin* folder, then open the

Figure 5-23 Opening the Friend.txt file in the *Open File* window

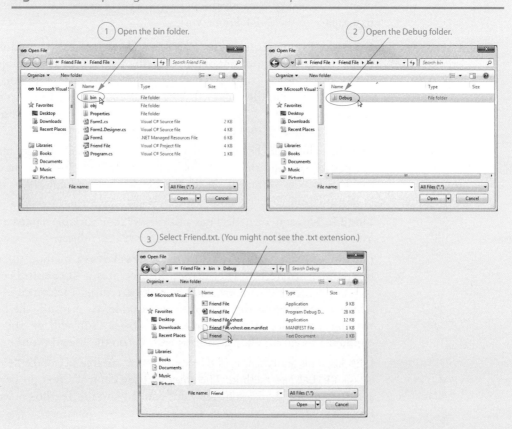

Debug folder, and then select the file *Friend.txt*. (You might not see the .txt extension, depending on how your system is set up.) Click the *Open* button.

Step 8: You should now see the contents of the Friend.txt file in Visual Studio, as shown in Figure 5-24. (The example in the figure shows the contents of the file after the user has written *Tim Owens* to the file.) When you are finished examining the contents of the file, you can close its tab. We come back to this project in the next tutorial.

Figure 5-24 Sample contents of the Friend.txt file shown in Visual Studio

Program 5-4 Completed Form1 code for the *Friend File* application

```
 1 using System;
 2 using System.Collections.Generic;
 3 using System.ComponentModel;
 4 using System.Data;
 5 using System.Drawing;
 6 using System.Linq;
 7 using System.Text;
 8 using System.Windows.Forms;
 9 using System.IO;
10
11 namespace Friend_File
12 {
13     public partial class Form1 : Form
14     {
15         public Form1()
16         {
17             InitializeComponent();
18         }
19
20         private void writeNameButton_Click(object sender, EventArgs e)
21         {
22             try
23             {
24                 // Declare a StreamWriter variable.
25                 StreamWriter outputFile;
26
27                 // Create a file and get a StreamWriter object.
28                 outputFile = File.CreateText("Friend.txt");
29
30                 // Write the friend's name to the file.
31                 outputFile.WriteLine(nameTextBox.Text);
32
33                 // Close the file.
34                 outputFile.Close();
```

```
35
36                          // Let the user know the name was written.
37                          MessageBox.Show("The name was written.");
38                      }
39              catch (Exception ex)
40              {
41                          // Display an error message.
42                          MessageBox.Show(ex.Message);
43              }
44          }
45
46          private void exitButton_Click(object sender, EventArgs e)
47          {
48              // Close the form.
49              this.Close();
50          }
51      }
52 }
```

Writing Numeric Data to a Text File

You can use the StreamWriter class's WriteLine or Write methods to write numbers (such as ints, doubles, and decimals) to a text file, but the numbers are converted to strings. For example, look at the following sample code (taken from the *Number File* project in the *Chap05* folder of the Student Sample Programs):

```
1 private void writeNumbersButton_Click(object sender, EventArgs e)
2 {
3     try
4     {
5         // Declare a StreamWriter variable.
6         StreamWriter outputFile;
7
8         // Create a file and get a StreamWriter object.
9         outputFile = File.CreateText("Numbers.txt");
10
11         // Write the numbers 1 through 10 to the file.
12         for (int count = 1; count <= 10; count++)
13         {
14             outputFile.WriteLine(count);
15         }
16
17         // Close the file.
18         outputFile.Close();
19     }
20     catch (Exception ex)
21     {
22         // Display an error message.
23         MessageBox.Show(ex.Message);
24     }
25 }
```

When this event handler executes, line 9 creates a text file named Numbers.txt, and the loop in lines 12–15 writes the numbers 1–10 to the file. Figure 5-25 shows how the file appears when opened with Notepad.

Figure 5-25 The Numbers.txt file opened in Notepad

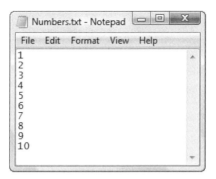

Appending Data to an Existing File

When you call the `File.CreateText` method to open a file and the file specified by the argument already exists, it is erased and a new empty file with the same name is created. For example, when you run the *Friend File* application that you completed in Tutorial 5-4, each time you click the *Write Name* button, the Friend.txt file is erased and a new file is created.

Sometimes you want to preserve an existing file and append new data to its current contents. To append data to an existing file, you open it with the `File.AppendText` method. It works like the `File.CreateText` method, but the file is not erased if it already exists. Any data written to the file is appended to the file's existing contents.

For example, assume the file Names.txt exists and contains the data shown in Figure 5-26:

Figure 5-26 Names.txt file

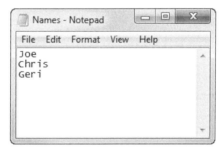

The following code opens the file and appends additional data to its existing contents:

```
1 StreamWriter outputFile;
2 outputFile = File.AppendText("Names.txt");
3
4 outputFile.WriteLine("Lynn");
5 outputFile.WriteLine("Steve");
6 outputFile.WriteLine("Bill");
7
8 outputFile.Close();
```

After this code executes, the Names.txt file contains the data shown in Figure 5-27:

Figure 5-27 Names.txt file after data has been appended

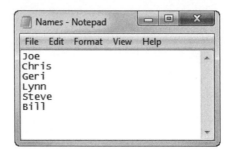

Tutorial 5-5:
Appending Data to the Friend.txt File

In this tutorial you will modify the *Friend File* application so it appends data to the Friend.txt file. When the user clicks the *Write Name* button, instead of erasing the file's current contents, the application adds the contents of the `nameTextBox` control to the Friend.txt file.

Step 1: If the *Friend File* project from Tutorial 5-4 is not currently open in Visual Studio (or Visual C# Express), open it now.

Step 2: Open the Form1 form's code in the code editor. You will make modifications to the `writeNameButton_Click` event handler. Program 5-5, at the end of this tutorial, shows how the event handler code will appear after you make the following changes:

Lines 8 and 9: Change the comments as shown to reflect the way that the Friend.txt file will be opened in line 10.

Line 10: Change this statement so it calls the `File.AppendText` method instead of the `File.CreateText` method.

Lines 21–25: Add the new comments and statements shown in these lines. Line 22 clears the `nameTextBox` control's contents, and line 25 gives the focus to the `nameTextBox` control. This makes the application more convenient for adding several names to the file.

Step 3: Save the project. Then, press F5 on the keyboard or click the *Start Debugging* button (▶) on the toolbar to compile and run the application.

Enter a name into the `nameTextBox` control and then click the *Write Name* button. You should see a message box letting you know that the name was written to the file. When you click the *OK* button to dismiss the message box, notice that the `nameTextBox` is cleared, and the focus is given to the TextBox. Enter another name, and click the *Write Name* button. Again, you see the message box. Click the *OK* button to dismiss the message box and then click the *Exit* button to end the application.

Step 4: Now you will look at the contents of the Friend.txt file.

• If you are using Visual Studio, click *File* on the menu bar, then click *Open*, and then click *File*.

• If you are using Visual C# Express, click *File* on the menu bar and then click *Open File*.

You should now see the *Open File* window, viewing the contents of the *Friend File* project folder. Open the *bin* folder, then open the *Debug* folder, and then select the file *Friend.txt*. (You might not see the .txt extension, depending on how your system is set up.) Click the *Open* button.

Step 5: You should now see the contents of the Friend.txt file in Visual Studio. Figure 5-28 shows an example. Notice that the names that you entered were appended to the file each time you clicked the *Write Name* button. When you are finished examining the contents of the file, you can close its tab. We come back to this project in the next tutorial.

Figure 5-28 Sample contents of the Friend.txt file shown in Visual Studio

Program 5-5 Partial code for Form1 in the *Friend File* application

```
 1 private void writeNameButton_Click(object sender, EventArgs e)
 2 {
 3     try
 4     {
 5         // Declare a StreamWriter variable.
 6         StreamWriter outputFile;
 7
 8         // Open the Friend.txt file for appending,
 9         // and get a StreamWriter object.
10         outputFile = File.AppendText("Friend.txt");
11
12         // Write the friend's name to the file.
13         outputFile.WriteLine(nameTextBox.Text);
14
15         // Close the file.
16         outputFile.Close();
17
18         // Let the user know the name was written.
19         MessageBox.Show("The name was written.");
20
21         // Clear the nameTextBox control.
22         nameTextBox.Text = "";
23
24         // Give the focus to the nameTextBox control.
25         nameTextBox.Focus();
26     }
27     catch (Exception ex)
28     {
29         // Display an error message.
30         MessageBox.Show(ex.Message);
31     }
32 }
```

Specifying the Location of an Output File

When you call the `File.CreateText` or `File.AppendText` methods to open a file, you pass the filename as a string argument. If the filename that you pass as an argument does not contain the file's path, the file's location will be the *bin\Debug* folder, under the application's project folder. You saw this in Tutorials 5-4 and 5-5 when you opened the Friend.txt file in Visual Studio.

If you want to open a file in a different location, you can specify a path as well as a filename in the argument that you pass to the `File.CreateText` or `File.AppendText` methods. If you specify a path in a string literal, be sure to prefix the string with the @ character. Here is an example:

```
StreamWriter outputFile;
outputFile = File.CreateText(@"C:\Users\Chris\Documents\Names.txt");
```

> **TIP:** You can also let the user specify the file location. See Section 5.7 for more information on the SaveFileDialog control.

Reading Data from a File with a `StreamReader` Object

To read data from a text file, you create a `StreamReader` object. You can then use the `StreamReader` class's **ReadLine** method to read a line of text from a file. For example, suppose a file named Students.txt exists and contains the four names shown in Figure 5-29.

Figure 5-29 Contents of the Students.txt file

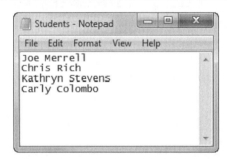

Let's suppose you want to write a program that reads the four names from the Students.txt file and displays them in message boxes. The following code sample shows how you can do this. (This code sample is taken from the *Student Names* project, in the *Chap05* folder of the Student Sample Programs that accompany this book.)

```
 1 try
 2 {
 3     // Declare a variable to hold an item read from the file.
 4     string studentName;
 5
 6     // Declare a StreamReader variable.
 7     StreamReader inputFile;
 8
 9     // Open the file and get a StreamReader object.
10     inputFile = File.OpenText("Students.txt");
11
```

```
12      // Read and display the first name.
13      studentName = inputFile.ReadLine();
14      MessageBox.Show(studentName);
15
16      // Read and display the second name.
17      studentName = inputFile.ReadLine();
18      MessageBox.Show(studentName);
19
20      // Read and display the third name.
21      studentName = inputFile.ReadLine();
22      MessageBox.Show(studentName);
23
24      // Read and display the fourth name.
25      studentName = inputFile.ReadLine();
26      MessageBox.Show(studentName);
27
28      // Close the file.
29      inputFile.Close();
30 }
31 catch (Exception ex)
32 {
33      // Display an error message.
34      MessageBox.Show(ex.Message);
35 }
```

Let's take a closer look at the code.

Line 1: This is the beginning of a `try-catch` statement. An exception will be thrown in the try block if a problem occurs while the file is being opened or while an item is being read from the file. If that happens, the program jumps to the `catch` clause in line 31.

Line 4: This statement declares a `string` variable named `studentName`. Each time we read a line of text from the file, we assign it to this variable.

Line 7: This statement declares a variable named `inputFile` that can be used to reference a `StreamReader` object.

Line 10: This statement opens the file from which we will be reading data. It does so by calling the `File.OpenText` method, passing the string `"Students.txt"` as an argument. The `File.OpenText` method does the following:

- It opens an existing text file with the name specified by the argument. If the file does not exist, an exception is thrown.
- It creates a `StreamReader` object in memory associated with the file.
- It returns a reference to the `StreamReader` object.

Notice that an assignment operator assigns the value returned from the `File.OpenText` method to the `inputFile` variable. This causes the `inputFile` variable to reference the `StreamReader` object that was created by the method.

Line 13: This statement calls the `inputFile.ReadLine` method, which reads a line of text from the file. The line of text is returned as a string from the method and assigned to the `studentName` variable. Since this statement reads the first line of text from the file, the `studentName` variable is assigned the string "Joe Merrell".

Line 14: This statement displays the contents of the `studentName` variable in a message box.

Lines 17 and 18: The statement in line 17 reads the next line of text from the file and assigns it to the `studentName` variable. After this line executes, the `studentName` variable is assigned the string "Chris Rich". The statement in line 18 displays the contents of the `studentName` variable in a message box.

Lines 21 and 22: The statement in line 21 reads the next line of text from the file and assigns it to the `studentName` variable. After this line executes, the `studentName` variable is assigned the string "Kathryn Stevens". The statement in line 22 displays the contents of the `studentName` variable in a message box.

Lines 25 and 26: The statement in line 25 reads the next line of text from the file and assigns it to the `studentName` variable. After this line executes, the `studentName` variable is assigned the string "Carly Colombo". The statement in line 26 displays the contents of the `studentName` variable in a message box.

Line 29: This statement closes the Students.txt file.

The Read Position

When a program works with an input file, a special value known as a **read position** is internally maintained for that file. A file's read position marks the location of the next item that will be read from the file. When an input file is opened, its read position is initially set to the first item in the file. As items are read from the file, the read position moves forward, toward the end of the file. Let's see how this works in the previous code sample (from the *Student Names* project) After the statement in line 10 executes, the read position for the Students.txt file is positioned as shown in Figure 5-30.

Figure 5-30 The initial read position

The `ReadLine` method call in line 13 reads an item from the file's current read position and assigns that item to the `studentName` variable. Once this statement executes, the `studentName` variable is assigned the string "Joe Merrell". In addition, the file's read position is advanced to the next item in the file, as shown in Figure 5-31.

Figure 5-31 Read position after the first `ReadLine` method call

The `ReadLine` method call in line 17 reads an item from the file's current read position and assigns that value to the `studentName` variable. Once this statement executes, the `studentName` variable is assigned the string "Chris Rich". The file's read position is advanced to the next item, as shown in Figure 5-32.

Figure 5-32 Read position after the second `ReadLine` method call

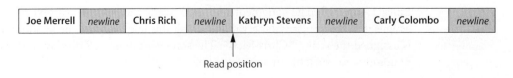

The `ReadLine` method call in line 21 reads an item from the file's current read position and assigns that value to the `studentName` variable. Once this statement executes, the `studentName` variable is assigned the string "Kathryn Stevens". The file's read position is advanced to the next item, as shown in Figure 5-33.

Figure 5-33 Read position after the third `ReadLine` method call

The last `ReadLine` method call appears in line 25. It reads an item from the file's current read position and assigns that value to the `studentName` variable. Once this statement executes, the `studentName` variable is assigned the string "Carly Colombo". The file's read position is advanced to the end of the file, as shown in Figure 5-34.

Figure 5-34 Read position after the fourth `ReadLine` method call

 NOTE: Did you notice that the previous code sample read the items in the Students.txt file in sequence, from the beginning of the file to the end of the file? Recall from our discussion at the beginning of the section that this is the nature of a sequential access file.

Reading Numeric Data from a Text File

Remember that when data is stored in a text file, it is encoded as text, using a scheme such as Unicode. Even if the file contains numbers, those numbers are stored in the file as a series of characters. Furthermore, when you read an item from a text file with the `StreamReader` class's `ReadLine` method, that item is returned as a string.

Suppose a text file contains numeric data, such as that shown in Figure 5-35. When we use the `ReadLine` method to read the items from the file, we get the strings "10", "20", and "30". If we need to perform math with these values, we must convert each value from a string to a numeric data type. We can use the `Parse` or `TryParse` families of methods that you already know about to perform this conversion.

Figure 5-35 A text file containing numeric data

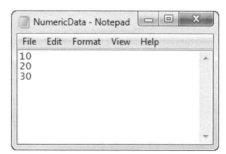

Let's suppose you want to write a program that reads the three numbers from the NumericData.txt file shown in Figure 5-35 and displays their total in a message box. The following code sample shows a simple demonstration. (This code sample is taken from the *Numeric Data* project in the *Chap05* folder of the Student Sample Programs that accompany this book.)

```
 1 try
 2 {
 3      // Variables to hold the numbers read from the file
 4      // and their total
 5      int number1, number2, number3, total;
 6
 7      // A StreamReader variable.
 8      StreamReader inputFile;
 9
10      // Open the file and get a StreamReader object.
11      inputFile = File.OpenText("NumericData.txt");
12
13      // Read three numbers from the file.
14      number1 = int.Parse(inputFile.ReadLine());
15      number2 = int.Parse(inputFile.ReadLine());
16      number3 = int.Parse(inputFile.ReadLine());
17
18      // Calculate the total of the numbers.
19      total = number1 + number2 + number3;
20
21      // Display the total.
22      MessageBox.Show("The total is " + total);
23
24      // Close the file.
25      inputFile.Close();
26 }
27 catch (Exception ex)
28 {
29      // Display an error message.
30      MessageBox.Show(ex.Message);
31 }
```

Let's take a closer look at the code.

Line 1: This is the beginning of a `try-catch` statement. Various exceptions can be thrown by the code in the try block, which cause the program to jump to the `catch` clause in line 27.

Line 5: This statement declares the `int` variables `number1`, `number2`, `number3`, and `total`. These variables hold the three values read from the file and their total.

Lines 8–11: After these statements have executed, the NumericData.txt file is opened for reading, and the `inputFile` variable references a `StreamReader` object that is associated with the file.

Line 14: This statement does the following:

- It calls the `inputFile.ReadLine` method to read a line of text from the file.

- The value that is returned from the `inputFile.ReadLine` method (a string), is passed as an argument to the `int.Parse` method.

- The value that is returned from the `int.Parse` method is assigned to the `number1` variable.

After this statement executes, the `number1` variable is assigned the first value read from the file, converted to an `int`. (The `number1` variable are assigned the value 10.)

Line 15: This statement reads the next value from the file, converts it to an `int`, and assigns the result to the `number2` variable. (The `number2` variable is assigned the value 20.)

Line 16: This statement reads the next value from the file, converts it to an `int`, and assigns the result to the `number3` variable. (The `number3` variable is assigned the value 30.)

Line 19: This statement calculates the sum of `number1`, `number2`, and `number3`, and assigns the result to `total`.

Line 22: This statement displays the sum of the numbers in a message box.

Line 25: This statement closes the file.

Reading a File with a Loop and Detecting the End of the File

Quite often a program must read the contents of a file without knowing the number of items that are stored in the file. For example, suppose you need to write a program that displays all the items in a file, but you do not know how many items the file contains. You can open the file and then use a loop to repeatedly read an item from the file and display it. However, an exception will be thrown if the program attempts to read beyond the end of the file. The program needs some way of knowing when the end of the file has been reached so it will not try to read beyond it. The following pseudocode shows the logic:

> *Open the file*
> *While not at the end of the file:*
>   *Read an item from the file*
>   *Display the item*
> *End While*
> *Close the file*

`StreamReader` objects have a Boolean property named EndOfStream that signals whether the end of the file has been reached. If the file's read position is at the end of the file (and there is no more data to read), the EndOfStream property is set to true. Otherwise, it is set to false. When you need to read all the items in a file without knowing how many items the file contains, you can write a loop that iterates as long as the EndOfStream property is false.

Let's assume `inputFile` references a `StreamReader` object that is associated with a file that is already open. You can write the loop in the following manner:

```
while (inputFile.EndOfStream == false)
{
    // Read an item from the file.
    // Process the item.
}
```

However, most programmers prefer the following logic, which uses the `!` operator:

```
while (!inputFile.EndOfStream)
{
    // Read an item from the file.
    // Process the item.
}
```

Recall that the `!` operator is the logical NOT operator. When you read the first line of this loop, you naturally think *while NOT at the end of the stream*. In Tutorial 5-6 you will complete an application that uses this technique to display all the items in a file.

Tutorial 5-6:
Using a Loop to Read to the End of a File

In this tutorial you complete the *South America* application that is found in the *Chap05* folder of the Student Sample Programs that accompany this book. The application's form has already been created and is shown in Figure 5-36. The application also has an accompany text file named Countries.txt that is stored in the *bin\Debug* folder under the project folder. The Countries.txt file contains the names of the countries of South America. Figure 5-37 shows the file as it appears in Notepad.

Figure 5-36 The *South America* application's form

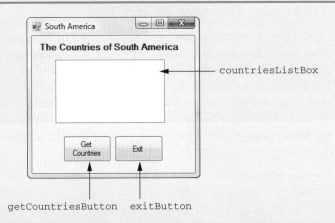

Figure 5-37 The Countries.txt file

When the completed application runs and the user clicks the *Get Countries* button, the application reads each country name from the file and adds each one to the countriesListBox control.

Step 1: Start Visual Studio (or Visual C# Express). Open the project named *South America* in the *Chap05* folder of the Student Sample Programs that accompany this book.

Step 2: Open the Form1 form's code in the code editor. Insert the **using System.IO;** directive shown in line 9 of Program 5-6 at the end of this tutorial. This statement is necessary because the **StreamReader** class is part of the **System.IO** namespace in the .NET Framework.

Step 3: Open the Form1 form in the *Designer*. The form is shown, along with the names of the important controls, in Figure 5-36. Double-click the getCountriesButton control. This opens the code editor, and you will see an empty event handler named getCountriesButton _Click. Complete the getCountriesButton _Click event handler by typing the code shown in lines 22–45 in Program 5-6. Let's take a closer look at the code:

Line 22: This is the beginning of a try-catch statement, which handles any exceptions that are thrown while the file is being processed. If an exception is thrown by any statement in the try block, the program jumps to the catch clause in line 49.

Line 25: This statement declares the string variable countryName, which holds the lines of text that are read from the file.

Lines 28–31: After these statements have executed, the Countries.txt file is opened for reading, and the inputFile variable references a StreamReader object that is associated with the file.

Line 34: This statement clears anything that might be displayed in the countriesListBox control. (This prevents the names of the countries from appearing multiple times in the ListBox if the user clicks the *Get Countries* button multiple times.)

Line 37: This is the beginning of a while loop that iterates as long as the end of the Countries.txt file has not been reached.

Line 40: This statement reads a line of text from the file and assigns it to the countryName variable.

Line 43: This statement adds the contents of the countryName variable to the ListBox.

Line 47: This statement closes the file.

Step 4: Switch your view back to the *Designer* and double-click the exitButton control. In the code editor you will see an empty event handler named exitButton_Click. Complete the exitButton_Click event handler by typing the code shown in lines 58–59 in Program 5-6.

Step 5: Save the project. Then, press F5 on the keyboard or click the *Start Debugging* button (▶) on the toolbar to compile and run the application. When the application runs, click the *Get Countries* button. This should fill the ListBox with the names of the countries from the Countries.txt file, as shown in Figure 5-38. Click the *Exit* button to exit the application.

Figure 5-38 The *South America* application displaying the list of countries

Program 5-6 Completed code for Form1 in the *South America* application

```
 1 using System;
 2 using System.Collections.Generic;
 3 using System.ComponentModel;
 4 using System.Data;
 5 using System.Drawing;
 6 using System.Linq;
 7 using System.Text;
 8 using System.Windows.Forms;
 9 using System.IO;
10
11 namespace South_America
12 {
13     public partial class Form1 : Form
14     {
15         public Form1()
16         {
17             InitializeComponent();
18         }
19
20         private void getCountriesButton_Click(object sender, EventArgs e)
21         {
22             try
23             {
24                 // Declare a variable to hold a country name.
25                 string countryName;
26
27                 // Declare a StreamReader variable.
28                 StreamReader inputFile;
29
30                 // Open the file and get a StreamReader object.
31                 inputFile = File.OpenText("Countries.txt");
32
33                 // Clear anything currently in the ListBox.
34                 countriesListBox.Items.Clear();
35
36                 // Read the file's contents.
37                 while (!inputFile.EndOfStream)
38                 {
39                     // Get a country name.
40                     countryName = inputFile.ReadLine();
41
42                     // Add the country name to the ListBox.
43                     countriesListBox.Items.Add(countryName);
44                 }
45
46                 // Close the file.
47                 inputFile.Close();
48             }
49             catch (Exception ex)
50             {
51                 // Display an error message.
52                 MessageBox.Show(ex.Message);
53             }
54         }
55
56         private void exitButton_Click(object sender, EventArgs e)
57         {
```

```
58              // Close the form.
59              this.Close();
60          }
61      }
62 }
```

Calculating a Running Total

Many programming tasks require you to calculate the total of a series of numbers. In this section you learn how to calculate the total of a series of numbers that are stored in a file. For example, suppose you have a file that contains a business's sales for each day of a week and you need to write a program that calculates the total of all the amounts in the file. The program would read the values in the file and keep a total of the values as they are read.

Programs that calculate the total of a series of numbers typically use two elements:

- A loop that reads each number in the series
- A variable that accumulates the total of the numbers as they are read

The variable that is used to accumulate the total of the numbers is called an **accumulator**. It is often said that the loop keeps a **running total** because it accumulates the total as it reads each number in the series. Figure 5-39 shows the general logic of a loop that calculates a running total.

Figure 5-39 Logic for calculating a running total

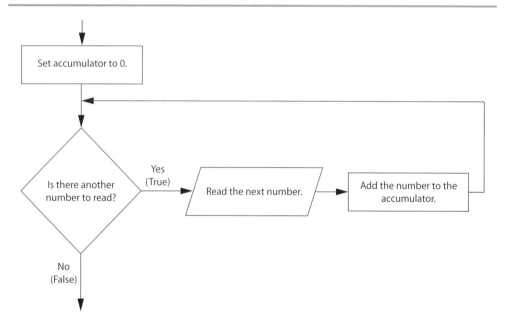

When the loop finishes, the accumulator will contain the total of the numbers that were read by the loop. Notice that the first step in the flowchart is to set the accumulator variable to 0. This is a critical step. Each time the loop reads a number, it adds it to the accumulator. If the accumulator starts with any value other than 0, it will not contain the correct total when the loop finishes.

In Tutorial 5-7 you will complete an application that calculates a running total of the values in a file.

Tutorial 5-7:
Calculating a Running Total

In this tutorial you complete the *Total Sales* application that is found in the *Chap05* folder of the Student Sample Programs that accompany this book. The application's form has already been created and is shown in Figure 5-40. The application also has an accompany text file named Sales.txt that is stored in the *bin\Debug* folder, under the project folder. The Sales.txt file contains the amounts shown in Figure 5-41.

Figure 5-40 The *Total Sales* application's form

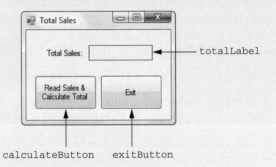

Figure 5-41 The *Total Sales* application's form

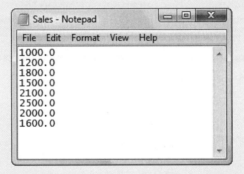

When the completed application runs and the user clicks the *Read Sales & Calculate Total* button, the application calculates the total of the values in the Sales.txt file and displays the total in the `totalLabel` control.

Step 1: Start Visual Studio (or Visual C# Express). Open the project named *Total Sales* in the *Chap05* folder of the Student Sample Programs that accompany this book.

Step 2: Open the Form1 form's code in the code editor. Insert the `using System.IO;` directive shown in line 9 of Program 5-7 at the end of this tutorial.

Step 3: Open the Form1 form in the *Designer*. The form is shown, along with the names of the important controls, in Figure 5-40. Double-click the `calculateButton` control. This opens the code editor, and you will see an empty event handler named `calculateButton_Click`. Complete the `calculateButton_Click` event handler by typing the code shown in lines 22–55 in Program 5-7. Let's take a closer look at the code:

Line 22: This is the beginning of a try-catch statement, which handles any exceptions that are thrown while the file is being processed. If an exception is thrown by any statement in the try block, the program jumps to the catch clause in line 51.

Lines 25–26: These statements declare the decimal variables sales and total. The sales variable holds each value that is read from the file, and the total variable is used as an accumulator. Notice that the total variable is explicitly initialized to 0.

Lines 29–32: After these statements have executed, the Sales.txt file is opened for reading, and the inputFile variable references a StreamReader object that is associated with the file.

Line 35: This is the beginning of a while loop that iterates as long as the end of the Countries.txt file has not been reached.

Line 38: This statement reads a line of text from the file, converts it to a decimal, and assigns the result to the sales variable.

Line 41: This statement adds the sales variable to the total variable.

Line 45: This statement closes the file.

Line 48: This statement displays the total, formatted as currency, in the totalLabel control.

Step 4: Switch your view back to the *Designer* and double-click the exitButton control. In the code editor you will see an empty event handler named exitButton_Click. Complete the exitButton_Click event handler by typing the code shown in lines 60–61 in Program 5-7.

Step 5: Save the project. Then, press F5 on the keyboard or click the *Start Debugging* button (▶) on the toolbar to compile and run the application. When the application runs, click the *Read Sales & Calculate Total* button. The total sales should be calculated and displayed, as shown in Figure 5-42. Click the *Exit* button to exit the application.

Figure 5-42 The *Total Sales* application displaying the total sales

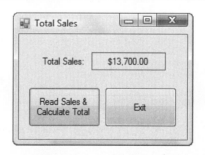

Program 5-7 Completed code for Form1 in the *Total Sales* application

```
1 using System;
2 using System.Collections.Generic;
3 using System.ComponentModel;
4 using System.Data;
5 using System.Drawing;
6 using System.Linq;
7 using System.Text;
```

```
 8 using System.Windows.Forms;
 9 using System.IO;
10
11 namespace Total_Sales
12 {
13     public partial class Form1 : Form
14     {
15         public Form1()
16         {
17             InitializeComponent();
18         }
19
20         private void calculateButton_Click(object sender, EventArgs e)
21         {
22             try
23             {
24                 // Variables
25                 decimal sales;        // To hold a sales amount
26                 decimal total = 0m;   // Accumulator, set to 0
27
28                 // Declare a StreamReader variable.
29                 StreamReader inputFile;
30
31                 // Open the file and get a StreamReader object.
32                 inputFile = File.OpenText("Sales.txt");
33
34                 // Read the file's contents.
35                 while (!inputFile.EndOfStream)
36                 {
37                     // Get a sales amount.
38                     sales = decimal.Parse(inputFile.ReadLine());
39
40                     // Add the sales amount to total.
41                     total += sales;
42                 }
43
44                 // Close the file.
45                 inputFile.Close();
46
47                 // Display the total.
48                 totalLabel.Text = total.ToString("c");
49
50             }
51             catch (Exception ex)
52             {
53                 // Display an error message.
54                 MessageBox.Show(ex.Message);
55             }
56         }
57
58         private void exitButton_Click(object sender, EventArgs e)
59         {
60             // Close the form.
61             this.Close();
62         }
63     }
64 }
```

✓ Checkpoint

5.18 What is an output file?

5.19 What is an input file?

5.20 What three steps must be taken by a program when it uses a file?

5.21 What is the difference between a text file and a binary file?

5.22 What are the two types of file access? What is the difference between these two?

5.23 What type of object do you create if you want to write data to a text file?

5.24 What type of object do you create if you want to read data from a text file?

5.25 If you call the `File.CreateText` method and the specified file already exists, what happens to the existing file?

5.26 If you call the `File.AppendText` method and the specified file already exists, what happens to the existing file?

5.27 What is the difference between the `WriteLine` and `Write` methods discussed in this chapter?

5.28 What method do you call to open a text file to read data from it?

5.29 What is a file's read position? Initially, where is the read position when an input file is opened?

5.30 How do you read a line of text from a text file?

5.31 How do you close a file?

5.32 Assume `inputFile` references a `StreamReader` object that is associated with an open file. Which of the following loops is written in the correct general format to read all of the items from the file?

Loop A:
```
while (inputFile.EndOfStream)
{
    // Read an item from the file.
}
```

Loop B:
```
while (!inputFile.EndOfStream)
{
    // Read an item from the file.
}
```

5.7 The OpenFileDialog and SaveFileDialog Controls

CONCEPT: The OpenFileDialog and SaveFileDialog controls allow your application to display standard Windows dialog boxes for opening and saving files. These allow the user to easily specify a file's name and location.

So far, the applications in this chapter that open a file specify the filename as a string literal. Most Windows users, however, are accustomed to using a dialog box to browse their disk for a file to open or for a location to save a file. You can use the OpenFileDialog and SaveFileDialog controls to equip applications with standard Windows dialog boxes for these purposes.

The OpenFileDialog Control

The **OpenFileDialog control** displays a standard Windows *Open* dialog box, such as the one shown in Figure 5-43. The ***Open* dialog box** is useful in applications that must open an existing file because it allows the user to browse the system and select the file.

Figure 5-43 Windows *Open* dialog box

Adding the OpenFileDialog Control to Your Project

To add an OpenFileDialog control to a form, double-click the OpenFileDialog tool under the *Dialogs* group in the *Toolbox* window. When the control is created, it does not appear on the form, but in an area at the bottom of the *Designer* known as the **component tray**. Figure 5-44 shows an example of how an OpenFileDialog control appears in the component tray. The control's default name is openFileDialog1. As with other controls, you can change the control's Name property to change its name.

Displaying an Open Dialog Box

In code, you can display an *Open* dialog box by calling the OpenFileDialog control's ShowDialog method. For example, assume that we have created an OpenFileDialog control and changed its name to openFile. The following statement calls the control's ShowDialog method:

```
openFile.ShowDialog();
```

In most cases, however, you will want to know whether the user clicked the *Open* button or the *Cancel* button to dismiss the *Open* dialog box. If the user clicked the *Open* button, it means that the user has selected a file and he or she can open it. If the user clicked the *Cancel* button, it means that the user does not want to proceed.

The ShowDialog method returns a value that indicates which button the user clicked to dismiss the dialog box. If the user clicked the *Open* button, the value DialogResult.OK is returned. If the user clicked the *Cancel* button, the value DialogResult.Cancel is

Figure 5-44 An OpenFileDialog control in the component tray

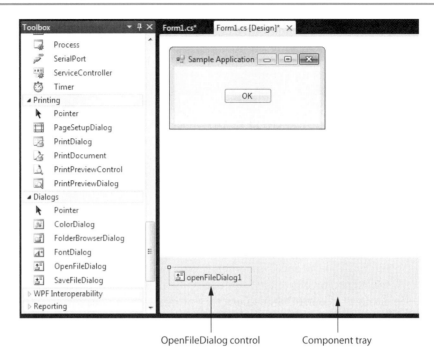

OpenFileDialog control   Component tray

returned. Assuming `openFile` is the name of an OpenFileDialog control, the following is an example of an `if-else` statement that calls the `ShowDialog` method and determines whether the user clicked the *Open* button or the *Cancel* button.

```
if (openFile.ShowDialog() == DialogResult.OK)
{
    MessageBox.Show("You clicked the Open button.");
}
else
{
    MessageBox.Show("You clicked the Cancel button.");
}
```

The Filename Property

When the user selects a file with the *Open* dialog box, the file's path and filename are stored in the control's **Filename property**. Assume `openFile` is the name of an Open-FileDialog control. The following code is an example of how you can display an *Open* dialog box and, if the user clicks the *Open* button to dismiss the dialog box, open the selected file.

```
 1 StreamReader inputFile;
 2
 3 if (openFile.ShowDialog() == DialogResult.OK)
 4 {
 5     // Open the selected file.
 6     inputFile = File.OpenText(openFile.Filename);
 7
 8     // Continue processing the file...
 9 }
10 else
11 {
12     MessageBox.Show("Operation cancelled.");
13 }
```

Let's take a closer look at the code. The statement in line 1 declares a `StreamReader` variable named `inputFile`. The `if` statement in line 3 calls the `openFile` control's `ShowDialog` method to display an *Open* dialog box. If the user clicks the *Open* button to dismiss the dialog box, the program continues to line 6, where the name of the selected file is retrieved from the control's Filename property and that file is opened. Otherwise (if the user clicks the *Cancel* button), the program jumps to the `else` clause in line 10.

> **TIP:** When you create an OpenFileDialog control, its Filename property is initially set to the control's default name. For example, if the control's default name is `openFileDialog1`, then the Filename property is also set to *openFileDialog1*. Always be sure to delete the default value of the Filename property.

The InitialDirectory Property

By default, the *Open* dialog box displays the contents of the user's *Documents* directory (or folder). You can specify another directory to be initially displayed by storing its path in the **InitialDirectory property**. For example, the following code stores the path *C:\Data* in the `openFile` control's InitialDirectory property before displaying an *Open* dialog box:

```
openFile.InitialDirectory = "C:\Data";

if (openFile.ShowDialog() == DialogResult.OK)
{
    // Continue to process the selected file...
}
else
{
    // The operation was cancelled.
}
```

In this example, when the *Open* dialog box is displayed it shows the contents of the directory *C:\Data*.

The Title Property

By default, the word Open is displayed in an Open dialog box's title bar. You can change the default text displayed in the title bar by changing the control's **Title property**.

The SaveFileDialog Control

The **SaveFileDialog control** displays a standard Windows *Save As* dialog box, such as the one shown in Figure 5-45. The **Save As dialog box** allows the user to browse the system and select a location and name for a file that is about to be saved.

Adding the SaveFileDialog Control to Your Project

The SaveFileDialog control has much in common with the OpenFileDialog control. To add a SaveFileDialog control to a form, double-click the SaveFileDialog tool under the *Dialogs* group in the *Toolbox* window. When the control is created, it appears in the component tray at the bottom of the *Designer*. The control will be given a default name such as saveFileDialog1, but you can change the name with the Name property.

Displaying a Save As Dialog Box

In code, you can display a *Save As* dialog box by calling the SaveFileDialog control's `ShowDialog` method. For example, assume that we have created a SaveFileDialog control

Figure 5-45 Windows *Save As* dialog box

and changed its name to `saveFile`. The following statement calls the control's `ShowDialog` method:

```
saveFile.ShowDialog();
```

The method returns a value indicating whether the user clicked the *Save* button or the *Cancel* button to dismiss the *Save As* dialog box. If the user clicks the *Save* button, the value `DialogResult.OK` is returned. If the user clicks the *Cancel* button, the value `DialogResult.Cancel` is returned. Assume `saveFile` is the name of a SaveFileDialog control. The following is an example of an `if-else` statement that calls the `ShowDialog` method and determines whether the user clicked the *Save* button or the *Cancel* button.

```
if (saveFile.ShowDialog() == DialogResult.OK)
{
    MessageBox.Show("You clicked the Save button.");
}
else
{
    MessageBox.Show("You clicked the Cancel button.");
}
```

The Filename Property

When the user specifies a location and filename with the *Save As* dialog box, the file's path and filename are stored in the control's Filename property. Assume `saveFile` is the name of a SaveFileDialog control. The following code is an example of how you can display a *Save As* dialog box, and if the user clicks the *Save* button to dismiss the dialog box, open the selected file.

```
1 StreamWriter outputFile;
2
3 if (saveFile.ShowDialog() == DialogResult.OK)
4 {
```

```
 5      // Create the selected file.
 6      outputFile = File.CreateText(openFile.Filename);
 7
 8      // Write data to the file...
 9 }
10 else
11 {
12      MessageBox.Show("Operation cancelled.");
13 }
```

Let's take a closer look at the code. The statement in line 1 declares a `StreamWriter` variable named `outputFile`. The `if` statement in line 3 calls the `saveFile` control's `ShowDialog` method to display a *Save As* dialog box. If the user clicks the *Save* button to dismiss the dialog box, the program continues to line 6, where the selected name and path are retrieved from the control's Filename property, and that file is created. Otherwise (if the user clicks the *Cancel* button), the program jumps to the `else` clause in line 10.

The InitialDirectory Property

By default, the *Save As* dialog box displays the contents of the user's *Documents* directory (or folder). You can specify another directory to be initially displayed by storing its path in the InitialDirectory property. The following code stores the path *C:\Data* in the `saveFile` control's InitialDirectory property before displaying a *Save As* dialog box:

```
saveFile.InitialDirectory = "C:\Data";

if (saveFile.ShowDialog() == DialogResult.OK)
{
    // Continue to process the file...
}
else
{
    // The operation was cancelled.
}
```

In this example, when the *Save As* dialog box is displayed, it shows the contents of the directory *C:\Data*.

The Title Property

By default the words *Save As* are displayed in a *Save As* dialog box's title bar. You can change the default text displayed in the title bar by changing the control's Title property.

 **Checkpoint**

5.33 What is the benefit of using an *Open* and/or *Save As* dialog box in an application that works with files?

5.34 What is the purpose of the following OpenFileDialog and SaveFileDialog properties?

InitialDirectory

Title

Filename

Random Numbers

> **CONCEPT:** Random numbers are used in a variety of applications. The .NET Framework provides the **Random** class that you can use in C# to generate random numbers.

Random numbers are useful for lots of different programming tasks. The following are just a few examples.

- Random numbers are commonly used in games. For example, computer games that let the player roll dice use random numbers to represent the values of the dice. Programs that show cards being drawn from a shuffled deck use random numbers to represent the face values of the cards.
- Random numbers are useful in simulation programs. In some simulations, the computer must randomly decide how a person, animal, insect, or other living being will behave. Formulas can be constructed in which a random number is used to determine various actions and events that take place in the program.
- Random numbers are useful in statistical programs that must randomly select data for analysis.
- Random numbers are commonly used in computer security to encrypt sensitive data.

The .NET Framework provides a class named `Random` that you can use in C# to generate random numbers. First you create an object from the `Random` class with a statement such as this:

```
Random rand = new Random();
```

Let's dissect the statement into two parts. The first part of the statement, appearing on the left side of the = operator, is as follows:

Random rand = new Random();

This declares a variable named rand
that can reference a Random object.

This declares a variable named `rand` that can be used to reference a `Random` object. The second part of the statement, appearing on the right side of the = operator, is as follows:

Random rand = new Random();

This creates a Random object
in memory.

The expression `new Random()` causes an object of the `Random` class to be created in memory. The = operator causes the `rand` variable to reference the `Random` object, as illustrated in Figure 5-46. After this statement has executed, we can use the `rand` variable to work with the `Random` object.

Figure 5-46 The rand variable references a Random object

The Next Method

Once you have created a Random object, you can call its Next method to get a random integer number. The following code shows an example:

```
// Declare an int variable.
int number;

// Create a Random object.
Random rand = new Random();

// Get a random integer and assign it to number.
number = rand.Next();
```

After this code executes, the number variable contains a random integer. If you call the Next method with no arguments, as shown in this example, the returned integer is somewhere between 0 and 2,147,483,647. Alternatively, you can pass an argument that specifies an upper limit to the generated number's range. In the following statement, the value assigned to number is somewhere between 0 and 99:

```
number = rand.Next(100);
```

The random integer's range does not have to begin at zero. You can add or subtract a value to shift the numeric range upward or downward. In the following statement, we call the Next method to get a random number in the range of 0 through 9, and then we add 1to it. So, the number assigned to number is somewhere in the range of 1 through 10:

```
number = rand.Next(10) + 1;
```

The following statement shows another example. It assigns a random integer to number between −50 and +49:

```
number = rand.Next(100) - 50
```

The NextDouble Method

You can call a Random object's NextDouble method to get a random floating-point number between 0.0 and 1.0 (not including 1.0). The following code shows an example:

```
// Declare a Double variable.
double number;

// Create a Random object.
Random rand = new Random();

// Get a random number and assign it to number.
number = rand.NextDouble();
```

After this code executes, the number variable will contain a random floating-point number in the range of 0.0 up to (but not including) 1.0.

In Tutorial 5-8 you will use random numbers to determine whether the heads or tails side of a coin is facing up after the coin has been tossed.

Tutorial 5-8:
Simulating Coin Tosses

In this tutorial you create an application that simulates the tossing of a coin. Each time the user tosses the coin, the application uses a Random object to get a random integer in the range of 0 through 1. If the random number is 0, it means the tails side of the coin is up, and if the random number is 1, it means the heads side is up. The application displays an image of a coin showing either heads or tails, depending on the value of the random number.

Step 1: Start Visual Studio (or Visual C# Express) and begin a new Windows Forms Application project named *Coin Toss*.

Step 2: Set up the application's form as shown in Figure 5-47. Notice that the form's Text property is set to *Coin Toss*. The names of the controls are shown in the figure. As you place each of the controls on the form, refer to Table 5-1 for the relevant property settings. (Make sure the headsPictureBox control's Visible property is set to True, and the tailsPictureBox control's Visible property is set to False. This will cause the coin to initially appear heads up when the application runs.)

Figure 5-47 Initial setup of the *Coin Toss* form

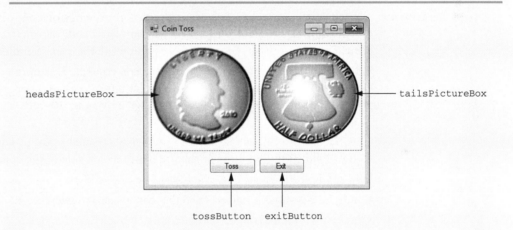

Table 5-1 Control property settings

Control Name	Control Type	Property Settings
headsPictureBox	PictureBox	**Image:** Select and import the Heads1.bmp file from the *Chap05* folder of the Student Sample Programs. **Size:** 170, 170 **SizeMode:** Zoom **Visible:** True
tailsPictureBox	PictureBox	**Image:** Select and import the Tails1.bmp file from the *Chap05* folder of the Student Sample Programs. **Size:** 170, 170 **SizeMode:** Zoom **Visible:** False
tossButton	Button	**Text:** *Toss*
exitButton	Button	**Text:** *Exit*

Step 3: After you have set all of the control properties as shown in Table 5-1, move the PictureBox controls so one is on top of the other, as shown in Figure 5-48. (In the figure, the `headsPictureBox` control is on top, but it really doesn't matter which is on top.) Also, reduce the width of the form and position the button controls as shown in the figure.

Figure 5-48 The controls repositioned and the form size adjusted

The `headsPictureBox` control is on top of the `tailsPictureBox` control

Step 4: Now you will create the Click event handlers for the Button controls. At the end of this tutorial, Program 5-8 shows the completed code for the form. You will be instructed to refer to Program 5-8 as you write the event handlers.

In the *Designer*, double-click the `tossButton` control. This opens the code editor, and you will see an empty event handler named `tossButton_Click`. Complete the `tossButton_Click` event handler by typing the code shown in lines 21–43 in Program 5-8. Let's take a closer look at the code:

Line 22: This statement declares an `int` variable named `sideUp`. This variable is used to hold a random number that indicates which side of the coin is up.

Line 25: This statement does the following:

- It declares a variable named `rand` that can be used to reference a `Random` object.
- It creates a `Random` object in memory.
- The = operator causes the `rand` variable to reference the `Random` object.

Line 29: This statement gets a random integer in the range of 0 through 1 and assigns it to the `sideUp` variable. The random integer represents which side of the coin is facing up. The value 0 means that the tails side is facing up, and the value 1 means that the heads side is facing up.

Lines 32–43: This `if-else` statement displays the side of the coin that is facing up. If `sideUp` equals 0, then the statements in lines 35 and 36 display the `tailsPictureBox` control and hide the `headsPictureBox` control. If `sideUp` equals 1, then the statements in lines 41 and 42 display the `headsPictureBox` control and hide the `tailsPictureBox` control.

Step 5: Switch your view back to the *Designer* and double-click the `exitButton` control. In the code editor you will see an empty event handler named `exitButton_Click`. Complete the `exitButton_Click` event handler by typing the code shown in lines 48–49 in Program 5-8.

Step 6: Save the project. Then, press F5 on the keyboard or click the *Start Debugging* button (▶) on the toolbar to compile and run the application. When the application runs, click the *Toss* button several times to simulate several coin tosses. When you are finished, click the *Exit* button to exit the application.

Program 5-8 Completed code for Form1 in the *Coin Toss* application

```
 1 using System;
 2 using System.Collections.Generic;
 3 using System.ComponentModel;
 4 using System.Data;
 5 using System.Drawing;
 6 using System.Linq;
 7 using System.Text;
 8 using System.Windows.Forms;
 9
10 namespace Coin_Toss
11 {
12     public partial class Form1 : Form
13     {
14         public Form1()
15         {
16             InitializeComponent();
17         }
18
19         private void tossButton_Click(object sender, EventArgs e)
20         {
21             // The sideUp variable will indicate which side is up.
22             int sideUp;
23
24             // Create a Random object.
25             Random rand = new Random();
26
27             // Get a random integer in the range of 0 through 1.
28             // 0 means tails up, 1 means heads up.
29             sideUp = rand.Next(2);
30
31             // Display the side that is up.
32             if (sideUp == 0)
33             {
34                 // Display tails up.
35                 tailsPictureBox.Visible = true;
36                 headsPictureBox.Visible = false;
37             }
38             else
39             {
40                 // Display heads up.
41                 headsPictureBox.Visible = true;
42                 tailsPictureBox.Visible = false;
43             }
44         }
45
46         private void exitButton_Click(object sender, EventArgs e)
47         {
48             // Close the form.
49             this.Close();
50         }
51     }
52 }
```

Random Number Seeds

The numbers that are generated by the Random class are not truly random. Instead, they are **pseudorandom numbers** that are calculated by a formula. The formula used to generate random numbers has to be initialized with a value known as a seed value. The **seed value** is used in the calculation that returns the next random number in the series. When a Random object is created in memory, it retrieves the system time from the computer's internal clock and uses that as the seed value. The system time is an integer that represents the current date and time, down to a hundredth of a second.

If a Random object uses the same seed value each time it is created, it always generates the same series of random numbers. Because the system time changes every hundredth of a second, it is the preferred value to use as the seed in most cases. However, you can specify a different integer value as the seed, if you desire, when you create a Random object. Here is an example:

```
Random rand = new Random(1000);
```

In this example, the Random object that is created uses 1000 as the seed value. Each time a Random object is created with this statement, it generates the same series of random numbers. That may be desirable in some applications, when you always want to produce the same set of pseudorandom numbers.

 Checkpoint

5.35 What does a Random object's Next method return?

5.36 What does a Random object's NextDouble method return?

5.37 Write code that creates a Random object and then assigns a random integer in the range of 1 through 100 to the variable randomNumber.

5.38 Write code that creates a Random object and then assigns a random integer in the range of 100 through 399 to the variable randomNumber.

5.39 What does a Random object use as its seed value if you do not specify one?

5.40 What happens if the same seed value is used each time a Random object is created?

 5.9 The Load Event

CONCEPT: When an application's form loads into memory, an event known as the Load event takes place. You can write an event handler for the Load event, and that handler will execute just before the form is displayed.

When you run an application, the application's form is loaded into memory and an event known as the **Load event** takes place. The Load event takes place before the form is displayed on the screen. If you want to execute some code at this point, you can write a Load event handler containing the desired code.

To create a Load event handler for a form, simply double-click any area of the form in the *Designer* window where there is no other control. The code editor will open with an empty Load event handler. If the form is named Form1, the event handler is named Form1_Load. Any code that you write inside the event handler executes when the form's Load event takes place. Here is an example of a Load event handler in a form named Form1:

```
private void Form1_Load(object sender, EventArgs e)
{
    MessageBox.Show("Prepare to see the form!");
}
```

Keep in mind that the Load event happens before the form is displayed on the screen. When the application containing this event handler runs, the message box is displayed before the form appears.

Load event handlers are useful for performing setup operations. In Tutorial 5-9 you will complete an application that uses a Load event handler to read items from a text file and add those items to a ListBox control.

Tutorial 5-9:
Creating a Load Event Handler

In this tutorial you complete the *Load Event* application that is found in the *Chap05* folder of the Student Sample Programs that accompany this book. This application is a variation of the *South America* application that you created in Tutorial 5-6. This version of the application uses a Load event handler to read the contents of the Countries.txt file and adds those items to a ListBox control.

The application's form has already been created and is shown in Figure 5-49. The application also has an accompanying text file named Countries.txt, that is stored in the *bin\Debug* folder, under the project folder. The Countries.txt file contains the names of the countries of South America.

Figure 5-49 The *Load Event* application's form

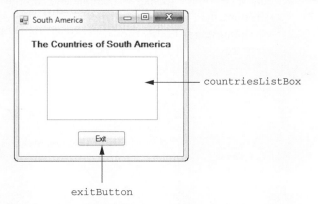

Step 1: Start Visual Studio (or Visual C# Express). Open the project named *Load Event* in the *Chap05* folder of the Student Sample Programs that accompany this book.

Step 2: Open the Form1 form's code in the code editor. Insert the **using System.IO;** directive shown in line 9 of Program 5-9 at the end of this tutorial. This statement is necessary because you will be using the **StreamReader** class, which is part of the **System.IO** namespace in the .NET Framework.

Step 3: Open the Form1 form in the *Designer*. The form is shown, along with the names of the important controls, in Figure 5-49. Double-click any part of the form that does not contain a control. (Be sure not to click the Label control, the ListBox control, or the Button control.) This opens the code editor, and you will see an empty event handler named Form1_Load. Complete the Form1_Load event handler by typing the code shown in lines 22–45 in Program 5-9. Let's take a closer look at the code:

Line 22: This is the beginning of a try-catch statement, which handles any exceptions that are thrown while the file is being processed. If an exception is thrown by any statement in the try block, the program jumps to the catch clause in line 46.

Line 25: This statement declares the string variable countryName, which holds the lines of text that are read from the file.

Lines 28–31: After these statements have executed, the Countries.txt file is opened for reading, and the inputFile variable references a StreamReader object that is associated with the file.

Line 34: This is the beginning of a while loop that iterates as long as the end of the Countries.txt file has not been reached.

Line 37: This statement reads a line of text from the file and assigns it to the countryName variable.

Line 40: This statement adds the contents of the countryName variable to the ListBox.

Line 44: This statement closes the file.

Step 4: Switch your view back to the *Designer* and double-click the exitButton control. In the code editor you will see an empty event handler named exitButton_Click. Complete the exitButton_Click event handler by typing the code shown in lines 55–56 in Program 5-9.

Step 5: Save the project. Then, press F5 on the keyboard or click the *Start Debugging* button (▶) on the toolbar to compile and run the application. When the application runs, the ListBox should appear filled with the names of the countries from the Countries.txt file, as shown in Figure 5-50. Click the *Exit* button to exit the application.

Figure 5-50 The *Load Event* application displaying the list of countries

Program 5-9 Completed code for Form1 in the *Load Event* application

```
 1 using System;
 2 using System.Collections.Generic;
 3 using System.ComponentModel;
 4 using System.Data;
 5 using System.Drawing;
 6 using System.Linq;
 7 using System.Text;
 8 using System.Windows.Forms;
 9 using System.IO;
10
```

```
11 namespace Load_Event
12 {
13     public partial class Form1 : Form
14     {
15         public Form1()
16         {
17             InitializeComponent();
18         }
19
20         private void Form1_Load(object sender, EventArgs e)
21         {
22             try
23             {
24                 // Declare a variable to hold a country name.
25                 string countryName;
26
27                 // Declare a StreamReader variable.
28                 StreamReader inputFile;
29
30                 // Open the file and get a StreamReader object.
31                 inputFile = File.OpenText("Countries.txt");
32
33                 // Read the file's contents.
34                 while (!inputFile.EndOfStream)
35                 {
36                     // Get a country name.
37                     countryName = inputFile.ReadLine();
38
39                     // Add the country name to the ListBox.
40                     countriesListBox.Items.Add(countryName);
41                 }
42
43                 // Close the file.
44                 inputFile.Close();
45             }
46             catch (Exception ex)
47             {
48                 // Display an error message.
49                 MessageBox.Show(ex.Message);
50             }
51         }
52
53         private void exitButton_Click(object sender, EventArgs e)
54         {
55             // Close the form.
56             this.Close();
57         }
58     }
59 }
```

Checkpoint

5.41 When does the Load event take place?

5.42 How do you create an event handler for the Load event?

Key Terms

accumulator	output file
binary file	postfix mode
body	posttest loop
component tray	prefix mode
counter variable	pretest loop
decrement	pseudorandom numbers
direct access file	random access file
file object	read position
filename	`ReadLine` method
filename extensions	running total
Filename property	*Save As* dialog box
increment	SaveFileDialog control
InitialDirectory property	seed value
initialization expression	sequential access file
input file	`StreamReader` class
`Items.Add` method	`StreamWriter` class
Items.Clear method	test expression
Items.Count property	text file
Iteration	Title property
Load event	update expression
newline character	`while` clause
`Next` method	`Write` method
Open dialog box	`WriteLine` method
OpenFileDialog control	

Review Questions

Multiple Choice

1. ListBox controls have an _____ method that erases all the items in the Items property.
   a. Items.Erase
   b. Items.Remove
   c. Items.Clear
   d. Items.Empty

2. A _____ is commonly used to control the number of times that a loop iterates.
   a. counter variable
   b. test expression
   c. `while` clause
   d. controlled variable

3. A(n) _____ tests its condition *before* performing an iteration.
   a. preemptive loop
   b. pretest loop
   c. infinite loop
   d. logical loop

4. The term _____ is used to describe a file that data is written to.
   a. input file
   b. output file
   c. saved file
   d. user file

5. The term _____ is used to describe a file that data is read from.

   a. data file
   b. write file
   c. read file
   d. input file

6. A _____ contains data that has been encoded as text, using a scheme such as Unicode.

   a. text file
   b. character file
   c. Unicode file
   d. system file

7. When you work with a, _____ you access data from the beginning of the file to the end of the file.

   a. direct access file
   b. random access file
   c. sequential access file
   d. binary access file

8. Files on a disk are identified by a _____.

   a. unique identifier
   b. filename
   c. binary sequencer
   d. file extension

9. A _____ is an object that is associated with a specific file and provides a way for the program to work with that file.

   a. data object
   b. directory object
   c. stream object
   d. file object

10. When a program works with an input file, a special value known as a(n) _____ is internally maintained for that file and marks the location of the next item that will be read from the file.

    a. input locator
    b. accumulator
    c. read position
    d. sequential read value

11. When the user selects a file with the *Open* dialog box, the file's path and filename are stored in the control's _____.

    a. Filename property
    b. FilePath property
    c. Pathname property
    d. Text property

12. The _____ displays a standard Windows *Save As* dialog box.

    a. SaveAsDialog control
    b. FileDialog control
    c. SaveFileDialog control
    d. StandardDialog control

13. Once you have created a `Random` object, you can call its _____ to get a random integer number.
    a. `Generate` method
    b. `Rand` method
    c. `NextInteger` method
    d. `Next` method

14. The _____ is used in the calculation that returns the next random number in the series.
    a. `Start` value
    b. seed value
    c. `Next` value
    d. sequence value

15. When you run an application, the application's form is loaded into memory and an event known as the _____ takes place.
    a. Startup event
    b. Begin event
    c. Load event
    d. Initialize event

True or False

1. If the ListBox is empty, the Items.Count property equals −1.

2. The `while` loop is known as a pretest loop, which means it tests its condition *before* performing an iteration.

3. To increment a variable means to increase its value and to decrement a variable means to decrease its value.

4. When a variable is declared in the initialization expression of a `for` loop, the scope of the variable is limited to the loop.

5. The `while` loop always performs at least one iteration, even if its Boolean expression is false to begin with.

6. The term read file is used to describe a file that data is read from

7. To append data to an existing file, you open it with the `File.AppendText` method.

8. As items are read from the file, the read position moves forward, toward the end of the file.

9. The numbers that are generated by the `Random` class are truly random.

10. The Load event takes place after the form is displayed on the screen.

Short Answer

1. What is contained in the body of a loop?

2. Write a programming statement that uses postfix mode to increment a variable named `count`.

3. How many iterations will occur if the test expression of a `for` loop is false to begin with?

4. What are filename extensions? What do they indicate about a file?

5. When an input file is opened, what is its read position initially set to?

6. How can you read all of the items in a file without knowing how many items the file contains?

7. What is a variable that is used to accumulate a total called?

8. By default, the *Open* dialog box displays the contents of the user's *Documents* directory. How can you specify another directory to be initially displayed?

9. Why is the system time the preferred seed value for a Random object?

10. What kind of code should be placed in the Load event?

Algorithm Workbench

1. Write a loop that displays your name 10 times.

2. Write a loop that displays all the odd numbers from 1 through 49.

3. Write a loop that displays every fifth number from 0 through 100.

4. Write a code sample that uses a loop to write the numbers from 1 through 10 to a file.

5. Assume that a file named People.txt contains a list of names. Write a code sample that uses a `while` loop to read the file and display its contents in a ListBox control.

Programming Problems

1. **Distance Calculator**

    If you know a vehicle's speed and the amount of time it has traveled, you can calculate the distance it has traveled as follows:

    $$Distance = Speed \times Time$$

    For example, if a train travels 40 miles per hour for 3 hours, the distance traveled is 120 miles. Create an application with a form similar to the one shown in Figure 5-51. The user enters a vehicle's speed and the number of hours traveled into text boxes. When the user clicks the *Calculate* button, the application should use a loop to display in a list box the distance the vehicle has traveled for each hour of that time period.

Figure 5-51 The *Distance Calculator* application

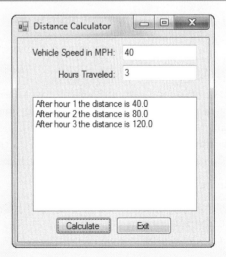

2. **Distance File**

   Modify the Distance Calculator program that you wrote for Programming Exercise 1 so it writes its output to a file instead of displaying it in a ListBox control. Open the file in Notepad or Visual Studio to confirm the output.

3. **Celsius-to-Fahrenheit Table**

   Assuming that *C* is a Celsius temperature, the following formula converts the temperature to a Fahrenheit temperature (*F*):

   $$F = \frac{9}{5}C + 32$$

   Create an application that displays a table of the Celsius temperatures 0–20 and their Fahrenheit equivalents. The application should use a loop to display the temperatures in a list box.

4. **Population**

   Create an application that predicts the approximate size of a population of organisms. The application should use text boxes to allow the user to enter the starting number of organisms, the average daily population increase (as a percentage), and the number of days the organisms will be left to multiply. For example, assume the user enters the following values:

   Starting number of organisms: 2

   Average daily increase : 30%

   Number of days to multiply: 10

   The application should display the following table of data in a ListBox control.

Day	Approximate Population
1	2
2	2.6
3	3.38
4	4.394
5	5.7122
6	7.42586
7	9.653619
8	12.5497
9	16.31462
10	21.209

5. **Pennies for Pay**

   Susan is hired for a job, and her employer agrees to pay her every day. Her employer also agrees that Susan's salary is 1 penny the first day, 2 pennies the second day, 4 pennies the third day, continuing to double each day. Create an application that allows the user to enter the number of days that Susan will work and calculates the total amount of pay she will receive over that period of time.

6. **Ocean Levels**

   Assuming the ocean's level is currently rising at about 1.5 millimeters per year, create an application that displays the number of millimeters that the ocean will have risen each year for the next 10 years. Display the output in a ListBox control.

7. **Calories Burned**

   Running on a particular treadmill, you burn 3.9 calories per minute. Create an application that uses a loop to display the number of calories burned after 10, 15, 20, 25, and 30 minutes. Display the output in a ListBox control.

8. **Tuition Increase**

   At one college the tuition for a full-time student is $6000 per semester. It has been announced that the tuition will increase by 2 percent each year for the next five years. Create an application with a loop that displays the projected semester tuition amount for the next 5 years in a ListBox control.

9. **Dice Simulator**

   Create an application that simulates rolling a pair of dice. When the user clicks a button, the application should generate two random numbers, each in the range of 1 through 6, to represent the value of the dice. Use PictureBox controls to display the dice. (In the student sample programs, in the *Chap05* folder, you will find six images named Die1.bmp, Die2.bmp, Die3.bmp, Die4.bmp, Die5.bmp, and Die6.bmp that you can use in the PictureBoxes.)

10. **Addition Tutor**

    Create an application that generates two random integers, each in the range of 100 through 500. The numbers should be displayed as addition problems on the application's form, such as

    $$247 + 129 = ?$$

    The form should have a text box for the user to enter the problem's answer. When a button is clicked, the application should do the following:

    - Check the user's input and display a message indicating whether it is the correct answer.
    - Generate two new random numbers and display them in a new problem on the form.

11. **Random Number Guessing Game**

    Create an application that generates a random number in the range of 1 through 100 and asks the user to guess what the number is. If the user's guess is higher than the random number, the program should display "Too high, try again." If the user's guess is lower than the random number, the program should display "Too low, try again." If the user guesses the number, the application should congratulate the user and then generate a new random number so the game can start over.

    Optional Enhancement: Enhance the game so it keeps count of the number of guesses that the user makes. When the user correctly guesses the random number, the program should display the number of guesses.

12. **Calculating the Factorial of a Number**

    In mathematics, the notation $n!$ represents the factorial of the nonnegative integer n. The factorial of n is the product of all the nonnegative integers from 1 through n. For example,

    $$7! = 1 \times 2 \times 3 \times 4 \times 5 \times 6 \times 7 = 5{,}040$$

    and

    $$4! = 1 \times 2 \times 3 \times 4 = 24$$

    Create an application that lets the user enter a nonnegative integer and then uses a loop to calculate the factorial of that number. Display the factorial in a label or a message box.

13. **Random Number File Writer**

Create an application that writes a series of random numbers to a file. Each random number should be in the range of 1 through 100. The application should let the user specify how many random numbers the file will hold and should use a SaveFileDialog control to let the user specify the file's name and location.

14. **Random Number File Reader**

This exercise assumes you have completed Programming Exercise 13, *Random Number File Writer*. Create another application that uses an OpenFileDialog control to let the user select the file that was created by the application that you wrote for Exercise 13. This application should read the numbers from the file, display the numbers in a ListBox control, and then display the following data:

- The total of the numbers
- The number of random numbers read from the file

6 Modularizing Your Code with Methods

TOPICS

6.1 Introduction to Methods

CONCEPT: Methods can be used to break a complex program into small, manageable pieces. A **void** method simply executes a group of statements and then terminates. A value-returning method returns a value to the statement that called it.

In a general sense, a method is a collection of statements that performs a specific task. So far you have experienced methods in two ways:

- You have created event handlers. An event handler is a special type of method that responds to events.
- You have executed predefined methods from the .NET Framework, such as `MessageBox.Show`, and the `TryParse` methods.

In this chapter you will learn how to create your own methods that can be executed just as you execute the .NET Framework methods.

Methods are commonly used to break a problem into small, manageable pieces. Instead of writing one long method that contains all the statements necessary to solve a problem, you can write several small methods that each solve a specific part of the problem. These small methods can then be executed in the desired order to solve the problem. This approach is sometimes called **divide and conquer** because a large problem is divided into several smaller problems that are easily solved. Figures 6-1 and 6-2 illustrates this idea by comparing two programs: one that uses a long, complex event handler containing all the statements necessary to solve a problem and another that divides a problem into smaller problems, each of which are handled by a separate method.

Figure 6-1 Using one long sequence of statements to perform a task

```
namespace Example
{
    public partial class Form1 : Form
    {
        private void myButton_Click(object sender, EventArgs e)
        {
            statement;
            statement;
            statement;
            statement;
            statement;              In this program the task is performed
            statement;              by one long seqeunce of statements in
            statement;                      an event handler.
            statement;
            statement;
            statement;
            statement;
            statement;
            statement;
            ... and so on.
        }
    }
}
```

Figure 6-2 Using methods to divide and conquer a problem

```
namespace Example
{
    public partial class Form1 : Form
    {
        private void myButton_Click(object sender, EventArgs e)
        {
            Method2();
            Method3();              Event
            Method4();              Handler
        }

        private void Method2()
        {
            statement;
            statement;  Method 2          In this program the task has
            statement;                  been divided into smaller tasks,
        }                               each of which is performed
                                            by a separate method.
        private void Method3()
        {
            statement;
            statement;  Method 3
            statement;
        }

        private void Method4()
        {
            statement;
            statement;  Method 4
            statement;
        }
    }
}
```

In general terms, a program that is broken into smaller units of code, such as methods, is known as a **modularized program**. Modularization tends to simplify code. If a specific task is performed in several places in a program, a method can be written once to perform that task and then be executed any time it is needed. This benefit of using methods is known as **code reuse** because you are writing the code to perform a task once and then reusing it each time you need to perform the task.

`void` Methods and Value-Returning Methods

In this chapter you will learn to write two types of methods: `void` methods and value-returning methods. When you call a **void method**, it simply executes the statements it contains and then terminates. When you call a **value-returning method**, it executes the statements that it contains and then it returns a value back to the statement that called it. The `Parse` methods are good examples of value-returning methods. The first type of method that you will learn to write is the `void` method.

6.2 void Methods

CONCEPT: A `void` method performs a task and then terminates. It does not return a value back to the statement that called it.

To create a method you write its definition. A method definition has two parts: a header and a body. The **method header**, which appears at the beginning of a method definition, lists several important things about the method, including the method's name. The **method body** is a collection of statements that are performed when the method is executed. These statements are enclosed inside a set of curly braces. Here is an example of a method definition:

```
private void DisplayMessage()
{
    MessageBox.Show("This is the DisplayMessage method.");
}
```

The Method Header

Using the previously shown method definition, Figure 6-3 points out the different parts of the method header, which is the first line.

Figure 6-3 Parts of the method header

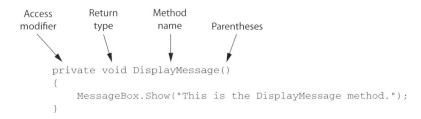

Let's take a closer look at the parts identified in the figure:

- **Access modifier**—The key word `private` is an access modifier. When a method is declared as `private`, it can be called only by code inside the same class as the method. Alternatively, a method that is declared as `public` can be called by code that is outside the class. This is important because some applications have multiple classes, and unless you specifically intend a method to be available to code outside the class, you should declare it `private`.
- **Return type**—Recall our previous discussion of `void` and value-returning methods. When the key word `void` appears here, it means that the method is a `void` method, and does not return a value. As you will see later in this chapter, a value-returning method lists a data type here.
- **Method name**—You should give each method a descriptive name. In general, the same rules that apply to variable names also apply to method names. The method in this example is named `DisplayMessage`, so we can easily guess what the method does: It displays a message.

In this book we use **Pascal case** for method names. Pascal case is like camelCase (the convention we have been using for variable names), except in a Pascal case name the first character is always uppercase. It is a standard convention among C# programmers to use Pascal case for method names because it differentiates method names from variable and field names.

- **Parentheses**—In the header, the method name is always followed by a set of parentheses. As you will see later in this chapter, you sometimes write declarations inside the parentheses, but for now, the parentheses will be empty.

> **NOTE:** The method header is never terminated with a semicolon.

The Method Body

Beginning at the line after the method header, one or more statements appear inside a set of curly braces ({ }). These statements are the method's body and are performed any time the module is executed.

When you write a method definition, Visual Studio automatically indents the statements in the method body. The indentation is not required, but it makes the code easier to read and debug. By indenting the statements in the body of the method, you visually set them apart from the surrounding code. This allows you to tell at a glance what part of the program is part of the method.

Declaring Methods Inside a Class

Methods usually belong to a class, so you must write a method's definition inside the class to which it is supposed to belong. In this chapter, all the methods that you will write will belong to an application's `Form1` class. When you write a method's definition, you write it inside the `Form1` class, as shown in Figure 6-4.

Figure 6-4 Write method definitions inside the `Form1` class

```
using System;
using System.Collections.Generic;
using System.ComponentModel;
using System.Data;
using System.Drawing;
using System.Linq;
using System.Text;
using System.Windows.Forms;

namespace Example
{
    public partial class Form1 : Form
    {
        public Form1()
        {
            InitializeComponent();
        }

                              ←————————————  Your method definitions will appear
                                             here, inside the Form1 class.

    }
}
```

Calling a Method

A method executes when it is called. Event handlers are called when specific events take place, but other methods are executed by method call statements. When a method is called, the program branches to that method and executes the statements in its body. Here is an example of a method call statement that calls the `DisplayMessage` method we previously examined:

```
DisplayMessage();
```

The statement is simply the name of the method followed by a set of parentheses. Because it is a complete statement, it is terminated with a semicolon.

Let's look at a complete program that uses the `DisplayMessage` method. In the *Chap06* folder of the Student Sample Programs that accompany this book is a project named *Simple Method*. Figure 6-5 shows the application's form, and Program 6-1 shows the form's code.

Figure 6-5 The *Simple Method* application's form

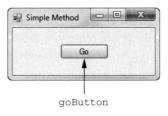

goButton

Program 6-1 Code for the *Simple Method* application's `Form1` form

```
 1 using System;
 2 using System.Collections.Generic;
 3 using System.ComponentModel;
 4 using System.Data;
 5 using System.Drawing;
 6 using System.Linq;
 7 using System.Text;
 8 using System.Windows.Forms;
 9
10 namespace Simple_Method
11 {
12    public partial class Form1 : Form
13    {
14       public Form1()
15       {
16          InitializeComponent();
17       }
18
19       private void goButton_Click(object sender, EventArgs e)
20       {
21          MessageBox.Show("This is the goButton_Click method.");
22          DisplayMessage();
23          MessageBox.Show("Back in the goButton_Click method.");
24       }
25
26       private void DisplayMessage()
27       {
28          MessageBox.Show("This is the DisplayMessage method.");
29       }
30    }
31 }
```

Let's step through the code. When the user clicks the *Go* button, the `goButton_Click` event handler executes. Inside the event handler the statement in line 21 displays *This is the goButton_Click method* in a message box. Then, line 22 calls the `DisplayMessage` method. As a shown in Figure 6-6, the program jumps to the `DisplayMessage` method and executes the statements in its body. There is only one statement in the body of the `DisplayMessage` method, which is line 28. This statement displays *This is the DisplayMessage method,* and then the method ends. As shown in Figure 6-7, the program jumps back to the part of the program that called the `DisplayMessage` method and resumes execution from that point. In this case, the program resumes execution at line 23, which displays *Back in the goButton_Click method*. The `goButton_Click` event handler ends at line 24.

Figure 6-6 Calling the `DisplayMessage` method

The program jumps to the `DisplayMessage` method and executes the statement in its body.

```
private void goButton_Click(object sender, EventArgs e)
{
    MessageBox.Show("This is the goButton_Click method.");
    DisplayMessage();
    MessageBox.Show("Back in the goButton_Click method.");
}

private void DisplayMessage()
{
    MessageBox.Show("This is the DisplayMessage method.");
}
```

Figure 6-7 The `DisplayMessage` method returns

When the `DisplayMessage` method ends, the program returns to the part of the program that called it, and resumes execution at the point.

```
private void goButton_Click(object sender, EventArgs e)
{
    MessageBox.Show("This is the goButton_Click method.");
    DisplayMessage();
    MessageBox.Show("Back in the goButton_Click method.");
}

private void DisplayMessage()
{
    MessageBox.Show("This is the DisplayMessage method.");
}
```

When a method is called, some operations are performed "behind the scenes" so the system will know to where the program should return after the method ends. First, the system saves the memory address of the location to which it should return. This is typically the statement that appears immediately after the method call. This memory location is known as the **return point**. Then, the system jumps to the method and executes the statements in its body. When the method ends, the system jumps back to the return point and resumes execution.

NOTE: When a program calls a method, programmers commonly say that the *control* of the program transfers to that method. This simply means that the method takes control of the program's execution.

In Tutorial 6-1 you will get hands-on practice writing and calling methods.

Tutorial 6-1:
Creating and Calling Methods

The *Chap06* folder in the Student Sample Programs that accompany this book contains a partially created project named *Lights*. In this tutorial you complete the project so it simulates a light being turned off or on. The project's form, in its initial setup, is shown in Figure 6-8.

Figure 6-8 The *Lights* project's form in its initial setup

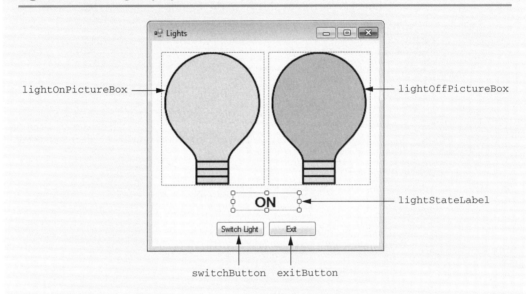

Here are some details about specific property settings:

- The `lightOnPictureBox` control's Visible property is initially set to True.
- The `lightOffPictureBox` control's Visible property is initially set to False.
- The `lightStateLabel` displays either *ON* or *OFF* while the application runs to indicate whether the light is on or off. Initially, this control's Text property is set to *ON*.

At run time, when the user clicks the *Switch Light* button, the state of the light is reversed. In other words, if the light is currently on, it will be turned off. If the light is currently off, it will be turned on.

When the light is turned on, the following actions take place:

- The `lightOnPictureBox` control's Visible property is set to `true`.
- The `lightOffPictureBox` control's Visible property is set to `false`.
- The `lightStateLabel` label's Text property is assigned the string `"ON"`.

When the light is turned off, the following actions take place:

- The `lightOffPictureBox` control's Visible property is set to `true`.
- The `lightOnPictureBox` control's Visible property is set to `false`.
- The `lightStateLabel` label's Text property is assigned the string `"OFF"`.

To modularize the code, you create a method named `TurnLightOn` (containing the code to turn the light on), and another method named `TurnLightOff` (containing the code to turn the light off). When you need to turn the light on, you call the `TurnLightOn` method and when you need to turn the light off you call the `TurnLightOff` method.

Step 1: Start Visual Studio (or Visual C# Express). Open the project named *Lights* in the *Chap06* folder of the Student Sample Programs that accompany this book.

Step 2: Open the Form1 form in the *Designer*. The form is shown, along with the names of the important controls, in Figure 6-8.

Step 3: Move the PictureBox controls so one is on top of the other, as shown in Figure 6-9. (In the figure, the `lightOnPictureBox` control is on top, but it really does not matter which is on top.) Also, reduce the width of the form and position the button controls as shown in the figure.

Figure 6-9 The controls repositioned and the form size adjusted

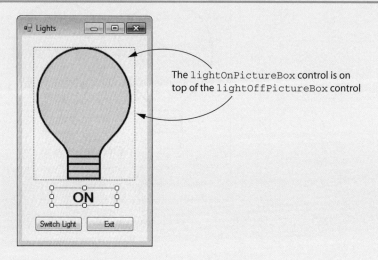

Step 4: Program 6-2, at the end of this tutorial, shows the form's completed code. Open the code editor and type the code for the `TurnLightOn` and the `TurnLightOff` methods, shown in lines 19–41 of Program 6-2.

Let's take a closer look at the code. Line 19 is the beginning of a method named `TurnLightOn`. The purpose of this method is to simulate the light turning on. When this method executes, line 22 makes the `lightOnPictureBox` control visible, line 25 makes the `lightOffPictureBox` control invisible, and line 28 sets the `lightStateLabel` control's Text property to `"ON"`.

Line 31 is the beginning of a method named `TurnLightOff`. The purpose of this method is to simulate the light turning off. When this method executes, line 34 makes the `lightOffPictureBox` control visible, line 37 makes the `lightOnPictureBox` control invisible, and line 40 sets the `lightStateLabel` control's Text property to `"OFF"`.

Step 5: Next, you create the Click event handlers for the Button controls. Switch back to the *Designer* and double-click the `switchButton` control. This opens the code editor, and you will see an empty event handler named `switchButton_Click`. Complete the `switchButton_Click` event handler by typing the code shown in lines 45–53 in Program 6-2.

Let's review this code. The `if` statement in line 46 determines whether the `lightOnPictureBox` control is visible. If it is, it means the light is turned on, so the statement in line 48 calls the `TurnLightOff` method to turn the light off.

Otherwise, the `else` clause in line 50 takes over, and the `TurnLightOn` method is called on line 52 to turn the light on.

Step 6: Switch your view back to the *Designer* and double-click the `exitButton` control. In the code editor you will see an empty event handler named `exitButton_Click`. Complete the `exitButton_Click` event handler by typing the code shown in lines 58–59 in Program 6-2.

Step 7: Save the project. Then, press F5 on the keyboard, or click the *Start Debugging* button (▶) on the toolbar to compile and run the application. When the application runs, click the *Switch Light* button several times to simulate several coin tosses. When you are finished, click the *Exit* button to exit the application.

Program 6-2 Completed code for Form1 in the *Lights* application

```
 1 using System;
 2 using System.Collections.Generic;
 3 using System.ComponentModel;
 4 using System.Data;
 5 using System.Drawing;
 6 using System.Linq;
 7 using System.Text;
 8 using System.Windows.Forms;
 9
10 namespace Lights
11 {
12     public partial class Form1 : Form
13     {
14         public Form1()
15         {
16             InitializeComponent();
17         }
18
19         private void TurnLightOn()
20         {
21             // Display the "light on" image.
22             lightOnPictureBox.Visible = true;
23
24             // Hide the "light off" image.
25             lightOffPictureBox.Visible = false;
26
27             // Display the light's state.
28             lightStateLabel.Text = "ON";
29         }
30
31         private void TurnLightOff()
32         {
33             // Display the "light off" image.
34             lightOffPictureBox.Visible = true;
35
36             // Hide the "light on" image.
37             lightOnPictureBox.Visible = false;
38
39             // Display the light's state.
40             lightStateLabel.Text = "OFF";
41         }
42
43         private void switchButton_Click(object sender, EventArgs e)
```

```
44          {
45              // Reverse the state of the light.
46              if (lightOnPictureBox.Visible == true)
47              {
48                  TurnLightOff();
49              }
50              else
51              {
52                  TurnLightOn();
53              }
54          }
55
56          private void exitButton_Click(object sender, EventArgs e)
57          {
58              // Close the form.
59              this.Close();
60          }
61      }
62 }
```

Top-Down Design

In this section, we have discussed and demonstrated how methods work. You have seen how the program jumps to a method when it is called and returns to the part of the program that called the method when the method ends. It is important that you understand these mechanical aspects of methods.

Just as important as understanding how methods work is understanding how to use methods to modularize a program. Programmers commonly use a technique known as **top-down design** to break down an algorithm into methods. The process of top-down design is performed in the following manner:

- The overall task that the program is to perform is broken down into a series of subtasks.
- Each subtask is examined to determine whether it can be further broken down into more subtasks. This step is repeated until no more subtasks can be identified.
- Once all of the subtasks have been identified, they are written in code.

This process is called top-down design because the programmer begins by looking at the topmost level of tasks that must be performed and then breaks down those tasks into lower levels of subtasks.

> **NOTE:** The top-down design process is sometimes called **stepwise refinement**.

 ## Checkpoint

6.1   What is the difference between a void method and a value-returning method?

6.2   What two parts does a method definition have?

6.3   What does the phrase "calling a method" mean?

6.4   When a void method is executing, what happens when the end of the method is reached?

6.5   Describe the steps involved in the top-down design process.

6.3 Passing Arguments to Methods

CONCEPT: An argument is any piece of data that is passed into a method when the method is called. A parameter is a variable that receives an argument that is passed into a method.

Sometimes it is useful not only to call a method, but also to send one or more pieces of data into the method. Pieces of data that are sent into a method are known as **arguments**. The method can use its arguments in calculations or other operations.

You are already familiar with how to use arguments in a method call. For example, look at the following statement:

```
MessageBox.Show("Hello");
```

This statement calls the `MessageBox.Show` method and passes the string `"Hello"` as an argument. Here is another example:

```
number = int.Parse(str);
```

Assume that number is an `int` variable and `str` is a `string` variable. This statement calls the `int.Parse` method, passing the `str` variable as an argument.

If you are writing a method and you want it to receive arguments when it is called, you must equip the method with one or more parameter variables. A **parameter variable**, often simply called a **parameter**, is a special variable that receives an argument when a method is called. Here is an example of a method that has a parameter variable:

```
private void DisplayValue(int value)
{
    MessageBox.Show(value.ToString());
}
```

Notice the `int` variable declaration that appears inside the parentheses (`int value`). This is the declaration of a parameter variable, which enables the `DisplayValue` method to accept an `int` value as an argument. Here is an example of a call to the `DisplayValue` method, passing 5 as an argument:

```
DisplayValue(5);
```

This statement executes the `DisplayValue` method. The argument that is listed inside the parentheses is assigned to the method's parameter variable, `value`. This is illustrated in Figure 6-10.

Figure 6-10 Passing the value 5 to the `DisplayValue` method

```
DisplayValue(5);            The value 5 is assigned
                           to the value parameter.


private void DisplayValue(int value)
{
    MessageBox.Show(value.ToString());
}
```

Inside the `DisplayValue` method, the variable `value` will contain the value of whatever argument was passed into it. If we pass 5 as the argument, the method will display the value 5 in a message box.

You may also pass the contents of variables and the values of expressions as arguments. For example, the following statements call the `DisplayValue` method with various arguments passed:

```
DisplayValue(x);
DisplayValue(x * 4);
DisplayValue(int.Parse("700"));
```

The first statement is simple. It passes the value of the variable x as the argument to the `DisplayValue` method. The second statement is also simple, but it does a little more work: it passes the result of the expression x * 4 as the argument to the `DisplayValue` method. The third statement does even more work. It passes the value returned from the `int.Parse` method as the argument to the `DisplayValue` method. (The `int.Parse` method is called first, and its return value is passed to the `DisplayValue` method.)

In the *Chap06* folder of the Student Sample Programs that accompany this book, you will find a project named *Argument Demo* that demonstrates this method. Figure 6-11 shows the application's form, and Program 6-3 shows the form's code.

Figure 6-11 The *Argument Demo* application's form

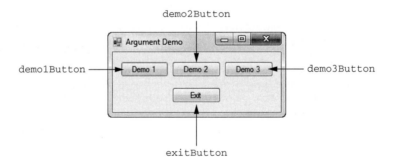

Program 6-3 Code for the *Argument Demo* application's `Form1` form

```
 1 using System;
 2 using System.Collections.Generic;
 3 using System.ComponentModel;
 4 using System.Data;
 5 using System.Drawing;
 6 using System.Linq;
 7 using System.Text;
 8 using System.Windows.Forms;
 9
10 namespace Argument_Demo
11 {
12     public partial class Form1 : Form
13     {
14         public Form1()
15         {
16             InitializeComponent();
17         }
18
19         private void DisplayValue(int value)
20         {
21             MessageBox.Show(value.ToString());
```

```
22            }
23
24            private void demo1Button_Click(object sender, EventArgs e)
25            {
26                // Call DisplayValue passing 5 as an argument.
27                DisplayValue(5);
28            }
29
30            private void demo2Button_Click(object sender, EventArgs e)
31            {
32                // Call DisplayValue passing the expression 3 + 5
33                // as an argument.
34                DisplayValue(3 + 5);
35            }
36
37            private void demo3Button_Click(object sender, EventArgs e)
38            {
39                // Use a loop to call DisplayValue 5 times.
40                for (int count = 0; count < 5; count++)
41                {
42                    DisplayValue(count);
43                }
44            }
45
46            private void exitButton_Click(object sender, EventArgs e)
47            {
48                // Close the form.
49                this.Close();
50            }
51        }
52 }
```

The form has four button controls, and a Click event handler has been written for each one. In addition to the event handlers, the code contains the DisplayValue method, which we discussed earlier, in lines 19–22.

If you run the application and click the *Demo 1* button, the demo1Button_Click event handler executes. Notice that in line 27 the DisplayValue method is called, passing 5 as an argument. This causes a message box to appear showing the value 5.

If you click the *Demo 2* button, the demo2Button_Click event handler executes. In line 34 the DisplayValue method is called, passing the expression 3 + 5 as an argument. This causes a message box to appear showing the value 8.

If you click the *Demo 3* button, the demo3Button_Click event handler executes. In line 40 a for loop executes five times, each time passing the count variable as an argument. This causes a message box to appear five times, showing the values 0 through 4.

NOTE: When calling a method and passing a variable as an argument, simply write the variable name inside the parentheses of the method call. Do *not* write the data type of the argument variable in the method call. For example, the following statement causes an error:

```
DisplayValue(int x); // Error!
```

The method call should appear as follows:

```
DisplayValue(x); // Correct
```

NOTE: In this text, the values that are passed into a method are called *arguments*, and the variables that receive those values are called *parameters*. There are several variations of these terms in use. In some circles these terms are switched in meaning. Also, some call the arguments *actual parameters* and call the parameters *formal parameters*. Others use the terms *actual argument* and *formal argument*. Regardless of which set of terms you use, it is important to be consistent.

In Tutorial 6-2 you will complete an application that calls a method and passes an argument to it.

Tutorial 6-2:
Passing an Argument to a Method

In this tutorial you complete the *Cards* project in the *Chap06* folder of the Student Sample Programs that accompany this book. The project's form, shown in Figure 6-12, has already been created for you. The PictureBox controls show the images of three cards. Each PictureBox control's Visible property is set to False, so they do not initially appear when the application runs. After you complete the application, the user can select a card's name from the ListBox, click the *Show Card* button, and the image of the selected card will appear.

Figure 6-12 The *Cards* project's form

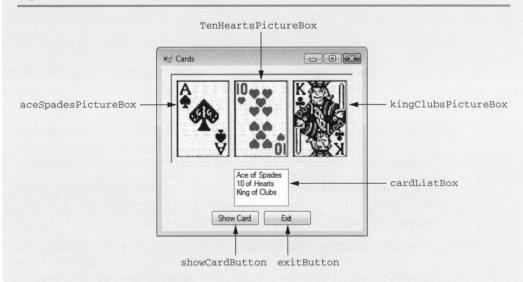

Step 1: Start Visual Studio (or Visual C# Express). Open the project named *Cards* in the *Chap06* folder of the Student Sample Programs that accompany this book.

Step 2: Program 6-4, at the end of this tutorial, shows the form's completed code. Open the code editor and type the comments and code for the `ShowCard` method, shown in lines 19–35 of Program 6-4.

The purpose of the `ShowCard` method is to display one of the card PictureBox controls. Let's take a closer look at the code.

Line 21: This is the beginning of the method. The method has a `string` parameter named `card`. When we call the method, we pass the item that the user selected in the ListBox as an argument, and the method displays the specified card.

> **Lines 23–34:** This is a `switch` statement that tests the value of the `card` parameter. If `card` is equal to `"Ace of Spades"`, the program jumps to the `case` statement in line 25 and calls the `ShowAceSpades` method in line 26. If `card` is equal to `"10 of Hearts"`, the program jumps to the `case` statement in line 28 and calls the `ShowTenHearts` method in line 29. If `card` is equal to `"King of Clubs"`, the program jumps to the `case` statement in line 31 and calls the `ShowKingClubs` method in line 32.

Step 3: Type the comments and code for the `ShowAceSpades` method, shown in lines 37–44 of Program 6-4. This method makes the `aceSpadesPictureBox` control visible, and the other PictureBox controls invisible.

Step 4: Type the comments and code for the `ShowTenHearts` method, shown in lines 46–53 of Program 6-4. This method makes the `tenHeartsPictureBox` control visible and the other PictureBox controls invisible.

Step 5: Type the comments and code for the `ShowKingClubs` method, shown in lines 55–62 of Program 6-4. This method makes the `kingClubsPictureBox` control visible, and the other PictureBox controls invisible.

Step 6: Next you create the Click event handlers for the Button controls. Switch back to the *Designer* and double-click the `showCardButton` control. This opens the code editor, and you will see an empty event handler named `showCardButton_Click`. Complete the `showCardButton_Click` event handler by typing the code shown in lines 66–75 in Program 6-4.

Let's review this code. The `if` statement in line 67 determines whether the user has selected an item in the `cardListBox`. If a value has been selected, line 69 calls the `ShowCard` method. Notice that the item that was selected in the ListBox (converted to a string) is passed as an argument. If the user has not selected an item in the `cardListBox` control, the `else` clause in line 71 takes over, and lines 73–74 display a message box telling the user to select a card.

Step 7: Switch your view back to the *Designer* and double-click the `exitButton` control. In the code editor you will see an empty event handler named `exitButton_Click`. Complete the `exitButton_Click` event handler by typing the code shown in lines 80–81 in Program 6-4.

Step 8: Save the project. Then, press F5 on the keyboard or click the *Start Debugging* button (▶) on the toolbar to compile and run the application. Test the application by selecting each card's name in the ListBox and clicking the *Show Card* button. When you are finished, click the *Exit* button to exit the application.

Program 6-4 Completed code for Form1 in the *Lights* application

```
 1 using System;
 2 using System.Collections.Generic;
 3 using System.ComponentModel;
 4 using System.Data;
 5 using System.Drawing;
 6 using System.Linq;
 7 using System.Text;
 8 using System.Windows.Forms;
 9
10 namespace Cards
11 {
12     public partial class Form1 : Form
```

```
13    {
14        public Form1()
15        {
16            InitializeComponent();
17        }
18
19        // The ShowCard method accepts a string that names
20        // the selected card, and displays that card.
21        private void ShowCard(string card)
22        {
23            switch (card)
24            {
25                case "Ace of Spades" :
26                    ShowAceSpades();
27                    break;
28                case "10 of Hearts":
29                    ShowTenHearts();
30                    break;
31                case "King of Clubs":
32                    ShowKingClubs();
33                    break;
34            }
35        }
36
37        // The ShowAceSpades method makes the Ace of Spades
38        // visible and the other cards invisible.
39        private void ShowAceSpades()
40        {
41            aceSpadesPictureBox.Visible = true;
42            tenHeartsPictureBox.Visible = false;
43            kingClubsPictureBox.Visible = false;
44        }
45
46        // The ShowTenHearts method makes the Ten of Hearts
47        // visible and the other cards invisible.
48        private void ShowTenHearts()
49        {
50            tenHeartsPictureBox.Visible = true;
51            aceSpadesPictureBox.Visible = false;
52            kingClubsPictureBox.Visible = false;
53        }
54
55        // The ShowKingClubs method makes the King of Clubs
56        // visible and the other cards invisible.
57        private void ShowKingClubs()
58        {
59            kingClubsPictureBox.Visible = true;
60            aceSpadesPictureBox.Visible = false;
61            tenHeartsPictureBox.Visible = false;
62        }
63
64        private void showCardButton_Click(object sender, EventArgs e)
65        {
66            // If a card is selected in the ListBox, display it.
67            if (cardListBox.SelectedIndex != -1)
68            {
69                ShowCard(cardListBox.SelectedItem.ToString());
70            }
71            else
72            {
```

```
73                    MessageBox.Show("Please select a card from " +
74                                     "the list box.");
75            }
76        }
77
78        private void exitButton_Click(object sender, EventArgs e)
79        {
80            // Close the form.
81            this.Close();
82        }
83    }
84 }
```

Argument and Parameter Data Type Compatibility

When you pass an argument to a method, the argument's data type must be assignment compatible with the receiving parameter's data type. Otherwise, an error occurs when you try to compile the code. We discussed assignment compatibility in Chapter 3. Here is a summary of how it applies to argument passing when using strings, ints, doubles, and decimals:

- You can pass only string arguments into string parameters.
- You can pass int arguments into int parameters, but you cannot pass double or decimal arguments into int parameters.
- You can pass either double or int arguments into double parameters, but you cannot pass decimal values into double parameters.
- You can pass either decimal or int arguments to decimal parameters, but you cannot pass double arguments into decimal parameters.

Parameter Variable Scope

Recall from Chapter 3 that a variable's scope is the part of the program where the variable may be accessed. A variable is visible only to statements inside the variable's scope. A parameter variable's scope is the method in which the parameter is declared. No statement outside the method can access the parameter variable.

Passing Multiple Arguments

Often it is useful to pass more than one argument to a method. The following code sample shows a method that accepts two arguments. The name of the method is ShowMax. It accepts two int arguments and displays the value of the argument that is the greatest. If the arguments are equal, it displays a message saying so. (This method can be found in the *Max* project in the *Chap06* folder of the Student Sample Programs that accompany this book.)

```
1 private void ShowMax(int num1, int num2)
2 {
3     if (num1 == num2)
4     {
5         MessageBox.Show("The numbers are equal.");
6     }
7     else if (num1 > num2)
8     {
9         MessageBox.Show(num1 + " is the greatest.");
```

```
10       }
11       else
12       {
13           MessageBox.Show(num2 + " is the greatest.");
14       }
15  }
```

Notice that two parameter variables, num1 and num2, are declared inside the parentheses in the method header (line 1). This is often referred to as a parameter list. Also notice that a comma separates the declarations. Here is an example of a statement that calls the method:

```
ShowMax(5, 10);
```

This statement passes the arguments 5 and 10 to the method. The arguments are passed into the parameter variables according to their positions. In other words, the first argument is passed into the first parameter variable, the second argument is passed into the second parameter variable, and so forth. So, this statement causes 5 to be passed into the num1 parameter and 10 to be passed into the num2 parameter. This is illustrated in Figure 6-13.

Figure 6-13 Two arguments passed according to position to a method

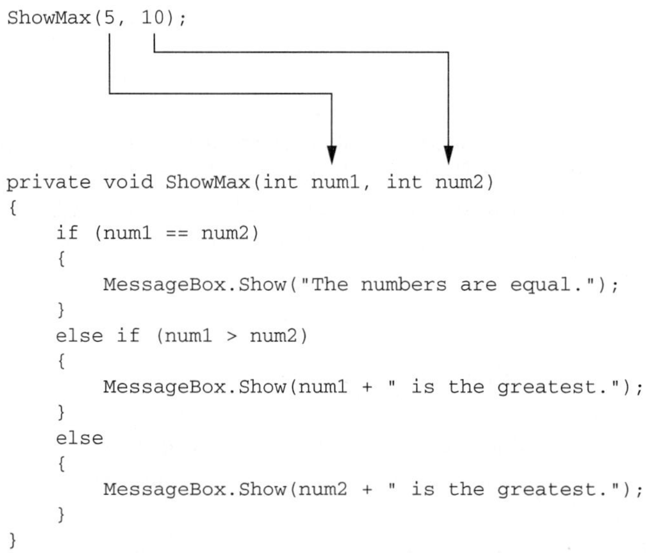

```
ShowMax(5, 10);



private void ShowMax(int num1, int num2)
{
    if (num1 == num2)
    {
        MessageBox.Show("The numbers are equal.");
    }
    else if (num1 > num2)
    {
        MessageBox.Show(num1 + " is the greatest.");
    }
    else
    {
        MessageBox.Show(num2 + " is the greatest.");
    }
}
```

Suppose we were to reverse the order in which the arguments are listed in the method call, as shown here:

```
ShowMax(10, 5);
```

This causes 10 to be passed into the num1 parameter and 5 to be passed into the num2 parameter. The following code sample shows one more example. This time we are passing variables as arguments.

```
int value1 = 2;
int value2 = 3;
ShowMax(value1, value2);
```

When the ShowMax method executes as a result of this code, the num1 parameter contains 2 and the num2 parameter contains 3.

NOTE: You have to write the data type for each parameter variable that is declared in a parameter list. For example, a compiler error would occur if the parameter list for the ShowMax method were written as shown here:

```
private void ShowMax(int num1, num2) // Error!
```

A data type for both the num1 and num2 parameter variables must be listed, as shown here:

```
private void ShowMax(int num1, int num2)
```

Named Arguments

In addition to the conventional approach of positional argument passing (where the first argument is passed into the method's first parameter, the second argument is passed into the method's second parameter, and so forth), C# also allows you to specify which parameter an argument should be passed into. To specify which parameter variable the argument should be passed to, you use the following format to write the argument in the method call:

```
parameterName : value
```

In this format *parameterName* is the name of a parameter variable and *value* is the value being passed to that parameter. An argument that is written using this syntax is known as a **named argument**. To demonstrate, look at the following method:

```
private void ShowName(string firstName, string lastName)
{
    MessageBox.Show(firstName + " " + lastName);
}
```

The following statement shows how the method can be called using named arguments:

```
ShowName(lastName : "Smith", firstName : "Suzanne");
```

This statement specifies that "Smith" should be passed into the lastName parameter and "Suzanne" should be passed into the firstName parameter. You get the same results as if you had called the method like this, using positional arguments:

```
ShowName("Suzanne", "Smith");
```

NOTE: Named arguments were introduced in Visual C# 2010. You cannot use them in older versions of C#.

Default Arguments

C# allows you to provide a **default argument** for a method parameter. When a default argument is provided for a parameter, it becomes possible to call the method without explicitly passing an argument into the parameter. Here is an example of a method that has a parameter with a default argument:

```
private void ShowTax(decimal price, decimal taxRate = 0.07m)
{
    // Calculate the tax.
    decimal tax = price * taxRate;

    // Display the tax.
    MessageBox.Show("The tax is " + tax.ToString("c"));
}
```

In this method definition, a default argument is provided for the `taxRate` parameter. Notice that the parameter name is followed by an equal sign and a value. The value that follows the equal sign is the default argument. In this case, the value is `0.07m` is the default argument for the `taxRate` parameter. Because the `taxRate` parameter has a default argument, we have the option of omitting an argument for it when we call the method. Here is an example:

```
ShowTax(100.0m);
```

This statement calls the `ShowTax` method, passing the value `100.0m` as the argument for the `price` parameter. Because we did not pass an argument into the `taxRate` parameter, its value will be `0.07m`. If we want the `taxRate` parameter to have a different value, we can specify an argument for it when we call the method, as shown here:

```
ShowTax(100.0m, 0.08m);
```

This statement calls the `ShowTax` method, passing `100.0m` as the argument for the `price` parameter and `0.08m` as the argument for the `taxRate` parameter.

Here are some details to keep in mind when using default arguments:

- Default arguments must be literals or constants. You cannot specify a variable as a default argument.
- You can provide default arguments for all of the parameters in a method. However, when only some of the parameters have a default argument (as in the previous example), you must declare the parameters with the default arguments last. For example, a compiler error would occur if we were to write the `ShowTax` method header as shown here:

  ```
  // Illegal method header!
  private void ShowTax(decimal taxRate = 0.07m, decimal price)
  ```

- When a method has several parameters with default arguments and you leave out one of the arguments when you call the method, you have to leave out all the arguments that come after it as well.

 NOTE: Default arguments were introduced in Visual C# 2010. You cannot use them in older versions of C#.

Passing Arguments by Value

All the example programs that you have looked at so far pass arguments by value. Arguments and parameter variables are separate items in memory. When an argument is **passed by value**, only a copy of the argument's value is passed into the parameter variable. If the contents of the parameter variable are changed inside the method, it has no effect on the argument in the calling part of the program.

For example, the following code comes from the *Pass By Value* project in the *Chap06* folder of the Student Sample Programs. When you run the application and click the *Go* button, you see the sequence of message boxes shown in Figure 6-14.

```
1 private void goButton_Click(object sender, EventArgs e)
2 {
3     int number = 99;
4
5     // Display the value of number.
6     MessageBox.Show("The value of number is " + number);
7
8     // Call ChangeMe, passing number as an argument.
9     ChangeMe(number);
```

```
10
11     // Display the value of number again.
12     MessageBox.Show("The value of number is " + number);
13 }
14
15 private void ChangeMe(int myValue)
16 {
17     // Change the value of the myValue parameter.
18     myValue = 0;
19
20     // Display the value of myValue.
21     MessageBox.Show("In ChangeMe, myValue is " + myValue);
22 }
```

Figure 6-14 Sequence of messages displayed by the *Pass By Value* application

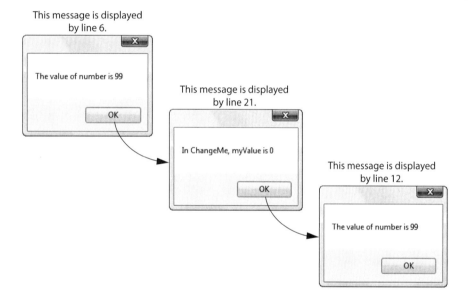

Inside the goButton_Click event handler, a local variable named number is declared in line 3, and initialized with the value 99. As a result, the statement in line 6 displays *The value of number is 99*. The number variable's value is then passed as an argument to the ChangeMe method in line 9. This means that in the ChangeMe method, the value 99 is assigned to the myValue parameter variable.

Inside the ChangeMe method, line 18 assigns the value 0 to the myValue parameter variable. This overwrites the value 99 that was passed into the parameter when the method was called. Line 21 displays the message *In ChangeMe, myValue is 0*.

After the ChangeMe method finishes, control of the program returns to the goButton_Click event handler. When the statement in line 12 executes, the message *The value of number is 99* is displayed. Even though the parameter variable myValue was changed in the ChangeMe method, the number variable in the goButton_Click event handler was not modified.

Passing by value works in most situations because arguments are usually sent to methods for informational purposes only. Typically, when you pass a variable as an argument to a method, you want that variable to have the same value before *and* after the method call. Passing an argument by value guarantees that the argument will not be changed by the method it is passed into. Sometimes, however, you want a method to be able to change the value of a variable that was passed as an argument to it. This requires a slightly different type of argument passing, which is discussed in the next section.

Checkpoint

> 6.6 What is the purpose of an argument?
>
> 6.7 Briefly summarize how assignment compatibility applies to argument passing.
>
> 6.8 What is the scope of a parameter variable?
>
> 6.9 What is a named argument?
>
> 6.10 What does it mean when an argument is passed by value?

6.4 Passing Arguments by Reference

CONCEPT: When an argument is passed by reference to a method, the method can change the value of the argument in the calling part of the program.

When you want a method to be able to change the value of a variable that is passed to it as an argument, the variable must be **passed by reference**. In C# there are two ways to pass an argument by reference:

- You can use a reference parameter in the method.
- You can use an output parameter in the method.

Using Reference Parameters

A **reference parameter** is a special type of parameter variable. When you pass an argument into a reference parameter, the reference parameter does not receive a copy of the argument's value. Instead, it becomes a *reference* to the argument that was passed into it. Anything that is done to the reference parameter is actually done to the argument that it references.

Reference parameters are useful for establishing two-way communication between methods. When a method calls another method and passes an argument by reference, communication between the methods can take place in the following ways:

- The calling method can communicate with the called method by passing an argument.
- The called method can communicate with the calling method by modifying the value of the argument via the reference parameter.

In C#, you declare a reference parameter by writing the `ref` keyword before the parameter variable's data type. For example, look at the following method:

```
private void SetToZero(ref int number)
{
    number = 0;
}
```

Inside the parentheses, the keyword `ref` indicates that `number` is a reference variable. The method assigns 0 to the `number` parameter. Because `number` is a reference parameter, this action is actually performed on the variable that was passed to the method as an argument.

When you call a method that has a reference parameter, you must also write the keyword `ref` before the argument. The following code sample shows an example.

```
int myVar = 99;
SetToZero(ref myVar);
```

The first statement declares myVar as an int variable, initialized with the value 99. The second statement calls the SetToZero method, passing myVar by reference. After the method call, the myVar variable is set to the value 0.

When you pass an argument to a ref parameter, that argument must already be set to some value. For example, if a variable has not been initialized or assigned a value, you cannot pass it as an argument into a ref parameter. The following code sample causes a compiler error:

```
int myVar;            // Declare myVar with no initial value.
SetToZero(ref myVar); // Error! myVar is not set to a value.
```

Let's look at a complete program that uses the SetToZero method. In the *Chap06* folder of the Student Sample Programs that accompany this book, you will find a project named *Pass By Ref*. Figure 6-15 shows the application's form, and Program 6-5 shows the form's code.

Figure 6-15 The *Pass By Ref* application's form

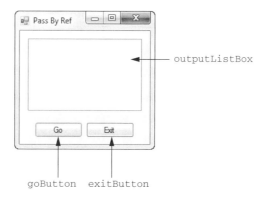

Program 6-5 Code for the *Pass By Ref* application's Form1 form

```
 1 using System;
 2 using System.Collections.Generic;
 3 using System.ComponentModel;
 4 using System.Data;
 5 using System.Drawing;
 6 using System.Linq;
 7 using System.Text;
 8 using System.Windows.Forms;
 9
10 namespace Pass_By_Ref
11 {
12     public partial class Form1 : Form
13     {
14         public Form1()
15         {
16             InitializeComponent();
17         }
18
19         // The SetToZero method accepts an int argument
20         // by reference and sets it to zero.
21         private void SetToZero(ref int number)
22         {
23             number = 0;
24         }
25
```

```
26          private void goButton_Click(object sender, EventArgs e)
27          {
28              // Declare some local int variables.
29              int x = 99, y = 100, z = 101;
30
31              // Display the values in those variables.
32              outputListBox.Items.Clear();
33              outputListBox.Items.Add("x is set to " + x);
34              outputListBox.Items.Add("y is set to " + y);
35              outputListBox.Items.Add("z is set to " + z);
36
37              // Pass each variable to SetToZero.
38              SetToZero(ref x);
39              SetToZero(ref y);
40              SetToZero(ref z);
41
42              // Display the values in those variables again.
43              outputListBox.Items.Add("--------------------");
44              outputListBox.Items.Add("x is set to " + x);
45              outputListBox.Items.Add("y is set to " + y);
46              outputListBox.Items.Add("z is set to " + z);
47          }
48
49          private void exitButton_Click(object sender, EventArgs e)
50          {
51              // Close the form.
52              this.Close();
53          }
54      }
55 }
```

Notice that the form has a ListBox control named outputListBox. This ListBox is used to display the program's output. The SetToZero method that we previously discussed appears in lines 21–24. The method accepts an int argument by reference and assigns the value 0 to the argument.

In the goButton_Click method, line 29 declares the int variables x, y, and z and initializes them to the values 99, 100, and 101, respectively. Line 32 clears the outputListBox control, and lines 33–35 display the values of the x, y, and z variables in the ListBox.

In lines 38–40 x, y, and z variables are passed as arguments, by reference, to the SetToZero method. Each time SetToZero is called, the variable that is passed as an argument is assigned the value 0. This is shown when the x, y, and z variables are displayed again in lines 44–46. Figure 6-16 shows the application's form after the *Go* button has been clicked.

Figure 6-16 The *Pass By Ref* application's output

Using Output Parameters

An **output parameter** works like a reference parameter. When you pass an argument into an output parameter, the output parameter becomes a reference to the argument that is passed into it. Anything that is done to the output parameter is actually done to the argument that it references. Output parameters are different from reference parameters in the following ways:

- An argument does not have to be set to a value before it is passed into an output parameter. For example, an uninitialized variable can be passed into an output parameter.
- A method that has an output parameter must set the output parameter to some value before it finishes executing.

In C#, you declare an output parameter by writing the `out` keyword before the parameter variable's data type. For example, we could modify the `SetToZero` method in the following way to make the `number` parameter an output parameter:

```
private void SetToZero(out int number)
{
    number = 0;
}
```

When you call a method that has an output parameter, you must also write the keyword out before the argument. The following code sample shows an example.

```
int myVar;
SetToZero(out myVar);
```

The first statement declares `myVar` as an uninitialized `int` variable. The second statement calls the `SetToZero` method, passing `myVar` into the output parameter. After the method call, the `myVar` variable is set to the value 0.

Tutorial 6-3 gives you some experience writing a method that uses an ouput parameter.

Tutorial 6-3:
Using an Output Parameter

In this tutorial you complete the *North America* application that is found in the *Chap06* folder of the Student Sample Programs that accompany this book. The application's form has already been created and is shown in Figure 6-17. The application also has an accompanying text

Figure 6-17 The *North America* application's form

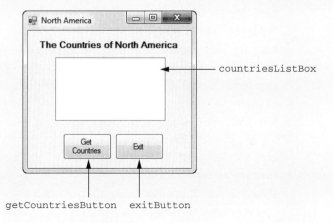

file named NorthAmerica.txt that is stored in the *Chap06* folder. The NorthAmerica. txt file contains the names of the countries of North America.

When the completed application runs and the user clicks the *Get Countries* button, the application uses an OpenFileDialog control to let the user select a file. The application reads each country name from the file and adds each one to the `countriesListBox` control.

Step 1: Start Visual Studio (or Visual C# Express). Open the project named *North America* in the *Chap06* folder of the Student Sample Programs that accompany this book.

Step 2: Open Form1 in the *Designer* and add an OpenFileDialog control to the form. Change the control's name to `openFile` and clear the contents of the control's Filename property.

Step 3: Open the Form1 form's code in the code editor. Insert the **using System.IO;** directive shown in line 9 of Program 6-6 at the end of this tutorial. This statement is necessary because you will be using the `StreamReader` class, which is part of the `System.IO` namespace in the .NET Framework.

Step 4: Type the comments and code for the `GetFileName` method, shown in lines 20–33 of Program 6-6. The purpose of the `GetFileName` method is to let the user select the file that should be opened. Let's take a closer look at the code.

Line 23: This is the beginning of the method. The method has a `string` output parameter named `selectedFile`. When we call the method, we pass a `string` variable as an argument. The method lets the user select the file that should be opened and stores its filename and path in the `selectedFile` parameter.

Lines 25–32: This `if` statement calls the `openFile` control's `ShowDialog` method. If the user clicks the *Open* button, the method returns the value `DialogResult.OK`, and line 27 assigns the name of the selected file to the `selectedFile` parameter. If the user clicks the *Cancel* button, line 31 assigns an empty string to the `selectedFile` parameter.

Step 5: Type the comments and code for the `GetCountries` method, shown in lines 35–69 of Program 6-6. In a nutshell, this method accepts a filename as an argument, reads the contents of the specified file, and adds them to the `countriesListBox` control. Here is a more detailed description of each part of the method:

Line 40: This is the beginning of a `try-catch` statement, which handles any exceptions that are thrown while the file is being processed. If an exception is thrown by any statement in the try block, the program will jump to the `catch` clause in line 67.

Line 43: This statement declares the `string` variable `countryName`, which holds the lines of text that are read from the file.

Line 46: This statement declares the `StreamReader` variable `inputFile`.

Line 49: After this statement has executed, the file specified by the `filename` parameter is opened for reading, and the `inputFile` variable references a `StreamReader` object that is associated with the file.

Line 52: This statement clears anything that might be displayed in the `countriesListBox` control.

Line 55: This is the beginning of a `while` loop that iterates as long as the end of the file has not been reached.

Line 58: This statement reads a line of text from the file and assigns it to the `countryName` variable.

Line 61: This statement adds the contents of the `countryName` variable to the ListBox.

Line 65: This statement closes the file.

Step 6: Open the Form1 form in the *Designer*. Double-click the `getCountriesButton` control. This opens the code editor, and you will see an empty event handler named `getCountriesButton _Click`. Complete the `getCountriesButton _Click` event handler by typing the code shown in lines 76–82 in Program 6-6. Let's take a closer look at the code:

Line 76: This statement declares a `string` variable named `filename`.

Line 79: This statement calls the `GetFileName` method, passing the `filename` variable as an argument. When the method returns, the `filename` variable contains the name of the file selected by the user.

Line 82: This statement calls the `GetCountries` method, passing the `filename` variable as an argument. The method opens the specified file and fills the `countriesListBox` control with its contents.

Step 7: Switch your view back to the *Designer* and double-click the `exitButton` control. In the code editor you will see an empty event handler named `exitButton_Click`. Complete the `exitButton_Click` event handler by typing the code shown in lines 87–88 in Program 6-6.

Step 8: Save the project. Then, press F5 on the keyboard or click the *Start Debugging* button (▶) on the toolbar to compile and run the application. When the application runs, click the *Get Countries* button. An *Open* dialog box should appear. Navigate to the *Chap06* folder in the Student Sample Programs, select the NorthAmerica.txt file, and click the *Open* button. This should fill the ListBox with the names of the countries from the selected file, as shown in Figure 6-18. Click the *Exit* button to exit the application.

Figure 6-18 The *North America* application displaying the list of countries

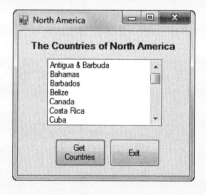

Program 6-6 Completed code for Form1 in the *North America* application

```
1 using System;
2 using System.Collections.Generic;
3 using System.ComponentModel;
4 using System.Data;
5 using System.Drawing;
6 using System.Linq;
7 using System.Text;
```

```
 8 using System.Windows.Forms;
 9 using System.IO;
10
11 namespace North_America
12 {
13     public partial class Form1 : Form
14     {
15         public Form1()
16         {
17             InitializeComponent();
18         }
19
20         // The GetFileName method gets a filename from the
21         // user and assigns it to the variable passed as
22         // an argument.
23         private void GetFileName(out string selectedFile)
24         {
25             if (openFile.ShowDialog() == DialogResult.OK)
26             {
27                 selectedFile = openFile.FileName;
28             }
29             else
30             {
31                 selectedFile = "";
32             }
33         }
34
35         // The GetCountries method accpets a filename as an
36         // argument. It opens the specified file and displays
37         // its contents in the countriesListBox control.
38         private void GetCountries(string filename)
39         {
40             try
41             {
42                 // Declare a variable to hold a country name.
43                 string countryName;
44
45                 // Declare a StreamReader variable.
46                 StreamReader inputFile;
47
48                 // Open the file and get a StreamReader object.
49                 inputFile = File.OpenText(filename);
50
51                 // Clear anything currently in the ListBox.
52                 countriesListBox.Items.Clear();
53
54                 // Read the file's contents.
55                 while (!inputFile.EndOfStream)
56                 {
57                     // Get a country name.
58                     countryName = inputFile.ReadLine();
59
60                     // Add the country name to the ListBox.
61                     countriesListBox.Items.Add(countryName);
62                 }
63
64                 // Close the file.
65                 inputFile.Close();
66             }
67             catch (Exception ex)
```

```
68                  {
69                      // Display an error message.
70                      MessageBox.Show(ex.Message);
71                  }
72              }
73
74          private void getCountriesButton_Click(object sender, EventArgs e)
75          {
76              string filename;     // To hold the filename
77
78              // Get the filename from the user.
79              GetFileName(out filename);
80
81              // Get the countries from the file.
82              GetCountries(filename);
83          }
84
85          private void exitButton_Click(object sender, EventArgs e)
86          {
87              // Close the form.
88              this.Close();
89          }
90      }
91 }
```

 Checkpoint

6.11 What is a reference parameter?

6.12 How can methods communicate using reference parameters?

6.13 What keyword is used to specify a reference parameter?

6.14 What is an output parameter?

6.5 Value-Returning Methods

CONCEPT: A value-returning method is a method that returns a value to the part of the program that called it.

A value-returning method is like a void method in the following ways:

- It contains a group of statements that perform a specific task.
- When you want to execute the method, you call it.

When a value-returning method finishes, however, it returns a value to the statement that called it. The value that is returned from a method can be used like any other value: It can be assigned to a variable, displayed on the screen, used in a mathematical expression (if it is a number), and so on.

You have already used many of the value-returning methods that are in the .NET Framework. For example, the int.Parse method accepts a string as an argument and returns the value of the string converted to an int. Let's review how that method works. In the following statement, assume number is an int variable:

```
number = int.Parse("100");
```

The part of the statement that reads int.Parse("100") is a call to the int.Parse method, with the string "100" passed as an argument. Figure 6-19 illustrates this part of the statement.

Figure 6-19 A statement that calls the int.Parse method

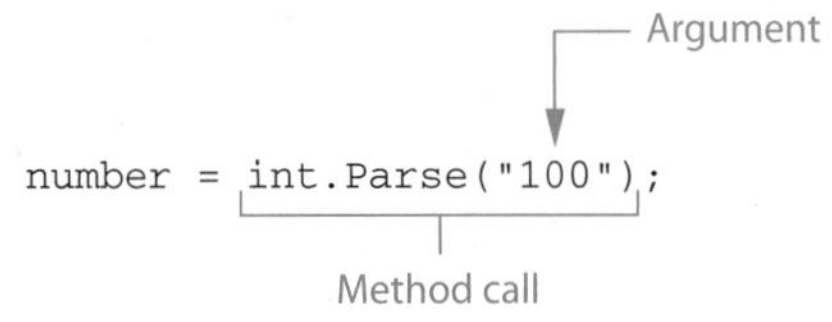

Notice that the call to the int.Parse method appears on the right side of an = operator. When the method is called, it returns an integer. The integer that is returned is assigned to the number variable, as shown in Figure 6-20.

Figure 6-20 The int.Parse method returns a value

```
                         100
            number = int.Parse("100");

        The value 100 is returned from the
        method and assigned to number.
```

Writing Your Own Value-Returning Functions

You write a value-returning method in the same way that you write a void method, with two exceptions:

- You must specify a data type for a value-returning method. The value that is returned from the method must be of the specified data type.
- A value-returning method must have a return statement. The return statement causes a value to be returned from the method.

Here is the general format of a value-returning method definition in C#:

```
AccessModifier DataType MethodName(ParameterList)
{
    statement;
    statement;
    etc.
    return expression;
}
```

- *AccessModifier* is an access modifier such as private or public.
- *DataType* is the data type of the value that the method returns. We commonly call this the method's **return type**. For example, if the method returns an integer, the word int appears here. If the method returns a double value, then the word double appears here. Likewise, if the method returns a decimal value, the word decimal appears here.
- *MethodName* is the name of the method.
- *ParameterList* is an optional parameter list. If the method does not accept arguments, then an empty set of parentheses appears.

One of the statements inside the method must be a `return` statement, which takes the following form:

```
return expression;
```

The value of the *expression* that follows the key word `return` is sent back to the statement that called the method. This can be any value, variable, or expression that has a value (such as a math expression). The value that is returned must be of the same data type as that specified in the method header or a compiler error will occur.

Here is an example of a value-returning method:

```
private int Sum(int num1, int num2)
{
    return num1 + num2;
}
```

Figure 6-21 illustrates the various parts of the method header. Notice that the method returns an `int`, the method's name is `sum`, and the method has two `int` parameters named `num1` and `num2`.

Figure 6-21 Parts of the method header

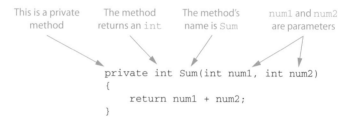

The purpose of this method is to accept two `int` values as arguments and return their sum. Notice that the `return` statement returns the value of the expression `num1 + num2`. When the `return` statement executes, the method ends its execution and sends the value of `num1 + num2` back to the part of the program that called the method.

Let's look at a complete program that demonstrates the `sum` method. In the *Chap06* folder of the Student Sample Programs that accompany this book, you will find a project named *Sum*. Figure 6-22 shows the application's form, and Program 6-7 shows the form's code. When you run the application, you enter two integers into the `age1TextBox` and `age2TextBox` controls. When you click the *Calculate Combined Age* button, the sum of the two integers is displayed in the `combinedAgeLabel` control.

Figure 6-22 The *Sum* application's form

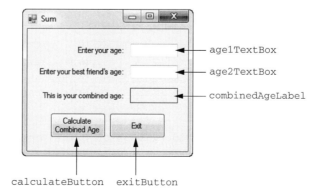

Program 6-7 Code for the *Sum* application's `Form1` form

```
 1 using System;
 2 using System.Collections.Generic;
 3 using System.ComponentModel;
 4 using System.Data;
 5 using System.Drawing;
 6 using System.Linq;
 7 using System.Text;
 8 using System.Windows.Forms;
 9
10 namespace Sum
11 {
12     public partial class Form1 : Form
13     {
14         public Form1()
15         {
16             InitializeComponent();
17         }
18
19         // The Sum method accepts two int arguments
20         // and returns the sum of the arguments.
21         private int Sum(int num1, int num2)
22         {
23             return num1 + num2;
24         }
25
26         private void calculateButton_Click(object sender, EventArgs e)
27         {
28             // Declare variables to hold two ages and their sum.
29             int userAge, friendAge, combinedAge;
30
31             // Get the user's age.
32             if (int.TryParse(age1TextBox.Text, out userAge))
33             {
34                 // Get the best friend's age age.
35                 if (int.TryParse(age2TextBox.Text, out friendAge))
36                 {
37                     // Get the sum of the ages.
38                     combinedAge = Sum(userAge, friendAge);
39
40                     // Display the combined age.
41                     combinedAgeLabel.Text = combinedAge.ToString();
42                 }
43                 else
44                 {
45                     // Display an error message.
46                     MessageBox.Show("Enter an integer for your age.");
47                 }
48             }
49             else
50             {
51                 // Display an error message.
52                 MessageBox.Show("Enter an integer for your age.");
53             }
54         }
55
56         private void exitButton_Click(object sender, EventArgs e)
57         {
```

```
58              // Close the form.
59              this.Close();
60          }
61      }
62 }
```

In line 32, the value entered into the `age1TextBox` control is converted to an `int` and stored in the `userAge` variable. In line 35, the value entered into the `age2TextBox` control is converted to an `int` and stored in the `friendAge` variable. Line 38 passes the `userAge` and `friendAge` variables as arguments to the `Sum` method. The sum of the two variables is returned from the method and assigned to the `combinedAge` variable. In line 41 the value of the `combinedAge` variable is converted to a string and displayed in the `combinedAgeLabel` control.

Let's assume the `userAge` variable is set to the value 23 and the `friendAge` variable is set to the value 25. Figure 6-23 shows how the arguments are passed to the method and how a value is returned from the method.

Figure 6-23 Arguments passed to `Sum` and a value returned

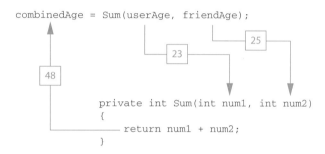

When you call a value-returning method, you usually want to do something meaningful with the value it returns. In line 38 of Program 6-7 the value that is returned from the `Sum` method is assigned to a variable. This is commonly how return values are used, but you can do many other things with them. For example, the following code shows a math expression that uses a call to the `Sum` method:

```
int x = 10, y = 15;
double average;
average = Sum(x, y) / 2.0;
```

In the last statement, the `Sum` method is called with `x` and `y` as its arguments. The method's return value, which is 25, is divided by 2.0. The result, 12.5, is assigned to `average`. Here is another example:

```
int x = 10, y = 15;
MessageBox.Show("The sum is " + Sum(x, y));
```

This code sends the `Sum` method's return value to `MessageBox.Show`, so it can be displayed on the screen. The message *The sum is 25* is displayed. Remember, a value-returning method returns a value of a specific data type. You can use the method's return value anywhere that you can use a regular value of the same data type. This means that anywhere an `int` value can be used, a call to an `int` value-returning method can be used. Likewise, anywhere a `double` value can be used, a call to a `double` value-returning method can be used. The same is true for all other data types.

In Tutorial 6-4 you complete an application that converts a value from one unit of measurement to another. The code will use a value-returning method to perform the conversion.

Tutorial 6-4:
Writing a Value-Returning Method

Cups and fluid ounces are common units of measurement for food items. Sometimes, when a recipe calls for an item measured in cups, you find that in the grocery store the item is sold in fluid ounces. To know how much you need to purchase for the recipe, you need to convert the required number of cups to fluid ounces. The formula is:

$$ounces = cups \times 8$$

In this tutorial you complete the *Cups To Ounces* application that is found in the *Chap06* folder of the Student Sample Programs that accompany this book. The application's form has already been created and is shown in Figure 6-24. When you complete the application, you will be able to enter a number of cups into the `cupsTextBox` control, click the *Convert* button, and see the equivalent number of fluid ounces in the `ouncesLabel` control.

Figure 6-24 The *Cups To Ounces* application's form

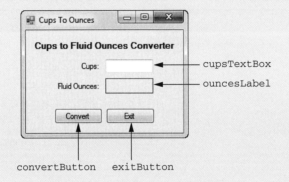

Step 1: Start Visual Studio (or Visual C# Express). Open the project named *Cups To Ounces* in the *Chap06* folder of the Student Sample Programs that accompany this book.

Step 2: Open the Form1 form in the *Designer*. The form is shown, along with the names of the important controls, in Figure 6-24.

Step 3: Program 6-8, at the end of this tutorial, shows the form's completed code. Open the code editor and type the comments and code for the `CupsToOunces` method shown in lines 19–25 of Program 6-8. The purpose of the method is to accept a number of cups as an argument and return that value converted to fluid ounces. You can see in line 22 that the method has a `double` parameter named `cups`, and in line 24 the method returns the value of `cups` multiplied by 8.

Step 4: Now you will create the Click event handlers for the Button controls. Switch back to the *Designer* and double-click the `convertButton` control. This opens the code editor, and you will see an empty event handler named `convertButton_Click`. Complete the `convertButton_Click` event handler by typing the code shown in lines 29–45 in Program 6-8. Let's review this code:

Line 30: This statement declares the `cups` and `ounces` variables, which hold the number of cups and ounces.

Lines 33–45: The `if` statement in line 33 converts the `cupsTextBox` control's Text property to a `double`, and the result is stored in the `cups` variable. If the conversion is successful, line 36 calls the CupsToOunces method, passing cups as an argument. The value that is returned from the method is assigned to the ounces variable, and in line 39 the value of the ounces variable is displayed in the ouncesLabel control. If the conversion is not successful, line 44 displays an error message.

Step 5: Switch your view back to the *Designer* and double-click the exitButton control. In the code editor you will see an empty event handler named exitButton_Click. Complete the exitButton_Click event handler by typing the code shown in lines 50–51 in Program 6-8.

Step 6: Save the project. Then, press F5 on the keyboard, or click the *Start Debugging* button (▶) on the toolbar to compile and run the application. When the application runs, enter the value 1 into the cupsTextBox control and click the *Convert* button. The application should display 8.0 as the number of fluid ounces. Continue to test the application with other values. When you are finished, click the *Exit* button to exit the application.

Program 6-8 Completed code for Form1 in the *Cups To Ounces* application

```
 1 using System;
 2 using System.Collections.Generic;
 3 using System.ComponentModel;
 4 using System.Data;
 5 using System.Drawing;
 6 using System.Linq;
 7 using System.Text;
 8 using System.Windows.Forms;
 9
10 namespace Cups_To_Ounces
11 {
12     public partial class Form1 : Form
13     {
14         public Form1()
15         {
16             InitializeComponent();
17         }
18
19         // The CupsToOunces method accepts a number
20         // of cups as an argument and returns the
21         // equivalent number of fluid ounces.
22         private double CupsToOunces(double cups)
23         {
24             return cups * 8.0;
25         }
26
27         private void convertButton_Click(object sender, EventArgs e)
28         {
29             // Variables to hold cups and ounces
30             double cups, ounces;
31
32             // Get the number of cups.
33             if (double.TryParse(cupsTextBox.Text, out cups))
34             {
35                 // Convert the cups to ounces.
36                 ounces = CupsToOunces(cups);
```

```
37
38                    // Display the ounces.
39                    ouncesLabel.Text = ounces.ToString("n1");
40              }
41              else
42              {
43                    // Display an error message.
44                    MessageBox.Show("Enter a valid number.");
45              }
46          }
47
48          private void exitButton_Click(object sender, EventArgs e)
49          {
50              // Close the form.
51              this.Close();
52          }
53      }
54 }
```

Boolean Methods

A Boolean method returns either `true` or `false`. You can use a Boolean method to test a condition, and then return either `true` or `false` to indicate whether the condition exists. Boolean methods are useful for simplifying complex conditions that are tested in decision and repetition structures.

For example, suppose you are writing a program that will ask the user to enter a number and then determine whether that number is even or odd. The following code shows how you can make that determination. Assume `number` is an `int` variable containing the number entered by the user.

```
if (number % 2 == 0)
{
    MessageBox.Show("The number is even.");
}
else
{
    MessageBox.Show("The number is odd.");
}
```

The meaning of the Boolean expression being tested by this `if-else` statement is not clear, so let's take a closer look at it:

```
number % 2 == 0
```

This expression uses the `%` operator, which was introduced in Chapter 2. Recall that the `%` operator divides two integers and returns the remainder of the division. So, this code is saying, If the remainder of `number` divided by 2 is equal to 0, then display a message indicating the number is even, or else display a message indicating the number is odd.

Because dividing an even number by 2 always gives a remainder of 0, this logic works. The code would be easier to understand, however, if you could somehow rewrite it to say, If the number is even, then display a message indicating it is even, or else display a message indicating it is odd. As it turns out, this can be done with a Boolean method. In this example, you could write a Boolean method named `IsEven` that accepts an `int` as an argument and returns `true` if the number is even or `false` otherwise. Here is an example how the `IsEven` method might be written:

```
private bool IsEven(int number)
{
    // Local variable to hold true or false
    bool numberIsEven;

    // Determine whether the number is even.
    if (number % 2 == 0)
    {
        numberIsEven = true;
    }
    else
    {
        numberIsEven = false;
    }

    // Return the result.
    return numberIsEven;
}
```

Then you can rewrite the `if-else` statement so it calls the `IsEven` method to determine whether `number` is even:

```
if (IsEven(number))
{
    MessageBox.Show("The number is even.");
}
else
{
    MessageBox.Show("The number is odd.");
}
```

Not only is this logic easier to understand, but now you have a method that you can call in the program any time you need to test a number to determine whether it is even. (The *Chap06* folder of the Student Sample Programs that accompany this book has a project named *Even Number* that demonstrates the `IsEven` method.)

Using a Boolean Method to Modularize Input Validation

Boolean methods can be useful for modularizing input validation. When a form has multiple TextBox controls, the input validation usually requires multiple, nested `if` statements. In many cases, you can simplify the code by creating a Boolean method that performs all the input validation and returns `true` if all of the input is valid or `false` if any of it is invalid. In Tutorial 6-5 you will complete an application that uses this approach.

Tutorial 6-5:
Modularizing Input Validation with a Boolean Method

In addition to regular pay, a company pays its employees an annual bonus. The company also contributes 5 percent of an employee's total compensation (gross pay plus bonus) to a retirement account. In this tutorial you complete an application that lets you enter an employee's gross pay and bonus amount and calculates the amount of retirement contribution. The project is named *Pay and Bonus* and is found in the *Chap06* folder of the Student Sample Programs. Figure 6-25 shows the application's form, which has already been created for you.

Figure 6-25 The *Pay and Bonus* application's form

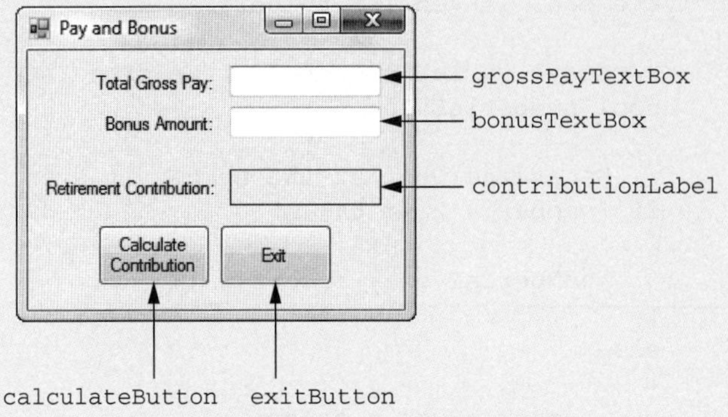

Step 1: Start Visual Studio (or Visual C# Express). Open the project named *Pay and Bonus* in the *Chap06* folder of the Student Sample Programs that accompany this book.

Step 2: Open the Form1 form's code in the code editor. Insert the comment and constant field declaration shown in lines 14 and 15 of Program 6-9. This constant, which is set to the value 0.05, is used in the calculation of the retirement account contribution.

Step 3: Type the comments and code for the `InputIsValid` method, shown in lines 22 through 53 of Program 6-9. Notice in line 26 that the method has reference parameters for gross pay and the bonus amount. The purpose of the method is to get the values entered by the user, convert them to `decimal` values, and assign them to the parameter variables. If the input is successfully converted, the method returns `true`. Otherwise, an error message is displayed and the method returns `false` to indicate that the input is not valid.

Step 4: Open the Form1 form in the *Designer*. Double-click the `calculateButton` control. This opens the code editor, and you will see an empty event handler named `calculateButton_Click`. Complete the `calculateButton_Click` event handler by typing the code shown in lines 57–67 in Program 6-9. Let's take a closer look at the code:

Line 58: This statement declares `decimal` variables to hold the gross pay, bonus amount, and contribution amount.

Lines 60–67: This `if` statement calls the `InputIsValid` method, passing the `grosspay` and `bonus` variables, by reference, as arguments. If the method returns true, the variables will contain the gross pay and bonus amount entered by the user. In that case, line 63 calculates the amount of contribution to the retirement account, and line 66 displays that amount.

Step 5: Switch your view back to the *Designer* and double-click the `exitButton` control. In the code editor you will see an empty event handler named `exitButton_Click`. Complete the `exitButton_Click` event handler by typing the code shown in lines 72–73 in Program 6-9.

Step 6: Save the project. Then, press F5 on the keyboard or click the *Start Debugging* button (▶) on the toolbar to compile and run the application. When the application runs, enter 80000 for the gross pay and 20000 for the bonus amount. Click the *Calculate Contribution* button. The application should display $5,000.00 as the amount of contribution. Try other values if you wish. Click the *Exit* button to exit the application.

Program 6-9 Completed code for Form1 in the *Pay and Bonus* application

```
 1 using System;
 2 using System.Collections.Generic;
 3 using System.ComponentModel;
 4 using System.Data;
 5 using System.Drawing;
 6 using System.Linq;
 7 using System.Text;
 8 using System.Windows.Forms;
 9
10 namespace Pay_and_Bonus
11 {
12     public partial class Form1 : Form
13     {
14         // Constant field for the contribution rate
15         private const decimal CONTRIB_RATE = 0.05m;
16
17         public Form1()
18         {
19             InitializeComponent();
20         }
21
22         // The InputIsValid method converts the user input and stores
23         // it in the arguments (passed by reference). If the conversion
24         // is successful, the method returns true. Otherwise it returns
25         // false.
26         private bool InputIsValid(ref decimal pay, ref decimal bonus)
27         {
28             // Flag variable to indicate whether the input is good
29             bool inputGood = false;
30
31             // Try to convert both inputs to decimal.
32             if (decimal.TryParse(grossPayTextBox.Text, out pay))
33             {
34                 if (decimal.TryParse(bonusTextBox.Text, out bonus))
35                 {
36                     // Both inputs are good.
37                     inputGood = true;
38                 }
39                 else
40                 {
41                     // Display an error message for the bonus.
42                     MessageBox.Show("Bonus amount is invalid.");
43                 }
44             }
45             else
46             {
47                 // Display an error message for gross pay.
48                 MessageBox.Show("Gross pay is invalid.");
49             }
50
51             // Return the result.
52             return inputGood;
53         }
54
55         private void calculateButton_Click(object sender, EventArgs e)
56         {
```

```
57                    // Variables for gross pay, bonus, and contributions
58                    decimal grossPay = 0m, bonus = 0m, contributions = 0m;
59
60                    if (InputIsValid(ref grossPay, ref bonus))
61                    {
62                        // Calculate the amount of contribution.
63                        contributions = (grossPay + bonus) * CONTRIB_RATE;
64
65                        // Display the contribution.
66                        contributionLabel.Text = contributions.ToString("c");
67                    }
68                }
69
70                private void exitButton_Click(object sender, EventArgs e)
71                {
72                    // Close the form.
73                    this.Close();
74                }
75            }
76        }
```

Returning a String from a Method

So far you've seen examples of methods that return numbers and Boolean values. You can write methods that return any type of data. Let's look at an example program that uses a string-returning method. The *Chap06* folder of the Student Sample Programs that accompany this book contains a project named *Full Name*. Figure 6-26 shows the application's form, and Program 6-10 shows the form's code. When you run the application, you enter your first name, middle name, and last name into the TextBox controls. When you click the *Show Full Name* button, your full name is displayed in the fullNameLabel control.

Figure 6-26 The *Full Name* application's form

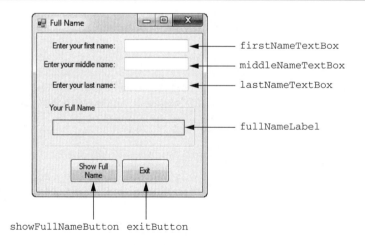

Program 6-10 Code for the *Full Name* application's Form1 form

```
1 using System;
2 using System.Collections.Generic;
3 using System.ComponentModel;
4 using System.Data;
```

```
 5 using System.Drawing;
 6 using System.Linq;
 7 using System.Text;
 8 using System.Windows.Forms;
 9
10 namespace Full_Name
11 {
12     public partial class Form1 : Form
13     {
14         public Form1()
15         {
16             InitializeComponent();
17         }
18
19         // The FullName method accepts arguments for a first
20         // name, a middle name, and a last name. It returns
21         // the full name.
22         private string FullName(string first, string middle, string last)
23         {
24             return first + " " + middle + " " + last;
25         }
26
27         private void showFullNameButton_Click(object sender, EventArgs e)
28         {
29             // Variables to hold the first, middle, last, and full names
30             string first, middle, last, full;
31
32             // Get the first, middle, and last names.
33             first = firstNameTextBox.Text;
34             middle = middleNameTextBox.Text;
35             last = lastNameTextBox.Text;
36
37             // Get the full name.
38             full = FullName(first, middle, last);
39
40             // Display the full name.
41             fullNameLabel.Text = full;
42         }
43
44         private void exitButton_Click(object sender, EventArgs e)
45         {
46             // Close the form.
47             this.Close();
48         }
49     }
50 }
```

Lines 22–25 define a method named `FullName`. Notice the following things about the method:

- Its return type is `string`.
- It has three `string` parameters: `first`, `middle`, and `last`. When we call the method we pass a first name, a middle name, and a last name as arguments.
- In line 24 it returns a string that is the concatenation of the `first`, `middle`, and `last` parameters, with spaces inserted between each.

Figure 6-27 shows an example of the application's form after the user has entered names into each TextBox and clicked the *Show Full Name* button.

Figure 6-27 Example output of the Full Name application

Checkpoint

6.15 What is a value-returning method? How is it used?

6.16 What is returned by a Boolean method?

6.17 Can a method be written to return any type of data?

Key Terms

arguments

code reuse

default argument

divide and conquer

method body

method header

modularized program

named argument

output parameter

parameter

parameter variable

Pascal case

passed by reference

passed by value

reference parameter

return point

return type

stepwise refinement

top-down design

value-returning method

`void` method

Review Questions

Multiple Choice

1. In general terms, a program that is broken into smaller units of code, such as methods, is known as a(n) _____.

   a. object-oriented program
   b. modularized program
   c. procedural program
   d. method-driven program

2. Writing the code to perform a task once and then reusing it each time you need to perform the task is a benefit of using methods called _____.

   a. code reuse
   b. the single-use philosophy
   c. method recycling
   d. code reprocessing

3. When you call a(n) _____, it simply executes the statements it contains and then terminates.

   a. intrinsic method
   b. `empty` method
   c. logical method
   d. `void` method

4. The _____, which appears at the beginning of a method definition, lists several important things about the method, including the method's name.

   a. method title
   b. method description
   c. method header
   d. method declaration

5. The _____ is a collection of statements enclosed inside a set of curly braces that are performed when the method is executed.

   a. method body
   b. method designation
   c. method code
   d. method classification

6. The _____ is the memory address that is saved by the system when a method is called and is the location to which the system should return after a method ends.

   a. calling address
   b. method address

    c.   return point

    d.   come back position

7. Programmers commonly use a technique known as _____ to break down an algorithm into methods.

    a.   prototyping

    b.   method modeling

    c.   algorithm division

    d.   top-down design

8. Pieces of data that are sent into a method are known as _____.

    a.   arguments

    b.   references

    c.   method variables

    d.   data entries

9. A(n) _____ is a special variable that receives an argument when a method is called.

    a.   reference variable

    b.   argument variable

    c.   parameter variable

    d.   method variable

10. A _____ specifies which parameter an argument should be passed into.

    a.   named argument

    b.   special argument

    c.   constant argument

    d.   literal argument

11. When a(n)_____ is provided for a parameter, it becomes possible to call the method without explicitly passing an argument into the parameter.

    a.   local argument

    b.   empty argument

    c.   default argument

    d.   expressional argument

12. When an argument is _____, only a copy of the argument's value is passed into the parameter variable.

    a.   a named constant

    b.   passed by association

    c.   passed by reference

    d.   passed by value

13. When you want a method to be able to change the value of a variable that is passed to it as an argument, the variable must be _____.

    a.   passed by reference

    b.   a local variable

    c.   passed by value

    d.   a named constant

14. A _____ a special type of parameter variable that is useful for establishing two-way communication between methods.

    a.   communication variable

    b.   reference parameter

    c.   method parameter

    d.   global variable

15. A(n) _____ can have an uninitialized value passed into it, but it must be set to some value before the method it belongs to finishes executing.

    a. input parameter
    b. reference parameter
    c. output parameter
    d. default parameter

16. A method's _____ is the type of value that the method returns.

    a. data type
    b. return type
    c. value type
    d. method type

True or False

1. Dividing a large problem into several smaller problems that are easily solved is sometimes called divide and conquer.

2. In a Pascal case name, the first character is always uppercase.

3. If a method belongs to a class, then you must write a method's definition inside the class.

4. The contents of variables and the values of expressions cannot be passed as arguments.

5. You do not have to write the data type for each parameter variable that is declared in a parameter list if they are all of the same data type.

6. An output parameter works like a by value parameter.

7. A value-returning function must contain a `return` statement.

8. A Boolean method returns either `yes` or `no`.

Short Answer

1. What do you call a method that executes the statements it contains and then returns a value back to the statement that called it?

2. What is the standard naming convention used among C# programmers for method names? Why?

3. What is another name for the top-down design process?

4. What is a parameter list?

5. How do you specify a named argument?

6. How are output parameters different from reference parameters?

7. How is a value-returning method like a `void` method? How is it different?

8. Can Boolean methods be used to modularize input validation? Why or why not?

Algorithm Workbench

1. Examine the following method header; then write an example call to the method.

```
private void ShowValue()
```

2. The following statement calls a method named `ShowHalf`. The `ShowHalf` method displays a value that is half that of the argument. Write the method.

```
ShowHalf(50);
```

3. Write the method header for a method named `ShowRetailPrice`. The method should include parameter variables for a list price and a markup percentage. Write the method so that the default argument for the markup percentage is set to 50 percent.

4. Examine the following method header; then write an example call to the method.

```
private void ResetValue(ref int value)
```

5. A program contains the following value-returning method.

```
private int Square(int value)
{
    return value * value;
}
```

Write a statement that passes the value 10 as an argument to this method and assigns its return value to the variable `result`.

Programming Problems

1. **Retail Price Calculator**

   Create an application that lets the user enter an item's wholesale cost and its markup percentage. It should then display the item's retail price. For example:

   - If an item's wholesale cost is $5.00 and its markup percentage is 100 percent, then the item's retail price is $10.00.
   - If an item's wholesale cost is $5.00 and its markup percentage is 50 percent, then the item's retail price is $7.50.

   The program should have a method named `CalculateRetail` that receives the wholesale cost and the markup percentage as arguments and returns the retail price of the item.

2. **Falling Distance**

   When an object is falling because of gravity, the following formula can be used to determine the distance the object falls in a specific time period:

   $$d = \frac{1}{2}gt^2$$

   The variables in the formula are as follows: d is the distance in meters, g is 9.8, and t is the amount of time in seconds that the object has been falling. Create an application that allows the user to enter the amount of time that an object has fallen and then displays the distance that the object fell. The application should have a function named `FallingDistance`. The `FallingDistance` function should accept an object's falling time (in seconds) as an argument. The function should return the distance in meters that the object has fallen during that time interval.

3. **Kinetic Energy**

   In physics, an object that is in motion is said to have kinetic energy. The following formula can be used to determine a moving object's kinetic energy:

   $$KE = \frac{1}{2}mv^2$$

   In the formula KE is the kinetic energy, m is the object's mass in kilograms, and v is the object's velocity in meters per second. Create an application that allows the user to enter an object's mass and velocity and then displays the object's kinetic energy. The application should have a function named `KineticEnergy` that accepts an object's mass (in kilograms) and velocity (in meters per second) as arguments. The function should return the amount of kinetic energy that the object has.

4. **Calories from Fat and Carbohydrates**

A nutritionist who works for a fitness club helps members by evaluating their diets. As part of her evaluation, she asks members for the number of fat grams and carbohydrate grams that they consume in a day. Then, she calculates the number of calories that result from the fat using the following formula:

Calories from fat = fat grams × 9

Next, she calculates the number of calories that result from the carbohydrates using the following formula:

Calories from carbs = carbs grams × 4

Create an application that will make these calculations. In the application, you should have the following methods:

- `FatCalories`—This method should accept a number of fat grams as an argument and return the number of calories from that amount of fat.
- `CarbCalories`—This method should accept a number of carbohydrate grams as an argument and return the number of calories from that amount of carbohydrates.

5. **Joe's Automotive**

Joe's Automotive performs the following routine maintenance services:

- Oil change—$26.00
- Lube job—$18.00
- Radiator flush—$30.00
- Transmission flush—$80.00
- Inspection—$15.00
- Muffler replacement—$100.00
- Tire rotation—$20.00

Joe also performs other nonroutine services and charges for parts and labor ($20 per hour). Create an application that displays the total for a customer's visit to Joe's. The form should resemble the one shown in Figure 6-28.

Figure 6-28 *Automotive* form

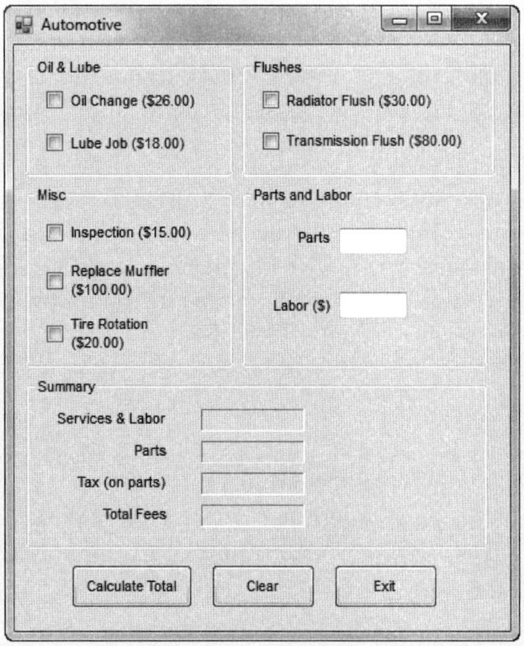

The application should have the following value-returning methods:

- `OilLubeCharges`—Returns the total charges for an oil change and/or a lube job, if any.
- `FlushCharges`—Returns the total charges for a radiator flush and/or a transmission flush, if any.
- `MiscCharges`—Returns the total charges for an inspection, muffler replacement, and/or a tire rotation, if any.
- `OtherCharges`—Returns the total charges for other services (parts and labor), if any.
- `TaxCharges`—Returns the amount of sales tax, if any. Sales tax is 6% and is charged only on parts. If the customer purchases services only, no sales tax is charged.
- `TotalCharges`—Returns the total charges.

The application should have the following `void` methods, called when the user clicks the *Clear* button:

- `ClearOilLube`—Clears the check boxes for oil change and lube job.
- `ClearFlushes`—Clears the check boxes for radiator flush and transmission flush.
- `ClearMisc`—Clears the check boxes for inspection, muffler replacement, and tire rotation.
- `ClearOther`—Clears the text boxes for parts and labor.
- `ClearFees`—Clears the labels that display the labels in the section marked *Summary*.

6. **Hospital Charges**

Create an application that calculates the total cost of a hospital stay. The daily base charge is $350. The hospital also charges for medication, surgical fees, lab fees, and physical rehab. The application should accept the following input:

- The number of days spent in the hospital
- The amount of medication charges
- The amount of surgical charges
- The amount of lab fees
- The amount of physical rehabilitation charges

Create and use the following value-returning methods in the application:

- `CalcStayCharges`—Calculates and returns the base charges for the hospital stay. This is computed as $350 times the number of days in the hospital.
- `CalcMiscCharges`—Calculates and returns the total of the medication, surgical, lab, and physical rehabilitation charges.
- `CalcTotalCharges`—Calculates and returns the total charges.

7. **Present Value**

Suppose you want to deposit a certain amount of money into a savings account and then leave it alone to draw interest for the next 10 years. At the end of 10 years you would like to have $10,000 in the account. How much do you need to deposit today to make that happen? You can use the following formula, which is known as the present-value formula, to find out:

$$P = \frac{F}{(1 + r)^n}$$

The terms in the formula are as follows:

- *P* is the *present value*, or the amount that you need to deposit today.
- *F* is the *future value* that you want in the account. (In this case, *F* is $10,000.)

- *r* is the *annual interest rate*.
- *n* is the *number of years* that you plan to let the money sit in the account.

Write a method named `PresentValue` that performs this calculation. The method should accept the future value, annual interest rate, and number of years as arguments. It should return the present value, which is the amount that you need to deposit today. Demonstrate the method in an application that lets the user experiment with different values for the formula's terms.

8. **Prime Numbers**

   A prime number is a number that can be evenly divided by only itself and 1. For example, the number 5 is prime because it can be evenly divided by only 1 and 5. The number 6, however, is not prime because it can be evenly divided by 1, 2, 3, and 6. Write a Boolean function named `IsPrime` that takes an integer as an argument and returns `true` if the argument is a prime number or `false` otherwise. Use the function in an application that lets the user enter a number and then displays a message indicating whether the number is prime.

> **TIP:** Recall that the `%` operator divides one number by another and returns the remainder of the division. In an expression such as num1 `%` num2, the `%` operator returns 0 if num1 is evenly divisible by num2.

9. **Prime Number List**

   This exercise assumes you have already written the `IsPrime` function in Exercise 8. Create another application that uses this function to display all the prime numbers from 1 through 100 in a list box. The program should have a loop that calls the `IsPrime` function.

10. **Rock, Paper, Scissors Game**

    Create an application that lets the user play the game of Rock, Paper, Scissors against the computer. The program should work as follows.

    1. When the program begins, a random number in the range of 1 through 3 is generated. If the number is 1, then the computer has chosen rock. If the number is 2, then the computer has chosen paper. If the number is 3, then the computer has chosen scissors. (Do not display the computer's choice yet.)
    2. The user selects his or her choice of rock, paper, or scissors. To get this input you can use Button controls, or clickable PictureBox controls displaying some of the artwork that you will find in the student sample files.
    3. The computer's choice is displayed.
    4. A winner is selected according to the following rules:
       - If one player chooses rock and the other player chooses scissors, then rock wins. (The rock smashes the scissors.)
       - If one player chooses scissors and the other player chooses paper, then scissors wins. (Scissors cuts paper.)
       - If one player chooses paper and the other player chooses rock, then paper wins. (Paper wraps rock.)
       - If both players make the same choice, the game must be played again to determine the winner.

    Be sure to modularize the program into methods that perform each major task.

7 Arrays and Lists

TOPICS

7.1 Value Types and Reference Types

CONCEPT: The data types in C# and the .NET Framework fall into two categories: value types and reference types.

In this chapter you will gain more experience working with objects. Specifically, you will work with arrays and collections, which are objects that store groups of data. Before we go into the details of creating and working with those objects, it will be helpful for you to understand how objects are stored in memory. In this section we discuss the ways that different types of objects are internally stored by the .NET Framework. As a result, you will better understand the concepts presented in this chapter, and chapters to come.

All the data types in C#—and the underlying .NET Framework—fall into two categories: **value types** and **reference types.** Of the C# data types that you have used so far, the following are value types: `int`, `double`, `decimal`, and `bool`. (There are other value types in addition to these, but these are the ones we focus on in this book.)

When you declare a value type variable, the compiler sets aside, or allocates, a chunk of memory that is big enough for that variable. For example, look at the following variable declarations:

```
int wholeNumber;
double realNumber;
decimal moneyNumber;
```

Recall from Chapter 3 that an `int` uses 32 bits of memory (4 bytes), a `double` uses 64 bits of memory (8 bytes), and a `decimal` uses 128 bits of memory (16 bytes). These declaration statements cause memory to be allocated as shown in Figure 7-1.

Figure 7-1 Memory allocated

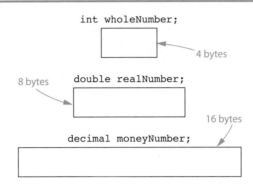

The memory that is allocated for a value type variable is the actual location that will hold any value that is assigned to that variable. For example, suppose we use the following statements to assign values to the variables shown in Figure 7-1:

```
wholeNumber = 99;
realNumber = 123.45;
moneyNumber = 800.0m;
```

Figure 7-2 shows how the assigned values are stored in each variable's memory location.

Figure 7-2 Values assigned to the variables

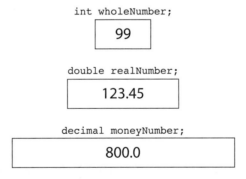

As you can see from these illustrations, value types are very straightforward. When you are working with a value type, you are using a variable that holds a piece of data.

This is different from the way that reference types work. When you are working with a reference type, you are using two things:

- An object that is created in memory
- A variable that references the object

The object that is created in memory holds data of some sort and performs operations of some sort. (Exactly what the data and operations are depends on what kind of object it is.) In order to work with the object in code, you need some way to refer to it. That's where the variable comes in. The variable does not hold an actual piece of data with which your program will work. Instead, it holds a special value known as a **reference,** which links the variable to the object.[1] When you want to work with the object, you use the variable that references it.

---

[1]A reference is similar to a memory address. It is a value that identifies the object's memory location.

A variable that is used to reference an object is commonly called a **reference variable.** Reference variables can be used only to reference objects. Figure 7-3 illustrates two objects that have been created in memory, each referenced by a variable.

Figure 7-3 Two objects referenced by variables

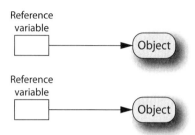

To understand how reference variables and objects work together, think about flying a kite. In order to fly a kite, you need a spool of string attached to it. When the kite is airborne, you use the spool of string to hold onto the kite and control it. This is similar to the relationship between an object and the variable that references the object. As shown in Figure 7-4, the object is like the kite, and the variable that references the object is like the spool of string.

Figure 7-4 The kite and string metaphor

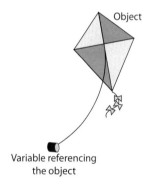

Creating a reference type object typically requires the following two steps:

1. You declare a reference variable.
2. You create the object and associate it with the reference variable.

After you have performed these steps, you can use the reference variable to work with the object. Let's look at an example that you have already learned about: creating objects of the Random class. Recall from Chapter 5 that the Random class allows your program to generate random numbers. Here is an example of how you create an object from the Random class:

```
Random rand = new Random();
```

Let's look at the different parts of this statement:

- The first part of the statement, appearing on the left side of the = operator, reads `Random rand`. This declares a variable named `rand` that can be used to reference an object of the `Random` type.
- The second part of the statement, appearing on the right side of the = operator, reads `new Random()`. The new **operator** creates an object in memory and returns a reference

to that object. So, the expression new Random() creates an object from the Random class and returns a reference to that object.

- The = operator assigns the reference that was returned from the new operator to the rand variable.

After this statement executes, the rand variable references a Random object, as shown in Figure 7-5. The rand variable can then be used to perform operations with the object, such as generating random numbers.

Figure 7-5 The rand variable referencing a Random object

 Checkpoint

7.1 Into what two categories do the data types in C# and the underlying .NET Framework fall?

7.2 What is the difference in the way you work with value types and reference types?

7.3 How is the relationship between an object and a reference variable similar to a kite and a spool of string?

7.4 Is a variable of the Random class a reference type or a value type?

 7.2 Array Basics

CONCEPT: An array allows you to store a group of items of the same data type together in memory. Processing a large number of items in an array is usually easier than processing a large number of items stored in separate variables.

In the programs you have written so far, you have used variables to store data in memory. The simplest way to store a value in memory is to store it in a variable. Variables work well in many situations, but they have limitations. For example, they can hold only one value at a time. Consider the following variable declaration:

```
int number = 99;
```

This statement declares an int variable named number, initialized with the value 99. Consider what happens if the following statement appears later in the program:

```
number = 5;
```

This statement assigns the value 5 to number, replacing the value 99 that was previously stored there. Because number is an ordinary variable, it can hold only one value at a time.

Because variables hold only a single value, they can be cumbersome in programs that process lists of data. For example, suppose you are asked to write a program that holds the names of 50 employees. Imagine declaring 50 variables to hold all those names:

```
string employee1;
string employee2;
string employee3;
```

and so on ...

```
string employee50
```

Then, imagine writing the code to process all 50 names. For example, if you wanted to display the contents of the variables in a ListBox, you would write code such as this:

```
employeeListBox.Items.Add(employee1);  // Display employee 1
employeeListBox.Items.Add(employee2);  // Display employee 2
employeeListBox.Items.Add(employee3);  // Display employee 3
```

and so on . . .

```
employeeListBox.Items.Add(employee50);  // Display employee 50
```

As you can see, variables are not well suited for storing and processing lists of data. Each variable is a separate item that must be declared and individually processed.

Fortunately, you can use an array as an alternative to a group of variables. An **array** is an object that can hold a group of values that are all the same data type. You can have an array of `int` values, an array of `double` values, and array of `decimal` values, or an array of `string` values, but you cannot store a mixture of data types in an array. Once you create an array, you can write simple and efficient code to process the values that are stored in it.

Arrays are reference type objects. Recall from Section 6.1 that two steps are required to create and use a reference type object:

1. You declare a reference variable.
2. You create the object and associate it with the reference variable.

Suppose you want to create an array that can hold `int` values. Here is an example of how you might declare a reference variable for the array:

```
int[] numbersArray;
```

This statement declares a reference variable named `numbersArray`. Notice that this statement looks like a regular `int` variable declaration except for the set of brackets (`[ ]`) that appear after the keyword `int`. The expression `int[]` indicates that this variable is a reference to an `int` array. So, we cannot use this variable to store an `int` value. Rather, we can use it to reference an `int` array.

The next step in the process is to create the array object and associate it with the `numbersArray` variable. The following statement shows an example:

```
numbersArray = new int[6];
```

As previously mentioned, the `new` keyword creates an object in memory. The expression that appears after the `new` keyword specifies what type of object to create. In this case, the expression `int[6]` specifies that the object should be an array large enough to hold six `int` values. The number inside the brackets is the array's **size declarator.** It indicates the number of values that the array should be able to hold.

The `new` keyword also returns a reference to the object that it creates. In the previously shown statement, the `new` keyword creates an `int` array and returns a reference to that array. The = operator assigns the reference to the `numbersArray` variable. After this statement executes, the `numbersArray` variable will reference an `int` array that can hold six values. This is shown in Figure 7-6.

Figure 7-6 The `numbersArray` variable referencing an `int` array

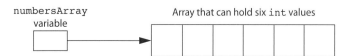

In the previous example we used two statements to (1) declare a reference variable and (2) create an array object. These two steps can be combined into one statement, as shown here:

```
int[] numbersArray = new int[6];
```

You can create arrays of any data. The following are all valid array declarations:

```
double[] temperatures = new double[100];
decimal[] prices = new decimal[50];
string[] nameArray = new string[1200];
```

An array's size declarator must be a nonnegative integer expression. It can be a literal value, as shown in the previous examples, or a variable. It is a preferred practice to use a named constant as a size declarator, however. Here is an example:

```
const int SIZE = 6;
int[] numbersArray = new int[SIZE];
```

This practice can make programs easier to maintain. As you will see later in this chapter, many array-processing techniques require you to refer to the array's size. When you use a named constant as an array's size declarator, you can use the constant to refer to the size of the array in your algorithms. If you ever need to modify the program so the array is a different size, you need only change the value of the named constant.

Array Elements and Subscripts

The storage locations in an array are known as **elements.** In memory, an array's elements are located in consecutive memory locations. Each element in an array is assigned a unique number known as a **subscript.** Subscripts are used to identify specific elements in an array. The first element is assigned the subscript 0, the second element is assigned the subscript 1, and so forth. For example, suppose a program has the following declarations:

```
const int SIZE = 5;
int[] numbersArray = new int[SIZE];
```

As shown in Figure 7-7, the array referenced by numbersArray has five elements. The elements are assigned the subscripts 0–4. (Because subscript numbering starts at 0, the subscript of the last element in an array is 1 less than the total number of elements in the array.)

Figure 7-7 Array subscripts

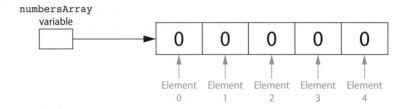

Array Element Default Values

Notice that Figure 7-7 shows each element of the array containing the value 0. When you create a numeric array in C#, its elements are set to the value 0 by default.

Remember, you can create an array to hold any type of value. It is possible to create an array of reference type objects. If you create an array of reference type objects, each element of the array acts as a reference variable. By default, the elements of an array of reference type objects are set to the special value null. The value null indicates that a reference variable is not set to a valid object and cannot be used for any meaningful purpose.

> **NOTE:** As you will see in Chapter 8, strings are actually reference types, so the default value of a `string` array's elements is `null`.

Working with Array Elements

You access the individual elements in an array by using their subscripts. For example, the following code creates an `int` array with five elements and assigns values to each of its elements.

```
const int SIZE = 5;
int[] numbersArray = new int[SIZE];
numbersArray[0] = 20;
numbersArray[1] = 30;
numbersArray[2] = 40;
numbersArray[3] = 50;
numbersArray[4] = 60;
```

This code assigns the value 20 to element 0, the value 30 to element 1, and so forth. Figure 7-8 shows the contents of the array after these statements execute.

Figure 7-8 Values assigned to each element

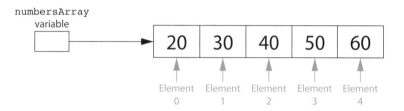

> **NOTE:** The expression `numbersArray[0]` is pronounced "numbersArray sub zero."

The following code shows another example. It creates a `string` array with three elements and assigns strings to each of its elements.

```
const int SIZE = 3;
string[] names = new string[SIZE];
names[0] = "Chris";
names[1] = "Laurie";
names[2] = "Joe";
```

The following code sample shows how values can be assigned from TextBox controls to array elements. Assume that an application's form has three TextBox controls named `amount1TextBox`, `amount2TextBox`, and `amount3TextBox` and that the user has entered a numeric value into each one. The following code creates a `decimal` array named `amounts` and assigns each of the TextBox control's input value to an array element.

```
const int SIZE = 3;
decimal[] amounts = new decimal[SIZE];
amounts[0] = decimal.Parse(amount1TextBox.Text);
amounts[1] = decimal.Parse(amount2TextBox.Text);
amounts[2] = decimal.Parse(amount3TextBox.Text);
```

Let's look at a complete program that demonstrates how to assign values to an array and then display the values in the array. In the *Chap07* folder of the Student Sample Programs that accompany this book you will find a project named *Display Elements*. Figure 7-9 shows the application's form.

Figure 7-9 The *Display Elements* application's form

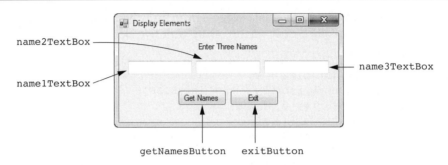

Here is the code for the `getNamesButton_Click` event handler:

```
 1 private void getNamesButton_Click(object sender, EventArgs e)
 2 {
 3     // Create an array to hold three strings.
 4     const int SIZE = 3;
 5     string[] names = new string[SIZE];
 6
 7     // Get the names.
 8     names[0] = name1TextBox.Text;
 9     names[1] = name2TextBox.Text;
10     names[2] = name3TextBox.Text;
11
12     // Display the names.
13     MessageBox.Show(names[0]);
14     MessageBox.Show(names[1]);
15     MessageBox.Show(names[2]);
16 }
```

Run the application, enter a name into each of the TextBox controls and then click the *Get Names* button. The following actions take place:

- In line 5, an array to hold three strings is created.
- In lines 8–10, the names that you entered into the TextBox controls are assigned to the array elements.
- In lines 13–15, each element of the array is displayed in a message box.

The *Display Elements* application displays the contents of a `string` array. Because the array's elements are strings, we can pass each element directly to the `MessageBox.Show` method without performing a data type conversion. If you want to pass a numeric array element to the `MessageBox.Show` method, however, you will have to call the element's `ToString` method. The following code sample demonstrates:

```
1 // Create an array to hold three integers.
2 const int SIZE = 3;
3 int[] myValues = new int[SIZE];
4
5 // Assign some values to the array elements.
6 myValues[0] = 10;
7 myValues[1] = 20;
8 myValues[2] = 30;
9
```

```
10 // Display the array elements.
11 MessageBox.Show(myValues[0].ToString());
12 MessageBox.Show(myValues[1].ToString());
13 MessageBox.Show(myValues[2].ToString());
```

Array Initialization

When you create an array, you can optionally initialize it with a group of values. Here is an example:

```
const int SIZE = 5;
int[] numbersArray = new int[SIZE] { 10, 20, 30, 40, 50 };
```

The series of values inside the braces and separated with commas is called an **initialization list.** These values are stored in the array elements in the order they appear in the list. (The first value, 10, is stored in numbersArray[0], the second value, 20, is stored in numbersArray[1], and so forth.)

When you provide an initialization list, the size declarator can be left out. The compiler determines the size of the array from the number of items in the initialization list. Here is an example:

```
int[] numbersArray = new int[] { 10, 20, 30, 40, 50 };
```

In this example, the compiler determines that the array should have five elements because five values appear in the initialization list.

You can also leave out the new operator and its subsequent expression when an initialization list is provided. Here is an example:

```
int[] numbersArray = { 10, 20, 30, 40, 50 };
```

Here are three separate examples that declare and initialize a string array named days. Each of these examples results in the same array:

```
// Example 1
const int SIZE = 7;
string[] days = new string[SIZE] = { "Sunday", "Monday",
                 "Tuesday", "Wednesday", "Thursday",
                 "Friday", "Saturday" };

// Example 2
string[] days = new string[] = { "Sunday", "Monday",
                "Tuesday", "Wednesday", "Thursday",
                "Friday", "Saturday" };

// Example 3
string[] days = { "Sunday", "Monday", "Tuesday",
                 "Wednesday", "Thursday", "Friday",
                 "Saturday" };
```

Using a Loop to Step Through an Array

You can store a number in an int variable and then use that variable as a subscript. This makes it possible to use a loop to step through an array, performing the same operation on each element. For example, look at the following code sample:

```
1 // Create an array to hold three integers.
2 const int SIZE = 3;
3 int[] myValues = new int[SIZE];
4
5 // Assign 99 to each array element.
```

```
6 for (int index = 0; index < SIZE; index++)
7 {
8     myValues[index] = 99;
9 }
```

Line 3 creates an `int` array named `myValues` with three elements. The `for` loop that starts in line 6 uses an `int` variable named `index` as its counter. The `index` variable is initialized with the value 0 and is incremented after each loop iteration. The loop iterates as long as `index` is less than 3. So, the loop will iterate three times. As it iterates, the `index` variable is assigned the values 0, 1, and 2.

Inside the loop, the statement in line 8 assigns the value 99 to an array element, using the index variable as the subscript. This is what happens as the loop iterates:

- The first time the loop iterates, `index` is set to 0, so 99 is assigned to `myValues[0]`.
- The second time the loop iterates, `index` is set to 1, so 99 is assigned to `myValues[1]`.
- The third time the loop iterates, `index` is set to 2, so 99 is assigned to `myValues[2]`.

Invalid Subscripts

When working with an array, it is important that you do not use an invalid subscript. You cannot use a subscript that is less than 0 or greater than the size of the array minus 1. For example, suppose an array has 100 elements. The valid subscripts for the array are the integers 0 through 99. If you try to use any value outside this range, an exception will be thrown at runtime. The following code sample demonstrates how a loop that is not carefully written can cause such an exception to be thrown:

```
1 // Create an array to hold three integers.
2 const int SIZE = 3;
3 int[] myValues = new int[SIZE];
4
5 // Will this loop cause an exception?
6 for (int index = 0; index <= SIZE; index++)
7 {
8     myValues[index] = 99;
9 }
```

Notice that the `for` loop iterates as long as `index` is less than *or equal to* 3. During the loop's last iteration, `index` is set to 3, so the statement in line 8 attempts to make an assignment to `myValues[3]`. There is no element in the array with the subscript 3, so an exception will be thrown.

The Length Property

In C#, all arrays have a **Length property** that is set to the number of elements in the array. For example, consider an array created by the following statement:

```
double[] temperatures = new double[25];
```

The `temperatures` array's Length property will be set to 25. If we executed the following statement, it would display the message "The temperatures array has 25 elements."

```
MessageBox.Show("The temperatures array has " +
    temperatures.Length + " elements.");
```

The Length property can be useful when processing the entire contents of an array with a loop. The subscript of the last element is always 1 less than the array's Length property. Here is an example:

```
for (int index = 0; index < temperatures.Length; index++)
{
    MessageBox.Show(temperatures[index].ToString());
}
```

> **NOTE:** An array's Length property is read only, so you cannot change its value.

In Tutorial 7-1 you complete an application that generates a set of random numbers similar to those used in lotteries. The numbers will be stored in an array.

Tutorial 7-1:
Using an Array to Hold a List of Random Lottery Numbers

In this tutorial you complete an application that randomly generates lottery numbers. The application's form is shown in Figure 7-10. When the *Generate Numbers* button is clicked, the application will generate five two-digit integer numbers and store them in an array. The contents of the array will then be displayed in Label controls.

Figure 7-10 The *Lottery Numbers* application's form

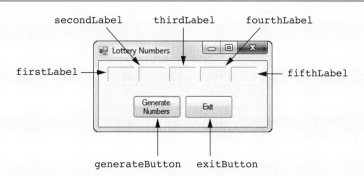

Step 1: Start Visual Studio (or Visual C# Express). Open the project named *Lottery Numbers* in the *Chap07* folder of the Student Sample Programs that accompany this book.

Step 2: Open the Form1 form in the *Designer*. Double-click the `generateButton` control. This will open the code editor, and you will see an empty event handler named `generateButton _Click`. Complete the `generateButton _Click` event handler by typing the code shown in lines 21–40 in Program 7-1. Let's take a closer look at the code:

Line 22: This statement declares an `int` constant named `SIZE`, set to the value 5. This is used as an array size declarator.

Line 23: This statement creates an `int` array named `lotteryNumbers` with five elements.

Line 26: This statement creates a `Random` object, referenced by a variable named `rand`.

Line 30: This `for` loop uses an `int` variable named `index` as its counter. The `index` variable is initialized with the value 0 and is incremented after each loop iteration. The loop iterates as long as `index` is less than `lotteryNumbers.Length` (which is 5). So, the loop will iterate five times. As it iterates, the `index` variable is assigned the values 0, 1, 2, 3, and 4.

Line 32: This statement gets a random number in the range of 0 through 99 and assigns it to `lotteryNumbers[index]`. The first time the loop iterates, this statement assigns a random number to lotteryNumbers[0]. The second time the loop iterates, this statement assigns a random number to lotteryNumbers[1]. This continues until the loop is finished. At that time, each element in the array is assigned a random number.

Lines 36–40: These statements display the array elements in the firstLabel, secondLabel, thirdLabel, fourthLabel, and fifthLabel controls.

Step 3: Switch your view back to the *Designer* and double-click the exitButton control. In the code editor you will see an empty event handler named exitButton_Click. Complete the exitButton_Click event handler by typing the code shown in lines 45–46 in Program 7-1.

Step 4: Save the project. Then, press F5 on the keyboard, or click the *Start Debugging* button (▶) on the toolbar to compile and run the application. When the application runs, click the *Generate Numbers* button. The application should display a set of random numbers in the Label controls. Click the *Generate Numbers* button several more times to see different sets of random numbers. When you are finished, click the *Exit* button to exit the application.

Program 7-1 Completed code for Form1 in the *Lottery Numbers* application

```
1  using System;
2  using System.Collections.Generic;
3  using System.ComponentModel;
4  using System.Data;
5  using System.Drawing;
6  using System.Linq;
7  using System.Text;
8  using System.Windows.Forms;
9
10 namespace Lottery_Numbers
11 {
12     public partial class Form1 : Form
13     {
14         public Form1()
15         {
16             InitializeComponent();
17         }
18
19         private void generateButton_Click(object sender, EventArgs e)
20         {
21             // Create an array to hold the numbers.
22             const int SIZE = 5;
23             int[] lotteryNumbers = new int[SIZE];
24
25             // Create a Random object.
26             Random rand = new Random();
27
28             // Fill the array with random numbers, in the range
29             // of 0 through 99.
30             for (int index = 0; index < lotteryNumbers.Length; index++)
31             {
32                 lotteryNumbers[index] = rand.Next(100);
33             }
34
35             // Display the array elements in the Label controls.
36             firstLabel.Text = lotteryNumbers[0].ToString();
```

```
37              secondLabel.Text = lotteryNumbers[1].ToString();
38              thirdLabel.Text = lotteryNumbers[2].ToString();
39              fourthLabel.Text = lotteryNumbers[3].ToString();
40              fifthLabel.Text = lotteryNumbers[4].ToString();
41          }
42
43          private void exitButton_Click(object sender, EventArgs e)
44          {
45              // Close the form.
46              this.Close();
47          }
48      }
49 }
```

Watching for Off-by-One Errors

Because array subscripts start at 0 rather than 1, you have to be careful not to perform an off-by-one error. An **off-by-one error** occurs when a loop iterates one time too many or one time too few. For example, look at the following code sample:

```
1 // Create an array to hold three integers.
2 const int SIZE = 100;
3 int[] myValues = new int[SIZE];
4
5 // Assign 99 to each array element.
6 for (int index = 1; index < myValues.Length; index++)
7 {
8     myValues[index] = 99;
9 }
```

The intent of this code is to create an int array with 100 elements and assign the value 99 to each element. However, this code has an off-by-one error. During the loop's execution, the index variable is assigned the values 1 through 99 when it should be assigned the values 0 through 99. As a result, the first element, which is at subscript 0, is skipped.

Using the foreach Loop with Arrays

C# provides a special loop that, in many circumstances, simplifies array processing. It is known as the **foreach loop**. When you use the foreach loop with an array, the loop automatically iterates once for each element in the array. For example, if you use the foreach loop with an eight-element array, the loop will iterate eight times. Because the foreach loop automatically knows the number of elements in an array, you do not have to use a counter variable to control its iterations, as with a regular for loop.

The foreach loop is designed to work with a temporary, read-only variable known as the **iteration variable**. Each time the foreach loop iterates, it copies an array element to the iteration variable. For example, the first time the loop iterates, the iteration variable will contain the value of element 0, the second time the loop iterates, the iteration variable will contain the value of element 1, and so forth.

Here is the general format of the foreach loop:

```
foreach(Type VariableName in ArrayName)
{
    statement;
    statement;
    etc.
}
```

The statements that appear inside the curly braces are the body of the loop. These are the statements executed each time the loop iterates. As with other control structures, the curly braces are optional if the body of the loop contains only one statement, as shown in the following general format:

```
foreach(Type VariableName in ArrayName)
    statement;
```

Let's take a closer look at the items appearing inside the parentheses:

- *Type* is the data type of the values in the array.
- *VariableName* is the name of the iteration variable.
- *in* is a keyword that must appear after the *VariableName*.
- *ArrayName* is the name of an array.

Suppose we have the following array declaration:

```
int[] numbers = { 3, 6, 9 };
```

We can use the following foreach loop to display the contents of the numbers array:

```
foreach (int val in numbers)
{
    MessageBox.Show(val.ToString());
}
```

Because the numbers array has three elements, this loop will iterate three times. The first time it iterates, val will contain the value of numbers[0], so a message box will display the value 3. During the second iteration, val will contain the value of numbers[1], so a message box will display the value 6. During the third iteration, val will contain the value of numbers[2], so a message box will display the value 9.

The foreach Loop versus the for Loop

When you need to read the values that are stored in an array from the first element to the last element, the foreach loop is simpler to use than the for loop. With the foreach loop, you do not have to be concerned about the size of the array, and you do not have to create a counter variable to hold subscripts. However, because the iteration variable is read only, there are circumstances in which the foreach loop is not adequate. You cannot use the foreach loop if you need to do any of the following:

- Change the contents of an array element
- Work through the array elements in reverse order
- Access some, but not all, of the array elements
- Simultaneously work with two or more arrays within the loop

In any of these circumstances, you should use the for loop to process the array.

Reassigning an Array Reference Variable

It is possible to reassign an array reference variable to a different array, as demonstrated by the following code sample:

```
1 // Create an array referenced by the numbers variable.
2 int[] numbers = new int[6];
3
4 // Reassign the numbers variable to a new array.
5 numbers = new int[3];
```

The statement in line 2 creates a six-element int array. A reference to the array is assigned to the numbers variable. Figure 7-11 shows how the numbers variable references the six-element array after this statement executes.

Figure 7-11 The `numbers` variable referencing a six-element array

Then, the statement in line 5 creates a new, three-element `int` array. A reference to the new array is assigned to the `numbers` variable. When line 5 executes, the reference that is currently stored in the `numbers` variable will be replaced by a reference to the three-element array. After this statement executes, the `numbers` variable will reference the three-element array instead of the six-element array. This is illustrated in Figure 7-12.

Figure 7-12 The `numbers` variable referencing a three-element array

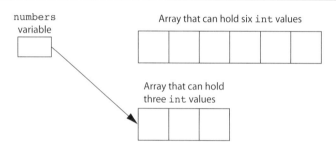

Notice in Figure 7-12 that the six-element array still exists in memory, but it is no longer referenced by any variables. Because it is no longer referenced, it cannot be accessed. When an object is no longer referenced, it becomes eligible for garbage collection. **Garbage collection** is a process that periodically runs, removing all unreferenced objects from memory.

 Checkpoint

7.5 Write a statement that declares a reference variable named `monthlyPay` for an array that can hold `decimal` values.

7.6 Write a statement so that the `monthlyPay` variable from Checkpoint 7.5 references a `decimal` array that can hold 12 values.

7.7 Combine the statements from Checkpoints 7.5 and 7.6 into a single statement, and use a named constant for a size declarator.

7.8 Write a statement that creates an array of 3 `string` values referenced by a variable named `fullName`. Provide an initialization list for the array using string values for a first, middle, and last name.

7.9 Under what circumstances should you use a `for` loop rather than a `foreach` loop to process data stored in an array?

7.10 What happens when an object such as an array is no longer referenced by a variable?

7.3 Working with Files and Arrays

CONCEPT: For some problems, files and arrays can be used together effectively. You can easily write a loop that saves the contents of an array to a file, and vice versa.

Some tasks may require you to save the contents of an array to a file so the data can be used at a later time. Likewise, some situations may require you to read the data from a file into an array. For example, suppose you have a file that contains a set of values and you want to reverse the order of the values. One technique for doing this is to read the file's values into an array and then write the values in the array back to the file from the end of the array to the beginning.

Writing an Array's Contents to a File

Writing the contents of an array to a file is a straightforward procedure: Open the file and use a loop to step through each element of the array, writing its contents to the file. For example, in the *Chap07* folder of the Student Sample Programs, you will find a project named *Array To File*. When you click the *OK* button, the application writes the contents of an int array to a file. The following code shows the Click event handler for the *OK* button.

```
1 private void okButton_Click(object sender, EventArgs e)
2 {
3     try
4     {
5         // Create an array with some values.
6         int[] numbers = { 10, 20, 30, 40, 50 };
7
8         // Declare a StreamWriter variable.
9         StreamWriter outputFile;
10
11        // Create the file and get a StreamWriter object.
12        outputFile = File.CreateText("Values.txt");
13
14        // Write the array's contents to the file.
15        for (int index = 0; index < numbers.Length; index++)
16        {
17            outputFile.WriteLine(numbers[index]);
18        }
19
20        // Close the file.
21        outputFile.Close();
22
23        // Let the user know it's done.
24        MessageBox.Show("Done");
25    }
26    catch (Exception ex)
27    {
28        // Display an error message.
29        MessageBox.Show(ex.Message);
30    }
31 }
```

The try-catch statement handles any file-related errors. Here is a summary of the code inside the try block:

- Line 6 creates an int array with five elements, initialized to the values 10, 20, 30, 40, and 50.
- Line 9 declares a StreamWriter variable named outputFile. (You do not see it in this code sample, but the directive using System.IO; appears at the top of the file. This is required for the StreamWriter declaration in line 9.)
- Line 12 creates a file named Values.txt for writing. After this statement executes, the outputFile variable will reference a StreamWriter object that is associated with the file.
- Line 15 is the beginning of a for loop. The loop iterates once for each element of the array. During the loop's iterations, the index variable will be assigned the values 1, 2, 3, 4 and 5.
- Inside the loop, line 17 writes the array element numbers[index] to the file.
- Line 21 closes the file.
- Line 24 displays a message box letting the user know the operation is done.

Figure 7-13 shows the contents of the Values.txt file, opened in Notepad, after the OK button has been clicked.

Figure 7-13 Contents of the Values.txt file

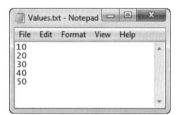

Reading Values from a File and Storing Them in an Array

Reading the contents of a file into an array is also straightforward: Open the file and use a loop to read each item from the file, storing each item in an array element. The loop should iterate until either the array is filled or the end of the file is reached. For example, in the *Chap07* folder of the Student Sample Programs, you will find a project named *File To Array*. When you click the *Get Values* button, the application reads values from a file named Values.txt into an int array. The contents of the array are then displayed in a list box. The following code shows the Click event handler for the *Get Values* button.

```
1 private void getValuesButton_Click(object sender, EventArgs e)
2 {
3     try
4     {
5         // Create an array to hold items read from the file.
6         const int SIZE = 5;
7         int[] numbers = new int[SIZE];
8
9         // Counter variable to use in the loop
10        int index = 0;
```

```
11
12              // Declare a StreamReader variable.
13              StreamReader inputFile;
14
15              // Open the file and get a StreamReader object.
16              inputFile = File.OpenText("Values.txt");
17
18              // Read the file's contents into the array.
19              while (index < numbers.Length && !inputFile.EndOfStream)
20              {
21                  numbers[index] = int.Parse(inputFile.ReadLine());
22                  index++;
23              }
24
25              // Close the file.
26              inputFile.Close();
27
28              // Display the array elements in the list box.
29              foreach (int value in numbers)
30              {
31                  outputListBox.Items.Add(value);
32              }
33          }
34      catch (Exception ex)
35      {
36              // Display an error message.
37              MessageBox.Show(ex.Message);
38      }
39 }
```

The `try-catch` statement handles any file-related errors. Here is a summary of the code inside the try block:

- Lines 6 and 7 create an `int` array with five elements.
- Line 10 declares an `int` variable named `index`, initialized with the value 0. This variable will be used in a loop to hold subscript values.
- Line 13 declares a `StreamReader` variable named `inputFile`. (You do not see it in this code sample, but the directive using `System.IO;` appears at the top of the file. This is required for the `StreamReader` declaration in line 13.)
- Line 16 opens a file named Values.txt for reading. After this statement executes, the `inputFile` variable references a `StreamReader` object that is associated with the file.
- Line 19 is the beginning of a `while` loop that reads items from the file and assigns them to elements of the `numbers` array. Notice that the loop tests two Boolean expressions connected by the `&&` operator. The first expression is `index < numbers.Length`. The purpose of this expression is to prevent the loop from writing beyond the end of the array. When the array is full, the loop stops. The second expression is `!inputFile.EndOfStream`. The purpose of this expression is to prevent the loop from reading beyond the end of the file. When there are no more values to read from the file, the loop stops.
- Inside the loop, line 21 reads a line of text from the file, converts it to an `int`, and assigns the `int` to `numbers[index]`. Then, line 22 increments `index`.
- Line 26 closes the file.
- The `foreach` loop in lines 29–32 displays the array elements in the `outputListBox` control.

Figure 7-14 shows the application's form after the *Get Values* button has been clicked.

Figure 7-14 The *File To Array* form

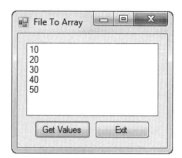

7.4 Passing Arrays as Arguments to Methods

CONCEPT: An array can be passed as an argument to a method. To pass an array, you pass the variable that references the array.

Sometimes you will want to write a method that accepts an entire array as an argument, and performs an operation on the array. For example, the following code shows a method named ShowArray. The method accepts an array of strings as an argument and displays each element in a message box.

```
1 private void ShowArray(string[] strArray)
2 {
3     foreach (string str in strArray)
4     {
5         MessageBox.Show(str);
6     }
7 }
```

Notice in line 1 that the method has a parameter variable named strArray and that the parameter's data type is string[]. The expression string[] indicates that this parameter variable is a reference to a string array. When you call this method, you must pass a string array as an argument.

When you call a method and pass an array as an argument, you simply pass the variable that references the array. The following code shows an example of how the ShowArray method (previously shown) might be called:

```
1 // Create an array of strings.
2 string[] people = { "Bill", "Jill", "Phil", "Will" };
3
4 // Pass the array to the ShowArray method.
5 ShowArray(people);
```

Line 2 creates an array of strings named people and initializes it with four strings. Line 5 calls the ShowArray method passing the people array as an argument.

Keep in mind that arrays are *always* passed by reference. When you pass an array as an argument, the thing that is passed into the parameter variable is a reference to the array. This is illustrated in Figure 7-15. As shown in the figure, the people variable contains a reference to an array. When the people variable is passed to the ShowArray method, the reference to the array is passed into the strArray parameter variable. Figure 7-16 shows that while the ShowArray method is executing, the people variable and the strArray parameter variable reference the same array in memory.

Figure 7-15 An array passed as an argument

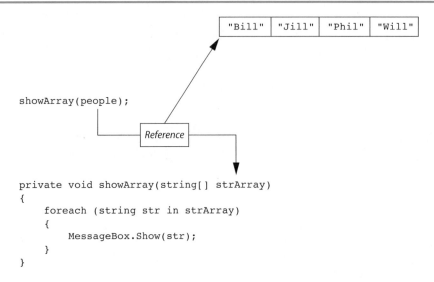

Figure 7-16 The `people` and `strArray` variables referencing the same array

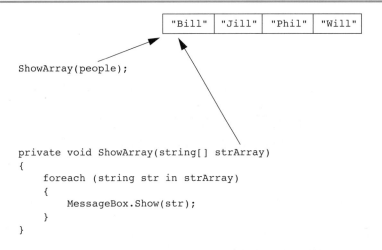

Because arrays are always passed by reference, a method that receives an array as an argument has access to the actual array (not a copy of the array). For example, in the *Chap07* folder of the Student Sample Programs, you will find a project named *Array Argument*. Figure 7-17 shows the application's form just after the user has clicked the

Figure 7-17 The *Array Argument* application

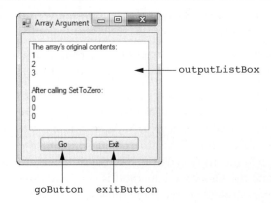

Go button. The following code shows the Click event handler for the *Go* button, and a method named `SetToZero`:

```
1 // Click event handler for the goButton control.
2 private void goButton_Click(object sender, EventArgs e)
3 {
4     // Create an int array.
5     int[] numbers = { 1, 2, 3 };
6
7     // Display the array in the list box.
8     outputListBox.Items.Add("The array's original contents:");
9     foreach (int number in numbers)
10    {
11        outputListBox.Items.Add(number);
12    }
13
14    // Pass the array to the SetToZero method.
15    SetToZero(numbers);
16
17    // Display the array in the list box again.
18    outputListBox.Items.Add("");
19    outputListBox.Items.Add("After calling SetToZero:");
20    foreach (int number in numbers)
21    {
22        outputListBox.Items.Add(number);
23    }
24 }
25
26 // The SetToZero method accepts an int array as an
27 // argument and sets its elememts to 0.
28 private void SetToZero(int[] iArray)
29 {
30     for (int index = 0; index < iArray.Length; index++)
31     {
32         iArray[index] = 0;
33     }
34 }
```

Let's take a closer look at the `goButton_Click` event handler:

- Line 5 creates an `int` array named `numbers`, initialized with the values 1, 2, and 3.
- Line 8 displays the string `"The array's original contents:"` in the `outputListBox` control.
- The `foreach` loop in lines 9–12 displays the contents of the `numbers` array in the `outputListBox` control. Look at Figure 7-17 and notice that the arrays values are 1, 2, and 3.
- Line 15 calls the `SetToZero` method, passing the `numbers` array as an argument.
- Line 18 displays a blank line in the `outputListBox` control, and line 19 displays the string `"After calling SetToZero:"`.
- The `foreach` loop in lines 9–12 displays the contents of the `numbers` array in the `outputListBox` control. Look at Figure 7-17 and notice that the array's values are now 0, 0, and 0.

As you can see from Figure 7-17, the `SetToZero` method changed the values stored in the `numbers` array. Let's look at the `SetToZero` method:

- Notice in line 28 that the method accepts an `int` array as an argument. The parameter variable's name is `iArray`.

- Line 30 is the beginning of a `for` loop that steps through the array. As the loop iterates, the `index` variable is assigned the values 0, 1, 2, and so forth. The loop iterates as long as `index` is less than `iArray.Length`.
- The statement in line 32 assigns 0 to the array element `iArray[index]`.

Because the `iArray` parameter is a reference to the array that was passed as an argument, the statement in line 32 assigns 0 to an element of the `numbers` array.

Using `ref` and `out` with Array Parameters

You saw in the previous example that arrays are always passed by reference. When you pass an array as an argument to a method, the method has direct access to the array through its parameter variable. However, the method cannot access the original reference variable that was used to pass the array. For example, in the *Chap07* folder of the Student Sample Programs, you will find a project named *Change Array 1*. Figure 7-18 shows the application's form just after the user has clicked the *Go* button. The following code shows the Click event handler for the *Go* button and a method named `ChangeArray`:

Figure 7-18 The *Change Array 1* application

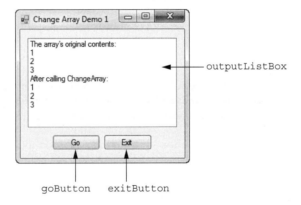

```
1   private void goButton_Click(object sender, EventArgs e)
2   {
3       // Create an int array.
4       int[] numbers = { 1, 2, 3 };
5
6       // Display the numbers array's contents.
7       outputListBox.Items.Add("The array's original contents:");
8       foreach (int value in numbers)
9       {
10          outputListBox.Items.Add(value);
11      }
12
13      // Pass the numbers array to the ChangeArray method.
14      ChangeArray(numbers);
15
16      // Display the numbers array's contents.
17      outputListBox.Items.Add("After calling ChangeArray:");
18      foreach (int value in numbers)
19      {
20          outputListBox.Items.Add(value);
21      }
22  }
23
```

```
24   private void ChangeArray(int[] iArray)
25   {
26       const int NEW_SIZE = 5;
27
28       // Make iArray reference a different array.
29       iArray = new int[NEW_SIZE];
30
31       // Set the new array's elements to 99.
32       for (int index = 0; index < iArray.Length; index++)
33       {
34           iArray[index] = 99;
35       }
36   }
```

Let's take a closer look at the goButton_Click event handler:

- Line 4 creates an int array named numbers, initialized with the values 1, 2, and 3.
- Lines 7–11 display the array's contents in the outputListBox control. Look at Figure 7-18 and notice that the arrays values are 1, 2, and 3.
- Line 14 calls the ChangeArray method, passing the numbers array as an argument.
- Lines 17–21 display the contents of the numbers array in the outputListBox control after the ChangeArray method has executed. Look at Figure 7-18 and notice that the array's values are still 1, 2, and 3. Apparently the method did not change the array.

Let's look at the ChangeArray method:

- Notice in line 24 that the method accepts an int array as an argument. The parameter variable's name is iArray. Keep in mind that when we call this method in line 14, passing numbers as an argument, the iArray parameter and the numbers variable reference the same array in memory.
- Line 26 declares an int constant named NEW_SIZE, set to the value 5.
- Line 29 creates a new int array in memory with five elements. A reference to the array is assigned to the iArray parameter variable. As shown in Figure 7-19, this

Figure 7-19 After line 29 executes

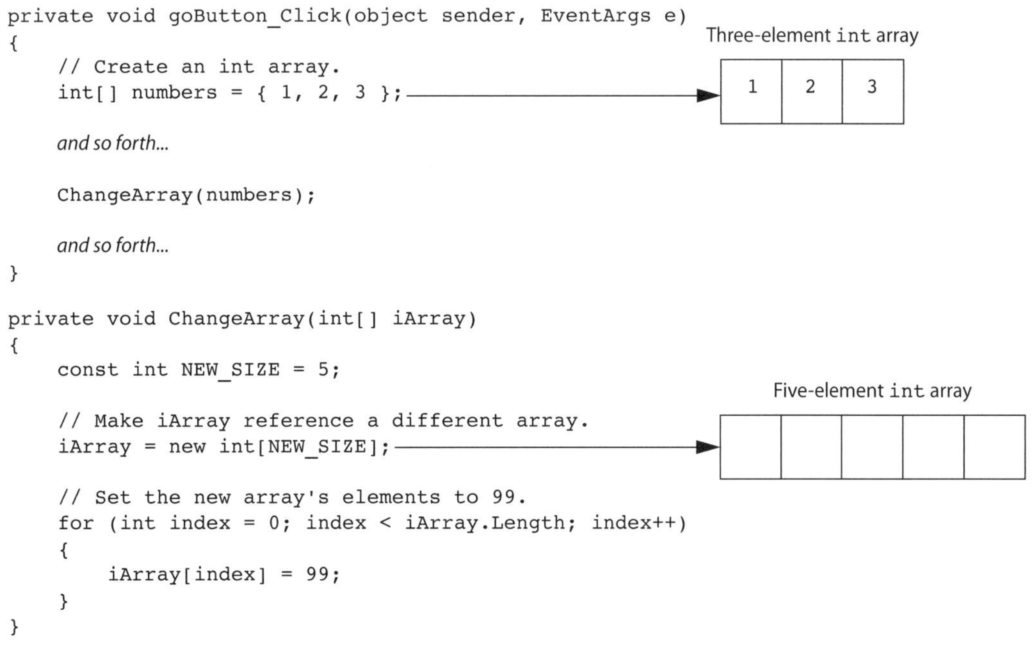

causes the `iArray` parameter variable to no longer reference the array that was passed as an argument. Instead, the `iArray` parameter references the new array.

- The `for` loop in lines 32–35 assigns the value 99 to each element of array referenced by `iArray`. This does not affect the `numbers` array.

When you use either the `ref` or `out` keywords with an array parameter, the receiving method not only has access to the array, but it also has access to the reference variable that was used to pass the array. For example, the *Change Array 2* project, in the *Chap07* folder of the Student Sample Programs, is identical to the *Change Array 1* project, except that the `iArray` parameter is declared with the `ref` keyword in the `ChangeArray` method. The following code shows the Click event handler for the *Go* button, and the `ChangeArray` method.

```
 1 private void goButton_Click(object sender, EventArgs e)
 2 {
 3     // Create an int array.
 4     int[] numbers = { 1, 2, 3 };
 5
 6     // Display the number array's contents.
 7     outputListBox.Items.Add("The array's original contents:");
 8     foreach (int value in numbers)
 9     {
10         outputListBox.Items.Add(value);
11     }
12
13     // Pass the number array to the ChangeArray method.
14     ChangeArray(ref numbers);
15
16     // Display the number array's contents.
17     outputListBox.Items.Add("After calling ChangeArray:");
18     foreach (int value in numbers)
19     {
20         outputListBox.Items.Add(value);
21     }
22 }
23
24 private void ChangeArray(ref int[] iArray)
25 {
26     const int NEW_SIZE = 5;
27
28     // Make iArray reference a different array.
29     iArray = new int[NEW_SIZE];
30
31     // Set the new array's elements to 99.
32     for (int index = 0; index < iArray.Length; index++)
33     {
34         iArray[index] = 99;
35     }
36 }
```

Notice that in line 24 the `iArray` parameter is declared with the `ref` keyword, and in line 14 the `ref` keyword is used to pass `numbers` as an argument to the `ChangeArray` method. In this code, the `iArray` parameter refers to the `numbers` variable. Anything that is done to the `iArray` parameter is actually done to the `numbers` variable. Figure 7-20 shows how line 29 causes the `numbers` variable to reference the new five-element array.

Figure 7-20 After line 29 executes in the *Change Array 2* application

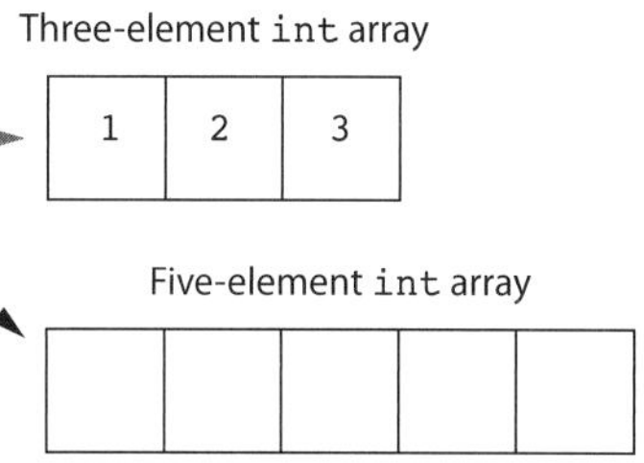

```
private void goButton_Click(object sender, EventArgs e)
{
    // Create an int array.
    int[] numbers = { 1, 2, 3 };

    and so forth...

    ChangeArray(ref numbers);

    and so forth...
}

private void ChangeArray(ref int[] iArray)
{
    const int NEW_SIZE = 5;

    // Make iArray reference a different array.
    iArray = new int[NEW_SIZE];

    // Set the new array's elements to 99.
    for (int index = 0; index < iArray.Length; index++)
    {
        iArray[index] = 99;
    }
}
```

Three-element `int` array

1	2	3

Five-element `int` array

Figure 7-21 shows the application's form just after the user has clicked the *Go* button. Notice from the program's output that after the `ChangeArray` method has been called, the `numbers` variable references a five-element array, and each element's value is 99.

Figure 7-21 The *Change Array 1* application

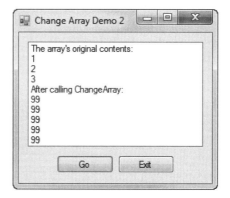

```
Change Array Demo 2

The array's original contents:
1
2
3
After calling ChangeArray:
99
99
99
99
99

    Go        Exit
```

 **Checkpoint**

7.11 When you pass an array as an argument, what is passed into the parameter variable?

7.12 Does a method that receives an array as an argument have access to the actual array or only a copy of the array?

7.13 What is the result when you use either the `ref` or `out` keywords with an array parameter?

7.5 Some Useful Array Algorithms

The Sequential Search

Programs commonly need to search for data that is stored in an array. Various techniques known as **search algorithms** have been developed to locate a specific item in a larger collection of data, such as an array. In this section we discuss the simplest of all search algorithms—the sequential search. The **sequential search algorithm** uses a loop to sequentially step through an array, starting with the first element. It compares each element with the value being searched for and stops when the value is found or the end of the array is encountered. If the value being searched for is not in the array, the algorithm unsuccessfully searches to the end of the array.

Let's look at an example. In the *Chap07* folder of the Student Sample Programs, you will find a project named *Colonies*. The application is a game that tests your knowledge of U.S. history. As shown in Figure 7-22, the application's form displays a list of states in a ListBox control. Only one of the states shown in the ListBox was an original American colony. You select the state that you believe was a colony and click the *OK* button to see if you were correct.

Figure 7-22 The *Colonies* application

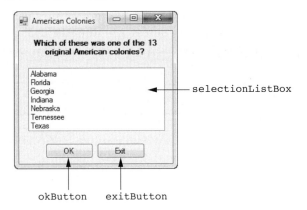

The following code is taken from the application. It shows a method named `SequentialSearch` and the Click event handler for the *OK* button.

```
 1 // The SequentialSearch method searches a string array
 2 // for a specified value. If the value is found, its
 3 // position is returned. Otherwise, -1 is returned.
 4 private int SequentialSearch(string[] sArray, string value)
 5 {
 6     bool found = false;   // Flag indicating search results
 7     int index = 0;        // Used to step through the array
 8     int position = -1;    // Position of value, if found
 9
10     // Search the array.
11     while (!found && index < sArray.Length)
12     {
13         if (sArray[index] == value)
14         {
15             found = true;
16             position = index;
17         }
18
19         index++;
```

```
20      }
21
22      // Return
23      return position;
24 }
25
26 private void okButton_Click(object sender, EventArgs e)
27 {
28      string selection;    // To hold the user's selection
29
30      // Create an array with the colony names.
31      string[] colonies = { "Delaware", "Pennsylvania", "New Jersey",
32                            "Georgia", "Connecticut", "Massachusetts",
33                            "Maryland", "South Carolina", "New Hampshire",
34                            "Virginia", "New York", "North Carolina",
35                            "Rhode Island" };
36
37      if (selectionListBox.SelectedIndex != -1)
38      {
39          // Get the selected item.
40          selection = selectionListBox.SelectedItem.ToString();
41
42          // Determine if the item is in the array.
43          if (SequentialSearch(colonies, selection) != -1)
44          {
45              MessageBox.Show("Yes, that was one of the colonies.");
46          }
47          else
48          {
49              MessageBox.Show("No, that was not one of the colonies.");
50          }
51      }
52 }
```

The `SequentialSearch` method, which begins in line 4, searches a `string` array for a specified value. It accepts a `string` array and a `string` search value as arguments. If the search value is found in the array, the method returns the value's subscript. If the search value is not found in the array, the method returns −1. Let's take a closer look at the method:

- Line 6 declares a `bool` variable named `found`. The `found` variable is used as a flag. Setting `found` to `false` indicates that the search value has not been found. Setting `found` to `true` indicates that the search value has been found. Notice that `found` is initialized with `false`.
- Line 7 declares an `int` variable named `index`, that will be used to step through the elements of the array. Notice that `index` is initialized with the value 0.
- Line 8 declares an `int` variable named `position`. If the search value is found in the array, we save its subscript in the `position` variable. Notice that the `position` variable is initialized with the value −1.
- The `while` loop that begins in line 11 searches the array for the specified value. It iterates as long as `found` is not `true` and `index` is less than the array's length.
- The `if` statement in line 13 determines whether `sArray[index]` is equal to `value`. If this is true, then the search value has been found in the array. In that case, line 15 sets `found` to `true`, and line 16 assigns `index` to `position`.
- Line 19 increments `index`.
- When the loop finishes, line 23 returns the value of the `position` variable. If the search value was found in the array, the `position` variable will contain the value's subscript. If the search value was not found in the array, the `position` variable will still be set to −1.

The Click event handler for the *OK* button begins in line 26. Let's take a closer look at the event handler's code:

- Line 28 declares a `string` variable named `selection`. This variable will hold the item that is selected from the ListBox control.
- Lines 31–35 declare a `string` array named `colonies`. The array is initialized with the names of the U.S. colonies.
- The `if` statement that begins in line 37 determines whether an item has been selected in the `selectionListBox` control. If an item has been selected, the following actions take place:
    - Line 40 gets the selected item and assigns it to the `selection` variable.
    - The `if` statement in line 43 calls the `SequentialSearch` method, passing the `colonies` array and the `selection` variable as arguments. If the value of the `selection` variable is found in the `colonies` array, the method returns a value other than −1, and line 45 displays a message box informing the user that the selected item was one of the colonies. However, if the value of the `selection` variable is not found in the `colonies` array, the method will return −1, and line 49 displays a message box informing the user that the selected item was not one of the colonies.

Copying an Array

Because an array is an object, there is a distinction between an array and the variable that references it. The array and the reference variable are two separate entities. This is important to remember when you wish to copy the contents of one array to another. You might be tempted to write something like the following code, thinking that you are copying an array:

```
int[] array1 = { 2, 4, 6, 8, 10 };
int[] array2 = array1; // This does not copy array1.
```

The first statement creates an array referenced by the `array1` variable. The second statement assigns `array1` to `array2`. This does not make a copy of the array referenced by `array1`. Rather, it assigns the reference that is in `array1` to `array2`. After this statement executes, both the `array1` and `array2` variables will reference the same array. This type of assignment operation is called a **reference copy**. Only a reference to the array object is copied, not the contents of the array object. This is illustrated in Figure 7-23.

Figure 7-23 Both `array1` and `array2` referencing the same array

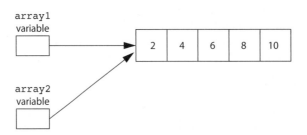

If you want to make a copy of an array, you must create the second array in memory and then copy the individual elements of the first array to the second. This is usually best done with a loop, such as the following:

```
1 const int SIZE = 5;
2 int[] firstArray = { 5, 10, 15, 20, 25 };
3 int[] secondArray = new int[SIZE];
4
```

```
5 for (int index = 0; index < firstArray.length; index++)
6 {
7     secondArray[index] = firstArray[index];
8 }
```

The loop in this code copies each element of `firstArray` to the corresponding element of `secondArray`.

Comparing Arrays

You cannot use the == operator to compare two array reference variables and determine whether the arrays are equal. For example, the following code appears to compare two arrays, but in reality it does not:

```
1 int[] firstArray  = { 5, 10, 15, 20, 25 };
2 int[] secondArray = { 5, 10, 15, 20, 25 };
3
4 if (firstArray == secondArray) // This is a mistake.
5 {
6     MessageBox.Show("The arrays are the same.");
7 }
8 else
9 {
10     MessageBox.Show("The arrays are not the same.");
11 }
```

When you use the == operator with reference variables, the operator compares the references that the variables contain, not the contents of the objects referenced by the variables. Because the `firstArray` and `secondArray` variables in this example reference different objects in memory, the result of the Boolean expression `firstArray == secondArray` is false, and the code reports that the arrays are not the same.

To compare the contents of two arrays, you must compare the elements of the two arrays. For example, look at the following code:

```
1 int[] firstArray  = { 2, 4, 6, 8, 10 };
2 int[] secondArray = { 2, 4, 6, 8, 10 };
3 boolean arraysEqual = true; // Flag variable
4 int index = 0;              // To hold array subscripts
5
6 // First determine whether the arrays are the same size.
7 if (firstArray.length != secondArray.length)
8 {
9     arraysEqual = false;
10 }
11
12 // Next determine whether the elements contain the same data.
13 while (arraysEqual && index < firstArray.length)
14 {
15     if (firstArray[index] != secondArray[index])
16     {
17         arraysEqual = false;
18     }
19     index++;
20 }
21
22 if (arraysEqual)
23 {
24     MessageBox.Show("The arrays are equal.");
25 }
26 else
```

```
27 {
28     MessageBox.Show("The arrays are not equal.");
29 }
```

This code determines whether firstArray and secondArray (declared in lines 1 and 2) contain the same values. A Boolean flag variable, arraysEqual, is declared and initialized to true, is declared in line 3. The arraysEqual variable used to signal whether the arrays are equal. Another variable, index, is declared and initialized to 0 in line 4. The index variable is used in a loop to step through the arrays.

First, the if statement in line 7 determines whether the two arrays are the same length. If they are not the same length, then the arrays cannot be equal, so the flag variable arraysEqual is set to false in line 9. Then a while loop begins in line 13. The loop executes as long as arraysEqual is true and the index variable is less than firstArray.length. During each iteration, it compares a different set of corresponding elements in the arrays. When it finds two corresponding elements that have different values, the flag variable arraysEqual is set to false.

After the loop finishes, an if statement examines the arraysEqual variable in line 22. If the variable is true, then the arrays are equal and a message indicating so is displayed in line 24. Otherwise, they are not equal, so a different message is displayed in line 28.

Totaling the Values in an Array

To calculate the total of the values in a numeric array, you use a loop with an accumulator variable. First, the accumulator is initialized with 0. Then, the loop steps through the array, adding the value of each array element to the accumulator.

```
1  // Create an int array.
2  int[] numbers = { 2, 4, 6, 8, 10 };
3
4  // Declare and initialize an accumulator variable.
5  int total = 0;
6
7  // Step through the array, adding each element to
8  // the accumulator.
9  for (int index = 0; index < units.Length; index++)
10 {
11     total += units[index];
12 }
13
14 // Display the total.
15 MessageBox.Show("The total is " + total);
```

Averaging the Values in an Array

The first step in calculating the average of all the values in a numeric array is to get the total of the values. The second step is to divide the total by the number of elements in the array. The following code shows an example:

```
1  // Create an array.
2  double[] scores = { 92.5, 81.6, 65.7, 72.8 }
3
4  // Declare and initialize an accumulator variable.
5  double total = 0.0;
6
7  // Declare a variable to hold the average.
8  double average;
```

```
 9
10 // Step through the array, adding each element to
11 // the accumulator.
12 for (int index = 0; index < scores.Length; index++)
13 {
14     total += scores[index];
15 }
16
17 // Calculate the average.
18 average = total / scores.Length;
19
20 // Display the average.
21 MessageBox.Show("The average is " + average);
```

When this code finishes, the average variable will contain the average of the values in the scores array. Notice that the last statement, which divides total by scores.length, is not inside the loop. This statement should execute only once, after the loop has finished its iterations.

Finding the Highest and Lowest Values in an Array

Some programming tasks require you to find the highest value in a set of data. Examples include programs that report the highest sales amount for a given time period, the highest test score in a set of test scores, the highest temperature for a given set of days, and so forth.

The algorithm for finding the highest value in an array works like this: You create a variable to hold the highest value (the following example names this variable highest). Then, you assign the value at element 0 to the highest variable. Next, you use a loop to step through the rest of the array elements, beginning at element 1. Each time the loop iterates, it compares an array element to the highest variable. If the array element is greater than the highest variable, then the value in the array element is assigned to the highest variable. When the loop finishes, the highest variable will contain the highest value in the array. The flowchart in Figure 7-24 illustrates this logic.

The following code demonstrates this algorithm:

```
 1 // Create an array.
 2 int[] numbers = { 8, 1, 12, 6, 2 };
 3
 4 // Declare a variable to hold the highest value, and
 5 // initialize it with the first value in the array.
 6 int highest = numbers[0];
 7
 8 // Step through the rest of the array, beginning at
 9 // element 1. When a value greater than highest is found,
10 // assign that value to highest.
11 for (int index = 1; index < numbers.Length; index++)
12 {
13     if (numbers[index] > highest)
14     {
15         highest = numbers[index];
16     }
17 }
18
19 // Display the highest value.
20 MessageBox.Show("The highest value is " + highest);
```

Figure 7-24 Flowchart for finding the highest value in an array

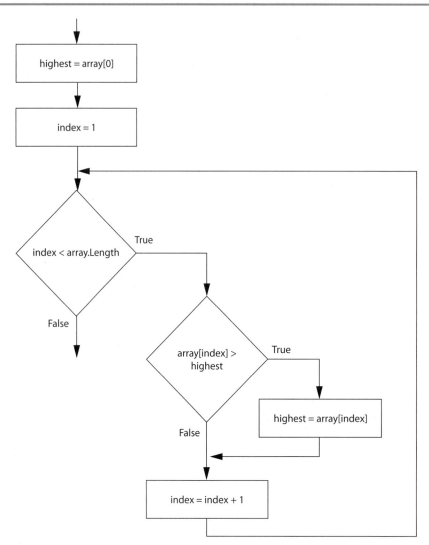

In some programs you are more interested in finding the lowest value than the highest value in a set of data. For example, suppose you are writing a program that stores several players' golf scores in an array and you need to find the best score. In golf, the lower the score the better, so you need an algorithm that finds the lowest value in the array.

The algorithm for finding the lowest value in an array is very similar to the algorithm for finding the highest score. It works like this: You create a variable to hold the lowest value (the following example names this variable lowest). Then, you assign the value at element 0 to the lowest variable. Next, you use a loop to step through the rest of the array elements, beginning at element 1. Each time the loop iterates, it compares an array element to the lowest variable. If the array element is less than the lowest variable, then the value in the array element is assigned to the lowest variable. When the loop finishes, the lowest variable contains the lowest value in the array. The flowchart in Figure 7-25 illustrates this logic.

Figure 7-25 Flowchart for finding the lowest value in an array

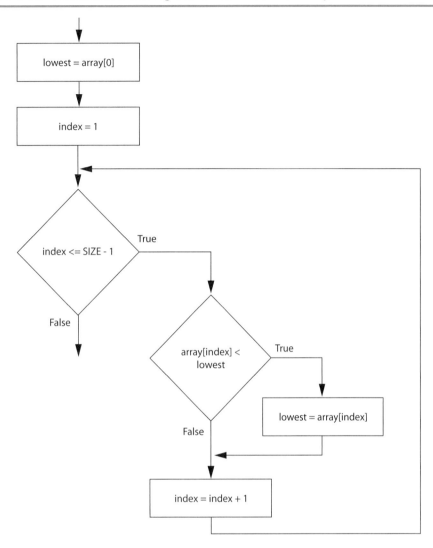

The following code demonstrates this algorithm:

```
 1 // Create an array.
 2 int[] numbers = { 8, 1, 12, 6, 2 };
 3
 4 // Declare a variable to hold the lowest value, and
 5 // initialize it with the first value in the array.
 6 int lowest = numbers[0];
 7
 8 // Step through the rest of the array, beginning at
 9 // element 1. When a value less than lowest is found,
10 // assign that value to lowest.
11 for (int index = 1; index < numbers.Length; index++)
12 {
13     if (numbers[index] < lowest)
14     {
15         lowest = numbers[index];
16     }
17 }
18
19 // Display the lowest value.
20 MessageBox.Show("The lowest value is " + lowest);
```

Partially Filled Arrays

Sometimes you need to store a series of items in an array, but you do not know the number of items in the series. As a result, you do not know the exact number of elements needed for the array. One solution is to make the array large enough to hold the largest possible number of items. This can lead to another problem, however. If the actual number of items stored in the array is less than the number of elements, the array will be only partially filled. When you process a partially filled array, you must process only the elements that contain valid data items.

A partially filled array is normally used with an accompanying integer variable that holds the number of items that are actually stored in the array. If the array is empty, then 0 is stored in this variable because there are no items in the array. Each time an item is added to the array, the variable is incremented. When code steps through the array's elements, the value of this variable is used instead of the array's size to determine the maximum subscript.

For example, in the *Chap07* folder of the Student Sample Programs, you will find a project named *Partially Filled Array*. When you click the *Go* button, the application reads up to 100 values from a file named Values.txt and stores them in a 100-element int array. If the file contains fewer than 100 values, the application will partially fill the array. The contents of the array are then displayed in a list box. Figure 7-26 shows the application's form just after the user has clicked the *Go* button. The following code shows the Click event handler for the *Get Values* button.

Figure 7-26 The *Partially Filled Array* application

```
 1 private void goButton_Click(object sender, EventArgs e)
 2 {
 3     try
 4     {
 5         // Create an array to hold items read from the file.
 6         const int SIZE = 100;
 7         int[] numbers = new int[SIZE];
 8
 9         // Variable to hold the number of items stored in
10         // the array
11         int count = 0;
12
13         // Declare a StreamReader variable.
14         StreamReader inputFile;
15
16         // Open the file and get a StreamReader object.
17         inputFile = File.OpenText("Values.txt");
```

```
18
19          // Read the file's contents into the array until the
20          // end of the file is reached, or the array is full.
21          while (!inputFile.EndOfStream && count < numbers.Length)
22          {
23              // Read the next item from the file.
24              numbers[count] = int.Parse(inputFile.ReadLine());
25
26              // Increment count.
27              count++;
28          }
29
30          // Close the file.
31          inputFile.Close();
32
33          // Display the array elements in the list box.
34          outputListBox.Items.Add("The file contains " + count +
35              " items:");
36
37          for (int index = 0; index < count; index++)
38          {
39              outputListBox.Items.Add(numbers[index]);
40          }
41      }
42      catch (Exception ex)
43      {
44          // Display an error message.
45          MessageBox.Show(ex.Message);
46      }
47 }
```

Let's examine the code in detail:

- Line 3 is the beginning of a `try-catch` statement that handles any errors that might result while reading data from the file.
- Line 6 declares a constant, `SIZE`, initialized with the value 100.
- Line 7 declares an `int` array named `numbers` using `SIZE` as the size declarator. As a result, the values array has 100 elements.
- Line 11 declares an `int` variable named `count`, which holds the number of items that are stored in the `numbers` array. Notice that `count` is initialized with 0 because there are no values stored in the array.
- Line 14 declares a `StreamReader` variable named `inputFile`. (You do not see it in this code sample, but the directive using `System.IO;` appears at the top of the file. This is required for the `StreamReader` declaration in line 14.)
- Line 17 opens a file named Values.txt for reading. After this statement executes, the `inputFile` variable references a `StreamReader` object that is associated with the file.
- Line 21 is the beginning of a `while` loop that reads items from the file and assigns them to elements of the `numbers` array. Notice that the loop tests two Boolean expressions connected by the `&&` operator. The first expression is `!inputFile.EndOfStream`. The purpose of this expression is to prevent the loop from reading beyond the end of the file. When there are no more values to read from the file, the loop stops. The second expression is `count < numbers.Length`. The purpose of this expression is to prevent the loop from writing beyond the end of the array. When the array is full, the loop will stop.
- Inside the loop, line 24 reads a line of text from the file, converts it to an `int`, and assigns the `int` to `numbers[index]`.
- Then, line 27 increments the `count` variable. Each time a number is assigned to an array element, the `count` variable is incremented. As a result, the `count` variable holds the number of items that are stored in the array.

- Line 31 closes the file.
- The `for` loop in lines 37–40 displays the array elements in the `outputListBox` control. Rather than stepping through all the elements in the array, however, the loop steps through only the elements that contain values. Notice that the loop iterates as long as `index` is less than `count`. Because `count` contains the number of items stored in the array, the loop stops when the element containing the last valid value has been displayed.

Now that you've seen several algorithms for processing the contents of an array, you should practice writing some of them yourself. Tutorial 7-2 takes you through the process of writing an application that reads data from a file into an `int` array and then determines the highest, lowest, and average values in the array.

Tutorial 7-2:
Processing an Array

In this tutorial you complete an application that reads five test scores from a file and stores the test scores in an array. The application displays the test scores as well as the highest score, the lowest score, and the average score. Figure 7-27 shows the application's form, which has already been created for you. A set of five test scores is stored in a file named TestScores.txt, which has also been created for you.

Figure 7-27 The *Test Average* application's form

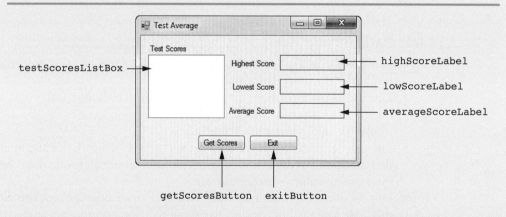

Step 1: Start Visual Studio (or Visual C# Express). Open the project named *Test Average* in the *Chap07* folder of the Student Sample Programs.

Step 2: Open the Form1 form's code in the code editor. Insert the `using System.IO;` directive shown in line 9 of Program 7-2 at the end of this tutorial. This statement is necessary because we will be using the `StreamReader` class, and it is part of the `System.IO` namespace in the .NET Framework.

Step 3: With the code editor still open, type the comments and code for the `Average` method, shown in lines 20–39 of Program 7-2. The purpose of the `Average` method is to accept an `int` array as an argument and return the average of the values in the array. This method uses an algorithm similar to the array averaging you saw earlier in this chapter.

Step 4: Type the comments and code for the `Highest` method, shown in lines 41–62 of Program 7-2. The purpose of the `Highest` method is to accept an `int` array as an argument and return the highest value in the array. This method uses an algorithm similar to the algorithm that you saw earlier in this chapter for finding the highest value in an array.

Step 5: Type the comments and code for the Lowest method, shown in lines 64–85 of Program 7-2. The purpose of the Lowest method is to accept an int array as an argument and return the lowest value in the array. This method uses an algorithm similar to the algorithm that you saw earlier in this chapter for finding the lowest value in an array.

Step 6: Now you create the Click event handlers for the Button controls. Switch back to the *Designer* and double-click the getScoresButton control. This opens the code editor, and you will see an empty event handler named getScoresButton_Click. Complete the getScoresButton_Click event handler by typing the code shown in lines 89–133 in Program 7-2. Let's review this code:

Line 89: This is the beginning of a try-catch statement that handles any exceptions that are thrown while reading and processing data from the file. If an exception occurs in the try block (lines 91–127), the program jumps to the catch block, and line 132 displays an error message.

Lines 92–98: The following declarations appear in these lines:

- SIZE—a constant, set to 5, for the number of test scores
- scores—an int array that holds the test scores
- index—an int variable, initialized to 0, that is used in a loop to step through the elements of the scores array
- highestScore—an int that holds the highest score
- lowestScore—an int that holds the lowest score
- averageScore—a double that holds the average score
- inputFile—a variable that references the StreamReader object that is used to read data from the file

Line 101: After this statement executes, the TestScores.txt file will be opened for reading, and the inputFile variable will reference a StreamReader object that is associated with the file.

Line 104: This is the beginning of a while loop that iterates as long as the end of the TestScores.txt file has not been reached and as long as index is less than scores.Length. (Recall that index starts with the value 0.)

Line 106: This statement reads a line of text from the file and assigns it to the array element scores[index].

Line 107: This statement increments the index variable.

Line 111: This statement closes the TestScores.txt file.

Lines 114—117: This foreach loop displays the contents of the scores array in the testScoresListBox control.

Line 120: This statement calls the Highest method, passing the scores array as an argument. The method returns the highest value in the array, which is assigned to the highestScore variable.

Line 121: This statement calls the Lowest method, passing the scores array as an argument. The method returns the lowest value in the array, which is assigned to the lowestScore variable.

Line 122: This statement calls the Average method, passing the scores array as an argument. The method returns the average of the values in the array, which is assigned to the averageScore variable.

Lines 125–127: These statements display the highest score, lowest score, and average score.

Step 7: Switch your view back to the *Designer* and double-click the `exitButton` control. In the code editor you will see an empty event handler named `exitButton_Click`. Complete the `exitButton_Click` event handler by typing the code shown in lines 138–139 in Program 7-2.

Step 8: Save the project. Then, press [F5] on the keyboard or click the *Start Debugging* button (▶) on the toolbar to compile and run the application. When the application runs, click the *Get Scores* button. This should display a set of test scores in ListBox as well as the highest, lowest, and average of the test scores, as shown in Figure 7-28. Click the *Exit* button to exit the application.

Figure 7-28 The *Test Average* application

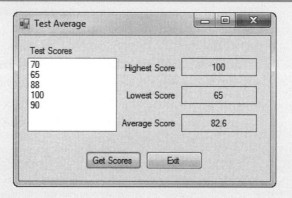

Program 7-2 Completed code for Form1 in the *Test Average* application

```
1 using System;
2 using System.Collections.Generic;
3 using System.ComponentModel;
4 using System.Data;
5 using System.Drawing;
6 using System.Linq;
7 using System.Text;
8 using System.Windows.Forms;
9 using System.IO;
10
11 namespace Test_Average
12 {
13     public partial class Form1 : Form
14     {
15         public Form1()
16         {
17             InitializeComponent();
18         }
19
20         // The Average method accepts an int array argument
21         // and returns the average of the values in the array.
22         private double Average(int[] iArray)
23         {
24             int total = 0;    // Accumulator, initialized to 0
```

```
25              double average;  // To hold the average
26
27              // Step through the array, adding each element to
28              // the accumulator.
29              for (int index = 0; index < iArray.Length; index++)
30              {
31                  total += iArray[index];
32              }
33
34              // Calculate the average.
35              average = (double) total / iArray.Length;
36
37              // Return the average.
38              return average;
39          }
40
41          // The Highest method accepts an int array argument
42          // and returns the highest value in that array.
43          private int Highest(int[] iArray)
44          {
45              // Declare a variable to hold the highest value, and
46              // initialize it with the first value in the array.
47              int highest = iArray[0];
48
49              // Step through the rest of the array, beginning at
50              // element 1. When a value greater than highest is found,
51              // assign that value to highest.
52              for (int index = 1; index < iArray.Length; index++)
53              {
54                  if (iArray[index] > highest)
55                  {
56                      highest = iArray[index];
57                  }
58              }
59
60              // Return the highest value.
61              return highest;
62          }
63
64          // The Lowest method accepts an int array argument
65          // and returns the lowest value in that array.
66          private int Lowest(int[] iArray)
67          {
68              // Declare a variable to hold the lowest value, and
69              // initialize it with the first value in the array.
70              int lowest = iArray[0];
71
72              // Step through the rest of the array, beginning at
73              // element 1. When a value less than lowest is found,
74              // assign that value to lowest.
75              for (int index = 1; index < iArray.Length; index++)
76              {
77                  if (iArray[index] < lowest)
78                  {
79                      lowest = iArray[index];
80                  }
81              }
82
83              // Return the lowest value.
```

```
 84                return lowest;
 85          }
 86
 87          private void getScoresButton_Click(object sender, EventArgs e)
 88          {
 89              try
 90              {
 91                  // Local variables
 92                  const int SIZE = 5;          // Number of tests
 93                  int[] scores = new int[SIZE]; // Array of test scores
 94                  int index = 0;              // Loop counter
 95                  int highestScore;           // The highest score
 96                  int lowestScore;            // The lowest score
 97                  double averageScore;        // The average score
 98                  StreamReader inputFile;     // For file input
 99
100                  // Open the file and get a StreamReader object.
101                  inputFile = File.OpenText("TestScores.txt");
102
103                  // Read the test scores into the array.
104                  while (!inputFile.EndOfStream && index < scores.Length)
105                  {
106                      scores[index] = int.Parse(inputFile.ReadLine());
107                      index++;
108                  }
109
110                  // Close the file.
111                  inputFile.Close();
112
113                  // Display the test scores.
114                  foreach (int value in scores)
115                  {
116                      testScoresListBox.Items.Add(value);
117                  }
118
119                  // Get the highest, lowest, and average scores.
120                  highestScore = Highest(scores);
121                  lowestScore = Lowest(scores);
122                  averageScore = Average(scores);
123
124                  // Display the values.
125                  highScoreLabel.Text = highestScore.ToString();
126                  lowScoreLabel.Text = lowestScore.ToString();
127                  averageScoreLabel.Text = averageScore.ToString("n1");
128              }
129              catch (Exception ex)
130              {
131                  // Display an error message.
132                  MessageBox.Show(ex.Message);
133              }
134          }
135
136          private void exitButton_Click(object sender, EventArgs e)
137          {
138              // Close the form.
139              this.Close();
140          }
141      }
142  }
```

7.6 Advanced Algorithms for Sorting and Searching Arrays

CONCEPT: A sorting algorithm is used to arrange data into some order. A search algorithm is a method of locating a specific item in a larger collection of data. The selection sort and the binary search are popular sorting and searching algorithms.

The Selection Sort Algorithm

Often the data in an array must be sorted in some order. Customer lists, for instance, are commonly sorted in alphabetical order. Student grades might be sorted from highest to lowest. Product codes could be sorted so all the products of the same color are stored together. In this section we explore how to write your own sorting algorithm. A sorting algorithm is a technique for scanning through an array and rearranging its contents in some specific order. The algorithm that we explore is called the selection sort.

The **selection sort** works like this: The smallest value in the array is located and moved to element 0. Then the next smallest value is located and moved to element 1. This process continues until all the elements have been placed in their proper order. Let's see how the selection sort works when arranging the elements of the array in Figure 7-29.

Figure 7-29 Values in an array

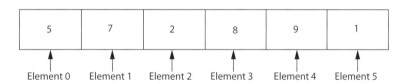

The selection sort scans the array, starting at element 0, and locates the element with the smallest value. Then, the contents of this element are swapped with the contents of element 0. In this example, the 1 stored in element 5 is swapped with the 5 stored in element 0. After the swap, the array appears as shown in Figure 7-30.

Figure 7-30 Values in the array after the first swap

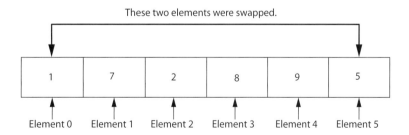

Then, the algorithm repeats the process, but because element 0 already contains the smallest value in the array, it can be left out of the procedure. This time, the algorithm begins the scan at element 1. In this example, the value in element 2 is swapped with the value in element 1. Then, the array appears as shown in Figure 7-31.

Figure 7-31 Values in the array after the second swap

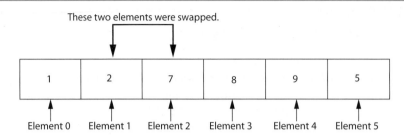

Once again, the process is repeated, but this time the scan begins at element 2. The algorithm will find that element 5 contains the next smallest value. This element's value is swapped with that of element 2, causing the array to appear as shown in Figure 7-32.

Figure 7-32 Values in the array after the third swap

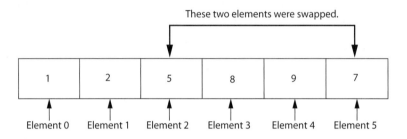

Next, the scanning begins at element 3. Its value is swapped with that of element 5, causing the array to appear as shown in Figure 7-33.

Figure 7-33 Values in the array after the fourth swap

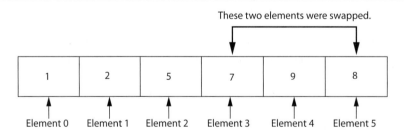

At this point there are only two elements left to sort. The algorithm finds that the value in element 5 is smaller than that of element 4, so the two are swapped. This puts the array in its final arrangement, as shown in Figure 7-34.

Figure 7-34 Values in the array after the fifth swap

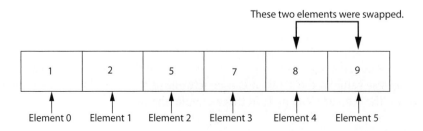

Swapping Array Elements

As you saw in the description of the selection sort algorithm, certain elements are swapped as the algorithm steps through the array. Let's briefly discuss the process of swapping two items in computer memory. Assume we have the following variable declarations:

```
int a = 1;
int b = 9;
```

Suppose we want to swap the values in these variables so the variable a contains 9 and the variable b contains 1. At first, you might think that we need only assign the variables to each other, like this:

```
// ERROR! The following does NOT swap the variables.
a = b;
b = a;
```

To understand why this does not work, let's step through the code. The first statement is a = b. This causes the value 9 to be assigned to a. But, what happens to the value 1 that was previously stored in a? Remember, when you assign a new value to a variable, the new value replaces any value that was previously stored in the variable. So, the old value, 1, is thrown away. Then the next statement is b = a. Since the variable a contains 9, this assigns 9 to b. After these statements execute, the variables a and b both contain the value 9.

To successfully swap the contents of two variables, we need a third variable that can serve as a temporary storage location:

```
int temp;
```

Then we can perform the following steps to swap the values in the variables a and b:

- Assign the value of a to temp.
- Assign the value of b to a.
- Assign the value of temp to b.

Figure 7-35 shows the contents of these variables as we perform each of these steps. Notice that after the steps are finished, the values in a and b are swapped.

Figure 7-35 Swapping the values of a and b

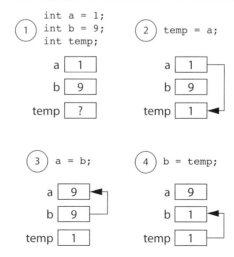

Here is the code for a Swap method that we can use to swap to int values:

```
1 private void Swap(ref int a, ref int b)
2 {
3     int temp = a;
4     a = b;
5     b = temp;
6 }
```

> **NOTE:** It is critical that we use reference parameters in the Swap method, because the method must be able to change the values of the items that are passed to it as arguments.

Let's look at a complete program that demonstrates the Selection Sort algorithm. In the *Chap07* folder of the Student Sample Programs, you will find a project named *Selection Sort*. Figure 7-36 shows the application's form. On the left, you see the form with the names of various controls. On the right you see the form after the *Go* button has been clicked. When you click the Go button, the following actions take place:

- An int array is created, initialized with unsorted values.
- The contents of the array are displayed in the originalListBox control.
- The array is passed as an argument to the SelectionSort method. The method uses the Selection Sort algorithm to sort the array.
- The contents of the array are displayed in the sortedListBox control.

Program 7-3 shows the complete code for the *Selection Sort* application.

Figure 7-36 The *Selection Sort* application's form

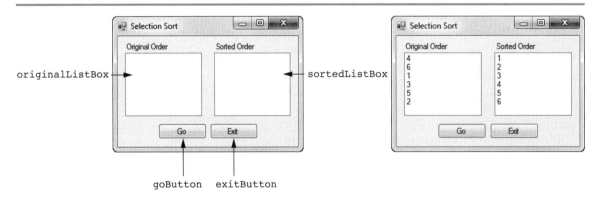

Program 7-3 Complete code for Form1 in the *Selection Sort* application

```
1 using System;
2 using System.Collections.Generic;
3 using System.ComponentModel;
4 using System.Data;
5 using System.Drawing;
6 using System.Linq;
7 using System.Text;
8 using System.Windows.Forms;
9
10 namespace Selection_Sort
```

```csharp
11  {
12      public partial class Form1 : Form
13      {
14          public Form1()
15          {
16              InitializeComponent();
17          }
18
19          // The SelectionSort method accepts an int array as an argument.
20          // It uses the Selection Sort algorithm to sort the array.
21          private void SelectionSort(int[] iArray)
22          {
23              int minIndex;   // Subscript of smallest value in scanned area
24              int minValue; // Smallest value in the scanned area
25
26              // The outer loop steps through all the array elements,
27              // except the last one. The startScan variable marks the
28              // position where the scan should begin.
29              for (int startScan = 0; startScan < iArray.Length - 1; startScan++)
30              {
31                  // Assume the first element in the scannable area
32                  // is the smallest value.
33                  minIndex = startScan;
34                  minValue = iArray[startScan];
35
36                  // Scan the array, starting at the 2nd element in the
37                  // scannable area, looking for the smallest value.
38                  for (int index = startScan + 1; index < iArray.Length; index++)
39                  {
40                      if (iArray[index] < minValue)
41                      {
42                          minValue = iArray[index];
43                          minIndex = index;
44                      }
45                  }
46
47                  // Swap the element with the smallest value with the
48                  // first element in the scannable area.
49                  Swap(ref iArray[minIndex], ref iArray[startScan]);
50              }
51          }
52
53          // The Swap method accepts two integer arguments, by reference,
54          // and swaps their contents.
55          private void Swap(ref int a, ref int b)
56          {
57              int temp = a;
58              a = b;
59              b = temp;
60          }
61
62          private void goButton_Click(object sender, EventArgs e)
63          {
64              // Create an array of integers.
65              int[] numbers = { 4, 6, 1, 3, 5, 2 };
66
67              // Display the array in original order.
68              foreach (int value in numbers)
69              {
70                  originalListBox.Items.Add(value);
71              }
```

```
72
73                      // Sort the array.
74                      SelectionSort(numbers);
75
76                      // Display the array in sorted order.
77                      foreach (int value in numbers)
78                      {
79                          sortedListBox.Items.Add(value);
80                      }
81              }
82
83              private void exitButton_Click(object sender, EventArgs e)
84              {
85                      // Close the form.
86                      this.Close();
87              }
88      }
89 }
```

The Binary Search Algorithm

Previously in this chapter we discussed the sequential search algorithm, which uses a loop to step sequentially through an array, starting with the first element. It compares each element with the value being searched for and stops when the value is found or the end of the array is encountered. If the value being searched for is not in the array, the algorithm unsuccessfully searches to the end of the array.

The advantage of the sequential search is its simplicity: It is very easy to understand and implement. Furthermore, it does not require the data in the array to be stored in any particular order. Its disadvantage, however, is its inefficiency. If the array being searched contains 20,000 elements, the algorithm has to look at all 20,000 elements in order to find a value stored in the last element.

In an average case, an item is just as likely to be found near the beginning of an array as near the end. Typically, for an array of n items, the sequential search locates an item in $n/2$ attempts. If an array has 50,000 elements, the sequential search makes a comparison with 25,000 of them in a typical case. This is assuming, of course, that the search item is consistently found in the array. ($n/2$ is the average number of comparisons. The maximum number of comparisons is always n.

When the sequential search fails to locate an item, it must make a comparison with every element in the array. As the number of failed search attempts increases, so does the average number of comparisons. Although the sequential search algorithm is adequate for small arrays, it should not be used on large arrays if speed is important.

The **binary search** is a clever algorithm that is much more efficient than the sequential search. Its only requirement is that the values in the array must be sorted in ascending order. Instead of testing the array's first element, this algorithm starts with the element in the middle. If that element happens to contain the desired value, then the search is over. Otherwise, the value in the middle element is either greater than or less than the value being searched for. If it is greater, then the desired value (if it is in the list) will be found somewhere in the first half of the array. If it is less, then the desired value (again, if it is in the list) will be found somewhere in the last half of the array. In either case, half of the array's elements have been eliminated from further searching.

If the desired value is not found in the middle element, the procedure is repeated for the half of the array that potentially contains the value. For instance, if the last half of the array is to be searched, the algorithm tests *its* middle element. If the desired value is not found there, the search is narrowed to the quarter of the array that resides before or after that element. This process continues until the value being searched for is either found or there are no more elements to test.

Here is the pseudocode for a method that performs a binary search on an array:

Method BinarySearch(array, searchValue)
  Set first to 0
  Set last to the last subscript in the array
  Set position to −1
  Set found to false

  While found is not true and first is less than or equal to last
    Set middle to the subscript half way between array[first]and array[last]
    If array[middle] equals searchValue
      Set found to true
      Set position to middle
    Else If array[middle] is greater than searchValue
      Set last to middle −1
    Else
      Set first to middle + 1
    End If
  End While

  Return position
End Method

This algorithm uses three variables to mark positions within the array: *first*, *last*, and *middle*. The *first* and *last* variables mark the boundaries of the portion of the array currently being searched. They are initialized with the subscripts of the array's first and last elements. The subscript of the element halfway between first and last is calculated and stored in the *middle* variable. If the element in the middle of the array does not contain the search value, the *first* or *last* variable is adjusted so that only the top or bottom half of the array is searched during the next iteration. This cuts the portion of the array being searched in half each time the loop fails to locate the search value.

The following C# method performs a binary search on an integer array. The first parameter, iArray, is searched for an occurrence of the number stored in value. If the number is found, its array subscript is returned. Otherwise, −1 is returned, indicating the value did not appear in the array.

```
 1 private int BinarySearch(int[] iArray, int value)
 2 {
 3     int first = 0;                 // First array element
 4     int last = iArray.Length - 1;  // Last array element
 5     int middle;                    // Midpoint of search
 6     int position = -1;             // Position of search value
 7     bool found = false;            // Flag
 8
 9     // Search for the value.
10     while (!found && first <= last)
11     {
12         // Calculate the midpoint.
13         middle = (first + last) / 2;
14
15         // If value is found at midpoint...
16         if (iArray[middle] == value)
17         {
18             found = true;
19             position = middle;
```

```
20            }
21            // else if value is in lower half...
22            else if (iArray[middle] > value)
23            {
24                last = middle - 1;
25            }
26            // else if value is in upper half....
27            else
28            {
29                first = middle + 1;
30            }
31        }
32
33        // Return the position of the item, or -1
34        // if it was not found.
35        return position;
36  }
```

If you want to see a complete application that uses the binary search algorithm, look at the *Binary Search* project, located in the *Chap07* folder of the Student Sample Programs. It loads a list of names from a file into an array and then performs a binary search to find a specific name in the array.

 Checkpoint

7.14 What is a search algorithm?

7.15 What is the purpose of a sorting algorithm?

7.16 What is the only requirement of the binary search algorithm?

 7.7 **Two-Dimensional Arrays**

CONCEPT: A two-dimensional array is like several identical arrays put together. It is useful for storing multiple sets of data.

The arrays that you have studied so far are known as one-dimensional arrays. They are called **one-dimensional** arrays because they can hold only one set of data. **Two-dimensional** arrays, which are also called *2D arrays*, can hold multiple sets of data. Think of a two-dimensional array as having rows and columns of elements, as shown in Figure 7-37. This figure shows a two-dimensional array having three rows and four columns. Notice that the rows are numbered 0, 1, and 2, and the columns are numbered 0, 1, 2, and 3. There is a total of 12 elements in the array.

Figure 7-37 A two-dimensional array

	Column 0	Column 1	Column 2	Column 3
Row 0				
Row 1				
Row 2				

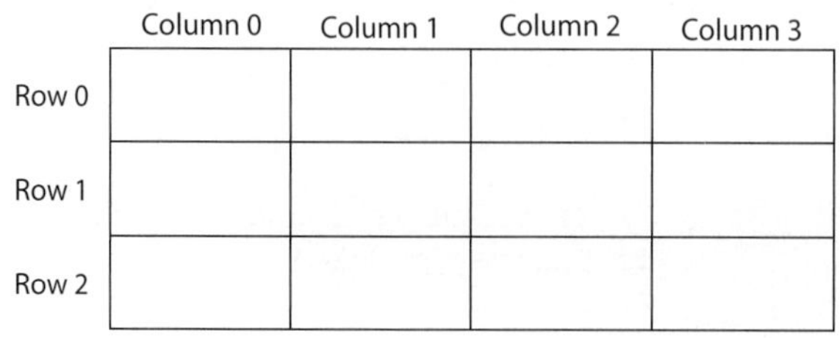

Two-dimensional arrays are useful for working with multiple sets of data. For example, suppose you are designing a grade-averaging program for a teacher. The teacher has six students, and each student takes five exams during the semester. One approach would be to create six one-dimensional arrays, one for each student. Each of these arrays would have five elements, one for each exam score. This approach would be cumbersome, however, because you would have to separately process each of the arrays. A better approach would be to use a two-dimensional array with six rows (one for each student) and five columns (one for each exam score), as shown in Figure 7-38.

Figure 7-38 Two-dimensional array with six rows and five columns

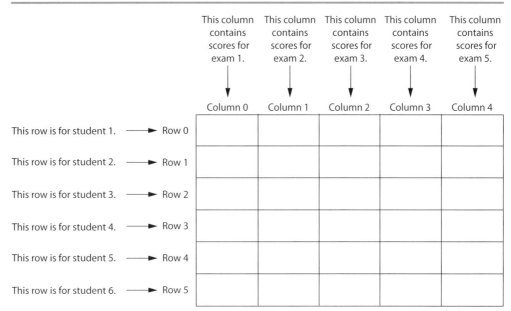

Declaring a Two-Dimensional Array

To declare a two-dimensional array, two size declarators are required: The first one is for the number of rows, and the second one is for the number of columns Here is an example declaration of a two-dimensional array with three rows and four columns:

```
double[,] scores = new double[3, 4];
```

Notice the comma that appears inside the first set of brackets. This indicates that the `scores` variable references a two-dimensional array. The numbers 3 and 4 are size declarators. The first size declarator specifies the number of rows, and the second size declarator specifies the number of columns. Notice that the size declarators are separated by a comma.

As with one-dimensional arrays, it is best to use named constants as the size declarators. Here is an example:

```
const int ROWS = 3;
const int COLS = 4;
int[,] scores = new int[ROWS, COLS];
```

When processing the data in a two-dimensional array, each element has two subscripts: one for its row and another for its column. In the `scores` array, the elements in row 0 are referenced as follows:

```
scores[0,0]
scores[0,1]
scores[0,2]
scores[0,3]
```

The elements in row 1 are referenced as follows:

```
scores[1,0]
scores[1,1]
scores[1,2]
scores[1,3]
```

And, the elements in row 2 are referenced as follows:

```
scores[2,0]
scores[2,1]
scores[2,2]
scores[2,3]
```

Figure 7-39 illustrates the array with the subscripts shown for each element.

Figure 7-39 Subscripts for each element of the `scores` array

	Column 0	Column 1	Column 2	Column 3
Row 0	scores[0,0]	scores[0,1]	scores[0,2]	scores[0,3]
Row 1	scores[1,0]	scores[1,1]	scores[1,2]	scores[1,3]
Row 2	scores[2,0]	scores[2,1]	scores[2,2]	scores[2,3]

Accessing the Elements in a Two-Dimensional Array

To access one of the elements in a two-dimensional array, you must use two subscripts. For example, suppose we have the following declarations in a program:

```
const int ROWS = 5;
const int COLS = 10;
int[,] values = new int[ROWS, COLS];
```

The following statement assigns the number 95 to `values[2,1]`:

```
values[2,1] = 95;
```

Programs often use nested loops to process two-dimensional arrays. For example, the following code assigns a random number to each element of the `values` array:

```
 1 // Create a Random object.
 2 Random rand = new Random();
 3
 4 // Create a two-dimensional int array.
 5 const int ROWS = 5;
 6 const int COLS = 10;
 7 int[,] values = new int[ROWS, COLS];
 8
 9 // Fill the array with random numbers.
10 for (int row = 0; row < ROWS; row++)
11 {
12     for (int col = 0; col < COLS; col++)
13     {
14         values[row, col] = rand.Next(100);
15     }
16 }
```

And the following set of nested loops displays all the elements of the `values` array in a ListBox control named `outputListBox`:

```
1 // Display the array contents.
2 for (int row = 0; row < ROWS; row++)
3 {
4     for (int col = 0; col < COLS; col++)
5     {
6         outputListBox.Items.Add(values[row, col].ToString());
7     }
8 }
```

Implicit Sizing and Initialization of Two-Dimensional Arrays

As with a one-dimensional array, you may provide an initialization list for a two-dimensional array. Recall that when you provide an initialization list for an array, you cannot provide the upper subscript numbers. When initializing a two-dimensional array, you must provide the comma to indicate the number of dimensions. The following is an example of a two-dimensional array declaration with an initialization list:

```
int[,] values = { {1, 2, 3},
                  {4, 5, 6},
                  {7, 8, 9} };
```

Initialization values for each row are enclosed in their own set of braces. In this example, the initialization values for row 0 are `{1, 2, 3}`, the initialization values for row 1 are `{4, 5, 6}`, and the initialization values for row 2 are `{7, 8, 9}`. So, this statement declares an array with three rows and three columns. The values are assigned to the `values` array in the following manner:

`values[0, 0]` is set to 1.

`values[0, 1]` is set to 2.

`values[0, 2]` is set to 3.

`values[1, 0]` is set to 4.

`values[1, 1]` is set to 5.

`values[1, 2]` is set to 6.

`values[2, 0]` is set to 7.

`values[2, 1]` is set to 8.

`values[2, 2]` is set to 9.

Tutorial 7-3 gives you hands-on practice working with a two-dimensional array.

Tutorial 7-3:
Completing the *Seating Chart* Application

In this tutorial, you complete the *Seating Chart* application. The application's form, which is shown in Figure 7-40, uses a PictureBox control to display an airplane seating chart that is arranged in rows and columns. When completed, the application allows the user to enter valid row and column numbers in the `rowTextBox` and `colTextBox` text

Figure 7-40 The *Seating Chart* application's form

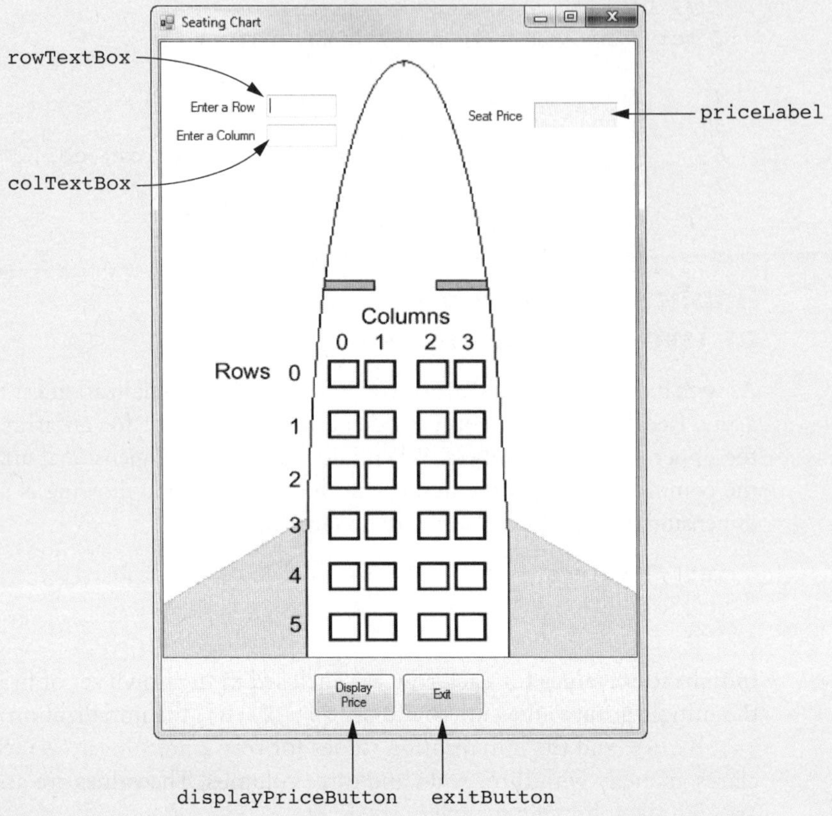

boxes and then click the *Display Price* button. The price of the selected seat will be displayed in the `priceLabel` control. The following table shows the seat prices:

Columns	0	1	2	3
Row 0	$450	$450	$450	$450
Row 1	$425	$425	$425	$425
Row 2	$400	$400	$400	$400
Row 3	$375	$375	$375	$375
Row 4	$375	$375	$375	$375
Row 5	$350	$350	$350	$350

When you write the code for the application, you will create a two-dimensional array to hold these values.

Step 1: Start Visual Studio (or Visual C# Express). Open the project named *Seating Chart* in the *Chap07* folder of the Student Sample Programs that accompany this book.

Step 2: Open the Form1 form in the *Designer*. Double-click the `displayPriceButton` control. This opens the code editor, and you will see an empty event handler named `displayPriceButton _Click`. Complete the event handler by typing the code shown in lines 21–77 in Program 7-4. Let's take a closer look at the code:

Line 22: This statement declares two `int` variables, `row` and `col`, to hold the row and column selected by the user.

Lines 25–26: These statements declare `int` constants named `MAX_ROW` and `MAX_COL`, set to the values 5 and 3, respectively. These are used as array size declarators.

Lines 29–35: This statement creates a two-dimensional `decimal` array named `prices`, initialized with the seat prices previously shown.

Line 38: This `if` statement converts the value entered into the `rowTextBox` control to an `int` and stores the result in the `row` variable. If the conversion is successful, the program continues. If the conversion fails, the program jumps to the `else` clause in line 73, and then line 76 displays an error message.

Line 41: This `if` statement converts the value entered into the `colTextBox` control to an `int` and stores the result in the `col` variable. If the conversion is successful, the program continues. If the conversion fails, the program jumps to the `else` clause in line 67, and then line 70 displays an error message.

Line 44: This `if` statement determines whether `row` is in the range of 0 through `MAX_ROW`. If so, the program continues. Otherwise, the program jumps to the `else` clause in line 60, and then lines 63–64 display an error message.

Line 47: This `if` statement determines whether `col` is in the range of 0 through `MAX_COL`. If so, the program continues. Otherwise, the program jumps to the `else` clause in line 53, and then lines 56–57 display an error message.

Lines 50–51: This statement uses `row` and `col` as subscripts to retrieve the selected seat's price from the `prices` array and then displays that value in the `priceLabel` control.

Step 3: Switch your view back to the *Designer* and double-click the `exitButton` control. In the code editor you will see an empty event handler named `exitButton_Click`. Complete the event handler by typing the code shown in lines 82–83 in Program 7-4.

Step 4: Save the project. Then, press F5 on the keyboard or click the *Start Debugging* button (▶) on the toolbar to compile and run the application. When the application runs, experiment by entering row and column numbers for different seats and comparing the displayed price with the table previously shown. When you are finished, click the *Exit* button to end the application.

Program 7-4 Completed code for Form1 in the *Seating Chart* application

```
 1 using System;
 2 using System.Collections.Generic;
 3 using System.ComponentModel;
 4 using System.Data;
 5 using System.Drawing;
 6 using System.Linq;
 7 using System.Text;
 8 using System.Windows.Forms;
 9
10 namespace Seating_Chart
11 {
12     public partial class Form1 : Form
13     {
14         public Form1()
15         {
16             InitializeComponent();
17         }
18
```

```
19         private void displayPriceButton_Click(object sender, EventArgs e)
20         {
21             // Variables for the selected row and column
22             int row, col;
23
24             // Constants for the maximum row and column subscripts
25             const int MAX_ROW = 5;
26             const int MAX_COL = 3;
27
28             // Create an array with the seat prices.
29             decimal[,] prices = { {450m, 450m, 450m, 450m},
30                                   {425m, 425m, 425m, 425m},
31                                   {400m, 400m, 400m, 400m},
32                                   {375m, 375m, 375m, 375m},
33                                   {375m, 375m, 375m, 375m},
34                                   {350m, 350m, 350m, 350m}
35                                 };
36
37             // Get the selected row number.
38             if (int.TryParse(rowTextBox.Text, out row))
39             {
40                 // Get the selected column number.
41                 if (int.TryParse(colTextBox.Text, out col))
42                 {
43                     // Make sure the row is within range.
44                     if (row >= 0 && row <= MAX_ROW)
45                     {
46                         // Make sure the column is within range.
47                         if (col >= 0 && col <= MAX_COL)
48                         {
49                             // Display the selected seat's price.
50                             priceLabel.Text =
51                                 prices[row, col].ToString("c");
52                         }
53                         else
54                         {
55                             // Error message for invalid column.
56                             MessageBox.Show("Column must be 0 through " +
57                                 MAX_COL);
58                         }
59                     }
60                     else
61                     {
62                         // Error message for invalid row.
63                         MessageBox.Show("Row must be 0 through " +
64                             MAX_ROW);
65                     }
66                 }
67                 else
68                 {
69                     // Display an error message for noninteger column.
70                     MessageBox.Show("Enter an integer for the column.");
71                 }
72             }
73             else
74             {
75                 // Display an error message for noninteger row.
76                 MessageBox.Show("Enter an integer for the row.");
77             }
78         }
79
```

```
80          private void exitButton_Click(object sender, EventArgs e)
81          {
82              // Close the form.
83              this.Close();
84          }
85      }
86  }
```

Summing All the Elements of a Two-Dimensional Array

To sum all the elements of a two-dimensional array, you can use a pair of nested loops to add the contents of each element to an accumulator. The following code shows an example:

```
1  const int ROWS = 3;
2  const int COLS = 3;
3  int[,] numbers = { {1, 2, 3, 4},
4                     {5, 6, 7, 8},
5                     {9, 10, 11, 12}
6                   };
7
8  int total = 0; // Accumulator, set to 0
9
10 // Sum the array elements.
11 for (int row = 0; row < ROWS; row++)
12 {
13     for (int col = 0; col < COLS; col++)
14     {
15         total += numbers[row, col];
16     }
17 }
18 // Display the sum.
19 MessageBox.Show("The total is " + total);
```

Summing the Rows of a Two-Dimensional Array

Sometimes you may need to calculate the sum of each row in a two-dimensional array. For example, suppose a two-dimensional array is used to hold a set of test scores for a set of students. Each row in the array is a set of test scores for one student. To get the sum of a student's test scores (perhaps so an average may be calculated), you use a loop to add all the elements in one row. The following code shows an example:

```
1  const int ROWS = 3;
2  const int COLS = 3;
3  int[,] numbers = { {1, 2, 3, 4},
4                     {5, 6, 7, 8},
5                     {9, 10, 11, 12}
6                   };
7
8  int total;  // Accumulator
9
10 // Sum each row in the array.
11 for (int row = 0; row < ROWS; row++)
12 {
13     // Set the accumulator to 0.
14     total = 0;
15
16     // Total the row.
17     for (int col = 0; col < COLS; col++)
```

```
18     {
19         total += numbers[row, col];
20     }
21
22     // Display the row's total.
23     MessageBox.Show("The total of row " + row +
24                     " is " + total);
25 }
```

Summing the Columns of a Two-Dimensional Array

Sometimes you may need to calculate the sum of each column in a two-dimensional array. For example, suppose a two-dimensional array is used to hold a set of test scores for a set of students and you wish to calculate the class average for each of the test scores. To do this, you calculate the average of each column in the array. This is accomplished with a set of nested loops. The outer loop controls the column subscript, and the inner loop controls the row subscript. The inner loop calculates the sum of a column, which is stored in an accumulator. The following code demonstrates:

```
 1 const int ROWS = 3;
 2 const int COLS = 4;
 3 int[,] numbers = { {1, 2, 3, 4},
 4                    {5, 6, 7, 8},
 5                    {9, 10, 11, 12}
 6                  };
 7
 8 int total;    // Accumulator
 9
10 // Sum each column in the array.
11 for (int col = 0; col < COLS; col++)
12 {
13     // Set the accumulator to 0.
14     total = 0;
15
16     // Total the column.
17     for (int row = 0; row < ROWS; row++)
18     {
19         total += numbers[row, col];
20     }
21
22     // Display the column's total.
23     MessageBox.Show("The total of column " + col +
24                     " is " + total);
25 }
```

Checkpoint

7.17 How many rows and how many columns are in the following array?

```
int[,] values = new decimal[200, 100];
```

7.18 Write a statement that assigns the value 50 to the very last element in the `values` array declared in Checkpoint 7.17.

7.19 Write a declaration for a two-dimensional `int` array initialized with the following table of data:

12	24	32	21	42
99	8	68	32	92
95	34	21	11	7

7.8 Jagged Arrays

CONCEPT: A jagged array is similar to a two-dimensional array, but the rows in a jagged array can have different lengths.

In a traditional two-dimensional array, each row has the same number of columns. Mentally, we visualize a two-dimensional array as a rectangular structure. Figure 7-37, previously shown, is an example. For this reason, two-dimensional arrays are sometimes referred to as **rectangular arrays**.

A **jagged array** is similar to a two-dimensional array, but the rows in a jagged array can have different numbers of columns. This is possible because a jagged array is actually an array of arrays. To be more specific, a jagged array is a one-dimensional array, and each element of the array is also a one-dimensional array. Figure 7-41 shows an example. In the figure, row 0 has four columns, row 1 has three columns, and row 2 has five columns.

Figure 7-41 A jagged array

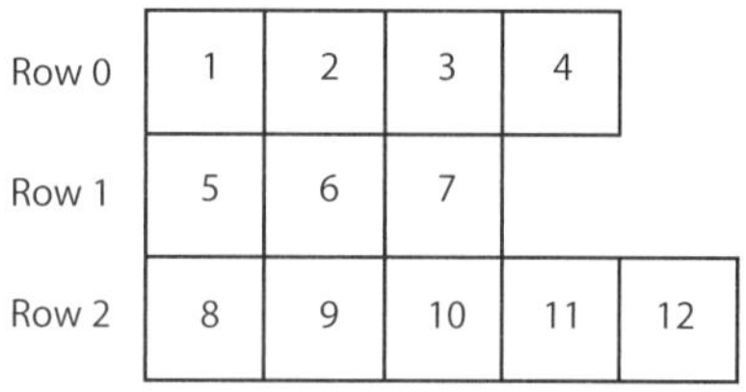

Because a jagged array is an array of arrays, you set it up differently than a two-dimensional array. First you create an array, and then you create each of the arrays that are the elements of the first array. The following code shows an example of how the jagged array in Figure 7-41 might be created and initialized.

```
1   // Create an array of 3 int arrays.
2   int[][] jaggedArray = new int[3][];
3
4   // Create each array that is an element
5   // of the jagged array.
6   jaggedArray[0] = new int[4] { 1, 2, 3, 4 };
7   jaggedArray[1] = new int[3] { 5, 6, 7 };
8   jaggedArray[2] = new int[5] { 8, 9, 10, 11, 12 };
```

Let's take a closer look at the code:

- Line 1 declares an array named `jaggedArray`. Notice that the data type is `int[][]`, with two sets of brackets. This indicates that we are declaring an array of `int` arrays. Also notice that the expression `new int[3][]` uses only one size declarator, specifying the number of rows. The column sizes must be set individually.
- Line 6 creates element 0, which is an `int` array with four columns. The columns are initialized with the values 1, 2, 3, and 4.
- Line 7 creates element 1, which is an `int` array with three columns. The columns are initialized with the values 5, 6, and 7.
- Line 8 creates element 2, which is an `int` array with five columns. The columns are initialized with the values 8, 9, 10, 11, and 12.

To access an item that is stored at a particular row and column in a jagged array, you enclose the row and column subscripts in their own sets of brackets. For example, the following statement displays the value stored at row 1, column 2, of the `jaggedArray` that was previously declared:

```
MessageBox.Show(jaggedArray[1][2].ToString());
```

The following statement shows another example. It assigns the value 99 to row 0, column 3, of `jaggedArray`:

```
jaggedArray[0][3] = 99;
```

A jagged array has a Length property that holds the number of rows, and then each row has its own Length property. You can use a row's Length property to determine the number of columns in that row. For example, the following set of nested loops displays all the values stored in the `jaggedArray` that was previously declared:

```
1 for (int row = 0; row < jaggedArray.Length; row++)
2 {
3     for (int col = 0; col < jaggedArray[row].Length; col++)
4     {
5         MessageBox.Show(jaggedArray[row][col].ToString());
6     }
7 }
```

 Checkpoint

7.20 Why are two-dimensional arrays sometimes referred to as rectangular arrays?

7.21 Write a statement that declares a jagged array of `int` values and initialize the columns of each row with the values in the following table of data:

2	4	6		
3	5	7	9	
5	9	11	17	21

 7.9 The List Collection

CONCEPT: `List` is a class in the .NET Framework that is similar to an array. Unlike an array, a `List` object's size is automatically adjusted to accommodate the number of items being stored in it.

The .NET Framework provides a class named `List`, which can be used for storing and retrieving items. Once you create a `List` object, you can think of it as a container for holding other objects. A `List` object is similar to an array but offers many advantages over an array. Here are a few:

- When you create a `List` object, you do not have to know the number of items that you intend to store in it.
- A `List` object automatically expands as items are added to it.
- In addition to adding items to a `List`, you can remove items as well.
- A `List` object automatically shrinks as items are removed from it.

Creating a List

Here is an example of how you create a `List` object that can be used to hold strings:

```
List<string> nameList = new List<string>();
```

This statement creates a `List` object, referenced by the `nameList` variable. Notice that in this example the word `string` is written inside angled brackets `<>` immediately after the word `List`. This specifies that the `List` can hold objects of the `string` data type. If you try to store any other type of object in this `List`, an error occurs.

Here is an example of how you create a `List` object that can be used to hold integers:

```
List<int> numberList = new List<int>();
```

This statement creates a `List` object, referenced by the `numberList` variable. Notice that in this example the word `int` is written inside angled brackets `<>` immediately after the word `List`.

Initializing a `List`

You can optionally initialize a `List` object when you declare it. Here is an example:

```
List<int> numberList = new List<int>() { 1, 2, 3 };
```

This statement creates a `List` object that can hold integers and initializes it with the values 1, 2, and 3. Here is an example that creates a `List` object to hold strings, and initializes it with three strings:

```
List<string> nameList = new List<string>() { "Chris",
    "Kathryn", "Bill" };
```

Adding Items to a `List`

To add items to an existing `List` object, you use the **Add method**. For example, the following statements create a List object and add a series of strings to it:

```
List<string> nameList = new List<string>();
nameList.Add("Chris");
nameList.Add("Kathryn");
nameList.Add("Bill");
```

After these statements execute, the `nameList` object will hold the three strings `"Chris"`, `"Kathryn"`, and `"Bill"`.

The items that are stored in a `List` have a corresponding index. The index specifies the item's location in the `List`, so it is much like an array subscript. The first item that is added to a `List` is stored at index 0. The next item that is added to the `List` is stored at index 1, and so forth. After the previously shown statements execute, `"Chris"` is stored at index 0, `"Kathryn"` is stored at index 1, and `"Bill"` is stored at index 2.

The Count Property

A `List` object has a **Count property** that holds the number of items stored in the `List`. For example, the following statement uses the Count property to display the number of items stored in `nameList`:

```
MessageBox.Show("The List has " + nameList.Count +
                " objects stored in it.");
```

Assuming that `nameList` holds the strings `"Chris"`, `"Kathryn"`, and `"Bill"`, the following statement will be displayed in a message box:

```
The List has 3 objects stored in it.
```

Accessing Items in a `List`

You can use subscript notation to access the items in a `List`, just as you can with an array. For example, the following `for` loop displays the items in the `nameList` object:

```
for (int index = 0; index < nameList.Count; index++)
{
    MessageBox.Show(nameList[index]);
}
```

Notice that the loop uses the `List` object's Count property in the test expression to control the number of iterations. Here is an example that reads values from a text file and adds them to a `List`:

```
 1 // Open the Names.txt file.
 2 StreamReader inputFile = File.OpenText("Names.txt");
 3
 4 // Create a List object to hold strings.
 5 List<string> nameList = new List<string>();
 6
 7 // Read the file's contents.
 8 while (!inputFile.EndOfStream)
 9 {
10     // Read a line and add it to the List.
11     nameList.Add(inputFile.ReadLine());
12 }
```

Let's take a closer look at this code:

- Line 2 opens a file named Names.txt and associates it with a `StreamReader` object that is referenced by the `inputFile` variable.
- Line 5 creates a `List` object, referenced by the `nameList` variable. The object can hold strings.
- The `while` loop that starts in line 8 iterates until the end of the file is reached.
- The statement in line 11 reads a line from the file and adds it to the `nameList` object.

After this code executes, the `nameList` object contains all the lines that were read from the Names.txt file.

You can also use the `foreach` loop to iterate over the items in a `List`, just as you can with an array. Here is an example:

```
foreach (string str in nameList)
{
    MessageBox.Show(str);
}
```

Passing a `List` to a Method

Sometimes you will want to write a method that accepts a `List` as an argument and performs an operation on the `List`. For example, the following code shows a method named `DisplayList`. The method accepts a `List` of strings as an argument and displays each item in `List`.

```
 1 private void DisplayList(List<string> sList)
 2 {
 3     foreach (string str in sList)
 4     {
 5         MessageBox.Show(str);
 6     }
 7 }
```

Notice in line 1 that the method has a parameter variable named sList and that the parameter's data type is List<string>. The parameter variable is a reference to a List<string> object. When you call this method, you must pass a List<string> object as an argument.

When you call a method and pass a List<string> object as an argument, you simply pass the variable that references the List. The following code shows an example of how the DisplayList method (previously shown) might be called:

```
1 // Create a List of strings.
2 List<string> nameList = new List<string>() { "Chris",
3     "Kathryn", "Bill" };
4
5 // Pass the List to the DisplayList method.
6 DisplayList(nameList);
```

The statement in lines 2 and 3 creates a List containing the strings "Chris", "Kathryn", and "Bill". Line 6 calls the DisplayList method, passing the nameList object as an argument.

> **NOTE:** List objects, like arrays, are always passed by reference.

Removing Items from a List

You can use the **RemoveAt** method to remove an item at a specific index in a List. The following code shows an example:

```
1 // Create a List of strings.
2 List<string> nameList = new List<string>() { "Chris",
3     "Kathryn", "Bill" };
4
5 // Remove the item at index 0.
6 nameList.RemoveAt(0);
```

The statement in lines 2 and 3 creates a List containing the strings "Chris", "Kathryn", and "Bill". Then, the statement in line 6 removes the string at index 0. After this statement executes, the List contains the strings "Kathryn" and "Bill".

If you know the value of the item that you want to remove from a List, but you do not know the item's index, you can use the **Remove method.** You pass the item that you want to remove as an argument, and the Remove method searches for that item in the List. If the item is found, it is removed. Here is an example:

```
1 // Create a List of strings.
2 List<string> nameList = new List<string>() { "Chris",
3     "Kathryn", "Bill" };
4
5 // Remove "Bill" from the List.
6 nameList.Remove("Bill");
```

The statement in lines 2 and 3 creates a List containing the strings "Chris", "Kathryn", and "Bill". Then, the statement in line 6 removes "Bill" from the List. After this statement executes, the List contains the strings "Chris" and "Kathryn".

The Remove method returns a Boolean value indicating whether the item was actually removed from the List. If the specified item was found in the List and removed, the Remove method returns true. If the item was not found in the List, the Remove method returns false. The following code demonstrates how you can use the value returned from the method:

```
1 // Create a List of strings.
2 List<string> nameList = new List<string>() { "Chris",
3     "Kathryn", "Bill" };
4
5 // Remove "Susan".
6 if (!nameList.Remove("Susan"))
7 {
8     MessageBox.Show("Susan was not found.");
9 }
```

The statement in lines 2 and 3 creates a List containing the strings "Chris", "Kathryn", and "Bill". Then, the statement in line 6 attempts to remove "Susan" from the List. The List does not contain the string "Susan", so the Remove method returns false. The message "Susan was not found" is displayed. After this code executes, the List still contains the strings "Chris", "Kathryn", and "Bill".

NOTE: The Remove method performs a sequential search to locate the specified item. If the List contains a large number of items, its performance will be slow.

If you want to remove all the items from a List, you can call the **Clear method**. Here is an example:

```
nameList.Clear();
```

After this statement executes, the nameList object is empty.

Inserting an Item

You can use the **Insert method** to insert an item at a specific index in a List. The following code shows an example:

```
1 // Create a List of strings.
2 List<string> nameList = new List<string>() { "Chris",
3     "Kathryn", "Bill" };
4
5 // Insert an item at index 0.
6 nameList.Insert("Joanne", 0);
```

The statement in lines 2 and 3 creates a List containing the strings "Chris", "Kathryn", and "Bill". Then, the statement in line 6 inserts the string "Joanne" at index 0. After this statement executes, the List contains the strings "Joanne", "Chris", "Kathryn", and "Bill".

NOTE: An exception will occur if the specified index is less than 0 or greater than the List object's Count property.

Searching for Items in a List

Because you can use subscript notation to access the items in a List, you can adapt any of the array-processing algorithms that you saw earlier in this chapter so they work with a List. For example, you can write code that performs a sequential search, binary search, selection sort, and so on, on a List.

An easy way to search for item in a List, however, is to use the IndexOf method. The IndexOf method accepts a value as an argument, and it searches for that value in the List. If the value is found, the method returns its index. If the value is not found, the method returns −1. The following code shows an example:

```
 1 // Create a List of strings.
 2 List<string> nameList = new List<string>() { "Chris",
 3     "Kathryn", "Bill" };
 4
 5 // Search for "Kathryn".
 6 int position = nameList.IndexOf("Kathryn");
 7
 8 // Was Kathryn found in the List?
 9 if (position != -1)
10 {
11     MessageBox.Show("Kathryn was found at index " +
12                     position);
13 }
14 else
15 {
16     MessageBox.Show("Kathryn was not found.");
17 }
```

The statement in lines 2 and 3 creates a List containing the strings "Chris", "Kathryn", and "Bill". The statement in line 6 calls the IndexOf method to search for "Kathryn" in the List. The value that is returned from the method is assigned to the position variable. After this statement executes, the position variable contains the index of "Kathryn" or −1 if "Kathryn" was not found in the List. The if statement in lines 9–17 displays one of two possible messages, depending on whether "Kathryn" was found. (If this code were executed, it would display the message "Kathryn was found at index 1".)

There are two additional versions of the IndexOf method that allow you to specify the area of the List that should be searched. The following statement shows an example of one of these:

```
position = nameList.IndexOf("Diane", 2);
```

Notice that two arguments are passed to the IndexOf method. The first argument, "Diane", is the item to search for. The second argument, 2 is the starting index of the search. This specifies that the search should begin at index 2 and end at the last item in the List. (The beginning index is included in the search. If you pass an invalid index as an argument, an exception occurs.)

Here is an example of another version of the IndexOf method:

```
position = nameList.IndexOf("Diane", 2, 5);
```

In this example, three arguments are passed to the IndexOf method. The first argument, "Diane", is the item to search for. The second argument, 2 is the starting index of the search. The third argument, 5, is the ending index of the search. This specifies that the search should begin at index 2, and end at index 5. (The beginning and ending indices are included in the search. If either index is invalid, an exception occurs.)

 NOTE: The IndexOf method performs a sequential search to locate the specified item. If the List contains a large number of items, its performance will be slow.

In Tutorial 7-4 you will complete an application that reads the contents of a file into a List, and then performs various operations on the List.

Tutorial 7-4:
Completing the *Test Score List* Application

In this tutorial, you complete the *Test Score List* application. The application's form, which is shown in Figure 7-42, has already been created for you. When you complete the application, it will read a set of test scores from a file into a List. (The file has also been created for you.) The test scores are displayed in the ListBox control. The average test score is calculated and displayed, as well as the number of above-average test scores and below-average test scores.

Figure 7-42 The *Test Score List* application's form

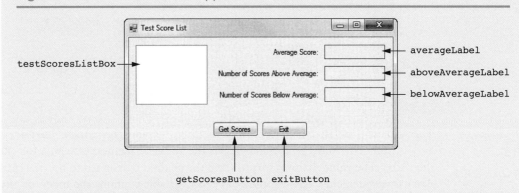

Step 1: Start Visual Studio (or Visual C# Express). Open the project named *Test Score List* in the *Chap07* folder of the Student Sample Programs.

Step 2: Open the Form1 form's code in the code editor. Insert the using System.IO; directive shown in line 9 of Program 7-5 at the end of this tutorial. This statement is necessary because we will be using the StreamReader class, and it is part of the System.IO namespace in the .NET Framework.

Step 3: With the code editor still open, type the comments and code for the ReadScores method, shown in lines 20–43 of Program 7-5. The purpose of the ReadScores method is to accept a List<int> object as an argument and read the contents of the TestScores.txt file into the list.

Step 4: Type the comments and code for the DisplayScores method, shown in lines 45–53 of Program 7-5. The purpose of the DisplayScores method is to accept a List<int> object as an argument and display its contents in the testScoresListBox control.

Step 5: Type the comments and code for the Average method, shown in lines 55–73 of Program 7-5. The purpose of the Average method is to accept a List<int> object as an argument and return the average of the values in the List.

Step 6: Type the comments and code for the AboveAverage method, shown in lines 75–95 of Program 7-5. The purpose of the AboveAverage method is to accept a List<int> object as an argument and return the number of above average scores it contains.

Step 7: Type the comments and code for the BelowAverage method, shown in lines 97–117 of Program 7-5. The purpose of the BelowAverage method is to accept a List<int> object as an argument and return the number of below average scores it contains.

Step 8: Next, you create the Click event handlers for the Button controls. Switch back to the *Designer* and double-click the getScoresButton control. This opens the code editor, and you will see an empty event handler named getScoresButton_Click. Complete the getScoresButton_Click event handler by typing the code shown in lines 121–144 in Program 7-5. Let's review this code:

Lines 121–123: These statements declare the following variables:

- averageScore—This variable is used to hold the average test score.

- numAboveAverage—This variable is used to hold the number of above-average test scores.

- numBelowAverage—This variable is used to hold the number of below-average test scores.

Line 126: This statement creates a List<int> object, referenced by the scoresList variable.

Line 129: This statement calls the ReadScores method, passing the scoresList object as an argument. After this statement executes, the scoresList object contains the test scores that are in the TestScores.txt file.

Line 132: This statement calls the DisplayScores method, passing the scoresList object as an argument. After this statement executes, the items in the scoresList object are displayed in the testScoresListBox control.

Line 135: This statement calls the Average method, passing the scoresList object as an argument. The method returns the average of the values in the scoresList object, which is assigned to the averageScore variable.

Line 136: This statement displays the average score in the averageLabel control.

Line 139: This statement calls the AboveAverage method, passing the scoresList object as an argument. The method returns the number of above-average scores in the scoresList object, which is assigned to the numAboveAverage variable.

Line 140: This statement displays the number of above-average scores in the aboveAverageLabel control.

Line 143: This statement calls the BelowAverage method, passing the scoresList object as an argument. The method returns the number of below-average scores in the scoresList object, which is assigned to the numBelowAverage variable.

Line 144: This statement displays the number of below-average scores in the belowAverageLabel control.

Step 9: Switch your view back to the *Designer* and double-click the exitButton control. In the code editor you will see an empty event handler named exitButton_Click. Complete the event handler by typing the code shown in lines 149–150 in Program 7-5.

Step 10: Save the project. Then, press F5 on the keyboard or click the *Start Debugging* button (▶) on the toolbar to compile and run the application. When the application runs, click the *Get Scores* button. This should display a set of test scores in the ListBox, as well as the average score, the number of above-average scores, and the number of below-average scores, as shown in Figure 7-43. Click the *Exit* button to exit the application.

Figure 7-43 The *Test Score List* application

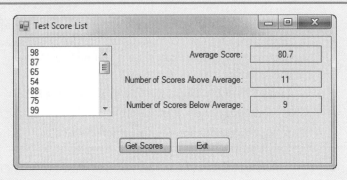

Program 7-5 Completed code for Form1 in the *Test Scores List* application

```
 1 using System;
 2 using System.Collections.Generic;
 3 using System.ComponentModel;
 4 using System.Data;
 5 using System.Drawing;
 6 using System.Linq;
 7 using System.Text;
 8 using System.Windows.Forms;
 9 using System.IO;
10
11 namespace Test_Score_List
12 {
13     public partial class Form1 : Form
14     {
15         public Form1()
16         {
17             InitializeComponent();
18         }
19
20         // The ReadScores method reads the scores from the
21         // TestScores.txt file into the scoresList parameter.
22         private void ReadScores(List<int> scoresList)
23         {
24             try
25             {
26                 // Open the TestScores.txt file.
27                 StreamReader inputFile = File.OpenText("TestScores.txt");
28
29                 // Read the scores into the list.
30                 while (!inputFile.EndOfStream)
31                 {
32                     scoresList.Add(int.Parse(inputFile.ReadLine()));
33                 }
34
35                 // Close the file.
36                 inputFile.Close();
37             }
38             catch (Exception ex)
39             {
40                 // Display an error message.
41                 MessageBox.Show(ex.Message);
```

```
42                  }
43              }
44
45              // The DisplayScores method displays the contents of the
46              // scoresList parameter in the ListBox control.
47              private void DisplayScores(List<int> scoresList)
48              {
49                  foreach (int score in scoresList)
50                  {
51                      testScoresListBox.Items.Add(score);
52                  }
53              }
54
55              // The Average method returns the average of the values
56              // in the scoresList parameter.
57              private double Average(List<int> scoresList)
58              {
59                  int total = 0;        // Accumulator
60                  double average;       // To hold the average
61
62                  // Calculate the total of the scores.
63                  foreach (int score in scoresList)
64                  {
65                      total += score;
66                  }
67
68                  // Calculate the average of the scores.
69                  average = (double)total / scoresList.Count;
70
71                  // Return the average.
72                  return average;
73              }
74
75              // The AboveAverage method returns the number of
76              // above average scores in scoresList.
77              private int AboveAverage(List<int> scoresList)
78              {
79                  int numAbove = 0;         // Accumulator
80
81                  // Get the average score.
82                  double avg = Average(scoresList);
83
84                  // Count the number of above average scores.
85                  foreach (int score in scoresList)
86                  {
87                      if (score > avg)
88                      {
89                          numAbove++;
90                      }
91                  }
92
93                  // Return the number of above average scores.
94                  return numAbove;
95              }
96
97              // The BelowAverage method returns the number of
98              // below average scores in scoresList.
99              private int BelowAverage(List<int> scoresList)
100             {
```

```
101                  int numBelow = 0;           // Accumulator
102
103              // Get the average score.
104              double avg = Average(scoresList);
105
106              // Count the number of below average scores.
107              foreach (int score in scoresList)
108              {
109                  if (score < avg)
110                  {
111                      numBelow++;
112                  }
113              }
114
115              // Return the number of below average scores.
116              return numBelow;
117          }
118
119          private void getScoresButton_Click(object sender, EventArgs e)
120          {
121              double averageScore;     // To hold the average score
122              int numAboveAverage;     // Number of above average scores
123              int numBelowAverage;     // Number of below average scores
124
125              // Create a List to hold the scores.
126              List<int> scoresList = new List<int>();
127
128              // Read the scores from the file into the List.
129              ReadScores(scoresList);
130
131              // Display the scores.
132              DisplayScores(scoresList);
133
134              // Display the average score.
135              averageScore = Average(scoresList);
136              averageLabel.Text = averageScore.ToString("n1");
137
138              // Display the number of above average scores.
139              numAboveAverage = AboveAverage(scoresList);
140              aboveAverageLabel.Text = numAboveAverage.ToString();
141
142              // Display the number of below average scores.
143              numBelowAverage = BelowAverage(scoresList);
144              belowAverageLabel.Text = numBelowAverage.ToString();
145          }
146
147          private void exitButton_Click(object sender, EventArgs e)
148          {
149              // Close the form.
150              this.Close();
151          }
152      }
153 }
```

Checkpoint

7.22 Write a statement that initializes a List with 4 values of the double data type.

7.23 Write a statement that adds a new value to the List object created in Checkpoint 7.22.

7.24 Write a statement that clears the contents of the List object created in Checkpoint 7.22.

7.25 Is it possible to write code that performs a sequential search, binary search, selection sort, and so on, on a List? Why or why not?

Key Terms

`Add` method
array
binary search
`Clear` method
Count property
elements
`foreach` loop
garbage collection
`IndexOf` method
initialization list
`Insert` method
iteration variable
jagged array
Length property
`List`
new operator

off-by-one error
one-dimensional
rectangular arrays
reference
reference copy
reference types
reference variable
`Remove` method
`RemoveAt` method
search algorithms
selection sort
sequential search algorithm
size declarator
subscript
Two-dimensional
value types

Review Questions and Exercises

Multiple Choice

1. The memory that is allocated for a _____ variable is the actual location that will hold any value that is assigned to that variable.

   a. reference type
   b. general type
   c. value type
   d. framework type

2. A variable that is used to reference an object is commonly called a(n) _____.

   a. reference variable
   b. resource variable
   c. object variable
   d. component variable

3. When you want to work with an object, you use a variable that holds a special value known as a(n) _____ to link the variable to the object.

   a. union
   b. reference
   c. object linker
   d. data coupling

4. The _____ creates an object in memory and returns a reference to that object.

   a. = operator
   b. object allocator
   c. reference variable
   d. new operator

5. A(n) _____ is an object that can hold a group of values that are all of the same data type.

   a. array
   b. collection
   c. container
   d. set

6. The _____ indicates the number of values that the array should be able to hold.

    a. allocation limit
    b. size declarator
    c. data type
    d. compiler

7. The storage locations in an array are known as _____.

    a. elements
    b. sectors
    c. pages
    d. blocks

8. Each element in an array is assigned a unique number known as a(n) _____.

    a. element identifier
    b. subscript
    c. index
    d. sequencer

9. When you create an array, you can optionally initialize it with a group of values called a(n) _____.

    a. default value group
    b. initialization list
    c. defined set
    d. value list

10. In C#, all arrays have a _____ that is set to the number of elements in the array.

    a. Limit property
    b. Size property
    c. Length property
    d. Maximum property

11. A(n) _____ occurs when a loop iterates one time too many or one time too few.

    a. general error
    b. logic error
    c. loop count error
    d. off-by-one error

12. C# provides a special loop that, in many circumstances, simplifies array processing. It is known as the _____.

    a. `for` loop
    b. `foreach` loop
    c. `while` loop
    d. `do-while` loop

13. The `foreach` loop is designed to work with a temporary, read-only variable that is known as the _____.

    a. element variable
    b. loop variable
    c. index variable
    d. iteration variable

14. _____ is a process that periodically runs, removing all unreferenced objects from memory.

    a. Systematic reallocation
    b. Memory cleanup

c. Garbage collection

d. Object maintenance

15. Various techniques known as _____ have been developed to locate a specific item in a larger collection of data, such as an array.

 a. seek functions

 b. request methods

 c. traversal procedures

 d. search algorithms

16. The _____ uses a loop to step through an array, starting with the first element, searching for an item.

 a. sequential search algorithm

 b. top-down method

 c. ascending search algorithm

 d. basic search function

17. A(n) _____ is a type of assignment operation that copies a reference to an array and not the contents of the array.

 a. object copy

 b. reference copy

 c. double reference

 d. parallel copy

18. The _____ is a clever algorithm that is much more efficient than the sequential search.

 a. linear search

 b. bubble sort

 c. binary search

 d. selection sort

19. A _____ is similar to a two-dimensional array, but the rows can have different numbers of columns.

 a. one-dimensional array

 b. columnar array

 c. jagged array

 d. split row array

20. The .NET Framework provides a class named _____, which can be used for storing and retrieving items.

 a. `Matrix`

 b. `Database`

 c. `Container`

 d. `List`

True or False

1. When you are working with a value type, you are using a variable that holds a piece of data.

2. Reference variables can be used only to reference objects.

3. Individual variables are well suited for storing and processing lists of data.

4. Arrays are reference type objects.

5. You can store a mixture of data types in an array.

6. When you create a numeric array in C#, its elements are set to the value 0 by default.

7. The subscript of the last element will always be one less than the array's Length property.

8. You use the == operator to compare two array reference variables and determine whether the arrays are equal.

9. A jagged array is similar to a two-dimensional array, but the rows in a jagged array can have different numbers of columns.

10. When you create a `List` object, you do not have to know the number of items that you intend to store in it.

Short Answer

1. How much memory is allocated by the compiler when you declare a value type variable?

2. What type of variable is needed to work with an object in code?

3. What two steps are typically required for creating a reference type object?

4. Are variables well suited for processing lists of data? Why or why not.

5. What value is returned by the Length property of an array?

6. What can cause an off-by-one error when working with an array?

7. How do you keep track of elements that contain data in a partially filled array?

8. Briefly describe the selection sort algorithm.

9. How is the binary search more efficient that the sequential search algorithm?

10. What advantages does a `List` have over an array?

Algorithm Workbench

1. Assume `names` is a variable that references an array of 20 `string` values. Write a `foreach` loop that displays each of the elements of the array in a ListBox control.

2. The variables `numberArray1` and `numberArray2` reference arrays that have 100 elements each. Write code that copies the values from `numberArray1` to `numberArray2`.

3. Write code for a sequential search that determines whether the value -1 is stored in an array with a reference variable named `values`. The code should display a message indicating whether the value was found.

4. Write a declaration statement that creates a two-dimensional array referenced by a variable named `grades`. The array should store `int` values using 18 rows and 12 columns.

5. Write code that sums each column in the array in Question 4.

6. Create a `List` object that uses the binary search algorithm to search for the string `"A"`. Display a message box indicating whether the value was found.

Programming Problems

1. **Total Sales**

   In the *Chap07* folder of the Student Sample Programs, you will find a file named Sales.txt. Figure 7-44 shows the file's contents displayed in Notepad. Create an application that reads this file's contents into an array, displays the array's contents in a ListBox control, and calculates and displays the total of the array's values.

Figure 7-44 The Sales.txt file

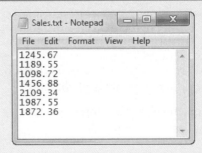

2. **Sales Analysis**

Modify the application that you created in Programming Exercise 1 so it also displays the following:

- The average of the values in the array
- The largest value in the array
- The smallest value in the array

3. **Charge Account Validation**

In the *Chap07* folder of the Student Sample Programs, you will find a file named ChargeAccounts.txt. The file contains a list of a company's valid charge account numbers. There are a total of 18 charge account numbers in the file, and each one is a 7-digit number, such as 5658845.

Create an application that reads the contents of the file into an array or a `List`. The application should then let the user enter a charge account number. The program should determine whether the number is valid by searching for it in the array or `List` that contains the valid charge account numbers. If the number is in the array or `List`, the program should display a message indicating the number is valid. If the number is not in the array or `List`, the program should display a message indicating the number is invalid.

4. **Driver's License Exam**

The local driver's license office has asked you to create an application that grades the written portion of the driver's license exam. The exam has 20 multiple-choice questions. Here are the correct answers:

1. B	2. D	3. A	4. A	5. C
6. A	7. B	8. A	9. C	10. D
11. B	12. C	13. D	14. A	15. D
16. C	17. C	18. B	19. D	20. A

Your program should store these correct answers in an array. The program should read the student's answers for each of the 20 questions from a text file and store the answers in another array. (Create your own text file to test the application.) After the student's answers have been read from the file, the program should display a message indicating whether the student passed or failed the exam. (A student must correctly answer 15 of the 20 questions to pass the exam.) It should then display the total number of correctly answered questions, the total number of incorrectly answered questions, and a list showing the question numbers of the incorrectly answered questions.

5. **World Series Champions**

In the *Chap07* folder of the Student Sample Programs, you will find the following files:

- Teams.txt—This file contains a list of several Major League baseball teams in alphabetical order. Each team listed in the file has won the World Series at least once.

- WorldSeriesWinners.txt—This file contains a chronological list of the World Series' winning teams from 1903 through 2009. (The first line in the file is the name of the team that won in 1903, and the last line is the name of the team that won in 2009. Note that the World Series was not played in 1904 or 1994.)

Create an application that displays the contents of the Teams.txt file in a ListBox control. When the user selects a team in the ListBox, the application should display the number of times that team has won the World Series in the time period from 1903 through 2009.

TIP: Read the contents of the WorldSeriesWinners.txt file into a List or an array. When the user selects a team, an algorithm should step through the list or array counting the number of times the selected team appears.

6. **Name Search**

   In the *Chap07* folder of the Student Sample Programs, you will find the following files:

   - GirlNames.txt—This file contains a list of the 200 most popular names given to girls born in the United States from 2000 through 2009.
   - BoyNames.txt—This file contains a list of the 200 most popular names given to boys born in the United States from 2000 through 2009.

   Create an application that reads the contents of the two files into two separate arrays or Lists. The user should be able to enter a boy's name, a girl's name, or both, and the application should display messages indicating whether the names were among the most popular.

7. **Population Data**

   In the *Chap07* folder of the Student Sample Programs, you will find a file named USPopulation.txt. The file contains the midyear population of the United States, in thousands, during the years 1950 through 1990. The first line in the file contains the population for 1950, the second line contains the population for 1951, and so forth.

   Create an application that reads the file's contents into an array or a List. The application should display the following data:

   - The average annual change in population during the time period
   - The year with the greatest increase in population during the time period
   - The year with the least increase in population during the time period

8. **Tic-Tac-Toe Simulator**

   Create an application that simulates a game of tic-tac-toe. Figure 7-45 shows an example of the application's form. The form shown in the figure uses eight large Label controls to display the Xs and Os.

   The application should use a two-dimensional int array to simulate the game board in memory. When the user clicks the *New Game* button, the application should step through the array, storing a random number in the range of 0 through 1 in each element. The number 0 represents the letter O, and the number 1 represents the letter X. The form should then be updated to display the game board. The application should display a message indicating whether player X won, player Y won, or the game was a tie.

Figure 7-45 The tic-tac-toe application

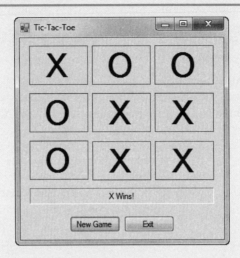

9. **Jagged Array of Exam Scores**

    Dr. Hunter teaches three sections of her Intro to Computer Science class. She has 12 students in section 1, 8 students in section 2, and 10 students in section 3. In the *Chap07* folder of the Student Sample Programs, you will find the following files:

    *   Section1.txt—This file contains the final exam scores for each student in section 1. (There are 12 integer scores in the file.)
    *   Section2.txt—This file contains the final exam scores for each student in section 2. (There are 8 integer scores in the file.)
    *   Section3.txt—This file contains the final exam scores for each student in section 3. (There are 10 integer scores in the file.)

    Create an application that reads these three files and stores their contents in a jagged array. The array's first row should hold the exam scores for the students in section 1, the second row should hold the exam scores for the students in section 2, and the third row should hold the exam scores for the students in section 3.

    The application should display each section's exam scores in a separate ListBox control and then use the jagged array to determine the following:

    *   The average exam score for each individual section
    *   The average exam score for all the students in the three sections
    *   The highest exam score among all three sections and the section number in which that score was found
    *   The lowest exam score among all three sections and the section number in which that score was found

8 More about Processing Data

8.1 Introduction

This chapter presents several diverse topics. Now that you have studied the fundamentals of programming using Visual C#, you can use the topics presented in this chapter to perform more advanced operations. First, we discuss various string and character processing techniques that are useful in applications that work extensively with text. Then we discuss structures, which allow you to encapsulate several variables into a single item. After that we discuss enumerated types, which are data types that you can create, consisting of specified values. Last, we discuss the ImageList control, which is a data structure for storing and retrieving images.

8.2 String and Character Processing

CONCEPT: Some programming tasks require that you manipulate strings at a detailed level. C# and the .NET Framework provide tools that let you work with individual characters and sets of characters within strings.

Sometimes the data with which a program must work comes in the form of text. Word processors, text messaging programs, e-mail applications, Web browsers, and spell-checkers are just a few examples of programs that work extensively with text. The earlier chapters in this book have demonstrated some simple text processing techniques, such as comparing strings and converting strings to other data types. Sometimes, however, you need to operate on strings at a more detailed level. Some operations require that you access or manipulate the individual characters in a string.

For example, you have probably used programs or Web sites that require you to set up a password that meets certain requirements. Some systems require that passwords have a minimum length and contain at least one uppercase letter, at least one lowercase letter, and at least one numeric digit. These requirements are intended to prevent ordinary words from being used as passwords and thus make the passwords more secure. When a new password is created, the system has to examine each of the password's characters to determine whether it meets the requirements. In the next section you will see an example of an algorithm that performs this very operation. First, however, we discuss the `char` data type and the process of retrieving the individual characters in a string.

The `char` Data Type

So far in this book, we have used the `string` data type to store text. C# also provides the `char` data type, which is used to store individual characters. A variable of the `char` data type can hold only one character at a time. Here is an example of how you might declare a `char` variable:

```
char letter;
```

This statement declares a `char` variable named `letter`, which can store one character. In C#, **character literals** are enclosed in single quotation marks. Here is an example showing how we would assign a character to the `letter` variable:

```
letter = 'g';
```

This statement assigns the character `'g'` to the `letter` variable. Because `char` variables can hold only one character, they are not compatible with strings. For example, you cannot assign a string to a `char` variable, even if the string contains only one character. The following statement, for example, will not compile because it attempts to assign a string literal to a `char` variable.

```
letter = "g";  // ERROR! Cannot assign a string to a char
```

It is important that you do not confuse character literals, which are enclosed in single quotation marks, with string literals, which are enclosed in double quotation marks.

When you need to convert a `char` variable to a string, you can call its `ToString` method. For example, the following statement displays the value of the `letter` variable in a message box:

```
MessageBox.Show(letter.ToString());
```

The following statement shows another example. Assume that `letter` is a `char` variable and `outputLabel` is the name of a Label control:

```
outputLabel.Text = letter.ToString();
```

Retrieving the Individual Characters in a String

C# allows you to access the individual characters in a string using subscript notation. This makes it possible to work with a string as if it were an array of characters. You use subscript 0 to access the first character, subscript 1 to access the second character, and so on. The subscript of the last character is 1 less than the string's length. The following code shows an example.

```
1 // Declare a string and a char.
2 string name = "Jacob";
3 char letter;
4
5 // Get the first character (at position 0).
```

```
6 letter = name[0];
7
8 // Display the character.
9 MessageBox.Show(letter.ToString());
```

In this code, line 2 declares a `string` variable named `name`, initialized with the string `"Jacob"`. Line 3 declares a `char` variable named `letter`. Line 6 gets the character at position 0 in `name` (the first character in the string) and assigns it to the `letter` variable. Line 9 displays the value of the `letter` variable in a message box. If this code were executed, a message box would appear showing the character J.

 NOTE: As with arrays, an exception occurs if you attempt to use an invalid subscript with a string. String subscripts must be at least 0, and they must be less than the length of the string.

The following code sample shows how a loop can be used to step through the characters in a string. Notice that in the `for` loop, the `index` variable has a starting value of 0 and is incremented after each iteration, and the loop iterates as long as `index` is less than `name.Length`. If this code were executed, a series of message boxes would appear displaying the characters J, a, c, o, and b.

```
 1 // Declare a string and a char.
 2 string name = "Jacob";
 3 char letter;
 4
 5 // Display the characters in the string.
 6 for (int index = 0; index < name.Length; index++)
 7 {
 8     letter = name[index];
 9     MessageBox.Show(letter.ToString());
10 }
```

Keep in mind that subscripts provide read-only access to the characters in a string. You cannot use a subscript to change the value of a character. For example, the following code will not compile because the second statement attempts to use a subscript expression to change the value of the first character in the `name` variable:

```
string name = "Jill";
name[0] = 'B';              // ERROR! This will not work!
```

You can also use the `foreach` loop to retrieve the individual characters in a string. The following code shows an example. If this code were executed, a series of message boxes would appear displaying the characters J, a, c, o, and b.

```
 1 // Declare a string and a char.
 2 string name = "Jacob";
 3 char letter;
 4
 5 // Display the characters in the string.
 6 foreach (char letter in name)
 7 {
 9     MessageBox.Show(letter.ToString());
10 }
```

Character Testing and Conversion Methods

The `char` data type provides several methods for testing the value of a character. Some of the methods are listed in Table 8-1. Note that each of the methods listed in the table returns a Boolean value of `true` or `false`.

Table 8-1 Some of the Character Testing Methods

Method	Description

char.IsDigit(*ch*)	The argument *ch* is a character. The method returns true if *ch* is a digit (0 through 9) or false otherwise.
	
	Example:
	
	``csharp
	string str = "12345";
	if (char.IsDigit(str[0]))
	{
	    MessageBox.Show("Character 0 is " +
	                    "a digit.");
	}
	``

char.IsDigit(*str*, *index*)	The argument *str* is a string, and *index* is the position of a character within *str*. The method returns true if the specified character is a digit (0 through 9) or false otherwise.
	
	Example:
	
	``csharp
	string str = "12345";
	if (char.IsDigit(str, 0))
	{
	    MessageBox.Show("Character 0 is " +
	                    "a digit.");
	}
	``

char.IsLetter(*ch*)	The argument *ch* is a character. The method returns true if *ch* is an alphabetic letter or false otherwise.
	
	Example:
	
	``csharp
	string str = "Hello World";
	if (char.IsLetter(str[0]))
	{
	    MessageBox.Show("Character 0 is " +
	                    "a letter.");
	}
	``

char.IsLetter(*str*, *index*)	The argument *str* is a string, and *index* is the position of a character within *str*. The method returns true if the specified character is an alphabetic letter or false otherwise.
	
	Example:
	
	``csharp
	string str = "Hello World";
	if (char.IsLetter(str, 0))
	{
	    MessageBox.Show("Character 0 is " +
	                    "a letter.");
	}
	``

char.IsLetterOrDigit(*ch*)	The argument *ch* is a character. The method returns true if *ch* is either an alphabetic letter or a numeric digit. Otherwise, the method returns false.

(continued)

Table 8-1 Some of the Character Testing Methods (*continued*)

Method	Description
	Example:

	`string str = "Hello World";`
	`if (char.IsLetterOrDigit(str[0]))`
	`{`
	    `MessageBox.Show("Character 0 is " +`
	                   `"either a letter " +`
	                   `"or a digit.");`
	`}`

`char.IsLetterOrDigit(str, index)`	The argument *str* is a string, and *index* is the position of a character within *str*. The method returns `true` if the specified character is either an alphabetic letter or a numeric digit. Otherwise, the method returns `false`.
	
	Example:
	`string str = "12345";`
	`if (char.IsLetterOrDigit(str, 0))`
	`{`
	    `MessageBox.Show("Character 0 is " +`
	                   `"either a letter " +`
	                   `"or a digit.");`
	`}`

`char.IsLower(ch)`	The argument *ch* is a character. The method returns `true` if *ch* is a lowercase letter or `false` otherwise.
	
	Example:
	`string str = "hello world";`
	`if (char.IsLower(str[0]))`
	`{`
	    `MessageBox.Show("Character 0 is " +`
	                   `"lowercase.");`
	`}`

`char.IsLower(str, index)`	The argument *str* is a string, and *index* is the position of a character within *str*. The method returns `true` if the specified character is a lowercase letter or `false` otherwise.
	
	Example:
	`string str = "hello world";`
	`if (char.IsLower(str, 0))`
	`{`
	    `MessageBox.Show("Character 0 is " +`
	                   `"lowercase.");`
	`}`

`char.IsPunctuation(ch)`	The argument *ch* is a character. The method returns `true` if *ch* is categorized as a punctuation mark or `false` otherwise.

(continued)

Table 8-1 Some of the Character Testing Methods *(continued)*

Method	Description
	Example:
| | ```csharp
string str = "Hello!";
if (char.IsPunctuation(str[5]))
{
    MessageBox.Show("Character 5 is a " +
                    "punctuation mark.");
}
``` |
| `char.IsPunctuation(str, index)` | The argument *str* is a string, and *index* is the position of a character within *str*. The method returns `true` if the specified character is categorized as a punctuation mark or `false` otherwise. |
| | *Example:* |
| | ```csharp
string str = "Hello!";
if (char.IsPunctuation(str, 5))
{
    MessageBox.Show("Character 5 is a " +
                    "punctuation mark.");
}
``` |
| `char.IsUpper(ch)` | The argument *ch* is a character. The method returns `true` if *ch* is an uppercase letter or `false` otherwise. |
| | *Example:* |
| | ```csharp
string str = "Hello World";
if (char.IsUpper(str[0]))
{
    MessageBox.Show("Character 0 is " +
                    "uppercase.");
}
``` |
| `char.IsUpper(str, index)` | The argument *str* is a string, and *index* is the position of a character within *str*. The method returns `true` if the specified character is an uppercase letter or `false` otherwise. |
| | *Example:* |
| | ```csharp
string str = "Hello World";
if (char.IsUpper(str, 0))
{
    MessageBox.Show("Character 0 is " +
                    "uppercase.");
}
``` |
| `char.IsWhiteSpace(ch)` | The argument *ch* is a character. The method returns `true` if *ch* is a white-space character or `false` otherwise. (White-space characters are the space, tab, linefeed, carriage-return, formfeed, vertical-tab, and newline characters.) |

(continued)

Table 8-1 Some of the Character Testing Methods (*continued*)

Method	Description
	Example: ```string str = " ";\nif (char.IsWhiteSpace(str[0]))\n{\n MessageBox.Show("Character 0 is " +\n "whitespace.");\n}```
`char.IsWhiteSpace(str, index)`	The argument *str* is a string, and *index* is the position of a character within *str*. The method returns `true` if the specified character is a white-space character or `false` otherwise. (White-space characters are the space, tab, linefeed, carriage-return, formfeed, vertical-tab, and newline characters.) *Example:* ```string str = " ";\nif (char.IsWhiteSpace(str, 0))\n{\n MessageBox.Show("Character 0 is " +\n "whitespace.");\n}```

In Tutorial 8-1 you use several of the character testing methods in an application that validates passwords.

Tutorial 8-1:
Completing the Password Validation Application

Many password-protected systems allow users to set up their own passwords. When a user creates a password, the system examines the password to determine whether it meets the minimum requirements. If it does not, the system rejects the password and requires the user to create another, more secure, password.

In this tutorial you complete the *Password Validation* application. The application's form, which has already been created for you, is shown in Figure 8-1. When the application is complete, the user will enter a password and then click the *Check Password* button. The application will check the password to make sure it meets the following requirements:

- The password must be at least eight characters long.
- The password must contain at least one uppercase character.
- The password must contain at least one lowercase character.
- The password must contain at least one numeric digit.

Figure 8-1 The *Password Validation* application's form

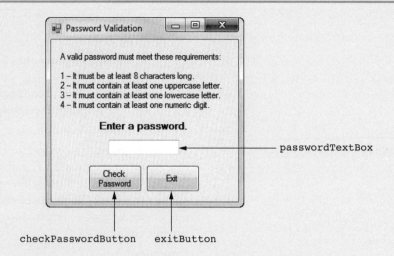

Step 1: Start Visual Studio (or Visual C# Express). Open the project named *Password Validation* in the *Chap08* folder of the Student Sample Programs.

Step 2: Open the Form1 form's code in the code editor. Type the comments and code for the NumberUpperCase method, shown in lines 19–36 of Program 8-1. The purpose of the NumberUpperCase method is to accept a string as an argument and return the number of uppercase letters contained in the string.

Step 3: Type the comments and code for the NumberLowerCase method, shown in lines 38–55 of Program 8-1. The purpose of the NumberLowerCase method is to accept a string as an argument and return the number of lowercase letters contained in the string.

Step 4: Type the comments and code for the NumberDigits method, shown in lines 57–74 of Program 8-1. The purpose of the NumberDigits method is to accept a string as an argument and return the number of numeric digits contained in the string.

Step 5: Next you create the Click event handlers for the Button controls. Switch back to the *Designer* and double-click the checkPasswordButton control. This opens the code editor, and you will see an empty event handler named checkPasswordButton_Click. Complete the event handler by typing the code shown in lines 78–95 in Program 8-1. Let's review this code:

Lines 78–81: The statement in line 78 declares a constant for the minimum password length. Line 81 declares the password variable and initializes it with the value entered by the user.

Line 84: The if-else statement that begins in line 84 evaluates a compound Boolean expression. In plain English, the statement should be interpreted like this:

If the password's length is at least 8 and
> *the number of uppercase letters in the password is at least 1 and*
> *the number of lowercase letters in the password is at least 1 and*
> *the number of numeric digits in the password is at least 1,*

Then the password is valid.
Else
> *The password does not meet the requirements.*

Step 6: Switch your view back to the *Designer* and double-click the `exitButton` control. In the code editor you will see an empty event handler named `exitButton_Click`. Complete the event handler by typing the code shown in lines 100–101 in Program 8-1.

Step 7: Save the project. Then, press F5 on the keyboard or click the *Start Debugging* button (▶) on the toolbar to compile and run the application. When the application runs, test various passwords to confirm that the application works properly. When you are finished, click the *Exit* button to exit the application.

Program 8-1 Completed code for Form1 in the *Password Validation* application

```
1  using System;
2  using System.Collections.Generic;
3  using System.ComponentModel;
4  using System.Data;
5  using System.Drawing;
6  using System.Linq;
7  using System.Text;
8  using System.Windows.Forms;
9
10 namespace Password_Validation
11 {
12     public partial class Form1 : Form
13     {
14         public Form1()
15         {
16             InitializeComponent();
17         }
18
19         // The NumberUpperCase method accepts a string argument
20         // and returns the number of uppercase letters it contains.
21         private int NumberUpperCase(string str)
22         {
23             int upperCase = 0;   // The number of uppercase letters
24
25             // Count the uppercase characters in str.
26             foreach (char ch in str)
27             {
28                 if (char.IsUpper(ch))
29                 {
30                     upperCase++;
31                 }
32             }
33
34             // Return the number of uppercase characters.
35             return upperCase;
36         }
37
38         // The NumberLowerCase method accepts a string argument
39         // and returns the number of lowercase letters it contains.
40         private int NumberLowerCase(string str)
41         {
42             int lowerCase = 0;   // The number of lowercase letters
43
44             // Count the lowercase characters in str.
45             foreach (char ch in str)
```

```
46                  {
47                      if (char.IsLower(ch))
48                      {
49                          lowerCase++;
50                      }
51                  }
52
53              // Return the number of lowercase characters.
54              return lowerCase;
55          }
56
57          // The NumberDigits method accepts a string argument
58          // and returns the number of numeric digits it contains.
59          private int NumberDigits(string str)
60          {
61              int digits = 0;   // The number of digits
62
63              // Count the digits in str.
64              foreach (char ch in str)
65              {
66                  if (char.IsDigit(ch))
67                  {
68                      digits++;
69                  }
70              }
71
72              // Return the number of digits.
73              return digits;
74          }
75
76          private void checkPasswordButton_Click(object sender, EventArgs e)
77          {
78              const int MIN_LENGTH = 8;   // Password's minimum length
79
80              // Get the password from the TextBox.
81              string password = passwordTextBox.Text;
82
83              // Validate the password.
84              if (password.Length >= MIN_LENGTH &&
85                  NumberUpperCase(password) >= 1 &&
86                  NumberLowerCase(password) >= 1 &&
87                  NumberDigits(password) >= 1)
88              {
89                  MessageBox.Show("The password is valid.");
90              }
91              else
92              {
93                  MessageBox.Show("The password does not meet " +
94                      "the requirements.");
95              }
96          }
97
98          private void exitButton_Click(object sender, EventArgs e)
99          {
100             // Close the form.
101             this.Close();
102         }
103     }
104 }
```

Character Case Conversion

The char data type also provides the ToLower and ToUpper methods listed in Table 8-2 for converting the case of a character. Each method accepts a char argument and returns a char value.

Table 8-2 Character Case Conversion Methods

Method	Description
char.ToLower(*ch*)	The argument *ch* is a character. The method returns the lowercase equivalent of *ch*.
char.ToUpper(*ch*)	The argument *ch* is a character. The method returns the uppercase equivalent of *ch*.

If the ToLower method's argument is an uppercase character, the method returns the lowercase equivalent. For example, look at the following code. The statement in line 2 assigns the character 'a' to the letter variable.

```
1 string str = "ABC";
2 char letter = char.ToLower(str[0]);
```

If the argument is already lowercase, the ToLower method returns it unchanged.

If the ToUpper method's argument is a lowercase character, the method returns the uppercase equivalent. For example, look at the following code. The statement in line 2 assigns the character 'A' to the letter variable.

```
1 string str = "abc";
2 char letter = char.ToUpper(str[0]);
```

If the argument is already uppercase, the ToUpper method returns it unchanged.

Searching For Substrings

Some tasks require you to search for a specific string of characters within a string. A string within a string is called a **substring**. Objects of the string data type have several methods that allow you to search for substrings. Table 8-3 summarizes the **Contains, StartsWith,** and **EndsWith methods**. Each of the methods in Table 8-3 returns a Boolean value indicating whether the substring was found.

Table 8-3 Some of the Substring-Searching Methods

Method	Description
stringVar.Contains(*substring*)	*stringVar* is the name of a string variable or is a string expression. The argument *substring* is also a string. The method returns true if *stringVar* contains the string *substring* or false otherwise.
	Example:

	```// The following code displays```
	 ```// "ice was found."```
	 ```string str = "chocolate ice cream";```
	 ```if (str.Contains("ice"))```
	 ```{```
	 ``` MessageBox.Show("ice was found.");```
	 ```}```

(continued)

Table 8-3 Some of the Substring-Searching Methods *(continued)*

Method	Description

stringVar.Contains(*ch*)	*stringVar* is the name of a string variable or is a string expression. The argument *ch* is a character. The method returns true if *stringVar* contains the character *ch* or false otherwise.
	
	Example:
	<pre>// The following code displays
	// "b was found."
	string str = "abcd";
	if (str.Contains('b'))
	{
	    MessageBox.Show("b was found.");
	}</pre>

stringVar.StartsWith(*substring*)	*stringVar* is the name of a string variable or is a string expression. The argument *substring* is also a string. The method returns true if *stringVar* starts with the string *substring* or false otherwise.
	
	Example:
	<pre>// The following code displays "The string
	// starts with choc."
	string str = "chocolate ice cream";
	if (str.StartsWith("choc"))
	{
	    MessageBox.Show("The string starts " +
	                    "with choc.");
	}</pre>

stringVar.EndsWith(*substring*)	*stringVar* is the name of a string variable or is a string expression. The argument *substring* is also a string. The method returns true if *stringVar* ends with the string *substring* or false otherwise.
	
	Example:
	<pre>// The following code displays "The string
	// ends with cream."
	string str = "chocolate ice cream";
	if (str.EndsWith("cream"))
	{
	    MessageBox.Show("The string ends " +
	                    "with cream.");
	}</pre>

The methods shown in Table 8-3 let you know whether a specified substring is found within a string. Sometimes you also want to know the position of the substring. When that is the case, you can use one of the **IndexOf** or **LastIndexOf** methods shown in Table 8-4. Note that each method in Table 8-4 returns an int.

Table 8-4 Methods for Getting a Character or Substring's Position

Method	Description
stringVar.IndexOf(*substring*)	*stringVar* is the name of a string variable or is a string expression. The argument *substring* is also a string. If *substring* is found in *stringVar*, the method returns the integer position of *substring*'s first occurrence. If *substring* is not found in *stringVar*, the method returns −1. *Example:* ```// The following code displays "10"
string str = "chocolate ice cream";
int position = str.IndexOf("ice");
if (position != -1)
{
MessageBox.Show(position.ToString());
}
else
{
MessageBox.Show("ice was not found.");
}```
stringVar.IndexOf(*substring*, *start*)	*stringVar* is the name of a string variable or is a string expression. The argument *substring* is a string, and the argument *start* is an integer. The method searches *stringVar* for *substring*, starting at the position specified by *start* and going to the end of *stringVar*. If *substring* is found in this portion of *stringVar*, the method returns the integer position of its first occurrence. If *substring* is not found, the method returns −1. *Example:* ```// The following code displays "2"
string str = "cocoa beans";
int position = str.IndexOf("co", 2);
if (position != -1)
{
MessageBox.Show(position.ToString());
}
else
{
MessageBox.Show("co was not found.");
}```
stringVar.IndexOf(*substring*, *start*, *count*)	*stringVar* is the name of a string variable or is a string expression. The argument *substring* is a string, the argument *start* is an integer, and the argument *count* is also an integer. The method searches *stringVar* for *substring*, starting at the position specified by *start* and continuing for *count* characters. If *substring* is found in this portion of *stringVar*, the method returns the integer position of its first occurrence. If *substring* is not found, the method returns −1.

(continued)

Table 8-4 Methods for Getting a Character or Substring's Position *(continued)*

Method	Description
	Example:
| | ```csharp
// The following code displays "6"
string str = "xx oo xx oo xx";
int position = str.IndexOf("xx", 3, 8);
if (position != -1)
{
    MessageBox.Show(position.ToString());
}
else
{
    MessageBox.Show("xx was not found.");
}
``` |
| *stringVar*.IndexOf(*ch*) | *stringVar* is the name of a string variable or is a string expression. The argument *ch* is a character. If *ch* is found in *stringVar*, the method returns the integer position of *ch*'s first occurrence. If *ch* is not found in *stringVar*, the method returns −1. |
| | *Example:* |
| | ```csharp
// The following code displays "2"
string str = "chocolate ice cream";
int position = str.IndexOf('o');
if (position != -1)
{
    MessageBox.Show(position.ToString());
}
else
{
    MessageBox.Show("o was not found.");
}
``` |
| *stringVar*.IndexOf(*ch*, *start*) | *stringVar* is the name of a string variable or is a string expression. The argument *ch* is a character, and the argument *start* is an integer. The method searches *stringVar* for *ch*, starting at the position specified by *start* and going to the end of *stringVar*. If *ch* is found in this portion of *stringVar*, the method returns the integer position of its first occurrence. If *ch* is not found, the method returns −1. |
| | *Example:* |
| | ```csharp
// The following code displays "4"
string str = "chocolate ice cream";
int position = str.IndexOf('o', 3);
if (position != -1)
{
    MessageBox.Show(position.ToString());
}
else
{
    MessageBox.Show("o was not found.");
}
``` |

(continued)
```

Table 8-4 Methods for Getting a Character or Substring's Position *(continued)*

Method	Description
`stringVar.IndexOf(ch, start, count)`	`stringVar` is the name of a string variable or is a string expression. The argument `ch` is a character, the argument `start` is an integer, and the argument `count` is also an integer. The method searches `stringVar` for `ch`, starting at the position specified by `start` and continuing for `count` characters. If `ch` is found in this portion of `stringVar`, the method returns the integer position of its first occurrence. If `substring` is not found, the method returns −1.

	Example:
	```// The following code displays "12"```
	```string str = "chocolate ice cream";```
	```int position = str.IndexOf('e', 10, 4);```
	```if (position != -1)```
	```{```
	``` MessageBox.Show(position.ToString());```
	```}```
	```else```
	```{```
	``` MessageBox.Show("e was not found.");```
	```}```

`stringVar.LastIndexOf(substring)`	`stringVar` is the name of a string variable or is a string expression. The argument `substring` is also a string. If `substring` is found in `stringVar`, the method returns the integer position of `substring`'s last occurrence. If `substring` is not found in `stringVar`, the method returns −1.

	Example:
	```// The following code displays "11".```
	```string str = "blue green blue";```
	```int position = str.LastIndexOf("blue");```
	```if (position != -1)```
	```{```
	``` MessageBox.Show(position.ToString());```
	```}```
	```else```
	```{```
	``` MessageBox.Show("blue was not found.");```
	```}```

`stringVar.LastIndexOf(substring, start)`	`stringVar` is the name of a string variable or is a string expression. The argument `substring` is a string, and the argument `start` is an integer. The method searches `stringVar` for `substring`, starting at the position specified by `start` and proceeding backward toward the beginning of `stringVar`. If `substring` is found in this portion of `stringVar`, the method returns its integer position. If `substring` is not found, the method returns −1.

(continued)

Table 8-4 Methods for Getting a Character or Substring's Position *(continued)*

Method	Description
	Example:
| | ```
// The following code displays "6".
string str = "xx oo xx oo xx";
int position = str.LastIndexOf("xx", 10);
if (position != -1)
{
    MessageBox.Show(position.ToString());
}
else
{
    MessageBox.Show("xx was not found.");
}
``` |
| *stringVar*.LastIndexOf(*substring, start, count*) | *stringVar* is the name of a string variable or is a string expression. The argument *substring* is a string, the argument *start* is an integer, and the argument *count* is also an integer. The method searches *stringVar* for *substring*, starting at the position specified by *start* and proceeding backward toward the beginning of *stringVar* for *count* characters. If *substring* is found in this portion of *stringVar*, the method returns its integer position. If *substring* is not found, the method returns −1. |
| | *Example:* |
| | ```
// The following code displays "6".
string str = "oo xx oo xx oo";
int position = str.LastIndexOf("oo", 10, 8);
if (position != -1)
{
    MessageBox.Show(position.ToString());
}
else
{
    MessageBox.Show("oo was not found.");
}
``` |
| *stringVar*.LastIndexOf(*ch*) | *stringVar* is the name of a string variable or is a string expression. The argument *ch* is a character. If *ch* is found in *stringVar*, the method returns the integer position of *ch*'s last occurrence. If *ch* is not found in *stringVar*, the method returns −1. |
| | *Example:* |
| | ```
// The following code displays "14".
string str = "chocolate ice cream";
int position = str.LastIndexOf('c');
if (position != -1)
{
    MessageBox.Show(position.ToString());
}
else
{
    MessageBox.Show("c was not found.");
}
``` |

(continued)
```

Table 8-4 Methods for Getting a Character or Substring's Position *(continued)*

Method	Description
`stringVar.LastIndexOf(ch, start)`	*stringVar* is the name of a string variable or is a string expression. The argument *ch* is a character, and the argument *start* is an integer. The method searches *stringVar* for *ch*, starting at the position specified by *start* and proceeding backward toward the beginning of *stringVar*. If *ch* is found in this portion of *stringVar*, the method returns its integer position. If *ch* is not found, the method returns −1.

Example:

```
// The following code displays "12".
string str = "chocolate ice cream";
int position = str.LastIndexOf('e', 14);
if (position != -1)
{
    MessageBox.Show(position.ToString());
}
else
{
    MessageBox.Show("e was not found.");
}
```

Method	Description
`stringVar.LastIndexOf(ch, start, count)`	*stringVar* is the name of a string variable or is a string expression. The argument *ch* is a character, the argument *start* is an integer, and the argument *count* is also an integer. The method searches *stringVar* for *ch*, starting at the position specified by *start* and proceeding backward for *count* characters. If *ch* is found in this portion of *stringVar*, the method returns its integer position. If *substring* is not found, the method returns −1.

Example:

```
// The following code displays "12".
string str = "chocolate ice cream";
int position = str.LastIndexOf('e', 14, 8);
if (position != -1)
{
    MessageBox.Show(position.ToString());
}
else
{
    MessageBox.Show("e was not found.");
}
```

Sometimes you need to retrieve a specific set of characters from a string. For example, suppose a string contains a U.S. telephone number, such as `"(919)555-1212"` and you are interested in getting the area code. You need a way to retrieve the characters in positions 1 through 3. You can use the **Substring method,** as shown in Table 8-5. Note that the Substring method returns a string.

Table 8-5 The Substring Method

Method	Description

stringVar.Substring(*start*)	*stringVar* is the name of a string variable or is a string expression. The argument *start* is an integer that specifies a position in *stringVar*. The method returns a string containing the characters beginning at *start*, continuing to the end of *stringVar*.
	
	Example:
	
	`// The following code displays "beans".`
	`string str = "cocoa beans";`
	`MessageBox.Show(str.Substring(6));`

stringVar.Substring(*start*,*count*)	*stringVar* is the name of a string variable or is a string expression. The argument *start* is an integer that specifies a position in *stringVar*, and *count* is an integer that specifies a number of characters. The method returns a string containing the characters beginning at *start* and continuing for *count* characters.
	
	Example:
	
	`// The following code displays "cocoa".`
	`string str = "cocoa beans";`
	`MessageBox.Show(str.Substring(0, 5));`

Methods For Modifying a String

Table 8-6 describes several methods that string objects have for modifying the contents of a string in the following ways:

- The Insert method inserts a string into another string.
- The Remove methods remove specified characters from a string.
- The ToLower method converts a string to all lowercase characters.
- The ToUpper method converts a string to all uppercase characters.
- The Trim method removes all leading and trailing spaces from a string. (**Leading spaces** are spaces that appear at the beginning of a string, and **trailing spaces** are spaces that appear at the end of a string.)
- The TrimStart method removes all leading spaces from a string.
- The TrimEnd method removes all trailing spaces from a string.

It is important to remember that the methods shown in Table 8-6 do not actually modify the calling string object. They return a modified copy of the calling string object. For example, look at the following code, which demonstrates the Remove method:

```
1 string str1 = "sunshine";
2 string str2 = str1.Remove(3);
3 MessageBox.Show(str1);
4 MessageBox.Show(str2);
```

Line 1 declares a string variable named str1, initialized with the string "sunshine". Line 2 calls the str1.Remove method, passing 3 as an argument. The method returns a copy of str1 with all the characters from position 3 to the end of the string removed. (The method returns the string "sun".) The string that is returned is assigned to the str2 variable. Line 3 displays the str1 variable, which is "sunshine", and line 4 displays the str2 variable, which is "sun".

Table 8-6 Methods For Modifying a String

Method	Description

`stringVar.Insert(start, strItem)`	`stringVar` is the name of a string variable or is a string expression. The `start` argument is an integer that specifies a position in `stringVar`, and the `strItem` argument is a string that is to be inserted. The method returns a string containing a copy of `stringVar` with `strItem` inserted into it beginning at the position specified by `start`. *Example:*
	
	`// The following displays "New York City".`
	`string str1 = "New City";`
	`string str2 = str1.Insert(4, "York ");`
	`MessageBox.Show(str2);`

`stringVar.Remove(start)`	`stringVar` is the name of a string variable or is a string expression. The `start` argument is an integer that specifies a position in `stringVar`. The method returns a string containing a copy of `stringVar` with all the characters from the position specified by `start` to the end removed. *Example:*
	
	`// The following displays "blue".`
	`string str1 = "blueberry";`
	`string str2 = str1.Remove(4);`
	`MessageBox.Show(str2);`

`stringVar.Remove(start, count)`	`stringVar` is the name of a string variable or is a string expression. The `start` argument is an integer that specifies a position in `stringVar`, and `count` is an integer that specifies a number of characters. The method returns a string containing a copy of `stringVar` with `count` characters removed, beginning at the position specified by `start`. *Example:*
	
	`// The following displays "jelly doughnuts".`
	`string str1 = "jelly filled doughnuts";`
	`string str2 = str1.Remove(6, 7);`
	`MessageBox.Show(str2);`

`stringVar.ToLower()`	`stringVar` is the name of a string variable or is a string expression. The method returns a string containing a copy of `stringVar` converted to lowercase. *Example:*
	
	`// The following displays "abc".`
	`string str1 = "ABC";`
	`string str2 = str1.ToLower();`
	`MessageBox.Show(str2);`

`stringVar.ToUpper()`	`stringVar` is the name of a string variable or is a string expression. The method returns a string containing a copy of `stringVar` converted to uppercase. *Example:*
	
	`// The following displays "ABC".`
	`string str1 = "abc";`
	`string str2 = str1.ToUpper();`

(continued)

Table 8-6 Methods For Modifying a String *(continued)*

Method	Description
	`MessageBox.Show(str2);`
`stringVar.Trim()`	*stringVar* is the name of a `string` variable or is a `string` expression. The method returns a string containing a copy of *stringVar* with all leading and trailing spaces removed.
	Example:

	`// The following displays ">Hello<".`
	`string str1 = "    Hello    ";`
	`string str2 = str1.Trim();`
	`MessageBox.Show(">" + str2 + "<");`

`stringVar.TrimStart()`	*stringVar* is the name of a `string` variable or is a `string` expression. The method returns a string containing a copy of *stringVar* with all leading spaces removed.
	Example:

	`// The following displays ">Hello<".`
	`string str1 = "    Hello";`
	`string str2 = str1.TrimStart();`
	`MessageBox.Show(">" + str2 + "<");`

`stringVar.TrimEnd()`	*stringVar* is the name of a `string` variable or is a `string` expression. The method returns a string containing a copy of *stringVar* with all trailing spaces removed.
	Example:

	`// The following displays ">Hello<".`
	`string str1 = "Hello    ";`
	`string str2 = str1.TrimEnd();`
	`MessageBox.Show(">" + str2 + "<");`

In Tutorials 8-2 and 8-3 you use several of the `string` methods that we have discussed in applications that format and unformat U.S. telephone numbers.

Tutorial 8-2:
Completing the *Telephone Format* Application

Telephone numbers in the United States are commonly formatted to appear in the following manner:

`(XXX)XXX-XXXX`

In the format, x represents a digit. The three digits that appear inside the parentheses are the area code. The three digits following the area code are the prefix, and the four digits after the hyphen are the line number. Here is an example:

`(919)555-1212`

Although the parentheses and the hyphen make the number easier for people to read, those characters are unnecessary for processing by a computer. In a computer system, a telephone number is commonly stored as an unformatted series of digits, as shown here:

`9195551212`

Programs that work with telephone numbers sometimes need to unformat numbers that have been entered by the user. This means that the parentheses and the hyphen must be removed prior to storing the number in a file or processing it in some other way. In addition, such programs need the ability to format a number so it contains the parentheses and the hyphen before displaying it on the screen or printing it on paper.

In this tutorial you complete the *Telephone Format* application. The application's form, which has already been created for you, is shown in Figure 8-2. When the application is complete, you will be able to enter a string of 10 digits into the `numberTextBox` control and click the Format button to see the string of digits formatted as a telephone number.

Figure 8-2 The *Telephone Format* application's form

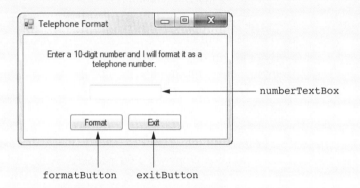

Step 1: Start Visual Studio (or Visual C# Express). Open the project named *Telephone Format* in the *Chap08* folder of the Student Sample Programs.

Step 2: Open the Form1 form's code in the code editor. Type the comments and code for the `IsValidNumber` method, shown in lines 19–49 of Program 8-2. The method accepts a string as an argument and return `true` if the string is 10 characters long and contains only digits. Otherwise, the method returns `false`. You use this method to make sure that the user has entered a valid string of digits. Let's take a closer look at the code.

> **Line 24:** This statement declares the constant `VALID_LENGTH`, initialized with the value 10, to represent the length of a valid string.
>
> **Line 25:** This statement declares a `bool` variable named `valid`, initialized with the value `true`. The `valid` variable is used as a flag to indicate whether the `str` parameter is a valid number.
>
> **Line 28:** This `if` statement determines whether the `str` parameter's length is valid. If so, the program continues at line 31. Otherwise, the program jumps to the `else` clause in line 41, and line 44 assigns `false` to the `valid` variable.
>
> **Line 31:** This `foreach` loop steps through each of the characters in the `str` parameter. If the statement in line 35 determines that a character is *not* a digit, then the statement in line 37 assigns `false` to the `valid` variable.
>
> **Line 48:** This statement returns the value of the `valid` variable.

Step 3: Type the comments and code for the `TelephoneFormat` method, shown in lines 51–63 of Program 8-2. The `TelephoneFormat` method accepts a string as an argument, passed by reference, and inserts the parentheses and the hyphen at the proper locations so it appears in the form `(XXX)XXX-XXXX`. Let's take a closer look at the code.

Line 53: Notice that the `ref` keyword is used in the declaration of the `str` parameter variable.

Line 56: This statement calls the `Insert` method to insert `"("` at position 0. All the characters in the string are automatically shifted right one space to accommodate the inserted character.

Line 59: This statement calls the `Insert` method to insert `")"` at position 4, shifting the characters that previously appeared beginning at position 4 to the right one space.

Line 62: This statement calls the `Insert` method to insert `"-"` at position 8, shifting the characters that previously appeared beginning at position 8 to the right one space. After this statement executes, the string referenced by `str` is formatted as `(XXX)XXX-XXXX`.

Step 4: Next you create the Click event handlers for the Button controls. Switch back to the *Designer* and double-click the `formatButton` control. This opens the code editor, and you will see an empty event handler named `formatButton_Click`. Complete the event handler by typing the code shown in lines 67–81 in Program 8-2. Let's review this code:

Line 68: Notice the expression on the right side of the = operator is `numberTextBox.Text.Trim()`. This expression calls the `Trim` method on the Text property of the `numberTextBox` control. The method returns a copy of the `numberTextBox` control's Text property with all leading and trailing spaces removed. The result is assigned to the `input` variable.

Line 72: This `if` statement calls the `IsValidNumber` method, passing the `input` variable as an argument. If the value of the `input` variable is a valid number, the method returns `true` and the program continues to line 74. In line 74 the `TelephoneFormat` method is called, passing `input` by reference as an argument, and then line 75 displays the value of the `input` variable in a message box.

If the value of the `input` variable is not a valid number, the `IsValidNumber` method returns `false`, and the program jumps to the `else` clause in line 77. Then, line 80 displays an error message.

Step 5: Switch your view back to the *Designer* and double-click the `exitButton` control. In the code editor you will see an empty event handler named `exitButton_Click`. Complete the event handler by typing the code shown in lines 86–87 in Program 8-2.

Step 6: Save the project. Then, press F5 on the keyboard or click the *Start Debugging* button (▶) on the toolbar to compile and run the application. When the application runs, test various input values to confirm that the application works property. For example, if you enter `9195551212`, the application should display `(919)555-1212`, and if you enter `abc5551212`, the application should display `"Invalid input"`. When you are finished, click the *Exit* button to exit the application.

Program 8-2 Completed code for Form1 in the *Telephone Format* application

```
1 using System;
2 using System.Collections.Generic;
3 using System.ComponentModel;
4 using System.Data;
5 using System.Drawing;
```

```
 6 using System.Linq;
 7 using System.Text;
 8 using System.Windows.Forms;
 9
10 namespace Telephone_Format
11 {
12     public partial class Form1 : Form
13     {
14         public Form1()
15         {
16             InitializeComponent();
17         }
18
19         // The IsValidNumber method accepts a string and
20         // returns true if it contains 10 digits or false
21         // otherwise.
22         private bool IsValidNumber(string str)
23         {
24             const int VALID_LENGTH = 10;  // Length of a valid string
25             bool valid = true;   // Flag to indicate validity
26
27             // Check the string's length.
28             if (str.Length == VALID_LENGTH)
29             {
30                 // Check each character in str.
31                 foreach (char ch in str)
32                 {
33                     // If this character is not a digit, the
34                     // string is not valid.
35                     if (!char.IsDigit(ch))
36                     {
37                         valid = false;
38                     }
39                 }
40             }
41             else
42             {
43                 // Incorrect length.
44                 valid = false;
45             }
46
47             // Return the status.
48             return valid;
49         }
50
51         // The TelephoneFormat method accepts a string argument
52         // by reference and formats it as a telephone number.
53         private void TelephoneFormat(ref string str)
54         {
55             // First, insert the left paren at position 0.
56             str = str.Insert(0, "(");
57
58             // Next, insert the right paren at position 4.
59             str = str.Insert(4, ")");
60
61             // Next, insert the hyphen at position 8.
62             str = str.Insert(8, "-");
63         }
64
```

```
65          private void formatButton_Click(object sender, EventArgs e)
66          {
67              // Get a trimmed copy of the user's input.
68              string input = numberTextBox.Text.Trim();
69
70              // If the input is a valid number, format it
71              // and display it.
72              if (IsValidNumber(input))
73              {
74                  TelephoneFormat(ref input);
75                  MessageBox.Show(input);
76              }
77              else
78              {
79                  // Display an error message.
80                  MessageBox.Show("Invalid input");
81              }
82          }
83
84          private void exitButton_Click(object sender, EventArgs e)
85          {
86              // Close the form.
87              this.Close();
88          }
89      }
90 }
```

Tutorial 8-3:
Completing the *Telephone Unformat* Application

In this tutorial you complete the *Telephone Unformat* application. The application's form, which has already been created for you, is shown in Figure 8-3. When the application is complete, you will be able to enter a telephone number in the format (XXX)XXX–XXXX into the numberTextBox control and click the *Unformat* button to see it with the parentheses and the hyphen removed.

Figure 8-3 The *Telephone Unformat* application's form

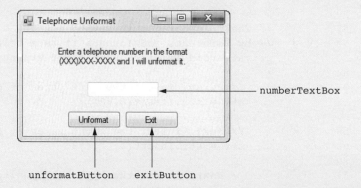

Step 1:   Start Visual Studio (or Visual C# Express). Open the project named *Telephone Unformat* in the *Chap08* folder of the Student Sample Programs.

Step 2:   Open the Form1 form's code in the code editor. Type the comments and code for the `IsValidFormat` method, shown in lines 19–43 of Program 8-3. The method accepts a string as an argument and returns `true` if the string is formatted as `(XXX)XXX-XXXX`. Otherwise, the method returns `false`. You use this method to make sure that the user has entered a properly formatted telephone number. Let's take a closer look at the code:

Line 27: This statement declares the constant `VALID_LENGTH`, initialized with the value 13, to represent the length of a properly formatted telephone number.

Line 28: This statement declares a `bool` variable named `valid`, initialized with the value `true`. The `valid` variable is used as a flag to indicate whether the `str` parameter is properly formatted.

Lines 31–32: The `if-else` statement that begins in these lines determines whether the `str` parameter is properly formatted. In plain English, the statement should be interpreted like this:

If the string's length is 13 and the character at position 0 is `"("` and the character at position 4 is `")"` and the character at position 8 is `"-"` Then
  Set `valid` to `true`.
Else
  Set `valid` to `false`.

After the `if-else` statement executes, the `valid` variable will be set to either `true` or `false`. indicating whether `str` is properly formatted. The statement in line 38 returns the value of the `valid` variable.

Line 42: This statement returns the value of the `valid` variable.

Step 3:   Type the comments and code for the `Unformat` method, shown in lines 45–64 of Program 8-3. The `Unformat` method accepts a string as an argument, passed by reference. The method assumes that the string is formatted as `(XXX)XXX-XXXX`. When the method is finished, the parentheses and the hyphen will be removed from the string. Let's take a closer look at the code:

Line 53: This statement deletes the character at position 0, which is the `"("` character. All the remaining characters are automatically shifted left by one position to occupy the space left by the deleted character.

Line 58: This statement deletes the character at position 3, which is the `")"` character. The characters that previously appeared beginning at position 4 are automatically shifted left to occupy the space left by the deleted character.

Line 63: This statement deletes character at position 6, which is the hyphen. The characters previously appearing to the right of the hyphen are automatically moved left by one position. After this statement executes, the string referenced by `str` will be unformatted, appearing simply as a string of digits.

Step 4:   Next you create the Click event handlers for the Button controls. Switch back to the *Designer* and double-click the `unformatButton` control. This opens the code editor, and you will see an empty event handler named `unformatButton_Click`. Complete the event handler by typing the code shown in lines 68−82 in Program 8-3. Let's review this code:

Line 69: Notice the expression on the right side of the = operator is `numberTextBox.Text.Trim()`. This expression calls the `Trim` method on the Text property of the `numberTextBox` control. The method returns a copy of the `numberTextBox` control's Text property with all leading and trailing spaces removed. The result is assigned to the `input` variable.

Line 73: This `if` statement calls the `IsValidFormat` method, passing the `input` variable as an argument. If the value of the `input` variable is properly formatted, the method returns `true`, and the program continues to line 75. In line 75 the `Unformat` method is called, passing `input` by reference as an argument, and then line 76 displays the value of the `input` variable in a message box.

If the value of the `input` variable is not properly formatted, the `IsValidFormat` method returns `false`, and the program jumps to the `else` clause in line 78. Then, line 81 displays an error message.

Step 5: Switch your view back to the *Designer* and double-click the `exitButton` control. In the code editor you will see an empty event handler named `exitButton_Click`. Complete the event handler by typing the code shown in lines 87–88 in Program 8-3.

Step 6: Save the project. Then, press F5 on the keyboard or click the *Start Debugging* button (▶) on the toolbar to compile and run the application. When the application runs, test various input values to confirm that the application works properly. For example, if you enter `(919)555-1212`, the application should display `9195551212`, and if you enter `919-555-1212`, the application should display `"Invalid input"`. When you are finished, click the *Exit* button to exit the application.

Program 8-3 Completed code for Form1 in the *Telephone Unformat* application

```
1 using System;
2 using System.Collections.Generic;
3 using System.ComponentModel;
4 using System.Data;
5 using System.Drawing;
6 using System.Linq;
7 using System.Text;
8 using System.Windows.Forms;
9
10 namespace Telephone_Unformat
11 {
12     public partial class Form1 : Form
13     {
14         public Form1()
15         {
16             InitializeComponent();
17         }
18
19         // The IsValidFormat method accepts a string argument
20         // and determines whether it is properly formatted as
21         // a U.S. telephone number in the following manner:
22         // (XXX)XXX-XXXX
23         // If the argument is properly formatted, the method
24         // returns true, otherwise false.
25         private bool IsValidFormat(string str)
26         {
27             const int VALID_LENGTH = 13; // Length of a valid string
28             bool valid;                  // Flag to indicate validity
29
30             // Determine whether str is properly formatted.
31             if (str.Length == VALID_LENGTH && str[0] == '(' &&
32                 str[4] == ')' && str[8] == '-')
```

```
33              {
34                  valid = true;
35              }
36              else
37              {
38                  valid = false;
39              }
40
41              // Return the value of valid.
42              return valid;
43          }
44
45          // The unformat method accepts a string, by reference,
46          // assumed to contain a telephone number formatted in
47          // this manner: (XXX)XXX-XXXX.
48          // The method unformats the string by removing the
49          // parentheses and the hyphen.
50          private void Unformat(ref string str)
51          {
52              // First, delete the left paren at position 0.
53              str = str.Remove(0, 1);
54
55              // Next, delete the right paren. Because of the
56              // previous deletion it is now located at
57              // position 3.
58              str = str.Remove(3, 1);
59
60              // Next, delete the hyphen. Because of the
61              // previous deletions it is now located at
62              // position 6.
63              str = str.Remove(6, 1);
64          }
65
66          private void unformatButton_Click(object sender, EventArgs e)
67          {
68              // Get a trimmed copy of the user's input.
69              string input = numberTextBox.Text.Trim();
70
71              // If the input is properly formatted, then unformat it
72              // and display it.
73              if (IsValidFormat(input))
74              {
75                  Unformat(ref input);
76                  MessageBox.Show(input);
77              }
78              else
79              {
80                  // Display an error message.
81                  MessageBox.Show("Invalid input");
82              }
83          }
84
85          private void exitButton_Click(object sender, EventArgs e)
86          {
87              // Close the form.
88              this.Close();
89          }
90      }
91  }
```

Tokenizing Strings

Sometimes a string contains a series of words or other items of data separated by spaces or other characters. For example, look at the following string:

```
"peach raspberry strawberry vanilla"
```

This string contains the following four items of data: peach, raspberry, strawberry, and vanilla. In programming terms, items such as these are known as **tokens**. Notice that a space appears between the items. The character that separates tokens is known as a **delimiter**. Here is another example:

```
"17;92;81;12;46;5"
```

This string contains the following tokens: 17, 92, 81, 12, 46, and 5. Notice that a semi-colon appears between each item. In this example, the semicolon is used as a delimiter. Some programming problems require you to read a string that contains a list of items and then extract all the tokens from the string for processing. For example, look at the following string that contains a date:

```
"3-22-2012"
```

The tokens in this string are 3, 22, and 2012, and the delimiter is the hyphen character. Perhaps a program needs to extract the month, day, and year from such a string.

The process of breaking a string into tokens is known as **tokenizing**. In C#, string objects have a method named Split that is used to tokenize the string. When you call a string object's Split method, the method extracts tokens from the string and returns them as an array of strings. Each element in the array is one of the tokens.

We discuss two ways that you can call the Split method. The first way is to pass the value null as an argument. When you pass null as an argument to the Split method, the method tokenizes the string using white-space characters as delimiters. (White-space characters are the space, tab, linefeed, carriage-return, formfeed, vertical-tab, and newline characters.) The method returns a string array, with each element of the array containing one of the tokens. The following code shows an example:

```
 1 // Create a String to tokenize.
 2 string str = "one two three four";
 3
 4 // Get the tokens from the string.
 5 string[] tokens = str.Split(null);
 6
 7 // Display each token.
 8 foreach (string s in tokens)
 9 {
10     MessageBox.Show(s);
11 }
```

Let's take a closer look at the code:

- Line 2 declares a string variable named str, initialized with the string "one two three four".
- Line 5 declares a string array named tokens. The tokens array is initialized with the array that is returned from the str.Split(null) method call. After this statement executes, the tokens array will have four elements, containing the strings "one", "two", "three", and "four".
- The foreach loop in lines 8–11 displays each of the token array's elements in message boxes. When the loop executes, four message boxes will be displayed, one after the other, showing the strings "one", "two", "three", and "four".

The second way that we call the `Split` method is to pass a `char` array as an argument. Each element of the `char` array is used as a delimiter. The following code shows an example:

```
 1 // Create a String to tokenize.
 2 string str = "one;two;three;four";
 3
 4 // Create an array of delimiters.
 5 char[] delim = { ';' };
 6
 7 // Get the tokens from the string.
 8 string[] tokens = str.Split(delim);
 9
10 // Display each token.
11 foreach (string s in tokens)
12 {
13     MessageBox.Show(s);
14 }
```

Let's take a closer look at the code:

- Line 2 declares a `string` variable named `str`, initialized with the string `"one;two;three;four"`.
- Line 5 declares a `char` array named `delim`. Notice that the initialization list contains only one character. The `delim` array has one element, containing the `';'` character.
- Line 8 declares a `string` array named `tokens`. The `tokens` array is initialized with the array that is returned from the `str.Split(delim)` method call. After this statement executes, the `tokens` array will have four elements, containing the strings `"one"`, `"two"`, `"three"`, and `"four"`.
- The `foreach` loop in lines 11–14 displays each of the `token` array's elements in message boxes. When the loop executes, four message boxes will be displayed, one after the other, showing the strings `"one"`, `"two"`, `"three"`, and `"four"`.

Some situations require that you use multiple characters as delimiters in the same string. For example, look at the following e-mail address:

```
joe@gaddisbooks.com
```

This string uses two delimiters: `@` (the *at* symbol) and `.` (the period). To extract the tokens from this string, we must specify both characters as delimiters. Here is an example:

```
 1 // Create a String to tokenize.
 2 string str = "joe@gaddisbooks.com";
 3
 4 // Create an array of delimiters.
 5 char[] delim = { '@', '.' };
 6
 7 // Get the tokens from the string.
 8 string[] tokens = str.Split(delim);
 9
10 // Display each token.
11 foreach (string s in tokens)
12 {
13     MessageBox.Show(s);
14 }
```

Let's take a closer look at the code:

- Line 2 declares a `string` variable named `str`, initialized with the string `"joe@gaddisbooks.com"`.
- Line 5 declares a `char` array named `delim.`, initialized with the characters `'@'` and `'.'`.

- Line 8 declares a `string` array named `tokens`. The `tokens` array is initialized with the array that is returned from the `str.Split(delim)` method call. After this statement executes, the `tokens` array will have three elements, containing the strings `"joe"`, `"gaddisbooks"`, and `"com"`.
- The `foreach` loop in lines 11–14 displays each of the `token` array's elements in message boxes. When the loop executes, four message boxes will be displayed, one after the other, showing the strings `"joe"`, `"gaddisbooks"`, and `"com"`.

Trimming a String before Tokenizing

When you are tokenizing a string that was entered by the user and you are using characters other than white spaces as delimiters, you probably want to trim the string before tokenizing it. Otherwise, if the user enters leading white-space characters, they will become part of the first token. Likewise, if the user enters trailing white-space characters, they will become part of the last token. For example, look at the following code:

```
1 // Create a string with leading and trailing whitespaces.
2 String str = "   one;two;three   ";
3
4 // Create a char array containing the semicolon.
5 char[] delim = { ';' };
6
7 // Get the tokens from the string.
8 string[] tokens = str.Split(delim);
9
10 // Display each token.
11 foreach (string s in tokens)
12 {
13     MessageBox.Show("*" + s + "*");
14 }
```

This code produces three message boxes, displaying the following output:

```
*   one*
*two*
*three   *
```

Notice that the first token contains the leading spaces and the last token contains the trailing spaces. To prevent leading and/or trailing white-space characters from being included in the first and last tokens, use the `Trim` method to remove them. Here is the same code, modified to use the `Trim` method:

```
1 // Create a string with leading and trailing white spaces.
2 String str = "   one;two;three   ";
3
4 // Create a char array containing the semicolon.
5 char[] delim = { ';' };
6
7 // Trim the string.
8 str = str.Trim();
9
10 // Get the tokens from the string.
11 string[] tokens = str.Split(delim);
12
13 // Display each token.
14 foreach (string s in tokens)
15 {
16     MessageBox.Show("*" + s + "*");
17 }
```

This code produces three message boxes, displaying the following output:

```
*one*
*two*
*three*
```

In Tutorial 8-4 you complete an application that reads and tokenizes data from a file that has been exported by Microsoft Excel.

Tutorial 8-4:
Completing the *CSV Reader* Application

A professor keeps her students' test scores in a Microsoft Excel spreadsheet. Figure 8-4 shows a set of five test scores for five students. Each column holds a test score, and each row represents the scores for one student.

Figure 8-4 Microsoft Excel spreadsheet

	A	B	C	D	E	F
1	87	79	91	82	94	
2	72	79	81	74	88	
3	94	92	81	89	96	
4	77	56	67	81	79	
5	79	82	85	81	90	
6						

Suppose the professor wants you to write a C# application that reads the test scores from the Excel spreadsheet and performs some operation with them. Excel, like many commercial applications, has the ability to export data to a text file. When the data in a spreadsheet is exported, each row is written to a line, and the values of the cells are separated by commas. For example, when the data shown in Figure 8-4 is exported, it will be written to a text file in the following format:

```
87,79,91,82,94
72,79,81,74,88
94,92,81,89,96
77,56,67,81,79
79,82,85,81,90
```

This is called the **comma separated value**, or CSV, file format. When you save a spreadsheet in this format, Excel saves it to a file with the *.csv* extension. In a C# application, you can read a line from the file into a `string` variable and then use the `Split` method to extract the cell values as tokens.

To learn how this is done, you will complete the *CSV Reader* application. The application's form, which has already been created for you, is shown in Figure 8-5. A file named Grades.csv, which contains the test scores shown in Figure 8-4, has also been created for you. When you run the completed application and click the *Get Scores* button, it will read the test scores from the Grades.csv file. Each student's average test score will be calculated and displayed in the `averagesListBox` control.

Figure 8-5 The *CSV Reader* application's form

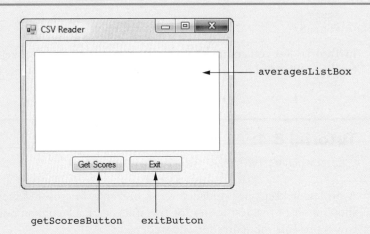

Step 1: Start Visual Studio (or Visual C# Express). Open the project named *CSV Reader* in the *Chap08* folder of the Student Sample Programs.

Step 2: Open the Form1 form's code in the code editor. Type the `using System.IO;` directive shown in line 9 of Program 8-4. This directive is necessary because we will create a `StreamReader` object to read input from a file.

Step 3: Next you create the Click event handlers for the Button controls. Switch back to the *Designer* and double-click the `getScoresButton` control. This opens the code editor, and you will see an empty event handler named `getScoresButton_Click`. Complete the event handler by typing the code shown in lines 22–73 in Program 8-4. Let's review this code:

Line 22: This is the beginning of a `try-catch` statement. The try block appears in lines 24–67, and the catch block appears in lines 71–72. If an exception is thrown by any statement in the try block, the program will jump to the catch block, and line 72 will display an error message.

Lines 24–28: These statements declare the following variables:

- `inputFile`, a `StreamReader` variable that will be used to read file input
- `line`, a `string` variable to hold a line that has been read from the file
- `count`, an `int` that will be used to count the number of students as a loop iterates (Notice that the `count` variable is initialized with the value 0.)
- `total`, an `int` that will hold the total of a student's test scores
- `average`, a `double` that will hold the average of a student's test scores

Line 31: This statement creates a `char` array named `delim`. The array has one element containing the character `','`.

Line 34: This statement opens the Grades.csv file. After the statement executes, the `inputFile` variable references a `StreamReader` object that is associated with the file.

Line 36: This is the beginning of a `while` loop that reads the contents of the Grades.csv file.

Line 39: This statement increments the `count` variable, which keeps count of the number of students. This statement will cause `count` to be set to 1 during the loop's first iteration, 2 during the loop's 2nd iteration, and so forth.

Line 42: This statement reads a line from the Grades.csv file and assigns it to the `line` variable.

Line 45: This statement tokenizes the `line` variable, using the `','` character as a delimiter. After this statement executes, the tokens are stored in the `tokens` array's elements. (The first test score is stored in `tokens[0]`, the second test score is stored in `tokens[1]`, etc.)

Line 48: This statement sets the `total` variable to 0. This is necessary because `total` is about to be used as an accumulator in calculating the total of the test scores that are in the `tokens` array.

Lines 52–55: This `foreach` loop steps through the elements of the `tokens` array. In line 54 each element is converted to an `int` and then added to the `total` variable. After the loop finishes, the total variable will contain the total of the test scores that are in the `tokens` array.

Line 59: This statement calculates the average of the test scores and assigns the result to the `average` variable. Note that the `(double)` cast operator is used to prevent integer division.

Lines 62–63: This statement displays the average, along with the student number, in the `averageListBox` control.

Line 67: This statement closes the Grades.csv file.

Step 4: Switch your view back to the *Designer* and double-click the `exitButton` control. In the code editor you see an empty event handler named `exitButton_Click`. Complete the event handler by typing the code shown in lines 78–79 in Program 8-4.

Step 5: Save the project. Then press [F5] on the keyboard or click the *Start Debugging* button (▶) on the toolbar to compile and run the application. When the application runs, click the *Get Scores* button. The student averages should appear as shown in Figure 8-6. When you are finished examining the averages, click the *Exit* button to exit the application.

Figure 8-6 Test averages displayed

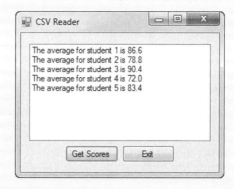

Program 8-4 Completed code for Form1 in the *CSV Reader* application

```
1 using System;
2 using System.Collections.Generic;
3 using System.ComponentModel;
4 using System.Data;
5 using System.Drawing;
6 using System.Linq;
7 using System.Text;
8 using System.Windows.Forms;
```

```
 9  using System.IO;
10
11  namespace CSV_Reader
12  {
13      public partial class Form1 : Form
14      {
15          public Form1()
16          {
17              InitializeComponent();
18          }
19
20          private void getScoresButton_Click(object sender, EventArgs e)
21          {
22              try
23              {
24                  StreamReader inputFile;  // To read the file
25                  string line;             // To hold a line from the file
26                  int count = 0;           // Student counter
27                  int total;               // Accumulator
28                  double average;          // Test score average
29
30                  // Create a delimiter array.
31                  char[] delim = { ',' };
32
33                  // Open the CSV file.
34                  inputFile = File.OpenText("Grades.csv");
35
36                  while (!inputFile.EndOfStream)
37                  {
38                      // Increment the student counter.
39                      count++;
40
41                      // Read a line from the file.
42                      line = inputFile.ReadLine();
43
44                      // Get the test scores as tokens.
45                      string[] tokens = line.Split(delim);
46
47                      // Set the accumulator to 0.
48                      total = 0;
49
50                      // Calculate the total of the
51                      // test score tokens.
52                      foreach (string str in tokens)
53                      {
54                          total += int.Parse(str);
55                      }
56
57                      // Calculate the average of these
58                      // test scores.
59                      average = (double)total / tokens.Length;
60
61                      // Display the average.
62                      averagesListBox.Items.Add("The average for student " +
63                          count + " is " + average.ToString("n1"));
64                  }
65
```

```
66                  // Close the file.
67                  inputFile.Close();
68              }
69              catch (Exception ex)
70              {
71                  // Display an error message.
72                  MessageBox.Show(ex.Message);
73              }
74          }
75
76          private void exitButton_Click(object sender, EventArgs e)
77          {
78              // Close the form.
79              this.Close();
80          }
81      }
82 }
```

Checkpoint

8.1 Declare a char variable named letter and assign the letter 'A' to the variable.

8.2 Write a statement that displays the value of a char variable named letterGrade in a message box.

8.3 Write a statement that declares a char variable named lastLetter and stores the last character of a string named alphabet in the variable.

8.4 Write a foreach loop that displays each character of a string variable named serialNumber in a message box.

8.5 Write the first line of an if statement that calls the char.IsPuncuation method and passes the last character of a string variable named sentence as an argument.

8.6 Write the first line of an if statement that calls the char.IsUpper method, passing a string variable named sentence and the index value for the first character of the sentence variable as arguments.

8.7 Write a statement that calls the char.ToUpper method, passes a char variable named lowercase as an argument, and stores the result in a char variable named uppercase.

8.8 What value does the char.ToLower function return if the argument is already lowercase?

8.9 Write a statement that calls the StartsWith method of a string named dessert, passes the string "strawberry" as an argument, and stores the result in a Boolean variable named found.

8.10 What value is returned by the IndexOf and LastIndexOf methods if the substring being searched for is not found?

8.11 A program has two string variables named str1 and str2. Write a statement that trims the leading and trailing whitespace characters from the str1 variable and assigns the result to the str2 variable.

8.12 A program has two string variables named vegetable and veggie. Write a statement that assigns an all lowercase copy of the vegetable variable to the veggie variable.

8.13 Declare a `char` array named `delimiters` and initialize it with the comma and semicolon characters.

8.14 What delimiter is used to separate data in a spreadsheet that has been exported to a text file with the .csv file extension?

8.3 Structures

CONCEPT: C# allows you to group several variables together into a single item known as a structure.

So far you have created applications that keep data in individual variables. Sometimes a relationship exists between different items of data. For example, a used-car dealer's inventory system might use the variables shown in the following declaration statements:

```
string make;      // The car's make
int year;         // The car's year model
double mileage;   // The car's mileage
```

All these variables are related because they will hold data about the same car. Their declaration statements, however, do not make it clear that they belong together. To create a relationship between variables, C# gives you the ability to package them together into a single item known as a structure. A **structure** is a data type you can create that contains one or more variables known as fields. The fields can be of different data types.

Before a structure can be used, it must be declared. Here is the general format that we use for declaring a structure:

```
struct StructureName
{
   Field Declarations
}
```

The first line of the structure declaration begins with the keyword `struct`, followed by the structure name. A set of braces appears next, and the braces contain one or more field declarations. Here is an example of a structure declaration:

```
1 struct Automobile
2 {
3     public string make;
4     public int year;
5     public double mileage;
6 }
```

The name of this structure is `Automobile`. In this book we always begin structure names with an uppercase letter. This is not required, but many programmers follow this practice because it helps distinguish structure names from variable names.

Lines 3, 4, and 5 declare three fields. Line 3 declares a `string` field named `make`, line 4 declares an `int` field named `year`, and line 5 declares a `double` field named `mileage`. Notice that each declaration begins with the keyword `public`. The keyword `public` is an access modifier that specifies the field can be directly accessed by statements outside the structure.

NOTE: Structures in C# are capable of much more than we discuss in this book. For example, in addition to declaring fields, you can also write methods inside of structures. We use structures for their simplest purpose only: to encapsulate a set of variables into a single item. If you find yourself using a structure for more than this, you should probably use a class instead. We discuss classes in Chapter 9.

In Chapter 2 we discussed the way that C# code is organized in namespaces, classes, and methods. Structure declarations can be written in a variety of places. For example, a structure declaration can appear in these locations:

- Outside the application's namespace
- Inside the application's namespace
- Inside a class
- Inside another structure

In this book we always declare structures inside an application's namespace but not inside of a class. Figure 8-7 shows where, in a form's code, that we typically write structure declarations. In the figure we have written the declaration of the `Automobile` structure inside the application's namespace but not inside the `Form1` class.

Figure 8-7 Where we typically write structure declarations

```
using System;
using System.Collections.Generic;
using System.ComponentModel;
using System.Data;
using System.Drawing;
using System.Linq;
using System.Text;
using System.Windows.Forms;

namespace Example
{
    struct Automobile
    {
        public string make;          We will write structure
        public int year;               declarations here.
        public double mileage;
    }

    public partial class Form1 : Form
    {
        public Form1()
        {
            InitializeComponent();
        }
    }
}
```

Keep in mind that a structure declaration does not create anything in memory. It simply tells the C# compiler what the structure is made of. Before you can use the structure to store data, you must create an **instance** of the structure in memory. (In programming terms, an *instance* and an *object* are the same thing. When you create an instance of a structure, you are creating an object.)

At the beginning of Chapter 7, we discussed value types and reference types. Structures are value types, so creating an instance of a structure is as simple as declaring a variable. For example, suppose we want to create an instance of the `Automobile` structure and we want the name of the instance to be `sportsCar`. We would write this:

```
Automobile sportsCar;
```

After this statement executes, an instance of the `Automobile` structure exists in memory. The name of the instance is `sportsCar`. As illustrated in Figure 8-8, the `sportsCar` object has three fields: `make`, `year`, and `mileage`.

Figure 8-8 The sportsCar object as an instance of the Automobile structure

sportsCar object

```
          make [                    ]
          year [                    ]
       mileage [                    ]
```

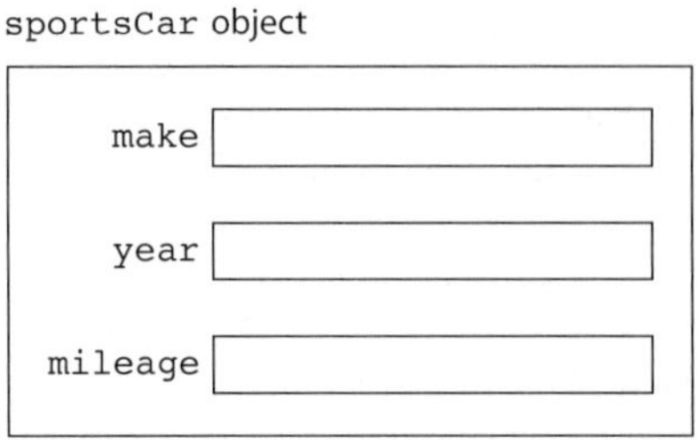

You can create multiple instances of a structure with a declaration statement, as shown here:

```
    Automobile sportsCar, pickupTruck;
```

This statement creates two instances of the Automobile structure. The objects are named sportsCar and pickupTruck. As illustrated in Figure 8-9, each object has its own make, year, and mileage fields.

Figure 8-9 Two instances of the Automobile structure

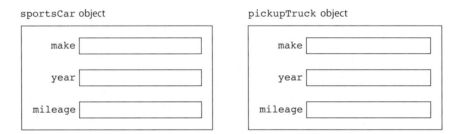

Using the new Operator to Create Structure Instances

When you create a structure object with a simple declaration statement, as previously shown, the object's fields are uninitialized, and if you attempt to use any of them before assigning them a value, a compiler error occurs. As an alternative, you can use the new operator to create an instance of a structure, as shown here:

```
    Automobile sportsCar = new Automobile();
```

This is the recommended technique for creating structure instances because the new operator not only creates the instance in memory, it also initializes the object's fields with the default value of 0. (If the structure contains any fields that are reference variables, they are initialized with the special value null.) Here is an example of creating two instances of the Automobile structure using the new operator:

```
    Automobile sportsCar = new Automobile();
    Automobile pickupTruck = new Automobile();
```

Accessing a Structure's Fields

Once you have created an instance of a structure, you can access its fields using the dot operator (a period). For example, suppose an application contains the Automobile structure declaration previously shown and the following code appears in a method:

```
1 Automobile sportsCar = new Automobile();
2 sportsCar.make = "Ford Mustang";
3 sportsCar.year = 1965;
4 sportsCar.mileage = 67500.0;
```

Line 1 creates an instance of the `Automobile` structure in memory. The object's name is `sportsCar`. Line 2 assigns the string `"Ford Mustang"` to the `sportsCar` object's make field. Line 3 assigns the value 1965 to the `sportsCar` object's year field. Line 4 assigns the value 67,500.0 to the `sportsCar` object's mileage field.

The following code shows another example using the same `sportsCar` object. These statements display the values of the object's fields in message boxes.

```
1 MessageBox.Show(sportsCar.make);
2 MessageBox.Show(sportsCar.year.ToString());
3 MessageBox.Show(sportsCar.mileage.ToString());
```

The following is another example. This statement displays a message such as `"1965 Ford Mustang with 67500 miles."`

```
MessageBox.Show(sportsCar.year + " " + sportsCar.make +
    " with " + sportsCar.mileage + " miles.");
```

Assigning One Structure Object to Another

You can use the assignment operator (=) to assign one structure object to another. For example, assume that `car1` and `car2` are both instances of the `Automobile` structure. The following statement assigns `car1` to `car2`:

```
car2 = car1;
```

After this statement executes, the `car2` object's fields contain the same values as the `car1` object's fields.

Passing Structure Objects to Methods

As with other types of objects, you can pass a structure object as an argument to a method. The following code shows a method named `DisplayAuto` that has been written to accept an instance of the `Automobile` structure as an argument:

```
1 private void DisplayAuto(Automobile auto)
2 {
3     MessageBox.Show(auto.year + " " + auto.make +
4         " with " + auto.mileage + " miles.");
5 }
```

Notice in line 1 that the method has a parameter variable named `auto`, and its data type is `Automobile`. When we call this method, we pass an `Automobile` object as an argument, as shown in the following code:

```
 1 // Create an instance of the Automobile structure.
 2 Automobile sportsCar = new Automobile();
 3
 4 // Assign values to the object's fields.
 5 sportsCar.make = "Chevy Corvette";
 6 sportsCar.year = 1970;
 7 sportsCar.mileage = 50000.0;
 8
 9 // Display the object's fields.
10 DisplayAuto(sportsCar);
```

In line 10 the `sportsCar` object is passed as an argument to the `DisplayAuto` method. Inside the `DisplayAuto` method, the `auto` parameter contains a copy of the `sportsCar` object.

Structure objects can be passed by value or by reference. Normally, structure objects are passed by value. The parameter variable contains a copy of the argument, and any changes that are made to the parameter do not affect the original argument. If the receiving method needs to change the contents of the original argument, however, the `ref` or `out` keywords can be used in the parameter declaration. The following code shows a method that uses a reference parameter of the `Automobile` type. Assume that the application's form has `TextBox` controls named `makeTextBox`, `yearTextBox`, and `mileageTextBox`.

```
 1 private void GetData(ref Automobile auto)
 2 {
 3     try
 4     {
 5         // Get the data from the TextBoxes.
 6         auto.make = makeTextBox.Text;
 7         auto.year = int.Parse(yearTextBox.Text);
 8         auto.mileage = double.Parse(mileageTextBox.Text);
 9     }
10     catch (Exception ex)
11     {
12         // Display the exception message.
13         MessageBox.Show(ex.Message);
14     }
15 }
```

Notice that the `auto` parameter is declared with the `ref` keyword. The statements in lines 6–8 get data from the TextBox controls and assign that data to the fields of the `auto` parameter. Since `auto` is a `ref` parameter, the values are actually assigned to the object that is passed as an argument to the method.

When we call this method, we pass an `Automobile` object by reference, as shown here:

```
1 // Create an instance of the Automobile structure.
2 Automobile car = new Automobile();
3
4 // Get data for the object.
5 GetData(ref car);
```

After the method executes, the `car` object contains the data that was entered into the TextBox controls.

Comparing Structure Objects

You cannot perform comparison operations directly on structure objects. For example, assume that `sportsCar` and `raceCar` are instances of the `Automobile` structure. The following statement will cause an error.

```
if (sportsCar == raceCar) // Error!
```

In order to compare two structure objects, you must compare the individual fields, as shown in the following code.

```
if (sportsCar.make == raceCar.make &&
    sportsCar.year == raceCar.year &&
    sportsCar.mileage == raceCar.mileage)
{
    MessageBox.Show("The two are equal.");
}
```

Arrays of Structure Objects

Structure objects can be stored in an array. For example, assume the `Automobile` structure previously shown exists in an application. The following code creates an array of five `Automobile` objects:

```
const int SIZE = 5;
Automobile[] cars = new Automobile[SIZE];
```

When you create a structure array, each element of the array is a structure instance and the fields of each instance are initialized to 0. (If any field is a reference variable, it is initialized to the value `null`.)

Each element of a structure array may be accessed through a subscript. For example, `cars[0]` is the first object in the array, `cars[1]` is the second, and so forth. To access a field of any element, simply place the dot operator and field name after the subscript. For example, the following expression refers to the `mileage` member of `cars[2]`:

```
cars[2].mileage
```

The following `for` loop steps through the `cars` array, displaying the data stored in each element:

```
for (int index = 0; index < cars.Length; index++)
{
    MessageBox.Show(cars[index].year + " " +
        cars[index].make + " with " +
        cars[index].mileage + " miles.");
}
```

You can also use the `foreach` loop to iterate over all of the elements in a structure array, as shown in the following code:

```
foreach (Automobile aCar in cars)
{
    MessageBox.Show(aCar.year + " " +
        aCar.make + " with " +
        aCar.mileage + " miles.");
}
```

Storing Structure Objects in a `List`

In Chapter 7 we discussed the `List` class, which is a container for storing a collection of objects. Here is an example of how you would create a `List` that can hold `Automobile` objects:

```
List<Automobile> carList = new List<Automobile>();
```

This statement creates a `List` object, referenced by the `carList` variable. Notice that the word `Automobile` is written inside angled brackets, `<>`, immediately after the word `List`. This specifies that the `List` can hold only objects of the `Automobile` data type.

To add a structure object to a `List`, you use the `Add` method. The following code shows an example:

```
1 // Create a List to hold Automobile objects.
2 List<Automobile> carList = new List<Automobile>();
3
4 // Create an instance of the Automobile structure.
5 Automobile sportsCar = new Automobile();
6
7 // Assign values to the object's fields.
```

```
 8 sportsCar.make = "Chevy Corvette";
 9 sportsCar.year = 1970;
10 sportsCar.mileage = 50000.0;
11
12 // Add the object to the List.
13 carList.Add(sportsCar);
```

The statement in line 2 creates a List named carList that can hold Automobile objects. Line 5 creates an instance of the Automobile structure named sportsCar, and lines 8–10 assign values to the object's fields. Line 13 adds the object to the List.

Keep in mind that structure instances are value type objects, and when you add a value type object to a List, the List will contain a copy of the object. For example look at the following code:

```
 1 // Create a List to hold Automobile objects.
 2 List<Automobile> carList = new List<Automobile>();
 3
 4 // Create an instance of the Automobile structure.
 5 Automobile sportsCar = new Automobile();
 6
 7 // Assign values to the object's fields.
 8 sportsCar.make = "Chevy Corvette";
 9 sportsCar.year = 1970;
10 sportsCar.mileage = 50000.0;
11
12 // Add the object to the List.
13 carList.Add(sportsCar);
14
15 // Assign new values to the object's fields.
16 sportsCar.make = "Ford Mustang";
17 sportsCar.year = 1965;
18 sportsCar.mileage = 67500.0;
19
20 // Add the object to the List.
21 carList.Add(sportsCar);
```

The statement in line 2 creates a List named carList that can hold Automobile objects. Lines 5–10 create an Automobile object named sportsCar and assign values to the object's fields. Line 13 adds the sportsCar object to the List. When line 13 executes, a copy of the sportsCar object is made and stored in the List. (This happens because the sportsCar object is a value type object.) At this point, two instances of the Automobile structure exist: the sportsCar object and the copy of the sportsCar object that is in the List.

Lines 16–18 assign new values to the sportsCar object's fields, and then line 21 adds the sportsCar object to the List again. Once more, a copy of the sportsCar object is made and added to the List. At this point, three instances of the Automobile structure exist: the sportsCar object and the two objects that are in the List.

Let's look at a complete program that demonstrates structure objects can be added to a List. In the *Chap08* folder of the Student Sample Programs that accompany this book, you will find a project named *Car List*. Figure 8-10 shows the application's form.

Figure 8-10 The *Car List* application's form

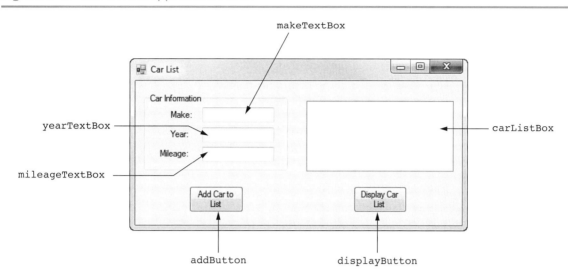

makeTextBox

yearTextBox

mileageTextBox

carListBox

addButton

displayButton

When you run the application, you can enter data about a car into the TextBox controls. When you click the addButton control, that data is assigned to an Automobile object and then added to a List. You can do this as many times as you wish. When you click the displayButton control, the data from each object in the List is displayed in the carListBox control. Figure 8-11 shows an example of the application's form after four objects have been added to the List and the displayButton control has been clicked.

Figure 8-11 The *Car List* application's form with data displayed

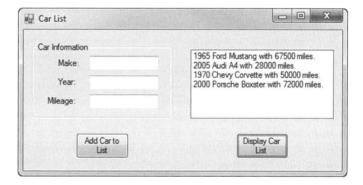

Program 8-5 shows the application's Form1 code. Let's take a closer look:

Lines 12–17: The Automobile structure is declared in these lines.

Line 22: This statement creates a List that can hold Automobile objects. Notice that the List is declared as a field in the Form1 class. All the methods in the class can access it.

Lines 32–46: The GetData method appears in these lines. The method accepts an Automobile object, by reference, as an argument. The data that has been entered into the form's TextBox controls is assigned to the object's fields.

Lines 48–66: The addButton_Click event handler appears in these lines. Here is a summary of the event handler's code:

- Line 51 creates the car object, which is an instance of the Automobile structure.
- Line 54 calls the GetData method, passing the car object, by reference, as an argument. After this statement executes, the car object's fields contain the data that was entered into the form's TextBoxes by the user.

- Line 57 adds a copy of the car object to the carList.
- Lines 60–62 clear the contents of the TextBoxes.
- Line 65 gives the focus to the makeTextBox control.

Lines 68–86: The displayButton_Click event handler appears in these lines. Here is a summary of the event handler's code:

- Line 71 declares a string variable named output. This is used to hold a line of output that is displayed in the ListBox control.
- Line 74 clears the ListBox control's current contents.
- The foreach loop in lines 77–85 displays data about each object in the carList.
  - The statement in lines 80–81 creates a line of output and assigns it to the output variable.
  - Line 84 adds the output variable to the carListBox control.

Program 8-5 Code for Form1 in the *Car List* application

```
 1 using System;
 2 using System.Collections.Generic;
 3 using System.ComponentModel;
 4 using System.Data;
 5 using System.Drawing;
 6 using System.Linq;
 7 using System.Text;
 8 using System.Windows.Forms;
 9
10 namespace Car_List
11 {
12     struct Automobile
13     {
14         public string make;
15         public int year;
16         public double mileage;
17     }
18
19     public partial class Form1 : Form
20     {
21         // Create a List as a field.
22         private List<Automobile> carList = new List<Automobile>();
23
24         public Form1()
25         {
26             InitializeComponent();
27         }
28
29         // The GetData method gets the data entered
30         // by the user and assigns it to the parameter
31         // object's fields.
32         private void GetData(ref Automobile auto)
33         {
34             try
35             {
36                 // Get the data from the TextBoxes.
37                 auto.make = makeTextBox.Text;
38                 auto.year = int.Parse(yearTextBox.Text);
39                 auto.mileage = double.Parse(mileageTextBox.Text);
40             }
41             catch (Exception ex)
42             {
43                 // Display the exception message.
44                 MessageBox.Show(ex.Message);
45             }
```

```
46              }
47
48          private void addButton_Click(object sender, EventArgs e)
49          {
50              // Create an instance of the Automobile structure.
51              Automobile car = new Automobile();
52
53              // Get the data entered by the user.
54              GetData(ref car);
55
56              // Add the car object to the List.
57              carList.Add(car);
58
59              // Clear the TextBoxes.
60              makeTextBox.Clear();
61              yearTextBox.Clear();
62              mileageTextBox.Clear();
63
64              // Reset the focus.
65              makeTextBox.Focus();
66          }
67
68          private void displayButton_Click(object sender, EventArgs e)
69          {
70              // Declare a string to hold a line of output.
71              string output;
72
73              // Clear the ListBox's current contents.
74              carListBox.Items.Clear();
75
76              // Display the car info in the ListBox.
77              foreach (Automobile aCar in carList)
78              {
79                  // Make a line of output.
80                  output = aCar.year + " " + aCar.make +
81                      " with " + aCar.mileage + " miles.";
82
83                  // Add the line of output to the ListBox.
84                  carListBox.Items.Add(output);
85              }
86          }
87      }
88 }
```

In Tutorial 8-5 you complete a phone book application that uses a `List` of structure objects.

Tutorial 8-5:
Completing the *Phonebook* Application

In this tutorial you complete the *Phonebook* application. When the application is complete, it will let you select a person's name from a ListBox control, and then it will display that person's phone number. Figure 8-12 shows an example of how the form will appear at run time. In the figure, Kevin Brown has been selected in the ListBox control, and Kevin's phone number is displayed in a Label control. The application's form has already been created for you and is shown in Figure 8-13 with the names of some of its controls.

Figure 8-12 The *Phonebook* application's form with a name selected

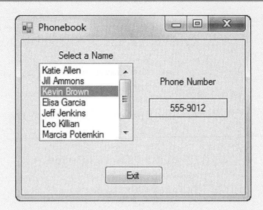

Figure 8-13 The *Phonebook* application's form

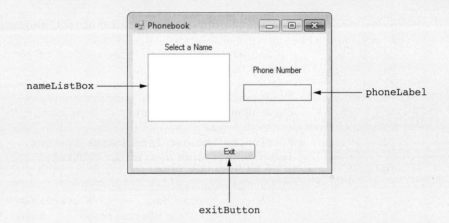

Before you start writing code, let's go over a summary of how the application will work. A file named PhoneList.txt, containing several names and corresponding phone numbers, has been created for you. (It is located in the project's *bin\debug* folder.) Its contents are shown in Figure 8-14. Notice that each line in the file contains a name, followed by a comma, followed by a phone number.

Figure 8-14 The contents of the PhoneList.txt file

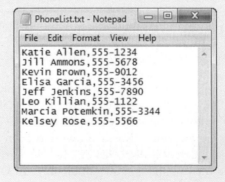

When the application starts, the form's Load event handler calls a method named ReadFile. The ReadFile method reads the contents of the PhoneList.txt file. Each line that is read from the file will be tokenized, using the comma character as a delimiter. This will result in two string tokens: one containing a person's name and the other containing a phone number. The tokens are stored in an instance of the following PhoneBookEntry structure:

```
struct PhoneBookEntry
{
    public string name;
    public string phone;
}
```

The PhoneBookEntry object is then added to a List. When the ReadFile method is finished, the List will contain a PhoneBookEntry object for each line in the PhoneList.txt file.

The Load event handler then calls another method named DisplayNames. The DisplayNames method steps through the List, getting the name field of each object and adding the name to the ListBox control. When the DisplayNames method is finished, the ListBox control will display all the names that are contained in the List.

When the user clicks a name in the ListBox control, a SelectedIndexChanged event occurs. You are to write an event handler that responds to this event. The event handler gets the index of the selected item in the ListBox control, and it uses that index to retrieve an object from the List. The object contains the phone number for the selected name, which is displayed in a Label control.

Step 1: Start Visual Studio (or Visual C# Express). Open the project named *Phonebook* in the *Chap08* folder of the Student Sample Programs.

Step 2: Open the Form1 form's code in the code editor. Type the using System.IO; directive shown in line 9 of Program 8-6. This directive is necessary because we will create a StreamReader object to read input from a file.

Step 3: Write the declaration of the PhoneBookEntry structure, shown in lines 13–17. Make sure you write the declaration inside the Phonebook namespace, exactly as shown in Program 8-6.

Step 4: Next you write the comment and the declaration for phoneList, which appears in lines 21–23 in Program 8-6. Notice that phoneList is declared as a field in the Form1 class. It is available to all the methods in the class.

Step 5: Write the comments and code for the ReadFile method, shown in lines 30–71 of Program 8-6. The ReadFile method opens the PhoneList.txt file. The while loop that begins in line 50 iterates until the end of the file is reached. In each iteration of the loop, the following lines of code are executed:

Line 53: This statement reads a line from the file and assigns it to the line variable.

Line 56: This statement tokenizes the line variable, using the comma character as a delimiter. The tokens are assigned to the tokens array. (After this statement executes, tokens[0] will contain a name and tokens[1] will contain a phone number.)

Lines 59–60: These statements assign the tokens to the name and phone fields of the entry object (which is an instance of the PhoneBookEntry structure).

Line 63: This statement adds the entry object to the phoneList collection.

Figure 8-15 illustrates the steps performed in these lines of code. After the loop is finished, `phoneList` will contain a `PhoneBookEntry` object for each line in the PhoneList.txt file.

Figure 8-15 A summary of lines 53–63

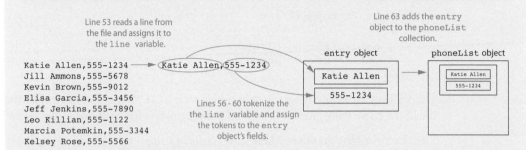

Step 6: Write the comments and code for the `DisplayNames` method, shown in lines 73–81 of Program 8-6. The `foreach` loop in line 77 steps through all the objects in `phoneList`. For each object in `phoneList`, line 79 adds the `name` field to the `nameListBox` control.

Note that the names are added to the ListBox control in the same order that they appear in `phoneList`. For example,

- The name "Katie Allen" is at index 0 in the ListBox, and the object containing "Katie Allen" is at index 0 in `phoneList`.
- The name "Jill Ammons" is at index 1 in the ListBox, and the object containing " Jill Ammons " is at index 1 in `phoneList`.

Figure 8-16 illustrates how the objects in `phoneList` and the names in the `nameListBox` control are related by their indexes. You take advantage of this relationship in Step 7 when you write the code to retrieve an object from `phoneList`.

Figure 8-16 Objects in `phoneList` and names in `nameListBox` as related by their indexes

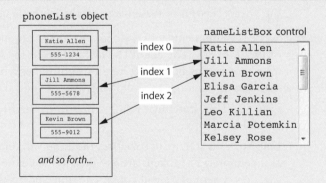

 NOTE: When the items in two data structures are related by their indexes, it is said that a **parallel relationship** exists between the data structures.

Step 7: Next you create the form's Load event handler. Switch back to the *Designer* and double-click any part of the form that does not contain a control. This opens the code editor, and you will see an empty event handler named `Form1_Load`. Complete the event handler by typing the code shown in lines 85–89 in Program 8-6. The statement in line 86 calls the `ReadFile` method, and line 89 calls the `DisplayNames` method.

Step 8: Now you create the SelectedIndexChange event handler for the `nameListBox` control. Switch back to the *Designer* and double-click the `nameListBox` control. This opens the code editor, and you will see an empty event handler named `nameListBox_ SelectedIndexChange`. Complete the event handler by typing the code shown in lines 94–98 in Program 8-6.

We mentioned in Step 6 that the names in the ListBox and the objects in `phoneList` are related by their indexes. When the user selects a name from the ListBox, all we have to do is get that item's index and then use that same index to retrieve the corresponding object from `phoneList`. That is exactly what happens in this event handler. Line 95 gets the index of the selected item in the `nameListBox` control and assigns it to the `index` variable. Line 98 uses the `index` variable to get an object from `phoneList`. The retrieved object's `phone` field is assigned to `phoneLabel.Text`.

Step 9: Switch your view back to the *Designer* and double-click the `exitButton` control. In the code editor you will see an empty event handler named `exitButton_Click`. Complete the event handler by typing the code shown in lines 103–104 in Program 8-6.

Step 10: Save the project. Then, press F5 on the keyboard or click the *Start Debugging* button (▶) on the toolbar to compile and run the application. When the application runs, select various names in the ListBox to confirm that the application works property. When you are finished, click the *Exit* button to exit the application.

Program 8-6 Completed code for Form1 in the *Phonebook* application

```
 1 using System;
 2 using System.Collections.Generic;
 3 using System.ComponentModel;
 4 using System.Data;
 5 using System.Drawing;
 6 using System.Linq;
 7 using System.Text;
 8 using System.Windows.Forms;
 9 using System.IO;
10
11 namespace Phonebook
12 {
13     struct PhoneBookEntry
14     {
15         public string name;
16         public string phone;
17     }
18
19     public partial class Form1 : Form
20     {
21         // Field to hold a list of PhoneBookEntry objects.
```

```
22          private List<PhoneBookEntry> phoneList =
23              new List<PhoneBookEntry>();
24
25          public Form1()
26          {
27              InitializeComponent();
28          }
29
30          // The ReadFile method reads the contents of the
31          // PhoneList.txt file and stores it as PhoneBookEntry
32          // objects in the phoneList.
33          private void ReadFile()
34          {
35              try
36              {
37                  StreamReader inputFile; // To read the file
38                  string line;            // To hold a line from the file
39
40                  // Create an instance of the PhoneBookEntry structure.
41                  PhoneBookEntry entry = new PhoneBookEntry();
42
43                  // Create a delimiter array.
44                  char[] delim = { ',' };
45
46                  // Open the PhoneList file.
47                  inputFile = File.OpenText("PhoneList.txt");
48
49                  // Read the lines from the file.
50                  while (!inputFile.EndOfStream)
51                  {
52                      // Read a line from the file.
53                      line = inputFile.ReadLine();
54
55                      // Tokenize the line
56                      string[] tokens = line.Split(delim);
57
58                      // Store the tokens in the entry object.
59                      entry.name = tokens[0];
60                      entry.phone = tokens[1];
61
62                      // Add the entry object to the List.
63                      phoneList.Add(entry);
64                  }
65              }
66              catch (Exception ex)
67              {
68                  // Display an error message.
69                  MessageBox.Show(ex.Message);
70              }
71          }
72
73          // The DisplayNames method displays the list of names
74          // in the namesListBox control.
75          private void DisplayNames()
76          {
77              foreach (PhoneBookEntry entry in phoneList)
78              {
79                  nameListBox.Items.Add(entry.name);
80              }
```

```
 81                }
 82
 83            private void Form1_Load(object sender, EventArgs e)
 84            {
 85                // Read the PhoneList.txt file.
 86                ReadFile();
 87
 88                // Display the names.
 89                DisplayNames();
 90            }
 91
 92            private void nameListBox_SelectedIndexChanged(object sender, EventArgs e)
 93            {
 94                // Get the index of the selected item.
 95                int index = nameListBox.SelectedIndex;
 96
 97                // Display the corresponding phone number.
 98                phoneLabel.Text = phoneList[index].phone;
 99            }
100
101            private void exitButton_Click(object sender, EventArgs e)
102            {
103                // Close the form.
104                this.Close();
105            }
106        }
107 }
```

Checkpoint

8.15 When a structure is declared, what is created in memory?

8.16 What does the keyword `public` specify about a field declared in a structure?

8.17 When you create an instance of a structure, what are you creating?

8.18 What effect does the `new` operator have when creating an instance of a structure?

8.19 Once you have created an instance of a structure, how can you access its fields?

8.20 Suppose an application contains a structure named `Engine` and that `motor1` and `motor2` are instances of the `Engine` structure. Write a statement that assigns `motor1` to `motor2`.

8.21 Write a statement that creates an array named `motors` that can hold 100 `Engine` objects.

8.22 What causes a parallel relationship to exist between data structures?

8.4 Enumerated Types

CONCEPT: An enumerated data type is a programmer-defined data type. It consists of predefined constants, known as enumerators, that represent integer values.

Sometimes, in a program, you need a way to represent values that cannot be stored in memory in a straightforward manner. For example, suppose you are writing a program that works with the days of the week (Sunday, Monday, Tuesday, etc.), and you need some way to represent each day of the week in memory. One solution is to let the integers 0 through 6 represent the days of the week; 0 could represent Sunday, 1 could represent Monday, and so forth. Although this approach will work, it has some drawbacks.

For example, it may not be clear to anyone else reading the code that the values 0 through 6 represent the days of the week. Also, you might decide that Sunday is the first day of the week, whereas someone else assumes that Monday is the first day of the week. When that other person sees the value 0, he or she might think that it represents Monday.

A better solution for dealing with this type of data is to create an enumerated data type. An **enumerated data type** is a data type that you can create. When you create an enumerated data type, you specify a set of symbolic values that belong to that data type. Here is an example of an enumerated data type declaration:

```
enum Day { Sunday, Monday, Tuesday, Wednesday,
           Thursday, Friday, Saturday }
```

An enumerated data type declaration begins with the keyword `enum`, followed by the name of the type, followed by a list of identifiers inside braces. The example declaration creates an enumerated data type named `Day`. The identifiers `Sunday`, `Monday`, `Tuesday`, `Wednesday`, `Thursday`, `Friday`, and `Saturday`, which are listed inside the braces, are known as **enumerators**. They represent the values that belong to the `Day` data type.

NOTE: Notice that the enumerators are not enclosed in quotation marks; therefore, they are not strings. Enumerators must be legal C# identifiers.

The enumerators are constants that represent integer values. When you declare an enumerated type, the enumerators are assigned integer values, starting with 0. For example, in the `Day` data type, the `Day.Sunday` enumerator is assigned the value 0, the `Day.Monday` enumerator is assigned the value 1, and so forth.

An enum declaration can appear in any of the following places:

- Outside the application's namespace
- Inside the application's namespace
- Inside a class

In this book we always write `enum` declarations in the same region that we write structure declarations: inside an application's namespace but not inside a class.

Once you have created an enumerated data type in your program, you can declare variables of that type. For example, the following statement declares `workDay` as a variable of the `Day` type:

```
Day workDay;
```

We refer to this as an enum variable. Because `workDay` is a variable of the `Day` type, the values that we can assign to it are the `Day` type's enumerators. For example, the following statement assigns the value `Day.Wednesday` to the `workDay` variable:

```
workDay = Day.Wednesday;
```

Notice that we assigned `Day.Wednesday` instead of just `Wednesday`. The name `Day.Wednesday` is the fully qualified name of the `Day` type's `Wednesday` enumerator. You have to use an enumerator's fully qualified name because it is possible to have the same enumerator appear in multiple enumerated types. Here is another example:

```
Day weekendDay = Day.Saturday;
```

This statement declares a `Day` variable named `weekendDay` and initializes it with the value `Day.Saturday`.

The following code shows another example. (Assume the application's form has a radio button control named `mondayRadioButton`.)

```
1 Day selectedDay;
2 if (mondayRadioButton.Checked)
3 {
4     selectedDay = Day.Monday;
5 }
```

In this code, line 1 declares a `Day` variable named `selectedDay`. The `if` statement in line 2 determines whether the `mondayRadioButton` control is selected. If it is, the statement in line 4 assigns `Day.Monday` to the `selectedDay` variable.

You can make comparisons with enum variables and enumerators. The following code shows an example. (Assume `selectedDay` is a `Day` variable.)

```
1 if (selectedDay == Day.Wednesday)
2 {
3     MessageBox.Show("Halfway through the week!");
4 }
```

The `if` statement in line 1 determines whether the `selectedDay` variable is equal to `Day.Wednesday`. If it is, line 3 displays a message box.

The following code shows how an enum variable can be tested in a `switch` statement. (Assume `selectedDay` is a `Day` variable.)

```
1 switch (selectedDay)
2 {
3     case Day.Sunday:
4         MessageBox.Show("Rest.");
5         break;
6     case Day.Monday:
7         MessageBox.Show("Back to work.");
8         break;
9     case Day.Tuesday:
10        MessageBox.Show("Just a regular work day.");
11        break;
12    case Day.Wednesday:
13        MessageBox.Show("Halfway through the week.");
14        break;
15    case Day.Thursday:
16        MessageBox.Show("Almost there.");
17        break;
18    case Day.Friday:
19        MessageBox.Show("Last day!");
20        break;
21    case Day.Saturday:
22        MessageBox.Show("Sleep late today.");
23        break;
24 }
```

In line 1 the `switch` statement tests the `selectedDay` variable. Depending on the value of the variable, the program branches to the appropriate `case` statement.

Using an Enumerator's or `enum` Variable's `ToString` Method

Enumerators and `enum` variables have a `ToString` method. When you call an enumerator's `ToString` method, it returns the name of the enumerator as a string. For example, the following code will display the string `"Sunday"` in a message box:

```
MessageBox.Show(Day.Sunday.ToString());
```

When you call an `enum` variable's `ToString` method, it returns the name of the value that the variable contains, as a string. For example, the following code will display the string `"Thursday"` in a message box:

```
Day today = Day.Thursday;
MessageBox.Show(today.ToString());
```

When you use the + operator with a string and an `enum` variable, the `enum` variable's `ToString` method is implicitly called. (The same thing happens when you use the + operator with an `int` variable. The `int` variable's `ToString` method is implicitly called.) Here is an example:

```
Day today = Day.Thursday;
MessageBox.Show("Today is " + today);
```

This code will display the string `"Today is Thursday"` in a message box.

In Tutorial 8-6 you complete an application that uses an enumerated type to represent the colors of the spectrum.

Tutorial 8-6:
Completing the *Color Spectrum* Application

The mnemonic ROY G BIV is commonly used to help remember the following sequence of colors of the visible spectrum: red, orange, yellow, green, blue, indigo, and violet. In this tutorial you complete the *Color Spectrum* application, which shows these colors. The application will display the name of a color if you click it.

The application's form, which has already been created for you, is shown in Figure 8-17. The colors are actually a set of Label controls with their BackColor properties set to the appropriate color.

Figure 8-17 The *Color Spectrum* application's form

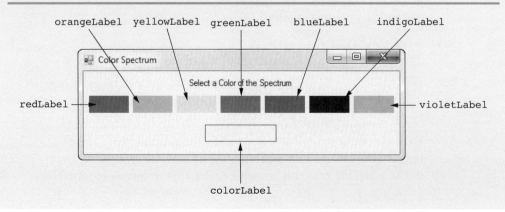

Step 1: Start Visual Studio (or Visual C# Express). Open the project named *Color Spectrum* in the *Chap08* folder of the Student Sample Programs.

Step 2: Open the Form1 form's code in the code editor. Write the declaration of the Spectrum enumerated type, shown in lines 12–16 of Program 8-7. Make sure you write the declaration inside the Color_Spectrum namespace, exactly as shown in Program 8-7. Notice that the enumerators in the Spectrum type represent the colors with which you will be working.

Step 3: Write the comments and code for the DisplayColor method, shown in lines 25–30 of Program 8-6. Notice in line 27 that this method has a parameter variable of the Spectrum type. When we call this method, we pass a Spectrum enumerator as an argument. In line 29, the name of the enumerator is displayed in the colorLabel control.

Step 4: Next you create the Click event handlers for the Label controls. Switch back to the *Designer* and double-click the redLabel control. This opens the code editor, and you will see an empty event handler named redLabel_Click. Complete the event handler by typing the statement shown in line 34 in Program 8-7. This statement calls the DisplayColor method, passing the Spectrum.Red eumerator as an argument.

Step 5: Repeat this process for the rest of the Label controls, writing the remaining Click event handlers shown in Program 8-7.

Step 6: Save the project. Then, press F5 on the keyboard, or click the *Start Debugging* button (▶) on the toolbar to compile and run the application. When the application runs, click the colors shown on the form to confirm that the application works property. When you are finished, click the *Exit* button to exit the application.

Program 8-7 Completed code for Form1 in the *Color Spectrum* application

```
1 using System;
2 using System.Collections.Generic;
3 using System.ComponentModel;
4 using System.Data;
5 using System.Drawing;
6 using System.Linq;
7 using System.Text;
8 using System.Windows.Forms;
9
10 namespace Color_Spectrum
11 {
12     enum Spectrum
13     {
14         Red, Orange, Yellow, Green,
15         Blue, Indigo, Violet
16     }
17
18     public partial class Form1 : Form
19     {
20         public Form1()
21         {
22             InitializeComponent();
23         }
24
```

```
25          // The DisplayColor method displays the
26          // name of a color.
27          private void DisplayColor(Spectrum color)
28          {
29              colorLabel.Text = color.ToString();
30          }
31
32          private void redLabel_Click(object sender, EventArgs e)
33          {
34              DisplayColor(Spectrum.Red);
35          }
36
37          private void orangeLabel_Click(object sender, EventArgs e)
38          {
39              DisplayColor(Spectrum.Orange);
40          }
41
42          private void yellowLabel_Click(object sender, EventArgs e)
43          {
44              DisplayColor(Spectrum.Yellow);
45          }
46
47          private void greenLabel_Click(object sender, EventArgs e)
48          {
49              DisplayColor(Spectrum.Green);
50          }
51
52          private void blueLabel_Click(object sender, EventArgs e)
53          {
54              DisplayColor(Spectrum.Blue);
55          }
56
57          private void indigoLabel_Click(object sender, EventArgs e)
58          {
59              DisplayColor(Spectrum.Indigo);
60          }
61
62          private void violetLabel_Click(object sender, EventArgs e)
63          {
64              DisplayColor(Spectrum.Violet);
65          }
66      }
67 }
```

Getting an Enumerator's or enum Variable's Integer Value

You cannot assign an enumerator directly to an int variable, but you can convert an enumerator to its underlying integer type by using a cast operator. Here is an example:

```
int value = (int)Day.Friday;
```

This statement declares an int variable named value and initializes it with the integer value of Day.Friday. After this statement executes, value will equal 5. Here is another example:

```
Day workDay = Day.Monday;
int value = (int)workDay;
```

The first statement declares a `Day` variable named `workDay`, initialized with `Day.Monday`. The second statement declares an `int` variable named `value` and initializes it with the integer value of the `workDay` variable. After this statement executes, `value` will equal 1.

Specifying Integer Values for Enumerators

By default, the enumerators in an enumerated data type are assigned the integer values 0, 1, 2, and so forth. If this is not appropriate, you can specify the values to be assigned, as in the following example.

```
enum Water { Freezing = 32, Boiling = 212 }
```

In this example, the `Water.Freezing` enumerator is assigned the integer value 32 and the `Water.Boiling` enumerator is assigned the integer value 212.

The integer values that you assign to enumerators do not have to be unique. For example, the following code shows an enumerated type named `MonthDays`. Its enumerators are `January`, `February`, `March`, and so forth. Notice that the values assigned to the enumerators are the days of the months (January has 31 days, February has 28 days, etc.) This data type might appear in an application that uses the days of each month.

```
1 enum MonthDays
2 {
3     January = 31, February = 28, March = 31,
4     April = 30, May = 31, June = 30,
5     July = 31, August = 31, September = 30,
6     October = 31, November = 30, December = 31
7 }
```

Comparing Enumerators and `enum` Variables

Previously you saw that enumerators and enum variables can be compared using the equality operator (==). You can also compare enumerators and enum variables with the other relational operators. For example, using the `Day` data type we have been discussing, the following expression is true.

```
Day.Friday > Day.Monday
```

The expression is true because the enumerator `Day.Friday` is stored in memory as 5 and the enumerator `Day.Monday` is stored as 1. The following code displays the message `"Friday is greater than Monday."`

```
1 if (Day.Friday > Day.Monday)
2 {
3   MessageBox.Show("Friday is greater than Monday.");
4 }
```

The following code shows another example that compares two enum variables. This code displays the message `"Friday is greater than Monday"`.

```
1 Day day1 = Day.Friday;
2 Day day2 = Day.Monday;
3
4 if (day1 > day2)
5 {
6     MessageBox.Show(day1 + " is greater than " + day2);
7 }
```

Enumerators and enum variables can be compared directly with integer values. For example, the following code displays the message `"Sunday is equal to zero."`

```
1 if (Day.Sunday == 0)
2 {
3   MessageBox.Show("Sunday is equal to zero.");
4 }
```

Using an `enum` Variable to Step Through an Array's Elements

Because enumerators represent integer values, they can be used in a loop to step through the elements of an array. For example, look at the following code:

```
1 decimal[] sales = { 1000, 2000, 3000, 4000,
2                     5000, 6000, 7000 };
3
4 for (Day dayCount = Day.Sunday; dayCount <= Day.Saturday; dayCount++)
5 {
6     MessageBox.Show("Sales for " + dayCount + " were " +
7         sales[(int)dayCount].ToString("c"));
8 }
```

Lines 1 and 2 create a `decimal` array named `sales`. The `for` loop that begins in line 4 uses an enum variable name `dayCount` as its counter variable. Notice the following about the loop:

- The `dayCount` variable is initialized with the value `Day.Sunday`.
- The loop iterates as long as `dayCount` is less than or equal to `Day.Saturday`.
- At the end of each iteration, `dayCount` is incremented.

In line 7 the expression `(int)dayCount` is used as an array subscript. As the loop executes, it displays the following messages:

- `"Sales for Sunday were $1,000.00"`
- `"Sales for Monday were $2,000.00"`
- `"Sales for Tuesday were $3,000.00"`
- `"Sales for Wednesday were $4,000.00"`
- `"Sales for Thursday were $5,000.00"`
- `"Sales for Friday were $6,000.00"`
- `"Sales for Saturday were $7,000.00"`

 Checkpoint

8.23 Look at the following declaration.

enum Flower { Rose, Daisy, Petunia }

a. What is the name of the data type?
b. In memory, what value will be stored for the enumerator `Flower.Rose`? For `Flower.Daisy`? For `Flower.Petunia`?
c. Write a statement that declares a variable of this enumerated type. The variable should be named `flora`. Initialize the variable with the `Flower.Petunia` enumerator.

8.24 What method do you use to display the string value of a enumerator?

8.25 How can you get the integer value of an enumerator?

8.5 The ImageList Control

CONCEPT: The ImageList control allows you to store a collection of images. At run time, you can retrieve an image from an ImageList control and display it in a PictureBox control.

The **ImageList control** is a container that can hold multiple images. As its name implies, it is a list of images. You can use an index to retrieve an image from an ImageList control and display the image in a PictureBox control.

There are a few guidelines that you should follow as you plan to use an ImageList control in an application:

- All the images stored in an ImageList control should be the same size.
- The images stored in an ImageList control can be no more than 256 by 256 pixels in size.
- All the images stored in an ImageList control should be in the same format (.bmp, .jpg, etc.)

Although these guidelines might seem restrictive, keep in mind that ImageList controls are designed to store small images such as icons or thumbnails. They also work well in game programs that display images such as cards.

You will find the ImageList control in the Components section of the Toolbox. When you double-click the ImageList tool in the Toolbox, an ImageList control is created in the component tray area, at the bottom of the *Designer*. (The ImageList control does not appear on the form.) Figure 8-18 shows an example. When you create ImageList controls, they are given default names such as `imageList1`, `imageList2`, and so on.

Figure 8-18 An ImageList control

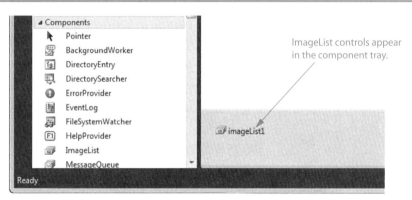

After you create an ImageList control, you should set its ImageSize property to the size of the images that you plan to store in the control. The default size is 16,16. You can set the ImageSize property to any value from 0,0 through 256,256. (If the value of the ImageSize property does not match the size of the images that are stored in the control, the images will appear distorted when you display them.)

Then, you can use the Images property to add images to the control. In the *Properties* window, click the ellipses button (⊡) that appears next to the Images property. This displays the *Images Collection Editor* window shown in Figure 8-19. Click the *Add* button, and an *Open* dialog box appears. Use the dialog box to locate and select the image file (or multiple image files) that you want to add to the ImageList control.

Figure 8-19 The *Images Collection Editor* window

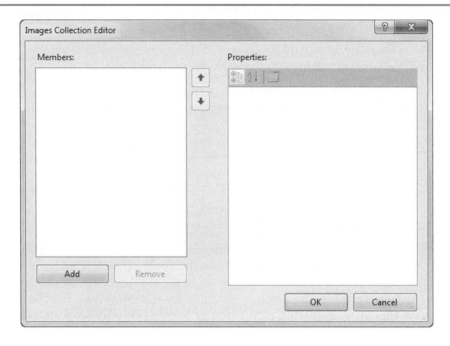

Figure 8-20 shows the *Images Collection Editor* window after four images have been added. The names of the images, which are shown in the *Members* list, are 2_Clubs.bmp, 2_Diamonds.bmp, 2_Hearts.bmp, and 2_Spades.bmp. Notice that an index value appears next to each image's name. You will use the index value later to retrieve images from the control. When you have added all the images that you want, click the *OK* button.

Figure 8-20 Four images added

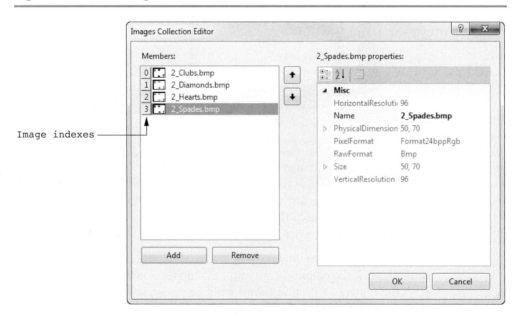

If you know the index value for a particular image, you can retrieve that image from the ImageList control and display it in a PictureBox. The following code shows an example. Assume `myImageList` is the name of an ImageList control and `myPictureBox` is the name of a PictureBox control.

```
myPictureBox.Image = myImageList.Images[5];
```

This statement gets the image at index 5 from `myImageList` and assigns it to the `myPictureBox` control's Image property. As a result, the image is displayed in the PictureBox.

In code, you can determine the number of images that are stored in an ImageList control by getting the value of the control's `Images.Count` property. The following code shows an example. Assume `myImageList` is the name of an ImageList control and `numberImages` is the name of an `int` variable.

```
numberImages = myImageList.Images.Count;
```

In Tutorial 8-7 you complete an application that randomly selects images from an ImageList control and displays them in a PictureBox.

Tutorial 8-7:
Completing the *Random Card* Application

In this tutorial you complete the *Random Card* application, which randomly displays images of poker cards selected from an ImageList control. The application's form, which has already been created for you, is shown in Figure 8-21. Notice that the PictureBox control is already displaying the image of a card's back.

Figure 8-21 The *Random Card* application's form

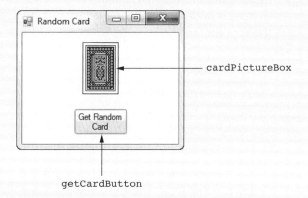

Step 1: Start Visual Studio (or Visual C# Express). Open the project named *Random Card* in the *Chap08* folder of the Student Sample Programs.

Step 2: Make sure the Form1 form is open in the *Designer*. Scroll down in the *Toolbox* until you see the *Components* section, and double-click the ImageList tool. This should create an ImageList control named `imageList1`, which you should see in the component tray.

Step 3: Change the name of the `imageList1` control to `cardImageList`.

Step 4: Each of the images that you will add to the `cardImageList` control are 50 by 70 pixels in size. Change the `cardImageList` control's ImageSize property to 50, 70.

Step 5: Next you add images to the `cardImageList` control. The images that you add are in the *Images/Cards/Poker Small* folder of the Student Sample Programs. In the *Properties* window, click the ellipses button (![...]) that appears next to the Images property. This displays the *Images Collection Editor* window.

Click the *Add* button, and an *Open* dialog box appears. Use the dialog box to select as many of the card image files as you want to add to the ImageList control. (You can use the Shift or Ctrl keys while clicking filenames to select multiple files.) When you have selected all the images that you want to add, click the *OK* button.

Step 6: Now you create the Click event handler for the getCardButton control. Double-click the getCardButton control in the *Designer*. This opens the code editor, and you will see an empty event handler named getCardButton_Click. Complete the event handler by typing the code shown in lines 21–28 in Program 8-8. Let's review this code.

Line 22: This statement creates a Random object, referenced by the rand variable.

Line 25: This statement declares an int variable named index. The variable is initialized with a random number that is returned from the rand.Next method. Notice that cardImageList.Images.Count is passed as an argument to the method. As a result, we get a random number in the range of 0 up to, but not including, the number of images in the control.

Line 28: This statement uses the index variable to retrieve an image from the cardImageList control and assigns it to the cardPictureBox control's Image property. As a result, the image is displayed in the PictureBox.

Step 7: Save the project. Then, press F5 on the keyboard or click the *Start Debugging* button (▶) on the toolbar to compile and run the application. When the application runs, click the *Get Random Card* button several times to see the images that are randomly selected. When you are finished, click the *Exit* button to exit the application.

Program 8-8 Completed code for Form1 in the *Random Card* application

```
1  using System;
2  using System.Collections.Generic;
3  using System.ComponentModel;
4  using System.Data;
5  using System.Drawing;
6  using System.Linq;
7  using System.Text;
8  using System.Windows.Forms;
9
10 namespace Random_Card
11 {
12     public partial class Form1 : Form
13     {
14         public Form1()
15         {
16             InitializeComponent();
17         }
18
19         private void getCardButton_Click(object sender, EventArgs e)
20         {
21             // Create a Random object.
22             Random rand = new Random();
23
24             // Get a random index.
25             int index = rand.Next(cardImageList.Images.Count);
```

```
26
27              // Display a card.
28              cardPictureBox.Image = cardImageList.Images[index];
29          }
30      }
31 }
```

Checkpoint

8.26 How you can determine the number of images that are stored in an ImageList control?

8.27 Under which section is the ImageList control located in the *Toolbox*?

8.28 There are a few guidelines that you should follow as you plan to use an ImageList control in an application. What are they?

8.29 How do you add images to an ImageList control?

8.30 What value determines which image from the ImageList will be displayed in a PictureBox?

Key Terms

character literals
comma separated value (CSV)
`Contains` method
delimiter
`EndsWith` method
enumerated data type
enumerators
ImageList control
`IndexOf` method
instance
`LastIndexOf` method

Leading spaces
parallel relationship
`StartsWith` method
structure
substring
`Substring` method
tokenizing
tokens
`ToLower` method
`ToUpper` method
trailing spaces

Review Questions

Multiple Choice

1. In C#, _____ are enclosed in single quotation marks.
   - a. strings
   - b. enumerators
   - c. tokens
   - d. character literals

2. The `char` data type provides the _____ for converting the case of a character.
   - a. `Lowercase` and `Uppercase` methods
   - b. `ToLower` and `ToUpper` methods
   - c. `IsDigit` and `IsLetter` methods
   - d. `IsWhiteSpace` and `IsPunctuation` methods

3. A string within a string is called a(n) _____.
   - a. character
   - b. inner string
   - c. substring
   - d. thread

4. The _____ of a `string` object allow you to search for substrings.
   - a. `TrimStart` and `TrimEnd` methods
   - b. `IndexOf` or `LastIndexOf` methods
   - c. `IsWhiteSpace` and `IsPunctuation` methods
   - d. `Contains`, `StartsWith`, and `EndsWith` methods

5. When you want to know the position of the substring, you can use one of the _____ of a `string` object.
   - a. `TrimStart` or `TrimEnd` methods
   - b. `IndexOf` or `LastIndexOf` methods
   - c. `ToLower` and `ToUpper` methods
   - d. `StartsWith` or `EndsWith` methods

6. The _____ of a `string` object can be used to retrieve a specific set of characters from a string.
   - a. `Substring` method
   - b. `IndexOf` method
   - c. `TrimStart` and `TrimEnd` methods
   - d. `StartsWith` and `EndsWith` methods

7. _____ are spaces that appear at the beginning of a string.

    a. Leading spaces
    b. Primary spaces
    c. Starting spaces
    d. Empty spaces

8. _____ are spaces that appear at the end of a string.

    a. Blank spaces
    b. Secondary spaces
    c. Ending spaces
    d. Trailing spaces

9. A series of words or other items of data contained in a string and separated by spaces or other characters are known as _____.

    a. substrings
    b. elements
    c. characters
    d. tokens

10. The character that separates tokens is known as a _____.

    a. partition
    b. literal
    c. delimiter
    d. symbol

11. The process of breaking a string into tokens is known as _____.

    a. extracting
    b. tokenizing
    c. delimiting
    d. parsing

12. The _____ file format is commonly used to export spreadsheet data to a text file.

    a. spreadsheet data volume, or SDV
    b. comma separated value, or CSV
    c. extensible markup language, or XML
    d. portable document format, or PDF

13. A _____ is a data type you can create that contains one or more variables known as fields.

    a. structure
    b. collection
    c. volume
    d. list

14. Before you can use a structure to store data, you must create a(n) _____ of the structure in memory.

    a. copy
    b. instance
    c. declaration
    d. reference

15. When the items in two data structures are related by their indexes, it is said that a _____ exists between the data structures.

    a. binary union
    b. parallel relationship
    c. unilateral bond
    d. virtual connection

16. When you create a(n) _____, you specify a set of symbolic values that belong to that data type.
    a. abstract data type
    b. symbolic data type
    c. enumerated data type
    d. cryptic data type

17. _____ are constants that represent integer values.
    a. Literals
    b. Enumerators
    c. Constants
    d. Tokens

18. The _____ is a container that can hold multiple images.
    a. ImageList control
    b. GroupBox control
    c. PictureBox control
    d. ComboBox control

True or False

1. You cannot store a string in a variable of the `char` data type.

2. C# allows you to access the individual characters in a string using subscript notation.

3. When you call a `string` object's `Split` method, the method divides the string into two substrings and returns them as an array of strings.

4. The fields contained in a structure must be of the same data type.

5. Before you can use the structure to store data, you must create an instance of the structure in memory.

6. Structure objects can be passed into a method only by reference.

7. You cannot perform comparison operations directly on structure objects.

8. Enumerators must be enclosed in quotation marks.

9. An `enum` declaration can only appear inside the application's namespace.

10. The integer values that you assign to enumerators do not have to be unique.

11. You can compare enumerators and `enum` variables with relational operators.

12. ImageList controls are designed to store small images such as icons or thumbnails.

Short Answer

1. What method can be used to convert a `char` variable to a string?

2. List the method you would use to determine whether each of the following is true or false for the value of a character.
    a. numeric digit
    b. alphabetic letter
    c. alphabetic letter or numeric digit
    d. punctuation mark
    e. white-space character
    f. uppercase letter
    g. lowercase letter

3. List the method you would use to determine each of the following about the value of a `string` object.

   a. starts with the substring "VENI"
   b. contains the substring "VIDI"
   c. ends with the substring "VICI"

4. Briefly describe each of the following `string` object methods.

   a. `Insert`
   b. `Remove`
   c. `ToLower`
   d. `ToUpper`
   e. `Trim`
   f. `TrimStart`
   g. `TrimEnd`

5. What characters are used as delimiters when you pass `null` as an argument to the `Split` method of a `string` object?

6. List the places that a structure can be declared in code.

7. Assume an application contains a structure named `Fruit`. Write a statement that demonstrates how you would create a `List` that can hold `Fruit` objects.

8. Can enumerators be used in a loop to step through the elements of an array? Why or why not.

9. Why should you use the `new` operator when creating instances of a structure?

10. What is the result if the value of the ImageSize property does not match the size of the images that are stored in the ImageList control.

Algorithm Workbench

1. Write a method that accepts a string as an argument and checks it for proper capitalization and punctuation. The method should determine if the string begins with an uppercase letter and ends with a punctuation mark. The method should return `true` if the string meets the criteria; otherwise it should return `false`.

2. Write a method that accepts a string as an argument and displays its contents backward. For instance, if the string argument is "gravity", the method should display "ytivarg".

3. Look at the following structure declaration:

```
struct Engine
{
    public int cylinders;
    public int horsepower;
    public int torque;
}
```

   Write a method that accepts two `Engine` structures as arguments, determines if the two structures are equal, and returns the Boolean value `true` if the structures are equal or `false` if the structures are not equal.

4. Declare an enumerated data type named `Direction` with enumerators for North, South, East, and West.

5. Write a statement that retrieves the image stored at index 0 from an ImageList control named `slideShowImageList` and displays it in a PictureBox control named `slideShowPictureBox`.

Programming Problems

1. **Word Counter**

   Create an application with a method that accepts a string as an argument and returns the number of words it contains. For instance, if the argument is "Four score and seven years ago," the method should return the number 6. The application should let the user enter a string, and then it should pass the string to the method. The number of words in the string should be displayed.

2. **Average Number of Letters**

   Modify the program you wrote for Problem 1 (Word Counter) so it also displays the average number of letters in each word.

3. **Sentence Capitalizer**

   Create an application with a method that accepts a string as an argument and returns a copy of the string with the first character of each sentence capitalized. For instance, if the argument is "hello. my name is Joe. what is your name?" the method should return the string "Hello. My name is Joe. What is your name?" The application should let the user enter a string and then pass it to the method. The modified string should be displayed.

4. **Vowels and Consonants**

   Create an application with a method that accepts a string as an argument and returns the number of vowels that the string contains. The application should have another method that accepts a string as an argument and returns the number of consonants that the string contains. The application should let the user enter a string, and should display the number of vowels and the number of consonants it contains.

5. **Most Frequent Character**

   Create an application that lets the user enter a string and displays the character that appears most frequently in the string.

6. **Word Separator**

   Create an application that accepts as input a sentence in which all the words are run together but the first character of each word is uppercase. Convert the sentence to a string in which the words are separated by spaces and only the first word starts with an uppercase letter. For example the string "StopAndSmellTheRoses." would be converted to "Stop and smell the roses."

7. **Pig Latin**

   Create an application that accepts a sentence as input and converts each word to "Pig Latin." In one version, to convert a word to Pig Latin you remove the first letter and place that letter at the end of the word. Then you append the string "ay" to the word. Here is an example:

   English: I SLEPT MOST OF THE NIGHT
   Pig Latin: IAY LEPTSAY OSTMAY FOAY HETAY IGHTNAY

8. **Sum of Numbers in a String**

   Create an application that lets the user enter a string containing series of numbers separated by commas. Here is an example of valid input:

   ```
   7,9,10,2,18,6
   ```

   The program should calculate and display the sum of all the numbers.

9. **Alphabetic Telephone Number Translator**

Many companies use telephone numbers like 555-GET-FOOD so the number is easier for their customers to remember. On a standard telephone, the alphabetic letters are mapped to numbers in the following fashion:

A, B, and C = 2
D, E, and F = 3
G, H, and I = 4
J, K, and L = 5
M, N, and O = 6
P, Q, R, and S = 7
T, U, and V = 8
W, X, Y, and Z = 9

Create an application that lets the user to enter a 10-character telephone number in the format XXX-XXX-XXXX. The application should display the telephone number with any alphabetic characters that appeared in the original translated to their numeric equivalent. For example, if the user enters 555-GET-FOOD, the application should display 555-438-3663.

10. **Morse Code Converter**

Design a program that asks the user to enter a string and then converts that string to Morse code. Morse code is a code where each letter of the English alphabet, each digit, and various punctuation characters are represented by a series of dots and dashes. Table 8-7 shows part of the code.

Table 8-7 Morse code

Character	Code	Character	Code	Character	Code	Character	Code
space	*space*	6	–....	G	––.	Q	––.–
comma	––..––	7	––...	H	....	R	.–.
period	.–.–.–	8	–––..	I	..	S	...
?	..––..	9	––––.	J	.–––	T	–
0	–––––	A	.–	K	–.–	U	..–
1	.––––	B	–...	L	.–..	V	...–
2	..–––	C	–.–.	M	––	W	.––
3	...––	D	–..	N	–.	X	–..–
4	....–	E	.	O	–––	Y	–.––
5	.....	F	..–.	P	.––.	Z	––..

11. **Drink Vending Machine Simulator**

Create an application that simulates a soft-drink vending machine. The application should let the user select one of the following soft drinks:

- Cola ($1.00 each)
- Root Beer ($1.00 each)
- Lemon Lime Soda ($1.00 each)
- Grape Soda ($1.50 each)
- Cream Soda ($1.50 each)

Figure 8-22 shows an example of the application's form. (The images that are displayed in the PictureBox controls are in the *Images\Drink Machine* folder of the

Figure 8-22 Drink vending machine simulator

Student Sample Programs.) When the application starts, the vending machine will have 20 of each type of soft drink. Each time the user selects a drink, the application should subtract 1 from the quantity of the selected drink. It should also update and display the total amount of sales. If the user selects a drink that is sold out, a message should be displayed indicating so.

In the application's code, create a structure that has fields for the following data:

Drink name
Drink cost
Number of drinks in machine

The program should create an array of five structure objects. Each element of the array should keep data for a specific type of soft drink.

12. **Slot Machine Simulation**

A slot machine is a gambling device into which the user inserts money and then pulls a lever (or presses a button). The slot machine then displays a set of random images. If two or more of the images match, the user wins an amount of money that the slot machine dispenses back to the user.

Create an application that simulates a slot machine. Figure 8-23 shows an example of how the form should look. The application should let the user enter into a

Figure 8-23 *Slot Machine* application

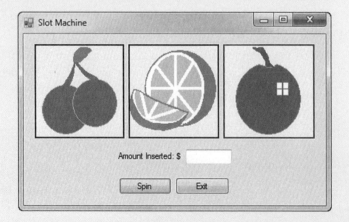

TextBox the amount of money he or she is inserting into the machine. When the user clicks the *Spin* button, the application should display three randomly selected symbols. (Slot machines traditionally display fruit symbols. You will find a set of fruit symbols in the *Images\Fruit Symbols* folder of the Student Sample Programs.)

If none of the randomly displayed images match, the program should inform the user that he or she has won $0. If two of the images match, the program should inform the user that he or she has won two times the amount entered. If three of the images match, the program should inform the user that he or she has won three times the amount entered. When the user clicks the Exit button to exit the application, the program should display the total amount of money entered into the slot machine and the total amount won.

9 Classes and Multiform Projects

TOPICS

9.1 Introduction to Classes

CONCEPT: A class is the blueprint for an object. It specifies the fields and methods a particular type of object has. From the class, one or more objects may be created.

As you have worked through this book, you have used objects extensively in all the programs that you have written. Some objects, such as the controls that you place on a form, are visual. Other objects, such as Random objects, arrays, List objects, and ImageList controls, cannot be seen on the screen but exist in memory and perform important tasks.

We mentioned in Chapter 1 that objects do not just magically appear in your program. Before a specific type of object can be used, that object has to be created in memory. And, before an object can be created in memory, you must have a class for the object.

A class is code that describes a particular type of object. It specifies the data that an object can hold (fields and properties) and the actions that an object can perform (methods). You can think of a class as a code "blueprint" that can be used to create a particular type of object. It serves a similar purpose as the blueprint for a house. The blueprint itself is not a house but is a detailed description of a house. When we use the blueprint to build an actual house, we could say we are building an instance of the house described by the blueprint. If we so desire, we can build several identical houses from the same blueprint. Each house is a separate instance of the house described by the blueprint. This idea is illustrated in Figure 9-1.

Figure 9-1 A blueprint and houses built from the blueprint

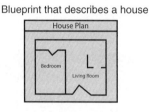

Blueprint that describes a house

Instances of the house described by the blueprint

So, a class is not an object but a description of an object. When the program is running, it can use the class to create, in memory, as many objects of a specific type as needed. Each object that is created from a class is called an **instance** of the class.

For example, Jessica is an entomologist (someone who studies insects), and she also enjoys writing computer programs. She designs a program to catalog different types of insects. As part of the program, she creates a class named `Insect`, which specifies fields, properties, and methods for holding and manipulating data common to all types of insects. The `Insect` class is not an object but a specification that objects may be created from. Next, she writes programming statements that create a `housefly` object, which is an instance of the `Insect` class. The `housefly` object is an entity that occupies computer memory and stores data about a housefly. It has the fields, properties, and methods specified by the `Insect` class. Then she writes programming statements that create a `mosquito` object. The `mosquito` object is also an instance of the `Insect` class. It has its own area in memory and stores data about a mosquito. Although the `housefly` and `mosquito` objects are two separate entities in the computer's memory, they were both created from the `Insect` class. This means that each object has the fields, properties, and methods described by the `Insect` class. This is illustrated in Figure 9-2.

Figure 9-2 The `housefly` and `mosquito` objects as instances of the `Insect` class

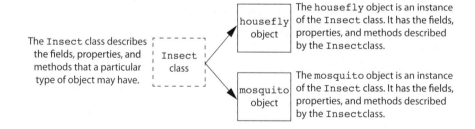

Creating a Class

You create a class by writing a **class declaration.** This is the general format of a class declaration:

```
class ClassName
{
    Member declarations go here...
}
```

The first line of a class declaration is known as the **class header.** It starts with the word `class`, followed by the name of the class. The same rules for naming variable apply to naming classes. Most programmers follow the convention of beginning class names with an uppercase letter. This helps to easily distinguish class names from variable names when reading code.

Following the class header is an opening curly brace. Next you write the class's **member declarations.** These are the statements that define the class's fields, properties, and methods. A closing curly brace appears at the end of the class declaration.

Let's look at a simple example. Suppose we are writing a program to simulate the tossing of a coin. In the program we need to repeatedly toss a coin and each time determine whether it landed heads up or tails up. First, we write a class named `Coin` that can perform the behaviors of the coin. The following code sample shows the `Coin` class. (Note that this class is only part of the application's code. In a moment you will see where it should appear in the project, but for now, we concentrate only on this class.)

```
 1 class Coin
 2 {
 3     // Field to represent the side facing up;
 4     private string sideUp;
 5
 6     // Constructor
 7     public Coin()
 8     {
 9         sideUp = "Heads";
10     }
11
12     // The toss method simulates tossing the coin.
13     public void Toss()
14     {
15         // Create a Random object.
16         Random rand = new Random();
17
18         // Use a random number to determine
19         // the side of the coin is facing up.
20         // 0 = Heads, 1 = Tails
21         if (rand.Next(2) == 0)
22         {
23             sideUp = "Heads";
24         }
25         else
26         {
27             sideUp = "Tails";
28         }
29     }
30
31     // The GetSideUp method returns the value
32     // of the sideUp field.
33     public string GetSideUp()
34     {
35         return sideUp;
36     }
37 }
```

The first line is the class header. It specifies that the name of the class is `Coin`. The curly braces that appear in lines 2 and 37 enclose the contents of the class. Let's take a closer look at the code inside the class:

Line 4: This statement declares a field named `sideUp`. The `sideUp` field is a `string` variable that indicates which side of the coin is facing up. If the heads side is facing up, the string `"Heads"` is assigned to this field. If the tails side is facing up, the string `"Tails"` is assigned to this field.

Notice that the field declaration begins with the keyword `private`. The keyword `private` is an access modifier that specifies the field cannot be directly accessed by statements outside the class.

By using the `private` access modifier, a class can hide its data from code outside the class. When a class's fields are hidden from outside code, the data is protected from accidental corruption. It is a common practice to make all a class's fields private and to provide access to those fields through methods only.

Lines 7–10: This code defines a special method known as a constructor. A **constructor** is a method that is automatically executed when an object is created. In most cases, a constructor is used to initialize an object's fields with starting values. It is called a constructor because it helps construct an object.

This constructor performs a simple task. In line 9 it assigns the string `"Heads"` to the `sideUp` field. As a result, any time we create an object of the `Coin` class, that object's `sideUp` field will initially be assigned the string `"Heads"`.

Notice the following about the constructor header in line 7:

- The name of the constructor is the same as the name of the class. In this case, the name of the constructor is `Coin`.
- The header does not specify a return type—not even `void`.
- The constructor header begins with the `public` access modifier. In most cases, a class's constructor is public. In this book we always use the `public` access modifier with constructors.

Lines 13–29: This code defines a `void` method named `Toss`. Notice that the `public` access modifier is used in the method header in line 13. Because the method is public, it can be called from code outside the `Coin` class.

The purpose of the `Toss` method is to simulate the tossing of the coin. When the method is called, line 16 creates a `Random` object, referenced by the `rand` variable. The `if` statement in line 21 gets a random number in the range of 0 through 1. If the number is 0, then line 23 assigns the string `"Heads"` to the `sideUp` field. Otherwise, line 27 assigns the string `"Tails"` to the `sideUp` field.

Lines 33–36: This code defines a method named `GetSideUp`. Notice that the `public` access modifier is used in line 33, which means that the method can be called from code outside the `Coin` class. Also notice that the method returns a `string`.

The purpose of the `GetSideUp` method is to return a string indicating which side of the coin is facing up. Notice that in line 35 the value of the `sideUp` field is returned.

Creating an Object

Remember, a class is not an object but a description of an object. The `Coin` class specifies what a `Coin` object is made of, but it does not create a `Coin` object in memory. To create a `Coin` object, we must write a statement such as this:

```
Coin myCoin = new Coin();
```

At this point in your studies, you have created plenty of objects, so this type of statement will be familiar to you. For example, `Random` objects, arrays, and `List`s are all created this way. Let's look at the different parts of this statement:

- The first part of the statement, appearing on the left side of the = operator, reads `Coin myCoin`. This declares a variable named `myCoin` that can be used to reference an object of the `Coin` class.

- The second part of the statement, appearing on the right side of the = operator, reads new Coin(). This expression creates an instance of the Coin class and calls the class's constructor. The new operator returns a reference to the object.
- The = operator assigns the reference that was returned from the new operator to the myCoin variable.

After this statement executes, the myCoin variable will reference a Coin object, as shown in Figure 9-3. Notice in the figure that the object's sideUp field is set to "Heads", as a result of the constructor.

Figure 9-3 The myCoin variable references a Coin object

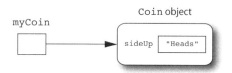

 NOTE: Classes are reference types. When you create an object from a class, you use a reference variable to reference that object. When you want to work with the object, you use the variable that references it.

Once we have created a Coin object, we can perform operations with it. For example, assuming the variable myCoin references a Coin object, the following statement calls the object's Toss method:

```
myCoin.Toss();
```

And, the following statement displays the side of the coin that is facing up:

```
MessageBox.Show(myCoin.GetSideUp());
```

Where to Write Class Declarations

In C# you have some flexibility in choosing where to write class declarations. When you start writing your own classes in a project, it is possible to write them in the same file that contains the form's class. Figure 9-4 shows an example of how the Coin class can be written in the same file as a project's Form1 class. Notice in the figure that the Coin class is written inside the project namespace. This is not required, but it is a good idea since the class is part of the project. (It does not matter if the class is written before or after the Form1 class.)

Although this approach might be acceptable for small classes, it is recommended that you write each class in its own separate file. Doing so makes your code more organized and helps keep your source code files to a manageable size. It also makes it easy for you to reuse classes in other projects. In this book, we always store classes in their own files.

Figure 9-4 The `Form1` class and the `Coin` class in the same source code file

```
using System;
using System.Collections.Generic;
using System.ComponentModel;
using System.Data;
using System.Drawing;
using System.Linq;
using System.Text;
using System.Windows.Forms;

namespace Example
{
    public partial class Form1 : Form
    {
        public Form1()
        {
            InitializeComponent();
        }

        Form1's methods and event handlers appear here.

    }

    class Coin
    {
        The Coin class's members appear here.

    }
}
```

Form1 class

Coin class

Visual Studio automates the process of adding a new class file to a project. When you are ready to write a new class, follow these steps to create a source file for the class:

1. With the project open in Visual Studio, click *Project* on the menu bar; then select *Add Class....* This is shown in Figure 9-5.

Figure 9-5 Selecting *Add Class...* on the *Project* menu

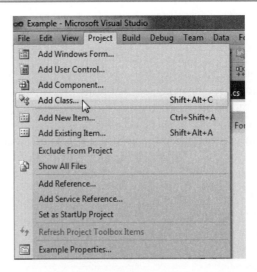

2. The *Add New Item* window, shown in Figure 9-6, should appear. Make sure *Class* is selected as the type of item. Notice in the figure that *Class1.cs* appears in the *Name* text box. This is the default filename that Visual Studio provides. Change the name

Figure 9-6 The *Add New Item* window

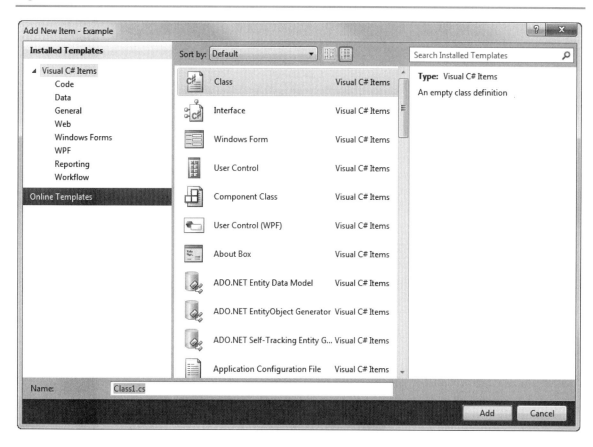

to match the name of the class that you are creating. For example, if you are creating a class named Coin, you change the name to *Coin.cs*. (Be sure that the filename ends with the .cs extension.)

3. Click the *Add* button.

After performing these steps, the specified source code file will be created in the project, and will be displayed in the code editor. The source code file already contains several using directives and an empty class declaration that you can edit. Figure 9-7 shows an example. You will also see an entry for the new source code file in the *Solution Explorer*, as shown in Figure 9-8.

Figure 9-7 A new class file displayed in the code editor

```
Coin.cs × Form1.cs      Form1.cs [Design]
Example.Coin
using System;
 using System.Collections.Generic;
 using System.Linq;
 using System.Text;

namespace Example
 {
     class Coin
     {
     }
 }
```

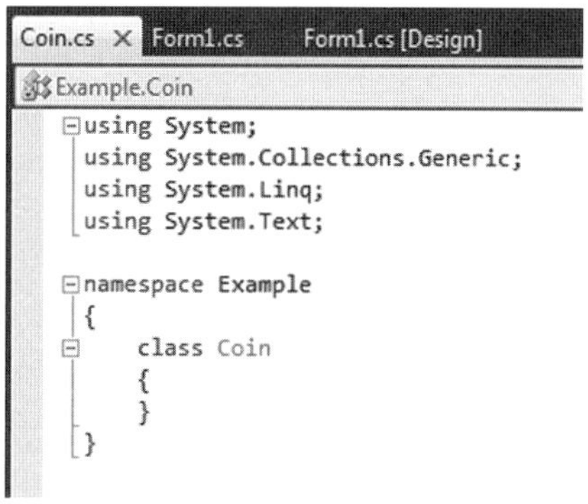

Figure 9-8 *Solution Explorer* window

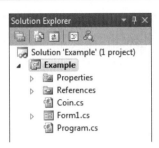

Tutorial 9-1 leads you through the process of creating the Coin class in an application that uses it to simulate a coin that can be tossed.

Tutorial 9-1:
Creating and Using the Coin Class

In this tutorial you complete the *Coin Toss* application. The application's form, which has already been created for you, is shown in Figure 9-9. When you run the completed application, you can click the *Toss Five Times* button and the application will simulate a coin being tossed five times. The results of each coin toss are displayed in the list box.

Figure 9-9 The *Coin Toss* application's form

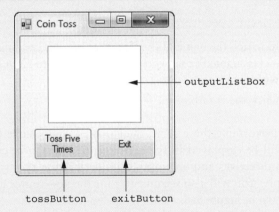

Step 1:   Start Visual Studio (or Visual C# Express). Open the project named *Coin Toss* in the *Chap09* folder of the Student Sample Programs.

Step 2:   Click *Project* on the Visual Studio menu bar; then select *Add Class....* The *Add New Item* window should appear. (See Figure 9-6 for an example.) Make sure *Class* is selected as the type of item. Notice that the default filename *Class1.cs* appears in the *Name* text box. Change the name to *Coin.cs*, as shown in Figure 9-10, and then click the *Add* button. This adds a source code file named Coin.cs to the project.

Step 3:   The Coin.cs file should now be displayed in the code editor, as shown in Figure 9-11. Notice that the file already contains several using directives and an empty Coin class has been created. Complete the code for the Coin class by typing lines 10–44 in Program 9-1.

Figure 9-10 The filename changed to Coin.cs

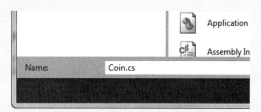

Figure 9-11 The Coin.cs file in the code editor

```
Coin.cs* ×  Form1.cs [Design]
Coin_Toss.Coin
    using System;
    using System.Collections.Generic;
    using System.Linq;
    using System.Text;

    namespace Coin_Toss
    {
        class Coin
        {                    ←────  You will add code to
        }                            the Coin class.
    }
```

Step 4: Next you create the Click event handlers for the Button controls. Click the tab that reads *Form1.cs [Design]* in the area just above the code editor to switch your view to the Form1 form in the Designer. (Alternatively, you can double-click the *Form1.cs* entry in the *Solution Explorer*.)

Step 5: Double-click the `tossButton` control. This opens the Form1.cs file in the code editor, and you will see an empty event handler named `tossButton_Click`. Complete the event handler by typing the code shown in lines 21–35 in Program 9-2. Let's review this code:

Line 22: This statement does the following:

- It declares a `Coin` reference variable named `myCoin`.
- It creates a `Coin` object in memory and calls its constructor.
- It assigns a reference to the `Coin` object to the `myCoin` variable.

After this statement executes, the `myCoin` variable will reference a `Coin` object. The object's `sideUp` field will be set to `"Heads"`.

Line 25: This statement clears the `outputListBox` control.

Lines 28–35: This `for` loop iterates five times, simulating five tosses of a coin. During each iteration, the following actions take place:

- Line 31 calls the `myCoin.Toss()` method.
- Line 34 calls the `myCoin.GetSideUp()` method to get the side of the coin that is facing up. The result of the method call is displayed in the `outputListBox` control.

Step 6: Switch your view back to the Form1 form in the *Designer* and double-click the `exitButton` control. In the code editor you will see an empty event handler named `exitButton_Click`. Complete the event handler by typing the code shown in lines 40–41 in Program 9-2.

Step 7: Save the project. Then, press ⌈F5⌉ on the keyboard or click the *Start Debugging* button (▶) on the toolbar to compile and run the application. When the application runs, click the *Toss Five Times* button and view the results. Figure 9-12 shows an example of the application's output. Click the button as many times as you wish to see different, random results. Click the *Exit* button when you are finished.

Figure 9-12 Example output of the *Coin Toss* application

Program 9-1 Completed code for the Coin.cs file in the *Coin Toss* application

```
 1 using System;
 2 using System.Collections.Generic;
 3 using System.Linq;
 4 using System.Text;
 5
 6 namespace Coin_Toss
 7 {
 8     class Coin
 9     {
10         // Field to represent the side facing up;
11         private string sideUp;
12         Random rand = new Random();
13
14         // Constructor
15         public Coin()
16         {
17             sideUp = "Heads";
18         }
19
20         // The toss method simulates tossing the coin.
21         public void Toss()
22         {
23             // Create a Random object.
24             //Random rand = new Random();
25
26             // Use a random number to determine
27             // the side of the coin is facing up.
28             // 0 = Heads, 1 = Tails
29             if (rand.Next(2) == 0)
30             {
31                 sideUp = "Heads";
32             }
33             else
34             {
35                 sideUp = "Tails";
```

```
36                }
37            }
38
39            // The GetSideUp method returns the value
40            // of the sideUp field.
41            public string GetSideUp()
42            {
43                return sideUp;
44            }
45        }
46  }
```

Program 9-2 Completed code for Form1 in the *Coin Toss* application

```
1  using System;
2  using System.Collections.Generic;
3  using System.ComponentModel;
4  using System.Data;
5  using System.Drawing;
6  using System.Linq;
7  using System.Text;
8  using System.Windows.Forms;
9
10 namespace Coin_Toss
11 {
12     public partial class Form1 : Form
13     {
14         public Form1()
15         {
16             InitializeComponent();
17         }
18
19         private void tossButton_Click(object sender, EventArgs e)
20         {
21             // Create a Coin object.
22             Coin myCoin = new Coin();
23
24             // Clear the ListBox.
25             outputListBox.Items.Clear();
26
27             // Toss the coin five times.
28             for (int count = 0; count < 5; count++)
29             {
30                 // Toss the coin.
31                 myCoin.Toss();
32
33                 // Display the side that is up.
34                 outputListBox.Items.Add(myCoin.GetSideUp());
35             }
36         }
37
38         private void exitButton_Click(object sender, EventArgs e)
39         {
40             // Close the form.
41             this.Close();
42         }
43     }
44 }
```

Passing an Object to a Method

When you are developing applications that work with objects, you often need to write methods that accept objects as arguments. For example, the following code shows a method named ShowCoinStatus that accepts a Coin object as an argument:

```
1 private void ShowCoinStatus(Coin coin)
2 {
3     MessageBox.Show("This side of the coin is up: " +
4                 coin.GetSideUp());
5 }
```

The following code sample shows how we might create a Coin object and then pass it as an argument to the ShowCoinStatus method:

```
Coin myCoin = new Coin();
ShowCoinStatus(myCoin);
```

Because classes are reference types, objects that are instances of a class are *always* passed by reference. When you pass an object that is an instance of a class as an argument, the thing that is passed into the parameter variable is a reference to the object. As a result, the method that receives the object as an argument has access to the actual object (not a copy of the object). For example, look at the following Flip method:

```
1 private void Flip(Coin coin)
2 {
3     coin.Toss();
4 }
```

This method accepts a Coin object as an argument, and it calls the object's Toss method. The following code demonstrates the method being called:

```
 1 // Create a Coin object.
 2 Coin myCoin = new Coin();
 3
 4 // This will display "Heads".
 5 MessageBox.Show(myCoin.GetSideUp());
 6
 7 // Pass the object to the Flip method.
 8 Flip(myCoin);
 9
10 // This might display "Heads", or it might
11 // display "Tails".
12 MessageBox.Show(myCoin.GetSideUp());
```

The statement in line 2 creates a Coin object, referenced by the variable myCoin. Line 5 displays the value of the myCoin object's sideUp field. Because the object's constructor set the sideUp field to "Heads", we know that line 5 will display the string "Heads". Line 8 calls the Flip method, passing the myCoin object as an argument, by reference. Inside the Flip method, the myCoin object's Toss method is called. Line 12 displays the value of the myCoin object's sideUp field again. This time, we cannot predict whether "Heads" or "Tails" will be displayed because the myCoin object's Toss method has been called.

Checkpoint

9.1 How is a class like a blueprint?

9.2 Briefly describe the process of writing a class declaration?

9.3 What is a constructor?

9.4 List the three steps for adding a new class file to a Visual C# project.

9.5 When you pass an object that is an instance of a class as an argument, what is passed into the parameter variable?

9.2 Properties

CONCEPT: A property is a class member that holds a piece of data about an object. Properties are implemented as special methods that set and get the values of corresponding fields.

A **property** is a special type of class member that allows an object to store and retrieve a piece of data. You are already familiar with properties because you have used them extensively when creating forms. GUI controls have properties that determine their characteristics. For example, a Label control's Text property determines the text that is displayed by the control.

In code, you work with properties in the same ways that you work with variables. For example, assume messageLabel is the name of a Label control. You can assign a specific value to the control's Text property, as shown here:

```
messageLabel.Text = "Hello";
```

Also, you can assign a property to a variable. The following statement initializes the variable str with the messageLabel control's Text property:

```
string str = messageLabel.Text;
```

From these examples, you can see that a property is a class member that behaves like a public field. A property is not a public field, however. It is a special set of methods, known as **accessors,** which work in conjunction with a private field. The private field, which is known as the property's **backing field,** holds any data that is assigned to the property. The accessors allow code outside the class to get the property's value and assign values to the property.

Let's look at an example of a simple class that has a property. Suppose you want to create a class named Pet that represents the family pet. The class will have a Name property to hold the pet's name. The following code shows how the Pet class might be written:

```
 1 class Pet
 2 {
 3     // Field for the pet's name
 4     private string _name;
 5
 6     // Constructor
 7     public Pet()
 8     {
 9         _name = "";
10     }
11
12     // Name property
13     public string Name
14     {
15         get
16         {
17             return _name;
18         }
19
20         set
21         {
```

```
22                        _name = value;
23              }
24       }
25  }
```

Let's take a closer look at the code inside the class:

Line 4: This statement declares a private `string` field named _name. The _name field is the backing field for the Name property. When a value is assigned to the Name property, it is stored in the _name field.

Notice that we have started the field's name with an underscore character. This is not a requirement, but some programmers begin the names of backing fields with an underscore to eliminate confusion between the field name and the property name. By following this practice, when you are reading the code and you see a variable name that begins with an underscore, you know immediately that it is a backing field for a property.

Lines 7–10: This is the class constructor. When an instance of the `Pet` class is created, this constructor assigns an empty string to the _name field.

Line 13: This is the beginning of a property declaration. It specifies three things about the property:

- `public`—The property is public, so it can be used by code outside the class. (Most properties are declared as public.)
- `string`—The property's data type is `string`.
- `Name`—The name of the property is Name.

Line 14: An opening curly brace appears in this line. The corresponding closing curly brace appears in line 24. Inside these braces are the Name property's accessors.

Lines 15–18: This is the property's `get` accessor. You can think of the `get` accessor as a method that returns the property's value. You can see that line 17 is a `return` statement, returning the value of the _name field. The `get` accessor is executed anytime the property is read.

Lines 20–23: This is the property's `set` accessor. The purpose of the `set` accessor is to set the property to a value. The `set` accessor has an implicit parameter named `value`. It is "implicit" because it is not declared, as the parameters in a regular method are. The **value parameter** is automatically created by the compiler, and its data type is the same as that of the property. In this case, the `value` parameter's data type is `string`.

Anytime a value is assigned to a property, the property's `set` accessor is executed, and the value being assigned is passed into the `value` parameter. Line 22 assigns the `value` parameter to the _name field.

The following code shows how you can use the `Pet` class's Name property.

```
1  // Create two Pet objects.
2  Pet myDog = new Pet();
3  Pet myCat = new Pet();
4
5  // Set their Name properties.
6  myDog.Name = "Fido";
7  myCat.Name = "Sylvester";
8
9  // Display their names.
10 MessageBox.Show("My dog's name is " + myDog.Name);
11 MessageBox.Show("My cat's name is " + myCat.Name);
```

Let's take a closer look at the code:

Line 2: This statement creates a `Pet` object, calls the `Pet` class constructor, and assigns a reference to the object to the `myDog` variable. After this statement executes, the `myDog` variable references a `Pet` object.

Line 3: This statement creates a `Pet` object, calls the `Pet` class constructor, and assigns a reference to the object to the `myCat` variable. After this statement executes, the `myCat` variable references a `Pet` object.

Line 6: This statement sets the `myDog` object's Name property to `"Fido"`. When this statement executes, the Name property's set accessor is executed, and the string `"Fido"` is passed into the `value` parameter. The `value` parameter is then assigned to the `myDog` object's _name field. This process is illustrated in Figure 9-13.

Figure 9-13 Setting the `myDog` object's Name property to `"Fido"`

```
                                    // Name property                      Pet  object
                                    public string Name
                                    {
                                        get
                                        {
                                            return _name;                _name    "Fido"
   myDog.Name = "Fido";                 }
                                        set
                                        {
                                            _name = value;
                                        }
                                    }
```

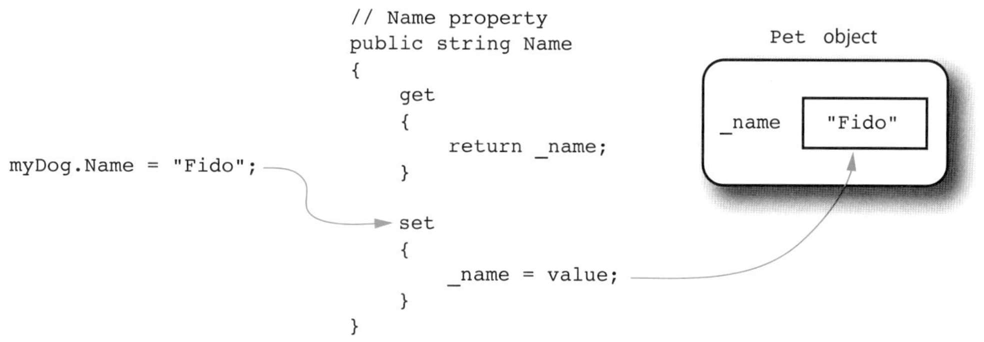

Line 7: This statement sets the `myCat` object's Name property to `"Sylvester"`. When this statement executes, the Name property's `set` accessor is executed, and the string `"Sylvester"` is passed into the `value` parameter. The `value` parameter is then assigned to the `myCat` object's _name field.

Line 10: This statement displays the message "My dog's name is Fido" in a message box. When the `myDog` object's Name property is retrieved, the `get` accessor returns the value of the object's _name field.

Line 11: This statement displays the message "My cat's name is Sylvester" in a message box. When the `myCat` object's Name property is retrieved, the `get` accessor returns the value of the object's _name field.

When an accessor contains only a single statement, many programmers prefer to write the entire accessor in one line of code. For example, the Name property in the `Pet` class could have been written like this:

```
// Name property
public string Name
{
    get { return _name; }
    set { _name = value; }
}
```

This concise style of writing accessors reduces the number of lines code in a class declaration without sacrificing the code's readability. From this point forward in the book, we will use this style when an accessor has only one statement.

Properties Versus Public Fields

At this point, you might be wondering why you should go to the trouble of creating a property when it would be easier to simply create a public field. For example, in the `Pet` class, couldn't we have just declared a public `string` field named `Name`? If the field is public, it can be directly accessed by code outside the class without the need for accessors.

It is possible to take that approach, but it is not recommended. Class fields are almost always declared `private` in order to protect them from accidental corruption. When code outside the class needs to access a field, it does so through public methods (or, in the case of a property, through accessors). This ensures that the object owning the fields is control of all changes being made to them.

Passing Properties as Arguments

You can pass a property as an argument to a method. For example, line 8 in the following code sample passes a `Pet` object's Name property as an argument to the `MessageBox.Show` method.

```
1 // Create a Pet object.
2 Pet myDog = new Pet();
3
4 // Set the object's Name property.
5 myDog.Name = "Fido";
6
7 // Display the Name property.
8 MessageBox.Show(myDog.Name);
```

When you pass a property as an argument to a method, there is one restriction: Properties can be passed only by value. If you try to pass a property to a `ref` or an out parameter, an error occurs.

Tutorial 9-2 leads you through the process of creating a class with properties. You use the class in a simple application that creates an object of the class and tests its properties.

Tutorial 9-2:

Creating and Using the `CellPhone` Class

Suppose you work as a programmer for a company that sells cell phones and wireless service. Your department is creating an application to manage the company's inventory of cells phones. You have been asked to create a class that represents a cell phone. The class should keep the following data about a cell phone:

- The phone's brand name
- The phone's model
- The phone's retail price

The class should have the following public properties:

- Brand—a `string` property that will store the phone's brand name
- Model—a `string` property that will store the phone's model
- Price—a `decimal` property that will store the phone's retail price

The class should have the following private fields:

- _brand—a `string` that serves as the backing field for the Brand property
- _model—a `string` that serves as the backing field for the Model property
- _price—a `decimal` that serves as the backing field for the Price property

The class should also have a constructor that initializes the private fields. The _brand and _model fields will be initialized with empty strings, and the _price field will be initialized with the value 0.

You create the `CellPhone` class in a project that will create an object of the class and test the object's properties. The project is named *Cell Phone Test* and has already been started for you; it is located in the *Chap09* folder of the Student Sample Programs. Figure 9-14 shows the application's form. At run time, you enter sample cell phone data into the text boxes and then click the *Create Object* button. The application creates an object of the `CellPhone` class and assigns the data from the text boxes to the object's properties. It then reads and displays the values of the object's properties in the `brandLabel`, `modelLabel`, and `priceLabel` controls.

Figure 9-14 The *Cell Phone Test* application's form

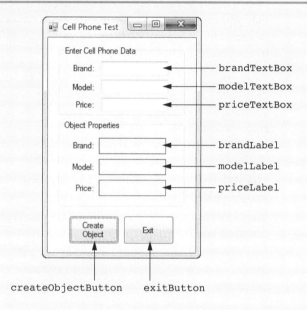

Step 1: Start Visual Studio (or Visual C# Express). Open the project named *Cell Phone Test* in the *Chap09* folder of the Student Sample Programs.

Step 2: Click *Project* on the Visual Studio menu bar and then select *Add Class...* The *Add New Item* window should appear. Make sure *Class* is selected as the type of item. Change the default filename to *CellPhone.cs* and then click the *Add* button. This adds a source code file named CellPhone.cs to the project.

Step 3: The CellPhone.cs file should now be displayed in the code editor. Complete the code for the `CellPhone` class by typing lines 10–42 in Program 9-3.

Step 4: Open the Form1.cs file in the code editor. Type the comments and code for the `GetPhoneData` method, shown in lines 19–43 of Program 9-4. Notice in line 22 that the method has a `CellPhone` parameter named `phone`. When we call this method, we pass a `CellPhone` object to it as an argument.

The purpose of the `GetPhoneData` method is to read the data that the user has entered into the form's text boxes and store that data in the `CellPhone` object's properties. Let's review this code:

Line 25: This statement declares a local `decimal` variable named `price`. This variable temporarily holds the value that the user entered for the phone's price while we perform input validation on that value.

Line 28: This statement assigns the `brandTextBox` control's Text property to the `phone` object's Brand property.

Line 31: This statement assigns the `modelTextBox` control's Text property to the `phone` object's Model property.

Lines 34–42: The `if` statement in line 34 calls the `decimal.TryParse` method to convert the `priceTextBox` control's Text property to a `decimal`, and it stores the result in the `price` variable. If the conversion is successful, line 36 assigns the `price` variable to the `phone` object's Price property. If the conversion is not successful, line 41 displays an error message.

You might be wondering why we need the `price` variable in this code. Why not simply pass the `phone.Price` property as the second argument to the `decimal.TryParse` method in line 34? The reason is that the second argument passed to the `decimal.TryParse` method is passed to an out parameter. Recall that you cannot pass a property to a `ref` or an `out` parameter. So, we pass the `price` variable, and if the conversion is successful, we assign the `price` variable to the `phone.Price` property.

Step 5: Next you create the Click event handlers for the Button controls. Switch your view to the Form1 form in the Designer. Double-click the `createObjectButton` control. This opens the Form1.cs file in the code editor, and you will see an empty event handler named `createObjectButton_Click`. Complete the event handler by typing the code shown in lines 47–56 in Program 9-4. Let's review this code:

Line 48: This statement creates a `CellPhone` object in memory, referenced by a variable named `myPhone`.

Line 51: This statement calls the `GetPhoneData` method, passing the `myPhone` object as an argument.

Lines 54–56: These statements display the values of the `myPhone` object's Brand, Model, and Price properties in the `brandLabel`, `modelLabel`, and `priceLabel` controls.

Step 6: Switch your view back to the Form1 form in the *Designer* and double-click the `exitButton` control. In the code editor you will see an empty event handler named `exitButton_Click`. Complete the event handler by typing the code shown in lines 61–62 in Program 9-4.

Step 7: Save the project. Then, press F5 on the keyboard or click the *Start Debugging* button (▶) on the toolbar to compile and run the application. When the application runs, enter some sample data in the TextBox controls and click the *Create Object* button. You should see the values that you entered displayed in the `brandLabel`, `modelLabel`, and `priceLabel` controls. Click the *Exit* button when you are finished.

Program 9-3 Completed code for the CellPhone.cs file in the *Cell Phone Test* application

```
 1 using System;
 2 using System.Collections.Generic;
 3 using System.Linq;
 4 using System.Text;
 5
 6 namespace Cell_Phone_Test
 7 {
 8     class CellPhone
 9     {
10         // Fields
11         private string _brand;    // The phone's brand
12         private string _model;    // The phone's model
```

```
13              private decimal _price;   // Retail price
14
15          // Constructor
16          public CellPhone()
17          {
18              _brand = "";
19              _model = "";
20              _price = 0m;
21          }
22
23          // Brand property
24          public string Brand
25          {
26              get { return _brand; }
27              set { _brand = value; }
28          }
29
30          // Model property
31          public string Model
32          {
33              get { return _model; }
34              set { _model = value; }
35          }
36
37          // Price property
38          public decimal Price
39          {
40              get { return _price; }
41              set { _price = value; }
42          }
43      }
44 }
```

Program 9-4 Completed code for Form1 in the *Cell Phone Test* application

```
1 using System;
2 using System.Collections.Generic;
3 using System.ComponentModel;
4 using System.Data;
5 using System.Drawing;
6 using System.Linq;
7 using System.Text;
8 using System.Windows.Forms;
9
10 namespace Cell_Phone_Test
11 {
12     public partial class Form1 : Form
13     {
14         public Form1()
15         {
16             InitializeComponent();
17         }
18
19         // The GetPhoneData method accepts a CellPhone object
20         // as an argument. It assigns the data entered by the
21         // user to the object's properties.
22         private void GetPhoneData(CellPhone phone)
```

```
23              {
24                  // Temporary variable to hold the price.
25                  decimal price;
26
27                  // Get the phone's brand.
28                  phone.Brand = brandTextBox.Text;
29
30                  // Get the phone's model.
31                  phone.Model = modelTextBox.Text;
32
33                  // Get the phone's price.
34                  if (decimal.TryParse(priceTextBox.Text, out price))
35                  {
36                      phone.Price = price;
37                  }
38                  else
39                  {
40                      // Display an error message.
41                      MessageBox.Show("Invalid price");
42                  }
43              }
44
45              private void createObjectButton_Click(object sender, EventArgs e)
46              {
47                  // Create a CellPhone object.
48                  CellPhone myPhone = new CellPhone();
49
50                  // Get the phone data.
51                  GetPhoneData(myPhone);
52
53                  // Display the phone data.
54                  brandLabel.Text = myPhone.Brand;
55                  modelLabel.Text = myPhone.Model;
56                  priceLabel.Text = myPhone.Price.ToString("c");
57              }
58
59              private void exitButton_Click(object sender, EventArgs e)
60              {
61                  // Close the form.
62                  this.Close();
63              }
64          }
65      }
```

Read-Only Properties

Sometimes it is useful to make a property read only. A **read-only property** can be read, but it cannot be modified. If you need to make a property read only, you simply do not write a set accessor for the property. The following Circle class shows an example:

```
1 class Circle
2 {
3      // Field
4      private double _diameter;
5
6      // Constructor
7      public Circle()
8      {
```

```
 9            _diameter = 0.0;
10      }
11
12      // Diameter property
13      public double Diameter
14      {
15          get { return _diameter; }
16          set { _diameter = value; }
17      }
18
19      // Radius property (read-only)
20      public double Radius
21      {
22          get { return _diameter / 2; }
23      }
24 }
```

This class has two properties: Diameter (defined in lines 13–17) and Radius (defined in lines 20–23). Notice that the Radius property has a `get` accessor but does not have a `set` accessor. The Radius property is read only. Therefore, if we create an object of the `Circle` class, we can get the value of the Radius property, but an error will occur if we try to assign a value to the Radius property.

Avoiding Stale Data

In the `Circle` class example, previously shown, notice that the Radius property does not have its own backing field, as the Diameter property does. Rather, the Radius property's `get` accessor returns the value of a calculation. The radius is not stored in a field because a circle's radius is dependent on the circle's diameter. If we store both the diameter and the radius in their own fields, the radius field will become incorrect as soon as the diameter field changes.

When a field's value is tightly dependent on other data and that field is not updated when the other data is changed, it is said that the field has become **stale**. When designing a class, you should take care not to store in a field any calculated data that can potentially become stale. Instead, provide a read-only property, or a method, that returns the value of the calculation.

 Checkpoint

9.6 What is a property?

9.7 When you pass a property as an argument to a method, there is one restriction. What is it?

9.8 How do you make a property read only?

9.9 What will happen if you try to assign a value to a read-only property?

9.10 What is stale data?

 9.3

Parameterized Constructors and Overloading

CONCEPT: A constructor that accepts arguments is known as a parameterized constructor. A class can have multiple versions of the same method, which are known as overloaded methods.

Constructors can accept arguments in the same way as other methods. A constructor that accepts arguments is known as a **parameterized constructor** because it has parameter variables. When a class has a parameterized constructor, you can pass initialization values to the constructor when you create an object. In Tutorial 9-3 you write a class that simulates a bank account. The class's constructor will accept an argument that specifies the account's starting balance.

Tutorial 9-3:

Creating and Using the BankAccount Class

In this tutorial you write a class named BankAccount that simulates a bank account. When you create an instance of the class, you pass the account's starting balance as an argument to the constructor. The class will have a Deposit method that adds an amount to the balance and a Withdraw method that subtracts an amount from the balance. The class will also have a read-only Balance property that reports the account's balance.

The BankAccount class is part of the Account Simulator application, which has already been started for you. Figure 9-15 shows the application's form. When the completed application runs, it creates a BankAccount object with a starting balance of $1,000.00. The balance is displayed in the balanceLabel control. If you want to make a deposit, you can enter the amount into the depositTextBox and click the *Deposit* button. If you want to make a withdrawal, you can enter the amount into the withdrawTextBox and click the *Withdraw* button. Each time you perform one of these actions, the new account balance is displayed.

Figure 9-15 The *Account Simulator* application's form

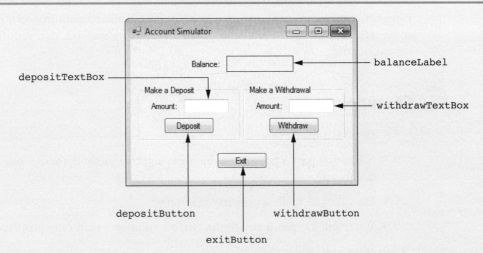

Step 1: Start Visual Studio (or Visual C# Express). Open the project named *Account Simulator* in the *Chap09* folder of the Student Sample Programs.

Step 2: Click *Project* on the Visual Studio menu bar and then select *Add Class...* The *Add New Item* window should appear. Make sure *Class* is selected as the type of item. Change the default filename to *BankAccount.cs* and then click the *Add* button. This adds a source code file named BankAccount.cs to the project.

Step 3: The BankAccount.cs file should now be displayed in the code editor. Complete the code for the `BankAccount` class by typing lines 10–35 in Program 9-5. Let's take a closer look at the code:

Line 11: This statement declares a private `decimal` field named `_balance`. The `_balance` field is the backing field for the Balance property.

Lines 14–17: These lines are the parameterized class constructor. When an instance of the class is created, an argument specifying the account's starting balance is passed into the `startingBalance` parameter. In line 16 the `startingBalance` parameter is assigned to the `_balance` field.

Lines 20–23: This is the code for the Balance property. Notice that the property does not have a `set` accessor, so it is read only.

Lines 26–29: This is the `Deposit` method, which accepts a `decimal` argument and adds the argument to the `_balance` field.

Lines 32–35: This is the `Withdraw` method, which accepts a `decimal` argument, and subtracts the argument from the `_balance` field.

Step 4: Open the Form1.cs file in the code editor. Type the comment and declaration shown in lines 14 and 15 of Program 9-6. The statement in line 15 does the following:

- It creates an object of the `BankAccount` class, passing the value 1000 as an argument to the constructor.
- It assigns a reference to the object to a field named `account`.

Because the `account` variable is declared as a field, all the methods in the `Form1` class have access to it.

Step 5: Next you create a Load event handler for the form. The Load event handler displays the account balance in the `balanceLabel` control. Switch your view to the Form1 form in the *Designer* and double-click any part of the form that does not contain a control. This opens the code editor, and you will see an empty event handler named `Form1_Load`. Complete the event handler by typing the code shown in lines 24 and 25 in Program 9-6. Notice that line 25 uses the `ToString` method to format the `account` object's Balance property as currency and assigns the result to the `balanceLabel` control's Text property.

Step 6: Now you create the Click event handlers for the Button controls. Switch your view back to the Form1 form in the *Designer* and double-click the `depositButton` control. This opens the code editor, and you will see an empty event handler named `depositButton_Click`. Complete the event handler by typing the code shown in lines 30–48 in Program 9-6. Let's look at the code:

Line 30: This statement declares a local `decimal` variable named `amount`. This holds the amount that the user wishes to deposit.

Lines 33–48: The `if` statement in line 33 calls the `decimal.TryParse` method to convert the `depositTextBox` control's Text property to a `decimal`, and it stores the result in the `amount` variable. If the conversion is successful, the following actions take place:

- Line 36 calls the `account` object's `Deposit` method, passing `amount` as an argument.
- Line 39 displays the account balance, formatted as currency.
- Line 42 clears the `depositTextBox` control.

If the conversion is not successful, line 47 displays an error message.

Step 7: Switch your view back to the Form1 form in the *Designer* and double-click the `withdrawButton` control. This opens the code editor, and you will see an empty event handler named `withdrawButton_Click`. Complete the event handler by typing the code shown in lines 53–71 in Program 9-6. Let's look at the code:

Line 53: This statement declares a local `decimal` variable named `amount`. This holds the amount that the user wishes to withdraw.

Lines 56–71: The `if` statement in line 56 calls the `decimal.TryParse` method to convert the `withdrawTextBox` control's Text property to a `decimal`, and it stores the result in the `amount` variable. If the conversion is successful, the following actions take place:

- Line 59 calls the `account` object's `Withdraw` method, passing `amount` as an argument.
- Line 62 displays the account balance, formatted as currency.
- Line 65 clears the `withdrawTextBox` control.

If the conversion is not successful, line 70 displays an error message.

Step 8: Switch your view back to the Form1 form in the *Designer* and double-click the `exitButton` control. In the code editor you will see an empty event handler named `exitButton_Click`. Complete the event handler by typing the code shown in lines 76–77 in Program 9-6.

Step 9: Save the project. Then, press [F5] on the keyboard or click the *Start Debugging* button (▶) on the toolbar to compile and run the application. When the application runs, experiment by depositing and withdrawing various amounts. Click the *Exit* button when you are finished.

Program 9-5 Completed code for the BankAccount.cs file in the *Account Simulator* application

```
1 using System;
2 using System.Collections.Generic;
3 using System.Linq;
4 using System.Text;
5
6 namespace Example
7 {
8     class BankAccount
9     {
10         // Field
11         private decimal _balance;
12
13         // Constructor
14         public BankAccount(decimal startingBalance)
15         {
16             _balance = startingBalance;
17         }
18
19         // Balance property (read-only)
20         public decimal Balance
21         {
22             get { return _balance; }
23         }
24
25         // Deposit method
26         public void Deposit(decimal amount)
```

```
27              {
28                  _balance += amount;
29              }
30
31              // Withdraw method
32              public void Withdraw(decimal amount)
33              {
34                  _balance -= amount;
35              }
36          }
37  }
```

Program 9-6 Completed code for Form1 in the *Account Simulator* application

```
 1  using System;
 2  using System.Collections.Generic;
 3  using System.ComponentModel;
 4  using System.Data;
 5  using System.Drawing;
 6  using System.Linq;
 7  using System.Text;
 8  using System.Windows.Forms;
 9
10  namespace Account_Simulator
11  {
12      public partial class Form1 : Form
13      {
14          // BankAccount field with a $1000 starting balance
15          private BankAccount account = new BankAccount(1000);
16
17          public Form1()
18          {
19              InitializeComponent();
20          }
21
22          private void Form1_Load(object sender, EventArgs e)
23          {
24              // Display the starting balance.
25              balanceLabel.Text = account.Balance.ToString("c");
26          }
27
28          private void depositButton_Click(object sender, EventArgs e)
29          {
30              decimal amount;   // To hold the amount of deposit
31
32              // Convert the amount to a decimal.
33              if (decimal.TryParse(depositTextBox.Text, out amount))
34              {
35                  // Deposit the amount into the account.
36                  account.Deposit(amount);
37
38                  // Display the new balance.
39                  balanceLabel.Text = account.Balance.ToString("c");
40
41                  // Clear the text box.
42                  depositTextBox.Clear();
43              }
44              else
```

```
45                    {
46                        // Display an error message.
47                        MessageBox.Show("Invalid amount");
48                    }
49            }
50
51        private void withdrawButton_Click(object sender, EventArgs e)
52        {
53            decimal amount;   // To hold the amount of withdrawal
54
55            // Convert the amount to a decimal.
56            if (decimal.TryParse(withdrawTextBox.Text, out amount))
57            {
58                // Withdraw the amount from the account.
59                account.Withdraw(amount);
60
61                // Display the new balance.
62                balanceLabel.Text = account.Balance.ToString("c");
63
64                // Clear the text box.
65                withdrawTextBox.Clear();
66            }
67            else
68            {
69                // Display an error message.
70                MessageBox.Show("Invalid amount");
71            }
72        }
73
74        private void exitButton_Click(object sender, EventArgs e)
75        {
76            // Close the form.
77            this.Close();
78        }
79    }
80 }
```

Overloaded Methods

Sometimes you need different ways to perform the same operation. For example, the BankAccount class that you wrote in Tutorial 9-3 has a Deposit method that accepts a decimal argument. Suppose you are using the class in an application that needs to pass a double variable to the method instead of a decimal variable. In this application, before you call the Deposit method, you have to convert the double variable to a decimal so it can be passed to the method. It would be nice if the Deposit method could accept either a decimal argument or a double argument. Then, it would be unnecessary to convert a double variable before passing it to the method. This can be accomplished with overloading.

When a method is **overloaded**, it means that multiple methods in the same class have the same name but use different types of parameters. Here is an example of how we might overload the Deposit method inside the BankAccount class:

```
1 // Deposit method
2 public void Deposit(decimal amount)
3 {
4     _balance += amount;
5 }
```

```
 6
 7 // Deposit method
 8 public void Deposit(double amount)
 9 {
10     _balance += (decimal)amount;
11 }
```

The first `Deposit` method (in lines 2–5) accepts a `decimal` argument, which is added to the _balance field in line 4. The second `Deposit` method (in lines 8–11) accepts a `double` argument. Line 10 uses a cast operator to convert its value to a `decimal`, and assigns the result to the _balance field.

When you write a call to the `Deposit` method, the compiler must determine which one of the overloaded methods you intended to call. The process of matching a method call with the correct method is known as **binding**. When an overloaded method is called, the compiler uses the method's name and parameter list to determine to which method to bind the call. If we call the `Deposit` method and pass a `decimal` argument, the version of the method that has a `decimal` parameter is called. Likewise, if we call the `Deposit` method and pass a `double` argument, the version of the method that has a `double` parameter is called.

The compiler uses a method's signature to distinguish it from other methods of the same name. A method's **signature** consists of the method's name and the data type and argument kind (by value, `ref`, or `out`) of the method's parameters, from left to right. For example, here are the signatures of the `Deposit` methods that we previously showed:

```
Deposit(decimal)
Deposit(double)
```

Note that the method's return type is *not* part of the signature. For this reason, you cannot overload methods by giving them different return types.

Overloaded Constructors

Constructors can also be overloaded, which means that a class can have more than one constructor. The rules for overloading constructors are the same for overloading other methods: Each version of the constructor must have a different parameter list. As long as each constructor has a unique signature, the compiler can tell them apart.

Here is an example of how we might overload the `BankAccount` class constructor:

```
 1 // Constructor
 2 public BankAccount()
 3 {
 4     _balance = 0;
 5 }
 6
 7 // Constructor
 8 public BankAccount(decimal startingBalance)
 9 {
10     _balance = startingBalance;
11 }
```

The first constructor (lines 2–5) is a **parameterless constructor**, which means it accepts no arguments. The following statement calls the parameterless constructor as it creates a `BankAccount` object:

```
BankAccount account = new BankAccount();
```

The second constructor (lines 8–11) accepts a `decimal` argument. The following statement calls this constructor as it creates a `BankAccount` object:

```
BankAccount account = new BankAccount(500m);
```

The following statement also calls the second constructor (lines 8–11) because an integer value can be implicitly converted to a `decimal`:

```
BankAccount account = new BankAccount(500);
```

The following code will cause an error, however, because there is no constructor that accepts a `double` argument:

```
// Error
BankAccount account = new BankAccount(500.0);
```

Default Constructors

It is perfectly legal to write a class without any constructors. If you write a class with no constructor whatsoever, the compiler provides a default constructor. The **default constructor** is a parameterless constructor (it accepts no arguments), and it initializes the object's fields with the value 0. (If any fields are reference variables, they are initialized with the special value `null`.)

 Checkpoint

9.11 What is a parameterized constructor?

9.12 What does it mean when a method is overloaded?

9.13 What is process of matching a method call with the correct method called?

9.14 What happens if you write a class with no constructor whatsoever?

9.15 Describe the purpose of the default constructor.

 9.4 ## Storing Class Type Objects in Arrays and `Lists`

CONCEPT: You can store a collection of class type objects in an array or a `List`.

Arrays of Class Type Objects

Objects that are instances of a class can be stored in an array. For example, assume the `CellPhone` class previously shown exists in an application. The following code creates a `CellPhone` array with four elements:

```
const int SIZE = 4;
CellPhone[] phones = new CellPhone[SIZE];
```

Although this code creates an array, it does not yet contain any objects. When you create an array of a class type, each element of the array is a reference variable. By default, each element will be initialized with the value `null`. The next step is to create the objects that each element will reference. This can be done one element at a time, as shown here:

```
phones[0] = new CellPhone();
phones[1] = new CellPhone();
phones[2] = new CellPhone();
phones[3] = new CellPhone();
```

Or, it can be done with a loop, as shown here:

```
for (int index = 0; index < phones.Length; index++)
{
```

```
            phones[index] = new CellPhone();
    }
```

Alternatively, you can initialize the array elements in the declaration statement:

```
CellPhone[] phones = {
                        new CellPhone(), new CellPhone(),
                        new CellPhone(), new CellPhone()
                    };
```

The following shows another example. This code creates a `BankAccount` array and initializes its elements with references to four `BankAccount` objects.

```
BankAccount[] accounts = {
                            new BankAccount(1000),
                            new BankAccount(2000),
                            new BankAccount(3000),
                            new BankAccount(4000)
                        };
```

Notice the arguments that are passed to the `BankAccount` constructor for each object. If the following code were executed, it would display "The balance is 1000", "The balance is 2000", and so forth:

```
for (int index = 0; index < accounts.Length; index++)
{
    MessageBox.Show("The balance is " +
                    accounts[index].Balance);
}
```

The following code performs the same operation using a `foreach` loop:

```
foreach (BankAccount acct in accounts)
{
    MessageBox.Show("The balance is " +
                    acct[index].Balance);
}
```

`Lists` of Class Type Objects

In Chapter 7 we discussed the `List` class, which is a container for storing a collection of objects. Here is an example of how you would create a `List` that can hold `CellPhone` objects:

```
List<CellPhone> phoneList = new List<CellPhone>();
```

This statement creates a `List` object, referenced by the `phoneList` variable. Notice that the word `CellPhone` is written inside angled brackets, `<>`, immediately after the word `List`. This specifies that the `List` can hold only objects of the `CellPhone` class type.

To add an object to a `List`, you use the `Add` method. The following code shows an example:

```
 1 // Create a List to hold CellPhone objects.
 2 List<CellPhone> phoneList = new List<CellPhone>();
 3
 4 // Create an instance of the CellPhone class.
 5 CellPhone myPhone = new CellPhone();
 6
 7 // Assign values to the object's properties.
 8 myPhone.Brand = "Acme Electronics";
 9 myPhone.Model = "M1000";
10 myPhone.Price = 199;
11
12 // Add the object to the List.
13 phoneList.Add(myPhone);
```

The statement in line 2 creates a `List` named `phoneList` that can hold `CellPhone` objects. Line 5 creates an instance of the `CellPhone` class, referenced by the `myPhone` variable. Lines 8–10 assign values to the object's properties. Line 13 adds the object to the `List`.

In Tutorial 9-4 you complete an application that uses a `List` to hold a collection of `CellPhone` objects.

Tutorial 9-4:
Completing the *Cell Phone Inventory* Application

In this tutorial you complete the *Cell Phone Inventory* application. Figure 9-16 shows the application's form, which has already been created for you. When you run the completed application, you can enter data about a cell phone into the TextBox controls. When you click the *Add Phone* button, that data is assigned to a `CellPhone` object's properties and then the object is added to a `List`. You can do this as many times as you wish. Each time you add a cell phone, its brand and model is displayed in the list box. If you select a phone in the list box, the application displays that phone's price.

Figure 9-16 The *Cell Phone Inventory* application's form

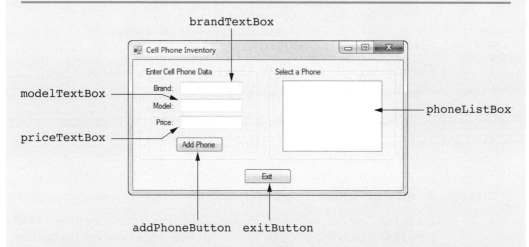

Figure 9-17 shows an example of the application at run time. In the figure, five cell phones have been added, and *Atlantic Mobile S2* has been selected in the list box. The selected phone's price is displayed in the message box.

Figure 9-17 The *Cell Phone Inventory* application's form

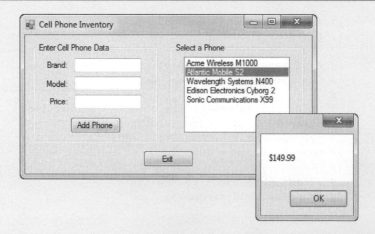

Step 1: Start Visual Studio (or Visual C# Express). Open the project named *Cell Phone Inventory* in the *Chap09* folder of the Student Sample Programs. Notice that the `CellPhone` class has already been added to the project for you in the file CellPhone.cs.

Step 2: Open the Form1.cs file in the code editor. Write the comment and the declaration for `phoneList`, which appears in lines 14 and 15 in Program 9-7. Notice that `phoneList` is declared as a field in the `Form1` class. It will be available to all the methods in the class.

Step 3: Type the comments and code for the `GetPhoneData` method, shown in lines 22–46 of Program 9-7. Notice that the method accepts a `CellPhone` object as an argument. The purpose of the `GetPhoneData` method is to read the data that the user has entered into the form's text boxes and store that data in the argument object's properties. (This method might look familiar. We used it in Tutorial 9-2.)

Step 4: Switch your view to the Form1 form in the *Designer* and double-click the `addPhoneButton` control. This opens the code editor, and you will see an empty event handler named `addPhoneButton_Click`. Complete the event handler by typing the code shown in lines 50–69 in Program 9-7. Let's look at the code:

Line 51: This statement creates a `CellPhone` object in memory, referenced by a variable named `myPhone`.

Line 54: This statement calls the `GetPhoneData` method, passing the `myPhone` object as an argument. After the method executes, the `myPhone` object's properties are set to the data entered by the user.

Line 57: This statement adds the `myPhone` object to the `phoneList`.

Lines 60–61: These statements add an entry to the `phoneListBox` control displaying the `myPhone` object's Brand and Model properties.

Lines 64–66: These statements clear the contents of the TextBox controls.

Line 69: This statement sets the focus to the `brandTextBox` control.

Note that each `CellPhone` object that is added to the `phoneList` has a corresponding item in the ListBox control. An object in the `phoneList` and its corresponding item in the ListBox share the same index. For example,

- The `CellPhone` object at index 0 in `phoneList` corresponds to the item at index 0 in the ListBox.
- The `CellPhone` object at index 1 in `phoneList` corresponds to the item at index 1 in the ListBox.

Recall from Chapter 8 that when the items in two data structures are related by their indexes, it is said that a parallel relationship exists between the data structures.

Step 5: Next you create the SelectedIndexChange event handler for the `phoneListBox` control. Switch back to the *Designer* and double-click the `phoneListBox` control. This opens the code editor, and you will see an empty event handler named `phoneListBox_SelectedIndexChange`. Complete the event handler by typing the code shown in lines 74–78 in Program 9-7.

We mentioned in Step 4 that the items in the list box and the objects in the `phoneList` are related by their indexes. When the user selects an item from the list box, all we have to do is get that item's index and then use that same index to retrieve the corresponding object from the `phoneList`. That is exactly what happens in this event handler. Line 75 gets the index of the selected item in the `phoneListBox` control and assigns it to the `index` variable. Line 78 uses the index variable to get an object from phoneList and display its Price property in a message box.

Step 6: Switch your view back to the *Designer* and double-click the exitButton control. In the code editor you will see an empty event handler named exitButton_Click. Complete the event handler by typing the code shown in lines 83 and 84 in Program 9-7.

Step 7: Save the project. Then, press F5 on the keyboard or click the *Start Debugging* button (▶) on the toolbar to compile and run the application. When the application runs, enter some sample data in the TextBox controls and click the *Add Phone* button. Repeat this with several different sets of data. Each time you add a phone, you should see its brand and model displayed in the list box. After you have entered data for several phones, click the entries that appear in the list box to see each phone's price. Click the *Exit* button when you are finished.

Program 9-7 Completed code for Form1 in the *Cell Phone Inventory* application

```csharp
1  using System;
2  using System.Collections.Generic;
3  using System.ComponentModel;
4  using System.Data;
5  using System.Drawing;
6  using System.Linq;
7  using System.Text;
8  using System.Windows.Forms;
9
10 namespace Cell_Phone_Inventory
11 {
12     public partial class Form1 : Form
13     {
14         // List to hold CellPhone objects
15         List<CellPhone> phoneList = new List<CellPhone>();
16
17         public Form1()
18         {
19             InitializeComponent();
20         }
21
22         // The GetPhoneData method accepts a CellPhone object
23         // as an argument. It assigns the data entered by the
24         // user to the object's properties.
25         private void GetPhoneData(CellPhone phone)
26         {
27             // Temporary variable to hold the price.
28             decimal price;
29
30             // Get the phone's brand.
31             phone.Brand = brandTextBox.Text;
32
33             // Get the phone's model.
34             phone.Model = modelTextBox.Text;
35
36             // Get the phone's price.
37             if (decimal.TryParse(priceTextBox.Text, out price))
38             {
39                 phone.Price = price;
40             }
```

```
41              else
42              {
43                  // Display an error message.
44                  MessageBox.Show("Invalid price");
45              }
46          }
47
48          private void addPhoneButton_Click(object sender, EventArgs e)
49          {
50              // Create a CellPhone object.
51              CellPhone myPhone = new CellPhone();
52
53              // Get the phone data.
54              GetPhoneData(myPhone);
55
56              // Add the CellPhone object to the List.
57              phoneList.Add(myPhone);
58
59              // Add an entry to the list box.
60              phoneListBox.Items.Add(myPhone.Brand + " " +
61                                     myPhone.Model);
62
63              // Clear the TextBox controls.
64              brandTextBox.Clear();
65              modelTextBox.Clear();
66              priceTextBox.Clear();
67
68              // Reset the focus.
69              brandTextBox.Focus();
70          }
71
72          private void phoneListBox_SelectedIndexChanged(object sender, EventArgs e)
73          {
74              // Get the index of the selected item.
75              int index = phoneListBox.SelectedIndex;
76
77              // Display the selected item's price.
78              MessageBox.Show(phoneList[index].Price.ToString("c"));
79          }
80
81          private void exitButton_Click(object sender, EventArgs e)
82          {
83              // Close the form.
84              this.Close();
85          }
86      }
87  }
```

Checkpoint

9.16 When you create a array of a class type, with what value will each element of the array be initialized?

9.17 How can you initialize an array of a class type with references to objects of the class?

9.18 How do you specify the class type that a `List` can hold?

9.5 Finding the Classes and Their Responsibilities in a Problem

When developing an object-oriented program, one of your first tasks is to identify the classes that you will need to create. Typically, your goal is to identify the different types of real-world objects that are present in the problem and then create classes for those types of objects within your application.

Over the years, software professionals have developed numerous techniques for finding the classes in a given problem. One simple and popular technique involves the following steps.

1. Get a written description of the problem domain.
2. Identify all the nouns (including pronouns and noun phrases) in the description. Each of these is a potential class.
3. Refine the list to include only the classes that are relevant to the problem.

Let's take a closer look at each of these steps.

Writing a Description of the Problem Domain

The **problem domain** is the set of real-world objects, parties, and major events related to the problem. If you adequately understand the nature of the problem you are trying to solve, you can write a description of the problem domain yourself. If you do not thoroughly understand the nature of the problem, you should have an expert write the description for you.

For example, suppose we are programming an application that the manager of Joe's Automotive Shop will use to print service quotes for customers. Here is a description that an expert, perhaps Joe himself, might have written:

> Joe's Automotive Shop services foreign cars and specializes in servicing cars made by Mercedes, Porsche, and BMW. When a customer brings a car to the shop, the manager gets the customer's name, address, and telephone number. The manager then determines the make, model, and year of the car and gives the customer a service quote. The service quote shows the estimated parts charges, estimated labor charges, sales tax, and total estimated charges.

The problem domain description should include any of the following:

- Physical objects such vehicles, machines, or products
- Any role played by a person, such as manager, employee, customer, teacher, student, and so on
- The results of a business event, such as a customer order or, in this case, a service quote
- Record-keeping items, such as customer histories and payroll records

Identify All of the Nouns

The next step is to identify all of the nouns and noun phrases. (If the description contains pronouns, include them, too.) Here's another look at the previous problem domain description. This time the nouns and noun phrases appear in bold.

> **Joe's Automotive Shop** services **foreign cars** and specializes in servicing **cars** made by **Mercedes**, **Porsche**, and **BMW**. When a **customer** brings a **car** to the **shop**, the **manager** gets the **customer's** **name**, **address**, and **telephone number**. The **manager** then determines the **make**, **model**, and **year** of the **car** and gives the **customer** a **service quote**. The **service quote** shows the **estimated parts charges**, **estimated labor charges**, **sales tax**, and **total estimated charges**.

Notice that some of the nouns are repeated. The following list shows all the nouns without duplicating any of them.

address

BMW

car

cars

customer

estimated labor charges

estimated parts charges

foreign cars

Joe's Automotive Shop

make

manager

Mercedes

model

name

Porsche

sales tax

service quote

shop

telephone number

total estimated charges

year

Refining the List of Nouns

The nouns that appear in the problem description are merely candidates to become classes. It might not be necessary to make classes for them all. The next step is to refine the list to include only the classes that are necessary to solve the particular problem at hand. We look at the common reasons that a noun can be eliminated from the list of potential classes.

1. **Some of the nouns really mean the same thing.**

   In this example, the following sets of nouns refer to the same thing:

   - **car, cars,** and **foreign cars**

   These all refer to the general concept of a car.

   - **Joe's Automotive Shop** and **shop**

   Both of these refer to the company "Joe's Automotive Shop."

We can settle on a single class for each of these. In this example we arbitrarily eliminate **cars** and **foreign cars** from the list and use the word **car**. Likewise, we eliminate **Joe's Automotive Shop** from the list and use the word **shop**. The updated list of potential classes is as follows:

address

BMW

car

~~cars~~

customer

estimated labor charges

estimated parts charges
~~foreign cars~~
~~Joe's Automotive Shop~~
make
manager
Mercedes
model
name
Porsche
sales tax
service quote
shop
telephone number
total estimated charges
year

Because **car**, **cars**, and **foreign cars** mean the same thing in this problem, we have eliminated **cars** and **foreign cars**. Also, because **Joe's Automotive Shop** and **shop** mean the same thing, we have eliminated **Joe's Automotive Shop**.

2. **Some nouns might represent items that we do not need to be concerned with in order to solve the problem.**

   A quick review of the problem description reminds us of what our application should do: print a service quote. In this example we can eliminate two unnecessary classes from the list:

   - We can cross **shop** off the list because our application needs to be concerned only with individual service quotes. It does not need to work with or determine any companywide information. If the problem description asked us to keep a total of all the service quotes, then it would make sense to have a class for the shop.
   - We will not need a class for the **manager** because the problem statement does not direct us to process any information about the manager. If there were multiple shop managers, and the problem description had asked us to record which manager generated each service quote, then it would make sense to have a class for the manager.

   The updated list of potential classes at this point is as follows:

   address
   BMW
   car
   ~~cars~~
   customer
   estimated labor charges
   estimated parts charges
   ~~foreign cars~~
   ~~Joe's Automotive Shop~~
   make
   ~~manager~~
   Mercedes
   model
   name
   Porsche
   sales tax
   service quote
   ~~shop~~
   telephone number
   total estimated charges
   year

Our problem description does not direct us to process any information about the **shop** or any information about the **manager**, so we have eliminated those from the list.

3. **Some of the nouns might represent objects, not classes.**

We can eliminate **Mercedes, Porsche,** and **BMW** as classes because, in this example, they all represent specific cars and can be considered instances of a **car** class. At this point the updated list of potential classes is as follows:

address
~~BMW~~
car
~~cars~~
customer
estimated labor charges
estimated parts charges
~~foreign cars~~
~~Joe's Automotive Shop~~   We have eliminated **Mercedes, Porsche,** and
~~manager~~   **BMW,** because they are all instances of a **car**
make   class. That means that these nouns identify
~~Mercedes~~   objects, not classes.
model
name
~~Porsche~~
sales tax
service quote
~~shop~~
telephone number
total estimated charges
year

4. **Some of the nouns might represent simple values that can be assigned to a variable and do not require a class.**

> **NOTE:** Some object-oriented designers take note of whether a noun is plural or singular. Sometimes a plural noun will indicate a class and a singular noun will indicate an object.

A class contains data attributes and methods. Data attributes are the fields and properties that define the object's state. Methods are actions or behaviors that can be performed by an object of the class. If a noun represents a type of item that would not have any identifiable data attributes or methods, then it can probably be eliminated from the list. To help determine whether a noun represents an item that would have data attributes and methods, ask the following questions about it:

• Would you use a group of related values to represent the item's state?
• Are there any obvious actions to be performed by the item?

If the answers to both of these questions are no, then the noun probably represents a value that can be stored in a simple variable. If we apply this test to each noun that remains in our list, we can conclude that the following are probably not classes: **address, estimated labor charges, estimated parts charges, make, model, name, sales tax, telephone number, total estimated charges,** and **year.** These are all simple string or numeric values that can be stored in variables. Here is the updated list of potential classes:

~~address~~
~~BMW~~
car
~~cars~~
customer
~~estimated labor charges~~
~~estimated parts charges~~
~~foreign cars~~
~~Joe's Automotive Shop~~
~~make~~
~~manager~~
~~Mercedes~~
~~model~~
~~name~~
~~Porsche~~
~~sales tax~~
service quote
~~shop~~
~~telephone number~~
~~total estimated charges~~
~~year~~

We have eliminated **address, estimated labor charges, estimated parts charges, make, model, name, sales tax, telephone number, total estimated charges,** and **year** as classes because they represent simple values that can be stored in variables.

As you can see from the list, we have eliminated everything except **car, customer,** and **service quote**. This means that in our application, we need classes to represent cars, customers, and service quotes. Ultimately, we will write a `Car` class, a `Customer` class, and a `ServiceQuote` class.

Identifying a Class's Responsibilities

Once the classes have been identified, the next task is to identify each class's responsibilities. A class's *responsibilities* are as follows

- The things that the class is responsible for knowing
- The actions that the class is responsible for doing

When you have identified the things that a class is responsible for knowing, then you have identified the class's fields and/or properties. Likewise, when you have identified the actions that a class is responsible for doing, you have identified its methods.

It is often helpful to ask these questions: In the context of this problem, what must the class know? What must the class do? The first place to look for the answers is in the description of the problem domain. Many of the things that a class must know and do will be mentioned. Some class responsibilities, however, might not be directly mentioned in the problem domain, so brainstorming is often required. Let's apply this methodology to the classes we previously identified from our problem domain.

The `Customer` class

In the context of our problem domain, what must the `Customer` class know? The description directly mentions the following items:

- The customer's name
- The customer's address
- The customer's telephone number

These are all values that can be represented as strings and stored as properties. The Customer class can potentially know many other things. One mistake that can be made at this point is to identify too many things that an object is responsible for knowing. In some applications, a Customer class might know the customer's e-mail address. This particular problem domain does not mention that the customer's e-mail address is used for any purpose, so we should not include it as a responsibility.

Now let's identify the class's methods. In the context of our problem domain, what must the Customer class do? The only obvious actions are these:

- Create and initialize an object of the Customer class.
- Get and set the customer's name.
- Get and set the customer's address.
- Get and set the customer's telephone number.

From this list we can see that the Customer class will have a constructor as well as fields and properties for the data attributes. The following code shows how the Customer class might be written:

```
 1 class Customer
 2 {
 3     // Fields
 4     private string _name;
 5     private string _address;
 6     private string _phone;
 7
 8     // Constructor
 9     public Customer(string name, string address, string phone)
10     {
11         _name = name;
12         _address = address;
13         _phone = phone;
14     }
15
16     // Name property
17     public string Name
18     {
19         get { return _name; }
20         set { _name = value; }
21     }
22
23     // Address property
24     public string Address
25     {
26         get { return _address; }
27         set { _address = value; }
28     }
29
30     // Phone property
31     public string Phone
32     {
33         get { return _phone; }
34         set { _phone = value; }
35     }
36 }
```

The `Car` Class

In the context of our problem domain, what must an object of the `Car` class know? The following items are all data attributes of a car and are mentioned in the problem domain:

- The car's make
- The car's model
- The car's year

Now let's identify the class's methods. In the context of our problem domain, what must the `Car` class do? Once again, the only obvious actions are the standard set of methods that we will find in most classes. Specifically, the actions are these:

- Create and initialize an object of the `Car` class.
- Get and set the car's make.
- Get and set the car's model.
- Get and set the car's year.

The following code shows how the `Car` class might be written:

```
 1 class Car
 2 {
 3     // Fields
 4     private string _make;
 5     private string _model;
 6     private int _year;
 7
 8     // Constructor
 9     public Car(string make, string model, int year)
10     {
11         _make = make;
12         _model = model;
13         _year = year;
14     }
15
16     // Make property
17     public string Make
18     {
19         get { return _make; }
20         set { _make = value; }
21     }
22
23     // Model property
24     public string Model
25     {
26         get { return _model; }
27         set { _model = value; }
28     }
29
30     // Year property
31     public int Year
32     {
33         get { return _year; }
34         set { _year = value; }
35     }
36 }
```

The `ServiceQuote` Class

In the context of our problem domain, what must an object of the `ServiceQuote` class know? The problem domain mentions the following items:

- The estimated parts charges
- The estimated labor charges

- The sales tax
- The total estimated charges

Careful thought and a little brainstorming reveals that two of these items are the results of calculations: sales tax and total estimated charges. Furthermore, in order to calculate the sales tax, the class must also know the sales tax rate.

Now let's identify the class's methods. In the context of our problem domain, what must the ServiceQuote class do? Once again, the only obvious actions are the standard set of methods that we will find in most classes. Specifically, the actions are these:

- Create and initialize an object of the ServiceQuote class.
- Get and set the estimated parts charges.
- Get and set the estimated labor charges.
- Get and set the sales tax rate.
- Get the sales tax.
- Get the total estimated charges.

The following code shows how the ServiceQuote class might be written:

```
1 class ServiceQuote
2 {
3      // Fields
4      private decimal _partsCharges;
5      private decimal _laborCharges;
6      private decimal _taxRate;
7
8      // Constructor
9      public ServiceQuote(decimal partsCharges,
10         decimal laborCharges, decimal taxRate)
11     {
12         _partsCharges = partsCharges;
13         _laborCharges = laborCharges;
14         _taxRate = taxRate;
15     }
16
17     // PartsCharges property
18     public decimal PartsCharges
19     {
20         get { return _partsCharges; }
21         set { _partsCharges = value; }
22     }
23
24     // LaborCharges property
25     public decimal LaborCharges
26     {
27         get { return _laborCharges; }
28         set { _laborCharges = value; }
29     }
30
31     // TaxRate property
32     public decimal TaxRate
33     {
34         get { return _taxRate; }
35         set { _taxRate = value; }
36     }
37
38     // SalesTax property (read-only)
39     public decimal SalesTax
40     {
41         get { return _partsCharges * _taxRate; }
```

```
42          }
43
44          // TotalCharges property (read-only)
45          public decimal TotalCharges
46          {
47              get
48              {
49                  return _partsCharges + _laborCharges +
50                      (_partsCharges * _taxRate);
51              }
52          }
53  }
```

This Is Only the Beginning

You should look at the process that we have discussed in this section merely as a starting point. It's important to realize that designing an object-oriented application is an iterative process. It may take you several attempts to identify all the classes that you will need and determine all their responsibilities. As the design process unfolds, you will gain a deeper understanding of the problem, and consequently you will see ways to improve the design.

 Checkpoint

9.19 What is a problem domain?

9.20 When designing an object-oriented application, who should write a description of the problem domain?

9.21 How do you identify the potential classes in a problem domain description?

9.22 What are a class's responsibilities?

9.23 What two questions should you ask to determine a class's responsibilities?

9.24 Will all a class's actions always be directly mentioned in the problem domain description?

 9.6   Creating Multiple Forms in a Project

CONCEPT: A Visual C# project can have multiple forms. Each form has its own class that can be instantiated and displayed on the screen.

The applications you have created so far have used only one form, named Form1. The Form1 form is displayed when the application runs, and when the Form1 form closes, the application ends. You are not limited to one form in a project, however. You may create multiple forms in a project to use as dialog boxes, to display error messages, and so on. Then you can display these forms as they are needed.

Every form in a Visual C# project has a class. For example, if a project has a form named Form1, then the project has a class named Form1, which is stored in a file named Form1.cs. When you add additional forms to a project, you add additional classes, which are stored in their own files. When you create event handlers for a specific form's controls, you write them as methods in that form's class.

Renaming the Form1 Form

When you add forms to a Visual C# project, they are given default names such as Form1, Form2, and so on. If you have only one form in a project, there is no compelling reason to change the form's name. However, when you have multiple forms in a project, you should give each form a meaningful name that describes its purpose.

Before you add a new form to a project, it is a good idea to change the name of the Form1 form. In this book, we always change the name of the Form1 form to MainForm because it is usually the main form in an application. To change the form's name, you use the Solution Explorer to change the name of the Form1.cs file to MainForm.cs. When you do this, Visual Studio automatically changes the name of the Form1 form to MainForm. Here is the procedure to follow:

1. Right-click the Form1.cs entry that appears in the Solution Explorer. The pop-up menu shown in Figure 9-18 should appear.

Figure 9-18 Right-clicking the form file in the *Solution Explorer*

2. Select *Rename* from the pop-up menu.
3. In the *Solution Explorer*, the form's filename should become highlighted. Type the new name, which is *MainForm.cs*, and press (Enter). (Be sure to type the .cs extension.)
4. The dialog box shown in Figure 9-19 will appear next. Click *Yes* to rename the form.

Figure 9-19 Clicking *Yes* to rename the form

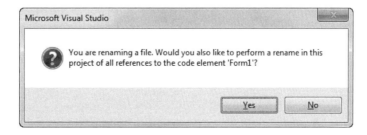

Figure 9-20 shows an example of the Solution Explorer after the Form1.cs file has been renamed MainForm.cs.

Figure 9-20 Form file renamed as MainForm.cs

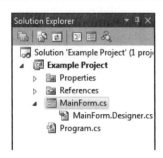

Adding a New Form to a Project

Follow these steps to add a new form to a project:

1. Click *Project* on the Visual Studio menu bar, and then select *Add Windows Form...* from the *Project* menu. The *Add New Item* window, shown in Figure 9-21, should appear.

Figure 9-21 *Add New Item* window

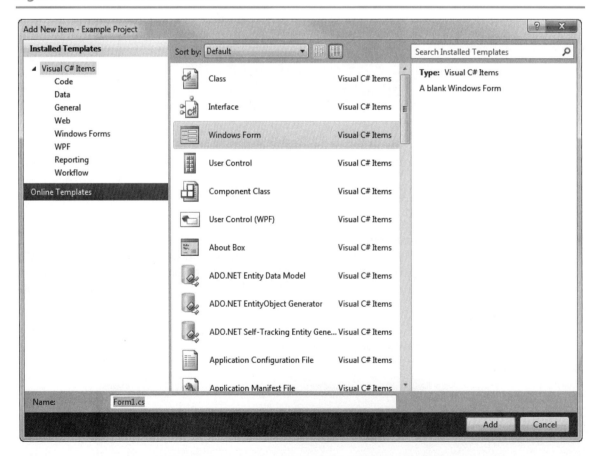

2. Near the bottom of the *Add New Item* window, a *Name* text box appears, where you can specify the new form's file name. Initially, a default name will appear here. (Notice that in Figure 9-21 the default name Form1.cs appears. The actual name that appears on your screen may be different.) Change the default name that is

displayed in the *Name* text box to a more descriptive name. For example, if you wish to name the new form ErrorForm, enter *ErrorForm.cs* in the *Name* text box. (Make sure you specify the *.cs* extension with the file name that you enter.)

3. Click the *Add* button.

After completing these steps, a new blank form is added to your project. The new form is displayed in the *Designer,* and an entry for the new form's file appears in the *Solution Explorer.* Figure 9-22 shows an example of the *Solution Explorer* with two form files: *ErrorForm.cs* and *MainForm.cs.* Once you have added a form to a project, you can place any controls on it that you desire and write the necessary event handlers for it.

Figure 9-22 *Solution Explorer* window showing two forms

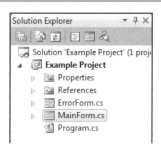

Switching between Forms and Form Code

In Visual Studio, you can easily switch your view to another form by double-clicking the form's entry in the *Solution Explorer* window. The form is then displayed in the *Designer.* You can also use the tabs that appear at the top of the *Designer* to display different forms or their code. For example, look at Figure 9-23. It shows the tabs that appear for a project with two forms: ErrorForm and MainForm. The tabs that display the *[Design]* designator cause a form to be displayed in the *Design* window. The tabs that appear without the designator cause a form's code to be displayed in the code editor.

Figure 9-23 *Designer* tabs

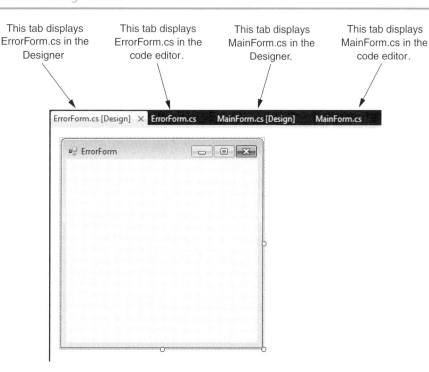

When you open a form in the code editor, you will see several using directives, a name-space declaration, and the form's class. Figure 9-24 shows an example. The file in the figure contains the code for a form named ErrorForm. Notice that the form's class is named ErrorForm.

Figure 9-24 A source code file containing a form class

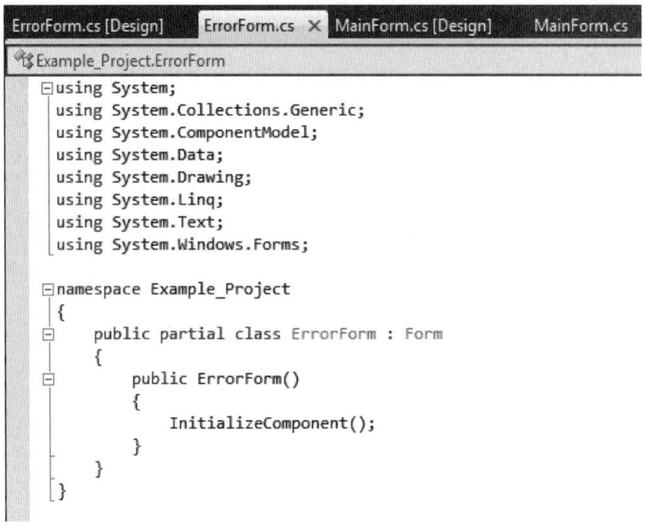

```
ErrorForm.cs [Design]    ErrorForm.cs  X   MainForm.cs [Design]    MainForm.cs
Example_Project.ErrorForm
using System;
using System.Collections.Generic;
using System.ComponentModel;
using System.Data;
using System.Drawing;
using System.Linq;
using System.Text;
using System.Windows.Forms;

namespace Example_Project
{
    public partial class ErrorForm : Form
    {
        public ErrorForm()
        {
            InitializeComponent();
        }
    }
}
```

Removing a Form

If you wish to remove a form from a project and delete its file from the disk, follow these steps.

1. Right-click the form's entry in the *Solution Explorer* window.
2. On the pop-up menu, click *Delete*.

If you wish to remove a form from a project but you do not want to delete its file from the disk, follow these steps.

1. Right-click the form's entry in the *Solution Explorer* window.
2. On the pop-up menu click *Exclude From Project*.

Displaying a Form

In your application's code, the first step in displaying a form is to create an instance of the form's class. For example, suppose a project has a form named ErrorForm. The following statement creates an instance of the ErrorForm class:

```
ErrorForm myErrorForm = new ErrorForm();
```

This statement declares a reference variable named myErrorForm. It also creates an object of the ErrorForm class in memory and assigns a reference to the object to the myErrorForm variable. After this statement executes, you will be able to use the myErrorForm variable to perform operations with the form.

Creating an instance of a form's class does not display the form on the screen. The next step is to call the form's ShowDialog method. Here is an example:

```
myErrorForm.ShowDialog();
```

The **ShowDialog** method displays a form on the screen, and it gives that form the focus. This means that control of the application transfers to the form. When the user closes the form, control of the application returns to the point where the ShowDialog method was called, and execution resumes.

Now that we've covered the basic concepts of creating and displaying a form, go through the steps in Tutorial 9-5. In the tutorial you create a simple application that has two forms.

Tutorial 9-5:
Creating an Application with Two Forms

Step 1: Start Visual Studio (or Visual C# Express). Create a new *Windows Forms Application* project named *Multiform Practice*.

Step 2: In the *Solutions Explorer* window, rename the *Form1.cs* file to *MainForm.cs*. (Right-click *Form1.cs* and then select *Rename* from the popup menu.) Changing the form's file name to *MainForm.cs* changes the form's name to MainForm. The *Solutions Explorer* window should appear as shown in Figure 9-25.

Figure 9-25 *Solution Explorer* after changing *Form1.cs* to *MainForm.cs*

Step 3: In the *Designer*, set up the MainForm form as shown in Figure 9-26.

Figure 9-26 MainForm

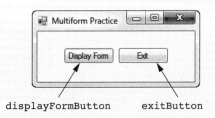

Step 4: Perform the following to create another form named MessageForm in the project:
- Click *Project* on the menu bar and then select *Add Windows Form...*
- The *Add New Item* window will appear. Enter *MessageForm.cs* as the name.
- Click the *Add* button.

As shown in Figure 9-27, a new form named MessageForm will appear in the *Designer*. Notice that an entry for *MessageForm.cs* appears in the *Solution Explorer*.

Figure 9-27 MessageForm added to the project

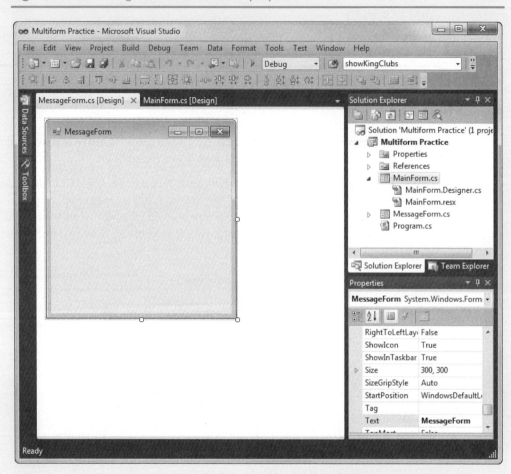

Step 5: In the *Designer*, set up the MessageForm as shown in Figure 9-28.

Figure 9-28 MessageForm

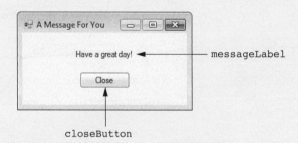

Step 6: Next you create the Click event handler for the `closeButton` control. In the *Designer*, double-click the `closeButton` control. This displays the MessageForm.cs file in the code editor, and you will see an empty event handler named `closeButton_Click`. Complete the event handler by typing the code shown in lines 21–22 in Program 9-8. When the user clicks the `closeButton` control, this event handler closes the form.

Step 7: Use the tabs at the top of the *Designer* to switch to *MainForm.cs [Design]*. This brings up the MainForm in the *Designer*.

Step 8: Now you create the Click event handler for the `displayFormButton` control. Double-click the `displayFormButton` control. This displays the MainForm.cs file in the code editor, and you will see an empty event handler named `displayFormButton_Click`. Complete the event handler by typing the code shown in lines 21–25 in Program 9-9. Let's review this code:

Line 22: This statement does the following:

- It declares a `MessageForm` reference variable named `myMessageForm`.
- It creates a `MessageForm` object in memory.
- It assigns a reference to the `MessageForm` object to the `myMessageForm` variable.

After this statement executes, the `myMessageForm` variable will reference a `MessageForm` object.

Line 25: This statement displays the MessageForm on the screen and transfers control of the application to the form.

Step 9: Switch your view back to the MainForm form in the *Designer* and double-click the `exitButton` control. In the code editor you will see an empty event handler named `exitButton_Click`. Complete the event handler by typing the code shown in lines 30–31 in Program 9-9.

Step 10: Save the project. Then, press F5 on the keyboard or click the *Start Debugging* button (▶) on the toolbar to compile and run the application. When the application runs, the MainForm should appear, as shown on the left in Figure 9-29. Click the *Display Form* button. The MessageForm form should appear, as shown on the right in Figure 9-29.

Figure 9-29 The MainForm and the MessageForm forms displayed

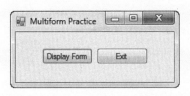

Step 11: On the MessageForm, click the *Close* button. This should close the Message-Form. Next, click the *Exit* button on the MainForm to end the application.

Program 9-8 Completed code for the MessageForm form

```
 1 using System;
 2 using System.Collections.Generic;
 3 using System.ComponentModel;
 4 using System.Data;
 5 using System.Drawing;
 6 using System.Linq;
 7 using System.Text;
 8 using System.Windows.Forms;
 9
10 namespace Multiform_Practice
11 {
12     public partial class MessageForm : Form
```

```
13    {
14        public MessageForm()
15        {
16            InitializeComponent();
17        }
18
19        private void closeButton_Click(object sender, EventArgs e)
20        {
21            // Close the form.
22            this.Close();
23        }
24    }
25 }
```

Program 9-9 Completed code for the MainForm form

```
1 using System;
2 using System.Collections.Generic;
3 using System.ComponentModel;
4 using System.Data;
5 using System.Drawing;
6 using System.Linq;
7 using System.Text;
8 using System.Windows.Forms;
9
10 namespace Multiform_Practice
11 {
12    public partial class MainForm : Form
13    {
14        public MainForm()
15        {
16            InitializeComponent();
17        }
18
19        private void displayFormButton_Click(object sender, EventArgs e)
20        {
21            // Create an instance of the MessageForm class.
22            MessageForm myMessageForm = new MessageForm();
23
24            // Display the form.
25            myMessageForm.ShowDialog();
26        }
27
28        private void exitButton_Click(object sender, EventArgs e)
29        {
30            // Close the form.
31            this.Close();
32        }
33    }
34 }
```

Accessing Controls on a Different Form

The controls that you place on a form have public access. Code that is outside the form's class can access the controls on that form. For example, suppose an application has a form named GreetingsForm and GreetingsForm has a Label control named `messageLabel`. The following code shows how you can create an instance of GreetingsForm, assign a value to the `messageLabel` control's Text property, and then display the form:

```
1 GreetingsForm greetingsForm = new GreetingsForm();
2 greetingsForm.messageLabel.Text = "Good day!"
3 greetingsForm.ShowDialog();
```

The statement in line 1 creates an instance of the `GreetingsForm` class, referenced by the `greetingsForm` variable. At this point the form exists in memory, but it has not been displayed on the screen. The statement in line 2 assigns the string `"Good day!"` to the `messageLabel` control's Text property. Notice that the control's name is preceded by `greetingsForm`, followed by a dot. This indicates that the control is not on the current form but on the form that is referenced by the `greetingsForm` variable. The statement in line 3 calls the form's `ShowDialog` method to display the form on the screen. When the form appears on the screen, the `messageLabel` control will display the text *Good Day!*

In Tutorial 9-6 you get a chance to create a multiform application in which code on one form creates an instance of another form and assigns values to controls on that form.

Tutorial 9-6:
Accessing a Control on a Different Form

In this tutorial you create an application that allows the user to select a food from the application's main form and then display a second form that shows the selected food's nutritional information.

Step 1: Start Visual Studio (or Visual C# Express). Create a new *Windows Forms Application* project named *Food Facts*.

Step 2: In the *Solutions Explorer* window, rename the *Form1.cs* file to *MainForm.cs*. (Right-click *Form1.cs* and then select *Rename* from the pop-up menu.) Changing the form's file name to *MainForm.cs* changes the form's name to MainForm.

Step 3: In the *Designer*, set up the MainForm form as shown in Figure 9-30.

Figure 9-30 MainForm

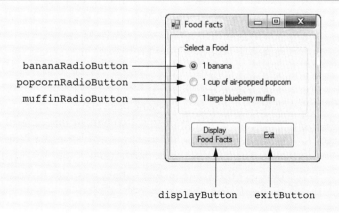

Step 4: Perform the following steps to create another form named NutritionForm in the project:

- Click *Project* on the menu bar and then select *Add Windows Form…*
- The *Add New Item* window will appear. Enter *NutritionForm.cs* as the name.
- Click the *Add* button.

Step 5: In the *Designer*, set up the NutritionForm form with the controls shown in Figure 9-31. The `foodLabel`, `caloriesLabel`, `fatLabel`, and `carbLabel` controls have the following property settings:

- *AutoSize* is set to *False*
- *BorderStyle* is set to *Fixed3D*

Figure 9-31 NutritionForm

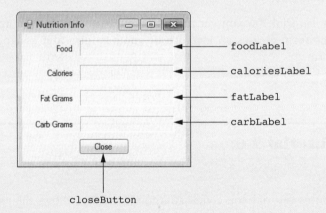

Step 6: Next you create the Click event handler for the `closeButton` control. In the *Designer*, double-click the `closeButton` control. This displays the NutritionForm.cs file in the code editor, and you will see an empty event handler named `closeButton_Click`. Complete the event handler by typing the code shown in lines 21–22 in Program 9-10. When the user clicks the `closeButton` control, this event handler will close the form.

Step 7: Use the tabs at the top of the *Designer* to switch to *MainForm.cs [Design]*. This brings up the MainForm in the *Designer*.

Step 8: Next you create the Click event handler for the `displayButton` control. Double-click the `displayButton` control. This displays the MainForm.cs file in the code editor, and you will see an empty event handler named `displayButton_Click`. Complete the event handler by typing the code shown in lines 21–48 in Program 9-11. Let's review this code:

Line 22: This statement creates an instance of the `NutritionForm` class, referenced by the `nutriForm` variable. Keep in mind that although the form has been created in memory, it has not yet been displayed on the screen.

Line 25: This `if` statement determines whether the `bananaRadioButton` control is selected. If so, the statements in lines 27–30 use the `nutriForm` variable to assign values to the Label controls on the NutritionForm form. The values that are assigned are the nutritional values for a banana.

Line 32: If the `bananaRadioButton` radio button is not selected, this `else if` clause determines whether the `popcornRadioButton` control is selected. If so, the statements in lines 34–37 use the `nutriForm` variable to assign values to the Label controls on the NutritionForm form. The values that are assigned are the nutritional values for 1 cup of air-popped popcorn.

Line 39: If neither the `bananaRadioButton` nor the `popcornRadioButton` radio buttons are selected, this `else if` clause determines whether the `muffinRadioButton` control is selected. If so, the statements in lines 41–44 use the `nutriForm` variable to assign values to the Label controls on the Nutrition-Form form. The values that are assigned are the nutritional values for one large blueberry muffin.

Line 48: This statement displays the NutritionForm on the screen and transfers control of the application to the form.

Step 9: Switch your view back to the MainForm form in the *Designer* and double-click the `exitButton` control. In the code editor you will see an empty event handler named `exitButton_Click`. Complete the event handler by typing the code shown in lines 53–54 in Program 9-11.

Step 10: Save the project. Then, press F5 on the keyboard or click the *Start Debugging* button (▶) on the toolbar to compile and run the application. When the application runs, the MainForm should appear, as shown on the left in Figure 9-32. With the *1 banana* radio button selected, click the *Display Food Facts* button. The NutritionForm form should appear, as shown on the right in the figure.

Figure 9-32 The MainForm and the NutritionForm forms displayed

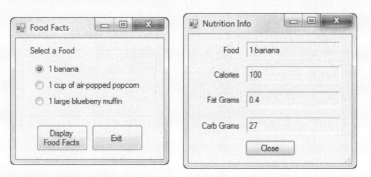

Step 11: On the NutritionForm, click the *Close* button. This should close the NutritionForm. Try selecting the other radio buttons on the MainForm form and clicking the *Display Food Facts* button to see each item's nutritional information. When you are finished, click the *Exit* button on the MainForm form to end the application.

Program 9-10 Completed code for the NutritionForm form

```
1 using System;
2 using System.Collections.Generic;
3 using System.ComponentModel;
4 using System.Data;
5 using System.Drawing;
6 using System.Linq;
7 using System.Text;
8 using System.Windows.Forms;
9
```

```
10 namespace Food_Facts
11 {
12     public partial class NutritionForm : Form
13     {
14         public NutritionForm()
15         {
16             InitializeComponent();
17         }
18
19         private void closeButton_Click(object sender, EventArgs e)
20         {
21             // Close the form
22             this.Close();
23         }
24     }
25 }
```

Program 9-11 Completed code for the MainForm form

```
 1 using System;
 2 using System.Collections.Generic;
 3 using System.ComponentModel;
 4 using System.Data;
 5 using System.Drawing;
 6 using System.Linq;
 7 using System.Text;
 8 using System.Windows.Forms;
 9
10 namespace Food_Facts
11 {
12     public partial class MainForm : Form
13     {
14         public MainForm()
15         {
16             InitializeComponent();
17         }
18
19         private void displayButton_Click(object sender, EventArgs e)
20         {
21             // Create an instance of the NutritionForm class.
22             NutritionForm nutriForm = new NutritionForm();
23
24             // Find the selected radio button.
25             if (bananaRadioButton.Checked)
26             {
27                 nutriForm.foodLabel.Text = "1 banana";
28                 nutriForm.caloriesLabel.Text = "100";
29                 nutriForm.fatLabel.Text = "0.4";
30                 nutriForm.carbLabel.Text = "27";
31             }
32             else if (popcornRadioButton.Checked)
33             {
34                 nutriForm.foodLabel.Text = "1 cup air-popped popcorn";
35                 nutriForm.caloriesLabel.Text = "31";
36                 nutriForm.fatLabel.Text = "0.4";
37                 nutriForm.carbLabel.Text = "6";
38             }
```

```
39                    else if (muffinRadioButton.Checked)
40                    {
41                        nutriForm.foodLabel.Text = "1 large blueberry muffin";
42                        nutriForm.caloriesLabel.Text = "385";
43                        nutriForm.fatLabel.Text = "9";
44                        nutriForm.carbLabel.Text = "67";
45                    }
46
47                    // Display the NutritionForm.
48                    nutriForm.ShowDialog();
49                }
50
51                private void exitButton_Click(object sender, EventArgs e)
52                {
53                    // Close the form.
54                    this.Close();
55                }
56            }
57 }
```

Modal and Modeless Forms

A form can be either modal or modeless. The ShowDialog method displays a form in modal fashion. When a **modal form** is displayed, no other form in the application can receive the focus until the modal form is closed. The user must close the modal form before he or she can work with any other form in the application. A **modeless form,** on the other hand, allows the user to switch focus to another form while it is displayed. The user does not have to close a modeless form to switch focus to another form. If you want to display a form in modeless fashion, call its **Show** method.

There is another important difference between modal and modeless forms. When you call the ShowDialog method to display a modal form, control of the program is transferred to the form, and no statements appearing after the ShowDialog method call will execute until the form is closed. Figure 9-33 illustrates this concept.

Figure 9-33 Execution of statements after displaying a modal form

```
statement;
statement;
messageForm.ShowDialog();
statement;
statement;
statement;
```
These statements will not execute until the messageForm form is closed.

When you call the Show method to display a modeless form, however, the statements that appear after the Show method call continue to execute while the form is displayed. The application does not wait until the modeless form is closed before executing these statements. Figure 9-34 illustrates this concept.

TIP: Modeless forms are typically used in special situations. In most multiform applications, you will want to display forms in modal fashion.

Figure 9-34 Execution of statements after displaying a modeless form

```
statement;
statement;
messageForm.ShowDialog();
statement;
statement;
statement;
```

These statements will execute immediately after the `messageForm` form is displayed.

Checkpoint

9.25 What steps should you follow to change a form's name?

9.26 What steps should you follow to add a new form to a project?

9.27 How do you remove a form from a project and delete its file from the disk?

9.28 What is the first step in displaying a form?

9.29 What access modifier do the controls that you place on a form have?

9.30 What happens after a form that has been displayed with the `ShowDialog` method is closed by the user?

Key Terms

accessors	overloaded
backing field	parameterized constructor
binding	parameterless constructor
class declaration	problem domain
class header	property
constructor	read-only property
default constructor	Show method
instance	ShowDialog method
member declarations	signature
modal form	stale
modeless form	value parameter

Review Questions

Multiple Choice

1. Each object that is created from a class is called a(n) _____ of the class.

   a. reference
   b. example
   c. instance
   d. event

2. You create a class by writing a(n) _____.

   a. blueprint
   b. class declaration
   c. initialization list
   d. object name

3. The first line of a class declaration is known as the _____.

   a. class preface
   b. class title
   c. class header
   d. class directive

4. The class's _____ are the statements that define the class's fields, properties, and methods.

   a. data agents
   b. body statements
   c. private definitions
   d. member declarations

5. A(n) _____ is a method that is automatically executed when an object is created.

   a. opener
   b. loader
   c. constructor
   d. assembler

6. A(n) _____ is a special type of class member that allows an object to store and retrieve a piece of data.

   a. property
   b. asset
   c. inserter/retriever
   d. accessory

7. A special set of methods, known as _____, work in conjunction with a private field and allow code outside the class to get the property's value, and assign values to the property.

   a. accessors
   b. imitators
   c. intermediates
   d. directives

8. The private field, which is known as the property's _____, holds any data that is assigned to the property.

   a. private data
   b. backing field
   c. holding value
   d. masked variable

9. The _____ parameter of the set accessor is automatically created by the compiler, and its data type is the same as that of the property.

   a. property
   b. value
   c. member
   d. detail

10. A _____ can be read, but it cannot be modified.

   a. limited property
   b. temporary value
   c. field value
   d. read-only property

11. When the value of an item is dependent on other data and that item is not updated when the other data is changed, what has the value become?

   a. bitter
   b. stale
   c. asynchronous
   d. moldy

12. A constructor that accepts arguments is known as a(n) _____.

   a. argumentative constructor
   b. changeable constructor
   c. parameterized constructor
   d. secondary constructor

13. When a method is _____, it means that multiple methods in the same class have the same name but use different types of parameters.

   a. emulated
   b. versioned
   c. threaded
   d. overloaded

14. The process of matching a method call with the correct method is known as _____.

   a. sorting
   b. matching
   c. styling
   d. binding

15. A method's _____ consists of the method's name and the data type and argument kind (by value, `ref`, or `out`) of the method's parameters, from left to right.

    a. appearance
    b. signature
    c. identifier
    d. footprint

16. A _____, is a constructor that accepts no arguments.

    a. parameterless constructor
    b. basic constructor
    c. primary constructor
    d. passive constructor

17. If you write a class with no constructor whatsoever, the compiler will provide a(n) _____.

    a. default constructor
    b. constructor list
    c. parameterized method
    d. error message

18. The _____ is the set of real-world objects, parties, and major events related to the problem.

    a. critical path
    b. problem domain
    c. solution set
    d. operation focus

19. A class's responsibilities are _____.

    a. the objects created from the class
    b. things the class knows
    c. actions the class performs
    d. both b and c

20. The _____ displays a form on the screen, and it gives that form the focus.

    a. `Show` method
    b. `ShowDialog` method
    c. `Clear` method
    d. `Focus` method

True or False

1. Objects that are instances of a class are always passed by value.

2. Class declarations must be written inside the project namespace.

3. A class is an object.

4. It is a common practice to make all a class's fields private and to provide access to those fields through methods.

5. The same rules for naming variables apply to naming classes.

6. If you need to make a property read only, you simply do not write a `set` accessor for the property.

7. If you try to pass a property to a `ref` or an `out` parameter, an error will occur.

8. Class fields are almost always declared `public` in order to make their values easily accessible to code outside of the class.

9. The get accessor can be thought of as a method that returns the class property's value.

10. Constructors can accept arguments in the same way as other methods.

11. It is legal to write a class without any constructors.

12. Objects that are instances of a class can be stored in an array.

13. The objects of a class can be stored in an array, but not in a List.

14. One way to find the classes needed for an object-oriented program is to identify all the verbs in a description of the problem domain.

15. Every form in a Visual C# project has a class.

Short Answer

1. When a method receives an object as an argument, does the method have access to the actual object or a copy of the object?

2. What are the advantages of storing classes in their own files?

3. How is a constructor used?

4. What is the difference between a class and an instance of a class?

5. What convention do most programmers follow when naming classes?

6. What is the value parameter? How is it created?

7. What is executed anytime a class property is read?

8. What is executed anytime a value is assigned to a class property?

9. How can you protect class fields from accidental corruption?

10. What is stale data?

11. Is it possible to pass initialization values to the constructor when you create an object? If so, how?

12. How does the compiler distinguish a method from other methods of the same name?

13. What do you call the constructor that is provided by the compiler, if no constructor is specified when a class is written?

14. In Visual Studio, how you can you switch your view to another form?

15. How do you remove a form from a project but keep its file on the disk?

16. What is the difference between a modal form and a modeless form?

Algorithm Workbench

1. Write a statement that creates an instance of the Transcript class.

2. Write the accessors for a property named CustomerNumber that assigns a string value to the _customerNumber field.

3. Suppose that an application declares an array of class objects with the following statement:

```
Employee[] employees = new Employee[9];
```

Write a loop that creates 10 instances of the class and assigns them to the elements of the array.

4. Look at the following description of a problem domain:

   The bank offers the following types of accounts to its customers: savings accounts, checking accounts, and money market accounts. Customers are allowed to deposit money into an account (thereby increasing its balance), withdraw money from an account (thereby decreasing its balance), and earn interest on the account. Each account has an interest rate.

   Assume that you are writing a program that will calculate the amount of interest earned for a bank account.

   a. Identify the potential classes in this problem domain.
   b. Refine the list to include only the necessary class or classes for this problem.
   c. Identify the responsibilities of the class or classes.

5. An application has two forms, named MainForm and SecondForm. The SecondForm form has a Label control named `readingLabel`, and the MainForm form has a TextBox control named `inputTextBox`. Assume the user has entered a value into the `inputTextBox` control on the MainForm form and an event handler executes the following statement:

   ```
   SecondForm secondForm = new SecondForm();
   ```

   Write a statement that executes after this statement and stores the value entered in the `inputTextBox` into the `readingLabel` control (in the SecondForm form).

Programming Problems

1. **`Pet` Class**

   Create a class named `Pet` (similar to the one discussed in this chapter), which has the following properties:

   - Name—The Name property holds the name of a pet.
   - Type—The Type property holds the type of animal that a pet is. Example values are "Dog", "Cat", and "Bird".
   - Age—The Age property holds the pet's age.

   Demonstrate the class in an application that creates an object of the class and lets the user enter the name, type, and age of his or her pet. This data should be stored in the object. Retrieve the pet's Name, Type, and Age properties and display their values on the screen.

2. **`Car` Class**

   Create a class named `Car` that has the following properties:

   - Year—The Year property holds the car's year model.
   - Make—The Make property holds the make of the car.
   - Speed—The Speed property holds the car's current speed.

   In addition, the class should have the following constructor and other methods.

   - **Constructor**—The constructor should accept the car's year and model and make them as arguments. These values should be assigned to the backing fields for the object's Year and Make properties. The constructor should also assign 0 to the backing field for the Speed property.
   - **`Accelerate`**—The `Accelerate` method should add 5 to the Speed property's backing field each time it is called.
   - **`Brake`**—The `Brake` method should subtract 5 from the Speed property's backing field each time it is called.

Demonstrate the class in an application that creates a Car object. The application's form should have an *Accelerate* button that calls the Accelerate method and then displays the car's current speed each time it is clicked. The application's form should also have a *Brake* button that calls the Brake method and then displays the car's current speed each time it is clicked.

3. **Personal Information Class**

   Create a class that holds the following personal data in properties: name, address, age, and phone number. Demonstrate the class in an application that creates three instances of the class. One instance should hold your information, and the other two should hold your friends' or family members' information. Display each object's properties on the application's form.

4. **Employee Class**

   Write a class named Employee that has the following properties:
   - **Name**—The Name property holds the employee's name.
   - **IdNumber**—The IdNumber property holds the employee's ID number.
   - **Department**—The Department property holds the name of the department in which the employee works.
   - **Position**—The Position property holds the employee's job title.

   The class should have the following overloaded constructors:
   - A constructor that accepts the following values as arguments and assigns them to the appropriate properties: employee's name, employee's ID number, department, and position
   - A constructor that accepts the following values as arguments and assigns them to the appropriate properties: employee's name and ID number. The Department and Position properties should be assigned an empty string ("")
   - A parameterless constructor that assigns empty strings ("") to the Name, Department, and Position properties, and 0 to the IdNumber property

   In an application, create three Employee objects to hold the following data:

Name	ID Number	Department	Position
Susan Meyers	47899	Accounting	Vice President
Mark Jones	39119	IT	Programmer
Joy Rogers	81774	Manufacturing	Engineer

   The application should store this data in the three objects and display the data for each employee on the screen.

5. **RetailItem Class**

   Write a class named RetailItem that holds data about an item in a retail store. The class should have the following properties:
   - **Description**—The Description property should hold a brief description of the item.
   - **UnitsOnHand**—The UnitsOnHand property should hold the number of units currently in inventory.
   - **Price**—The Price property should hold the item's retail price.

Write a constructor that accepts arguments for each property.

The application should create an array of three `RetailItem` objects containing the following data:

	Description	Units on Hand	Price
Item 1	Jacket	12	59.95
Item 2	Jeans	40	34.95
Item 3	Shirt	20	24.95

The application should have a loop that steps through the array, displaying each element's properties.

6. **Dorm and Meal Plan Calculator**

   A university has the following dormitories:

Allen Hall	$1,500 per semester
Pike Hall	$1,600 per semester
Farthing Hall	$1,800 per semester
University Suites	$2,500 per semester

   The university also offers the following meal plans:

7 meals per week	$ 600 per semester
14 meals per week	$1,200 per semester
Unlimited meals	$1,700 per semester

   Create an application with two forms. The main form should allow the user to select a dormitory and a meal plan. The application should show the total charges on the second form.

7. **E-Mail Address Book**

   Create an application with a class named `PersonEntry`. The `PersonEntry` class should have properties for a person's name, e-mail address, and phone number. Also, create a text file that contains the names, e-mail addresses, and phone numbers for at least five people. When the application starts, it should read the data from the file and create a `PersonEntry` object for each person's data. The `PersonEntry` objects should be added to a `List`, and each person's name should be displayed in a list box on the application's main form. When the user selects a name from the list box, a second form should appear displaying that person's name, e-mail address, and phone number.

10 Inheritance and Polymorphism

TOPICS

10.1 Inheritance

CONCEPT: Inheritance allows a new class to extend an existing class. The new class inherits the members of the class it extends.

Generalization and Specialization

In the real world you can find many objects that are specialized versions of other more general objects. For example, the term *insect* describes a very general type of creature with numerous characteristics. Because grasshoppers and bumblebees are insects, they have all the general characteristics of an insect. In addition, they have special characteristics of their own. For example, the grasshopper has its jumping ability, and the bumblebee has its stinger. Grasshoppers and bumblebees are specialized versions of an insect. This is illustrated in Figure 10-1.

Inheritance and the "Is a" Relationship

When one object is a specialized version of another object, there is an **"is a" relationship** between them. For example, a grasshopper is an insect. Here are a few other examples of the "is a" relationship:

- A poodle is a dog.
- A car is a vehicle.
- A flower is a plant.
- A rectangle is a shape.
- A football player is an athlete.

Figure 10-1 Bumblebees and grasshoppers, specialized versions of an insect

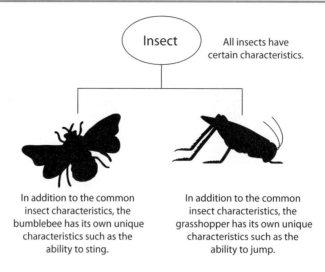

Insect — All insects have certain characteristics.

In addition to the common insect characteristics, the bumblebee has its own unique characteristics such as the ability to sting.

In addition to the common insect characteristics, the grasshopper has its own unique characteristics such as the ability to jump.

When an "is a" relationship exists between objects, it means that the specialized object has all of the characteristics of the general object, plus additional characteristics that make it special. In object-oriented programming, inheritance is used to create an "is a" relationship among classes. This allows you to extend the capabilities of a class by creating another class that is a specialized version of it.

Inheritance involves a base class and a derived class. The **base class** is the general class and the **derived class** is the specialized class. You can think of the derived class as an extended version of the base class. The derived class inherits fields, properties, and methods from the base class without any of them having to be rewritten. Furthermore, new fields, properties, and methods may be added to the derived class, and that is what makes it a specialized version of the base class.

NOTE: Base classes are sometimes called superclasses, and derived classes are sometimes called **subclasses**. Either set of terms is correct. For consistency, this text uses the terms *base class* and *derived class*.

Let's look at an example of how inheritance can be used. Suppose we are developing an application that a car dealership can use to manage its inventory of used cars. The dealership's inventory includes three types of automobiles: cars, pickup trucks, and sport-utility vehicles (SUVs). Regardless of the type, the dealership keeps the following data about each automobile:

- Make
- Year model
- Mileage
- Price

Each type of vehicle that is kept in inventory has these general characteristics plus its own specialized characteristics. For cars, the dealership keeps the following additional data:

- Number of doors (2 or 4)

For pickup trucks, the dealership keeps the following additional data:

- Drive type (two-wheel drive or four-wheel drive)

And, for SUVs, the dealership keeps the following additional data:

- Passenger capacity

In designing this program, one approach would be to write the following three classes:

- A `Car` class with properties for the make, year model, mileage, price, and the number of doors
- A `Truck` class with properties for the make, year model, mileage, price, and the drive type
- A `SportUtility` class with properties for the make, year model, mileage, price, and the passenger capacity

This is an inefficient approach, however, because all three classes have a large number of common properties. As a result, the classes would contain a lot of duplicated code. In addition, if we discover later that we need to add more common attributes, we would have to modify all three classes.

A better approach would be to write an `Automobile` base class to hold all the general data about an automobile and then write derived classes for each specific type of automobile. The following code shows the `Automobile` class:

```
 1 class Automobile
 2 {
 3     // Fields
 4     private string _make;
 5     private string _model;
 6     private int _mileage;
 7     private decimal _price;
 8
 9     // Constructor
10     public Automobile()
11     {
12         _make = "";
13         _model = "";
14         _mileage = 0;
15         _price = 0;
16     }
17
18     // Make property
19     public string Make
20     {
21         get { return _make; }
22         set { _make = value; }
23     }
24
25     // Model property
26     public string Model
27     {
28         get { return _model; }
29         set { _model = value; }
30     }
31
32     // Mileage property
33     public int Mileage
34     {
35         get { return _mileage; }
36         set { _mileage = value; }
37     }
38
39     // Price property
40     public decimal Price
```

```
41    {
42         get { return _price; }
43         set { _price = value; }
44    }
45 }
```

Lines 4–7 declare the backing fields for the Make, Model, Mileage, and Price properties. The parameterless constructor, which appears in lines 10–16, assigns empty strings to the _make and _model fields and 0 to the _mileage and _price fields. The code for the Make, Model, Mileage, and Price properties appears in lines 19–44.

The Automobile class is a complete class, from which we can create objects. However, the Automobile class holds only general data about an automobile. It does not hold any of the specific pieces of data that the dealership wants to keep about cars, pickup trucks, and SUVs. To hold data about those specific types of automobiles, we write derived classes that inherit from the Automobile class. The following code shows the Car class, which is derived from the Automobile class.

```
 1 class Car : Automobile
 2 {
 3      // Field
 4      private int _doors;
 5
 6      // Constructor
 7      public Car()
 8      {
 9           _doors = 0;
10      }
11
12      // Doors property
13      public int Doors
14      {
15           get { return _doors; }
16           set { _doors = value; }
17      }
18 }
```

Take a closer look at the class header in line 1:

```
class Car : Automobile
```

This line of code has some new notation. After the name of the class, Car, a colon appears, followed by the name of another class, Automobile. This line indicates that we are defining a class named Car, and it is derived from the Automobile class. The Car class is the derived class and the Automobile class is the base class. Figure 10-2 illustrates this notation. If we want to express the relationship between the Car class and the Automobile class, we can say that a Car is an Automobile.

Figure 10-2 Inheritance notation in the class header

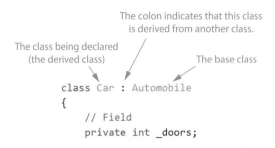

Because the `Car` class is derived from the `Automobile` class, the `Car` class inherits all the `Automobile` class's members, except its constructor. (The purpose of the base class's constructor is to create an instance of the base class, so it makes sense that the derived class does not inherit the base class's constructor.)

> **NOTE:** Although the derived class inherits the base class's private members, it cannot directly access them. Only methods in the base class can directly access the base class's private members.

The `Car` class has a parameterless constructor that appears in lines 7–10. In line 9, the constructor assigns the value 0 to the `_doors` field. Here is a summary of what happens when an object of the `Car` class is created:

- The base class constructor executes first. In this case, the `Automobile` class's constructor is called, and it assigns empty strings to the `_make` and `_model` fields and 0 to the `_mileage` and `_price` fields.
- The derived class constructor executes next. In this case, 0 is assigned to the `_doors` field.

The code for the Doors property appears in lines 13–17.

Before going any further, let's look at a complete application that demonstrates the `Automobile` and `Car` classes. In the *Chap10* folder of the Student Sample Programs you will find a project named *Car Demo*. This project contains a form named Form1, the `Automobile` class, and the `Car` class. Figure 10-3 shows the Form1 form.

Figure 10-3 The *Car Demo* project's Form1 form

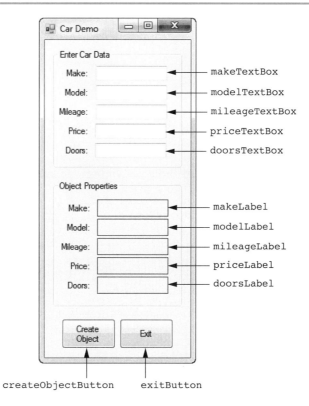

When you run the application, enter sample car data into the text boxes and then click the *Create Object* button. The application will create an object of the Car class and assign the data from the text boxes to the object's properties. It will then read and display the values of the object's properties in the makeLabel, modelLabel, , mileageLabel, , priceLabel, and doorsLabel controls. Figure 10-4 shows an example of the application's form after the user has entered some data and clicked the *Create Object* button.

Figure 10-4 The *Car Demo* application

Program 10-1 shows the code in the Form1.cs file.

Program 10-1 Form1 code in the *Car Demo* project

```
1 using System;
2 using System.Collections.Generic;
3 using System.ComponentModel;
4 using System.Data;
5 using System.Drawing;
6 using System.Linq;
7 using System.Text;
8 using System.Windows.Forms;
9
10 namespace Car_Demo
11 {
12     public partial class Form1 : Form
13     {
14         public Form1()
15         {
16             InitializeComponent();
17         }
18
19         // The GetCarData method accepts a Car object as an
20         // argument. It assigns the data entered by the
21         // user to the object's properties.
```

```
22          private void GetCarData(Car car)
23          {
24              // Temporary variables to hold mileage, price,
25              // and number of doors
26              int mileage;
27              decimal price;
28              int doors;
29
30              // Get the car's make.
31              car.Make = makeTextBox.Text;
32
33              // Get the car's model.
34              car.Model = modelTextBox.Text;
35
36              // Get the car's mileage.
37              if (int.TryParse(mileageTextBox.Text, out mileage))
38              {
39                  car.Mileage = mileage;
40
41                  // Get the car's price.
42                  if (decimal.TryParse(priceTextBox.Text, out price))
43                  {
44                      car.Price = price;
45
46                      // Get the number of doors.
47                      if (int.TryParse(doorsTextBox.Text, out doors))
48                      {
49                          car.Doors = doors;
50                      }
51                      else
52                      {
53                          // Display an error message.
54                          MessageBox.Show("Invalid number of doors");
55                      }
56                  }
57                  else
58                  {
59                      // Display an error message.
60                      MessageBox.Show("Invalid price");
61                  }
62              }
63              else
64              {
65                  // Display an error message.
66                  MessageBox.Show("Invalid mileage");
67              }
68          }
69
70          private void createObjectButton_Click(object sender, EventArgs e)
71          {
72              // Create a Car object.
73              Car myCar = new Car();
74
75              // Get the car data.
76              GetCarData(myCar);
77
78              // Display the car data.
79              makeLabel.Text = myCar.Make;
80              modelLabel.Text = myCar.Model;
81              mileageLabel.Text = myCar.Mileage.ToString();
82              priceLabel.Text = myCar.Price.ToString("c");
```

```
83                     doorsLabel.Text = myCar.Doors.ToString();
84             }
85
86         private void exitButton_Click(object sender, EventArgs e)
87         {
88             // Close the form.
89             this.Close();
90         }
91     }
92 }
```

Let's take a closer look at the code:

Lines 22–68: This is the code for the GetCarData method. The purpose of the method is to accept a Car object as an argument, get the car data entered by the user (performing input validation on the mileage, price, and doors), and store that data in the Car object's properties.

Line 73: This statement creates an instance of the Car class, referenced by the myCar variable.

Line 76: This statement calls the GetCarData method, passing the myCar object as an argument. After the method executes, the myCar object's properties will contain the data entered by the user.

Lines 79–83: These statements display the myCar object's properties.

Now let's take a look at the Truck and SportUtility classes, which are also derived from the Automobile class. Here is the code for the Truck class:

```
 1 class Truck : Automobile
 2 {
 3     // Field
 4     private string _drive;
 5
 6     // Constructor
 7     public Truck()
 8     {
 9         _drive = "";
10     }
11
12     // Drive property
13     public string Drive
14     {
15         get { return _drive; }
16         set { _drive = value; }
17     }
18 }
```

The Truck class has a string property named Drive. This property holds a value such as "Four-Wheel Drive" or "Two-Wheel Drive." The backing field for the property is named _drive and is declared in line 4. The code for the property is in lines 13–17. The constructor, which appears in lines 7–10, assigns an empty string to the _drive field.

Now, let's look at the SportUtility class, which is also derived from the Automobile class:

```
 1 class SportUtility : Automobile
 2 {
 3     // Field
 4     private int _passengers;
 5
```

```
 6        // Constructor
 7        public SportUtility()
 8        {
 9            _passengers = 0;
10        }
11
12        // Passengers property
13        public int Passengers
14        {
15            get { return _passengers; }
16            set { _passengers = value; }
17        }
18 }
```

The SportUtility class has an int property named Passengers. This property holds the vehicle's passenger capacity. The backing field for the property is named _passengers and is declared in line 4. The code for the property is in lines 13–17. The constructor, which appears in lines 7–10, assigns an empty string to the _passengers field.

Now, let's look at a program that demonstrates all four of these classes. In the *Chap10* folder of the Student Sample Programs, you will find a project named *Car Truck SUV Demo*. This project contains a form named Form1, the Automobile class, the Car class, the Truck class, and the SportUtility class. Figure 10-5 shows the Form1 form, and Program 10-2 shows the code in the Form1.cs file.

Figure 10-5 The *Car Truck SUV Demo* project's Form1 form

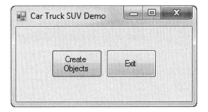

Program 10-2 Form1 code in the *Car Truck SUV Demo* project

```
 1 using System;
 2 using System.Collections.Generic;
 3 using System.ComponentModel;
 4 using System.Data;
 5 using System.Drawing;
 6 using System.Linq;
 7 using System.Text;
 8 using System.Windows.Forms;
 9
10 namespace Car_Truck_SUV_Demo
11 {
12     public partial class Form1 : Form
13     {
14         public Form1()
15         {
16             InitializeComponent();
17         }
18
19         private void createObjectsButton_Click(object sender, EventArgs e)
20         {
21             // Create a Car object for a used 2001 BMW with 70,000
22             // miles, priced at $15,000, with 4 doors.
```

```
23              Car myCar = new Car();
24              myCar.Make = "BMW";
25              myCar.Model = "2001";
26              myCar.Mileage = 70000;
27              myCar.Price = 15000;
28              myCar.Doors = 4;
29
30              // Create a Truck object for a used 2002 Toyota
31              // pickup with 40,000 miles, priced at $12,000,
32              // with four wheel drive.
33              Truck myTruck = new Truck();
34              myTruck.Make = "Toyota";
35              myTruck.Model = "2002";
36              myTruck.Mileage = 40000;
37              myTruck.Price = 12000;
38              myTruck.Drive = "Four Wheel Drive";
39
40              // Create a SportUtility object for a used 2000
41              // Volvo with 30,000 miles, priced at $15,500,
42              // with a passenger capacity of 5.
43              SportUtility mySUV = new SportUtility();
44              mySUV.Make = "Volvo";
45              mySUV.Model = "2000";
46              mySUV.Mileage = 30000;
47              mySUV.Price = 15500;
48              mySUV.Passengers = 5;
49
50              // Display data about the car.
51              MessageBox.Show(myCar.Model + " " + myCar.Make + " with " +
52                  myCar.Mileage + " miles, priced at " +
53                  myCar.Price.ToString("c") + ", with " + myCar.Doors +
54                  " doors.");
55
56              // Display data about the truck.
57              MessageBox.Show(myTruck.Model + " " + myTruck.Make +
58                  " with " + myTruck.Mileage + " miles, priced at " +
59                  myTruck.Price.ToString("c") + ", with " +
60                  myTruck.Drive);
61
62              // Display data about the SUV.
63              MessageBox.Show(mySUV.Model + " " + mySUV.Make + " with " +
64                  mySUV.Mileage + " miles, priced at " +
65                  mySUV.Price.ToString("c") + ", with " + mySUV.Passengers +
66                  " passengers.");
67          }
68
69      private void exitButton_Click(object sender, EventArgs e)
70      {
71          // Close the form.
72          this.Close();
73      }
74  }
75 }
```

Let's step through the code in the createObjectsButton_Click event handler. Line 23 creates an instance of the Car class, referenced by the myCar variable. Lines 24–28 assign values to the objects Make, Model, Mileage, Price, and Doors properties.

Line 33 creates an instance of the Truck class, referenced by the myTruck variable. Lines 34–38 assign values to the objects Make, Model, Mileage, Price, and Drive properties.

Line 43 creates an instance of the SportUtility class, referenced by the mySUV variable. Lines 44–48 assign values to the objects Make, Model, Mileage, Price, and Passengers properties.

Lines 51–54 display the properties of the myCar object in the topmost message box shown in Figure 10-6. Lines 57–60 display the properties of the myTruck object in the middle message box shown in Figure 10-6. Lines 63–66 display the properties of the mySUV object in the bottom message box shown in Figure 10-6.

Figure 10-6 Message boxes displayed by the *Car Truck SUV Demo* project

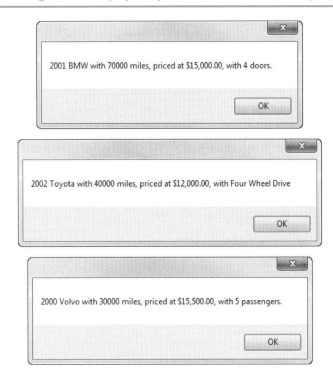

2001 BMW with 70000 miles, priced at $15,000.00, with 4 doors.

OK

2002 Toyota with 40000 miles, priced at $12,000.00, with Four Wheel Drive

OK

2000 Volvo with 30000 miles, priced at $15,500.00, with 5 passengers.

OK

In Tutorial 10-1 you create a base class for a savings account, and a derived class for a certificate of deposit.

Tutorial 10-1:
Creating and Testing the SavingsAccount and CDAccount Classes

Bank Financial Systems, Inc., develops financial software for banks and credit unions. The company is developing a new system that manages customer accounts. One of your tasks is to develop a class that represents a savings account. The data that must be held by an object of this class is

- The account number
- The interest rate
- The account balance

You must also develop a class that represents a certificate of deposit (CD) account. The data that must be held by an object of this class is

- The account number
- The interest rate
- The account balance
- The account maturity date

As you analyze these requirements, you realize that a CD account is really a specialized version of a savings account. The class that represents a CD will hold all the same data as the class that represents a savings account, plus an extra property for the maturity date. You decide to create a `SavingsAccount` class to represent a savings account and then create a class that is derived from `SavingsAccount`, named `CDAccount`, to represent a CD account.

To test the classes, you will use them in an application that lets the user enter data about a CD account, creates an object of the `CDAccount` class, sets the object's properties to the data that the user entered, and then displays the object's data. The application's form, which has already been created for you, is shown in Figure 10-7.

Figure 10-7 The *CD Account Test* application's form

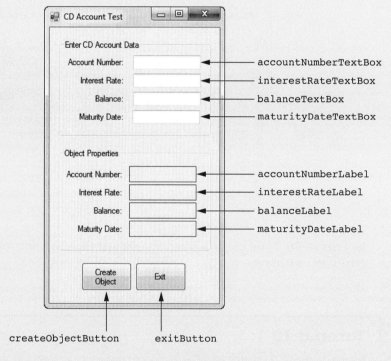

Step 1: Start Visual Studio (or Visual C# Express). Open the project named *CD Account Test* in the *Chap10* folder of the Student Sample Programs.

Step 2: Click *Project* on the Visual Studio menu bar and then select *Add Class...* The *Add New Item* window should appear. Make sure *Class* is selected as the type of item. Change the default filename to *SavingsAccount.cs* and then click the *Add* button. This adds a source code file named SavingsAccount.cs to the project.

Step 3: The SavingsAccount.cs file should now be displayed in the code editor. Complete the code for the `SavingsAccount` class by typing lines 10–42 in Program 10-3. The class code is very straightforward. It declares properties named

AccountNumber, InterestRate, and Balance, as well as the backing fields for the properties. The class also has a parameterless constructor that initializes the backing fields to default values.

Step 4: Click *Project* on the Visual Studio menu bar and then select *Add Class...* The *Add New Item* window should appear. Make sure *Class* is selected as the type of item. Change the default filename to *CDAccount.cs* and then click the *Add* button. This adds a source code file named CDAccount.cs to the project.

Step 5: The CDAccount.cs file should now be displayed in the code editor. Complete the code for the CDAccount class as follows:

- At the end of the class header type : SavingsAccount to indicate that this class is derived from the SavingsAccount class. (See line 8 in Program 10-4.)
- Type the code shown in lines 10–24 in Program 10-4. The class code is very straightforward. It declares a property named MaturityDate as well as the backing field for the property. The class also has a parameterless constructor that initializes the backing field to an empty string.

Step 6: Open the Form1.cs file in the code editor. Type the comments and code for the GetCDData method, shown in lines 19–56 of Program 10-5. Notice in line 22 that the method has a CDAccount parameter named account. When we call this method, we pass a CDAccount object to it as an argument.

The purpose of the GetCDData method is to read the data that the user has entered into the form's text boxes and store that data in the account object's properties. The values that have been entered for the interest rate and the balance are validated.

Step 7: Next you create the Click event handlers for the Button controls. Switch your view to the Form1 form in the Designer. Double-click the createObjectButton control. This opens the Form1.cs file in the code editor, and you will see an empty event handler named createObjectButton_Click. Complete the event handler by typing the code shown in lines 60–70 in Program 10-5. Let's review this code:

Line 61: This statement creates a CDAccount object in memory, referenced by a variable named myAccount.

Line 64: This statement calls the GetCDData method, passing the myAccount object as an argument. After the method executes, the myAccount object's properties will be set to the values entered by the user.

Lines 67–70: These statements display the values of the myAccount object's properties.

Step 8: Switch your view back to the Form1 form in the *Designer* and double-click the exitButton control. In the code editor you will see an empty event handler named exitButton_Click. Complete the event handler by typing the code shown in lines 75–76 in Program 10-5.

Step 9: Save the project. Then, press F5 on the keyboard or click the *Start Debugging* button (▶) on the toolbar to compile and run the application. When the application runs, enter some sample data in the TextBox controls and click the *Create Object* button. You should see the values that you entered displayed in the *Object Properties* group box. Figure 10-8 shows an example. Click the *Exit* button when you are finished.

Figure 10-8 The *CD Account Test* application

 NOTE: The MaturityDate property in the CDAccount class is implemented as a string. If you prefer, you can use the DateTime data type provided by the .NET Framework. We have not covered the DateTime data type in this book, but if you feel adventurous, you can explore it on your own and devise a way to implement the MaturityDate property as a DateTime instead of a string.

Program 10-3 Completed code for the SavingsAccount.cs file in the *CD Account Test* application

```
1 using System;
2 using System.Collections.Generic;
3 using System.Linq;
4 using System.Text;
5
6 namespace CD_Account_Test
7 {
8     class SavingsAccount
9     {
10         // Fields
11         private string _accountNumber;
12         private decimal _interestRate;
13         private decimal _balance;
14
15         // Constructor
16         public SavingsAccount()
17         {
18             _accountNumber = "";
19             _interestRate = 0;
20             _balance = 0;
21         }
22
23         // AccountNumber property
24         public string AccountNumber
```

```
25            {
26                get { return _accountNumber; }
27                set { _accountNumber = value; }
28            }
29
30            // InterestRate property
31            public decimal InterestRate
32            {
33                get { return _interestRate; }
34                set { _interestRate = value; }
35            }
36
37            // Balance property
38            public decimal Balance
39            {
40                get { return _balance; }
41                set { _balance = value; }
42            }
43        }
44 }
```

Program 10-4 Completed code for the CDAccount.cs file in the *CD Account Test* application

```
 1 using System;
 2 using System.Collections.Generic;
 3 using System.Linq;
 4 using System.Text;
 5
 6 namespace CD_Account_Test
 7 {
 8     class CDAccount : SavingsAccount
 9     {
10         // Field
11         private string _maturityDate;
12
13         // Constructor
14         public CDAccount()
15         {
16             _maturityDate = "";
17         }
18
19         // MaturityDate property
20         public string MaturityDate
21         {
22             get { return _maturityDate; }
23             set { _maturityDate = value; }
24         }
25     }
26 }
```

Program 10-5 Completed code for Form1 in the *CD Account Test* application

```
 1 using System;
 2 using System.Collections.Generic;
 3 using System.ComponentModel;
```

```csharp
 4 using System.Data;
 5 using System.Drawing;
 6 using System.Linq;
 7 using System.Text;
 8 using System.Windows.Forms;
 9
10 namespace CD_Account_Test
11 {
12     public partial class Form1 : Form
13     {
14         public Form1()
15         {
16             InitializeComponent();
17         }
18
19         // The GetCDData method accepts a CDAccount object
20         // as an argument. It assigns the data entered by
21         // the user to the object's properties.
22         private void GetCDData(CDAccount account)
23         {
24             // Temporary variables to hold interest rate
25             // and balance
26             decimal interestRate;
27             decimal balance;
28
29             // Get the account number.
30             account.AccountNumber = accountNumberTextBox.Text;
31
32             // Get the maturity date.
33             account.MaturityDate = maturityDateTextBox.Text;
34
35             // Get the interest rate.
36             if (decimal.TryParse(interestRateTextBox.Text, out interestRate))
37             {
38                 account.InterestRate = interestRate;
39
40                 // Get the balance.
41                 if (decimal.TryParse(balanceTextBox.Text, out balance))
42                 {
43                     account.Balance = balance;
44                 }
45                 else
46                 {
47                     // Display an error message.
48                     MessageBox.Show("Invalid balance");
49                 }
50             }
51             else
52             {
53                 // Display an error message.
54                 MessageBox.Show("Invalid interest rate");
55             }
56         }
57
58         private void createObjectButton_Click(object sender, EventArgs e)
59         {
60             // Create a CDAccount object.
61             CDAccount myAccount = new CDAccount();
62
```

```
63              // Get the CD account data.
64              GetCDData(myAccount);
65
66              // Display the CD account data.
67              accountNumberLabel.Text = myAccount.AccountNumber;
68              interestRateLabel.Text = myAccount.InterestRate.ToString("n2");
69              balanceLabel.Text = myAccount.Balance.ToString("c");
70              maturityDateLabel.Text = myAccount.MaturityDate;
71          }
72
73          private void exitButton_Click(object sender, EventArgs e)
74          {
75              // Close the form.
76              this.Close();
77          }
78      }
79 }
```

Base Class and Derived Class Constructors

When you create an instance of a derived class, the base class constructor is executed first, and then the derived class constructor is executed. In all the examples that we have discussed so far, the base class and the derived class have parameterless constructors. When you create an instance of a derived class, by default the base class's parameterless constructor is automatically executed.

But what happens if the base class's constructor has parameters? Or, what happens if the base class has multiple, overloaded constructors and you want to make sure a specific one is called? In either of these situations, the derived class constructor must explicitly call the base class constructor.

For example, look at the following `Rectangle` class:

```
1 class Rectangle
2 {
3      // Fields
4      private int _length;
5      private int _width;
6
7      // Constructor
8      public Rectangle()
9      {
10          _length = 0;
11          _width = 0;
12      }
13
14      // Constructor
15      public Rectangle(int length, int width)
16      {
17          _length = length;
18          _width = width;
19      }
20
21      // Length property
22      public int Length
23      {
24          get { return _length; }
25          set { _length = value; }
26      }
```

```
27
28      // Width property
29      public int Width
30      {
31          get { return _width; }
32          set { _width = value; }
33      }
34  }
```

This class holds data about a rectangle. It has Length and Width properties to store a rectangle's length and width. It also has two constructors: a parameterless constructor (lines 8–12) that initializes _length and _width to 0 and a constructor that accepts arguments for the length and the width (lines 15–19).

The following Box class is derived from the Rectangle class:

```
1  class Box : Rectangle
2  {
3      // Field
4      private int _height;
5
6      // Constructor
7      public Box()
8      {
9          _height = 0;
10     }
11
12     // Constructor
13     public Box(int length, int width, int height)
14         : base(length, width)
15     {
16         _height = height;
17     }
18
19     // Height property
20     public int Height
21     {
22         get { return _height; }
23         set { _height = value; }
24     }
25 }
```

The Box class holds data about a rectangular box, which has a length, width, and height. The class inherits the Length and Width properties from the Rectangle class, and it has its own Height property. Notice that the Box class has two constructors: a parameterless constructor (lines 7–10) and a parameterized constructor (lines 13–17).

If you create an instance of the Box class, calling its parameterless constructor, the Rectangle class's parameterless constructor will be executed. Here is an example:

```
Box myBox = new Box();
```

After this statement executes, the myBox object's Length, Width, and Height properties will be set to 0.

Now, let's look at the Box class's parameterized constructor. The following code appears in line 13:

```
public Box(int length, int width, int height)
```

This constructor has three parameters: length, width, and height. Notice the following code in line 14:

```
: base(length, width)
```

The **base keyword** refers to the base class. This is an explicit call to the base class's parameterized constructor, passing `length` and `width` as arguments. To understand how this works, consider the following statement:

```
Box myBox = new Box(100, 200, 300);
```

This statement creates an instance of the `Box` class, passing 100 into the `length` parameter, 200 into the `width` parameter, and 300 into the `height` parameter. The code in line 14 of the `Box` class calls the `Rectangle` class's parameterized constructor, passing `length` and `width` as arguments. After the `Rectangle` class's constructor executes, the `Box` class constructor resumes execution. The resulting `Box` object's Length property will be set to 100, its Width property will be set to 200, and its Height property will be set to 300.

Summary of Constructor Issues in Inheritance

- When you create an instance of a derived class, the base class constructor is executed first and then the derived class constructor is executed.
- When you create an instance of a derived class, by default the base class's parameterless constructor is automatically executed.
- If you want a parameterized constructor in the base class to execute, you must explicitly call it from the derived class's constructor. You do this by writing the notation : base(*parameterList*) in the derived class's constructor header.
- If the base class does not have a parameterless constructor, the derived class constructor must use the notation : base(*parameterList*) to call one of the base class's parameterized constructors.

 Checkpoint

10.1 In this section we discussed base classes and derived classes. Which is the general class and which is the specialized class?

10.2 What does it mean to say there is an "is a" relationship between two objects?

10.3 What does a derived class inherit from its base class?

10.4 Look at the following code, which is the first line of a class declaration. What is the name of the base class? What is the name of the derived class?
```
class Canary : Bird
```

10.5 Briefly summarize the constructor issues in inheritance.

 **Polymorphism**

CONCEPT: Polymorphism allows derived classes to have methods with the same names as methods in their base classes. It gives the ability for a program to call the correct method, depending on the type of object that is used to call it.

The term **polymorphism** refers to an object's ability to take different forms. It is a powerful feature of object-oriented programming. In this section, we look at two essential ingredients of polymorphic behavior:

1. The ability to define a method in a base class and then define a method with the same name in a derived class. When a derived class method has the same name as a

base class method, it is often said that the derived class method **overrides** the base class method.

2. The ability to call the correct version of an overridden method, depending on the type of object that is used to call it. If a derived class object is used to call an overridden method, then the derived class's version of the method is the one that executes. If a base class object is used to call an overridden method, then the base class's version of the method is the one that executes.

Perhaps the best way to describe polymorphism is to demonstrate it, so let's consider a simple example. Look at the following code for the `Animal` class:

```
 1 class Animal
 2 {
 3     // Field
 4     private string _species;
 5
 6     // Constructor
 7     public Animal(string species)
 8     {
 9         _species = species;
10     }
11
12     // Species property
13     public string Species
14     {
15         get { return _species; }
16         set { _species = value; }
17     }
18
19     // MakeSound method
20     public virtual void MakeSound()
21     {
22         MessageBox.Show("Grrrrrrr");
23     }
24 }
```

Line 4 declares the `string` field `_species`. This is the backing field for the Species property, defined in lines 13–17. The constructor in lines 7–10 takes an argument that is assigned to the `_species` field.

The class has a method named `MakeSound`, in lines 20–23. The method simply displays "Grrrrrrr" in a message box. Notice the `virtual` keyword that appears in the method header. The **virtual** keyword declares that a derived class is allowed to override this method.

Here is an example of code that uses an instance of the `Animal` class:

```
1 Animal myAnimal = new Animal("regular animal");
2 MessageBox.Show("The species is " + myAnimal.Species);
3 myAnimal.MakeSound();
```

The statement in line 1 creates an object of the `Animal` class, passing the string "regular animal" to the constructor. The object is referenced by the `myAnimal` variable. Line 2 displays "The species is regular animal" in a message box. Line 3 calls the `myAnimal` object's `MakeSound` method, which displays "Grrrrrrr" in a message box.

Next, look at the `Dog` class, which is derived from the `Animal` class:

```
1 class Dog : Animal
2 {
3     // Field
4     private string _name;
5
```

```
 6      // Constructor
 7      public Dog(string name) : base ("Dog")
 8      {
 9          _name = name;
10      }
11
12      // Name property
13      public string Name
14      {
15          get { return _name; }
16          set { _name = value; }
17      }
18
19      // MakeSound method
20      public override void MakeSound()
21      {
22          MessageBox.Show("Woof! Woof!");
23      }
24 }
```

Line 4 declares the `string` field _name. This is the backing field for the Name property, defined in lines 13–17. The constructor in lines 7–10 takes an argument for the dog's name. Notice that the constructor calls the base class constructor, passing the string `"Dog"` as an argument. The `Animal` class constructor assigns the string `"Dog"` to the _species field.

Although the `Dog` class is derived from the `Animal` class, the `Animal` class's `MakeSound` method is inadequate for the `Dog` class. So, the `Dog` class overrides the `Animal` class's `MakeSound` method. The `Dog` class's `MakeSound` method, in lines 20–23, displays `"Woof! Woof!"` in a message box, which is more appropriate for a dog. Notice the override keyword that appears in the method header. The **override keyword** declares that this method overrides a method in the base class.

Here is an example of code that uses an instance of the `Dog` class:

```
1 Dog myDog = new Dog("Fido");
2 MessageBox.Show("The species is " + myDog.Species);
3 MessageBox.Show("The animal's name is " + myDog.Name);
4 myDog.MakeSound();
```

The statement in line 1 creates an object of the `Dog` class, passing the string `"Fido"` to the constructor. The object is referenced by the myDog variable. Line 2 displays "The species is Dog" in a message box. Line 3 displays "The animal's name is Fido" in a message box. Line 4 calls the myDog object's `MakeSound` method. When we use a `Dog` object to call the `MakeSound` method, the version of the method that is in the `Dog` class is the one that executes. So, the statement in line 4 displays "Woof! Woof!" in a message box.

Next, look at the `Cat` class, which is also derived from the `Animal` class:

```
 1 class Cat : Animal
 2 {
 3      // Field
 4      private string _name;
 5
 6      // Constructor
 7      public Cat(string name) : base("Cat")
 8      {
 9          _name = name;
10      }
11
12      // Name property
13      public string Name
```

```
14      {
15          get { return _name; }
16          set { _name = value; }
17      }
18
19      // MakeSound method
20      public override void MakeSound()
21      {
22          MessageBox.Show("Meow");
23      }
24 }
```

Line 4 declares the string field _name. This is the backing field for the Name property, defined in lines 13–17. The constructor in lines 7–10 takes an argument for the cat's name. Notice that the constructor calls the base class constructor, passing the string "Cat" as an argument. The Animal class constructor assigns the string "Cat" to the _species field.

Although the Cat class is derived from the Animal class, the Animal class's MakeSound method is inadequate for the Cat class. So, the Cat class overrides the Animal class's MakeSound method. The Cat class's MakeSound method, in lines 20–23, displays "Meow" in a message box, which is more appropriate for a cat. Notice the override keyword that appears in the method header

Here is an example of code that uses an instance of the Cat class:

```
1 Cat myCat = new Cat("Kitty");
2 MessageBox.Show("The species is " + myCat.Species);
3 MessageBox.Show("The animal's name is " + myCat.Name);
4 myCat.MakeSound();
```

The statement in line 1 creates an object of the Cat class, passing the string "Kitty" to the constructor. The object is referenced by the myCat variable. Line 2 displays "The species is Cat" in a message box. Line 3 displays "The animal's name is Kitty" in a message box. Line 4 calls the myCat object's MakeSound method. When we use a Cat object to call the MakeSound method, the version of the method that is in the Cat class is the one that executes. So, the statement in line 4 displays "Meow" in a message box.

Because of the "is a" relationship between a base class and a derived class, an object of the Dog class is not just a Dog object. It is also an Animal object. (A dog is an animal.) Because of this relationship, we can use an Animal class variable to reference a Dog object. For example, look at the following code:

```
1 Animal myAnimal = new Dog("Fido");
2 MessageBox.Show("The species is " + myAnimal.Species);
3 myAnimal.MakeSound();
```

Line 1 declares myAnimal as a variable of the Animal type. It also creates an object of the Dog class and assigns a reference to the Dog object to the myAnimal variable. After this statement executes, we will have an Animal variable referencing a Dog object. This assignment is legal because a Dog object is also an Animal object. Line 2 displays "The species is Dog" in a message box. Line 3 calls the myAnimal object's MakeSound method, which displays "Woof! Woof!" in a message box.

Similarly, we can use an Animal variable to reference a Cat object, as shown in the following code:

```
1 Animal myAnimal = new Cat("Kitty");
2 MessageBox.Show("The species is " + myAnimal.Species);
3 myAnimal.MakeSound();
```

The statement in line 2 displays "The species is Cat" in a message box. Line 3 calls the myAnimal object's MakeSound method, which displays "Meow" in a message box.

Overriding Properties

Properties in a base class can be overridden in the same way that methods can be overridden. In the base class, you write the virtual keyword in the property declaration, as shown here:

```
public virtual double Weight
{
    get { return _weight; }
    set { _weight = value; }
}
```

This example declares a virtual property named Weight. To override the property in the derived class you write the override keyword in the property declaration. For example, suppose that in a derived class we want to override the Weight property so the get accessor returns the weight on the moon. Here is an example:

```
public override double Weight
{
    get { return _weight * 0.165; }
    set { _weight = value; }
}
```

Base Class Reference Variables Know about Base Class Members Only

A base class reference variable can reference an object of any class that is derived from the base class. However, there is a limit to what the base class variable can do with those objects. A base class reference variable knows only about the members that are declared in the base class. If the derived class introduces additional methods, properties, or fields, a base class reference variable cannot access them. For example, look at the following code:

```
1 Animal myAnimal = new Dog("Fido");
2 MessageBox.Show("The species is " + myAnimal.Species);
3 MessageBox.Show("The animal's name is " + myAnimal.Name); // ERROR!
4 myAnimal.MakeSound();
```

Line 3 in this code will not compile. The myAnimal variable is an Animal reference variable, and the Animal class does not have a Name property. Even though the myAnimal variable is referencing a Dog object, it cannot access the object's Name property.

The "Is a" Relationship Does Not Work in Reverse

It is important to understand that the "is a" relationship does not work in reverse. Although the statement "a dog is an animal" is true, the statement "an animal is a dog" is not true. This is because all dogs are animals, but not all animals are dogs. So, the following statement will not compile:

```
Dog myDog = new Animal("Dog");
```

You cannot assign an Animal reference to a Dog variable. This makes sense because Dog objects have capabilities that go beyond those of an Animal object.

> **NOTE:** Interestingly, the C# compiler will allow you to make such an assignment if you use a cast operator, as shown here:
>
> ```
> Dog myDog = (Dog) new Animal("Dog");
> ```
>
> However, an exception will be thrown at run time when the assignment takes place.

Passing Objects to Base Class Parameters

Polymorphism gives you a great deal of flexibility when designing applications. For example, look at the following method:

```
private void ShowAnimalInfo(Animal animal)
{
    MessageBox.Show("Species: " + animal.Species);
    animal.MakeSound();
}
```

This method displays information about an animal. Because it has an `Animal` variable as its parameter, you can pass an `Animal` object to the method when you call it. The method then displays the object's Species property and calls its `MakeSound` method.

The `ShowAnimalInfo` method works with an `Animal` object, but what if you also need methods that display the same information about `Dog` objects and `Cat` objects? Do you need to write additional methods for each of these types? Because of polymorphism, the answer is *no*. In addition to `Animal` objects, you can also pass `Dog` objects or `Cat` objects as arguments to the `ShowAnimalInfo` method previously shown.

In Tutorial 10-2 you complete an application that uses the `Animal`, `Dog`, and `Cat` classes to demonstrate polymorphism.

Tutorial 10-2:
Completing the *Polymorphism* Application

In this tutorial you complete the *Polymorphism* application, which demonstrates the `Animal`, `Dog`, and `Cat` classes shown in this section. The application also incorporates the `ShowAnimalInfo` method previously described.

The application's form, which has already been created for you, is shown in Figure 10-9. When you run the completed application, clicking the *Create an Animal* button creates an object of the `Animal` class and passes the object to the `ShowAnimalInfo` method. Clicking the *Create a Dog* button creates an object of the `Dog` class and passes that object to the `ShowAnimalInfo` method. Clicking the *Create a Cat* button creates an object of the `Cat` class and passes that object to the `ShowAnimalInfo` method.

Figure 10-9 The *Polymorphism* application's form

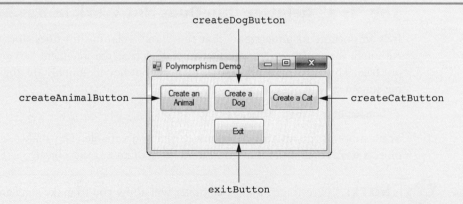

Step 1: Start Visual Studio (or Visual C# Express). Open the project named *Polymorphism* in the *Chap10* folder of the Student Sample Programs.

Step 2: Click *Project* on the Visual Studio menu bar and then select *Add Class...* The *Add New Item* window should appear. Make sure *Class* is selected as the type of item. Change the default filename to *Animal.cs* and then click the *Add* button. This adds a source code file named Animal.cs to the project.

Step 3: The Animal.cs file should now be displayed in the code editor. Add the `using` directive shown in line 5 of Program 10-6. This is necessary in order for the class to call the `MessageBox.Show` method. Next, complete the code for the `Animal` class by typing lines 11–31 in Program 10-6.

Step 4: Click *Project* on the Visual Studio menu bar and then select *Add Class…* The *Add New Item* window should appear. Make sure *Class* is selected as the type of item. Change the default filename to *Dog.cs* and then click the *Add* button. This adds a source code file named Dog.cs to the project.

Step 5: The Dog.cs file should now be displayed in the code editor. Add the `using` directive shown in line 5 of Program 10-7. This is necessary in order for the class to call the `MessageBox.Show` method. Next, add the `: Animal` notation to the class header, shown in line 9 of Program 10-7. Then, complete the code for the `Dog` class by typing lines 11–32 in Program 10-7.

Step 6: Click *Project* on the Visual Studio menu bar and then select *Add Class…* The *Add New Item* window should appear. Make sure *Class* is selected as the type of item. Change the default filename to *Cat.cs*, and then click the *Add* button. This adds a source code file named Cat.cs to the project.

Step 7: The Cat.cs file should now be displayed in the code editor. Add the `using` directive shown in line 5 of Program 10-8. This is necessary in order for the class to call the `MessageBox.Show` method. Next, add the `: Animal` notation to the class header, shown in line 9 of Program 10-8. Then, complete the code for the `Dog` class by typing lines 11–32 in Program 10-8.

Step 8: Open the Form1.cs file in the code editor. Type the comments and code for the `ShowAnimalInfo` method shown in lines 19–26 of Program 10-9.

Step 9: Next you create the Click event handlers for the Button controls. Switch your view to the Form1 form in the Designer. Double-click the `createAnimalButton` control. This opens the Form1.cs file in the code editor, and you will see an empty event handler named `createAnimalButton_Click`. Complete the event handler by typing the code shown in lines 30–31 in Program 10-9.

Let's review this code. Line 30 creates an object of the `Animal` class, passing `"Regular animal"` as an argument to the constructor. Line 31 passes the object to the `ShowAnimalInfo` method.

Step 10: Switch your view to the Form1 form in the Designer. Double-click the `createDogButton` control. This will open the Form1.cs file in the code editor, and you will see an empty event handler named `createDogButton_Click`. Complete the event handler by typing the code shown in lines 36–38 in Program 10-9.

Let's review this code. Line 36 creates an object of the `Dog` class, passing `"Fido"` as an argument to the constructor. Line 37 displays the object's Name property in a message box. Line 38 passes the object to the `ShowAnimalInfo` method.

Step 11: Switch your view to the Form1 form in the Designer. Double-click the `createCatButton` control. This opens the Form1.cs file in the code editor, and you will see an empty event handler named `createCatButton_Click`. Complete the event handler by typing the code shown in lines 43–45 in Program 10-9.

Let's review this code. Line 43 creates an object of the `Cat` class, passing `"Kitty"` as an argument to the constructor. Line 44 displays the object's Name property in a message box. Line 45 passes the object to the `ShowAnimalInfo` method.

Step 12: Switch your view back to the Form1 form in the *Designer* and double-click the exitButton control. In the code editor you will see an empty event handler named exitButton_Click. Complete the event handler by typing the code shown in lines 50–51 in Program 10-9.

Step 13: Save the project. Then, press F5 on the keyboard or click the *Start Debugging* button(▶) on the toolbar to compile and run the application. When the application runs, click the *Create an Animal* button. You should see the following messages displayed in message boxes:

Species: Regular animal

Grrrrrr

Next, click the *Create a Dog* button. You should see the following messages displayed in message boxes:

The dog's name is Fido

Species: Dog

Woof! Woof!

Next, click the *Create a Cat* button. You should see the following messages displayed in message boxes:

The cat's name is Kitty

Species: Cat

Meow

Click the *Exit* button when you are finished.

Program 10-6 Completed code for the Animal.cs file in the *Polymorphism* application

```
 1 using System;
 2 using System.Collections.Generic;
 3 using System.Linq;
 4 using System.Text;
 5 using System.Windows.Forms;  // Needed for MessageBox
 6
 7 namespace Polymorphism
 8 {
 9     class Animal
10     {
11         // Field
12         private string _species;
13
14         // Constructor
15         public Animal(string species)
16         {
17             _species = species;
18         }
19
20         // Species property
21         public string Species
22         {
23             get { return _species; }
24             set { _species = value; }
25         }
26
27         // MakeSound method
28         public virtual void MakeSound()
```

```
29          {
30              MessageBox.Show("Grrrrrrr");
31          }
32      }
33 }
```

Program 10-7 Completed code for the Dog.cs file in the *Polymorphism* application

```
1 using System;
2 using System.Collections.Generic;
3 using System.Linq;
4 using System.Text;
5 using System.Windows.Forms;  // Needed for MessageBox
6
7 namespace Polymorphism
8 {
9     class Dog : Animal
10    {
11        // Field
12        private string _name;
13
14        // Constructor
15        public Dog(string name)
16            : base("Dog")
17        {
18            _name = name;
19        }
20
21        // Name property
22        public string Name
23        {
24            get { return _name; }
25            set { _name = value; }
26        }
27
28        // MakeSound method
29        public override void MakeSound()
30        {
31            MessageBox.Show("Woof! Woof!");
32        }
33    }
34 }
```

Program 10-8 Completed code for the Cat.cs file in the *Polymorphism* application

```
1 using System;
2 using System.Collections.Generic;
3 using System.Linq;
4 using System.Text;
5 using System.Windows.Forms;  // Needed for MessageBox
6
7 namespace Polymorphism
8 {
9     class Cat : Animal
10    {
11        // Field
12        private string _name;
13
```

```
14          // Constructor
15          public Cat(string name)
16              : base("Cat")
17          {
18              _name = name;
19          }
20
21          // Name property
22          public string Name
23          {
24              get { return _name; }
25              set { _name = value; }
26          }
27
28          // MakeSound method
29          public override void MakeSound()
30          {
31              MessageBox.Show("Meow");
32          }
33      }
34 }
```

Program 10-9 Completed code for Form1 in the *Polymorphism* application

```
 1 using System;
 2 using System.Collections.Generic;
 3 using System.ComponentModel;
 4 using System.Data;
 5 using System.Drawing;
 6 using System.Linq;
 7 using System.Text;
 8 using System.Windows.Forms;
 9
10 namespace Polymorphism
11 {
12     public partial class Form1 : Form
13     {
14         public Form1()
15         {
16             InitializeComponent();
17         }
18
19         // The ShowAnimalInfo method accepts an Animal
20         // object as an argument. It displays the object's
21         // species and calls its MakeSound method.
22         private void ShowAnimalInfo(Animal animal)
23         {
24             MessageBox.Show("Species: " + animal.Species);
25             animal.MakeSound();
26         }
27
28         private void createAnimalButton_Click(object sender, EventArgs e)
29         {
30             Animal myAnimal = new Animal("Regular animal");
31             ShowAnimalInfo(myAnimal);
32         }
33
34         private void createDogButton_Click(object sender, EventArgs e)
```

```
35        {
36            Dog myDog = new Dog("Fido");
37            MessageBox.Show("The dog's name is " + myDog.Name);
38            ShowAnimalInfo(myDog);
39        }
40
41        private void createCatButton_Click(object sender, EventArgs e)
42        {
43            Cat myCat = new Cat("Kitty");
44            MessageBox.Show("The cat's name is " + myCat.Name);
45            ShowAnimalInfo(myCat);
46        }
47
48        private void exitButton_Click(object sender, EventArgs e)
49        {
50            // Close the form.
51            this.Close();
52        }
53    }
54 }
```

Checkpoint

10.6 Look at the following class definitions:

```
class Vegetable
{
    public virtual void message()
    {
        MessageBox.Show("I'm a vegetable.");
    }
}

class Potato : Vegetable
{
    public override void message()
    {
        MessageBox.Show("I'm a potato.");
    }
}
```

Given these class declarations, what will the following code display?

```
Vegetable v = new Potato();
Potato p = new Potato();
v.message();
p.message();
```

10.7 Does the "is a" relationship work in reverse? Why or why not?

10.3 Abstract Classes

CONCEPT: An abstract class serves as a base class but is not instantiated itself. An abstract method has no body and must be overridden in a derived class.

Sometimes it does not make sense to instantiate a base class. For example, consider a factory that manufactures airplanes. The factory does not make a generic airplane but makes two specific types of airplanes: a prop-driven plane and a commuter jet. The computer software that catalogs the planes might use a class named `Airplane`. The `Airplane` class has members representing the common characteristics of all airplanes. In addition, the software has a class named `PropPlane` and a class named `CommuterJet`. These classes represent the two specific airplane models the factory manufactures and are derived from the `Airplane` class. The `Airplane` class is never instantiated but is used as a base class for the other classes.

A class that is not intended to be instantiated but is to be used only as a base class is called an **abstract class**. An abstract class serves as a starting point, providing some members for its derived classes. To declare a class as abstract, you use the **abstract** keyword in the class header. Here is the general format:

```
abstract class ClassName
{
    // Member declarations
}
```

The primary difference between an abstract class and a regular class (which is sometimes called a **concrete class**) is that the abstract class cannot be instantiated. A statement that tries to use the new operator to instantiate an abstract class will not compile.

Abstract classes can also contain abstract methods. An **abstract method** is a method that appears in a base class but expects to be overridden in a derived class. An abstract method has only a header and no body. In the header, the `abstract` keyword appears before the return type. Here is a very simple example of an abstract class that contains an abstract method:

```
abstract class Person
{
    public abstract void DoSomething();
}
```

When an abstract method appears in a class, it must be overridden in any class that is derived from the class. In this example, if a class is derived from the `Person` class, the derived class must override the `DoSomething` method.

Abstract classes can also contain abstract properties. An **abstract property** is a property that appears in a base class but expects to be overridden in a derived class. In the property header, the `abstract` keyword appears before the property type. Here is a very simple example of an abstract class that contains an abstract method:

```
abstract class Person
{
    public abstract string JobTitle
    {
        get;
        set;
    }
}
```

Notice that the abstract property shows `get` and `set` accessors, but it does not specify what those accessors do. When an abstract property appears in a class, it must be overridden in any class that is derived from the class. In this example, if a class is derived from the `Person` class, the derived class must override the `JobTitle` property.

NOTE: If you want to create an abstract read-only property, leave out the `set` accessor.

In Tutorial 10-3 you complete an application that uses an abstract base class with an abstract property.

Tutorial 10-3:
Completing the *Computer Science Student* Application

In this tutorial you write an abstract class named `Student`. The `Student` class holds data that is common to all students, but it does not hold all the data needed for students of specific majors. The `Student` class is intended to be a base class that can be derived by other classes that represent students of specific majors.

The `Student` class has a Name property to hold a student's name and an ID property to hold a student's ID number. It also has an abstract read-only property named Required-Hours. The purpose of the RequiredHours property is to hold the number of required hours for a specific major. Any class that is derived from the `Student` class must override the RequiredHours property.

You also write a class named `CompSciStudent`, which is derived from the Student class. The `CompSciStudent` class has a field named AcademicTrack, which holds the name of the student's academic track. It also overrides the RequiredHours property to calculate and return the number of hours required for a computer science major.

You will demonstrate the classes in the *Computer Science Student* application. The application's form, which has already been created for you, is shown in Figure 10-10. When you run the completed application, you will enter a student's name and ID number into the text boxes, and you will select an academic track using the radio buttons. When you click the *Get Required Hours* button, the application will create a `CompSciStudent` object, initialized with the data you entered. It will then get the value of the RequiredHours property and display it on the form.

Figure 10-10 The *Computer Science* application's form

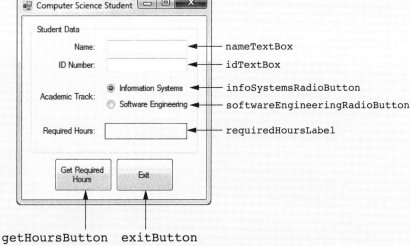

Step 1: Start Visual Studio (or Visual C# Express). Open the project named *Computer Science Student* in the *Chap10* folder of the Student Sample Programs.

Step 2: Click *Project* on the Visual Studio menu bar and then select *Add Class...*. The *Add New Item* window should appear. Make sure *Class* is selected as the type of item. Change the default filename to *Student.cs* and then click the *Add* button. This adds a source code file named Student.cs to the project.

Step 3: The Student.cs file should now be displayed in the code editor. Add the `abstract` keyword to the class header, shown in line 8 of Program 10-10. Next, complete the code for the `Student` class by typing lines 10–39 in Program 10-10.

Step 4: Click *Project* on the Visual Studio menu bar and then select *Add Class...* The *Add New Item* window should appear. Make sure *Class* is selected as the type of item. Change the default filename to *CompSciStudent.cs* and then click the *Add* button. This adds a source code file named CompSciStudent.cs to the project.

Step 5: The CompSciStudent.cs file should now be displayed in the code editor. Add the `:` `Student` notation to the class header, shown in line 8 of Program 10-11. Then, complete the code for the `CompSciStudent` class by typing lines 10–36 in Program 10-11.

Notice that the RequiredHours property, in lines 33–36, overrides the abstract RequiredHours property in the base class. This property calculates and returns the number of required hours.

Step 6: Now you will create the Click event handlers for the Button controls. Switch your view to the Form1 form in the Designer. Double-click the `getHoursButton` control. This opens the Form1.cs file in the code editor, and you will see an empty event handler named `getHoursButton_Click`. Complete the event handler by typing the code shown in lines 21–44 in Program 10-12. Let's review this code:

Line 22: This statement declares three local `string` variables: `name`, `id`, and `track`. They will be used to hold user input.

Lines 25–26: These statements get the name and ID number entered by the user and assigns those values to the `name` and `id` variables.

Lines 29–36: This `if-else` statement determines which radio button is selected and assigns a value to the `track` variable.

Lines 39–40: This statement creates a `CompSciStudent` object, referenced by the variable `csStudent`, and initializes it with the data entered by the user.

Lines 43–44: This statement gets the value of the `csStudent` object's Required-Hours property and displays it in the `requiredHoursLabel` control.

Step 7: Switch your view back to the Form1 form in the *Designer* and double-click the `exitButton` control. In the code editor you will see an empty event handler named `exitButton_Click`. Complete the event handler by typing the code shown in lines 49–50 in Program 10-12.

Step 8: Save the project. Then, press F5 on the keyboard or click the *Start Debugging* button (▶) on the toolbar to compile and run the application. When the application runs, enter some sample data in the TextBox controls, select a value with the radio buttons and click the *Get Required Hours* button. You should see the value 120.0 displayed as the number of required hours. Click the *Exit* button when you are finished.

Program 10-10 Completed code for the Student.cs file in the *Computer Science* application

```
1 using System;
2 using System.Collections.Generic;
3 using System.Linq;
4 using System.Text;
```

```
 5
 6 namespace Computer_Science_Student
 7 {
 8     abstract class Student
 9     {
10         // Fields
11         private string _name;
12         private string _id;
13
14         // Constructor
15         public Student(string name, string id)
16         {
17             _name = name;
18             _id = id;
19         }
20
21         // Name property
22         public string Name
23         {
24             get { return _name; }
25             set { _name = value; }
26         }
27
28         // ID property
29         public string ID
30         {
31             get { return _id; }
32             set { _id = value; }
33         }
631
35         // RequiredHours property (abstract)
36         public abstract double RequiredHours
37         {
38             get;
39         }
40     }
41 }
```

Program 10-11 Completed code for the CompSciStudent.cs file in the *Computer Science* application

```
 1 using System;
 2 using System.Collections.Generic;
 3 using System.Linq;
 4 using System.Text;
 5
 6 namespace Computer_Science_Student
 7 {
 8     class CompSciStudent : Student
 9     {
10         // Constants
11         private double MATH_HOURS = 20;
12         private double CS_HOURS = 40;
13         private double GEN_HOURS = 60;
14
15         // Fields
16         private string _academicTrack;
17
18         // Constructor
```

```
19          public CompSciStudent(string name, string id, string track)
20              : base(name, id)
21          {
22              _academicTrack = track;
23          }
24
25          // AcademicTrack property
26          public string AcademicTrack
27          {
28              get { return _academicTrack; }
29              set { _academicTrack = value; }
30          }
31
32          // RequiredHours property
33          public override double RequiredHours
34          {
35              get { return MATH_HOURS + CS_HOURS + GEN_HOURS; }
36          }
37      }
38 }
```

Program 10-12 Completed code for Form1 in the *Computer Science* application

```
1  using System;
2  using System.Collections.Generic;
3  using System.ComponentModel;
4  using System.Data;
5  using System.Drawing;
6  using System.Linq;
7  using System.Text;
8  using System.Windows.Forms;
9
10 namespace Computer_Science_Student
11 {
12     public partial class Form1 : Form
13     {
14         public Form1()
15         {
16             InitializeComponent();
17         }
18
19         private void getHoursButton_Click(object sender, EventArgs e)
20         {
21             // Variables to hold input
22             string name, id, track;
23
24             // Get the student's name and ID.
25             name = nameTextBox.Text;
26             id = idTextBox.Text;
27
28             // Get the student's academic track.
29             if (infoSystemsRadioButton.Checked)
30             {
31                 track = "Information Systems";
32             }
33             else
34             {
35                 track = "Software Engineering";
36             }
```

```
37
38              // Create a CompSciStudent object.
39              CompSciStudent csStudent =
40                  new CompSciStudent(name, id, track);
41
42              // Display the student's required hours.
43              requiredHoursLabel.Text =
44                  csStudent.RequiredHours.ToString("n1");
45          }
46
47          private void exitButton_Click(object sender, EventArgs e)
48          {
49              // Close the form.
50              this.Close();
51          }
52      }
53 }
```

Checkpoint

10.8 What is the purpose of an abstract class?

10.9 If a class is abstract, what cannot be done with the class?

10.10 If a class is derived from a base class that has an abstract method, what must the derived class do?

10.11 What must be done with an abstract property before it can be used?

10.12 How can you create an abstract read-only property?

Key Terms

abstract class	"is a" relationship
abstract keyword	override keyword
abstract method	overrides
abstract property	polymorphism
base class	subclasses
base keyword	superclasses
concrete class	virtual keyword
derived class	

Review Questions

1. When one object is a specialized version of another object, there is an _____ between them.

   a. "is a" relationship
   b. innate association
   c. inherent union
   d. unbreakable union

2. In an inheritance relationship, the _____ is the general class.

   a. derived class
   b. base class
   c. dependent class
   d. child class

3. In an inheritance relationship, the _____ is the specialized class.

   a. base class
   b. master class
   c. derived class
   d. parent class

4. Base classes are sometimes called _____.

   a. megaclasses
   b. primitive classes
   c. starter classes
   d. superclasses

5. Derived classes are sometimes called _____.

   a. refined classes
   b. subclasses
   c. child classes
   d. neoclasses

6. The _____ refers to the base class.

   a. friend keyword
   b. this keyword
   c. base keyword
   d. class keyword

7. The term _____ refers to an object's ability to take different forms.

   a. multi-instance
   b. by referencing
   c. polymorphism
   d. oligopoly

8. When a derived class method has the same name as a base class method, it is often said that the derived class method _____ the base class method.

    a. terminates
    b. cancels out
    c. overrides
    d. short circuits

9. The _____ declares that a derived class is allowed to override a method.

    a. `void` keyword
    b. `protected` keyword
    c. `base` keyword
    d. `virtual` keyword

10. The _____ declares that this method overrides a method in the base class.

    a. `override` keyword
    b. `class` keyword
    c. `virtual` keyword
    d. `base` keyword

11. A class that is not intended to be instantiated, but used only as a base class, is called a(n) _____.

    a. dummy class
    b. subclass
    c. virtual class
    d. abstract class

12. To declare a class as abstract, you use the _____ in the class header.

    a. `abstract` keyword
    b. `base` keyword
    c. `void` keyword
    d. `virtual` keyword

13. A regular, nonabstract class is sometimes called a _____.

    a. true class
    b. model class
    c. concrete class
    d. real class

14. A(n) _____ is a method that appears in a base class but expects to be overridden in a derived class.

    a. abstract method
    b. virtual method
    c. concrete method
    d. base method

15. A(n) _____ is a property that appears in a base class but expects to be overridden in a derived class.

    a. virtual property
    b. concrete property
    c. base property
    d. abstract property

16. _____ allows a base class reference variable to reference a derived class object.

    a. Polymorphism
    b. Inheritance
    c. Generalization
    d. Specialization

True or False

1. The base class inherits fields, properties, and methods from the derived class.

2. Polymorphism allows a class variable of the base class type to reference objects of either the base class or the derived class types.

3. Properties in a base class cannot be overridden in the same way that methods can be overridden.

4. A base class reference variable can reference an object of any class that is derived from the base class.

5. A statement that tries to use the new operator to instantiate an abstract class will not compile.

6. A class that is not intended to be instantiated, but used only as a base class, is called a concrete class.

7. When an abstract property appears in a class, it must be overridden in any class that is derived from the class.

Short Answer

1. What does a derived class inherit from its base class?

2. Look at the following code, which is the first line of a class declaration. What is the name of the base class? What is the name of the derived class?

    ```
    class Tiger : Felis
    ```

3. Can methods in the derived class directly access the base class's private members?

4. When you create an instance of a derived class, which constructor is called first?

5. In what kind of situation would you want to use an abstract class instead of a base class?

6. What is primary difference between an abstract class and a regular class?

7. Can abstract classes also contain abstract properties?

Algorithm Workbench

1. Write the first line of the definition for a Poodle class. The class should be derived from the Dog class.

2. Look at the following class declarations:

    ```
    class Plant
    {
        public virtual void Message()
        {
            MessageBox.Show("I'm a plant.");
        }
    }

    class Tree : Plant
    {
        public override void Message()
        {
            MessageBox.Show("I'm a tree.");
        }
    }
    ```

Given these class definitions, what will the following code display?

```
Plant p = new Tree();
p.Message();
```

3. Write a parameterized constructor for a base class named `Movie` with a `string` field named `_title` and an `int` field named `_runningTime`.

4. A class named `Wave` has a virtual property named Frequency. A class named `Sound` is derived from the `Wave` class. Write example code showing how the Frequency property might appear in the `Sound` class.

5. Create an abstract class called `Star`. Include an abstract method named `SolarMasses` that returns a value of the `double` data type.

Programming Problems

1. **`Employee` and `ProductionWorker` Classes**

   Create an `Employee` class that has properties for the following data:
   - Employee name
   - Employee number

   Next, create a class named `ProductionWorker` that is derived from the `Employee` class. The `ProductionWorker` class should have properties to hold the following data:
   - Shift number (an integer, such as 1, 2, or 3)
   - Hourly pay rate

   The workday is divided into two shifts: day and night. The Shift property will hold an integer value representing the shift that the employee works. The day shift is shift 1 and the night shift is shift 2.

   Create an application that creates an object of the `ProductionWorker` class and lets the user enter data for each of the object's properties. Retrieve the object's properties and display their values.

2. **`ShiftSupervisor` Class**

   In a particular factory, a shift supervisor is a salaried employee who supervises a shift. In addition to a salary, the shift supervisor earns a yearly bonus when his or her shift meets production goals. Create a `ShiftSupervisor` class that is derived from the `Employee` class you created in Programming Exercise 1. The `ShiftSupervisor` class should have a property that holds the annual salary and a property that holds the annual production bonus that a shift supervisor has earned. Demonstrate the class in an application.

3. **`TeamLeader` Class**

   In a particular factory, a team leader is an hourly paid production worker that leads a small team. In addition to hourly pay, team leaders earn a fixed monthly bonus. Team leaders are required to attend a minimum number of hours of training per year. Design a `TeamLeader` class that is derived from the `ProductionWorker` class you created in Programming Exercise 1. The `TeamLeader` class should have properties for the monthly bonus amount, the required number of training hours, and the number of training hours that the team leader has attended. Demonstrate the class in an application.

4. **`Person` and `Customer` Classes**

   Design a class named `Person` with properties for holding a person's name, address, and telephone number. Next, design a class named `Customer`, which is derived from the `Person` class. The `Customer` class should have a property for a customer number and a Boolean property indicating whether the customer wishes to be on a mailing list. Demonstrate an object of the `Customer` class in a simple application.

5. **PreferredCustomer** Class

A retail store has a preferred customer plan where customers can earn discounts on all their purchases. The amount of a customer's discount is determined by the amount of the customer's cumulative purchases in the store as follows:

- When a preferred customer spends $500, he or she gets a 5 percent discount on all future purchases.
- When a preferred customer spends $1,000, he or she gets a 6 percent discount on all future purchases.
- When a preferred customer spends $1,500, he or she gets a 7 percent discount on all future purchases.
- When a preferred customer spends $2,000 or more, he or she gets a 10 percent discount on all future purchases.

Design a class named **PreferredCustomer**, which is derived from the **Customer** class you created in Programming Exercise 4. The **PreferredCustomer** class should have properties for the amount of the customer's purchases and the customer's discount level. Demonstrate the class in a simple application.

11 Databases

TOPICS

11.1 Introduction to Database Management Systems

CONCEPT: A database management system (DBMS) is software that manages large collections of data.

If an application needs to store only a small amount of data, traditional files work well. These types of files are not practical, however, when a large amount of data must be stored and manipulated. Many businesses keep hundreds of thousands—or even millions—of data items in files. When a traditional file contains this much data, simple operations such as searching, inserting, and deleting become cumbersome and inefficient.

When developing applications that work with an intensive amount of data, most developers prefer to use a database management system. A **database management system (DBMS)** is software that is specifically designed to store, retrieve, and manipulate large amounts of data in an organized and efficient manner. Once the data is stored using the database management system, applications may be written in C# or other languages to communicate with the DBMS. Rather than retrieving or manipulating the data directly, applications can send instructions to the DBMS. The DBMS carries out those instructions and sends the results back to the application, as Figure 11-1 illustrates.

Although Figure 11-1 is simplified, it illustrates the layered nature of an application that works with a DBMS. The topmost layer of software, which—in this case—is written in

Figure 11-1 A C# application interacting with a DBMS, which manipulates data

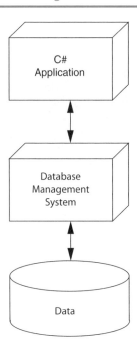

C#, interacts with the user. It also sends instructions to the next layer of software, the DBMS. The DBMS works directly with the data and sends the results of operations back to the application.

For example, suppose a company keeps all its product records in a database. The company has a C# application that allows the user to look up information on any product by entering its product ID number. The C# application instructs the DBMS to retrieve the record for the product with the specified product ID number. The DBMS retrieves the product record and sends the data back to the C# application. The C# application displays the data to the user.

The advantage of this layered approach to software development is that the C# programmer does not need to know about the physical structure of the data. He or she needs to know only how to interact with the DBMS. The DBMS handles the actual reading of, writing of, and searching for data.

SQL Server Express Edition

There are numerous DBMSs in use today, and Visual C# can interact with many of them. Some of the more popular ones are Microsoft SQL Server, Oracle, DB2, MySQL, and Microsoft Access. In this book we use Microsoft SQL Server Express Edition because it is automatically installed on your system when you install Visual Studio or Visual C# Express.

 Checkpoint

11.1 What is a database management system (DBMS)?

11.2 Why do most businesses use a DBMS to store their data instead of creating their own text files to hold the data?

11.3 When developing a C# application that uses a DBMS to store and manipulate data, why doesn't the programmer need to know specific details about the physical structure of the data?

Tables, Rows, and Columns

CONCEPT: Data that is stored in a database is organized into tables, rows, and columns.

A database management system stores data in a **database**. The data that is stored in a database is organized into one or more tables. Each **table** holds a collection of related data. The data that is stored in a table is then organized into rows and columns. A **row** is a complete set of information about a single item. The data that is stored in a row is divided into columns. Each **column** holds an individual piece of information about the item.

For example, suppose we are developing a phone book application and we want to store a list of names and phone numbers in a database. We initially store the following list:

Katie Allen	555-1234
Jill Ammons	555-5678
Kevin Brown	555-9012
Elisa Garcia	555-3456
Jeff Jenkins	555-7890
Leo Killian	555-1122
Marcia Potemkin	555-3344
Kelsey Rose	555-5566

Think about how this data would appear if we stored it as rows and columns in a spreadsheet. We would put the names in one column and the phone numbers in another column. Each row, then, would contain data about one person. Figure 11-2 shows how the third row contains the name and phone number for Kevin Brown.

Figure 11-2 The table

This row contains data about one person:
Name: Kevin Brown
Phone: 555-9012

Name	Phone
Katie Allen	555-1234
Jill Ammons	555-5678
Kevin Brown	555-9012
Elisa Garcia	555-3456
Jeff Jenkins	555-7890
Leo Killian	555-1122
Marcia Potemkin	555-3344
Kelsey Rose	555-5566

When we create a database table to hold this information, we organize it in a similar manner. We give the table a name, such as `Person`. In the table, we create a column for the names and a column for the phone numbers. Each column in a table must have a name, so we can name our columns `Name` and `Phone`, respectively.

Column Data Types

When you create a database table, you must specify a data type for the columns. The data types that you can choose from are not C# data types, however. They are the data types that are provided by the DBMS. In this book we are using Microsoft SQL Server, so we will select from the data types provided by that DBMS. Table 11-1 lists a few of the Microsoft SQL Server data types and shows the C# data type with which each is generally compatible.

> **NOTE:** Table 11-1 shows the data types that you will most often use while learning. These are only a small number of the data types provided by Microsoft SQL Server, however.

Table 11-1 A few of the Microsoft SQL Server data types

SQL Server Data Type	Description	Corresponding C# or .NET Framework Data Type
bit	True/false values	bool
datetime	A date and a time	DateTime
decimal(t, d)	A decimal value with t total digits and d digits appearing after the decimal point.	decimal
float	Real numbers	double
int	An integer number	int
money	Values that represent currency	decimal
nchar(n)	A fixed-length Unicode string with a maximum length of n characters.	string
nvarchar(n)	A variable-length Unicode string with a maximum length of n characters.	string

> **NOTE:** The nchar(n) and nvarchar(n) data types are both used to store strings. An nchar(n) column is fixed in length and will always use n characters of space in the database. An nvarchar(n) column is variable in length, and the amount of space it uses in the database will be enough to accommodate the piece of data it holds, up to n characters.

Primary Keys

Most database tables have a **primary key**, which is a column that can be used to identify a specific row. The column that is designated as the primary key must hold a unique value for each row. Here are some examples:

- A table stores employee data, and one of the columns holds employee ID numbers. Because each employee's ID number is unique, this column can be used as the primary key.
- A table stores product data, and one of the columns holds the product number. Because each product has a unique product number, this column can be used as the primary key.
- A table stores invoice data, and one of the columns holds invoice numbers. Each invoice has a unique invoice number, so this column can be used as a primary key.

Identity Columns

Sometimes the data that you want to store in a table does not contain any unique items that can be used as a primary key. For example, in the `Person` table that we previously described, neither the `Name` column nor the `Phone` column contains unique data. Two people can have the same name, so it is possible that a name might appear more than once in the `Name` column. Also, multiple people can share the same phone number, so it is possible that a phone number might appear more than once in the `Phone` column. Consequently, you cannot use the `Name` column or the `Phone` column as a primary key.

In a case such as this, it is necessary to create an identity column specifically to serve as the primary key. An **identity column** is a column that contains unique values that are generated by the DBMS. Identity columns typically contain integers. Each time a new row is added to the table, the DBMS automatically assigns a unique value to that row's identity column.

For example, when designing the `Person` table that we previously discussed, we could create an `int` column named `PersonID` and designate that column as an identity column. (As a result, the DBMS assigns a unique integer value to the `PersonID` column for each row.) Then we could designate the `PersonID` column as the table's primary key. Figure 11-3 shows an example of the `Person` table after we have created it and entered data into it.

Figure 11-3 The `Person` table with data entered

PersonID	Name	Phone
1	Katie Allen	555-1234
2	Jill Ammons	555-5678
3	Kevin Brown	555-9012
4	Elisa Garcia	555-3456
5	Jeff Jenkins	555-7890
6	Leo Killian	555-1122
7	Marcia Potemkin	555-3344
8	Kelsey Rose	555-5566

Allowing Null Values

If a column contains no data, it is said to be null. Sometimes it is okay for a column to be left empty. Some columns, however, such as primary keys, must contain a value. When you are designing a table, you can specify whether a column is allowed to be null. If a particular column is not allowed to be null, anytime you add a row of data to the table, the DBMS will require that a value be provided for the column. Leaving the column empty results in an error.

 Checkpoint

11.4 Describe each of the following terms:
   a. database
   b. table
   c. row
   d. column

11.5 Match the Microsoft SQL Server data type with the compatible C# data type.
   1. bit   a. double
   2. datetime   b. int
   3. float   c. bool
   4. int   d. DateTime
   5. money   e. string
   6. nchar   f. decimal

11.6 What is the purpose of a primary key?

11.7 What is an identity column?

11.8 If a particular column is not allowed to be null, what is the result if the column is left empty?

11.3 Creating a Database in Visual Studio

CONCEPT: A .NET application uses several components, arranged in layers, to connect to a database. Visual Studio provides tools that allow you to create a database and configure the various components that an application needs to connect to it.

Connecting an Application to a Database

A .NET application requires a set of special components that let it connect to, and work with, a database. The components are layered one on top of the other, as shown in Figure 11-4.

Figure 11-4 The components used by an application to connect to a database

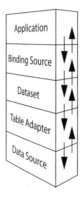

Here is a summary of the layers shown in the figure:

- **Data Source**—As its name implies, a **data source** is a source of data with which the application can work. Data sources are usually databases, but they can also be Excel spreadsheets, XML data, text files, or Web services.
- **Table Adapter**—A **table adapter** connects to a data source and can retrieve data from a table in a data source. It can also update the table in the data source.
- **Dataset**—A **dataset** gets a copy of a table from the table adapter and keeps the copy of the table in memory. Instead of working directly with the database, the application works with the dataset, modifying rows, deleting rows, adding new rows, etc. Then, the dataset can instruct the table adapter to write the changes back to the database.
- **Binding Source**—A **binding source** is a component that can connect user interface controls directly to a dataset.

Fortunately, Visual Studio provides wizards that make it easy to create and configure the necessary components. In Tutorial 11-1 you start a new C# project and use Visual Studio to perform the following:

- Create an SQL Server database
- Design a table in the database
- Add data to the table

Tutorial 11-1:

Starting the *Phone Book* Application and Creating the Phonelist.mdf Database

In the next two tutorials, you create an application that uses a database to store a list of names and phone numbers. In this tutorial you start the application by creating the database. In the next tutorial you connect the application to the database, add a dataset, and add a control to the form that allows the user to interact with the database.

Step 1: Start Visual Studio (or Visual C# Express). Create a new *Windows Forms Application* project named *Phone Book*.

Step 2: Change the Form1 form's Text property to *Phone Book*.

Step 3: Next you create a new database and add it to the project. Click *Project* on the Visual Studio menu bar and then select *Add New Item...*

Step 4: The *Add New Item* window will appear. Scroll down the list of items and select *Service-based Database*, as shown in Figure 11-5. You also need to specify the database's name in the *Name* text box at the bottom of the window. A default name, such as *Database1.mdf* appears there. Change the name to *Phonelist.mdf*. (Be sure to keep the .mdf file extension.)

Figure 11-5 The *Add New Item* window

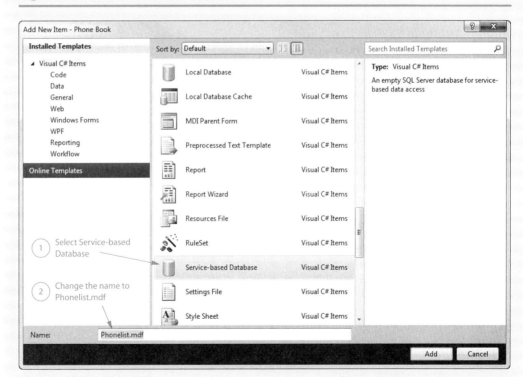

Step 5: Click the *Add* button in the *Add New Item* window. This adds an empty SQL Server database named Phonelist.mdf to your project.

Step 6: The *Data Source Configuration Wizard* window, shown in Figure 11-6, appears next. Click the *Cancel* button. (You are canceling the process at this point because the database that you just created is currently empty. You cannot configure a data source until you have created a database table.)

Figure 11-6 Clicking *Cancel* in the *Data Source Configuration Wizard* window

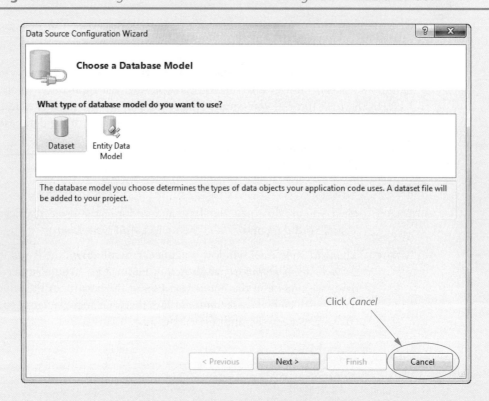

Step 7: Look at the *Solution Explorer*, shown in Figure 11-7, and notice that it now contains an entry for the Phonelist.mdf database. Double-click the entry for Phonelist.mdf database. Notice that a new window named *Server Explorer* is now open in the area where the Toolbox is located. (The window is named *Server Explorer* in Visual Studio. If you are using Visual C# Express, the window is named *Database Explorer*.) The *Server Explorer* is shown in Figure 11-8.

NOTE: For our purposes, it does not matter whether you are using the *Server Explorer* in Visual Studio or the *Database Explorer* in Visual C# Express. They both work the same way. The *Server Explorer* provides the added capability to locate databases across your network.

Figure 11-7 *Solution Explorer* entry for the Phonelist.mdf database

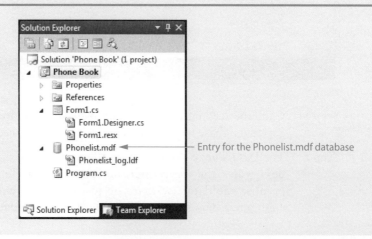

Figure 11-8 *Server Explorer*

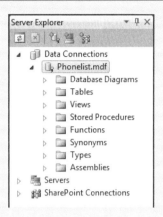

Step 8: Now you add a table to the Phonelist.mdf database. In the *Server Explorer* (or *Database Explorer*), make sure the Phonelist.mdf entry is expanded, as shown in Figure 11-8. Right-click on *Tables*, and as shown in Figure 11-9, click *Add New Table* on the menu.

Figure 11-9 Adding a Table to the Phonelist.mdf database

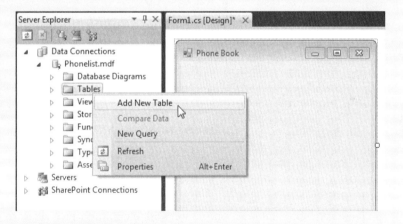

This displays the *Table Designer* and the *Column Properties* window, as shown in Figure 11-10. You use the *Table Designer* to specify the names and data types of the table's columns, and the *Column properties* window allows you to set various properties for each column.

Step 9: The first column that you add to the table is the `PersonID` column. The `PersonID` column is an identity column (the DBMS automatically generates unique integer values for it), and it will be the table's primary key.

In the *Table Designer*, under *Column Name*, type `PersonID`, and then press Tab. Under *Data Type*, select `int`. Remove the checkmark that appears under *Allow Nulls*. The *Table Designer* should appear as shown in Figure 11-11.

Figure 11-10 The *Table Designer* and the *Column Properties* window

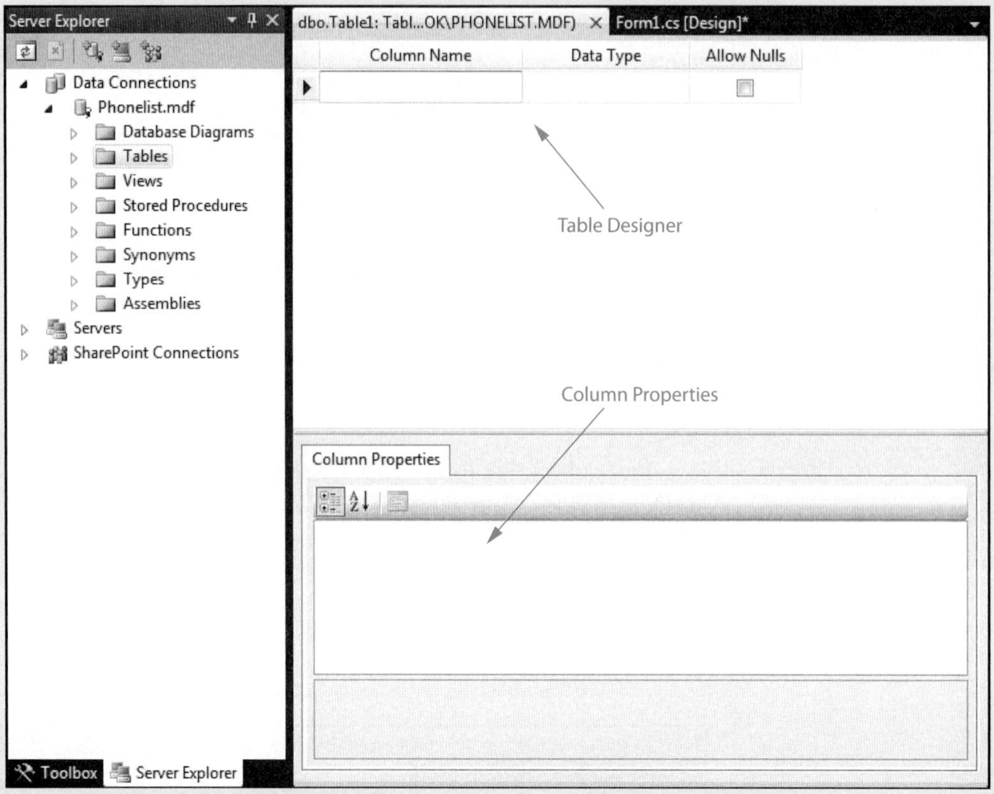

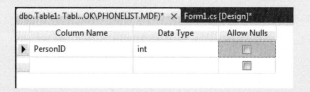

Figure 11-11 The `PersonID` column created in the *Table Designer*

Step 10: Now you must set the `PersonID` column's properties to designate it as an identity column. In the *Column Properties* window, scroll down until you see *Identity Specification*. Double-click *Identity Specification,* and you should see the (*Is Identity*), *Identity Increment*, and *Identity Seed* properties appear below it, as shown in Figure 11-12.

Figure 11-12 The column's *Identity Specification* properties displayed

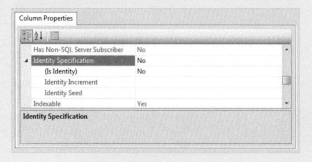

Step 11: Change the (*Is Identity*) property to *Yes*. This designates the column as an identity column. As a result, the column contains a unique, automatically generated value. Notice that the *Identity Increment* and *Identity Seed* properties are both now set to *1*, as shown in Figure 11-13. Leave these values as they are.

Figure 11-13 The *Identity Specification* properties set to the desired values

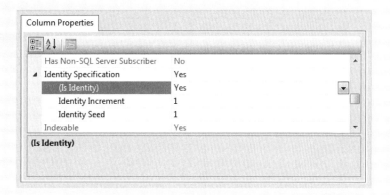

Step 12: Now you will designate the `PersonID` column as the primary key. Right-click the arrow button (▶) that appears next to the column name, as shown in the left image in Figure 11-14. A pop-up menu appears, as shown in the right image in Figure 11-14. Select *Set Primary Key*. (Alternatively, you can just click the key button (🔑) on the toolbar.) After doing this, you should see a small key icon appear next to the column name in the *Table Designer*, as shown in Figure 11-15.

Figure 11-14 Designating the `PersonID` column as the primary key

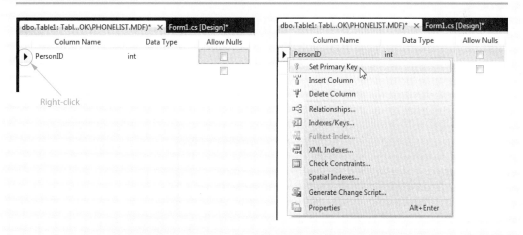

Figure 11-15 The `PersonID` column designated as the primary key

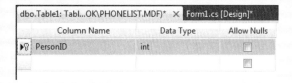

Step 13: In the *Table Designer*, add another column named `Name`. Select *nvarchar(50)* as the data type and remove the check under *Allow Nulls*.

Step 14: Add another column named `Phone`. Select *nvarchar(50)* as the data type and remove the check under *Allow Nulls*. The Table Designer should now appear as shown in Figure 11-16.

Figure 11-16 The `PersonID`, `Name`, and `Phone` columns created in the *Table Designer*

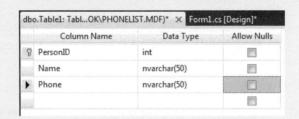

Step 15: You are finished designing the table, so now you can save it. Click *File* on the Visual Studio menu bar and then click *Save Table1*. The *Choose Name* dialog box, shown in Figure 11-17, appears. Enter `Person` as the name and click *OK*. The table has now been saved in the database.

Figure 11-17 The *Choose Name* dialog box

Step 16: The next step is to enter data into the table. In the *Server Explorer* (or *Database Explorer*), expand the *Tables* entry and then right-click the `Person` entry. You will see the pop-up menu shown in Figure 11-18. Click *Show Table Data* in the menu.

Figure 11-18 Clicking *Show Table Data*

Step 17: The table should now be opened and ready for input, as shown in Figure 11-19. Enter several names and phone numbers into the `Name` and the `Phone` columns. As you enter data, keep the following in mind:

- Do not enter values for the `PersonID` column. The system automatically generates a value for the `PersonID` column each time you add a new row.
- You must enter values for the `Name` and `Phone` columns. Recall that you removed the check from *Allow Nulls* for these columns when you designed the table. If you try to move away from a row without specifying values for these columns, you will see an error message.
- Exclamation points will appear next to the columns as you enter data. These simply mean that the data has not been saved to the database. When you move away from the row, the data is saved and the exclamation points disappear.

Figure 11-20 shows the table with sample data entered.

Figure 11-19 Ready to enter data into the `Person` Table

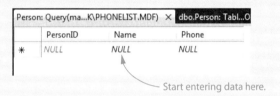

Figure 11-20 Sample data entered into the `Person` Table

Step 18: Once you have entered all the data, click *File* on the Visual Studio menu and then click *Save All*. The rows are saved to the Phonelist.mdf database.

Step 19: Close the table and the *Table Designer* so the Form1 form is displayed in the *Designer*.

Let's review what you have done up to this point:

- Created a SQL Server database named Phonelist.mdf
- Designed and created a table named `Person`
- Entered sample data into the table

In the next tutorial you connect the Phonelist.mdf database to the application's form and add a control to the form that lets the user interact with the database. If you intend to continue to the next tutorial at this time, leave the project open in Visual Studio.

The Database File's Location

When you use Visual Studio to create a database, as you did in Tutorial 11-1, the database file will be created in the project folder. For example, Figure 11-21 shows how the Phonelist.mdf database file was created in the *Phone Book* application's project folder.

 NOTE: When you create a SQL Server database, you will also see a file that ends with the .LDF extension. For example, in Figure 11-21 you see a file named Phonelist_log.LDF. This is a transaction log file. The SQL Server DBMS uses it to keep a log of all the operations that you perform on the database.

Figure 11-21 Location of the Phonelist.mdf database file

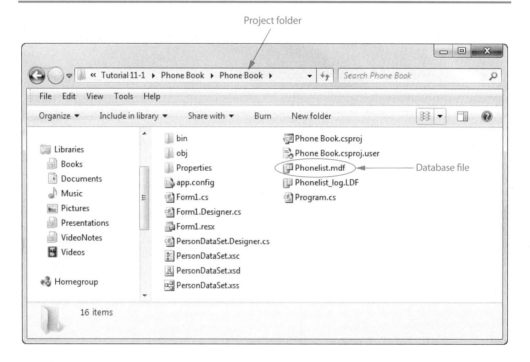

 Checkpoint

11.9 List each of the .NET components that allow an application connect to, and work with, a database in the order they are layered. Begin the list with the application as the topmost layer.

11.10 What is the relationship between the table adapter and data source components?

11.11 What component is used to connect interface controls to a dataset?

 11.4 **The DataGridView Control**

CONCEPT: A DataGridView control can display a database table in a scrollable grid.

A **data-bound control** is a user interface control that is connected to a data source. For example, a data-bound control can be connected to a column in a database table. Data-bound controls automatically display data from the data source and can be used to change the data that they are bound to. One of the simplest and most powerful data-bound controls is the DataGridView control. A **DataGridView control** can display an entire database table in a scrollable grid on an application's form.

In Tutorial 11-2 you continue working on the *Phone Book* application that you started in Tutorial 11-1. You connect the application's form to the Phonelist.mdf database and add a DataGridView control that can be used to view and update the Person table.

Tutorial 11-2:
Completing the *Phone Book* Application

In this tutorial you complete the *Phone Book* application. You add the Phonelist.mdf database to the project as a data source, create a dataset that is connected to the Person table, and add a DataGridView control that lets the user to interact with the database.

Step 1: Make sure the *Phone Book* project is open in Visual Studio (or Visual C# Express) from the previous tutorial.

Step 2: Click *Data* on the Visual Studio menu and then click *Add New Data Source....* You should see the *Data Source Configuration Wizard*, as shown in Figure 11-22.

Figure 11-22 The *Data Source Configuration Wizard—Choose a Data Source Type*

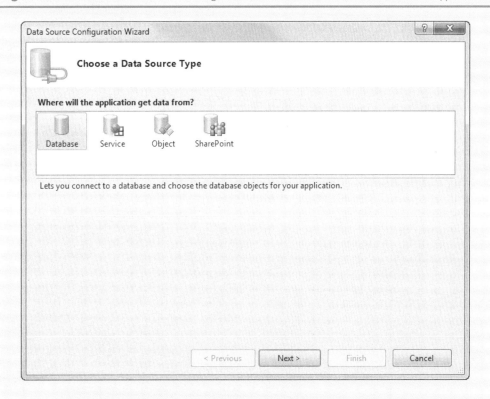

Step 3: The data source you are adding is a database, so make sure *Database* is selected and then click *Next >*. The window now appears, as shown in Figure 11-23.

Step 4: Make sure *Dataset* is selected, and click *Next >*. The window now appears, as shown in Figure 11-24.

Figure 11-23 The *Data Source Configuration Wizard—Choose a Database Model*

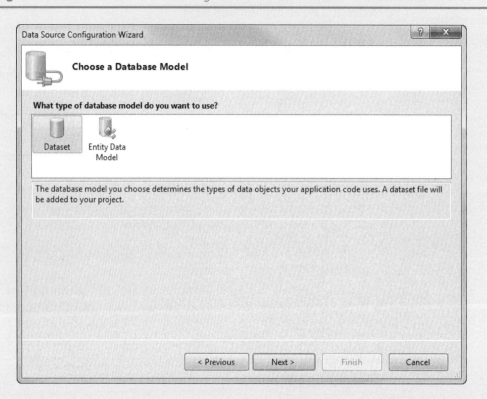

Figure 11-24 The *Data Source Configuration Wizard—Choose Your Data Connection*

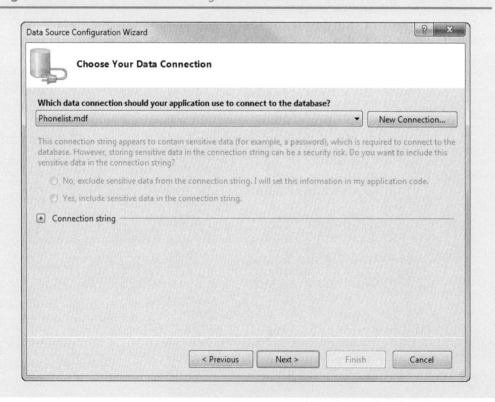

Step 5: In this window you are asked to choose a data connection, and the Phonelist .mdf database should be automatically selected, as shown in Figure 11-24. Simply click *Next >*. The window now appears, as shown in Figure 11-25.

Figure 11-25 The *Data Source Configuration Wizard—Save the Connection String*

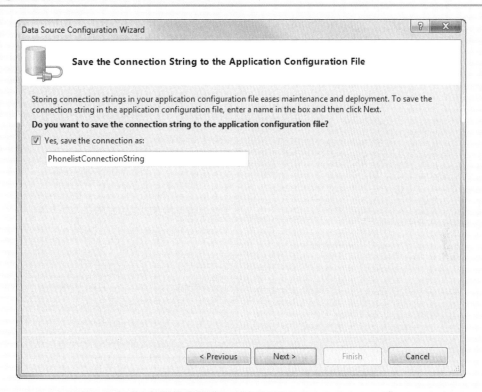

Step 6: In this window you are asked if you want to save a connection string. Leave the *Yes* box checked and click *Next >*.

Step 7: In the window that appears now, you are asked to choose the database objects that you want to include in the dataset. Expand the *Tables* entry, and place a check next to `Person`, as shown in Figure 11-26.

At the bottom of the window you can specify a name for the dataset. The default name `PhonelistDataSet` is already provided. Because you selected the `Person` table as the database object, change the dataset name to `PersonDataSet`. Click *Finish*.

Here is a summary of what you just did:

- You added the Phonelist.mdf database as a data source to the application.
- You created a dataset component that is connected to the `Person` table. The name of the dataset component is `PersonDataSet`.

Step 8: Visual Studio provides a *Data Sources* window that lets you see all the data sources in the current project. Click *Data* on the Visual Studio menu bar and then click *Show Data Sources*. The *Data Sources* window should be displayed, as shown in Figure 11-27. Notice that the window shows the name of the dataset, which is `PersonDataSet`, and the name of the table to which the dataset is connected, which is `Person`.

Figure 11-26 The *Data Source Configuration Wizard—Choose Your Database Objects*

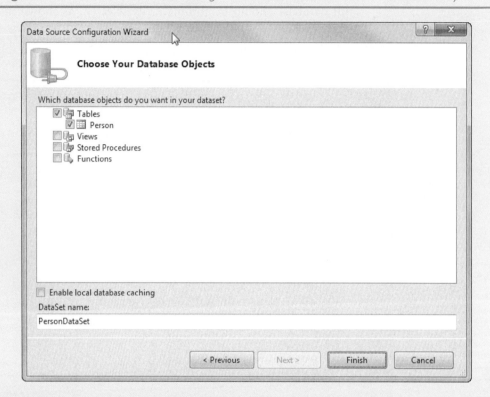

Figure 11-27 The *Data Sources* Window

Step 9: Next you select DataGridView as the default data-bound control for the `Person` table. In the *Data Sources* window, click the entry for the `Person` table, as shown in the image on the left in Figure 11-28. Then, click the down arrow (⊡), and select *DataGridView*, as shown in the image on the right.

Figure 11-28 Selecting DataGridView as the data-bound control for the `Person` table

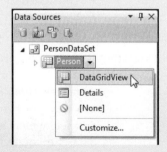

Select Person.

Click the down-arrow and select DataGridView.

Step 10: Now you add a DataGridView control to the form. As shown in Figure 11-29, click and drag the `Person` table from the *Data Sources* window onto the form. As shown in Figure 11-30, this creates a DataGridView control and a navigation bar on the form. (If necessary, adjust the size of the form and the size and position of the DataGridView control so they appear similar to Figure 11-30.)

Figure 11-29 Dragging the `Person` table onto the form

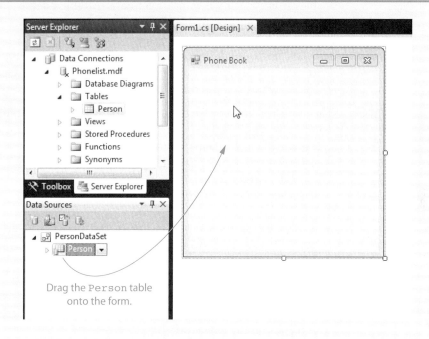

Figure 11-30 The DataGridView control placed on the form

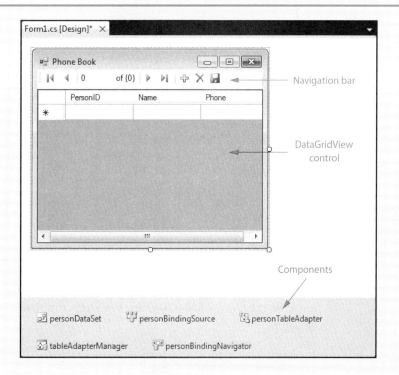

Notice that the component tray (the gray area at the bottom of the Designer) now contains several items. These are components that were automatically created when you placed the DataGridView control on the form. Here's a summary of the components:

- `personTableAdapter`—This is the table adapter. It gets data directly from the data source, which in this case is the Person.mdf database.
- `tableAdapterManager`—In many applications, the database has multiple tables from which we want to get data. A table adapter manager is a component that manages multiple tables.
- `personDataSet`—This is the dataset component. It gets a copy of the table from the table adapter and keeps it in memory. The application works with the dataset instead of working directly with the database.
- `personBindingSource`—This is the navigation bar.

Step 11: Save and run the application. The form will appear similar to Figure 11-31, with the rows of the `Person` table displayed in the DataGridView control. You can use the DataGridView control in the following ways:
- To change the value of a cell, click the cell with the mouse and then change its data as necessary.
- To select a row, click the button that appears next to it, along the left side of the control.
- To delete a row, select it; then either click the Delete button (✕) on the navigation bar or press [Delete] on the keyboard.
- To add a new row, scroll to the bottom of the grid, where you will see an empty row. Enter the new data in the empty row.
- The changes that you make affect only the in-memory copy of the table that is held in the dataset. To save the changes to the database, click the Save button (🖫) on the navigation bar.
- To sort the rows on a column value, click the column heading.

Figure 11-31 The *Phone Book* application running

Step 12: Use the DataGridView control to make several changes to the dataset. For example, change a value in an existing row, add a new row, and delete an existing row. Be sure to click the Save button (🖫) on the navigation bar to save your changes.

Step 13: Close the application and then rerun it to verify that your changes were saved. When you are finished, close the application.

Auto-Generated Code

When you place a data-bound control, such as the DataGridView, on a form, Visual Studio does a lot of work behind the scenes to make the control functions. In fact, you completed the application in Tutorial 11-2 without writing a single line of code! If you open the form in the code editor, however, you will see that Visual Studio generated some code, as shown in Program 11-1.

Program 11-1 Form1 code in the *Phone Book* application

```
 1 using System;
 2 using System.Collections.Generic;
 3 using System.ComponentModel;
 4 using System.Data;
 5 using System.Drawing;
 6 using System.Linq;
 7 using System.Text;
 8 using System.Windows.Forms;
 9
10 namespace Phone_Book
11 {
12     public partial class Form1 : Form
13     {
14         public Form1()
15         {
16             InitializeComponent();
17         }
18
19         private void personBindingNavigatorSaveItem_Click(object sender, EventArgs e)
20         {
21             this.Validate();
22             this.personBindingSource.EndEdit();
23             this.tableAdapterManager.UpdateAll(this.personDataSet);
24
25         }
26
27         private void Form1_Load(object sender, EventArgs e)
28         {
29             // TODO: This line of code loads data into the 'personDataSet.Person' table...
30             this.personTableAdapter.Fill(this.personDataSet.Person);
31
32         }
33     }
34 }
```

Visual Studio adds an event handler in lines 19–25 that executes when the user clicks the *Save* button on the navigation bar. In a nutshell, the statements in this method apply any changes that have been made to the DataGridView control to the dataset and then save the dataset to the database.

Visual Studio also adds a Load event handler for the form, in lines 27–32. In line 30, the event handler calls the table adapter's `Fill` method, passing a reference to the `Person` table (contained in the dataset) as an argument. This statement causes the table adapter to load data from the database into the dataset.

Checkpoint

11.12 What do you call a user interface control that is connected to a data source?

11.13 List the components that are automatically created when you place a DataGridView control on a form.

11.14 What is the purpose of the table adapter's `Fill` method?

11.15 What kind of information is displayed in the *Data Sources* window? How is it displayed?

11.5 Connecting to an Existing Database and Using Details View Controls

CONCEPT: You can easily connect an application to an existing database. The Details view controls are an alternative to the DataGridView control for interacting with a database.

In Tutorial 11-1 you used Visual Studio to create a database from scratch and populate its table with data. More often, programmers must create applications that connect to existing databases. In Tutorial 11-3 you create an application and connect it to a database that is provided in the Student Sample Program files. The database is named ProductDB.mdf, and you will find it in the Chap11 folder. The database has one table, named `Product`. Figure 11-32 shows the data that is stored in the `Product` table.

Figure 11-32 The `Product` table in the ProductDB.mdf database

Product_Number	Description	Units_On_Hand	Price
10-01	Oxford Cloth Shirt	100	39.9500
10-02	Poplin Shirt	150	38.5000
10-03	Plaid Flannel Shirt	80	34.7500
10-04	Canvas Shirt	200	32.9500
10-05	Cotton Shirt	250	28.9500
20-01	Chino Classic Fit Pants	100	28.9500
20-02	Chino Relaxed Fit Pants	100	28.9500
20-03	Denim Jeans	275	32.9500
20-04	Wool Trousers	75	78.9500
30-01	Warm-Up Jacket	125	59.9500
30-02	Fleece Pullover	150	28.9500
30-03	Parka	75	199.9500

Here are some things to know about the columns in the `Product` table:

- The `Product_Number` column is the primary key. Its data type is `nchar(5)`, and nulls are not allowed.
- The `Description` column's data type is `nvarchar(50)`, and nulls are not allowed.
- The `Units_On_Hand` column's data type is `int`, and nulls are not allowed.
- The `Price` column's data type is `money`, and nulls are not allowed.

In the tutorial you also learn how to create a Details view. A **Details view** is a set of individual controls that are bound to the columns in a single row. Rather than showing multiple rows at once, a Details view lets the user see one row at a time. Figure 11-33 shows an example of a form with a set of Details view controls. In the figure, the TextBox controls are bound to the columns of the `Product` table. Notice that the form also has a navigation bar. The navigation bar works just like the one that appears with a DataGridView control. It can be used to move forward and backward in the table, add new rows, delete the currently displayed row, and save the changes that have been made.

Notice in Figure 11-33 that each TextBox control has a Label controls next to it, identifying the column. When you create a Details view, these Label controls are created automatically. As you can see in the figure, the underscores in the column name are replaced by spaces in the Label controls.

Figure 11-33 Details view

Tutorial 11-3:
Creating the *Products* Application and Using a Details View

Step 1:   Start Visual Studio (or Visual C# Express). Create a new *Windows Forms Application* project named *Products*.

Step 2:   Change the Form1 form's Text property to *Products*.

Step 3:   Click *Data* on the Visual Studio menu bar and then click *Add New Data Source*.... You should see the *Data Source Configuration Wizard*, as shown in Figure 11-34. Make sure *Database* is selected and then click *Next >*.

Step 4:   The window now appears as shown in Figure 11-35. Make sure *Dataset* is selected, and click *Next >*.

Step 5:   The window now appears as shown in Figure 11-36. In this window you are asked to choose a data connection. Because you have not previously created any data connections in this project, none are available for you to choose from. So, you will have to create a new data connection. Click the *New Connection* button.

Figure 11-34 The *Data Source Configuration Wizard—Choose a Data Source Type*

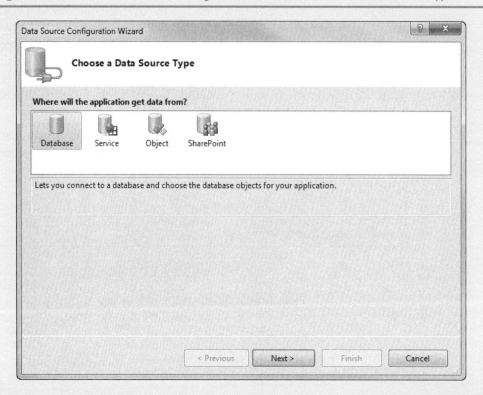

Figure 11-35 The *Data Source Configuration Wizard—Choose a Database Model*

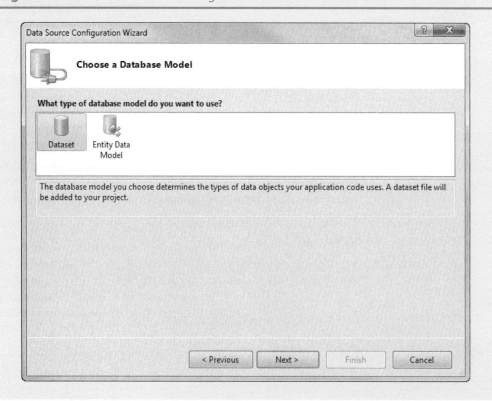

Figure 11-36 The *Data Source Configuration Wizard—Choose Your Data Connection*

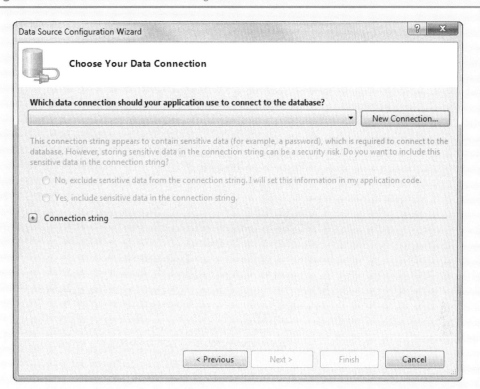

Step 6: You see the *Add Connection* dialog box next, as shown in Figure 11-37. (**Important:** The screens shown in Figures 11-37 and 11-38 were taken from Visual Studio. If you are using Visual C# Express, the dialog box will look slightly different. The steps given here will work regardless of the version you are using.)

Figure 11-37 The *Add Connection* Dialog Box (Visual Studio)

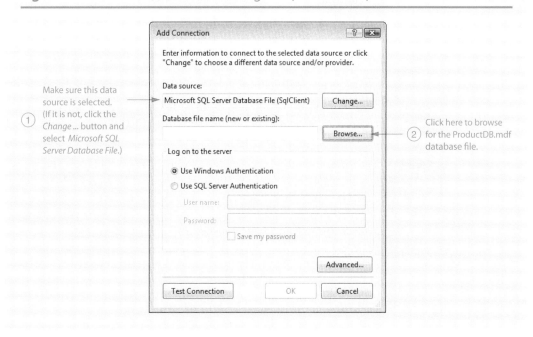

Figure 11-38 The data source and database file selected (Visual Studio)

Perform the following:

- Look *carefully* at the selected data source. Make sure *Microsoft SQL Server Database File (SqlClient)* is selected. If not, click the *Change...* button and select *Microsoft SQL Server Database File*. (You will have to do this if you are using Visual C# Express.)
- As indicated in the figure, click the *Browse...* button. Navigate to the *Chap11* folder in the Student Sample Programs and select the ProductDB .mdf file.

  Figure 11-38 shows how the dialog box should appear now. At this point, you can optionally click the *Test Connection* button to test the connection to the database. You should see the message *Test Connection Succeeded*.

Step 7: Click the *OK* button on the *Add Connection* dialog box to close the dialog box.

Step 8: You should be back at the *Data Source Configuration* window, as shown in Figure 11-39. As shown in the figure, ProductDB.mdf should be selected as the data connection. Click the *Next >* button to continue.

Step 9: You should see the dialog box shown in Figure 11-40. The message is telling you that the database file is located outside the project folder, and you are being asked if you want to copy it into the project. Unless your instructor has told you to do otherwise, click *Yes*. That will make it easier for you to copy the complete project to submit to your instructor.

Figure 11-39 *Data Source Configuration* window with ProductDB.mdf selected

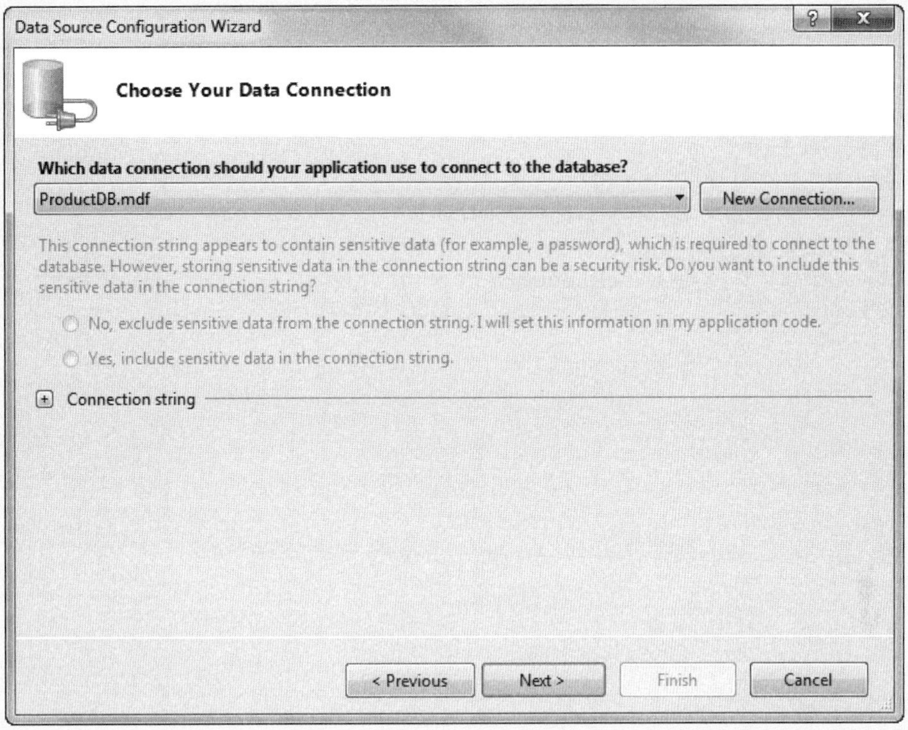

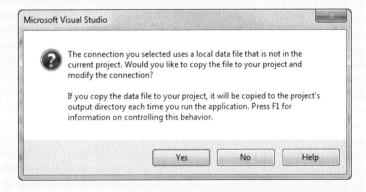

Figure 11-40 Message about copying the database to the project

Step 10: The *Data Source Configuration* window should now appear as shown in Figure 11-41. Click the *Next >* button to continue.

Step 11: The *Data Source Configuration* window should now appear, as shown in Figure 11-42. You are asked to choose the database objects that you want to include in the dataset. Expand the *Tables* entry and place a check next to `Product`, as shown in Figure 11-42.

At the bottom of the window, you can specify a name for the dataset. The default name `ProductDBDataSet` is already provided. Because you selected the `Product` table as the database object, change the dataset name to `ProductDataSet`. Click *Finish*.

Figure 11-41 *Data Source Configuration* window—*Save the Connection String*

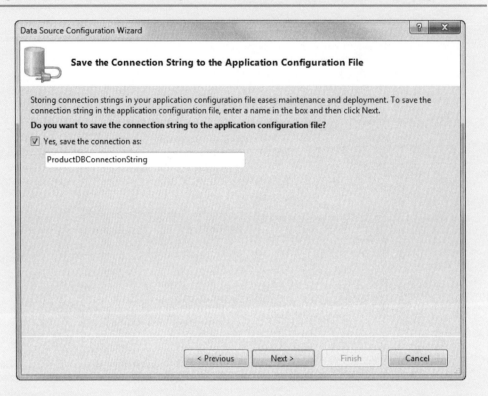

Figure 11-42 The *Data Source Configuration Wizard*—*Choose Your Database Objects*

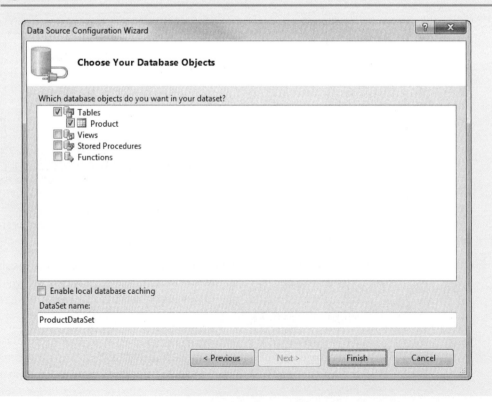

Here is a summary of what you just did:

- You added the ProductDB.mdf database as a data source to the application.
- You created a dataset component that is connected to the Product table. The name of the dataset component is ProductDataSet.

Step 12: Next you display the *Data Sources* window. Click *Data* on the Visual Studio menu bar and then click *Show Data Sources*. The *Data Sources* window should be displayed, as shown in Figure 11-43. Notice that the window shows the name of the dataset, which is ProductDataSet, and the name of the table that the dataset is connected to, which is Product.

Figure 11-43 The *Data Sources* Window

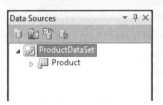

Step 13: Now you select Details as the default data-bound control for the Product table. In the *Data Sources* window, click the entry for the Product table, as shown in the image on the left in Figure 11-44. Then, click the down arrow ( ), and select *Details*, as shown in the image on the right.

Figure 11-44 Selecting Details as the data-bound control for the Product table

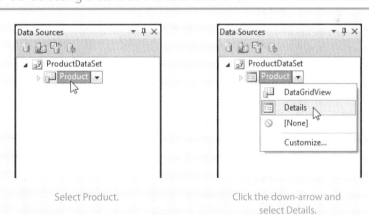

Select Product.   Click the down-arrow and
                                   select Details.

Step 14: Next you add a Details view onto the form. As shown in Figure 11-45, click and drag the Product table from the *Data Sources* window onto the form. As shown in Figure 11-46, this creates a set of Details view controls, complete with a navigation bar, on the form. (Adjust the size of the form and the size and position of the controls so they appear similar to Figure 11-46.)

Figure 11-45 Dragging the `Product` table onto the form

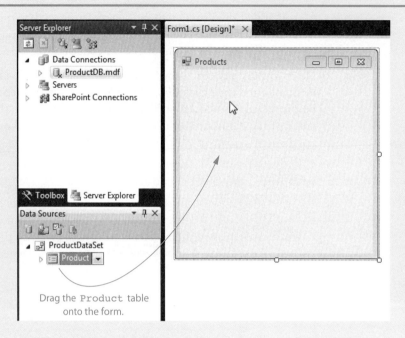

Figure 11-46 Placing the Details view controls on the form

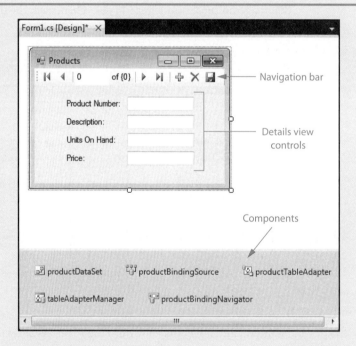

Step 15: Save and run the application. The form will appear similar to Figure 11-47, with data from the first row of the `Product` table displayed. You can use the form in the following ways:

- On the navigation bar, the *Move next* button (▶) moves your view to the next row, and the *Move last* button (▶|) moves your view to the last row.
- The *Move previous* button (◀) moves your view to the previous row, and the *Move first* button (|◀) moves your view to the first row.

Figure 11-47 The *Phone Book* application running

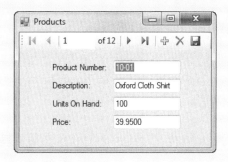

- The values of a row are displayed in text boxes. To change a value, simply click the text box with the mouse and then change its data as necessary.
- To add a new row, click the *Add new* button (✛). An empty row will be created and displayed. Enter data for the new row into the text boxes.
- To delete the row that is currently displayed, click the Delete button (✕) on the navigation bar.
- The changes that you make affect only the in-memory copy of the table that is held in the dataset. To save the changes to the database, click the *Save* button (🖫) on the navigation bar.

Step 16: Use the Details view controls to make several changes to the dataset. For example, change a value in an existing row, add a new row, and delete an existing row. Be sure to click the *Save* button (🖫) on the navigation bar to save your changes.

Step 17: Close the application and then rerun it to verify that your changes were saved. When you are finished, close the application.

Copies of the Database at Run Time

Recall that in Step 9 of Tutorial 11-3, Visual Studio displayed a message indicating that you had selected a database file located outside the project folder, and you were asked if you wanted to copy the file into the project. (See Figure 11-40.) You answered *Yes*, and, as a result, the database file was copied into the project folder.

Then, when you ran the application for the first time, Visual Studio copied the database file from the project folder to the project's **output folder**, which is the *bin\Debug* folder. Each subsequent time the application runs, it connects to the copy of the database in the output folder instead of the project folder.

Suppose you make a change to the application, such as repositioning a control, and you run it again. Because you modified the application, Visual Studio rebuilds the project (recompiles it). Visual Studio also copies the database file, once again, from the project folder to the output folder. As a side effect, any changes that you previously made to the database will be lost!

You can get around this behavior by answering *No* to the dialog box shown in Figure 11-40. That causes the application to always connect to the database in its external location. However, if you are being graded on the project, your instructor will have trouble running it on his or her computer because the database file will be missing. So, it is normally a good idea to answer *Yes* to the dialog box in Figure 11-40, as long as you are aware that rebuilding the project causes the database in the output folder to be overwritten.

670 Chapter 11 Databases

 Checkpoint

11.16 How can you create a form that shows the columns of only a single row of a database in an application?

11.17 What happens when you drag a table from the *Data Sources* window onto a form?

11.18 Where is a project's output folder located?

11.6 More About Data-Bound Controls

CONCEPT: The DataGridView control and the Details view may be customized in various ways. Other controls, such a list boxes, can be data-bound to allow interaction with a database.

Customizing the DataGridView Control

In the *Designer*, if you select a DataGridView control, you will see a small arrow in the upper-right corner of the control's bounding box. Figure 11-48 shows an example. This is called a **smart tag**. When you click on the smart tag, a tasks panel will pop up, giving you a number of options that you can perform with the DataGridView control. Figure 11-49 shows an example of the tasks panel.

Figure 11-48 A DataGridView control's smart tag

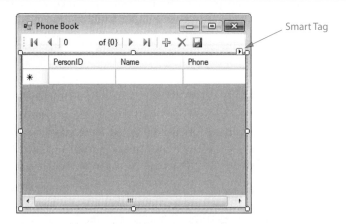

Notice in the figure that the tasks panel has the following check boxes:

- *Enable Adding*—When this item is checked, the user may add rows in the Data-GridView control. This item is checked by default.
- *Enable Editing*—When this item is checked, the user may change the contents of rows in the DataGridView control. This item is checked by default.
- *Enable Deleting*—When this item is checked, the user may delete rows from the DataGridView control. This item is checked by default.
- *Enable Column Reordering*—When this item is checked, the user may click and drag columns to rearrange them in the DataGridView control. This item is not checked by default.

Figure 11-49 A DataGridView control's tasks panel

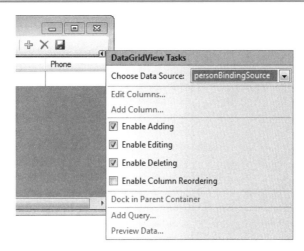

If you do not want the user to be able to add, edit, or delete rows in the DataGridView control, simply remove the appropriate checkmarks.

Keep in mind that the navigation bar has buttons that allow the user to add, delete, and save the data in the DataGridView control. These buttons will still work, even after you have disabled adding, editing, and deleting in the DataGridView control's task panel. To disable a button on the navigation bar, right-click it in the *Designer*. This will display the pop-up menu shown in Figure 11-50. Notice in the figure that *Enabled* is checked. Click *Enabled* to remove the checkmark, thus disabling the button. When a button is disabled, it will appear grayed-out on the navigation bar. Figure 11-51 shows an example with the *Add*, *Delete*, and *Save* buttons disabled.

Figure 11-50 Disabling the *Delete* button

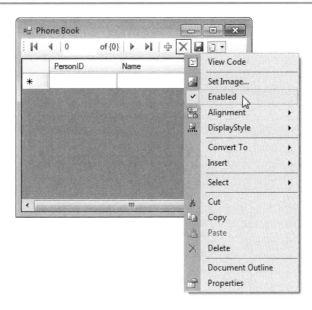

Figure 11-51 The *Add*, *Delete*, and *Save* buttons disabled (grayed-out)

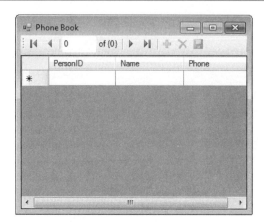

Customizing the Details View

In Tutorial 11-3 you saw how several controls are created automatically when you create Details view for a table. For example, TextBoxes were created and bound to the individual columns. Label controls that identify the columns were also created, as was a navigation bar.

When you create a Details view, the type of control that a column is automatically bound to is determined by the column's data type, as follows:

- Columns containing character data are bound to TextBox controls by default.
- Numeric columns are bound to TextBox controls by default.
- Bit columns are bound to CheckBox controls.
- Datetime columns are bound to DateTimePicker controls, which allow the user to select a date from a small pop-up calendar.

It is possible to change the type of control that a column is bound to in a Details view. For example, recall that the Product table in Tutorial 11-3 has a column named Product_Number. The Product_Number column contains character data, so a TextBox control was created for it when you placed the Details view on the form. However, the Product_Number column is the primary key for the table, so you might not want the user to be able to change it. A Label control might be a better option. That way, the user can see the product number but cannot change it.

Before you place a Details view on a form, you can select the type of control to which each column will be bound. In the *Data Sources* window, expand the table entry as shown in the image on the left in Figure 11-52. Then, select a column and click the down arrow

Figure 11-52 Selecting the type of data-bound control for a column

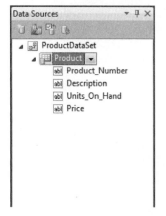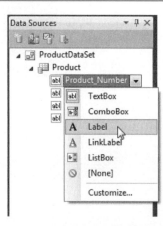

() that appears next to it, as shown in the image on the right in the figure. A menu will pop up that shows the types of controls that you can select. In the image on the right in Figure 11-52, we are selecting the Label control for the `Product_Number` column. Then, when we create the Details view, it appears as shown in Figure 11-53.

Figure 11-53 Details view with the product number displayed in a Label control

When you drag an entire table from the *Data Sources* window and drop it onto a form, the Details view that is created contains data-bound controls for all the columns. Sometimes you might not want all the columns displayed, however. Alternatively, you can drag the individual columns, one at a time, from the *Data Sources* window onto the form. Figure 11-54 shows an example of a Details view that displays only the product number and description. We created this Details view by dragging the `Product_Number` column and then the `Description` column from the *Data Sources* window onto the form.

Figure 11-54 Product number and description displayed

Binding Columns to ListBox Controls

A list box can be a convenient way to look up data in a table. You can bind a column to a ListBox control, which causes all the values in that column to be displayed in the list box. When the user selects an item from the list box, the rest of the columns from the selected row can be displayed.

To bind a ListBox control to a column, you must set two of the control's properties: DataSource and DisplayMember. The **DataSource property** identifies the table from which the ListBox will get its data. The **DisplayMember property** identifies the column. In Tutorial 11-4 you use this technique to create a data lookup form for the ProductDB.mdf database.

Tutorial 11-4:
Creating the *Product Lookup* Application

Step 1:   Start Visual Studio (or Visual C# Express). Create a new *Windows Forms Application* project named *Product Lookup*.

Step 2:   Change the Form1 form's Text property to *Product Lookup*.

Step 3:   Perform the following steps to connect the application to the ProductDB.mdf database, and select the Product table as the dataset:

- From the *Data* menu, select *Add New Data Source....*
- Select *Database* and click *Next >*.
- Select *Dataset* and click *Next >*.
- Click *New Connection....*
- In the *Add Connection* window, make sure *Microsoft SQL Server Database File (SqlClient)* is the selected data source.
- In the *Add Connection* window, click *Browse*, and go to the *Chap11* folder in the Student Sample Programs. Select the ProductDB.mdf file. Click *OK*.
- Click *Next >*, and when asked if you want to copy the file to the project, click *Yes*.
- Click *Next >*.
- Select the Product table as the database object, and change the name of the dataset to ProductDataSet. Click *Finish*.

> **NOTE:** This is the same procedure that you performed in Steps 3–11 in Tutorial 11-3. If you want more detailed guidance, go back to that tutorial to see the actual screens.

Step 4:   Create a ListBox control named productNumberListBox. Just above the List-Box, place a Label control that displays "Select a Product Number". The form should look similar to Figure 11-55.

Step 5:   Select the ListBox control. In the Properties window, select the DataSource property and then click the down arrow (⏷) that appears next to it. In the list that pops up, expand *Other Data Sources*, then expand *Project Data Sources*, then expand *ProductDataSet*, and then select *Product*. This is shown in Figure 11-56.

Figure 11-55 ListBox and Label created

Figure 11-56 Product table selected in the DataSource property

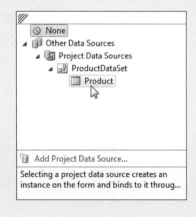

Step 6:   Select the ListBox control's DataMember property and then click the down arrow (▾) that appears next to it. In the list that pops up, select `Product_Number`.

Step 7:   In the *Data Sources* window, set the `Product` table's view to Details, as shown in Figure 11-57.

Step 8:   In the *Data Sources* window, expand the `Product` table so the column names are displayed, as shown in Figure 11-58.

Figure 11-57 Select Details   **Figure 11-58** Column names displayed

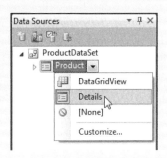
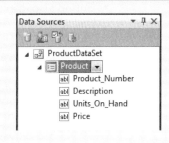

Step 9:   One at a time, drag the `Description`, `Units_On_Hand`, and `Price` columns from the *Data Sources* window onto the form. Place them as shown in Figure 11-59. Resize the form so it appears similar to that shown in the figure.

Figure 11-59 Column names displayed

Step 10:   Save the project and run the application. The application's form should appear similar to Figure 11-60. Notice that the list box contains a list of all the product numbers in the `Product` table. When you select a product number in the list box, that product's description, units on hand, and price are displayed in the TextBox controls. When you are finished, exit the application.

Figure 11-60 The Product Lookup application running

Having Data-Bound Controls on Multiple Forms

You have seen that when you place a data-bound control on a form, Visual Studio automatically creates a set of components that allow the form to connect to the database. These components include a dataset. When you place data-bound controls on multiple forms, keep in mind that each form has its own dataset. When you make changes to the dataset in one form, those changes do not automatically appear in other forms that have their own dataset. Consider the following scenario:

- Form1 displays a view of a database, perhaps in a DataGridView control.
- Some code in Form1 displays Form2.
- Form2 also displays a view of the same database, allowing the user to make changes and save those changes to the database. The user closes Form2.
- Form1 is still displaying its original copy of the data. Its dataset does not automatically update, so Form1 does not show the changes that were made by Form2.

To make sure that a dataset contains a current copy of the data, you need to write code that causes the table adapter to read the database table and fill the dataset. You do this by calling the table adapter's Fill method. In Tutorial 11-5 you learn how to do this by creating an application that correctly handles the scenario previously discussed.

Tutorial 11-5:
Creating the *Multiform Products* Application

Step 1: Start Visual Studio (or Visual C# Express). Create a new *Windows Forms Application* project named *Multiform Products*.

Step 2: Change the Form1 form's Text property to *Products*.

Step 3: In the Solution Explorer, change the name of Form1.cs to *MainForm.cs*. This changes the name of the Form1 form to MainForm.

Step 4: Perform the following steps to connect the application to the ProductDB.mdf database and select the Product table for the dataset:

- From the *Data* menu, select *Add New Data Source....*
- Select *Database* and click *Next >.*
- Select *Dataset* and click *Next >.*
- Click *New Connection....*
- In the *Add Connection* window, make sure *Microsoft SQL Server Database File (SqlClient)* is the selected data source.
- In the *Add Connection* window, click *Browse* and go to the *Chap11* folder in the Student Sample Programs. Select the ProductDB.mdf file. Click *OK.*
- Click *Next >*, and when asked if you want to copy the file to the project, click *Yes.*
- Click *Next >.*
- Select the Product table as the database object, and change the name of the dataset to ProductDataSet. Click *Finish.*

NOTE: This is the same procedure that you performed in Steps 3–11 in Tutorial 11-3. If you want more detailed guidance, go back to that tutorial to see the actual screens.

Step 5: Open the Data Sources window and, as shown in Figure 11-61, drag a Data-GridView control onto the form, bound to the `Product` table. After creating the DataGridView control, adjust size of the form and the control as shown in Figure 11-62.

Figure 11-61 Create a DataGridView control on the form

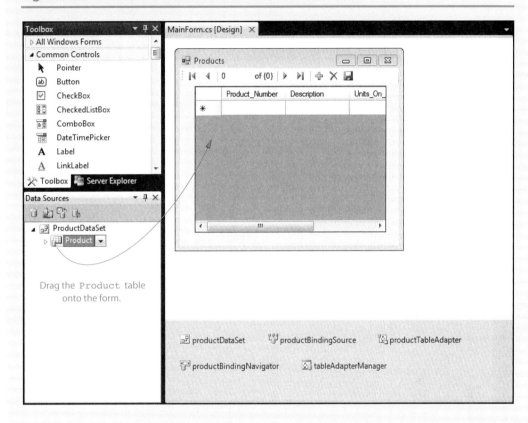

Figure 11-62 The form and DataGridView control resized

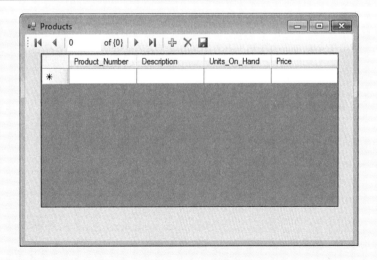

Step 6: Create the Button controls shown in Figure 11-63. (You write Click event handlers for these buttons later.)

Figure 11-63 Button controls placed on the MainForm

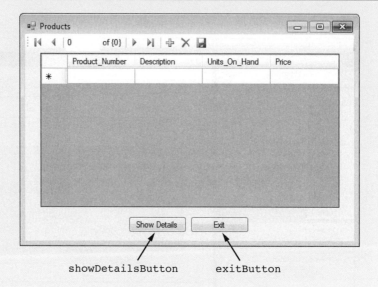

Step 7: Add another form named DetailsForm to the project. As a reminder, these are the steps:

- Click *Project* on the Visual Studio menu bar and then select *Add Windows Form....*
- In the *Add New Item* window, enter DetailsForm.cs as the name and click *Add*.

Step 8: Change the form's Text property to *Details*.

Step 9: In the *Data Sources* window, change the Product table's default view to *Details*, as shown in Figure 11-64. Then, as shown in Figure 11-65, drag a Details view onto the form.

Figure 11-64 Changing the Product table's default view to *Details*

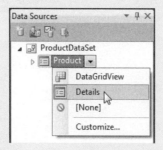

Step 10: Resize the DetailsForm form and create the button control shown in Figure 11-66.

Step 11: Double-click the closeButton control, and complete its Click event handler, as shown in lines 36–37 of Program 11-2.

Figure 11-65 Creating a Details view on the form

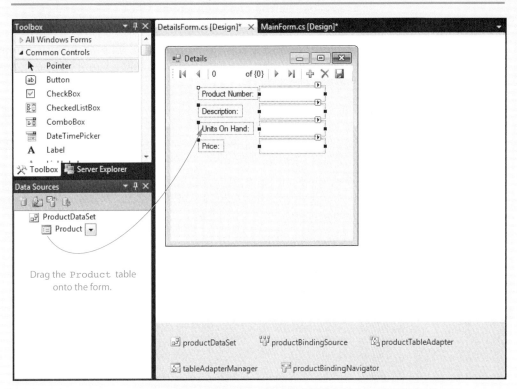

Figure 11-66 Form resized and *Close* button placed

closeButton

Step 12: Switch your view back to the MainForm form in the *Designer*. Double-click the showDetailsButton control, and complete its Click event handler, as shown in lines 36–43 of Program 11-3. Let's take a closer look at the code:

Line 37: This statement creates an instance of the DetailsForm class, referenced by the details variable.

Line 40: This statement displays the DetailsForm form. The user will be able to make changes to the product data using the DetailsForm and save those changes to the database.

Line 43: This statement calls the table adapter's Fill method, passing the dataset as an argument. As a result, the dataset will be filled with the current contents of the Product table, and the DataGridView control's contents will be updated.

Step 13: Switch your view back to the MainForm form in the *Designer*. Double-click the exitButton control, and complete its Click event handler, as shown lines 48 and 49 of Program 11-3.

Step 14: Save the project and run the application. The MainForm should show the Product table in the DataGridView control. Click the *Show Details* button to display the DetailsForm.

In the DetailsForm, make some changes to the data. For example, change the value of an existing piece of data, insert a new row, or delete an existing row. After making the changes, be sure to click the *Save* button (▣) on the navigation bar. Then, click the *Close* button to close the DetailsForm.

Back at the MainForm, browse the data in the DataGridView control to confirm that it shows the changes you just made. When you are finished, exit the application.

Program 11-2 Completed code for the DetailsForm

```
 1 using System;
 2 using System.Collections.Generic;
 3 using System.ComponentModel;
 4 using System.Data;
 5 using System.Drawing;
 6 using System.Linq;
 7 using System.Text;
 8 using System.Windows.Forms;
 9
10 namespace Multiform_Products
11 {
12     public partial class DetailsForm : Form
13     {
14         public DetailsForm()
15         {
16             InitializeComponent();
17         }
18
19         private void productBindingNavigatorSaveItem_Click(object sender, EventArgs e)
20         {
21             this.Validate();
22             this.productBindingSource.EndEdit();
23             this.tableAdapterManager.UpdateAll(this.productDataSet);
24
25         }
26
27         private void DetailsForm_Load(object sender, EventArgs e)
28         {
29             // TODO: This line of code loads data into the ...
30             this.productTableAdapter.Fill(this.productDataSet.Product);
31
32         }
33
34         private void closeButton_Click(object sender, EventArgs e)
35         {
36             // Close the form.
37             this.Close();
38         }
39     }
40 }
```

Program 11-3 Completed code for the MainForm form

```csharp
 1 using System;
 2 using System.Collections.Generic;
 3 using System.ComponentModel;
 4 using System.Data;
 5 using System.Drawing;
 6 using System.Linq;
 7 using System.Text;
 8 using System.Windows.Forms;
 9
10 namespace Multiform_Products
11 {
12     public partial class MainForm : Form
13     {
14         public MainForm()
15         {
16             InitializeComponent();
17         }
18
19         private void productBindingNavigatorSaveItem_Click(object sender, EventArgs e)
20         {
21             this.Validate();
22             this.productBindingSource.EndEdit();
23             this.tableAdapterManager.UpdateAll(this.productDataSet);
24
25         }
26
27         private void MainForm_Load(object sender, EventArgs e)
28         {
29             // TODO: This line of code loads data into ...
30             this.productTableAdapter.Fill(this.productDataSet.Product);
31
32         }
33
34         private void showDetailsButton_Click(object sender, EventArgs e)
35         {
36             // Create an instance of the DetailsForm.
37             DetailsForm details = new DetailsForm();
38
39             // Display the form.
40             details.ShowDialog();
41
42             // Update the dataset.
43             this.productTableAdapter.Fill(this.productDataSet.Product);
44         }
45
46         private void exitButton_Click(object sender, EventArgs e)
47         {
48             // Close the form.
49             this.Close();
50         }
51     }
52 }
```

Checkpoint

11.19 What happens when a control's smart tag is clicked in the *Designer*?

11.20 When you create a Details view, what determines the type of control to which a column is bound?

11.21 Which two properties must be set to bind a ListBox control to a column?

11.22 What is the name of the table adapter method that populates the dataset with a current copy of the data?

11.7 Selecting Data with the SQL Select Statement

CONCEPT: SQL is a standard language that most DBMS's support. The Select statement is used in SQL to retrieve data from a database.

SQL, which stands for **structured query language,** is a standard language for working with database management systems. It was originally developed by IBM in the 1970s. Since then, SQL has been adopted by almost all database software vendors as the language of choice for interacting with their DBMS.

SQL consists of several key words. You use the key words to construct statements, which are also known as **queries.** These statements, or queries, are submitted to the DBMS and are instructions directing the DBMS to carry out operations on its data. In this section you learn how to construct simple SQL statements and then pass them to the SQL Server DBMS.

 NOTE: Although SQL is a language, you do not use it to write applications. It is intended only as a standard means of interacting with a DBMS. You still need a general programming language, such as C#, to write an application for the ordinary user.

In SQL you use the **Select statement** to retrieve the rows in a table. As its name implies, the Select statement allows you to select specific rows. We start with a very simple form of the statement, as shown here:

```
Select Columns From Table
```

In the general form, `Columns` is one or more column names, and `Table` is a table name. Here is an example Select statement that we might execute on the ProductDB.mdf database:

```
Select Description From Product
```

This statement retrieves the Description column for every row in the Product table. You can specify more than one column in a Select statement by separating the column names with commas. Here is an example:

```
Select Description, Price From Product
```

This statement retrieves the Description column and the Price column for every row in the Product table. If you wish to retrieve every column in a table, you can use the * character instead of listing column names. Here is an example:

```
Select * From Product
```

This statement retrieves every column for every row in the `Product` table. SQL statements are free form, which means that tabs, newlines, and spaces between the key words are ignored. For example, the statement

```
Select * From Product
```

works the same as

```
Select
   *
From
   Product
```

In addition, SQL key words and table names are case insensitive. The previous statement could be written as

```
SELECT * FROM PRODUCT
```

Specifying a Search Criteria with the `Where` Clause

Sometimes you want to retrieve every row in a table. In many situations, however, you want to narrow the list down to only a few selected rows in the table. That is where the `Where` clause comes in. The `Where` clause can be used with the `Select` statement to specify a search criteria. When you use the `Where` clause, only the rows that meet the search criteria are returned. The general format of a `Select` statement with a `Where` clause is

```
Select Columns From Table Where Criteria
```

In the general format, `Criteria` is a conditional expression. Here is an example of a `Select` statement that uses the `Where` clause:

```
Select * From Product Where Price > 20.00
```

The first part of the statement, `Select * From Product`, specifies that we want to see every column. The `Where` clause specifies that we want only the rows in which the contents of the `Price` column are greater than 20.00. As a result, the `Select` statement retrieves only the rows in which `Price` is greater than 20.00.

SQL supports the relational operators listed in Table 11-2 for writing conditional expressions in a `Where` clause.

Table 11-2 SQL relational operators

Operator	Meaning
>	Greater than
<	Less than
>=	Greater than or equal to
<=	Less than or equal to
=	Equal to
<>	Not equal to

Notice that the equal to and not equal to operators in SQL are different from those in C#. The equal to operator is one equal sign, not two equal signs. The not equal to operator is <>.

Let's look at a few more examples of the `Select` statement. The following statement could be used to retrieve the product numbers and prices of all the items that are priced at $28.95:

```
Select Product_Number, Price From Product Where Price = 28.95
```

The following `Select` statement retrieves all the columns from only the rows where the description is "Denim Jeans".

```
Select * From Product Where Description = 'Denim Jeans'
```

If you look carefully at the previous statement, you will notice another difference between SQL syntax and C# syntax. In SQL, string literals are enclosed in single quotes, not double quotes.

TIP: If you need to include a single quote as part of a string, simply write two single quotes in its place. For example, suppose you wanted to search the `Product` table for Katy's Wool Cap. You could use the following statement:

```
Select * From Product Where Description = 'Katy''s Wool Cap'
```

String comparisons in SQL are case sensitive. If you ran the following statement against the `Product` table, you would not get any results:

```
Select * From Product Where Description = 'denim jeans'
```

However, you can use the `Lower()` function to convert a string to lowercase. Here is an example:

```
Select * From Product Where Lower(Description) = 'denim jeans'
```

This statement converts the `Description` column to all lowercase before performing the comparison. As a result, it will return all rows where `Description` equals "denim jeans" regardless of case. You could use the `Upper` function, which converts a string to uppercase, to achieve the same results:

```
Select * From Product Where Upper(Description) = 'DENIM JEANS'
```

Using the LIKE Operator

Sometimes searching for an exact string will not yield the results you want. For example, suppose the `Product` table contains the rows shown in Figure 11-67 and we want a list of all the shirts.

The following statement will not work. Can you see why?

```
Select * From Product Where Description = 'Shirt'
```

Figure 11-67 The `Product` table in the ProductDB.mdf database

Product_Number	Description	Units_On_Hand	Price
10-01	Oxford Cloth Shirt	100	39.9500
10-02	Poplin Shirt	150	38.5000
10-03	Plaid Flannel Shirt	80	34.7500
10-04	Canvas Shirt	200	32.9500
10-05	Cotton Shirt	250	28.9500
20-01	Chino Classic Fit Pants	100	28.9500
20-02	Chino Relaxed Fit Pants	100	28.9500
20-03	Denim Jeans	275	32.9500
20-04	Wool Trousers	75	78.9500
30-01	Warm-Up Jacket	125	59.9500
30-02	Fleece Pullover	150	28.9500
30-03	Parka	75	199.9500

This statement will search for rows where the Description column is equal to the string "Shirt". Unfortunately, it will find none because there are no rows in which the Description column is equal to "Shirt". However, the word "Shirt" does appear in the `Description` column of some of the rows. For example, in Figure 11-67 the first row's `Description` column is "Oxford Cloth Shirt", the second row's `Description` column is "Poplin Shirt", and so forth.

In order to find all the shirts, we need to search for rows where "Shirt" appears as a substring in the `Description` column. You can perform just such a search using the `Like` operator. Here is an example of how to use it.

```
Select * From Product Where Description Like '%Shirt%'
```

The `Like` operator is followed by a string that contains a character pattern. In this example, the character pattern is `'%Shirt%'`. The `%` symbol is used as wildcard character. It represents any sequence of zero or more characters. The pattern `'%Shirt%'` specifies that the string "Shirt" must appear with any sequence of characters before or after it. So, the statement previously shown would return all rows in which the `Description` column contains the string "Shirt".

Likewise, the following statement will result in all the rows where the `Description` column starts with the word "Chino".

```
Select * From Product Where Description Like 'Chino%'
```

The underscore character (_) is also used as a wildcard. Unlike the `%` character, the underscore represents a single character. For example, look at the following statement:

```
Select * From Product Where Product_Number Like '2_-0_'
```

This statement will result in all the rows where the `Product_Number` column begins with "2", followed by any one character, followed by "-0", followed by any one character.

You can use the `Not` operator to disqualify a character pattern in a search criteria. For example, suppose you want a list of all the items that are not shirts. The following statement will yield just those results.

```
Select * From Product Where Description Not Like '%Shirt%'
```

Using `And` and `Or`

You can use the `And` and `Or` logical operators to specify multiple search criteria in a `Where` clause. For example, look at the following statement:

```
Select * From Product Where Price > 20.00 And Price < 30.00
```

The `And` operator requires that both search criteria be true in order for a row to be qualified as a match. The only rows that will be returned from this statement are those where the `Price` column contains a value that is greater than 20.00 and less than 30.00.

Here's an example that uses the `Or` operator:

```
Select * From Product
Where Description Like '%Shirt%' or Product_Number Like '10-%'
```

The `Or` operator requires that either of the search criteria be true in order for a row to be qualified as a match. This statement searches for rows where the `Description` column contains the string "Shirt" at any position or where the `Product_Number` column starts with "10-".

Sorting the Results of a `Select` Query

If you wish to sort the results of a `Select` query, you can use the `Order By` clause. Here is an example:

```
Select * From Product Order By Price
```

This statement produces a list of all the rows in the `Product` table, ordered by the `Price` column. The list will be sorted in ascending order on the `Price` column, meaning that the lowest-priced coffees will appear first.

Here's a `Select` query that uses both a `Where` clause and an `Order By` clause:

```
Select * From Product
    Where Price > 20.00
    Order By Price
```

This statement produces a list of all the rows in the `Product` table where the `Price` column contains a value greater than 20.00, listed in ascending order by price.

If you want the list sorted in descending order (from highest to lowest), use the `Desc` operator, as shown here:

```
Select * From Product
    Where Price > 20.00
Order By Price Desc
```

Table Adapter Queries

A **table adapter query** is an SQL statement that is stored in a table adapter and can be executed simply by calling a method. For example, all table adapters contain a query that fills a dataset with data from a table. That query can be executed by calling the table adapter's `Fill` method. When you place a data-bound control, such as a DataGridView control, on a form, a Load event handler that calls the table adapter's `Fill` method is automatically created for the form.

Let's look at an example. In Visual Studio, open the *Multiform Products* project that you created in Tutorial 11-5, and open source code for the MainForm form. Look at the form's Load event handler, which is shown here (the comment that appears in line 3 has been shortened to fit on the page):

```
1 private void MainForm_Load(object sender, EventArgs e)
2 {
3     // TODO: This line of code loads data into ...
4     this.productTableAdapter.Fill(this.productDataSet.Product);
5
6 }
```

The statement in line 4 calls the `productTableAdapter`'s `Fill` method, passing the dataset's `Product` table as an argument. The `Fill` method fills the dataset table with rows that are returned from a SQL statement. Now let's look at the SQL statement that is executed by the `Fill` method. In the *Solution Explorer*, you should see an entry named *ProductDataSet.xsd*, as shown in Figure 11-68. This is the **schema definition file** that describes the contents of the `productDataSet`. Double-click the *ProductDataSet.xsd* entry to open it in an editor window, as shown in Figure 11-69. The area at the top of the diagram shows the columns that are included in the dataset, and the area at the bottom shows the table adapter query methods.

Figure 11-68 Schema Definition File entry in the *Solution Explorer*

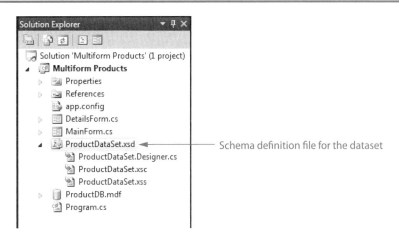

Figure 11-69 ProductDataSet.xsd opened for editing

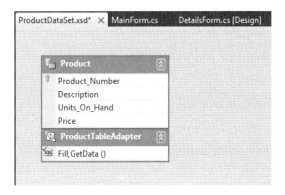

Right-click the area that reads *Fill, GetData()* and, as shown in Figure 11-70, select *Configure* from the pop-up menu. This displays the *Table Adapter Configuration Wizard* window shown in Figure 11-71. Notice the SQL query that appears in *Table Adapter Configuration Wizard* window. The dataset is filled with the rows that are returned by this `Select` statement. If you were to change this `Select` statement, for instance, by adding a `Where` clause and then by clicking the *Finish* button, the data that is initially displayed in the DataGridView control would change accordingly. When you are finished examining the window, click the *Cancel* button to close it.

Figure 11-70 Select *Configure* from the pop-up menu

Figure 11-71 *Table Adapter Configuration Wizard*

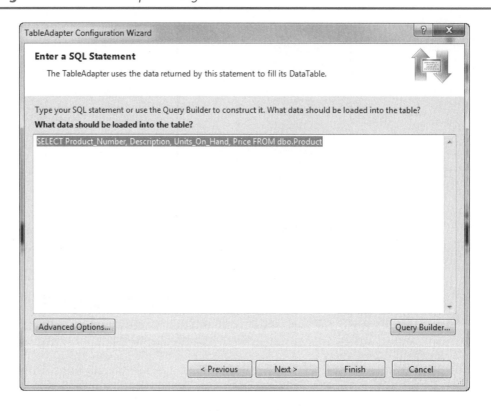

 NOTE: Notice that the table name in the Select statement is preceded with the dbo. prefix. The prefix dbo stands for database owner and is part of an SQL Server naming convention. In our example programs, the dbo prefix is optional.

Adding New Table Adapter Queries

You can add your own SQL queries to a table adapter and call them from your C# code. In Tutorial 11-6 you add several queries to a table adapter, and then you create buttons on the application's form that executes those queries.

Tutorial 11-6:
Creating the *Product Queries* Application

In this tutorial you create an application that displays the Product table from the ProductDB .mdf database in a DataGridView control. You also add two SQL queries to the table adapter. The queries perform the following:

- Return all the rows, sorted by price in ascending order
- Return only the rows with more than 100 units on hand

Then, you create buttons on the applications form that execute the queries.

Step 1: Start Visual Studio (or Visual C# Express). Create a new *Windows Forms Application* project named *Product Queries*.

Step 2: Change the Form1 form's Text property to *Product Queries*.

Step 3: Perform the following steps to connect the application to the ProductDB.mdf database and select the `Product` table for the dataset:

- From the *Data* menu, select *Add New Data Source....*
- Select *Database* and click *Next >.*
- Select *Dataset* and click *Next >.*
- Click *New Connection....*
- In the *Add Connection* window, make sure *Microsoft SQL Server Database File (SqlClient)* is the selected data source.
- In the *Add Connection* window, click *Browse* and go to the *Chap11* folder in the Student Sample Programs. Select the ProductDB.mdf file. Click *OK.*
- Click *Next >,* and when asked if you want to copy the file to the project, click *Yes.*
- Click *Next >.*
- Select the `Product` table as the database object, and change the name of the dataset to `ProductDataSet`. Click *Finish.*

 NOTE: This is the same procedure that you performed in Steps 3–11 in Tutorial 11-3. If you want more detailed guidance, go back to that tutorial to see the actual screens.

Step 4: Open the Data Sources window and drag a DataGridView control onto the form, bound to the `Product` table. After creating the DataGridView control, adjust the size of the form and the control, as shown in Figure 11-72.

Figure 11-72 The application's form

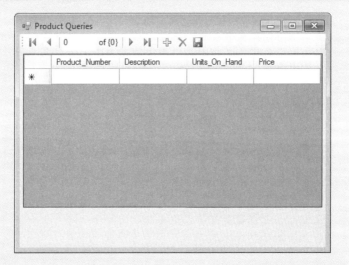

Step 5: Now you add the first query, which sorts the data in the dataset by price. In the Solution Explorer, double-click the *ProduceDataSet.xsd* entry. This opens the dataset schema description. Right-click the area that reads *ProductTableAdapter.* As shown in Figure 11-73, select *Add,* and then click *Query....*

 NOTE: It is possible that you will see *Add Query...* on the pop-up menu instead of *Add.* If that is the case, simply click *Add Query....*

Figure 11-73 Adding a query to the table adapter

Step 6: The *Table Adapter Configuration Wizard* appears next, as shown in Figure 11-74. Make sure *Use SQL Statements* is selected, and then click *Next >*.

Figure 11-74 *Table Adapter Configuration Wizard—Choose a Command Type*

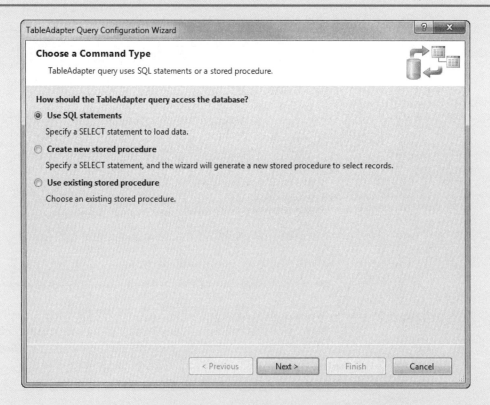

Step 7: The wizard now prompts you to choose a query type, as shown in Figure 11-75. Make sure *SELECT which returns rows* is selected, and then click *Next >*.

Figure 11-75 *Table Adapter Configuration Wizard—Choose a Query Type*

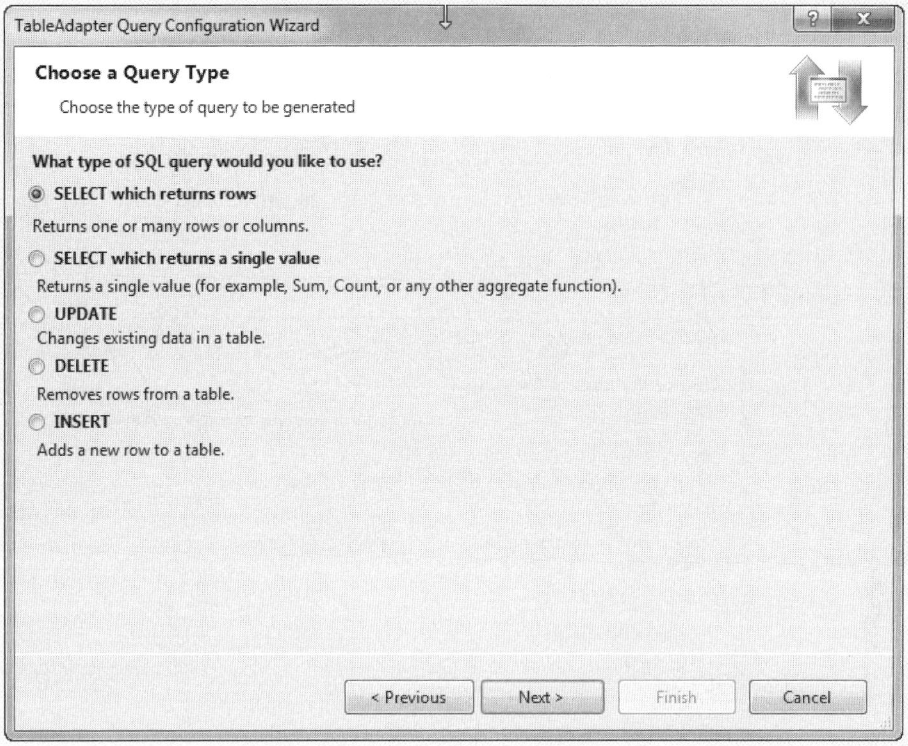

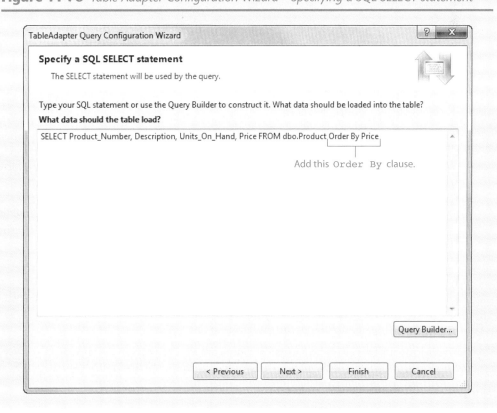

Step 8: The wizard now prompts you to *Specify a SQL SELECT statement*. A statement is already shown that returns every row in the `Product` table. Add the `Order By Price` clause to the end of the statement, as shown in Figure 11-76. Click *Next >*.

Figure 11-76 *Table Adapter Configuration Wizard—Specifying a SQL SELECT statement*

Step 9: The wizard now prompts you to *Choose Methods to Generate*. We are interested only in generating a method to fill the dataset with the results of our SQL statement. Make the following selections:

- Make sure *Fill a DataTable* is checked.
- Under *Fill a DataTable*, enter `FillByPrice` as the method name. This will be the name of the method that executes the SQL statement.
- Make sure *Return a DataTable* is not checked.

The window should now appear as shown in Figure 11-77. Click *Next >*.

Figure 11-77 *Table Adapter Configuration Wizard—Choose Methods to Generate*

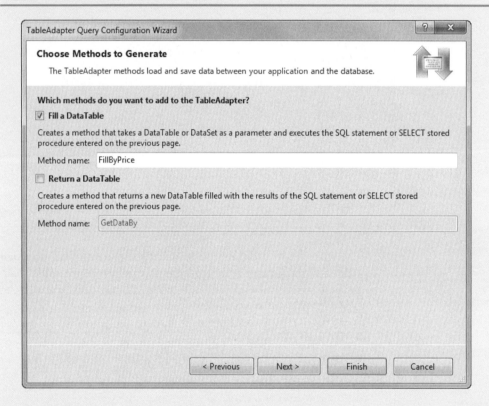

Step 10: The wizard now shows you the results, as shown in Figure 11-78. Click the *Finish* button.

The schema definition file (ProductDataSet.xsd) should now appear as shown in Figure 11-79. Notice that the method `FillByPrice()` now appears in the area at the bottom of the diagram.

> **NOTE:** After you have created a table adapter query, you can edit it by right-clicking its entry in the dataset schema definition and then clicking *Configure...* from the pop-up menu.

Step 11: Next you add the second query, which returns only the rows with units on hand greater than 100. Perform the following steps (most of these are the same as those you performed to add the previous query):

- In the schema definition, right-click the area that reads *ProductTableAdapter*.
- In the pop-up menu, select *Add*, and then click *Query....* (Or, if you see *Add Query...*, then select that.)

Figure 11-78 *Table Adapter Configuration Wizard—Wizard Results*

TableAdapter Query Configuration Wizard

Wizard Results

Review the list of tasks the wizard has performed. Click Finish to complete the wizard or click Previous to make changes.

TableAdapter query 'ProductTableAdapter' was configured successfully.

Details:

✔ Generated SELECT statement.
✔ Generated Fill method.

To apply these settings to your query, click Finish.

< Previous   Next >   Finish   Cancel

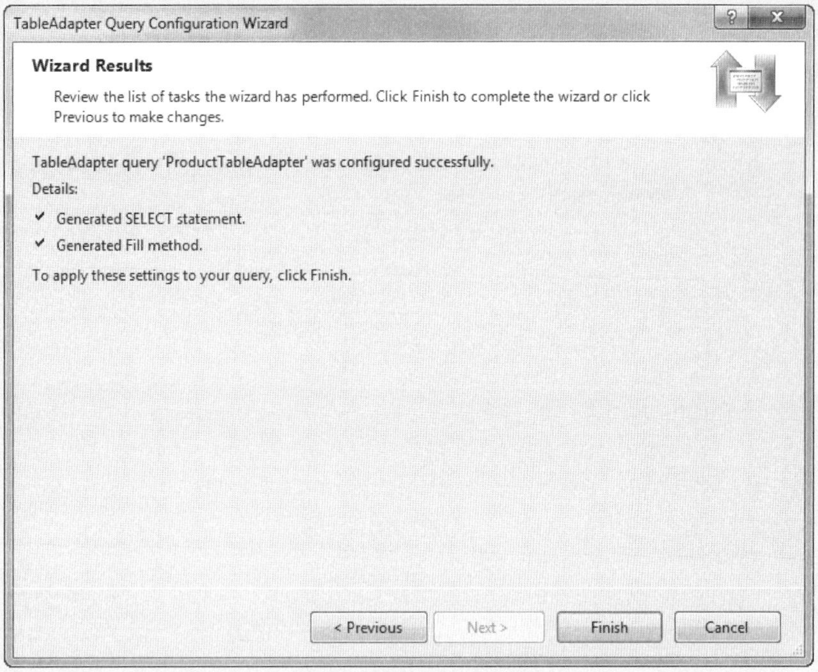

Figure 11-79 The `FillByPrice()` method appearing in the schema definition file

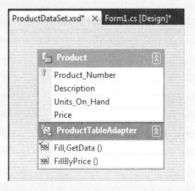

- The *Table Adapter Configuration Wizard* appears next. Make sure *Use SQL Statements* is selected and then click *Next >*.
- The wizard now prompts you to choose a query type. Make sure *SELECT which returns rows* is selected and then click *Next >*.
- The wizard now prompts you to *Specify a SQL SELECT statement*. A statement is already shown that returns every row in the `Product` table. Add the `WHERE Units_On_Hand > 100` clause to the end of the statement, as shown in Figure 11-80. Click *Next >*.
- The wizard now prompts you to *Choose Methods to Generate*. Make the following selections:

  Make sure *Fill a DataTable* is checked.
  Under *Fill a DataTable*, enter `FillByUnits` as the method name. This will be the name of the method that executes the SQL statement.
  Make sure *Return a DataTable* is not checked.

Figure 11-80 *Table Adapter Configuration Wizard—Specify a SQL SELECT statement*

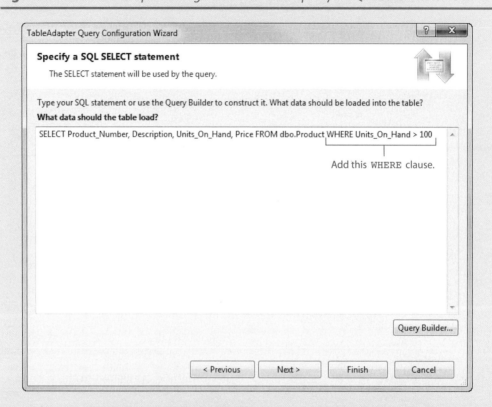

- The window should now appear as shown in Figure 11-81. Click *Next >*.
- The wizard now shows you the results. Click the *Finish* button.

Figure 11-81 *Table Adapter Configuration Wizard—Choose Methods to Generate*

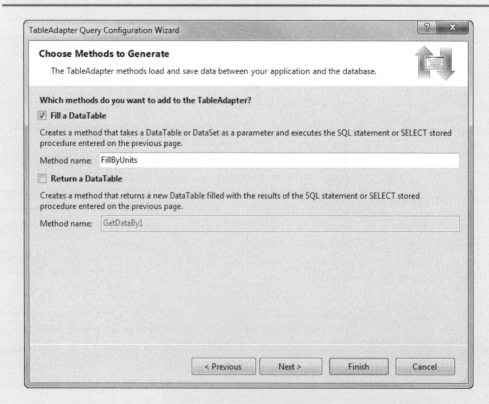

The schema definition file (ProductDataSet.xsd) should now appear as shown in Figure 11-82. Notice that the two methods you created, `FillByPrice()` and `FillByUnits()`, now appear in the area at the bottom of the diagram.

Figure 11-82 The `FillByPrice()` and `FillByUnits()` methods as they appear in the schema definition file

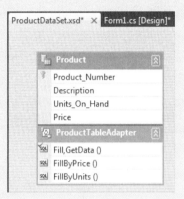

Step 12: Now you add button controls to the application's form that execute the SQL queries. Open Form1 in the Designer and add the two button controls shown in Figure 11-83.

Figure 11-83 Button controls added to the form

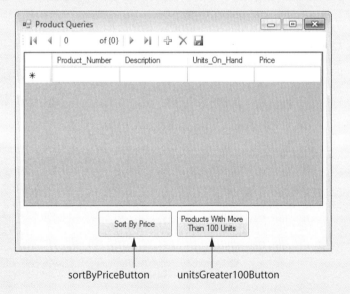

Step 13: Double-click the `sortByPriceButton` control. Complete `sortByPriceButton_Click` the event handler by typing the code in line 36 in Program 11-4. This statement calls the table adapter's `FillByPrice` method.

Step 14: Switch your view back to Form1 in the *Designer* and double-click the `unitsGreater100Button` control. Complete `unitsGreater100Button_Click` event handler by typing the code in line 41 in Program 11-4. This statement calls the table adapter's `FillByUnits` method.

Step 15: Save the project, and then run the application. When the form appears, it should show all the Product table's rows in the DataGridView control. When you click the *Sort By Price* button, the data should appear sorted by price. When you click the *Products With More Than 100 Units* button, you should see only the rows where Units_On_Hand is greater than 100. When you are finished, close the application's form to exit. (If you plan to immediately continue to the next tutorial, leave the project opened in Visual Studio. You continue to develop this application in the next tutorial.)

Program 11-4 Completed Form1 code in the *Product Queries* application

```
 1 using System;
 2 using System.Collections.Generic;
 3 using System.ComponentModel;
 4 using System.Data;
 5 using System.Drawing;
 6 using System.Linq;
 7 using System.Text;
 8 using System.Windows.Forms;
 9
10 namespace Product_Queries
11 {
12     public partial class Form1 : Form
13     {
14         public Form1()
15         {
16             InitializeComponent();
17         }
18
19         private void productBindingNavigatorSaveItem_Click(object sender, EventArgs e)
20         {
21             this.Validate();
22             this.productBindingSource.EndEdit();
23             this.tableAdapterManager.UpdateAll(this.productDataSet);
24
25         }
26
27         private void Form1_Load(object sender, EventArgs e)
28         {
29             // TODO: This line of code loads data into ...
30             this.productTableAdapter.Fill(this.productDataSet.Product);
31
32         }
33
34         private void sortByPriceButton_Click(object sender, EventArgs e)
35         {
36             this.productTableAdapter.FillByPrice(this.productDataSet.Product);
37         }
38
39         private void unitsGreater100Button_Click(object sender, EventArgs e)
40         {
41             this.productTableAdapter.FillByUnits(this.productDataSet.Product);
42         }
43     }
44 }
```

SQL Math Functions

SQL provides several functions for performing calculations. For example, the `Avg` function calculates the average value in a particular column. Here is an example `Select` statement using the `Avg` function:

```
Select Avg(Price) From Product
```

This statement produces a single value: the average of all the values in the `Price` column. Because we did not use a `Where` clause, it uses all the rows in the `Product` table in the calculation. Here is an example that calculates the average price of all the items having a product number that begins with "20":

```
Select Avg(Price)From Product Where Product_Number LIKE '20%'
```

Another of the mathematical functions is `Sum`, which calculates the sum of a column's values. The following statement, which is probably not very useful, calculates the sum of the values in the `Price` column:

```
Select Sum(Price) From Product
```

The `Min` and `Max` functions determine the minimum and maximum values found in a column. The following statement gives the minimum value in the `Price` column:

```
Select Min(Price) From Product
```

The following statement gives the maximum value in the `Price` column:

```
Select Max(Price) From Product
```

The `Count` function can be used to determine the number of rows in a table, as demonstrated by the following statement:

```
Select Count(*) From Product
```

The * simply indicates that you want to count entire rows. Here is another example, which gives the number of items with a price greater than 50.0:

```
Select Count(*) From Product Where Price > 50.0
```

In Tutorial 11-7 you will add another query to the table adapter in the Product Queries application. The new query will display average price of all the items in the database.

Tutorial 11-7:

Creating the *Product Queries* Application

In this tutorial you add a query to the Product Queries application that returns the average price of all the items in the Products table. You also add a button to the application's form that executes the query and displays its result.

Step 1: Make sure the *Product Queries* project is open in Visual Studio (or Visual C# Express) from the previous tutorial.

Step 2: In the Solution Explorer, double-click the *ProduceDataSet.xsd* entry. This opens the dataset schema description. Right-click the area that reads *ProductTableAdapter*. In the pop-up menu, select *Add* and then click *Query....* (Or, if you see *Add Query...* on the pop-up menu, select it.)

Step 3: The *Table Adapter Configuration Wizard* appears next. Make sure *Use SQL Statements* is selected and then click *Next >*.

Step 4: The wizard now prompts you to choose a query type. Make sure *SELECT which returns a single value* is selected and then click *Next >*.

Step 5: The wizard now prompts you to *Specify a SQL SELECT statement*. Delete the statement currently shown in the window and replace it with the following:

```
Select Avg(Price) From Product
```

The window should appear as shown in Figure 11-84. Click *Next >*.

Figure 11-84 Table Adapter Configuration Wizard—Specify a SQL SELECT statement

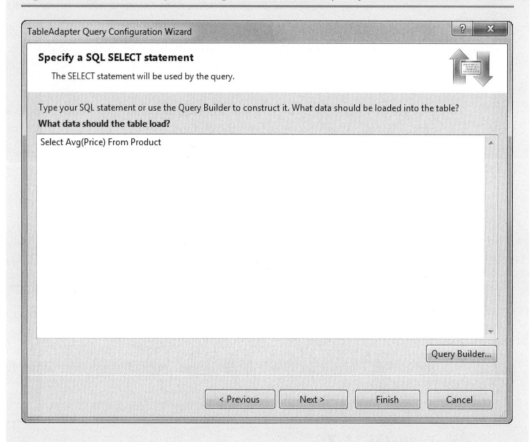

Step 6: The wizard now prompts you to *Choose Function Name*. The name that you specify in this window will be the name of the method that executes the query. As shown in Figure 11-85, change the name to `AveragePrice` and then click *Next >*.

Step 7: The wizard now shows you the results. Click the *Finish* button.

The schema definition file (ProductDataSet.xsd) should now appear, as shown in Figure 11-86. Notice that the `AveragePrice` method appears, along with the other methods that you previously created.

Figure 11-85 *Table Adapter Configuration Wizard—Choose Function Name*

TableAdapter Query Configuration Wizard

Choose Function Name

Choose the name of the function to be generated

What would you like to name the new function?

AveragePrice

[< Previous] [Next >] [Finish] [Cancel]

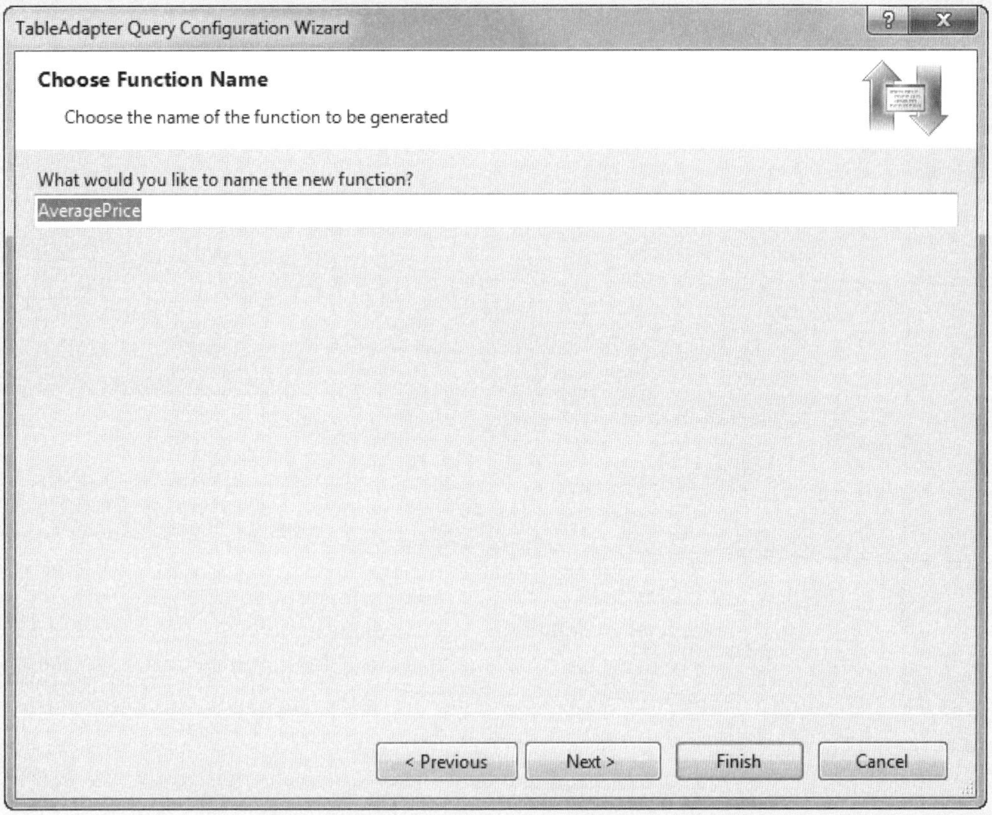

Figure 11-86 The `AveragePrice()` method as it appears in the schema definition file

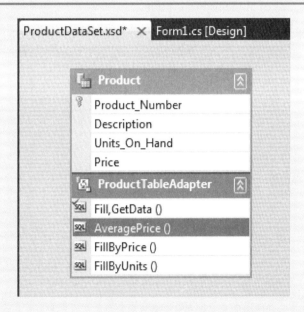

Step 8: Next you a add button control to the application's form that executes the table adapter's `AveragePrice` method. Open Form1 in the *Designer* and the `averagePriceButton` control shown in Figure 11-87.

Figure 11-87 The averagePriceButton control added to the form

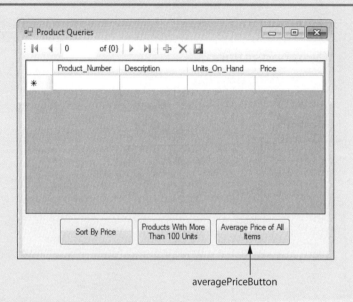

averagePriceButton

Step 9: Double-click the averagePriceButton control. Complete the averagePriceButton_Click event handler by typing the code in lines 46–54 in Program 11-5. Let's take a closer look at the code:

Line 47: This statement declares a local decimal variable named averagePrice.

Line 50: This statement calls the table adapter's AveragePrice method, which returns the result of the Select statement that you wrote in Step 4. The value that is returned is assigned to the averagePrice variable. Notice that we had to use a cast operator to explicitly convert the value to a decimal.

Lines 53–54: This statement displays a message box showing the average price of all items in the table.

Step 10: Save the project and then run the application. Click the *Average Price of All Items* button. You should see a message box displaying a message indicating the average price of all the items. When you are finished, close the application's form to exit.

Program 11-5 Completed Form1 code in the *Product Queries* application

```
 1 using System;
 2 using System.Collections.Generic;
 3 using System.ComponentModel;
 4 using System.Data;
 5 using System.Drawing;
 6 using System.Linq;
 7 using System.Text;
 8 using System.Windows.Forms;
 9
10 namespace Product_Queries
11 {
12     public partial class Form1 : Form
13     {
14         public Form1()
15         {
16             InitializeComponent();
17         }
```

```
18
19              private void productBindingNavigatorSaveItem_Click(object sender, EventArgs e)
20              {
21                  this.Validate();
22                  this.productBindingSource.EndEdit();
23                  this.tableAdapterManager.UpdateAll(this.productDataSet);
24
25              }
26
27              private void Form1_Load(object sender, EventArgs e)
28              {
29                  // TODO: This line of code loads data into the...
30                  this.productTableAdapter.Fill(this.productDataSet.Product);
31
32              }
33
34              private void sortByPriceButton_Click(object sender, EventArgs e)
35              {
36                      this.productTableAdapter.FillByPrice(this.productDataSet.Product);
37              }
38
39              private void unitsGreater100Button_Click(object sender, EventArgs e)
40              {
41                      this.productTableAdapter.FillByUnits(this.productDataSet.Product);
42              }
43
44              private void averagePriceButton_Click(object sender, EventArgs e)
45              {
46                  // Declare a variable to hold the average price.
47                  decimal averagePrice;
48
49                  // Get the average price.
50                  averagePrice = (decimal) this.productTableAdapter.AveragePrice();
51
52                  // Display the average price.
53                  MessageBox.Show("Average price of all items: " +
54                      averagePrice.ToString("c"));
55              }
56          }
57 }
```

Query Parameters

SQL queries can accept arguments. Just as with regular methods, arguments are passed into parameter variables. In an SQL statement, a parameter variable begins with the @ symbol. The following statement shows an example:

```
Select * From Product Where Price < @priceValue
```

This statement retrieves all the rows in which the Price column is less than the value of the priceValue parameter. Here is another example:

```
Select * From Product
Where Price < @priceValue And Units_On_Hand < @unitsValue
```

This statement retrieves all the rows in which the Price column is less than the value of the @priceValue parameter and the Units_On_Hand column is less than the value of the @unitsValue parameter.

When you call the table adapter method for an SQL query, you have to pass arguments for any parameters that are used in the query. In Tutorial 11-8 you create an application that gets a value from the user and passes that value as an argument to an SQL query.

Tutorial 11-8:
Creating the *Product Search* Application

In this tutorial you create an application that displays the Product table from the ProductDB.mdf database in a DataGridView control. The user will be able to enter a value into a text box and search for all items that contain that value in their description.

Step 1: Start Visual Studio (or Visual C# Express). Create a new *Windows Forms Application* project named *Product Search*.

Step 2: Change the Form1 form's Text property to *Product Search*.

Step 3: Perform the following steps to connect the application to the ProductDB.mdf database and select the `Product` table for the dataset:

- From the *Data* menu, select *Add New Data Source....*
- Select *Database* and click *Next >.*
- Select *Dataset* and click *Next >.*
- Click *New Connection....*
- In the *Add Connection* window, make sure *Microsoft SQL Server Database File (SqlClient)* is the selected data source.
- In the *Add Connection* window, click *Browse* and go to the *Chap11* folder in the Student Sample Programs. Select the ProductDB.mdf file. Click *OK.*
- Click *Next >*, and when asked if you want to copy the file to the project, click *Yes.*
- Click *Next >.*
- Select the `Product` table as the database object, and change the name of the dataset to `ProductDataSet`. Click *Finish.*

> **NOTE:** This is the same procedure that you performed in Steps 3–11 in Tutorial 11-3. If you want more detailed guidance, go back to that tutorial to see the actual screens.

Step 4: Open the Data Sources window and drag a DataGridView control onto the form, bound to the `Product` table.

Step 5: Adjust the size of the form and the DataGridView control, as shown in Figure 11-88. Then, place the group box, text box, and buttons as shown in the figure. Here is a summary of what the Button controls will do when the application is completed:

- The `searchButton` control will get the value that has been entered into the `searchTextBox`, and pass that as an argument to an SQL query. The query will return all rows in the `Product` table that contain the value that was passed as an argument. Those rows will be displayed in the DataGridView control.
- The `showAllButton` will display all the rows of the `Product` table in the DataGridView control.

Figure 11-88 The application's form

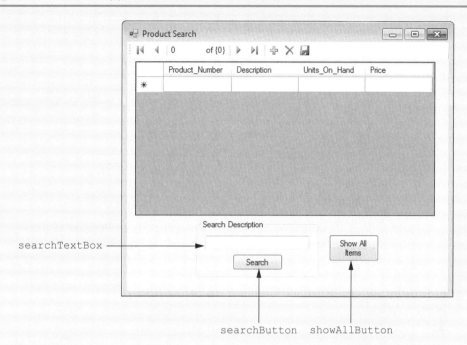

Step 6: In the Solution Explorer, double-click the *ProduceDataSet.xsd* entry. This opens the dataset schema description. Right-click the area that reads *ProductTableAdapter.* In the pop-up menu, select *Add* and then click *Query....* (Or, if you see *Add Query...* on the pop-up menu, select it.)

Step 7: The *Table Adapter Configuration Wizard* appears next. Make sure *Use SQL Statements* is selected and then click *Next >*.

Step 8: The wizard now prompts you to choose a query type. Make sure *SELECT which returns rows* is selected and then click *Next >*.

Step 9: The wizard now prompts you to *Specify a SQL SELECT statement*. Modify the default statement that is provided as shown here:

```
Select Product_Number, Description, Units_On_Hand, Price
From Product
Where Description Like '%' + @value + '%'
```

Notice that a parameter query named @value is used in the Where clause. Also, notice the use of the + operator for string concatenation. When this query executes, it will return all rows in which the Description column contains the value specified by the @value parameter. The window at this point should appear as shown in Figure 11-89.

Click *Next >*.

Step 10: The wizard now prompts you to *Choose Methods to Generate*. Make the following selections:

- Make sure *Fill a DataTable* is checked.
- Under *Fill a DataTable*, enter SearchDesc as the method name. This will be the name of the method that executes the SQL statement.
- Make sure *Return a DataTable* is not checked.

The window should now appear as shown in Figure 11-90. Click *Next >*.

Figure 11-89 *Table Adapter Configuration Wizard—Specify a SQL SELECT statement*

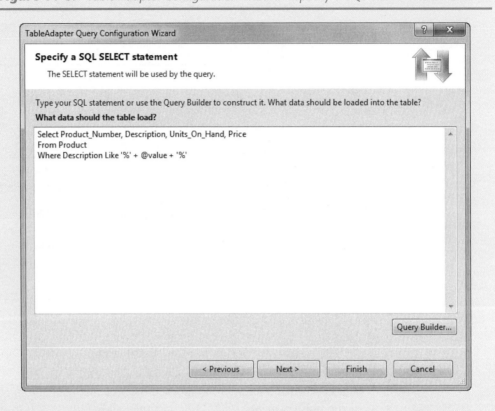

Figure 11-90 *Table Adapter Configuration Wizard—Choose Methods to Generate*

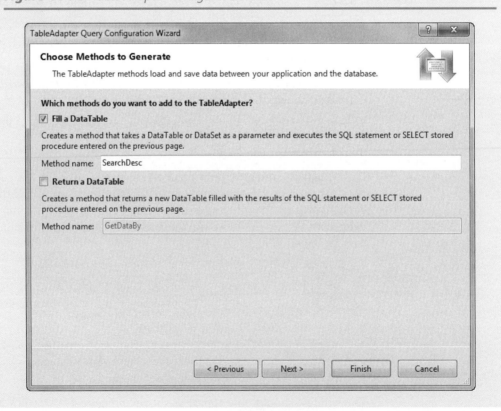

Step 11: The wizard now shows you the results. Click the *Finish* button.

The schema definition file (ProductDataSet.xsd) should now appear as shown in Figure 11-82. Notice that the `SearchDesc(@value)` now appears in the area at the bottom of the diagram.

Step 12: Open Form1 in the *Designer* and double-click the `searchButton` control. Complete the `searchButton_Click` event handler by typing the code shown in lines 36 and 37 in Program 11-6.

The statement in these lines calls the table adapter's `SearchDesc` method. The first argument is the dataset's `Product` table, and the second argument is the `searchTextBox` control's Text property. The second argument will be passed into the SQL query's `@value` parameter.

Step 13: Switch your view back to Form1 in the *Designer* and double-click the `showAllButton` control. Complete the `showAllButton_Click` event handler by typing the code shown in line 42 in Program 11-6. The statement this line calls the table adapter's `Fill` method. Recall that the `Fill` method fills the dataset table with all of the rows from the table.

Step 14: Save the project and then run the application. Enter a search term, such as *Shirt* or *Pants,* in the text box and click the *Search* button. You should see all the rows that contain that search term displayed in the DataGridView control. To reset the DataGridView control so it displays all of the rows, click the *Show All Items* button. Experiment with several search terms. When you are finished, close the application.

Program 11-6 Completed Form1 code in the *Product Search* application

```
 1 using System;
 2 using System.Collections.Generic;
 3 using System.ComponentModel;
 4 using System.Data;
 5 using System.Drawing;
 6 using System.Linq;
 7 using System.Text;
 8 using System.Windows.Forms;
 9
10 namespace Product_Search
11 {
12     public partial class Form1 : Form
13     {
14         public Form1()
15         {
16             InitializeComponent();
17         }
18
19         private void productBindingNavigatorSaveItem_Click(object sender, EventArgs e)
20         {
21             this.Validate();
22             this.productBindingSource.EndEdit();
23             this.tableAdapterManager.UpdateAll(this.productDataSet);
24
25         }
26
```

```
27          private void Form1_Load(object sender, EventArgs e)
28          {
29              // TODO: This line of code loads data into the...
30              this.productTableAdapter.Fill(this.productDataSet.Product);
31
32          }
33
34          private void searchButton_Click(object sender, EventArgs e)
35          {
36              this.productTableAdapter.SearchDesc(
37                  this.productDataSet.Product, searchTextBox.Text);
38          }
39
40          private void showAllButton_Click(object sender, EventArgs e)
41          {
42              this.productTableAdapter.Fill(this.productDataSet.Product);
43          }
44      }
45 }
```

Checkpoint

11.23 In SQL, what is the purpose of the Select statement?

11.24 What are the instructions for the DBMS to carry out operations on its data called?

11.25 How are the relational operators used in SQL different from those used in C#?

11.26 How do you write a single quote as part of a string in SQL?

11.27 What is the purpose of the Like operator in SQL?

11.28 How is the underscore character different from the % character in SQL?

11.29 How do you sort the results of a Select query in SQL?

11.30 In an SQL statement, with what symbol does a query parameter begin?

Key Terms

binding source	identity column
column	output folder
database	primary key
database management system	queries
(DBMS)	row
data-bound control	schema definition file
DataGridView control	`Select` statement
dataset	smart tag
data source	structured query language (SQL)
DataSource property	table
Details view	table adapter
DisplayMember property	table adapter query

Review Questions

Multiple Choice

1. A(n) _____ is software that is specifically designed to store, retrieve, and manipulate large amounts of data in an organized and efficient manner.

   a. software development kit (SDK)
   b. database management system (DBMS)
   c. application programming interface (API)
   d. driver development kit (DDK)

2. A _____ is a collection of tables that are stored using a database management system.

   a. data source
   b. dataset
   c. database
   d. spreadsheet

3. A _____ holds a collection of related data that is organized into rows and columns.

   a. table
   b. grid
   c. dataset
   d. worksheet

4. A _____ is a complete set of information about a single item in a table of a database.

   a. data source
   b. dataset
   c. column
   d. row

5. A(n) _____ holds an individual piece of information about the item in a row of a table in a database.

   a. column
   b. volume
   c. record
   d. entry

6. A _____ is a unique column value that can be used to identify a specific row in a table of a database.

   a. data cell
   b. primary key
   c. prime column
   d. lookup entry

7. A(n) _____ is a column that contains unique values that are generated by the DBMS.

   a. generated column
   b. pseudo-primary key
   c. identity column
   d. automatic entry

8. A _____ is a source of data with which the application can work.

   a. database communicator
   b. dataset
   c. data source
   d. parser

9. A _____ connects to a data source and can retrieve and update data from a table in a data source.

   a. source connection
   b. dataset
   c. binding source
   d. table adapter

10. A _____ gets a copy of a table from the table adapter and keeps the copy of the table in memory.

    a. connection
    b. dataset
    c. read-only table
    d. table adapter

11. A _____ is a component that can connect user interface controls directly to a dataset.

    a. controller
    b. source editor
    c. binding source
    d. component adapter

12. A _____ is a user interface control that is connected to a data source.

    a. DBMS component
    b. data-bound control
    c. source control
    d. database control

13. A _____ can display an entire database table in a scrollable grid on an application's form.

    a. scrollable data control
    b. Table control
    c. SmartGrid control
    d. DataGridView control

14. A _____ is a set of individual controls that are bound to the columns in a single row.

   a. data-bound control set
   b. data collection
   c. Details view
   d. Column view

15. In a Visual Studio project, the *bin\Debug* folder is known as the _____.

   a. input folder
   b. output folder
   c. build folder
   d. home folder

16. In the *Designer*, the _____ that appears in the upper-right corner of a control's bounding box can be clicked to display a tasks panel, which provides a number of options that can be performed with the control.

   a. double arrow
   b. smart tag
   c. resizing handle
   d. name

17. The _____ identifies the table from which to get data.

   a. DataSource property
   b. Table property
   c. DataBound property
   d. DataTable property

18. The _____ identifies the column of the table from which to display data.

   a. DisplayData property
   b. DataOutput property
   c. ShowColumn property
   d. DisplayMember property

19. _____, which stands for _____, is a standard language for working with database management systems.

   a. SQL, structured query language
   b. DBL, database language
   c. XML, extensible markup language
   d. HTML, hypertext markup language

20. _____ are instructions for the DBMS to carry out operations on its data.

   a. Command strings
   b. Queries
   c. Build statements
   d. Data tokens

21. In SQL, you use the _____ to retrieve the rows in a table.

   a. `Select` statement
   b. `Like` operator
   c. `%` symbol
   d. `Where` clause

22. A(n) _____ is an SQL statement that is stored in a table adapter and can be executed simply by calling a method.

   a. automated query
   b. dataset query

    c.   table adapter query

    d.   structured data query

23.   The _____ describes the contents of a dataset, and its name appears in the *Solution Explorer* ending with the .xsd file extension.

    a.   schema definition file

    b.   data markup file

    c.   table description file

    d.   DBMS protocol file

True or False

1.   When developing applications that work with an intensive amount of data, most developers prefer to use traditional files.

2.   The DBMS works directly with the data and sends the results of operations back to the application.

3.   The data that is stored in a database is organized into one or more tables.

4.   Each column in a table must have a name.

5.   When you create a database table, the data types that you can choose from are C# data types.

6.   When working with the data in a database table, the column that is designated as the primary key must hold a unique value for each row.

7.   If a column in a database table contains no data, it is said to be null.

8.   An application works directly with a database, modifying rows, deleting rows, adding new rows, and so on.

9.   Rather than showing multiple rows at once, a Details view lets the user see one row at a time.

10.   SQL is a language that can be used to write data intensive applications.

11.   String comparisons in SQL are case sensitive.

Short Answer

1.   In what situation do traditional files work well for storing data?

2.   Briefly describe the layered nature of an application that works with a DBMS.

3.   What is the data that is stored in a row of a table in a database divided into?

4.   Are the data types used when creating a database table C# data types? If not, what kind of data types are they?

5.   How do you create a primary key for a table with columns that could potentially contain the same values?

6.   What type of columns in a database table must always contain a value?

7.   Instead of working with the database directly, with what component does an application work?

8.   What control can be used to display an entire database table in a scrollable grid on an application's form?

9.   What is a Details view?

10.   In SQL, what statement do you use to retrieve specific rows from a table in a database?

11.   How do you sort the results of a `Select` query in descending order in SQL?

Algorithm Workbench

1. Look at the following SQL statement.

    ```
    Select Name From Employee
    ```

    a. What is the name of the table from which this statement is retrieving data?
    b. What is the name of the column that is being retrieved?

For Questions 2–8, assume that a database has a table named Stock, *with the following columns:*

Column Name	Type
Trading_Symbol	nchar(10)
Company_Name	nchar(25)
Num_Shares	int
Purchase_Price	money
Selling_Price	money

2. Write a Select statement that returns all the columns from every row in the table.

3. Write a Select statement that returns only the Trading_Symbol column from every row in the table.

4. Write a Select statement that returns the Trading_Symbol column and the Num_Shares column from every row in the table.

5. Write a Select statement that returns the Trading_Symbol column only from the rows where Purchase_Price is greater than $25.00.

6. Write a Select statement that returns all the columns from the rows where Trading_Symbol starts with "SU".

7. Write a Select statement that returns the Trading_Symbol column only from the rows where Selling_Price is greater than Purchase_Price and Num_Shares is greater than 100.

8. Write a Select statement that returns the Trading_Symbol column and the Num_Shares column only from the rows where Selling_Price is greater than Purchase_Price and Num_Shares is greater than 100. The results should be sorted by the Num_Shares column in ascending order.

Programming Problems

1. **Personnel Database**

    Use Visual Studio to create a database named Personnel.mdf. The database should have a table named Employee, with columns for employee ID, name, position, and hourly pay rate. The employee ID should be the primary key. Insert at least five sample rows of data into the Employee table. Create an application that displays the Employee table in a DataGridView control.

2. **Multiform Personnel Database Application**

    Create an application that connects to the Personnel.mdf database that you created in Programming Exercise 1. The application's main form should display the Employee table in a DataGridView control. The main form should also have a button that, when clicked, displays a second form. The second form should display the Employee table in a Details view. Make sure that when the second form is closed, the main form refills the dataset so the most current data is displayed.

3. **Hourly Pay Sorter**

   Create an application that connects to the Personnel.mdf database that you created in Programming Exercise 1. The application's form should display the `Employee` table in a DataGridView control. The form should also have the following controls:

   - A button that, when clicked, sorts the data in ascending order by hourly pay rate.
   - A button that, when clicked, sorts the data in descending order by hourly pay rate.

4. **Employee Search**

   Create an application that connects to the Personnel.mdf database that you created in Programming Exercise 1. The application's form should display the `Employee` table in a DataGridView control. The application should let the user specify a name in a text box and then search for that name in the `Employee` table. The application should display any rows that contain a full or partial match of the specified name.

5. **Highest and Lowest Pay Rate**

   Create an application that connects to the Personnel.mdf database that you created in Programming Exercise 1. The application's form should display the `Employee` table in a DataGridView control. The form should also have the following controls:

   - A button that, when clicked, displays a message indicating the highest (maximum) pay rate in the table.
   - A button that, when clicked, displays a message indicating the lowest (minimum) pay rate in the table.

6. **Population Database**

   In the *Chap11* folder of the Student Sample Programs, you will find a database file named PopulationDB.mdf. The database has a table named `City`. The `City` table has the following columns:

Column Name	Data Type
City	nvarchar(50) *Primary key*
Population	float

   The `City` column stores the name of a city and the `Population` column stores the population of that city. The database has 20 rows already entered.

   Create an application that connects to the PopulationDB.mdf database and allows the user to perform the following:

   - Use data-bound controls to add new rows to the database, change existing rows, and delete rows.
   - Sort the list of cities by population, in ascending order.
   - Sort the list of cities by population, in descending order.
   - Sort the list of cities by name.
   - Get the total population of all the cities.
   - Get the average population of all the cities.
   - Get the highest population.
   - Get the lowest population.

A C# Primitive Data Types

Data Type	Description
bool	A variable to store the Boolean values `true` and `false`.
byte	An unsigned 8-bit integer to store values in the range of 0 through 255.
sbyte	A signed 8-bit integer to store values in the range of -128 through 127.
char	A 16-bit variable to hold a Unicode character.
decimal	A 128-bit variable to hold real numbers, rounded to 28 digits of precision, in the range of -7.9228×10^{24} to 7.9228×10^{24}.
double	A 64-bit variable to hold real numbers, rounded to 15 digits of precision, in the range of $\pm 5.0 \times 10^{2324}$ to $\pm 1.7 \times 10^{308}$.
float	A 32-bit variable to hold real numbers rounded to 15 digits of precision, in the range of -3.4×10^{38} to $+3.4 \times 10^{38}$.
int	A signed 32-bit integer to store values in the range of $-2,147,483,648$ through $2,147,483,647$.
uint	An unsigned 32-bit integer to store values in the range of 0 through 4,294,967,295.
long	A signed 64-bit integer to store values in the range of $-9,223,372,036,854,775,808$ through 9,223,372,036,854,775,807.
ulong	An unsigned 64-bit integer to store values in the range of 0 through 18,446,744,073,709,551,615.
short	A signed 16-bit integer to store values in the range of $-32,768$ through 32,767.
ushort	An unsigned 16-bit integer to store values in the range of 0 through 65,535.
string	A variable to hold strings.

B Additional User Interface Controls

The chapters in this textbook have introduced you to the fundamental Visual C# controls. There are many more controls available in Visual C#, and this appendix introduces you to several of them. The examples discussed in this appendix can be found in the Student Sample Program Files.

ToolTips

A **ToolTip** is a small box displayed when the user holds the mouse cursor over a control. The box shows a short description of what the control does. Most Windows applications use ToolTips as a way of providing immediate and concise help to the user. Figure B-1 shows an example.

Figure B-1 A ToolTip displayed

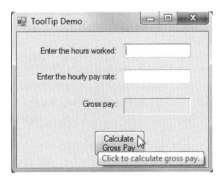

The **ToolTip control** allows you to create ToolTips for other controls on a form. Place a ToolTip control in your application by double-clicking the ToolTip icon in the Toolbox, just as you place other controls. When you do so, a ToolTip control appears in the component tray, the resizable area at the bottom of the *Designer* that holds invisible controls. Figure B-2 shows an example.

Figure B-2 ToolTip control

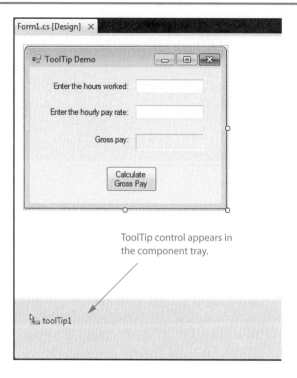

ToolTip control appears in the component tray.

When you add a ToolTip control to a form, a new property is added to all the other controls on that form. The new property is named ToolTip on *ToolTipControl,* where *ToolTipControl* is the name of the ToolTip control. For example, suppose you add a ToolTip control to a form and keep the default name ToolTip1. The new property added to the other controls is named ToolTip on ToolTip1.

The ToolTip on *ToolTipControl* property holds the string that is displayed as the control's ToolTip. Any text that you enter into a control's ToolTip on *ToolTipControl* property is displayed as that control's ToolTip when the user holds the mouse cursor over the control.

Other ToolTip Properties

ToolTip controls have other properties that affect their behavior. The InitialDelay property determines the amount of time, in milliseconds, that elapses between the user pointing the mouse at a control and the ToolTip's appearance. The default setting is 500. (One millisecond is one-thousandth second, so 500 milliseconds is one-half second.)

The AutoPopDelay property is also a measure of time in milliseconds. It determines how long a ToolTip remains on the screen once it is displayed. The default setting is 5000. The ReshowDelay property holds the number of milliseconds that elapse between the displaying of different ToolTips as the user moves the mouse from control to control. The default setting is 100.

You can set these properties individually or set them all at once with the AutomaticDelay property. When you store a value in the AutomaticDelay property, InitialDelay is set to the same value, AutoPopDelay is set to 10 times the value, and ReshowDelay is set to one-fifth the value.

Combo Boxes

A **combo box** is like a list box that has been combined with a text box. Figure B-3 shows an example of one style of combo box, known as a simple combo box.

Figure B-3 A simple combo box

Combo boxes and list boxes are similar in the following ways:

- They both display a list of items to the user.
- They both have Items, Items.Count, SelectedIndex, SelectedItem, and Sorted properties.
- They both have `Items.Add` and `Items.Clear` methods.
- All these properties and methods work the same with combo boxes and list boxes.

Additionally, a combo box has a rectangular area that works like a text box. The user may either select an item from the combo box's list or type text into the combo box's text input area.

Like a text box, the combo box has a Text property. If the user types text into the combo box, the text is stored in the Text property. Also, when the user selects an item from the combo box's list, the item is copied to the Text property.

Combo Box Styles

There are three different styles of combo boxes: the drop-down combo box, the simple combo box, and the drop-down list combo box. You can select a combo box's style with its DropDownStyle property. Let's look at the differences of each style.

- **Drop-Down Combo Box.** This is the default setting for the combo box DropDownStyle property. At run time, a drop-down combo box like the one shown on the left in Figure B-4 appears. When the user clicks the down arrow, a list drops down as shown in the image on the right in the figure. The user may either select an item from the list or type input into the text box that appears at the top of the control. The item that is selected or the text that is entered is assigned to the combo box's Text property.

Figure B-4 A drop-down combo box

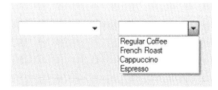

- **Simple Combo Box.** This is the style of combo box shown in Figure B-3. With the simple style of combo box, the list of items does not drop down but is always displayed. As with the drop-down combo box, this style allows the user to select an item from the list or type text directly into the text box area. When typing, the user is not restricted to the items that appear in the list. The item that is selected or the text that is entered is assigned to the combo box's Text property.
- **Drop-Down List Combo Box.** With the drop-down list combo box style, the user may not type text directly into the combo box. An item must be selected from the list. At run time, a drop-down list combo box appears, as shown the image on the left in Figure B-5. When the user clicks the down arrow, a list of items appears, as shown in the image on the right in the figure. The item that is selected is assigned to the combo box's Text property.

Figure B-5 A drop-down list combo box

Getting the User's Input from a Combo Box

As with the list box, you can determine which item has been selected from a combo box's list by retrieving the value in the SelectedIndex or SelectedItem properties. If the user has typed text into the combo box's text area, however, you cannot use the SelectedIndex or SelectedItem properties to get the text. The best way to get the user's input is with the Text property, which contains either the user's text input or the item selected from the list.

List Boxes Versus Combo Boxes

The following guidelines will help you decide when to use a list box and when to use a combo box.

- Use a drop-down or simple combo box when you want to provide the user a list of items from which to select but do not want to limit the user's input to the items on the list.
- Use a list box or a drop-down list combo box when you want to limit the user's selection to a list of items. The drop-down list combo box generally takes less space than a list box (because the list doesn't appear until the user clicks the down arrow), so use it when you want to conserve space on the form.

Scroll Bars

Scroll bars provide a visual way to adjust a value within a range of values. These types of controls display a slider that may be dragged along a track. Visual C# provides a horizontal scroll bar control named HScrollBar and a vertical scroll bar control named VScrollBar. Figure B-6 shows examples of each of these controls. You can find these controls in the Toolbox, in the *All Windows Forms* group.

Figure B-6 Horizontal and vertical scroll bars

Here is a summary of the important properties of each of these controls:

- The Value property is an integer value that is adjusted as the user moves the control's slider. (The default value is 0.)
- The Minimum property is the lower limit of the scrollable range. (The default value is 0.)

- The Maximum property is the upper limit of the scrollable range. (The default value is 100.)
- The LargeChange property is the integer amount by which the Value property changes when the user clicks the scroll bar area that lies to either side of the slider. This is also the amount by which the Value property changes when the user presses the Page Up or Page Down keys on the keyboard while the control has the focus. (The default value is 10.)
- The SmallChange property is the integer amount by which the Value property changes when the user clicks one of the arrows that appear at either end of a scroll bar control. (The default value is 1.)

When a horizontal scroll bar's slider is moved toward its left side, the Value property is decreased. When the slider is moved toward the scroll bar's right side, the Value property is increased. When a vertical scroll bar's slider is moved toward its top, the Value property is decreased. When the slider is moved toward the scroll bar's bottom, the Value property is increased.

When the user moves the slider on a scroll bar control, a Scroll event occurs. If you write a Scroll event handler for the control, the event handler will execute any time the slider is moved. To generate a code template for the Scroll event handler, simply double-click the scroll bar control in the *Designer*.

Figure B-7 shows the form in an example application that demonstrates the HScrollBar control. The HScrollBar control is named `hScrollBar`, and the label that displays the value is named `valueLabel`. The form's code is shown in Program B-1. This project can be found in the *Appendix B* folder in the Student Sample Programs. You will also find a similar project that demonstrates the VScrollBar control.

Figure B-7 HScrollBar Demo application form

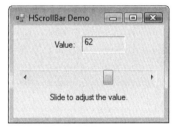

Program B-1 Form1 code in the *HScrollBar Demo* application

```
1 using System;
2 using System.Collections.Generic;
3 using System.ComponentModel;
4 using System.Data;
5 using System.Drawing;
6 using System.Linq;
7 using System.Text;
8 using System.Windows.Forms;
9
10 namespace HScrollBar_Demo
11 {
12     public partial class Form1 : Form
13     {
14         public Form1()
15         {
16             InitializeComponent();
17         }
18
```

```
19          private void Form1_Load(object sender, EventArgs e)
20          {
21              hScrollBar.Value = 0;
22              hScrollBar.Minimum = 0;
23              hScrollBar.Maximum = 100;
24              hScrollBar.LargeChange = 10;
25              hScrollBar.SmallChange = 1;
26
27              // Display the scroll bar's initial value
28              // in the label control.
29              valueLabel.Text = hScrollBar.Value.ToString();
30          }
31
32          private void hScrollBar_Scroll(object sender, ScrollEventArgs e)
33          {
34              // Display the scroll bar value.
35              valueLabel.Text = hScrollBar.Value.ToString();
36          }
37      }
38 }
```

Using a TabControl to Organize a Form

A TabControl allows you to create a user interface that is made of multiple pages, with each page containing its own set of controls. The TabControl appears as a container on a form, with one or more tabs positioned along its top edge. Each tab represents a different page, known as a TabPage. When the user clicks a tab, the control displays that page. You can find the TabControl in the Toolbox, in the *Containers* group.

When you insert a new TabControl, it will contain two TabPage controls named Tab-Page1 and TabPage2. This is shown in Figure B-8. Keep in mind that a TabControl is a container that contains TabPage controls. When you are working with a TabControl in the *Designer,* you can select the TabControl (the container) or you can select the individual TabPage controls that it contains. When you work with a TabControl for the first time, you should practice selecting each of the controls in the group so you know at all times which one you are working with.

Each of the TabPage controls has its own set of properties that can be changed in the *Properties* window. For example, to change the text that is displayed on a TabPage's tab, you change that TabPage control's Text property.

Figure B-8 A TabControl with two TabPages

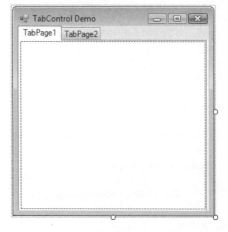

As previously mentioned, a TabControl contains two TabPage controls when first inserted in a form. To add more TabPages, select the TabControl and then select its Tab-Pages property. (Click the ellipses button [...] that appears next to the TabPages property window.) This opens the TabPage Collection Editor, shown in Figure B-9. This window allows you to add new TabPages, remove existing TabPages, and edit each TabPage properties.

Figure B-9 *TabPage Collection Editor* window

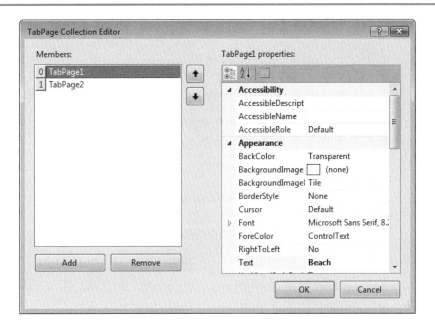

Figure B-10 shows an example application named *TabControl Demo* that can be found in the Student Sample Programs. The application's form has a TabControl with three Tab-Pages. Each TabPage contains a PicturePox control displaying an image. (There is no code in the application.)

Figure B-10 *TabControl Demo* application

The WebBrowser Control

The WebBrowser control (found in the *Common Controls* group in the *Toolbox*) allows you to display a Web page on an application's form. The control has a property named Url that can be set to a Web page's URL (Uniform Resource Locator). At run time, that Web page is displayed in the control.

At design time, you can use the Properties window to set the Url property. You simply type a valid URL such as http://www.gaddisbooks.com into the property's value box. If you want to set the Url property in code, you must create a Uri object (Uniform Resource Identifier) and assign that object to the property. Here is an example:

```
WebBrowser1.Url = new Uri("http://www.gaddisbooks.com");
```

Alternatively, you can call the control's Navigate method to display a Web page, as shown here:

```
WebBrowser1.Navigate(New Uri("http://www.gaddisbooks.com"));
```

In either of these approaches, an exception will be thrown if an invalid Web address is used.

When a Web page has finished loading, a DocumentCompleted event occurs. If you want to perform some action after a page has loaded, you can write a handler for this event. (Just double-click the WebBrowser control in the Designer window to create a code template for the DocumentCompleted event handler.)

Figure B-11 shows the *WebBrowser Demo* application in the Student Sample Programs. The application's form has a WebBrowser control named WebBrowser1, a TextBox control named urlTextBox, and a Button control named goButton. When the user clicks the goButton button, the application sets the WebBrowser1 control's Url property to the address that has been typed into the urlTextBox text box. The Form1 form's code is shown in Program B-2.

Figure B-11 *WebBrowser Demo* application

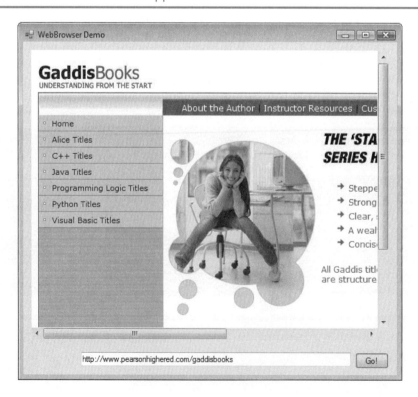

Program B-2 Form1 code in the *WebBrowser Demo* application

```
 1 using System;
 2 using System.Collections.Generic;
 3 using System.ComponentModel;
 4 using System.Data;
 5 using System.Drawing;
 6 using System.Linq;
 7 using System.Text;
 8 using System.Windows.Forms;
 9
10 namespace WebBrowser_Demo
11 {
12     public partial class Form1 : Form
13     {
14         public Form1()
15         {
16             InitializeComponent();
17         }
18
19         private void goButton_Click(object sender, EventArgs e)
20         {
21             try
22             {
23                 WebBrowser1.Url = new Uri(urlTextBox.Text);
24             }
25             catch (Exception ex)
26             {
27                 // Error message for an invalid Web address.
28                 MessageBox.Show(ex.Message);
29             }
30         }
31     }
32 }
```

The ErrorProvider Component

The ErrorProvider component (found in the *Components* group in the *Toolbox*) allows you to indicate that the user has entered an invalid value by displaying a blinking error icon (🔴) next to a specific control on the application's form. When the user hovers the mouse pointer over the icon, an error message is displayed as a tooltip.

When you insert an ErrorProvider component, it appears in the component tray at the bottom of the *Designer* window with a default name such as ErrorProvider1. In code, when the user enters an invalid value with a specific control, you call the ErrorProvider component's SetError method. Here is the general format for calling the method:

```
ErrorProviderName.SetError(ControlName, ErrorMessage);
```

In the general format, *ErrorProviderName* is the name of the ErrorProvider component, *ControlName* is the name of the control that you want to display the error icon next to, and *ErrorMessage* is the error message to associate with the error. Here is an example:

```
ErrorProvider1.SetError(payRateTextBox, "Invalid pay rate");
```

This statement uses the ErrorProvider1 component to display an error icon next to the payRateTextBox control. When the user hovers the mouse pointer over the error icon, the message *Invalid pay rate* is displayed as a tooltip.

The error icon will remain displayed next to the specified control until you call the `SetError` method again, passing the same control name as the first argument and an empty string as the second argument. Here is an example:

```
ErrorProvider1.SetError(payRateTextBox, "");
```

Figure B-12 shows the *ErrorProvider Demo* application in the Student Sample Programs. The user enters a number of hours in the `hoursTextBox` control, a numeric pay rate in the `payRateTextBox` control, and then clicks the `calcButton` control to calculate gross pay. If a nonnumeric value is entered for either the hours or the pay rate, an ErrorProvider component displays an error icon next to the control containing the invalid value. In Figure B-12 the user has entered an invalid value for the pay rate. The Form1 form's code is shown in Program B-3.

Figure B-12 *ErrorProvider Demo* application

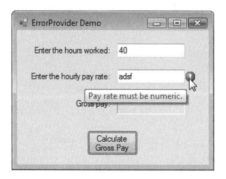

Program B-3 Form1 code in the *ErrorProvider Demo* application

```
 1 using System;
 2 using System.Collections.Generic;
 3 using System.ComponentModel;
 4 using System.Data;
 5 using System.Drawing;
 6 using System.Linq;
 7 using System.Text;
 8 using System.Windows.Forms;
 9
10 namespace ErrorProvider_Demo
11 {
12     public partial class Form1 : Form
13     {
14         public Form1()
15         {
16             InitializeComponent();
17         }
18
19         private void calcButton_Click(object sender, EventArgs e)
20         {
21             // Variables for hours, pay rate, and gross pay
22             decimal hours, payRate, grossPay;
23
24             // Clear any existing errors.
25             ErrorProvider1.SetError(hoursTextBox, "");
26             ErrorProvider1.SetError(payRateTextBox, "");
27
28             // Get values and calculate gross pay.
29             if (decimal.TryParse(hoursTextBox.Text, out hours))
```

```
30                    {
31                        if (decimal.TryParse(payRateTextBox.Text, out payRate))
32                        {
33                            // Calculate the gross pay.
34                            grossPay = hours * payRate;
35
36                            // Display the gross pay.
37                            grossPayLabel.Text = grossPay.ToString("c");
38                        }
39                        else
40                        {
41                            // Invalid pay rate
42                            ErrorProvider1.SetError(payRateTextBox,
43                                "Pay rate must be numeric.");
44                        }
45                    }
46                    else
47                    {
48                        // Invalid hours
49                        ErrorProvider1.SetError(hoursTextBox,
50                            "Hours must be numeric.");
51                    }
52                }
53            }
54 }
```

Using the SelectionStart and SelectionLength Properties to Select Text in a TextBox

TextBox controls have two properties, SelectionStart and SelectionLength, which you can use to make the process of correcting invalid input more convenient for the user. When the user enters an invalid value, you can display an error message and then use these properties to automatically select the invalid input for the user. Then, the user can immediately retype the input without having to use the mouse to select the TextBox.

The SelectionStart and SelectionLength properties can be used in code to automatically select the text in a text box. The SelectionStart property holds the position of the first selected character in the text box. The SelectionLength property holds the number of characters that are selected. For example, assume that nameTextBox is a text box and look at the following code.

```
nameTextBox.Focus();
nameTextBox.SelectionStart = 0;
nameTextBox.SelectionLength = 5;
```

The first statement gives nameTextBox the focus. The second statement establishes that the first character in nameTextBox (which is at position 0) is the first selected character. The next statement establishes that five characters will be selected. Together, the statements cause the first five characters in nameTextBox to be selected.

So, how do you use similar code to select all the text in a TextBox? You use the TextBox's Length property to get the length of the text and assign that value to the TextBox's SelectionLength property. Here is an example:

```
nameTextBox.Focus();
nameTextBox.SelectionStart = 0;
nameTextBox.SelectionLength = nameTextBox.Text.Length;
```

After these statements execute, all the contents of the nameTextBox control are selected. When the user types a key, that keystroke immediately erases all the selected text.

Figure B-13 shows the *Selected Text Demo* application in the Student Sample Program files. This is a modified version of the *ErrorProvider Demo* application previously shown. In this version, after the ErrorProvider displays an error icon, the content of the TextBox containing the invalid input is automatically selected. In the figure, the user has entered an invalid value for the hours. The application's code is shown in Program B-4.

Figure B-13 *Selected Text Demo* application

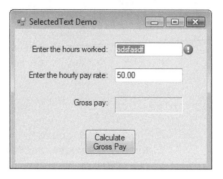

Program B-4 Form1 code in the *Selected Text Demo* application

```
1 using System;
2 using System.Collections.Generic;
3 using System.ComponentModel;
4 using System.Data;
5 using System.Drawing;
6 using System.Linq;
7 using System.Text;
8 using System.Windows.Forms;
9
10 namespace Selected_Text_Demo
11 {
12     public partial class Form1 : Form
13     {
14         public Form1()
15         {
16             InitializeComponent();
17         }
18
19         private void calcButton_Click(object sender, EventArgs e)
20         {
21             // Variables for hours, pay rate, and gross pay
22             decimal hours, payRate, grossPay;
23
24             // Clear any existing errors.
25             ErrorProvider1.SetError(hoursTextBox, "");
26             ErrorProvider1.SetError(payRateTextBox, "");
27
28             // Get values and calculate gross pay.
29             if (decimal.TryParse(hoursTextBox.Text, out hours))
30             {
31                 if (decimal.TryParse(payRateTextBox.Text, out payRate))
32                 {
33                     // Calculate the gross pay.
34                     grossPay = hours * payRate;
```

```
35
36                      // Display the gross pay.
37                      grossPayLabel.Text = grossPay.ToString("c");
38                  }
39                  else
40                  {
41                      // Invalid pay rate
42                      ErrorProvider1.SetError(payRateTextBox,
43                          "Pay rate must be numeric.");
44
45                      // Select the invalid input.
46                      payRateTextBox.Focus();
47                      payRateTextBox.SelectionStart = 0;
48                      payRateTextBox.SelectionLength =
49                          payRateTextBox.Text.Length;
50                  }
51              }
52              else
53              {
54                  // Invalid hours
55                  ErrorProvider1.SetError(hoursTextBox,
56                      "Hours must be numeric.");
57
58                  // Select the invalid input.
59                  hoursTextBox.Focus();
60                  hoursTextBox.SelectionStart = 0;
61                  hoursTextBox.SelectionLength =
62                      hoursTextBox.Text.Length;
63              }
64          }
65      }
66 }
```

Creating a Menu System

A **menu system** is a collection of commands organized in one or more drop-down menus. In Visual Studio, the **menu designer** allows you to visually create a custom menu system for any form in an application. Before you learn how to use the menu designer, you must learn about the typical components of a menu system. Look at the Example Menu System shown in Figure B-14.

Figure B-14 Example menu system

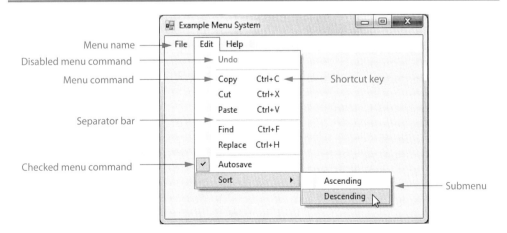

The menu system in the figure consists of the following items.

- **Menu names.** Each drop-down menu has a name. The menu names are listed on a menu strip that appears just below the form's title bar. The menu names in Figure B-14 are *File*, *Edit*, and *Help*. The user may activate a menu by clicking the menu name. In the figure, the *Edit* menu has been activated.
- **Menu command.** Menus have commands. The user selects a command by clicking it, entering its access key, or entering its shortcut key.
- **Shortcut key.** A shortcut key is a key or combination of keys that cause a menu command to execute. Shortcut keys are shown on a menu to the right of their corresponding commands. For example, in Figure B-14, Ctrl+C is the shortcut key for the *Copy* command.
- **Disabled menu command.** You can cause a menu command to be disabled when you do not want the user to select it. A disabled menu command appears in dim lettering (grayed out) and cannot be selected. In Figure B-14, the *Undo* command is disabled.
- **Checked menu command.** A checked menu command is usually one that turns an option on or off. A checkmark appears to the left of the command, indicating the option is turned on. When no checkmark appears to the left of the command, the option is turned off. The user toggles a checked menu command each time he or she selects it. In Figure B-14, *Autosave* is a checked menu command.
- **Submenu.** Some of the commands on a menu are actually the names of submenus. You can tell when a command is the name of a submenu because a right arrow appears to its right. Activating the name of a submenu causes the submenu to appear. For example, in Figure B-14, clicking the *Sort* command causes a submenu to appear.
- **Separator bar.** A separator bar is a horizontal bar used to separate groups of commands on a menu. In Figure B-14, separator bars are used to separate the *Copy*, *Cut*, and *Paste* commands into one group, the *Find* and *Replace* commands into another group, and the *Sort* command in a box by itself. Separator bars are used only as visual aids and cannot be selected by the user.

The MenuStrip Control

An application's menu system is constructed with a **MenuStrip control**. When your form is displayed in the *Designer*, find the *Menus & Toolbars* section of the *Toolbox* window and double-click the *MenuStrip* icon. A MenuStrip control will appear in the component tray at the bottom of the *Designer*, with a default name of MenuStrip1.

When the MenuStrip control is selected, you will see the words *Type Here* displayed in a strip at the top of the form. This is the **menu designer**, a tool that allows you to visually edit the contents of the menu. You simply click inside this strip and type the names of the items that you want to appear in the menu. Figure B-15 shows an example where a *File* menu has been added.

Figure B-15 Inserting text into a menu item

Each item that you create in a menu system is a **ToolStripMenuItem object**. When you select a menu item in the menu designer, you see its properties listed in the *Properties* window. The text that you typed for the item in the menu designer will appear in the object's Text property.

ToolStripMenuItem objects are given default names that are based on the text that you typed for the object in the menu designer. For example, if you type the text "File" for a menu item, the object's name will be `fileToolStripMenuItem`. For another example, it you type the text "Help" for a menu item, the object's name will be `helpToolStripMenuItem`.

ToolStripMenuItem objects also respond to events. You can make a menu functional by writing Click event procedures for its objects.

How to Use the Menu Designer

Once you have placed a MenuStrip control in a form's component tray, you can use the menu designer to create menu items. Start the menu designer by selecting the MenuStrip control. Figure B-16 shows a form with a MenuStrip control selected in the component tray, and the menu designer started. The menu designer appears on the form in the location that the menu system will appear.

Figure B-16 MenuStrip control selected and menu designer started

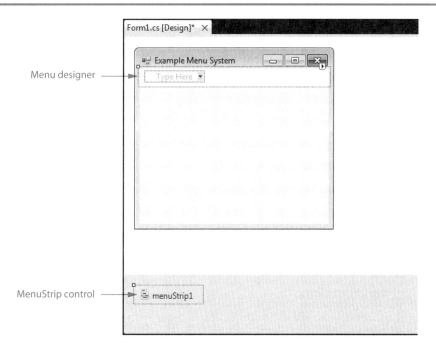

Notice in Figure B-16 that the words *Type Here* appear in a small box in the menu designer. This marks the position of the first menu item. A ToolStripMenuItem object is automatically created when you type text into the box. The text you type is stored in the item's Text property and is displayed on the menu strip. Figure B-17 shows the menu designer after the word *File* has been typed as the text for the first menu item.

Figure B-17 MenuStrip object with *File* as its text

Notice that the menu designer now shows two new *Type Here* boxes, one below and one to the right of the first object. Simply click in one of the boxes to select it and then type the text that you wish to appear at that position. Figure B-18 shows the menu designer with a more complete menu system. The menu system has *File*, *Edit*, and *Help* menus. The *Edit* menu is displayed.

Figure B-18 Menu designer with many items

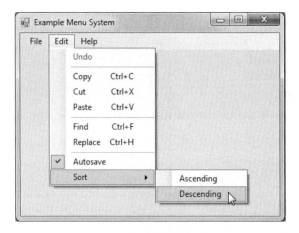

Shortcut Keys

As previously stated, a shortcut key is a key or combination of keys that cause a menu command to execute. Table B-1 lists some commonly used shortcut keys in Windows applications.

Table B-1 Some commonly used shortcut keys in Windows applications

Shortcut Key	Command
Ctrl + S	Save
Ctrl + P	Print
Ctrl + C	Copy
Ctrl + X	Cut
Ctrl + V	Paste

Shortcut keys are shown on a menu to the right of their corresponding commands. To create a shortcut key for a menu item, click the down arrow that appears next to the **ShortcutKeys** property in the *Properties* window. A dialog appears, as shown in Figure B-19. The *Key* drop-down list shows all the available shortcut keys, and allows you to select a key from the list. The dialog also allows you to select the Ctrl, Shift, or Alt key (or any combination of these). For example, if you want to assign Ctrl+S as a shortcut key, you would select the *S* key in the drop-down list and place a check next to *Ctrl*.

Figure B-19 The ShortcutKeys property

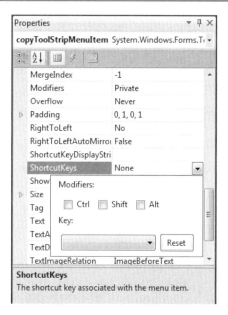

You must also make sure that the **ShowShortcut property** is set to *True*. When set to *False*, the item's shortcut key is not displayed.

Checked Menu Items

Some programs have menu items that simply turn a feature on or off. For example, suppose you are creating an application that functions as an alarm clock and you want the user to be able to turn the alarm on or off with a menu item. A common approach would be to have a checked menu item for the alarm. When a checkmark appears next to the menu item, it indicates that the alarm is on. When the checkmark is not displayed next to the menu item, it indicates that the alarm is off. When the user clicks the menu item, it toggles its state between on and off. This type of menu item is called a checked menu item.

To give a menu item the ability to become checked or unchecked when it is clicked by the user, you set the item's **CheckOnClick property** to *True*. You can then set the **Checked property** to either *True* or *False* to specify how the item should initially appear when the application runs. If you set the Checked property to *True*, the item will appear with a checkmark next to it. If you set the Checked property to *False*, no checkmark will be shown.

In code you can use the Checked property to determine whether a menu item is checked. If the Checked property is set to *True*, it means the item is checked. If the Checked property is set to *False*, it means the item is unchecked. The following code shows an example.

This code tests the Checked property of a menu item named `alarmToolStripMenuItem`. If the item is checked, a message box is displayed.

```
if (alarmToolStripMenuItem.Checked)
{
    MessageBox.Show("WAKE UP!");
}
```

Disabled Menu Items

A disabled menu item appears dimmed, or grayed out, and may not be selected by the user. You may disable a menu item by setting its Enabled property to *False*. For example, applications that provide *Cut*, *Copy*, and *Paste* commands usually disable the *Paste* command until something is cut or copied. So, the *Paste* menu item's Enabled property can be set to False at design time (in the *Properties* window) and then set to `true` in code after the *Cut* or *Copy* commands have been used. Assuming that the *Paste* menu item is named `pasteToolStripMenuItem`, the following code enables it:

```
pasteToolStripMenuItem.Enabled = true;
```

Separator Bars

You can insert a separator bar into a menu in either of the following ways:

- Right-click an existing menu item. On the pop-up menu that appears, select *Insert* and then select *Separator*. A separator bar is inserted above the menu item.
- Type a hyphen (-) as a menu item's Text property.

Submenus

When an existing menu item is selected in the menu designer, a *Type Here* box is displayed to its right. Figure B-20 shows an example. This box allows you to create a submenu item. When you create a submenu, a right arrow (▶) is automatically displayed next to the menu item that is the parent of the submenu.

Figure B-20 Creating a submenu

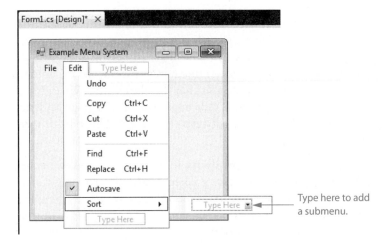

Type here to add a submenu.

Inserting Menu Items in an Existing Menu

If you need to insert a new menu item above an existing menu item, start the menu designer and then right-click the existing menu item. On the pop-up menu that appears, select *Insert* and then select *MenuItem*. A new menu item is inserted above the existing menu item. If you need to insert a new menu item at the bottom of an existing menu, start the menu designer and simply select the desired menu or submenu. A *Type Here* box automatically appears at the bottom.

Deleting Menu Items

To delete a menu item, start the menu designer and perform one of the following procedures:

- Right-click the menu item you wish to delete. On the pop-up menu, select *Delete*.
- Select the menu item you wish to delete and then press Delete on the keyboard.

Rearranging Menu Items

You can move a menu item by clicking and dragging. Simply select it in the menu designer and drag it to the desired location.

ToolStripMenuItem Click Events

You do not have to write code to display a menu or a submenu. When the user clicks a menu item that displays a menu or a submenu, Visual Studio automatically causes the menu or submenu to appear.

If a menu item does not have a menu or submenu to display, you make it functional by providing a Click event handler for it. For example, assume a menu system has a *File* menu with an *Exit* command, which causes the application to end. The menu item for the *Exit* command is named `exitToolStripMenuItem`. Here is the code for the object's Click event handler:

```
private void exitToolStripMenuItem_Click(object sender, EventArgs e)
{
    // Close the form.
    this.Close();
}
```

To write a Click event handler for a menu item, start the menu designer and then double-click the desired menu item. An empty event handler is created.

Standard Menu Items

Although not all applications have identical menu systems, it is standard for most applications to have the following menu items:

- A *File* menu as the leftmost item on the menu strip.
- An *Exit* command on the *File* menu. This command ends the application.
- A *Help* menu as the rightmost item on the menu strip.
- An *About* command on the *Help* menu. This command displays a window giving basic information about the application.

You should always add these items to your menu systems because most Windows users expect to see them. You should also assign shortcut keys to the most commonly used commands. Study the menu system in an application such as Microsoft Word or Microsoft Excel to become familiar with a typical menu design.

C   ASCII/Unicode Characters

The following table lists the ASCII (American Standard Code for Information Interchange) character set, which is the same as the first 127 Unicode character codes. This group of character codes is known as the *Latin Subset of Unicode*. The code columns show character codes and the character columns show the corresponding characters. For example, the code 65 represents the letter *A*. Note that the first 31 codes, and code 127, represent control characters that are not printable.

Code	Character	Code	Character	Code	Character	Code	Character	Code	Character
0	NUL	26	SUB	52	4	78	N	104	h
1	SOH	27	Escape	53	5	79	O	105	i
2	STX	28	FS	54	6	80	P	106	j
3	ETX	29	GS	55	7	81	Q	107	k
4	EOT	30	RS	56	8	82	R	108	l
5	ENQ	31	US	57	9	83	S	109	m
6	ACK	32	(Space)	58	:	84	T	110	n
7	BEL	33	!	59	;	85	U	111	o
8	Backspace	34	"	60	<	86	V	112	p
9	HTab	35	#	61	=	87	W	113	q
10	Line Feed	36	$	62	>	88	X	114	r
11	VTab	37	%	63	?	89	Y	115	s
12	Form Feed	38	&	64	@	90	Z	116	t
13	CR	39	'	65	A	91	[	117	u
14	SO	40	(	66	B	92	\	118	v
15	SI	41	)	67	C	93	]	119	w
16	DLE	42	*	68	D	94	^	120	x
17	DC1	43	+	69	E	95	_	121	y
18	DC2	44	,	70	F	96	`	122	z
19	DC3	45	-	71	G	97	a	123	{
20	DC4	46	.	72	H	98	b	124	|
21	NAK	47	/	73	I	99	c	125	}
22	SYN	48	0	74	J	100	d	126	~
23	ETB	49	1	75	K	101	e	127	DEL
24	CAN	50	2	76	L	102	f		
25	EM	51	3	77	M	103	g		

D Answers to Checkpoint Questions

Chapter 1

1.1 A program is a set of instructions that a computer follows to perform a task.

1.2 Hardware is all the physical devices, or components, that a computer is made of.

1.3 The central processing unit (CPU), main memory, secondary storage devices, input devices, and output devices

1.4 The CPU

1.5 Main memory

1.6 Secondary storage

1.7 Input device

1.8 Output device

1.9 Operating system

1.10 Utility program

1.11 Application software

1.12 1 byte

1.13 A bit

1.14 Binary

1.15 It is an encoding scheme that uses a set of 128 numeric codes to represent the English letters, various punctuation marks, and other characters. These numeric codes are used to store characters in a computer's memory. (ASCII stands for the American Standard Code for Information Interchange.)

1.16 Unicode

1.17 Digital data is data that is stored in binary, and a digital device is any device that works with binary data.

1.18 Machine language

1.19 Main memory, or RAM

1.20 The fetch-decode-execute cycle

1.21 It is an alternative to machine language. Instead of using binary numbers for instructions, assembly language uses short words that are known as mnemonics.

1.22 A high-level language

1.23 Syntax

1.24 A compiler

1.25 An interpreter

1.26 A syntax error

1.27 The part of the computer with which the user interacts

1.28 A command line interface requires the user to type commands. If a command is typed correctly, it is executed and the results are displayed. If a command is not typed correctly, an error message is displayed.

1.29 The program

1.30 A program that responds to events that are caused by the user, such as the clicking of a mouse

1.31 A program component that contains data and performs operations

1.32 Object oriented

1.33 An object can (1) store data in fields or properties and (2) perform operations called methods.

1.34 Controls

1.35 To perform some task

1.36 Code that describes a particular type of object

1.37 A collection of classes and other code that can be used, along with a programming language such as C#, to create programs for the Windows operating system

1.38 When a program needs specific objects that cannot be found in the .NET framework

1.39 1. *Understand the program's purpose*
      2. *Design the graphical user interface (GUI)*
      3. *Design the program's logic*
      4. *Write the code*
      5. *Correct syntax errors*
      6. *Test the program and correct logic errors*

1.40 A set of well-defined logical steps that must be taken to perform a task

1.41 An algorithm that is written out in this manner, in plain English statements

1.42 A diagram that graphically depicts the steps of an algorithm

1.43 • Oval—terminal symbol
      • Parallelogram—input or output
      • Rectangle—processing

1.49 A collection of files that belong to a single application

1.50 A container that holds one or more Visual C# projects

1.44 The *Solution Explorer* window allows you to navigate among the files in a Visual C# project.

1.45 When you are creating a Visual C# application, you use the *Properties* window to examine and change a control's properties.

1.46 The standard toolbar contains buttons that execute frequently used commands

1.47 The Toolbox is a window that allows you to select the controls that you want to use in an application's user interface. The toolbar contains buttons that execute frequently used Visual Studio commands.

1.48 A small rectangular box that pops up when you hover the mouse pointer over a button on the toolbar or in the *Toolbox* for a few seconds

1.49 A Visual C# project consists of several files. You can think of a project as a collection of files that belong to a single application.

1.50 A solution is a container that holds one or more Visual C# projects. If you are developing applications for a large organization, you might find it convenient to store several related projects together in the same solution.

Chapter 2

2.1 An empty form in the *Designer*

2.2 It is enclosed by a thin dotted line called a bounding box.

2.3 To resize an object's bounding box using the mouse

2.4 A name

2.5 To display the properties of the currently selected object

2.6 Causes the properties to be displayed in alphabetical order

2.7 Causes the properties to be displayed in groups

2.8 The text that is displayed in the form's title bar

2.9 The form's width and height in pixels

2.10 A scrollable list of controls that you can add to a form

2.11 To add a control to a form, you simply find it in the Toolbox and then double-click it

2.12 What the button will do when it is clicked

2.13 The first character must be one of the letters *a–z* or *A–Z* or an underscore character. After the first character, you may use the letters *a–z* or *A–Z*, the digits 0–9, or underscores. The name cannot contain spaces.

2.14 The camelCase naming convention

2.15 Source code

2.16 If you want your application to perform any meaningful actions you must write code.

2.17 The application's start-up code

2.18 Code that is associated with the Form1 form

2.19 Namespaces, classes, and methods

2.20 A container that holds classes

2.21 braces ({})

2.22 Click the tab for the desired window.

2.23 Double-click the button control in the *Designer.*

2.24 An event that occurs when an application is running and the user clicks a control

2.25 `MessageBox.Show`

2.26 Data that is literally written into a program

2.27 Double quotation marks

2.28 Press the F5 key on the keyboard, or click the *Start Debugging* button on the toolbar.

2.29 The *Common Controls* group

2.30 The Text property

2.31 The Font property

2.32 None

2.33 Click the down-arrow button that appears next to the property's value. Select the desired value from the list.

2.34 The AutoSize property

2.35 The TextAlign property

2.36 Place a Label control on the form at the location where you want the result to be displayed. Erase the contents of the Label control's Text property. In the application's code, you write the necessary statements to perform the calculation and then you store the result of the calculation in the Label control's Text property.

2.37 It clears the text that is displayed in a Label control.

2.38 To display a graphic image on a form

2.39 In the *Common Controls* group

2.40 Use its Image property to specify the image that it will display.

2.41 Normal

2.42 The image is uniformly resized to fit in the PictureBox without losing its original aspect ratio.

2.43 Create a Click event handler for the PictureBox control that displays the image.

2.44 Yes, if a control's Visible property is set to False, the control can still be seen at design time, but during run time, the control will not be visible.

2.45 Comments are brief notes that are placed in a program's source code to explain how parts of the program work.

2.46 A Line comment begins with two forward slashes and appears on one line. A Block comment starts with a forward slash and an asterisk and ends with an asterisk followed by a forward slash and can occupy multiple lines.

2.47 Be careful not to reverse the beginning and ending symbols, and don't forget the ending symbol.

2.48 Programmers commonly use blank lines and indentations in their code to create a sense of visual organization; this makes the code easier to understand and to read.

2.49 `this.Close();`

2.50 It is underlined with a jagged line in the code editor.

2.51 A description of the error will pop up in a tooltip window.

2.52 A window appears that displays the errors.

Chapter 3

3.1 A TextBox control

3.2 Retrieve the contents of the control's Text property

3.3 A string

3.4 Assign an empty string (`""`) to the Text property.

3.5 To store a value in memory

3.6 `string myFavoriteFood = "pizza";`

3.7 a. String
   b. Real number
   c. String
   d. Integer

3.8 a. Legal
   b. Illegal; spaces are not allowed in variable names.
   c. Legal
   d. Illegal; first character of the variable name cannot be a number.

3.9 The string `"Hello!"`

3.10 While the event is executing; then it is deleted.

3.11 The statement will result in an error.

3.12 Yes, `string` variables can be assigned only string values.

3.13 `string name, city, state;`

3.14 a. `decimal`
   b. `int`
   c. `double`
   d. `decimal`
   e. `int`

3.15 b, variables of the `int` data type can be assigned only whole-number values.

3.16 `int dollars = (int)deposit;`

3.17 6

3.18 `length` and `width`

3.19 1. Perform any operations that are enclosed in parentheses.
   2. Perform any multiplications, divisions, or modulus operations as they appear from left to right
   3. Perform any additions or subtractions as they appear from left to right.

3.20 ```
decimal pricePerFoot = 2.99m;
decimal boardLength = 10.5;
decimal totalCost = boardLength * pricePerFoot;
or
decimal pricePerFoot = 2.99m;
double boardLength = 10.5;
decimal totalCost = (decimal)boardLength * pricePerFoot;
```

3.21 9

3.22 70

3.23 2.5

3.24 a. `count += 1;`
b. `amount -= 5;`
c. `radius *= 10;`
d. `length /= 2;`

3.25 `int.Parse`

3.26 a. `decimal.Parse("90.5");`
b. `decimal.Parse(grandTotal);`
c. `decimal.Parse("50");`
d. `decimal.Parse(priceTextBox.Text);`

3.27 The result will be an error because numeric values cannot be assigned to strings.

3.28 a. `MessageBox.Show(grandTotal.ToString());`
b. `MessageBox.Show(highScore.ToString());`
c. `MessageBox.Show(sum.ToString());`
d. `MessageBox.Show(width.ToString());`

3.29 `resultLabel.Text = result.ToString();`

3.30 `MessageBox.Show(salary.ToString("c"));`

3.31 a. `"P"` or `"p"` for percent format
b. `"E"` or `"e"` for exponential scientific format
c. `"C"` or `"c"` for currency format
d. `"N"` or `"n"` for number format
e. `"F"` or `"f"` for fixed-point scientific format

3.32 12

3.33 `"d5"`

3.34 `millimeters.ToString("f4");`

3.35 An unexpected error that occurs while a program is running, such as user input that is not in the correct format

3.36 Click the Stop Debugging button or by pressing [Shift] + [F5].

3.37 Statements that can potentially throw an exception

3.38 If a statement in the try block throws an exception

3.39 Assign a name to the exception object when writing the catch clause of a `try-catch` statement and then use the Message property of the exception object in the catch block to display the default error message in a message box.
```

3.40
```
try
{
    int value1;    // To hold value 1.
    int value2;    // To hold value 2.
    int sum;       // To hold the sum.

    // Get the values as input from the user.
    value1 = int.Parse(value1TextBox.Text);
    value2 = int.Parse(value2TextBox.Text);

    // Calculate the sum of value 1 and value 2.
    sum = value1 + value2;

    // Display the result in the Label control.
    sumLabel.Text = sum.ToString();
}
catch (Exception ex)
{
    // Display the default error message.
    MessageBox.Show(ex.Message);
}
```

3.41 They make programs more self-explanatory and allow for widespread changes to easily be made to the program.

3.42 `const double DISCOUNT = 0.9;`

3.43 At the top of a class declaration, before any methods

3.44 It's a good programming practice to make fields `private` because `private` fields are hidden from code outside the class. That prevents code outside the class from changing the values of a class's fields and helps prevent bugs from creeping into your program.

3.45 A local variable exists only while the method in which it is declared is executing, but a field exists as long as the form exists.

3.46 `private const decimal INTEREST_RATE = 0.059m;`

3.47 `double product = Math.Pow(12.0, 2.0);`

3.48 `Math.Max`

3.49 `Math.Min`

3.50 The button's Click event handler will execute.

3.51 Click *View* on the Visual Studio menu bar and then click *Tab Order*. Exit tab order selection mode by pressing the Esc key.

3.52 `numberTextBox.Focus();`

3.53 In the Text property, place an ampersand (&) before the character you wish to use as the access key.

3.54 In the Text property, place two ampersand (&&) characters where you would like the single ampersand to appear on the Button control.

3.55 `resultLabel.BackColor = Color.White;`
`resultLabel.ForeColor = Color.Red;`

3.56 None, Tile, Center, Stretch, and Zoom

3.57 The controls inside the GroupBox control are also deleted.

3.58 The TabIndex values of controls inside a group box are organized relative to the GroupBox control's TabIndex property.

3.59 A Panel cannot display a title and does not have a Text property. A Panel's border can be specified by its BorderStyle property.

Chapter 4

4.1 A logical design that controls the order in which a set of statements execute

4.2 It is a program structure that can execute a set of statements only under certain circumstances.

4.3 A decision structure that provides a single alternative path of execution. If the condition that is being tested is true, the program takes the alternative path.

4.4 An expression that can be evaluated as either true or false

4.5 You can determine whether one value is greater than, less than, greater than or equal to, less than or equal to, equal to, or not equal to another value.

4.6
```
if (y == 20)
{
    x = 0;
}
```

4.7
```
if (sales >= 10000)
{
    commissionRate = 0.2;
}
```

4.8 A dual alternative decision structure has two possible paths of execution—one path is taken if a condition is true and the other path is taken if the condition is false.

4.9 When the Boolean expression is false

4.10
```
if (sales >= 50000)
{
    commissionRate = 0.2;
}
else
{
    commissionRate = 0.1;
}
```

4.11
```
if (number == 1)
{
    MessageBox.Show("One");
}
else if (number == 2)
{
    MessageBox.Show("Two");
}
else if (number == 3)
{
    MessageBox.Show("Three");
}
else
{
    MessageBox.Show("Unknown");
}
```

4.12 It is an expression that is created by using a logical operator to combine two Boolean subexpressions.

4.13 F; T; F; F; T; T; T; F; F; T

4.14 T; F; T; T; T

4.15 The `&&` operator: If the expression on the left side of the `&&` operator is false, the expression on the right side will not be checked.

The || operator: If the expression on the left side of the || operator is true, the expression on the right side will not be checked.

4.16
```
if (speed >= 0 && speed <= 200)
{
    MessageBox.Show("The number is valid");
}
```

4.17
```
if (speed < 0 || speed > 200)
{
    MessageBox.Show("The number is not valid");
}
```

4.18 `true` or `false`

4.19 A variable that signals when some condition exists in the program

4.20 z is not less than a.

4.21 Boston; New York

4.22 `true`

4.23 The variable specified by the second argument.

4.24 0

4.25 It specifies an output variable. An output variable is a variable that is passed as an argument to a method, and when the method is finished, a value is stored in the variable.

4.26 Only one

4.27 All of them can potentially be selected.

4.28 When a CheckBox or RadioButton control is selected, or checked, its Checked property is set to True.

4.29
```
switch (choice)
{
    case 1:
        MessageBox.Show("You chose 1.");
        break;
    case 2:
        MessageBox.Show("You chose 2.");
        break;
    case 3:
        MessageBox.Show("You chose 3.");
        break;
    default:
        MessageBox.Show("Make another choice.");
        break;
}
```

4.30 You select the Items property and then use the String Collection Editor to enter items.

4.31. When the user selects an item in a ListBox, the item is stored in the ListBox's SelectedItem property.

4.32 When the user selects an item in a ListBox, the item's index is stored in the ListBox's SelectedIndex property. If no item is selected in the ListBox, the SelectedIndex property is set to –1.

Chapter 5

5.1 You call the control's `Items.Add` method.

5.2 The control's Items.Count property holds the number of items stored in the ListBox.

5.3 You call the control's `Items.Clear` method.

5.4 An execution of the statements in the body of the loop

5.5 A variable that is used to store the number of iterations that a loop has performed

5.6 A loop that tests its Boolean expression before performing an iteration

5.7 Before

5.8 A loop that has no way of stopping and repeats until the program is interrupted

5.9 6; 5

5.10 Four times

5.11 Initialization, test, and update

5.12 Here is one possible set of answers:
```
a. count = 0;
b. count < 50;
c. count++
d. for (count = 0; count < 50; count++)
   {
       MessagaBox.Show("I love to program");
   }
```

Here is another possible set of answers:
```
a. count = 1;
b. count <= 50;
c. count++
d. for (count = 1; count <= 50; count++)
   {
       MessagaBox.Show("I love to program");
   }
```

5.13 It would display the numbers 1, 2, 3, 4, and 5 in message boxes.

5.14 It would display the numbers 0, 100, 200, 300, 400, and 500 in message boxes.

5.15 A loop that tests its Boolean expression after it performs an iteration

5.16 The `while` loop is a pretest loop, and the `do-while` loop is a posttest loop. The do-while loop will always iterate at least one time.

5.17 One time

5.18 A file that data is written to. It is called an output file because the program stores output in it.

5.19 A file from which data is read; it is called an input file because the program gets input from the file.

5.20 Open the file, process the file, and close the file.

5.21 A text file contains data that has been encoded as text, using a scheme such as Unicode. A binary file contains data that has not been converted to text.

5.22 Sequential and direct (or random) access. When you work with a sequential access file, you access data from the beginning of the file to the end of the file. When you work with a direct access file, you can jump directly to any piece of data in the file without reading the data that comes before it.

5.23 `StreamWriter`

5.24 `StreamReader`

5.25 Its contents are erased.

5.26 Its contents are not erased.

5.27 The `WriteLine` method writes an item of data to a file and then writes a newline character. The `Write` method writes an item of data to a text file without writing a newline character.

5.28 `File.OpenText`

5.29 A file's read position marks the location of the next item that will be read from the file. When an input file is opened, its read position is initially set to the first item in the file.

5.30 With the `StreamReader` class's `ReadLine` method

5.31 With the `StreamReader` or `StreamWriter` class's `Close` method

5.32 Loop B is written in the correct form.

5.33 Most users of Windows are accustomed to using a dialog box to browse their disk for a file to open or for a location to save a file. An *Open* and/or *Save As* dialog box allows the user of your application to easily specify a file's name and location.

5.34 *InitialDirectory*: Specifies the directory to be initially displayed

Title: Specifies the text displayed in the title bar

Filename: When the user selects a file with the *Open* dialog box, the file's path and filename are stored in the control's Filename property. When the user specifies a location and filename with the *Save As* dialog box, the file's path and filename are stored in the control's Filename property.

5.35 If you call the `Next` method with no arguments, the method returns an integer that is somewhere between 0 and 2,147,483,647. Alternatively, you can pass an argument that specifies an upper limit to the generated number's range.

5.36 A random floating-point number between 0.0 and 1.0 (not including 1.0)

5.37 ```
Random rand = new Random();
randomNumber = rand.Next(100) + 1;
```

5.38  ```
Random rand = new Random();
randomNumber = rand.Next(300) + 100;
```

5.39 The system time, retrieved from the computer's internal clock

5.40 It will always generate the same series of random numbers.

5.41 When a form is loaded into memory, before it is displayed.

5.42 Double-click any area of the form in the *Designer* window, where there is no other control.

Chapter 6

6.1 A `void` method simply executes a group of statements and then terminates. A value-returning method returns a value to the statement that called it.

6.2 A header and a body.

6.3 You are causing the method to execute.

6.4 Control of the program goes back to the part of the program that called the method.

6.5 • The overall task that the program is to perform is broken down into a series of subtasks.
   • Each subtask is examined to determine whether it can be further broken down into more subtasks. This step is repeated until no more subtasks can be identified.
   • Once all the subtasks have been identified, they are written in code.

6.6 A method uses arguments to pass data into the method using parameter variables.

6.7 Assignment compatibility applies to argument passing in the following ways:
   • You can pass only string arguments into `string` parameters.
   • You can pass `int` arguments into `int` parameters, but you cannot pass `double` or `decimal` arguments into `int` parameters.
   • You can pass either `double` or `int` arguments into `double` parameters, but you cannot pass `decimal` values into `double` parameters.
   • You can pass either `decimal` or `int` arguments to `decimal` parameters, but you cannot pass `double` arguments into `decimal` parameters.

6.8 The scope of a parameter variable is limited to the method in which it is declared.

6.9 A named argument is a parameter variable with a default value.

6.10 A copy is passed into the parameter variable, and it does not modify the original argument.

6.11 A reference parameter is a reference to the argument it was passed. Any changes done to the parameter are also done to the argument.

6.12 The calling method can communicate with the called method by passing an argument.

   The called method can communicate with the calling method by modifying the value of the argument via the reference parameter.

6.13 The `ref` keyword

6.14 An output parameter works like a reference parameter, but the value passed into it can be uninitialized and it must be set by the method before the method terminates.

6.15 A value-returning method returns a value to the caller. A value-returning method can be used to perform a calculation and then return the result.

6.16 The Boolean values `true` or `false`

6.17 Yes. A method can be written to return any type of data.

Chapter 7

7.1 Value types and reference types

7.2 When you are working with a value type, you are using a variable that holds a piece of data, but when you are working with a reference type, you are using two things:

- An object that is created in memory
- A variable that references the object

7.3 The object is like the kite, and the variable that references the object is like the spool of string.

7.4 Reference type

7.5 `decimal[] monthlyPay;`

7.6 `monthlyPay = new decimal[12];`

7.7 `const int SIZE = 12;`
`double[] monthlyPay = new decimal[SIZE];`

7.8 `string [] fullName = { "John", "Quincy", "Adams" };`

7.9 In any of the following circumstances, you should use a `for` loop to process the array:

- To change the contents of an array element
- To work through the array elements in reverse order
- To access some of but not all the array elements
- To simultaneously work with two or more arrays within the loop

7.10 When an object is no longer referenced, it becomes eligible for garbage collection.

7.11 A reference to the array

7.12 Because arrays are always passed by reference, a method that receives an array as an argument has access to the actual array.

7.13 The receiving method not only has access to the array, but it also has access to the reference variable that was used to pass the array.

7.14 A method of locating a specific item in a larger collection of data

7.15 A technique for scanning through an array and rearranging its contents in some specific order

7.16 The values in the array must be sorted in ascending order.

7.17 200 rows and 100 columns

7.18 `values[199][99] = 50;`

7.19 `int[,] values = { { 12, 24, 32, 21, 42 },`
`                    { 99,  8, 68, 32, 92 },`
`                    { 95, 34, 21, 11,  7 } };`

7.20 In a traditional two-dimensional array, each row has the same number of columns.

7.21 `int[][] values = new int [3][];`
`values[0] = new int[3] { 2, 4, 6 };`
`values[1] = new int[4] { 3, 5, 7, 9 };`
`values[2] = new int[5] { 5, 9, 11, 17, 21 };`

7.22 `List<double> valueList = new List<double>() { 1.0, 2.0, 3.0 };`

7.23 `valueList.Add(4.0);`

7.24 `valueList.Clear();`

7.25 Yes. You can use the subscript notation of a List to adapt any of the array-processing algorithms so they work with a `List`.

Chapter 8

8.1 `char letter = 'A';`

8.2 `MessageBox.Show(letterGrade.ToString());`

8.3 `char lastLetter = alphabet[alphabet.Length-1];`

8.4
```
foreach (char character in serialNumber)
{
     MessageBox.Show(character.ToString());
}
```

8.5 `if (char.IsPunctuation(sentence[sentence.Length-1]))`

8.6 `if (char.IsUpper(sentence, 0))`

8.7 `uppercase = char.ToUpper(lowercase);`

8.8 If the argument is already lowercase, the `ToLower` method returns it unchanged.

8.9 `found = dessert.StartsWith("Strawberry");`

8.10 If the substring is not found, the methods will return the integer value `-1`.

8.11 `city.Trim();`

8.12 `vegetable.ToLower();`

8.13 `char[] delimiters = { ',', ';' };`

8.14 A comma is used as the delimiter for files with the .csv extension.

8.15 Nothing

8.16 The keyword `public` is an access modifier that specifies the field can be directly accessed by statements outside the structure.

8.17 When you create an instance of a structure, you are creating an object.

8.18 The `new` operator creates an instance of the structure and initializes the object's fields with the default value of 0 or `null` if any of the fields are reference variables.

8.19 Once you have created an instance of a structure, you can access its fields using the dot operator.

8.20 `motor2 = motor1;`

8.21 `Engine [] motors = new Engine[100];`

8.22 When the items in two data structures are related by their indexes

8.23 a. `Flower`
b. 1, 2, 3
c. `Flower flora = Flower.Petunia;`

8.24 The `ToString` method

8.25 You can convert an enumerator to its underlying integer type by using a cast operator.

8.26 By getting the value of the control's `Images.Count` property

8.27 You will find the ImageList control in the Components section of the Toolbox.

8.28 • All the images stored in an ImageList control should be the same size.
   • The images stored in an ImageList control can be no more than 256 by 256 pixels in size.
   • All the images stored in an ImageList control should be in the same format (.bmp, .jpg, etc.).

8.29 In the *Properties* window, click the ellipses button that appears next to the Images property. Click the *Add* button, and an *Open* dialog box will appear. Use the dialog box to locate and select the image file that you want to add to the ImageList control.

8.30 If you know the index value for a particular image, you can retrieve that image from the ImageList control and display it in a PictureBox.

Chapter 9

9.1 A class is code that describes a particular type of object. You can think of a class as a code blueprint that can be used to create a particular type of object.

9.2 The first line of a class declaration is known as the class header. It starts with the word `class`, followed by the name of the class. Following the class header is an opening curly brace. Next, you write the class's member declarations. These are the statements that define the class's fields, properties, and methods. A closing curly brace appears at the end of the class declaration.

9.3 A constructor is a method that is automatically executed when an object is created. In most cases, a constructor is used to initialize an object's fields with starting values.

9.4 1. With the project open in Visual Studio, click *Project* on the menu bar and then select *Add Class....*
   2. Select *Class* as the type of item in the *Add New Item* window and then change the name that appears in the *Name* text box to match the name of the class that you are creating.
   3. Click the *Add* button.

9.5 When you pass an object that is an instance of a class as an argument, the thing that is passed into the parameter variable is a reference to the object.

9.6 A property is a special type of class member that allows an object to store and retrieve a piece of data.

9.7 Properties can be passed only by value.

9.8 If you need to make a property read only, you simply do not write a `set` accessor for the property.

9.9 An error will occur if you try to assign a value to a read-only property.

9.10 When field's value is tightly dependent on other data and that field is not updated when the other data is changed, it is said that the field has become stale.

9.11 A parameterized constructor is a constructor that accepts arguments.

9.12 When a method is overloaded, it means that multiple methods in the same class have the same name, but use different types of parameters.

9.13 Binding

9.14 If you write a class with no constructor whatsoever, the compiler will provide a default constructor.

9.15 The default constructor is a parameterless constructor (it accepts no arguments), and it initializes the object's fields with the value 0. (If any fields are reference variables, they are initialized with the special value `null`.)

9.16 When you create an array of a class type, each element of the array is a reference variable. By default, each element is initialized with the value `null`.

9.17 You can initialize the array element one element at a time, in a loop, or in the declaration statement of the array.

9.18 By writing the class type inside the angled brackets, `<>`, immediately after the word `List`

9.19 A written description of the real-world objects, parties, and major events related to the problem.

9.20 If you adequately understand the nature of the problem you are trying to solve, you can write a description of the problem domain yourself. If you do not thoroughly understand the nature of the problem, you should have an expert write the description for you.

9.21 First, identify the nouns, pronouns, and pronoun phrases in the problem domain description. Then, refine the list to eliminate duplicates, items that you do not need to be concerned with in the problem, items that represent objects instead of classes, and items that represent simple values that can be stored in variables.

9.22 The things that the class is responsible for knowing and the actions that the class is responsible for doing

9.23 In the context of this problem, what must the class know? What must the class do?

9.24 No

9.25 Follow these steps to rename a form:
1. Right-click the form's name in the Solution Explorer.
2. Select *Rename* from the pop-up menu.
3. In the *Solution Explorer*, the form's filename should become highlighted. Type the new name, and press Enter.
4. When the dialog box appears, click *Yes* to rename the form.

9.26 Follow these steps to add a new form to a project:
1. Click *Project* on the Visual Studio menu bar and then select *Add Windows Form...* from the *Project* menu. The *Add New Item* window should appear.
2. Near the bottom of the *Add New Item* window, a *Name* text box appears where you can specify the new form's file name. Initially, a default name will appear here. Change the default name that is displayed in the *Name* text box to a more descriptive name.
3. Click the *Add* button.

9.27 If you wish to remove a form from a project and delete its file from the disk, follow these steps:
1. Right-click the form's entry in the *Solution Explorer* window.
2. On the pop-up menu, click *Delete*.

9.28 In your application's code, the first step in displaying a form is to create an instance of the form's class.

9.29 The controls that you place on a form have public access.

9.30 When the user closes the form, control of the application returns to the point where the `ShowDialog` method was called, and execution resumes.

Chapter 10

10.1 The base class is the general class, and the specialized class is the derived class.

10.2 One object is a specialized version of the other object.

10.3 It inherits all the base class's members.

10.4 `Bird` is the base class and `Canary` is the derived class.

10.5 Summary of constructor issues in inheritance.

- When you create an instance of a derived class, the base class constructor is executed first, and then the derived class constructor is executed.
- When you create an instance of a derived class, by default the base class's parameterless constructor is automatically executed.
- If you want a parameterized constructor in the base class to execute, you must explicitly call it from the derived class's constructor. You do this by writing the notation : `base(`*`parameterList`*`)` in the derived class's constructor header.
- If the base class does not have a parameterless constructor, the derived class constructor must use the notation : `base(`*`parameterList`*`)` to call one of the base class's parameterized constructors.

10.6 I'm a potato.

I'm a potato.

10.7 No. An object of a base class is not a specialized version of a derived class. Although the statement "a dog is an animal" is true, the statement "an animal is a dog" is not true. This is because all dogs are animals, but not all animals are dogs.

10.8 An abstract class is meant to be a base class and never instantiated. It serves as a starting point, providing some members for its derived classes.

10.9 It cannot be instantiated.

10.10 It must override the abstract method.

10.11 It must be overridden in a derived class.

10.12 Simply leave out the `set` accessor.

Chapter 11

11.1 A database management system is software that is specifically designed to store, retrieve, and manipulate large amounts of data in an organized and efficient manner.

11.2 Most businesses use a DBMS instead of creating their own text files because a DBMS is specifically designed to store, retrieve, and manipulate large amounts of data in an organized and efficient manner. When traditional files contain large amounts of data, simple operations such as searching, inserting, and deleting become cumbersome and inefficient.

11.3 The programmer does not need to know specific details about the physical structure of the data because the DBMS handles the actual reading of, writing of, and searching for data. The programmer needs to know only how to interact with the DBMS.

11.4 a. A database is the data that is stored in a database management system and organized into one or more tables.
b. A table holds a collection of related data that is organized into rows and columns.
c. A row is a complete set of information about a single item in a table of a database.
d. A column holds an individual piece of information about the item in a row of a table in a database.

11.5 1. c
2. d
3. f
4. b
5. a
6. e

11.6 A primary key serves as a unique value that can be used to identify a specific row.

11.7 A column that contains unique values that are generated by the DBMS

11.8 Leaving the column empty will result in a error.

11.9 Application
Binding source
Dataset
Table adapter
Data source

11.10 A table adapter connects to a data source and can retrieve data from a table in a data source. It can also update the table in the data source.

11.11 A binding source is a component that can connect user interface controls directly to a dataset.

11.12 A user interface control that is connected to a data source is called a data-bound control.

11.13 Table adapter
Adapter manager
Data set
Binding source

11.14 The Fill method causes the table adapter to load data from the database into the dataset.

11.15 Visual Studio provides a *Data Sources* window that lets you see all the data sources in the current project. Click *Data* on the Visual Studio menu bar; then click *Show Data Sources* to display the *Data Sources* window.

11.16 Create a Details view to display on a single row of a database.

11.17 Dragging a table from the *Data Sources* window onto the form creates a DataGridView control (by default), complete with a navigation bar, on the form.

11.18 The project's output folder is the *bin\Debug* folder.

11.19 When you click the smart tag, a tasks panel will pop up, giving you a number of options that you can perform with the control.

11.20 The type of control to which a column is automatically bound is determined by the column's data type.

11.21 To bind a ListBox control to a column, you must set two of the control's properties: DataSource and DisplayMember.

11.22 The table adapter's `Fill` method

11.23 You use the `Select` statement to retrieve the rows in a table.

11.24 Queries

11.25 In SQL, the equal to operator is one equal sign, not two equal signs, and the not equal to operator is <>.

11.26 If you need to include a single quote as part of a string, simply write two single quotes in its place.

11.27 The `Like` operator can be used to search for a substring in a column.

11.28 Unlike the % character, the underscore represents a single character.

11.29 The `Order By` clause

11.30 The @ symbol

Index